DIE IN BATTLE, DO NOT DESPAIR

War and Military Culture in South Asia, 1757-1947

www.helion.co.uk/warandmilitarycultureinsouthasia

Series Editors

Professor Emeritus Raymond Callahan, University of Delaware

Alan Jeffreys, Imperial War Museum

Professor Daniel Marston, Australian National University

Editorial Advisory Board

Squadron Leader (Retired) Rana Chhina, Centre of Armed Forces Historical Research, United Service Institution of India

Professor Anirudh Deshpande, University of Delhi

Professor Ashley Jackson, King's College London

Dr Robert Johnson, Oxford University

Lieutenant Commander Kalesh Mohanan, Naval History Division, Ministry of Defence, India

Dr Tim Moreman

Dr David Omissi, University of Hull

Professor Peter Stanley, University of New South Wales, Canberra

Dr Chandar Sundaram, Department of Continuing Studies, University of Victoria

Dr Erica Wald, Goldsmiths, University of London

Submissions

The publishers would be pleased to receive submissions for this series. Please contact us via email (info@helion.co.uk), or in writing to Helion & Company Limited, 26 Willow Road, Solihull, West Midlands, B91 1UE.

Titles

No 1   *'Swords Trembling In Their Scabbards'. The Changing Status of Indian Officers in the Indian Army 1757-1947* Michael Creese (ISBN 978-1-909982-81-9)

No 2   *'Discipline, System and Style'. The Sixteenth Lancers and British Soldiering in India 1822-1846* John H. Rumsby (ISBN 978-1-909982-91-8)

No 3   *Die in Battle, Do not Despair. The Indians on Gallipoli, 1915* Peter Stanley (ISBN 978-1-910294-67-3)

No 4   *Brave as a Lion. The Life and Times of Field Marshal Hugh Gough, 1st Viscount Gough* Christopher Brice (ISBN 978-1-910294-61-1)

Die in Battle, Do Not Despair

The Indians on Gallipoli, 1915

War and Military Culture in South Asia, 1757-1947 No. 3

Peter Stanley

Published in association with the United Service Institution of India

Helion & Company Limited

Helion & Company Limited
26 Willow Road
Solihull
West Midlands
B91 1UE
England
Tel. 0121 705 3393
Fax 0121 711 4075
Email: info@helion.co.uk
Website: www.helion.co.uk
Twitter: @helionbooks
Visit our blog http://blog.helion.co.uk/

Published by Helion & Company in association with the United Service Institution of India 2015

Designed and typeset by Bookcraft Ltd, Stroud, Gloucestershire
Cover designed by Paul Hewitt, Battlefield Design (www.battlefield-design.co.uk)
Printed by Gutenberg Press Limited, Tarxien, Malta

Text © Peter Stanley 2015
Photographs © as individually credited
Maps © Barbara Taylor 2015

Front cover: A follower (left) with a Gurkha rifleman, who displays his kukri, perhaps at the photographer's invitation. (ATL 077916).
Rear cover: Sepoys of the 14th Sikhs in the trenches, 1915. (14th Sikhs album)

ISBN 978 1 910294 67 3

British Library Cataloguing-in-Publication Data.
A catalogue record for this book is available from the British Library.

All rights reserved. No part of this publication may be reproduced, stored in a retrieval system, or transmitted, in any form, or by any means, electronic, mechanical, photocopying, recording or otherwise, without the express written consent of Helion & Company Limited.

For details of other military history titles published by Helion & Company Limited contact the above address, or visit our website: http://www.helion.co.uk.

We always welcome receiving book proposals from prospective authors.

Contents

List of illustrations	vi
List of maps	x
Series Editor's Preface	xi
Foreword by Rana Chhina	xiii
Acknowledgments	xv
Explanatory notes	xviii
Introduction: 'A Song of the War will I make'	xxii
1 'To slay the enemy was the Master's order': the Indian Army, 1914	25
2 'O my lover, thou wilt leave me': mobilisation, 1914	40
3 'I came to the land of Egypt': defending the Canal, 1914-15	53
4 'Behold O Master the mighty host': the Mediterranean Expeditionary Force	68
5 'My friends and brothers dying': Anzac, April	83
6 'Be not weary and faint hearted': Anzac, May	97
7 'When the smoke of the guns falls like a mist': Gurkha Bluff, May	114
8 'Death roams about with its mouth open': Gully Ravine, June	134
9 'The soldier must suffer': Gully Spur, June	151
10 'When my body was weak and despaired': summer on Gallipoli	170
11 'May I die fighting in the thick of battle': Sari Bair, August	192
12 'Considering your duty as a warrior': Hill 60, August	217
13 'Shall we live to return to India?' Demakjelik Bair, September-October	238
14 'The sea wind blew away the hates': evacuation, October-December	265
15 'He is here today; he will be here hereafter': remembering Gallipoli	283
Appendices	
I Force G order of battle	303
II Indian army units represented on Gallipoli	305
III Sources of chapter quotations	307
IV Indians on Gallipoli today	308
V Strengths, reinforcements and losses	311
VI Indian dead of the Gallipoli campaign	315
Sources	359
Index	373

List of Illustrations

An infantry battalion of the Indian Army: the 2/10th Gurkha Rifles at Takdah in 1914. (Gurkha Museum, Winchester)	29
1/6th Gurkhas' khud racing team, 1913. (Gurkha Museum, Winchester)	36
Ceremonies in which recruits swore oaths under their regiments' colours confirmed the Gurkhas' loyalty to their units. (Gurkha Museum, Pokhara)	37
Officers: British and Gurkha officers of the 2/10th Gurkhas, grouped around Lieutenant-Colonel Francis Sutton, photographed at Takdah in 1914. While British and Gurkha officers were distributed evenly through the group, the names of only four of the nineteen Gurkhas were recorded. (Gurkha Museum, Pokhara)	46
A cartoon published in the Australian weekly magazine the *Bulletin* in 1914 demonstrates the esteem Sikh troops enjoyed in the empire. Here, David Low ridicules the possibility of German subversion. (National Library of Australia)	51
Indians in Cairo – a curiosity to the locals as well as to empire troops. (State Library of Victoria)	54
Life on the Canal Defences. Indian troops catching eels (top) and fishing. (*Mullaly, Bugle and Kukri*)	59
Captain Denis Ryan's drawing of the 14th Sikhs' and 6th Gurkhas' post on the eastern bank of the canal near Kantara. (*Historical Record of the 6th Gurkha Rifles*)	61
Sir William Birdwood's staff, photographed in Cairo. Among British and Australian officers, a New Zealander and a Canadian, the largest single group of officers were six of the Indian Army, including Charles Villiers-Stuart and Andrew Skeen. (AWM A01580)	61
An artist's imagining, published in the *Illustrated London News*, depicting the Indian defence of the Suez Canal. (National Library of Australia)	66
Indians and other empire troops on the bank of the Suez Canal. (State Library of Victoria)	67
Major-General Herbert Cox, commander of the 29th Indian Infantry Brigade in 1915. (*Mullaly, Bugle and Kukri*)	71
Punjabi Musalman troops meeting Australians in a railway truck in Egypt. Men of the two armies exhibited a strong curiosity about each other. (AWM PS0468)	71
General Sir William Birdwood meeting Punjabi Musalman troops, probably members of the mountain batteries. Birdwood could speak to Indian troops in Hindustani or Urdu. (AWM C02159)	76
Lionel Lindsay's cartoon of his character 'Chunder Loo' as an Indian mountain gunner, one of his advertisements for Cobra boot polish in the Australian magazine the *Bulletin*. (National Library of Australia)	79
Mountain gunners in 'mufti' (casual dress). The men come from the batteries' two main ethnic groups – Punjabi Musalman (left) and Sikh (right). (National Library of Australia)	81

List of Illustrations   vii

Army Headquarters, Simla; today still used as offices by the Indian Army in Shimla. (Author)	81
Troops of the 1st Australian Division landing at Anzac Cove late on the morning of 25 April 1915. (AWM A01090)	86
Mountain gunners unloading their guns from mules at Anzac. (AWM P00046)	86
The beach at what became Anzac Cove with men of the 1st Australian Division forming up beside gunners of Jacob's Battery. (ATL PAColl-7581-84)	87
An Australian gunner photographed what he called the '21st Indian Battery Guard', a sign of how the Indian mountain brigade maintained soldierly standards. (State Library of Victoria)	91
Indian gunners and Anzacs at one of the gunners' bivouacs at Anzac early in the campaign, evidence of the relationship between them. (AWM H00198)	91
Mountain gunners dragging a gun into position on Walker's Ridge. looking northward, toward Suvla Bay. (ATL 061508)	102
Mangat Rai, Heber Alexander's clerk in his Supply and Transport unit at Anzac, to whom Alexander may have dedicated his book *On Two Fronts*. (Heber Alexander, *On Two Fronts*)	106
A benevolent Britannia doles out alms to Muslim widows in a poster seeking donations in Britain. It is a reminder of the needs of soldiers' widows. (Mary Evans Picture Library)	109
An Indian follower cutting the hair of an Anzac; one of the ways Indians made money from their fellow soldiers at Anzac. (AWM C01139)	111
An Australian and a Hindu 'follower' (identifiable by his non-regulation clothing) photographed, perhaps while enjoying a chat at Anzac. (AWM C01544)	111
Sepoy Nanak Singh of the 89th Punjabis, photographed later in life, whose recollections of Gallipoli are both rare and valuable. (Dr Tajinderpal Singh, Perth)	116
Men of the 14th Sikhs arriving at Cape Helles, with Second Lieutenant Reginald Savory conspicuous in his pith helmet in the centre of the lighter. (14th Sikhs Album)	116
Charles Bruce's headquarters dug-outs on Gully Spur in May 1915, from the *Illustrated London News*. (*Illustrated London News*)	119
A clipping from the *Graphic* in September 1915, showing the Indians' rear area in Gully Ravine. It shows how broad and deep the gully was behind the front line. The tents (right) seem to house the 108th Indian Field Ambulance. (14th Sikhs album)	119
Looking south from Gurkha Bluff. (Author)	121
Gurkha Bluff, depicted in the *Illustrated London News* in August, showing the rugged terrain across which Bruce's 1/6th Gurkhas attacked. (National Library of Australia)	121
Punjabi Musalmans, possibly of one of the Punjabi battalions withdrawn at the end of May, inspecting fragments of Turkish shrapnel in a posed photograph. (IWM Q013372)	123
An advertisement for Gurkha 'sweetheart' brooches in the Allahabad *Pioneer* (a newspaper widely read across Bengal and the United Provinces), aimed at British officers' female relatives. (National Library of India)	126
Hindu drivers of the Supply and Transport corps cremating their dead later in the campaign on a specially constructed stone-built platform. (IWM Q013689)	129
Norman Wimbush's drawing of a 'langi' – a cook – delivering food to men of the 14th Sikhs in the regiment's front line trenches. (14th Sikhs album)	132
Three Australians and a Sikh photographed in Egypt, published in the *Sydney Mail* with the caption 'Best of Chums'. The Australians on either side of the Sikh were killed in France in 1916. The Sikh's face is blurred, perhaps because he moved at the moment of exposure, but its indistinctness symbolises our knowledge of these men and their relations with other empire troops. (*Sydney Mail*)	135

viii   Die In Battle, Do Not Despair

Gurkhas wounded in the hand: a reflection of the intensity of combat in the Gully Spur trenches. (ATL PA1-0-863-01-4) 140
Indian medical orderlies, including men from at least three Indian communities, with Australian or British orderlies and a nurse, beside a third-class railway carriage used to transport wounded in Egypt. (AWM C00545) 144
Indian troops bathing in the sea, probably at Cape Helles. (AWM C00805) 147
Sepoys of the 14th Sikhs in the trenches, 1915. (14th Sikhs album) 147
An 'Indian mule camp at Anzac', showing a muleteer at left donning his turban. Much of the domestic life of Indian soldiers remains obscure, revealed only in details of photographs. (*Sydney Mail*) 149
A follower (left) with a Gurkha rifleman, who displays his kukri, perhaps at the photographer's invitation. (ATL 077916) 152
Stretcher-bearers evacuating a man pose for a photograph. These men are of the Army Bearer Corps, who were generally Hindus from Ganges valley. (14th Sikhs album) 159
Sikh, Punjabi Musalman and Hindu wounded on a hospital ship carrying them to Malta, relieved to be away from the peninsula. The man on the right has been wounded in the hand: a common occurrence among Indian troops on Gallipoli. (*Sydney Mail*) 165
Orderlies and bearers at the Surgical Dressing Room of 108 Indian Field Ambulance later in the campaign, a photograph preserved in its war diary. (National Archives, UK) 167
A ward of the Lady Hardinge War Hospital in Bombay, where Indian wounded from Gallipoli would be treated through 1915. (*Illustrated London News*) 168
A muleteer of one of the Supply and Transport companies in a deep sap – possibly the now vanished 'Great Sap' – at Anzac. (ATL 077970) 171
Indian stretcher-bearers carrying wounded down from the firing line during the summer of 1915. (AWM P01116-055) 174
Gurkhas and Anzacs mixing, possibly on the island of Imbros during the Indian troops' rest there during the summer of 1915. (AWM P08678) 180
Indian troops, possibly Gurkhas, bathing using improvised showers, possibly on Imbros during the brigade's rest in July 1915. (AWM H00758) 182
Sikh officers, almost certainly of the Patiala Infantry–and probably Major Harban Singh on the left. (IWM Q013665) 185
A mule camp of the Supply and Transport Corps, which made such an important contribution to the maintenance of the British empire force on Gallipoli. (AWM J02706) 189
Three subedars who served with the 14th Sikhs on Gallipoli, from left to right, Subedar Major Sham Singh, Subedar Kishan Singh (transferred from the Burma Military Police) and Subedar Bhagat Singh of the Patiala Infantry. The Indian units' efficiency and everyday management largely depended upon men such as these. (14th Sikhs album) 191
Patiala sepoys wounded in the August offensive recuperating in hospital in Egypt. (*Patiala and the Great War*) 201
A Company, probably of the 14th Sikhs or the Patialas beside a barbed wire cage holding captured Turks. The soldiers wear the white armbands issued to those taking part in the August offensive. (ATL 077922) 205
Major Cecil Allanson, who commanded the 1/6th Gurkhas in the climactic assault on Sari Bair, and whose life was marked forever after by the ordeal. (Gurkha Museum, Winchester) 206
Looking from Hill Q, the scene of Allanson's attack, eastwards toward the Dardanelles, early one August morning. (Author) 207
Men of the 2/10th Gurkhas on Sari Bair ridge during the August offensive, one of the very few photographs of Indians in action on Gallipoli. (14th Sikhs album) 209

The Narrows, seen from Sari Bair soon after the war; the view seen by Allanson and his men on the morning of 9 August. (*The 5th Royal Gurkha Rifles*)	211
Sikh sepoys in the front line at Demakjelik Bair with a bomb catapult, a sign of how close Ottoman and Indian trenches were. (14th Sikhs album)	218
Anzac and Gurkha snipers. The dress of the two demonstrates their very different attitudes toward smartness. As regulars, the Gurkhas, despite serving in the front line, wear their uniform and kit correctly: the Australians or New Zealanders adopt a more casual approach. (AWM A05612)	219
A man of the 29th Indian Infantry Brigade in the front line near Hill 60 in August, one of the few photographs taken on Indians under fire on Gallipoli. Though in the 14th Sikhs' album, and standing beside Sikhs, the man does not seem to be a Sikh. (14th Sikhs album)	220
Demakjelik Bair, looking eastwards to roughly the site of the Indian brigade headquarters in 1915. (Author)	221
The second contingent of Patiala Sikhs to serve on Gallipoli undergoing kit inspection before departure from Egypt, September 1915. (Patiala album)	222
A folded print of a blurred photograph of no man's land looking toward Hill 60 in the late summer of 1915, showing the bare ground over which British empire troops attacked. (14th Sikhs album)	223
Norman Wimbush's drawings of men of the 14th Sikhs firing a periscope rifle (left) and of a sniping team operating (with a British officer observing and a sepoy firing) from the trenches at Demakjelik Bair. (14th Sikhs album)	229
Three men of the Patiala Rajindra Infantry who may have served on Gallipoli, showing the sepoys' uniform and kit. As Sikhs they wear the sacred 'kara', or metal ring, on the turban. (Patiala album)	231
Leslie Hore's water-colour, of 'Mule Gully'. (State Library of New South Wales)	235
The country around Demakjelik Bair in 2014. (Author)	241
A Gurkha machine-gun in the front line at Demakjelik Bair. At right is a periscope wrapped in hessian and an improvised gong, used as an alarm against attack. (14th Sikhs album)	241
Leslie Hore's depiction of Mule Gully. (State Library of New South Wales)	243
Looking down Mule Gully today. (author)	243
Two Indians (one Hindu, the other Musalman) pause for a snapshot with a group of Australian service corps men, suggesting the informal relationships between the two. (AWM C01174)	245
A Punjabi Musalman herds sheep imported from Egypt to provide halal meat for the mountain artillery's members. (AWM C01614)	246
Punjabi Musalman muleteers in a camp near Demakjelik Bair face the rigors of the approaching winter. (AWM H16578)	246
Leslie Hore's depiction of 'tea on the terrace', in which turbaned bearers serve tea to Supply and Transport and visiting light horse officers. (State Library of New South Wales)	249
Sikhs presenting their rifles for inspection in the trenches at Demakjelik Bair. The disciplined maintenance of their weapons, part of the regular army's routine, was one explanation for the Indian brigade's endurance. (14th Sikhs album)	251
Norman Wimbush's drawing of Sikhs, Anzacs and Gurkhas mixing in the trenches. In the centre an Anzac (with a curiously Asian cast of face) inspects a Gurkha's kukri. (14th Sikhs album)	259
A badly wounded Supply and Transport driver, his leg torn off by shrapnel, awaiting stretcher-bearers, a depiction by John Hargrave of the stoicism shown by many Indian soldiers. (John Hargrave, *At Suvla Bay*)	267

Gurkhas, cold, sick and fed-up but resigned, in the trenches at Demakjelik Bair later in the campaign. (14th Sikhs album)   267

'Crippled on Gallipoli': William Villiers-Stuart's annotation to a photograph of one of his beloved 1/5th Gurkhas. (Gurkha Museum, Winchester)   269

Frost-bitten Gurkhas and other Indian troops awaiting evacuation from behind the line at Demakjelik Bair, December 1915. (AWM C02448)   272

Norman Wimbush's drawing of men carrying supplies to the 14th Sikhs' flooded front line trenches early in December. (14th Sikhs album)   272

One of the piers at Anzac from which the Indians left the peninsula. (14th Sikhs album)   281

Men of the 14th Sikhs unpacking at Suez after the evacuation of the peninsula. (14th Sikhs album)   284

Rifleman Chandrabin Rana, 1/6th Gurkhas, who, as William Villiers-Stuart annotated in his album, 'did not return from Gallipoli'. (Gurkha Museum, Winchester)   288

The 'British' officers of the 14th Sikhs (including the MO, Herajee Cursetjee, at left), photographed at Peshawur in 1914. The annotations record that all but four of them died in the war, eight of them on Gallipoli in 1915. (14th Sikhs album)   289

Sikh veterans of Gallipoli with Reginald Savory in 1945. (Bamford, *1st King George's Own Battalion*)   293

Patiala veterans (including men who served on Gallipoli) greeting the Prince of Wales in Patiala in 1922, with His Highness Bupinder Singh mounted on the left. (Patiala album)   294

'In Memory of Gallant Warriors' – the war memorial erected at Patiala by the Maharajah Bupinder Singh, one of the few such war memorials in India, depicting the Patiala Rajendra Infantry on Sari Bair and listing the names of men of the regiment who died on Gallipoli. (Author)   296

The Commonwealth War Graves Commission memorial at Cape Helles, which commemorates 1500 Indian Army troops among 20,000 British Empire soldiers who died on Gallipoli but who have no known grave. (Author)   300

'He died for freedom and honour' – Rifleman Duble Gurung's medallion, preserved in the 2/10th (and later Royal Gurkha Rifles) officers' mess after his family in Nepal could not be traced. (Gurkha Museum, Pokhara)   302

List of Maps

1 Northern India, 1914
2 The Eastern Mediterranean
3 Suez Canal defences, 1914-15
4 The Gallipoli peninsula, 1915
5 Anzac area, 1915
6 Gully Ravine, 1915
7 The August offensive, 1915
8 Damakjelik Bair, 1915

War and Military Culture in South Asia, 1757-1947
Series Editor's Preface

The aim of this new academic historical series is to produce well-researched monographs on the armed forces of South Asia, concentrating mainly on the East India Company and the Indian armed forces from 1757 until 1947. Books in the series will examine the military history of the period as well as social, cultural, political and economic factors, although inevitably the armies of the East India Company and the Indian Army will dominate the series. In addition, edited volumes of conference papers, memoirs and campaign histories will also be published. It is hoped this series will be of interest to both serious historians and the general military history reader.

The foundation of the series coincides with the rise of academic interest in Indian military history over the last few years. In particular the series will contribute to the 'new military history' of South Asia. This came to prominence at an academic conference held in Cambridge in 1997 that was re-invigorated at two recent conferences held at the University of Greenwich and Jadavpur University, Kolkata in 2013-2014 with aim of 'Re-newing the Military History of Colonial South Asia'. The aim of this series is to harness this explosion of interest and channel it into a series of ground-breaking volumes that add to the growing historiography of the period. For example in the field of Second World War studies and the period until Partition, Daniel Marston and Tim Moreman have spearheaded this historical research with their volumes: *Phoenix from the Ashes: The Indian Army in the Burma Campaign* (2003) and *The Jungle, the Japanese and the Commonwealth Armies at War* (2005). These are complemented by Raymond Callahan's *Churchill and His Generals* (2007), a seminal work published in the United States that should be better known in the United Kingdom, and the wider study by Ashley Jackson on *The British Empire and the Second World War* (2006). Similarly there have been a number of relevant conferences such as one held at the Imperial War Museum in 2009, the papers of which were published as *The Indian Army, 1939-1947: Experience and Development* (2012). Daniel Marston's *The Indian Army and the End of the Raj* (2014) has also recently been published.

This interest has been mirrored in India as eight volumes of the official histories of the Indian Armed Forces during the Second World War were reprinted in India in 2012 and another four in 2014. They were originally published between 1954 and 1960. As Squadron Leader Rana Chhina stated at the launch of the reprints: 'As a resurgent India seeks to be a major player on the world stage, it behoves it to discard its narrow post-colonial world view, and to step up to reclaim the role that its armed forces played out on a global scale' during the Second World War. Anirudh Deshpande's *A Spring of Despair: Mutiny, Rebellion and Death in India, 1946* will be published in 2015. Similarly Rana Chhina and the United Service Institution of India are organising a number of events for the centenary of 'India and the Great War', including a number of detailed academic studies in partnership with this series. It is envisaged that monographs will be published on the role of the Indian Army in all the major First World War theatres as well as other aspects of the war such as the Indian State Forces and an edited volume of essays.

The series editors, members of the editorial advisory board and our publisher, Duncan Rogers of Helion, are all delighted to be involved in this series and we hope it will be of interest not only in the UK and India but globally, too.

Alan Jeffreys

Foreword

Many decades ago, the chance discovery of a khaki drill Great War tunic hanging on a peg on a village wall, buttressed by the subsequent find of two Victory medals in an old family trunk led to what would become a lifelong fascination with the exploits of the old Indian Army in general and its role in the Great War in particular. During school vacations and subsequent term-breaks from the National Defence Academy, I would prod an old kinsman who began his service career as a sowar in the Guides Cavalry and retired post-independence as a risaldar in the Scinde Horse, to take me to meet as many old soldiers who lived in the vicinity of our village as he could manage. In those days Punjab villages were full of men who had fought in the second world war. However, their stories did not excite the imagination as much as of those who had served before, and gone to war on horseback, and remembered using the lance and sword, not as ceremonial accoutrements but as weapons of war. To listen to these men recount tales of France, Basra, Baghdad and Kut-el-Amara, of Kanstantunia (Constantinople) and the Dardanelles; and of their fathers who had served in Tibet, China and Afghanistan, or their grandfathers, who rode to Delhi during the great 'Ghadr' (revolt) of 1857, was heady stuff indeed. The stories of those who had so 'recently' served in North Africa and the Western Desert, in Malaya, Burma and Italy, paled into insignificance in front of the then fast fading generation of the Great War.

Amongst the recollections of these Indian veterans of the "laam" or the "long war" as it was known in the Punjab, two stood out in particular: the siege of Kut, and the evacuation of Gallipoli. Even if they had not served in these theatres, these engagements still formed a part of the veterans' folklore of the war and were cited and remembered as such. Another passing anecdote related to me by my neighbor, the charming silver-haired Miss Felice Pereira, BEM, in the now long-vanished Alexandra Place "chummeries" in New Delhi added to my interest in the enigmatic Indian involvement at Gallipoli. Felice had begun her secretarial career as PS to the Adjutant-General in India during the Second World War. She would relate how she had instructions from the AG, Lieutenant General Reginald Savory, to usher in a tall distinguished looking retired Sikh soldier whenever he may call on him, no matter who else might be waiting for an audience. One day her curiosity got the better of her and she asked Savory the reason behind this special courtesy. "He saved my life at Gallipoli", was all that the general said in reply.

Later, for many years, the fact that the Indian Army's significant involvement in various theatres of the Great War found little or no mention in most accounts involving those campaigns was a source of constant personal irritation. Yet none suffered a neglect more glaring than that meted out to the Indian presence on Gallipoli. The most readily available book on the subject in India, *Gallipoli* by Alan Moorehead, was silent on the subject as were all others of that ilk.

Many years later in 2004, a chance meeting with the author in the library of the venerable United Service Institution of India led to a mutual consensus that "something needed to be done" to rectify this situation. However, it took nearly another decade before this resolve could ultimately fructify. The result is here for all to see, recorded for posterity in the ensuing pages of this book, a superb example of the historian's craft. Professor Stanley has nimbly surmounted the daunting obstacle faced by most scholars who seek to work on the Indian Army: a paucity of sources. Using a vast variety of sources from three continents, the author vividly brings to life the hitherto unknown story of the Indians at Gallipoli. This account is a fitting tribute to the exploits of a forgotten army, even more befittingly published in the centenary of the conflict in which they fought. The campaign at Gallipoli helped shape the national identities of Australia, New Zealand and modern Turkey. It is appropriate that the role and sacrifice of those Indian sepoys who fought and died on Gallipoli be remembered along with the Anzacs and Mehmets, and soldiers of other nationalities whose memory is intrinsically linked with the campaign.

This book forms the first of a sub-series that seeks to focus specifically on the Indian Army in the Great War; an initiative for which the publisher and editors deserve to be complimented. By his endeavours, Professor Stanley has set the bar very high for the others who will follow. I wish them luck, and place on record my grateful acknowledgment of the author's sterling contribution to the history of India's involvement in the Great War.

Before memory fades, we must remember.

Rana T.S. Chhina
New Delhi

Acknowledgments

My principal debt is to Duncan Rogers of Helion & Company, and the editorial board of its 'War and Military Culture in South Asia, 1757-1947' series, particularly Prof. Ray Callahan, Mr Alan Jeffreys, and Prof. Dan Marston, and to the publisher's reviewer, Mr Peter Hart.

I am grateful to the International Policy Division of the Department of Defence, and especially Mr. Andrew Craig and Captain Sheldon Williams, RAN, Australian Defence Attaché-designate in New Delhi, and Colonel Michael Collie, Australian Defence Attaché, who between them greatly assisted research in India. I am also very grateful to Ms Jasmine Jones, Ms Fe Donaghue, Ms Caitlin Atkinson, and especially Ms Kate Alexander, who swiftly and efficiently processed the orders for images for this book, which the Department of Defence generously funded. With the assistance of its 2014 'Indians and Anzacs on Gallipoli' grant I was able to travel to India, Nepal, Turkey and Britain to complete archival and field research.

The Department of Defence sponsored this publication to commemorate Australia and India's joint contribution to the Gallipoli campaign; however, the views expressed in this publication are solely those of the author in his private capacity and do not necessarily reflect the views of the Department of Defence.

In my own institution, UNSW Canberra, I am grateful to my colleagues Prof. Jeff Grey and A/Prof. Mesut Uyar. Jeff shared his insights into the British empire's war against the Ottoman empire, and Mesut, our Ottoman Fellow, once again generously shared his knowledge of and sources relating to British empire (and in this case Indian) troops captured by the Ottomans on Gallipoli. Without his aid I would never have found the words of Rifleman Kulbahadur Gurung. Mr Hayward Maberly and Ms Denise Shepherd of the ADFA Library provided invaluable help.

Also in Canberra I found ready interest from the Indian and Pakistan High Commissions, and wish to thank their respective Defence Advisors, Captain M. Paul Samuel and Brigadier Muhammed Asghar. Relations between Pakistan and India remain cool, but both can look back to a time when men from the precursor army of both nations – Muslim, Hindu and Sikh – served together as comrades.

Elsewhere in Australasia I am grateful to the staff of the Research Centre of the Australian War Memorial, the National Archives of Australia, the National Library of Australia, the State Library of New South Wales, the State Library of South

Australia and the State Library of Victoria, and in New Zealand to the Alexander Turnbull Library, Wellington (especially Ms Linda McGregor), the Queen Elizabeth II Army Memorial Library, Waiouru (especially Ms Dolores Ho) and Archives New Zealand. New Zealand participants of the 'Experience of a Lifetime' conference, held at Massey University in August 2014 were characteristically generous, and I thank especially Mr Neil Frances of the Wairarapa Archives, Ms Sarah Johnston of Nao Taonga and Sir Peter Jackson for their assistance with photographs.

Australia's Sikh community has supported my research and I express my gratitude to Mr. Bawa Jagdev, OAM and his colleagues on the National Australia Sikh Council, especially its president, Mr. Ajmer Singh Gill and his colleagues, and to Ms Manpreet Singh of SBS Radio, Melbourne. I am particularly grateful to members of the Australian Sikh community who brought to my attention family stories, including Mr. Amandeep Singh of Sydney, Dr Tajinderpal Singh of Perth, great-grandson of Sepoy Nanak Singh of the 69th Punjabis and Mr Balbir Singh Banwait, son of Havildar Waryam Singh, 14th Sikhs.

In Britain I am grateful to the staff of the Library of the Imperial War Museums (and especially Nigel Steel, who generously shared his work on Sikhs on Gallipoli, and Ms Jane Rosen, who surmounted the limitations of the IWM's system), the National Army Museum (especially Ms Kate Swann), the British Library and the National Archives, (UK), and the London Metropolitan Archives (which acted as a foster-repository for NAM records), all in London. In Winchester, Major Gerald Davis and especially Mr. Gavin Edgerley-Harris, former and present Curators of the Gurkha Museum, generously granted me access to its rich collection: an archive in which researchers are offered cups of tea, delivered to their desks by Gurkha orderlies. Mr Paul Evans, Librarian at the Royal Artillery Institution, Woolwich, supplied details that enabled me to identify mountain artillery officers. Glynn Proctor of the Commonwealth War Graves Commission responded promptly and helpfully to several appeals for details from the Commission's files. I am grateful to Mr. Harbakhsh Grewal and Mr Parmjit Singh of the UK Punjab Heritage Trust (curators of its excellent 2014 *War, Faith and Empire* exhibition) for its support. Mr Robert Baker of Blinded Veterans, UK, kindly provided a reference to Karam Singh at St Dunstan's, Dehra Dun. Mr. Foster Summerson, assisted my research by advertising in the Gallipoli Society's journal, *The Gallipolian*. I am grateful to Ms Jane Butler-Bryan for undertaking research on my behalf in London. In Ireland Anto O'Brien helped enormously by locating and sharing records of Major Harold Wilmer.

It has been a joy to work with Helion & Company on this book, and I particularly want to thank designer, Mrs Kim McSweeney, and cartographer, Ms Barbara Taylor, for their work in making the book as handsome as it is.

In India, I owe a great debt of gratitude to Squadron Leader (Retd) Rana Chhina of the United Service Institution of India, who generously shared his advice and sources. I appreciate the assistance of some of the staff of the National Archives of India, New Delhi, and especially Mr Ashok Kumar, and some of the staff of the National Library of India, Kolkata. I appreciate the assistance of the staff of the libraries of the

United Service Institution of India, the Nehru Memorial Library, the Archaeological Survey of India Library and the Library of the Indira Gandhi Centre for the Visual Image, New Delhi. Captain Amarinder Singh, His Highness the present Maharaja of Patiala, generously hosted a visit by my wife, Claire, and I to the New Moti Bagh Palace, Patiala, and willingly shared sources and knowledge. I am grateful to Mr Amardeep Singh and Mr Karen Singh of the staff at Patiala. I am grateful to Mr. Adil Chhina for conducting research on my behalf in New Delhi. The Australian High Commission in New Delhi was also helpful, and I thank Ms Sandra O'Malley and her staff particularly.

In Nepal, Lieutenant-Colonel Elton Davies of British Gurkhas Nepal, and Major James Arney and his staff at British Gurkhas Pokhara arranged an informative visit to the depot at Pokhara. I am grateful to Lieutenant-Colonel Garry Blewett, head of the Gurkha Welfare Scheme, who provided a useful briefing on the relationship between Britain and the Gurkhas historically and today They also introduced me to the Gurkha Museum at Pokhara, and Hon. Major Krishnabahadur Gurung, MVO, MBE and Hon. Major Damarbahadur Gurung, its manager, gave me a memorable and productive tour of the museum and allowed me to use its library, which also provided a cup of tea; a Gurkha tradition, it seems.

In Turkey the necessary field work for this book could not have been as successful as it was without the assistance of Mr Eric Goosens, the genial, knowledgeable and helpful proprietor of The Gallipoli Houses, Koçadere, who gave generously of advice and conducted me around parts of Gallipoli with which I was unfamiliar.

Presentations at several academic conferences have helped me to develop and test ideas and interpretations, and I am grateful to the organisers and participants at several gatherings: the United Service Institution of India seminar series, New Delhi, January 2014; the Jaipur Literature Festival, February 2014, the conference 'India and the Great War', United Service Institution of India, New Delhi, March 2014 (for all of which I especially thank Rana Chhina), the conferences 'Re-Newing the Military History of Colonial India', Javedpur University, Kolkata, January 2014 (for which I particularly thank Prof. Kaushik Roy), and 'The British Empire and the Great War', Nanyang Technical University, Singapore, February 2014 (for which I thank Dr Andrekos Varnava and especially Dr Ayhan Aktar, who alerted me to the existence of the crucial source *Çanakkale Muharebeleri'nin Esirleri*).

My friend and colleague Dr Mark Johnston has provided many examples of Australian and Indian encounters, sharing his research with a characteristic generosity. Other individuals assisted the project without necessarily knowing quite how, including: Dr Santanu Das, Dr Anirudh Deshpande, Mr Tom Donovan, Dr Jeff Doyle, Ms Linda Emery, Mr. Harry Fecitt, Dr Indivar Kamtekar, Dr Gavin Rand (who generously shared files he had located at Winchester), Dr Radhika Singha, and Prof. Sir Hew Strachan.

As ever, my journeys in researching this book, to Britain, India New Zealand and Turkey, have taken me away from Claire and my daughters Claire and Jane. I once again acknowledge their loving forbearance and support.

Explanatory Notes

The chapter headings are adapted from Gurkha verses, the hymns of the Sikh gurus, the *Bhagavad Gita* and the *Q'ran*, more or less in proportion to the composition of the Indian Army's contribution to the Gallipoli campaign. Ralph Turner of the 3rd Gurkha Rifles collected the Gurkha verses. While he and his battalion served in France and Palestine, and not Gallipoli, the sentiments are representative not only of Gurkhas but also of the rank and file of the old Indian Army.[1]

I am conscious that, as the Punjab government's history of the province in the war sternly put it, 'the Gurkhas, who come from Nepal, are not technically Indians' – eager to show that the Punjab provided the bulk of India's manpower in the war.[2] This was true in 1915 as today, but they were a part of the Indian Army, and on that basis are included in this book to references to 'Indian troops'. The spelling of 'Gurkha' evidently presented problems to many observers, who referred to 'Ghurkhas', 'Ghurkas' and Gurkas'. Likewise, contemporaries adopted a variety of spelling for believers in Islam, including 'Muhammadan', 'Mahommedan', 'Mahomedan', Muhammedans, etc., as well as the Indian Army's preferred form, Musalman. I refer to the names of places as used in 1915 (such as Constantinople or Maidos rather than Istanbul or Ecabat and Simla rather than Shimla). All quotations are verbatim, including where the sentiments of 1915 might be regarded as offensive to the sensibilities of a century later.

Unit titles often present difficulties for the uninitiated, and I have abbreviated them while (I hope) making them intelligible. The 14th King George's Own Ferozepore Sikhs will be called the 14th Sikhs or simply 'the Sikhs'. Gurkha regiments were numbered separately to their Indian counterparts, from 1 to 10, but each had two battalions. The Gurkha battalions that served on Gallipoli were the 1/4th, 1/5th 1/6th and 2/10th (or in some sources, 1-4th, 1-5th, etc.), pronounced, 'first fourth' and so on. Rather than use full titles (such as the 1st Battalion, 5th Gurkha Rifles (Frontier Force)), I will use simply 4th, 5th, 6th and 10th Gurkhas, unless needing to mention the regiments' other battalions. The two mountain artillery batteries will be called either 'Kohat' or 'Jacob's', rather than by their numbers (21st and 26th respectively).

---

1 Lowe, 'Gurkhas remember France and Palestine', *The Kukri*, No. 41, May 1989, p. 139.
2 Leigh, *The Punjab and the War*, p. 7.

The Indian Army had different names for some ranks, some with no counterparts in the British Army. Subedars and jemadars were Indian commissioned officers who, regardless of age or experience, ranked below the most junior British subaltern. Indian 'States Forces', the military forces of the princely states, did, however, have Indian commissioned officers, but who were usually treated as Indian officers. Comparative ranks were:

British	Indian
General	-
Lieutenant-General	-
Major-General	-
Brigadier-General	-
Colonel	-
Lieutenant-Colonel	-
Major	-
Captain	-
First Lieutenant	-
Second Lieutenant	-
-	Subedar-Major
-	Subedar
-	Jemadar/Ressaidar (the latter in Supply & Transport units until 1921)
Sergeant-Major	Havildar-Major
Sergeant	Havildar
Corporal	Naik
Lance-Corporal	Lance-Naik
Private/Rifleman/Gunner/Driver	Sepoy/Rifleman/Gunner/Driver

Then there were 'Followers' of various kinds, including Supply and Transport drivers and battalion servants, both 'private' (i.e. contracted by officers) and 'public'.

Battalions were commanded by a lieutenant-colonel, assisted by a dozen or so British officers, including a senior major and four double-company commanders, usually captains. They usually had an adjutant, a quartermaster (responsible for rations, equipment and supplies), a machine-gun officer and a medical officer (sometimes Indian) assisted by an assistant surgeon (invariably Indian). Each double company commander was assisted by a subaltern (a lieutenant), who sometimes took on additional duties such as adjutant or quartermaster. When the battalions lost British officers in action the neat distribution of duties was abandoned and the surviving officers shared them as best they could. Colonels were typically aged in their forties, captains in their thirties, lieutenants in their twenties. (Even in war promotion remained mysteriously slow

– Reginald Savory remained a second lieutenant throughout the Gallipoli campaign, despite at one point briefly commanding his battalion.)

Each company was commanded by a subedar, assisted by a jemadar; both native officers of considerable experience. Indian battalions nominally had a subedar-major, seven subedars, seven jemadars and often a jemadar adjutant. These were literally old soldiers, especially in Indian terms, all promoted from the ranks of senior NCOs and wise in the ways of the army. Mountain artillery batteries likewise had a subedar and two jemadars, carefully balancing the 'classes' from which they were recruited. They were all men in or approaching their mid-forties; old for soldiers; as old as their battalion commanders: twice the age of the subalterns who acted as second-in-command to a double company. In the 14th Sikhs, for instance, Subedar-Major Lal Singh, appointed to the rank just before the war's outbreak, had enlisted in 1887. In the 6th Gurkhas Subedar Gambirsing Pun had served for just over twenty years when he was promoted to subedar-major. The coming war would subject these men to severe challenges: some would meet them superbly.

Their companies of about 80 men comprised sections of about twenty, commanded by Indian havildars, (sergeants). Each company should have had five public followers: two *langris* (cooks), two *bhistis* (water-orderlies) and a sweeper, responsible for disposing of waste. 'Private' followers were servants employed by the officers individually or as a mess ('the average British officer is a person who wants a good deal of looking after', a Punjabi captain observed wryly).[3] Both sorts of followers wore nondescript clothes in a military style (sometimes sepoys' cast-offs; at least once an Australian uniform) and were listed on the unit's roll books. If wounded they were treated by the army medical system (though were not eligible for wound pensions) but if killed were listed on memorials.

Distances and quantities have been rendered, as seems appropriate, in imperial measurements, and monetary values remain necessarily unconverted. The sources of all direct quotations are given in footnotes, using short titles or abbreviated citations to archival sources, full details of which are given in the Sources.

---

3   Webster, 'The supply of followers on active service for a battalion of Indian infantry', *Journal of the United Service Institution of India*, Vol. XLV, 1916, p. 275.

As ever, I have attempted to limit the abbreviations, the curse of military history, used in the text. The following appear, mostly in footnotes:

2/Lt	Second Lieutenant
Brig-Gen	Brigadier-General
Capt	Captain
Cpl	Corporal
Lt	Lieutenant
Lt-Col	Lieutenant-Colonel
Maj	Major
MEF	Mediterranean Expeditionary Force
Pte	Private
Sgt	Sergeant

A list of abbreviations of archives and libraries can be found on p. 367.

Introduction: 'A Song of the War will I make'

Die in Battle, Do not Despair... represents a different kind of military history to the traditional model. While it includes maps with arrows showing the movements of units and formations and is structured around a familiar campaign narrative, it is (or aims to be) more than conventional military history. It seeks to bring to bear upon the operations of the Indian troops committed to the Gallipoli campaign of 1915 the evidence, analysis and insights of social history. It is, in short, military social history, of a kind I have been developing for some thirty years, which attempts to understand both what Indian troops contributed to the conduct and outcome of the Gallipoli campaign and how the nature of their army and the demands made upon them affected their experience of that part of the Great War.

It seeks to tell an Indian story; not without difficulty. One of the hallmarks of our understanding of the Great War has been that despite our best efforts it remains stubbornly that of literate Europeans. Scholars have made heroic efforts to incorporate the experience and memory of colonial peoples caught up in what was and has largely remained a 'Great European War'. While unavoidably drawing upon official and unofficial records created mainly by British officers this book seeks to encompass the words and experiences of Indian officers and other ranks, and includes Indian soldiers' voices. (Gurkha sources, however, 'are so rare as to be almost non-existent').[1] Though I have sought to obtain and express an 'Indian' perspective on the experience of Gallipoli, this book remains the product of an Australian historian and is partly based upon Australasian sources that other nations' historians may not have used. As a result it offers fresh insights into the relationship between Indian troops and the Anzacs whom they fought alongside in 1915.

It is incontrovertible that the Indian part in the Gallipoli campaign has been neglected. Peter Liddle's *Men of Gallipoli* (1976) made fewer than a dozen mentions of Indians, and they largely references to British officers such as Major Cecil Allanson or Second Lieutenant Reginald Savory. The limitations of language constrain historians just as they at first prevented Anzac troops from conversing freely with Indians on Gallipoli. This book tries to broaden the cast of notable Indian army individuals, including Arthur Fergusson, Heber Alexander, Subedar Gambirsing Pun, Naik Jan

---

1   Gould, *Imperial Warriors*, p. 4. For an exception see p. 240.

Mahomed, Lance-Naik Karam Singh, and many others with less prominent parts. Other, even recent books, though making impressive contributions to the understanding of the campaign as a whole (such as Tim Travers's *Gallipoli* or Robin Prior's *Gallipoli: the End of the Myth*) mention Indian units in passing, refer to them vaguely or get their names wrong (errors easy to make given the Indian army's complex lineage). Robin Prior, offering the most recent authoritative account, refers to the 'Indian Brigade' just seven times, and only to the 14th Sikhs and 1/6th Gurkhas – whom, emulating the Dardanelles Commission, he miscalls 'Ghurkas' – and in a caption misidentifies Hindu bearers as 'Sikhs'.

Rana Chhina, the only other scholar who has written about Indians on Gallipoli in any detail at all, remarked at the end of his excellent survey essay 'Their mercenary calling' in 2013 that the incidents he mentioned, describing incidents in the Indian experience of Gallipoli 'remind us that behind the dry statistics and official reports there lies another story that can perhaps now never be told'.[2] He referred to the experience of Indian other ranks, who appear in the mass or in the background in documents written by and photographs taken by their British officers. This book attempts to tell that story, trying to recover the experiences, attitudes and even the words of Indian other ranks as far as that is possible.

Until recently the history of the Indian Army in the Great War remained largely in the hands of British authors who tended to write largely (as the pioneering historians De Witt Ellinwood and S.D. Pradhan put it in 1974) 'in terms of purely military activity and military glory, usually with a strong British bias'.[3] As the work of a military social historian, while unashamedly dealing with military operations, this book also attempts to examine sepoys' and officers' experiences and to place them in the broader contexts of the Indian Army's history and that of the Gallipoli campaign. In writing military history honestly it will, I hope, avoid any suggestion of 'military glory'. There is, however, much more work to be done in re-interpreting the Indian contribution to the campaign, with the quantity of primary sources justifying further books on the Indian part in the Helles and August battles.

The nations of the sub-continent appear to have taken little interest in the history of the army of un-partitioned India. Gallipoli figures but briefly in several regimental histories published after 1947, and superficially in just a handful of secondary sources, a deficiency partially but handsomely rectified in 2013 with the appearance of Rana Chhina's essay, the first account of the Indian contribution to the campaign based on archival sources.

This book has been long in gestation but short in execution. Having an interest in India and its army, when I commenced work at the Australian War Memorial in 1980 I published an article in *Sabretache, the Journal of the Military Historical Society of Australia*, on the relationship between the Indian mountain gunners and Australians

---

2   Chhina, 'Their mercenary calling', p. 253.
3   Ellinwood & Pradhan, *India and World War I*, p. 5.

at Anzac, based almost entirely upon Arthur Fergusson's memoir.[4] Over the following thirty years I identified, collected (and often misplaced) further material relating to Indians on Gallipoli, in collections in Australia, Britain, New Zealand, India, and in fieldwork in Turkey. Though I occasionally tried out the idea on publishers, on the Indian High Commission in Canberra and on successive South Asia desk officers in the Australian Department of Foreign Affairs and Trade, I did not actually write a word. (To paraphrase Dr Johnson, none but a blockhead writes without a contract.) The approach of the present centenary of the Great War, the positive response of Duncan Rogers of Helion and his 'War and Military Culture in South Asia 1757-1947' editorial board, the actual help of the Australian Department of Defence and the encouragement of senior colleagues of my new institution, the University of New South Wales, Canberra, made the idea of a book on Indians on Gallipoli a reality. After being a remote prospect for so long, it was commissioned in March 2013 and researched and written in 2013-14, involving further research in Australia and trips to India, Britain, Nepal, New Zealand and Turkey. The Acknowledgments detail the many debts I have incurred in the course of the past eighteen months. Fittingly, the manuscript was completed while on Gallipoli.

Peter Stanley
The Gallipoli Houses,
Koçadere,
Turkey
31 August 2014

---

4   Stanley, '"An Entente ... most remarkable": Indians at Anzac', *Sabretache*, 1981.

1

'To slay the enemy was the Master's order': the Indian Army in 1914

The story this book tells mostly takes place on the scrubby hillsides of a peninsula in Turkey but it begins far from Gallipoli, on the rugged hillsides of Nepal and the plains of northern India, especially the Punjab. British adventurers, officials, soldiers and administrators created an empire – the British 'Sircar', as Indians called it – and in doing so forged unique relationships with two very different groups of its inhabitants: the people mainly of central Nepal who came to be called Gurkhas and the people of the Punjab who called themselves Sikhs.

'Martial races': British India's soldiers

At the turn of the eighteenth century, as the East India Company extended its power from Calcutta up the Ganges valley, defeating or co-opting Bengal's native princes, its governors encountered the vigorous kingdom of Nepal. Over the previous half-century the Gorkha dynasty had become paramount among the small, warring principalities of the vale of Kathmandu, suppressing and incorporating the surrounding minor chiefs. After an inconclusive encounter in the mid-eighteenth century, in 1814 the Gorkha state and the Sircar of the Governor-General Lord Hastings at last confronted each other in the foothills of the Himalayas. The sepoys of the Company Bahadur battled a native power that challenged its superior firepower and discipline in courage and fighting prowess in its own mountainous country. The Sircar narrowly defeated the Nepalese, but even before the war's end the Company had recruited troops it called Goorkhas.

Thirty years later the Company's inexorable advance to the north-west brought it into conflict with the Sikh kingdom. In the turbulent aftermath of the death of the great Sikh ruler Runjeet Singh, the Company twice clashed with the *Khalsa*, the Sikh army of the faithful. In two short but hard-fought wars, in 1845-46 and 1848-49, the two battled on the plains of the Punjab, the Khalsa the equal of the Company's mainly sepoy army, again narrowly defeated. Immediately after the Sikh defeat British officers, admiring their erstwhile enemy's courage, formed regiments of Sikhs.

25

Less than a decade later the Sikh and Gurkha regiments' loyalty enabled the British to withstand the shock of the mutiny of the Bengal Army and then to suppress the most significant rebellion they ever faced. Over the half-century following the great mutiny-rebellion of 1857 (which resulted in the re-building of the Indian armies in ways specifically intended to deter a recurrence) two related developments occurred. The British increasingly recruited from what they thought of as India's 'martial races'; and they drew them increasingly from British India's north-west. After 1857, the number of battalions drawn from the Punjab and the north-west grew from 28 in 1862 to 57 in 1914, with corresponding declines in recruits from Madras and Bombay. Gurkha troops saw an even greater increase, rising from five battalions in 1862 to twenty in 1914. By 1904 nearly two-thirds of the Indian Army came from the Punjab (especially Sikhs and what the army called Musalmans – Muslims), Nepal or the frontier: the homes of the Indian troops who were to serve on Gallipoli.[1]

India's diversity became one of the British Sircar's safeguards. Rather than recruit from a few ethnic groups (as the Bengal Army had before 1857) the army balanced ethnic and religious groups within and between units, in the belief that Musalmans, Hindus and various ethnic sub-groups would not make common cause. Under the sway of the 'martial race' theory formalised from the mid-1880s it had created units of two or more 'classes' (or ethnic or religious groups) as well as entire regiments of one group, the so-called 'class regiments'. While the Punjabi battalions sent to Gallipoli were organised on the 'class company' principle, all of the infantry which remained on Gallipoli belonged to the all-Sikh 14th Sikhs or the four Gurkha battalions. The mountain artillery batteries also included both Sikhs and Punjabi Musalmans, the mule corps included many Hindustani Musalmans, while Hindus from South India and even Bengalis served in the field ambulance, men rarely found in combatant units.

The chief theorist, or at least populariser, of martial race, George MacMunn (a long-serving Royal Artilleryman in India who in 1915 was to become responsible for supplies in the Dardanelles Army), described the basis of the idea succinctly in his *The Armies of India* in 1911:

> It is one of the essential differences between the East and the West that, that in the East, with exceptions, only certain clans and classes can bear arms; others have not the physical courage necessary for warfare.[2]

A great deal of pseudo-scientific mumbo-jumbo purported to validate this presumption. General O'Moore Creagh, for example, (Commander-in-Chief in India, 1909-14) claimed that hilly, cooler climates produced better soldiers than hot, flat ones – perhaps not recognising that this 'explained' the Gurkhas' quality – but not the

---

1   Omissi, *The Sepoy and the Raj*, pp. 11, 19.
2   MacMunn, *The Armies of India*, p. 129.

Sikhs'.[3] Perhaps the single most notable reservation necessary to emphasise is that the British officers who subscribed to or articulated the martial race theory qualified it by accepting that these races only exhibited the admirable qualities when led by British officer: as we will see a belief that was to influence the experience and use of Indian troops on Gallipoli. Officers who became a part of the Indian Gallipoli story had a hand in the documentation of India (and its army's) ethnography. Arthur Bingley, the author of the authoritative handbook, *Sikhs*, published in 1910, became responsible for the administrative command of Indian troops in Egypt and on Gallipoli in 1915.

It was not only British officers who embraced this theory. The first synoptic *Handbook to the Fighting Races of India* was written by P.D. Bonarjee, a clerk in the Military Department, of a group firmly excluded from the martial pantheon. Bonarjee, passing on judgments made by British officers of Gurkha battalions, praised the 'unemotional and unsentimental Gurkha' as 'much like the English', who like them was 'cool when in battle'.[4] The Jat Sikhs of the 14th Sikhs he described as 'an exceptionally fine type of Asiatic … the beau ideal of an Oriental soldier'.[5] Arthur Bingley thought that his Sikhs were the 'bravest and steadiest of soldiers … more faithful, more trustworthy, and far less liable to panic'.[6] But every ethnic group had its partisans, invariably officers who had commanded them. Second Lieutenant Herbert Winn thought that his 'Punjabis' (by which he meant Punjabi Musalmans, known in the army as 'PMs'), were 'fine men mostly six feet tall'. Like all Indian Army officers he began his service with a spell attached to a British regiment, but he wanted to soldier with the class he considered to be the finest in the army.[7] As a result the 'Indian' Army was not actually representative of India. It increasingly constituted a limited range of supposedly 'martial' groups.

A series of 'handbooks' defined the ethnographic characteristics of the army's various 'classes', written by officers with long experience and deep knowledge and affection for 'their' men. Officers' memoirs and the formal *Handbooks* portrayed Gurkhas as tough, loyal and resilient, but deprecated their intelligence; so much so that Gurkhas' alleged stolidity, not to say stupidity, became a standing joke. Their admirers intended this simple-mindedness as a compliment: throwing into relief their positive qualities as uncomplicated warriors. The ethnic characteristics ascribed to Gurkhas were to an extent manufactured (indeed, 'Gurkha' was no indigenous name, but was borrowed to describe the East India Company's Nepalese mercenaries). The various Gurkha regiments were recruited from men of particular tribes. Again, taking those that served on Gallipoli, the 4th, 5th and 6th were recruited from central western Nepal (comprising Magars and Gurungs), while the 10th ('the Cinderella', its

---

3   Creagh, *Indian Studies*, p. 233.
4   Bonarjee, *A Handbook to the Fighting Races of India*, p. 103.
5   Ibid., pp. 85-86.
6   Bingley, *Sikhs*, p. 126.
7   Letter, 21 December 1914, Herbert Winn, 97/18/1, 6508, IWM.

historian wrote) was drawn from the east (Rais and Limbus), though some men were merely *recruited* as Magars or Gurungs, an example of the bogus ethnography inspired by the celebrated *Handbooks*.[8]

While the martial race theory professed to define with ethnographic precision the characteristics of a given group, in fact it acted as a means for British officers to understand, explain and even shape their attributes and actions, in and out of battle; at the time and retrospectively. 'To predict a man's behaviour', the historian David Omissi wrote, 'it was necessary to know only the collective attributes of the group to which he belonged'.[9] For historians, this use of the theory – which pervades the military history of British India – represents a challenge. On the one hand regimental histories appear to demonstrate that Sikhs and Gurkhas exhibited the characteristics outlined in the various *Handbooks of the Indian Army*. On the other hand, they were written by officers who believed not only in the validity of the theory but also in their men's virtues. As a result, its history as traditionally told appears to confirm the theory. As this book seeks to show, the reality appears to be that the Sikh, Gurkha and Punjabi Musalman units that served on Gallipoli generally performed exceedingly well not because of their racial composition, but because they were well trained and led professional units, and when they did not perform well (as will be shown) there are military rather than racial explanations for their shortcomings.

Writing a century on from the great 'durbar' at Delhi in 1911 confronts the modern author with a dilemma. On the one hand, the reality of the old, pre-war Indian Army seems poignantly real. The writings of its admirers, its British officers above all, evoke the qualities of its constituent races and religious, regional and ethnic groups that composed it. No officer who did not fall in love with his men's qualities persisted, and almost every officer who served wrote lovingly of his men, both as individuals or (more often) as representative 'types' of the old Indian Army. The historian runs the risk of simply imbibing and repeating these encomiums. In any case, thirty odd years of post-colonial scholarship has exposed the pernicious workings of 'Orientalism' in the mentality of the empire's rulers, and it is no longer possible to simply accept and reproduce officers' appreciations of India's 'martial races'. It is clear that much of what passed as straightforward ethnography was in fact wishful thinking; but no less powerful for that.

'Fine but self-centered battalions': Kitchener's reforms

The India the army either protected or oppressed (depending on perspective) was changing. For nearly thirty years, since the formation (by a British civil servant) of the Indian National Congress, the Raj had faced Indian calls for a measure of self-rule. While its constitutional wing remained moderate and respectful for the time being,

---

8 Mullaly, *Bugle and Kukri*, p. 49.
9 Omissi, *The Sepoy and the Raj*, p. 31.

An infantry battalion of the Indian Army: the 2/10th Gurkha Rifles at Takdah in 1914. (Gurkha Museum, Winchester)

radical and revolutionary elements threatened the Sircar's equilibrium: 1912 saw the attempted assassination in Delhi of the Viceroy, Lord Hardinge (Viceroy 1910-16). Soldiers looked askance on these changes: even one of the most innovative British Gurkha officers wrote that 'certain educated Indians' in Bombay and Calcutta had 'humbugged our people at home' in fostering the 'cloven hoof' of nationalism.[10]

Seeking to align the army to the realities of these changes and the broader strategic reality the empire faced had brought reform to the Indian Army in the decade before the war. Horatio Herbert Kitchener, victor of Omdurman and in South Africa, became Commander-in-Chief in India in 1902, a position he held for seven crucial years. He drove through a reorganisation, creating a structure to form a field army (intended to meet a possible Russian advance through Afghanistan) as well forestalling or suppressing rebellion. He also changed command and logistic arrangements, in the process falling out with Lord Curzon (Viceroy 1899-1905) over the army's governance. After a decade of change (in which virtually every infantry battalion was allotted a new number and title and many reforms introduced) the army seemed ready to support the empire in war, though (with the entente with imperial Russia) the ostensible enemy seemed to have evaporated. Lord Hardinge later claimed that British India had been 'absolutely ready for war', though he also thought that General Sir O'Moore Creagh (Commander-in-Chief 1909-14) had 'failed as an administrator'.[11] Creagh, an easy-going Irishmen, retired in April 1914 having failed to consolidate Kitchener's changes. His successor, General Sir Beauchamp Duff, who

10   Maxwell, *Villiers-Stuart on the Frontier*, p. 35.
11   Hardinge, *My Indian Years 1910-1916*, pp. 103; 16.

had been Kitchener's Adjutant-General and protégé, India hands dismissed as merely 'an office clerk'.[12] That its two commanders-in-chief immediately before the war so much lacked dynamism it is surprising that the army performed as well as it did in mobilising to meet its greatest crisis yet.

Though organised by Lord Kitchener into nominal divisions in the decade before the Great War, the Indian Army, 200,000-strong in 1914, essentially comprised, as an officer conceded, a collection of 'fine but self-centered battalions'.[13] The Indian Army's organisation was full of the 'most terrible defects', as Charles Bruce wrote censoriously.[14] The system known mysteriously as 'half-mounting' obliged sepoys to pay for their uniforms, boots and food, meaning that men who wore their boots out in becoming efficient were, in effect, fined for it. Many soldiers wore their own clothing off duty (and around their lines), and cantonment hospitals were, even senior officers conceded, scandalously bad, O'Moore Creagh describing them as 'a disgrace to civilization'.[15] The sepoys' quarters – huts built by soldiers themselves (often reluctantly and badly) stood in 'lines', of grass-roofed mud huts, often squalid and insanitary. One of O'Moore Creagh's few initiatives as Commander-in-Chief was to advocate the construction of 'pucca' – that is, genuine brick – barrack buildings, a program interrupted by the war's outbreak.

The Indians' British officers often had deep family roots in British India. The full names of George Swinley, killed with the 14th Sikhs at Helles, was George Dighton Probyn Swinley – all surnames famous in the Indian Army – and they were also the family names of Leila, the wife of Arthur Tillard of the 4th Gurkhas. The father of Captain Henry Molloy, who served with the 5th Gurkhas on Gallipoli, had raised the regiment in 1886. Harold Wilmer, who was to die with the 14th Sikhs at Helles, was the son and grandson of Indian Army officers. Two Battye brothers served on Gallipoli – Rothney with 108th Field Ambulance for the entire campaign and Hedley, killed with the 5th Gurkhas in the disastrous attack on Gully Spur in its first days on the peninsula. (Hedley Battye's father and uncles had also died in battle, and with the 5th Gurkhas, a reminder of the costs that an imperial military career imposed on families across generations.) In the army's 'native' ranks it is notable in rolls of men killed how many came from the same villages. Many sepoys followed fathers or uncles into their regiments, as Gurkha photograph albums show.[16] The most telling illustration of the Indian Army's family links was William Birdwood, who commanded the corps in which most Indians on Gallipoli were to serve. He was one of 25 nephews in uniform of Sir George Birdwood, the Anglo-Indian naturalist, named in a list published in

---

12 Menezes, *Fidelity and Honour*, p. 243.
13 'Chameleon', 'Regimental Spirit in the Indian Army', *Journal of the United Services Institution of India*, 1932, p. 353.
14 Bruce, *Himalayan Wanderer*, p. 53.
15 Creagh, *Indian Studies*, p. 265.
16 Mercer, 'Shadows from the past history of Gurkhas', *The Kukri*, 1956, p. 52.

the *Pioneer*. By the time the list appeared in October 1915 no fewer than four of the Birdwoods had been killed and three wounded; one of each on Gallipoli.[17]

Indian mountain artillery officers differed from this, in that they were commissioned into the Royal Artillery (that is, were of the British Army and, indeed, nominally and incongruously of the Royal Garrison Artillery), and were attached to the Indian Army while posted to its mountain batteries. But service in mountain batteries required special skills, both in operating the guns and in commanding their units, so the mountain artillery tended to retain officers for years. A battery commander, usually a major, was often 'a man of considerable experience', as Arthur Fergusson's account of his Gallipoli service suggests.[18]

Indian units tended to be insular – the first officer from the 6th Gurkhas went to the Staff College at Camberley (revived in the 1870s and open to ambitious Indian Army officers for over twenty years) only in 1899. Officers left their regiments for extra-regimental and staff appointments, but for many the attraction of regimental soldiering, and the pleasures of its society, field sports and the life of their men, prevailed. Even the iconoclastic William Villiers-Stuart thought that 'the very best type' of British Indian Army officer was 'not vastly clever', but 'very sound'.[19] A damning report on promotion examinations in the last issue of the *Journal of the United Service Institution of India* before the outbreak of war provided evidence of a generally surprisingly low level of professional interest or attainment. Of 61 majors considered for 'Tactical Fitness for Command' only 32 passed, and only seven of the successful candidates reached 75%, a result described as with staggering understatement as 'a somewhat low standard'.[20] Not that Indian Army officers were untalented. To command a polyglot force they often excelled in languages – Harold Wilmer spoke Hindi, Pushtu, Punjabi and Baluchi (all at the higher levels), as well as French, Italian and (after service in Somaliland) Swahili.

Though unintellectual, Indian regiments' senior regimental officers who served on Gallipoli had long practical experience of war. Charles Bruce of the 6th Gurkhas had served in Burma in 1889, Hazara 1891, Waziristan 1894-95 and the Tirah 1897-98. Philip Palin of the 14th Sikhs had also served in Burma, Hazara and Tochi, 1897-98. Arthur Tillard of the 3rd and 4th Gurkhas had served in the Lushai campaign on the north-east frontier in 1892-93, in the Tirah, Waziristan and in the 1903-04 expedition to Tibet. Indian units trained regularly and realistically, and even when moving stations were effectively on active service: this was a peacetime army never truly at peace.

17   *Pioneer*, 22 October 1915, p. 8.
18   MacFetridge & Warren, (eds), *Tales of the Mountain Gunners*, p. 6.
19   Maxwell, *Villiers-Stuart on the Frontier*, p. 26.
20   'Summary of the more important general remarks', *Journal of the United Service Institution of India*, 1914, pp. 437-38.

Nor were regiments at peace internally. British officers could not assume that they would be obeyed automatically. They had to earn their men's respect and often faced either silent disdain or outright insubordination. Not surprisingly many developed what one called a 'personality leadership cult', exemplified by Charles Bruce's idiosyncratic command of the 1/6th Gurkhas.[21] Just as the army balanced ethnic and religious groups, so it paid due deference to its men's religious sensibilities within units. Their men's religious festivals became part of the military year. Gurkha battalions, for example, observed Hindu festivals, such as Dusserah, when the battalion paraded with its British officers, who ate with their men and their families and witnessed festivities. If numbers allowed, Musalman units included *maulvis* (priests) and in any case commanding officers maintained a watch on their men's religious feelings and respected the fasting demanded over Ramazan, and throughout the year, as far as possible, animals were slaughtered according to the rules of the army's respective faiths. Each Sikh battalion supported its own *Granthi* and *gurudwara* and travelled with a revered copy of the *Granth Sahib*, and British officers also respectfully witnessed their men's religious ceremonies. Students of Sikhism came to argue that Sikh regiments' sponsorship of Sikh formalities within the army (making the beard compulsory and regulating turbans and pagris, for example) ensured the survival and propagation of the faith. It was, so George MacMunn thought, 'British officers of the Sikh regiments ... who kept the sacred fire alive'.[22] This respect for religious observance was to affect the composition of the Indian force committed to the Gallipoli campaign.

The Indian Army's British officers held commissions identical to their counterparts in the British Army, in which, indeed, they had all spent a year before being posted to the Indian Army. All were expected to become proficient in the vernacular language (or languages) of their men – in the case of the Sikhs Punjabi, for Musalmans Urdu and in the Gurkhas a lingua franca of Nepalese dialects known as Gurkhali. Recruiting and training was highly de-centralised, and regimental recruiting parties periodically toured its defined area, seeking volunteers from specific ethnic and religious groups and often from particular villages and districts with which the regiment had developed a bond over the previous sixty-odd years. It was a system intended to create strong identities of loyalty, but ill-suited to sustain units suffering casualties on the scale of a world war.

Conventional wisdom in the Indian Army held that Indian units could not operate without British officers, and that Indian other ranks were devoted to them. In practice, as David Omissi found in his scrutiny of letters written by Indians wounded on the Western Front, sepoys rarely mentioned their British officers in their letters, an absence we might suspect applied also to Gallipoli. He concluded that 'the bond

---

21   Maxwell, *Villiers-Stuart on the Frontier*, p. 26.
22   MacMunn, 'The Story of the Sikhs and the Recent Troubles', unidentified article, pp. 576-77, MacMunn Papers, Folder 7, Special Collections, ADFA.

between British officers and Indian other ranks was not as intense as the imperialists liked to believe', but accepted that the relationship worked.[23] On the other hand their men gave officers affectionate nicknames – Charles Bruce was '*Bhalu*' (as readers of Kipling know, 'bear'), while Arthur Fergusson of the mountain artillery became 'Percussion Sahib'. There is also the example of Heber Alexander, who not only included in his memoir *On Two Fronts* a photograph of his chief clerk, Mangat Rai, but dedicated the book to him: 'D.M.R. for 'invaluable help in the production of this book'. A century on, in the absence of substantive evidence from the Indian side, it is hard to judge. But British officers tended to be anything but stand-offish. They became involved in their men's religious and cultural festivals and spent time with them on and off duty. This, an officer later reflected 'made them prone to too much interference in the duties of the [Indian] junior leaders', and speculated that 'this state of affairs may have been partly responsible for the heavy losses of British leaders later on'.[24] As we will see, the experience of Gallipoli sheds light on that relationship.

'Either a Gurkha or a Sikh': the Indian Army's élite infantry

Despite the great range of ethnic groups in the Indian Army's infantry – including Brahmans, Punjabi Musalmans, Rajputs, Mahrattas, Baluchis, Dogras, Jats or Garwhalis – the only two kinds of battalions to remain on Gallipoli comprised Gurkhas and Sikhs. Both were prominent in the popular image of the Indian Army – figures of both appear on Calcutta's Victoria Memorial (inaugurated in 1906 and opened in 1921) – its only military sculptures. 'To the English journalist', Heber Alexander complained, 'every Indian soldier is apparently either a Gurkha or a Sikh'.[25] In the case of the Indian infantry committed to Gallipoli this generalisation turned out to be true. (It became true because, as we will find, the Punjabis were withdrawn; perhaps unjustly.)

The Ferozepore Sikhs had been one of the first Sikh regiments formed in 1846 in the wake of the defeat of the independent Sikh state and then loyally fought for the British in the great sepoy mutiny-rebellion. In Kitchener's reorganisation it had been re-titled the 14th, becoming in 1910 King George's Own Ferozepore Sikhs. It recruited from villages in the southern Punjab district of Ferozepore, almost all volunteers, the sons of substantial farmers working plots irrigated by the newly established canal colonies, sharing in the Punjab's prosperity, some funded by the remittances of serving and ex-soldiers. The 14th Sikhs had taken part in some of the Indian Army's most evocative campaigns, the Black Mountain expedition of 1888, in Waziristan and Chitral in the mid-1890s and in Tochi in 1897. Soon after it had sent a detachment to East Africa and then served in the suppression of the 'Boxer' rebellion in

23 Omissi, *The Sepoy and the Raj*, p. 106.
24 Mullaly, *Bugle and Kukri*, p. 45.
25 Alexander, *On Two Fronts*, p. 47.

China in 1900-02. In the decade before the war it served on the frontier, at Multan, Ferozepore, Quetta, Loralai and, by 1914, Peshawur. Sikhs quickly adopted hockey after its introduction into the Indian Army in the early years of the twentieth century, the 14th Sikhs hotly contesting the Punjab Native Army Hockey Tournament with its rival the 15th. Under Lieutenant-Colonel Philip Palin, who took command in 1912, the regiment demonstrated a high standard of training, discipline and morale, 'nearly as perfect as is humanly possible', the regimental history later claimed.[26]

Or so it seemed: but the army's Sikhs had been susceptible to the unease that pervaded the Punjab in the decade before the war. In 1906-07 political unrest following changes to the management of the irrigation colonies, while Sikh political movements, notably the *Ghadr* movement, spread among ambitious Sikh migrants to the American Pacific coast and back to the Punjab. Both affected the army and its numerous Sikhs. In 1906 a meeting in Ferozepore called to protest against changes to the alienation of irrigated land involved 300 *serving* soldiers, and many returning migrants (some would-be migrants rejected by Canada) were ex-soldiers. In 1907 Sikh soldiers were reported to have attended a 'seditious meeting' in Multan – the 14th Sikhs' depot.[27] By 1914 senior army officers thought that 'a good many regiments were, we may say, tainted' by this unease.[28] Suspicion fell on all-Sikh 'class regiments', including the 14th Sikhs, which appears to have been one of the group of battalions 'it was necessary to break up and distribute' under Kitchener.[29] In 1913 the regiment had come under the notice of Army Headquarters for the wrong reasons when members of it engaged in an 'affray' with locals civilians.[30] Despite this volatility, the 14th Sikhs was militarily one of the army's most efficient units, among the first battalions to be mobilised in 1914, to its surprise – it expected to be left on the sensitive and unpredictable frontier.

Gurkha battalions exhibited a fierce, almost tribal, individuality, with each regiment having its own dress distinctions and traditions, competing with the others – innovations in kit or methods, rather than being shared were kept secret. The individuality extended from arcane matters of titles to improvements in equipment. The 2/10th Gurkhas, for example, insisted on using the archaic title 'Goorkha' until Lieutenant-Colonel Francis Sutton took over in 1914 and ordered that it be called the 'Gurkha Rifles' like the rest, while the innovations in machine-gun tactics developed by the 1/5th before 1914 remained within the battalion. Gurkhas mixed

---

26 Talbot, *The 14th King George's Own Sikhs*, p. 60.
27 Mazumder, *The Indian Army and the Making of Punjab*, pp. 206; 209; 232.
28 Proceedings of the Army in India Committee, 1912, Vol. II, Minutes of Evidence, p. 14.
29 MacMunn, 'The Story of the Sikhs and the Recent Troubles', unidentified article, p. 576, MacMunn Papers, Folder 7, Special Collections, ADFA.
30 'Serious affray between detachment 14th Sikhs at Toisar, and local people on 15 January, Army Proceedings, February 1915, Items 2156-86, NAI. Sadly, the papers were labeled 'confidential' and were possibly not incorporated in the Army Proceedings transferred to the National Archives.

unselfconsciously with British troops (their privates were 'Riflemen', not 'Sepoys') but as foreign mercenaries maintained their own insular communities in the Indian cantonments in which they lived. Many Gurkha soldiers were married, sending to Nepal for women in arranged marriages, women who, limited by language and their status as chattels, spoke to no one outside the battalion's 'lines'. Their male children, known as 'line boys' might be recruited into the regiment, though officers suspected (illogically and unfairly, but in accordance with the tenets of the martial race theory) that away growing up away from Nepal's hills diminished their 'fighting spirit': many became buglers.

Regarded (certainly self-regarded) as an élite (they were numbered separately to all the other 130-odd Indian battalions), the ten Gurkha regiments, organised in twenty battalions, revelled in their differences, competing with each other while sure of their superiority in the army generally. Sport, often competitive between units, formed a strong part of the army's ethos. The Gurkhas promoted a vigorous tradition of 'khud running' – fell-racing in the steep slopes and thin air of their hill cantonments. The 6th Gurkhas' champion from 1909 was a 1908 recruit named Tulbir Gurung, who won the Gurkha Brigade Khud Race for five years in a row, a unequalled record for successive wins. A silver statuette, the 'Little Man', presented to the winning battalion adorned the 6th's officers' mess at Abbottabad for years, surrendered only in 1914.

Command in the Gurkhas fostered 'characters', such as Major Charles Bruce (who had introduced khud running) took over the 6th Gurkhas in 1913, his own regiment, the 5th, farewelling him without regret because '"characters" are fine, but … in the battalion, except on active service, he was a damnable nuisance'.[31] Bruce, a noted mountaineer and Himalayan hunter, exemplified the idiosyncratic but effective command style the Indian Army's regimental system encouraged. (Bruce's other claim to fame was that he was credited with introducing the 'shorts, khaki, pairs' in which by 1914 Gurkhas fought.[32])

The 5th Gurkhas' depot had been at Abbottabad for a decade by the war's outbreak. 'During all that time', the regimental history admitted, 'there happened nothing of outstanding importance'.[33] But through the decade cumulative changes created the look of the Gurkhas who served on Gallipoli – the introduction of machine-guns (two Maxims per battalion), the short magazine Lee-Enfield rifles, rucksacks, aluminium water bottles, broad-brimmed hats and waterproof capes. Though the battalion saw no active service, it continued the Gurkhas' tradition of frequent and hard training, both in cantonment and on manoeuvres.

---

31 Ibid., p. 128. It was whispered over late-night brandy-panis in cantonment messes that Bruce had 'screwed every Gurkha wife in the regiment' (Chenevix-Trench, *The Indian Army and the King's Enemies*, p. 25). Whether this was or could be literally true, it reflected the insularity of the regiment in which the possibility could be contemplated and, indeed, condoned.
32 Woodyatt, *Under Ten Viceroys*, p. 164.
33 Regimental Committee, *History of the Royal Gurkha Rifles*, p. 165.

1/6th Gurkhas' khud racing team, 1913. (Gurkha Museum, Winchester)

Several of the regiments whose Gallipoli service forms the core of this book already commanded a respect verging on adulation, even among those who knew the Indian Army well. Kitchener had been 'very much attracted' by the 1/5th Gurkhas and favoured it often in inspections and reviews.[34] Ian Hamilton, who was to command the Dardanelles invasion force, had served as a subaltern on the trans-Indus frontier with the Gordon Highlanders beside the Hazara (later the 5th) Gurkha Battalion. Admiring their soldierly qualities. Hamilton became one of the Gurkhas' great advocates, and as we will see it was through his intercession that almost an entire brigade of Gurkhas fought in the Dardanelles. It must be said that even Hamilton thought of Gurkhas as unsophisticated hill-warriors, doubting that could they use modern weapons. He declared in the 5th Gurkhas mess that 'the Indian and Gurkha soldier can never be taught to use the backsight on his rifle as he will never be able to learn the numeric figures': this to officers who trained their men to use telephones, machine-guns and silent hand signals.[35]

34 Maxwell, *Villiers-Stuart on the Frontier*, pp. 181-82.
35 Maxwell, *Villiers-Stuart on the Frontier*, p. 155.

Ceremonies in which recruits swore oaths under their regiments' colours confirmed the Gurkhas' loyalty to their units. (Gurkha Museum, Pokhara)

'Izzat' and 'rizzat': honour and money

Though fitted for war, as the Indian Army's files testify it was also a supremely bureaucratic army, in which nothing occurred without the sanction of up to half-a-dozen levels of authority. The *Military Account Code* ran to over 680 heavily annotated and amended pages, governing every possible financial eventuality. In 1913-14, for example, the 'Payment of fees to tea-tasters employed by the Supply and Transport Corps' needed eight dockets of documents occupied offices in Burma, Secunderabad and Lucknow, and at least three functionaries in Army Headquarters, over nine months, all reported to the India Office, in printed proceedings. Procuring nine handcarts to clear ordure at Bangalore, costing 11 rupees per cart, occupied ten dockets over fifteen months, and in the end the question of from whose account the 100 rupees should come remained unresolved. To be fair, sometimes the Army Proceedings documented cases that decided precedents (e.g. 'whether the two wives of a deceased Indian soldier should have equal shares of the family pension' – the answer; they should). But most of the army's business entailed paperwork that moved between desks because centralised authority stymied initiative. So by 1915 a decision on 'corrections to the *Manual of Physical Training for the Indian Army* (price 4 annas) had consumed 31 dockets over nearly three years.[36] The Indian government, a veteran explained, was 'unreasonable and devastatingly inefficient', passing through cycles of morbid stagnation and febrile reform. When in a burst of energy he cleaned out forty years of records from his orderly room in six weeks he disposed of 8,000 pounds of 'useless old rubbish' – that is, precious regimental files.[37]

36 All cases from Army Proceedings, January 1915, NAI.
37 Maxwell, *Villiers-Stuart on the Frontier*, pp. 124; 142-43.

For Indian troops on Gallipoli, this bureaucratic tendency would have several consequences. It meant that the doings of a small force operating in a remote part of the Ottoman empire far from India would be documented in surprising detail. Though not all the relevant files survived the dismemberment and distribution of the Indian Army's records in 1947, or indeed the files' transfer to and movement within the National Archives of India, the Army Headquarters records supplement the often patchy unit war diaries. Second, it meant that decisions about the troops' conditions of service would be debated between London and headquarters in Simla, Cairo and the Dardanelles throughout the campaign, impeding decisions on, for example, matters of the troops' conditions of service, questions of vital interest to every sepoy relevant even as they fought the Ottoman Turks.

Though matters of a few rupees a month, the conditions of service mattered to sepoys; all the more because of the small amounts involved. The Indian Army's champions emphasised its tradition, longevity and the imperative of the sepoys' 'izzat', or sense of honour (one of the army's finest histories was entitled *A Matter of Honour*). But as important (in the view of those concerned with the army's recruitment) was 'rizzat', meaning the material conditions of service, and rizzat often trumped izzat for those contemplating enlistment.[38] Since 1913 sepoys basically received 13 rupees a month, increasing slightly with service, good conduct, proficiency pay and batta (or bonuses paid on active service), with havildars receiving up to 30 rupees and Indian officers a hundred. At the same time, sepoys paid for their food, uniforms and footwear, often costing them more than half of their pay. Still, military pay was assured (guaranteed by the Sircar) and long service or wounds were compensated by pensions, modest but certain. One of the great benefits of military service was the certainty of a pension, or the possibility of securing a grant of land, and the 'canal colonies' of the Punjab boomed in the forty years before the Great War as military pensioners settled the irrigated plains.

However blimpish topee-wearing, red-tabbed and mustachio'd British Indian officers may today appear, the most sensitive realised that India – and therefore its army – faced uncertain and potentially profound change. Colonel Arthur Bingley, author of the army's handbook on Sikhs who in 1914 was to take charge of the administration of Indian force in Egypt and later Gallipoli, acknowledged under the questioning of the Committee on the Army in India two years before 'the agitators" desires – 'to have a greater voice in the management of their own affairs … a national spirit is being evolved', he said.[39] Mohammedans felt perturbed over the turbulence in Turkey's revolution against the Sultan and looked to 'Pan-Islamic' movements; Sikhs had fallen under 'the teachings of political agitators'; radical and reformist Hindus decried cow-killing (British soldiers each ate a pound of beef daily) and called for religious renewal, and the exclusion of ambitious Indian (mainly Punjabi) would-be

---

38 O'Dwyer, 'India's Man-power in the War', *Army Quarterly*, Vol. 2, No. 2, July 1921, p. 259.
39 Proceedings of the Army in India Committee, 1912, Vol. II, Minutes of Evidence, p. 14.

emigrants from South Africa, Canada and Australia caused 'much ill-feeling', while the Indian National Congress sought a degree of self-determination, albeit respectfully and moderately; for now. Individually none were critical; collectively all were worrisome.

For an empire that as recently as December 1911 had celebrated the declaration of King George V as emperor of India, in a spectacular durbar (at which the monarch proclaimed Delhi as the new imperial capital, and made Indian soldiers eligible for the Victoria Cross), the confidential discussions of British India's rulers were full of foreboding. Witness after witness before the Army in India Committee just six months later spoke of 'agitators', 'sedition' and 'disloyalty', not just among India's rising but frustrated middle class, but among the army, their bulwark against a recurrence of the mutiny-rebellion of 1857, an epic nightmare still within living and all-too-vivid memory. Those responsible for the Indian Army knew that ultimately it was a mercenary force. 'They are all aliens', the Adjutant General, Major-General Sir Fenton Aylmer, confided, 'they have no patriotism. Their loyalty depends on their contentment' – and he thought that their reliability had been compromised by a gradual but clear reduction in the value of their pay and pensions, an issue he regarded as important as the army's rearmament and the introduction of aeroplanes, mechanical transport and wireless telegraphy.[40] The war was to defer consideration of the question of adjusting pensions – ironically, since it would result in the incapacitation of tens of thousands of sepoys and officers; over four thousand on Gallipoli. In the meantime, the Indian Army would be committed to war.

'Ressaldar' – an Indian officer – wrote to the *Pioneer* in 1915 responding to calls to increase sepoys' pensions. He argued that native soldiers should 'represent our case properly and strongly', but only after they 'finish the war with a glorious victory'. In the meantime, 'Ressaldar' affirmed, 'we the Indian soldiers are doing our best … to sacrifice our lives for our beloved Emperor and country, fighting against his enemies up to the last drop of our blood'.[41] It was a succinct an expression of the ethos of the old Indian Army, and in the Great War in general and on Gallipoli in particular it was be fully tested.

---

40   Proceedings of the Army in India Committee, 1912, Vol. II, Minutes of Evidence, p. 179.
41   *Pioneer*, 13 October 1915, p. 11.

2

'O my lover, thou wilt leave me': mobilisation 1914

The Allahabad *Pioneer* devoted a small paragraph on its crowded front page on Wednesday 1 July 1914 to news from the Balkans: 'HEIR OF AUSTRIA MURDERED ... HIS WIFE ALSO KILLED'.[1] News of the European crisis that followed the assassination of the Archduke Franz Ferdinand in Sarajevo in June 1914 arrived at the height of the north Indian summer and seemed very remote. Heber Alexander of the Supply and Transport Corps, described his station, Amballa, 125 miles north of the new imperial capital. It lay 'very hot and very dull' in the long, baking days and nights as the north Indian plain lay panting, waiting sullenly for the breaking of the monsoon.[2] The hot weather of 1914 was among the worst in living memory and the longed-for monsoon broke only gradually through July, with patchy rain spreading eastwards. The nights remained muggy and the days hot and humid. While the monsoon grew in strength newspapers reported on the 'European crisis', though few realised what a Balkan rupture might mean. Hardinge was advised of the probability of war just six days before receiving the cable announcing Britain's entry.

'When Sahib; today?': the outbreak of war

In the first week of August news of a European war galvanized even the sleepy members of Amballa's Sirhind Club. Discussions about the war, fuelled by cabled reports from London, distracted bridge and billiards players. Not that any of them expected that the Indian Army would take a part in operations in Europe, though by the year's end two infantry divisions were indeed in the trenches of Flanders. Though immediately caught up in responding to the crisis, staff officers at Army Headquarters continued to wear the blue patrol uniforms of the peacetime army, not adopting khaki until Beauchamp Duff's departure in 1916. Nevertheless, as soon as word of the European war reached Simla, the newspapers reported, the staff officers began

---

1   *Pioneer*, 1 July 1914, p. 1.
2   Alexander, *On Two Fronts*, p. 1.

working night and day, electric lights burning in the big white-painted headquarters blocks below Simla's fashionable ridge-top Mall, readying the Indian Army to take part in the conflict.

The news spread swiftly to the army's cantonments by telegraph, but men and officers on leave often learned belatedly of the news that would affect them all. Charles Bruce of the 1/6th Gurkhas was leading a climbing party in the peaks of Ladakh when in late July porters arrived carrying copies of newspapers to their remote camp. They read enough of the headlines, now weeks old, realising that they must return to their station, Abbottabad, arriving days after the declaration of war. The war's outbreak arrived at an inconvenient season. With the monsoon far advanced, many officers were on leave in the Hills or even in Britain while many men were on furlough far from their cantonments – as an army of peasant soldiers the Indian Army allowed men generous leave when needed on home farms. Not until early December were they expected back, to permit the training and manoeuvres that began in the cold weather. Now they were recalled, hindered by distance, the rains and flooded roads delaying their return. Runners travelled to villages across Nepal recalling men by 'halla' – word-of-mouth – to depots and cantonments. Orders went out recalling reservists and those on leave (though several hundred officers on leave in Britain were ordered to remain, and many found themselves posted to newly-formed battalions of Kitchener's Army). Despite rivers swollen by monsoon rain and muddy tracks, by November most men on furlough and reservists had made their way to their depots, and the battalions could at last go to war.

The Indian Army existed for war. A correspondent, 'J.S.', wrote to the *Pioneer* describing an encounter with a pensioner of Probyn's Horse, J.S.'s grandfather's regiment. 'The war has broken out!' the pensioner exclaimed. J.S. replied that it was 'terrible to think of the consequences, the loss of life ...' The pensioner reproached him, declaring that 'it opens the doors of glory'.[3] Captain Humphrey Gell of the 69th Punjabis, newly commissioned from the Isle of Man, recorded the 'childish delight' that his men displayed at the order to leave Jhelum to go to war. A member of one of the regiment's Sikh companies greeted the news with a grin and the eager question, 'When Sahib; today?'[4]

But the war's first year saw the Punjab, the most significant province for army recruiting, swept by unrest, plague, rising grain prices, Sikh frustration over restrictive migration policies in Australia and especially Canada and Mohammedan concern that the British empire fought the Ottoman, home of Islam's *Khalifate* and its most holy sites. Conflict brewed between Mohammedan peasants and Hindu moneylenders and with an active but unfocused *Ghadr* movement ('sedition-mongers', as Michael O'Dwyer, Lieutenant-Governor of the Punjab, described it). For a further year a 'constant series of explosions' swept the Punjab, in *Ghadr* bomb outrages,

3 *Pioneer*, 18 September 1914, p. 7.
4 Diary, 11 & 17 October 1914, Humphrey Gell, P158, 10048, IWM.

organised bank robberies, the murder of police and especially the killing and intimidation of 'loyal' Sikh leaders.[5] Rumours that Britain's war was not prospering unsettled the community that provided some of the Indian Army's most valuable troops.

Despite concerns over the reliability of Musalman troops and the reluctance of Sikh communities to offer recruits, the Viceroy in January 1915 praised publicly Indians volunteering in a 'remarkable manner'.[6] It might be thought 'remarkable' given the lack of concern Indians might have had in what might have been seen as an imperial war, but Hardinge's success as Viceroy since 1910 had been to build bridges with the moderate nationalist Congress, which saw loyalty in wartime as a means to generate confidence and gain concessions in the long term.) India's 'fighting races', Hardinge said, had 'had their appetites whetted by the stories of Indian successes' in battle – all of which had occurred in France (he ignored the disaster at Tanga, in German East Africa, when ill-prepared Indian battalions broke in the face of a smaller force of German-led Askaris). A Sydney editorial writer – probably Charles Bean, who in 1915 would land on Gallipoli with the Anzacs – anticipated that 'fighting side-by-side with Canada and Australia at Britain's side' would 'give India new ideals', though what those ideals might be he left vague: in 1914 they certainly did not extend to independence.[7]

India's 300 million people were committed to war by the Viceroy's order and most long remained ignorant of or indifferent to it. Michael O'Dwyer condescendingly but honestly acknowledged that 'one is apt to forget that the wider issues in the war could not be fully understood by the sturdy peasants to whom the Army looked for its man-power'.[8] (Or perhaps this was a back-handed admission that the war was not actually India's fight.) But three significant protagonists immediately responded positively. India's British communities – military, official, commercial and unofficial – all immediately committed to the war effort, even though at first little could be contributed besides charitable subscriptions for Belgian orphans or the Indian Soldiers Fund. The leaders of the nationalist movement, especially the Indian National Congress, declared its favour, seeing in loyalty a route to securing concessions; all it sought at the time. Thirdly, the princely states immediately and spectacularly seized on the war as a way to demonstrate their loyalty. Within weeks the princes had offered money to charter hospital ships and men from their state forces. The Maharaja of Patiala, whose forces would enter the Indian Gallipoli story, not only readied his two regiments for service, but accompanied them as far as Aden, when illness forced his return. But from Patiala he supported the imperial war effort. Having prospered under the 'wise administration of this benign Government', he told a rally in February 1915, 'it is our bounden duty to help the Government' and urged his state and village officials

---

5 O'Dwyer, *India as I knew it*, pp. 197-206.
6 *Sydney Morning Herald*, 19 January 1915, p. 9.
7 Ibid., 11 September 1914, p. 6.
8 O'Dwyer, 'India's Man-power in the War', *Army Quarterly*, Vol. 2, No. 2, July 1921, p. 260.

to 'bring before us for enlistment as many fit men as possible'.[9] (The maharaja's tone suggested that though formally a matter of individual choice, for rural and especially princely India enlistment may have been a matter of directed voluntarism.)

'If we can get the men': recruiting

'India has little to think of', the *Pioneer*'s Simla correspondent gushed in September 1914, 'save the leaving of her troops for the front': a perspective peculiar to Simla, perhaps; but one certainly apparent in cantonments across India.[10] The first Indian formations had mobilised within days of the war's outbreak, and before the month's end the first battalions had sailed for Europe. On 10 October, recognising the empire's need in an expanding war, the India Office ordered the mobilisation of a further twenty battalions, organised into five brigades for service in Egypt. They included the 14th Sikhs, the 69th and 89th Punjabis and the 1/6th Gurkhas, which were designated the 29th Indian Infantry Brigade.[11] With the arrival of mobilisation orders the Indian battalion opened war diaries, as *Field Service Regulations* directed, but their busy adjutants failed to record much detail. The 14th Sikhs' records 'Orders received for Regiment to mobilize' at 4p.m. on 12 October and 'mobilization complete' on 27 October, with nothing in between.[12]

Because British regular battalions of India's pre-war garrison left for Europe (many to form the 29th Infantry Division, which we will encounter on Gallipoli) these new brigades comprised four Indian battalions. This expedient breached a practice that had been imposed since 1857, in that an 'Indian' brigade usually included a British battalion, as a condescending 'stiffener' and a none-too-subtle warning against the perils of mutiny. The crisis of 1914 saw this rule jettisoned, and the Indian brigades in Egypt including the 29th Brigade included no British battalions. The significance of this has unaccountably been overlooked. Later in 1915 the Viceroy's military staff stressed to the Marquess of Crewe (the Secretary of State for India) 'the importance of retaining … in the brigades in which Indian troops are serving, at least one battalion of regular British troops'.[13] Why this did not also apply to the Indian brigades in Egypt and the Dardanelles is unclear, but in a sense the formation of a modern wholly Indian Army symbolically can be dated from 1914.

Despite the reforms Kitchener had forced through the Indian Army's senior officers knew before its outbreak that a major war would subject their army to severe strain. As soon as word of war reached Simla Fenton Aylmer wrote a paper proving that it immediately faced 'a most impossible state of affairs'. Even as mobilisation began he

9   History of Patiala State Forces, Part III, p. 45, Maharaja of Patiala collection.
10 *Pioneer*, 17 September 1914, p. 3.
11 Tel. 8 October 1914, Chamberlain to Hardinge, WWI/286/H, NAI.
12 War diary, 14th Sikhs, October 1914, WO95/4432, NAUK.
13 Tel., 6 July 1915, Hardinge to Chamberlain, WWI/295/H, NAI.

showed that most battalions faced a deficit of several hundred men before the wastage of illness and battle would further reduce their fighting strengths. Naturally the answer was to recruit vigorously – '*if we can get the men*'. In the meantime, men would need to be drafted from units in India to feed the first twenty battalions earmarked for active service. Aylmer remained pessimistic. '*If* we can enlist … men during the first six months and they take 6 months to train, we may hope to supply war wastage …' This he described at best as '*a makeshift arrangement*'. The Commander-in-Chief, Sir Beauchamp Duff, remained sanguine. Accepting groundless War Office advice that the war would not last six months, he breezily minuted that 'I don't think we need detailed calculations', and thought that active recruiting would solve the problem. 'That will do to begin with'.[14]

While leave men trekked to join their battalions across the hills and valleys of Nepal – the country had no roads at all, but tracks threaded up ranges and along the bunds fringing rice-fields – the country's Prime Minister pondered how it might respond to the war, and how it might gain from it. Nepal and the government of British India had concluded a treaty exactly a century before, an important aspect of which governed the recruitment of Nepalese soldiers, 'Gurkhas', for the Indian Army. 'For some time past I have been thinking of how I might further help the Gurkha soldiers in the British Army', Maharaja Sir Chandra Shumshere Jang wrote in late October to the British Resident in Kathmandu, Colonel John Manners-Smith (who had been awarded the Victoria Cross with the 5th Gurkhas after a clash in Kashmir in 1891). Nepal benefitted economically from the remittances Gurkhas sent home and, as with the princely states, increased recruitment solidified its position with the Sircar.

From the war's outset Gurkha recruiting remained strong because Shumshere Jung urged his recruiting officers – known as 'gallawallahs' – to entice men to volunteer, extending the groups traditionally accepted, paying men to travel to depots and offering cash bonuses to volunteers and their families. The gallawallahs, with their velvet waistcoats and silver buttons, cut a dash, enticing young men from a life of drudgery. The Nepal Durbar promulgated measures intended to 'set the minds of Gurkha soldiers at ease about their domestic affairs and encourage them to do their duty with whole-hearted zeal'. Because Nepal remained a nominally independent kingdom it employed its own recruiting parties: British officers were forbidden from recruiting directly within its borders until 1951. This made the Nepal Durbar's recruiting agents both influential and wealthy. Within a month, they began scouring the villages for young men, paying them subsistence money and their families a bonus of 24 rupees – a considerable sum – to release their young men. The government made lists of soldiers' dependents, who were promised allowances and immunity from

---

14 Adjutant General's Branch Notes – Recruiting – Indian Army, Foreign and Political Department, External-B April 1915, Nos 171-203, 'Arrangements made by the Nepal Durbar to provide recruits for the Gurkha regiments of the Indian Army' (NAI) (Aylmer's emphasis).

dispossession or legal suits.[15] Already, the recruiters began looking beyond the traditional castes of Magars, Gurungs, Rais and Limbus. Some, pushed into volunteering by their families, took the bonus and deserted, but most remained, becoming the reinforcements who would find themselves on Gallipoli within the year.

Despite the intimidation by Ghadr activists and unease among India's Mohammedans, volunteering – or at least recruitment – continued. By the end of 1914 the target of 21,000 recruits set for the war's first four months had been exceeded by 7,000, 14,000 of them from the Punjab, most Punjabi Musalmans. But reports of heavy casualties in France dismayed many in India, and letters from men in France deterred potential recruits from offering themselves. A letter intercepted from a sepoy serving in France discouragingly described the predicament in an easily broken code: 'all the white pepper [British troops] has gone, and there is only a little black pepper [Indians] left'.[16]

'Magic and electrifying word': mobilisation

Mobilisation and movement orders reached the Ferozepore Sikhs at Peshawur on 12 October 1914. It had a relatively leisurely two weeks to prepare for its departure, calling up reservists (that is, men who had recently completed their service but with obligations to be recalled) and accepting men transferred from the 45th Sikhs, with which it was linked through its regimental centre – a sign that the Indian Army's reinforcement system was already under stress. Some 30 officers (13 British and 17 Indian) and almost 800 other ranks (and 85 followers) left Peshawur by train amid scenes of 'great enthusiasm'.[17] They arrived in Karachi to board the *City of Manchester* on 3 November. While the regiment's train chugged the length of the Indus valley Britain and Ottoman Turkey went to war, a decision that would affect, and for many end, the lives of every man aboard.

Of the Gurkha battalions to serve on Gallipoli, the 1/4th had been among the first to mobilise, leaving Bakloh within just a week of the war's outbreak to embark on 24 August for France. The 2/10th Gurkhas was a thousand miles east, at Takdah, in the hills east of Darjeeling, a station built on the cloud line and dripping wet most of the year (its 'so-called rifle range' could not be used for weeks at a time for mist).[18] Formed only in 1890, the regiment felt 'its fighting reputation yet to be established': the Great War would see its first active service. It marched out of Takdah on 22 October, boarded the celebrated 'toy train' of the Darjeeling railway and made for Bombay and the war. The 1/5th and 1/6th Gurkhas were both stationed at Abbottabad, in Hazara

---

15 'Steps taken by the Nepal Durbar to protect the interests of the Gurkha soldiers … Religious prohibition against Gurkhas on active service eating tinned mutton', Foreign and Political Department, Internal – B, May 1915, Nos 1214-1220, NAI.
16 O'Dwyer, 'India's Man-power in the War', *Army Quarterly*, Vol. 2, No. 2, July 1921, p. 261.
17 Talbot, *The 14th King George's Own Sikhs*, p. 63.
18 Mullaly, *Bugle and Kukri*, p. 44.

Officers: British and Gurkha officers of the 2/10th Gurkhas, grouped around Lieutenant-Colonel Francis Sutton, photographed at Takdah in 1914. While British and Gurkha officers were distributed evenly through the group, the names of only four of the nineteen Gurkhas were recorded. (Gurkha Museum, Pokhara)

province 80 miles north of Rawalpindi in the scenic Orash valley. A large, healthy cantonment, Abbottabad was home to four Gurkha battalions. The 1/6th Gurkhas left Abbottabad on 28 October farewelled by the other battalions in garrison, British residents of the cantonments and even by 'a strong contingent from the Bazar'; clearly sad at farewelling business.[19] Two weeks later the 5th Gurkhas entrained for Karachi, embarking on 17 November and finally joining a big convoy from Bombay steaming for Egypt. (The presence of German raiders in the Indian Ocean made convoys and escorts prudent.)

In the meantime the infantry battalion of the Maharaja of Patiala's little army left India on 1 November, also to go to Egypt. Britain shared the rule of its Indian empire with dozens of princely states, small and large. The princely states immediately supported the Sirdar by offering 'Imperial Service Troops'. At a time of increasing, if peaceful, moderate but, it has to be said, ineffective nationalist agitation by the Indian

---

19   Regimental Committee, *History of the 5th Royal Gurkha Rifles*, p. 204.

National Congress, the princes saw the war as an opportunity to confirm their special relationship with the Sircar.

From Dehra Dun in the Himalayan foothills came the two batteries of the 7th Indian Mountain Artillery Brigade, 21st (Kohat) and 26th (Jacob's) Batteries. These, two of the just twelve mountain batteries permitted to the Indian Army, were among the longest-established Indian units to serve on Gallipoli. Jacob's Battery had originally been raised in 1843 as part of the Bombay Foot Artillery, and Kohat in 1851 from former gunners of the Sikh army. Both had served in Afghanistan in the 1878-80 war, and Kohat had seen action in the Tirah expedition of 1897-98. Each had five British officers, commissioned in the Royal Artillery but serving in India for much of their careers, three native officers and about 300 gunners, drivers, ancillary tradesmen such as fitters and saddlers and followers – Sikhs and Hindus but with a majority of Punjabi Musalmans. Each battery needed some 300 mules – 'of a superior class, sturdy and stout ... with good straight backs', drawn from the United States, Argentina, China, Cyprus and the Punjab, usually unshod for work in rough country.[20] Each battery's six 10-pounder guns could fire a ten-pound shell just over three miles (with accuracy diminishing with distance) and could be broken down into four mule-loads of some 200 pounds each.

Mules were also vital to the Supply and Transport Corps units. Though wearing a uniform, a Supply and Transport driver was 'not a "soldier" within the meaning of' army regulations.[21] They were not combatant troops but 'followers' – on a par with the dhobies and bhistis, and paid less than sepoys. Though looked down upon by the army's combat units, the Supply and Transport Corps excelled in *bandobast* – organisation. When George Aylmer's corps at Sialkote received the 'magic and electrifying word "Mobilise"' he was able to reply within three days that his train was ready to go anywhere ordered.[22] Heber Alexander's mule corps was mobilised at Amballa on 9 August. As with the infantry, its constituent units were scattered and orderlies and telegrams recalled detachments and sub-units from all over the Simla foothills, from Kalka, Dugshai and Simla. It was only possible to meet the mobilisation schedule by commandeering men, mules and carts from neighbouring corps.

Each mule corps had a small British cadre: an officer, several 'conductors' – warrant officers – and staff sergeants (two each). The British personnel took responsibility for the inevitable paperwork, leaving Indian NCOs to organise and lead the supply columns, but the Supply and Transport officers appear to have been more than mere functionaries. As Heber Alexander acknowledged, 'the personal factor ... is so essential in all dealings with Indian troops' in order to get the most from them in unsung,

---

20 Moore, 'Merits and demerits of the various breeds of animals used in war', *Journal of the United Service Institution of India*, Vol. L, 1921, p. 145.
21 'Summary of the more important general remarks', *Journal of the United Service Institution of India*, July 1914, p. 441.
22 Aylmer, 'Lecture delivered Deputy Assistant Director of Transport, ...', *Journal of the United Service Institution of India*, 1917, p. 298.

unending and poorly paid work.[23] Supply and Transport Corps mules were a mixture of Argentine, Chinese or 'country-bred' (that is, Indian) animals, able to carry 2 maunds (160 pounds) or draw ten (800 pounds) in a two-wheeled Ammunition Transport (AT) cart.

'As I had never dreamed of': embarkation for overseas service

The Indian Army would be deployed outside India, performing several vital services for the empire within months of the war's outbreak. Over the previous century Indian troops had been used in small numbers in imperial campaigns, in Asia (China, 1860), Africa (Abyssinia, 1867), and in the Mediterranean as an imperial reserve, garrisoning Malta in 1878. Kitchener's reforms as Commander-in-Chief had created an army intended to meet internal rebellion (the nightmare since 1857) and a threat from imperial Russia from the north-west, but also a reservoir for overseas service, a decision made just a few years before the Great War's outbreak. The awareness had not percolated thoroughly – Heber Alexander won a sovereign from a Gurkha colonel, who had stated that 'nothing would induce him to believe that an Indian Division was going to fight in France', though he conceded that they might be useful in minor overseas expeditions.[24] In fact, before the end of 1914 the two Indian divisions in the trenches around Ypres arguably saved the decimated British Expeditionary Force from disaster. The Gurkha colonel was not alone in guessing that while Indian troops might serve in East Africa or Egypt (as they did) they would not be required to fight a European enemy; but such was the empire's need of trained troops they were.

Organised in nominal brigades in groups of the cantonments in which they served in peace-time, the formations picked to serve overseas the Indian Army's brigades assembled. The 29th Infantry Brigade's battalions mostly came from the Punjab and the north-west frontier – the 14th Sikhs (from Peshawur), the 1/6th Gurkhas (Abbottabad) the 69th Punjabis (Jhelum) and the 89th Punjabis (Dinapore, in Bihar). They were to be commanded by Major-General Herbert Cox.

Herbert Cox (1860-1923), the son of an Anglican minister, had been educated at Charterhouse and Sandhurst. Commissioned into King's Own Scottish Borderers in 1880, he joined the Indian Army in 1883 and by 1914 was commanding the 2nd (Nowshera) Brigade, on India's North-West frontier, one of the Indian Army's most critical commands. Of him, a junior officer of the 69th Punjabis wrote, 'one couldn't wish for a better Gen¹ to go on active service with'. Like many, they thought that they were destined for France but found they were now in E Force 'whatever that is'.[25] It was one of the five Expeditionary Forces dispatched from India in 1914. A, at first the largest, went to France; B and C to East Africa, D to Mesopotamia and E to Egypt.

---

23 Alexander, *On Two Fronts*, p. 4.
24 Ibid., p. 11.
25 Diary, 2 November 1914, Humphrey Gell, P158, 10048, IWM.

Like officers of other empire forces (and indeed, members of the Imperial War Council) senior Indian officers were convinced that the main enemy would be Germany, and they regarded Ottoman Turkey as a distraction. Humphrey Gell learned of the outbreak of war with Turkey while the *City of Manchester* completed taking aboard the 69th Punjabis and the 14th Sikhs at Karachi. He confided his hope that 'this show with Turkey now doesn't spoil our chances of going to France'.[26] Even before serious fighting began to affect its strength, the Indian Army was compelled to cross-post officers and men to meet the needs of the several expeditionary forces. Reginald Savory left Peshawur with a draft in January 1915. Not only did he think he was to serve in Europe ('I am off to France at last', he told his family) but he thought that he and his draft of 75 Sikh sepoys was destined for the 15th Ludhiana Sikhs. Both were diverted to their sister regiment, the 14th Ferozepore Sikhs.[27]

The Indian Army's administrative weaknesses became apparent even in the transport of troops to Karachi and Bombay, the ports of embarkation. Though the journey took up to two-and-a-half days, several accounts describe drafts not being fed adequately on the way, with men living on 'sweets' bought on station platforms.[28] Despite the want of bandobast the troops' entraining revealed their delight in what they faced. The 69th Punjabis' signalling officer described the scene at Jhelum, when 'they all sang and laughed marching into the station & cheered on leaving'. He was surprised to observe 'no depressing scenes', even though the regiment recruited around Jhelum and many of the men's relations came to see them off. The next day, presumably having spoken to some of his men, he qualified this, noting that the family of Gurdit Singh, one of the regiment's clerks, had been 'much more downhearted', and that 'he had to cheer them up'.[29] At Karachi docks the (British) 'Ladies Patriotic League of Karachi' served out chilies, cigarettes, tea and dried fruit to Indian troops, a sign of how the war had already disturbed accustomed dealings between memsahibs and sepoys.

Despite its lack of an effective cadre of general staff officers the trains rolled into the docks at Karachi and Bombay to board merchant vessels and passenger ships requisitioned or contracted as troopships. While the Indian Army was being used as an imperial reserve, few of its men had served overseas. As the 69th Punjabis' signalling officer observed, his men 'haven't the smallest idea of what a ship looks like'.[30] George Aylmer's mule drivers had never seen the sea and when they saw their ship wanted to know how many mules were going to pull it; other troops speculated that ships ran on rails under the water, like trains.

The voyage presented more challenges, mysteries and wonders. In the 6th Gurkhas men objected to their drinking water being rationed, arguing that there was an

26 Ibid.
27 Letter, Reginald Savory, 28 January 1915, 7603-93, NAM.
28 Letter, Herbert Winn, 20 May 1915, 97/18/1, 6508, IWM.
29 Diary, 29 & 30 October 1914, Humphrey Gell, P158, 10048, IWM.
30 Ibid., 30 October 1914.

abundance of water all around. Subedar Gambirsing Pun, who had travelled by ship to attend George V's coronation in 1910, demonstrated that the sea was salt by dispensing a bucket of sea water to the sceptics. (Gambirsing Pun, soon to be promoted to be the 6th's subedar major is a figure of great stature in its Gallipoli history, and a tragic illustration of what his devoted service brought.) Several accounts of their voyages, even over the generally placid Indian Ocean, Arabian and Red Seas describe Gurkhas especially feeling 'horribly sea sick'. Sea-sickness afflicted Indian medical staff too. On the voyage of a draft of 5th Gurkhas in May the officer commanding the draft took to examining and prescribing medicines for sick soldiers in front of the medical officer, who lay prostrate in a deck-chair. The uncomfortable conditions (the men were 'packed like herrings', a Punjabi officer wrote) did not affect their determination – they remained 'quite cheery'.[31] Many no doubt would have agreed with the Sikh soldier who sailed from Bombay at the same time who wrote home that 'on the voyage ... I saw on land and sea such wonderful things as I had never dreamed of'.[32]

Charles Bruce was aboard the *Teesta*, which had sailed from Karachi on 1 November, with the 1/6th Gurkhas. As its 25 ships steamed in two columns 28 ships from Bombay joined it, the giant convoy shaking into three parallel lines as the cruiser HMS *Swiftsure* and armed merchant cruisers of the Royal Indian Marine steamed ahead and abeam. It was a sight that Bruce was sure he would 'never forget', a demonstration of the empire's military and naval might.[33] Over the following months further transports left Bombay and Karachi carrying troops to France and Egypt. (At the very same docks in Bombay at the same time, in January 1915, Mohandas Gandhi would arrive in India from South Africa. Gandhi was to join Congress in supporting both the war and recruitment (incongruously for a man already committed to non-violence) but would in time change his and India's mind on war and on India's place in the empire.)

Arriving at Aden on 9 November, the convoy provided a detachment sent to seize the Ottoman fort at Sheik Syed, its newness to war suggested by the operation orders, drafted by Charles Villiers-Stuart on City Line notepaper, in pen.[34] Three transports, escorted by the cruiser HMS *Duke of Edinburgh*, landed troops – three of the four infantry units of which were to first serve on Gallipoli – the 14th Sikhs and 69th and 89th Punjabis, along with the 23rd Pioneers. About half of the fort's 400-strong garrison was captured with the loss of four 'IORs' – Indian Other Ranks – killed and eleven wounded, including a British officer. (The Indian Army's casualty figures are complicated to detail, including as they do wounded, killed, missing and captured for British and Indian officers and IORs.) The operation, directed by Herbert Cox, tested the units' readiness for active service. The occupation of Sheik Syed provided useful

---

31 Ibid., 2 November 1914.
32 Letter, quoted in Mazumder, *The Indian Army and the Making of Punjab*, p. 44.
33 Bruce, *Himalayan Wanderer*, p. 246.
34 Humphrey Gell Papers, P158, 10048, IWM.

A THIN PRETENCE.

A cartoon published in the Australian weekly magazine the *Bulletin* in 1914 demonstrates the esteem Sikh troops enjoyed in the empire. Here, David Low ridicules the possibility of German subversion. (National Library of Australia)

experience – it was the first time most of the units' men had seen action; indeed, it was the first time they had seen each other. Cox's 29th Indian Infantry Brigade were regulars but also, effectively, tyros at war. Of the officers of his tiny staff at least three – Villiers-Stuart, Leopold Poynder (his signalling officer) and Harold Wilmer (staff captain) – would die, one in Mesopotamia, two on Gallipoli.)

With the Ottoman empire now an enemy the Suez Canal became vulnerable as well as vital. Many of the units in the convoy, including Cox's brigade, were held in Egypt. Indian troops, enough to form two infantry divisions, the 10th and 11th, and a brigade of Imperial Service cavalry, constituted the largest single component of the army in Egypt.

Soon after the Indian troops' arrival the 38-ship convoy reached Egypt carrying the first contingents of Australians and New Zealand volunteers, the nucleus of what was to become the Australian and New Zealand Army Corps with which the Indians were to serve on Gallipoli. As the Australasian ships steamed slowly up the canal (bound for Alexandria, where they would disembark) they passed the camps of the Indian formations deployed to protect the waterway. Anzac diaries and letters testify to the effect this encounter with the military force of the empire. The Australian brigadier, John Monash, who was to serve alongside Indians on Gallipoli, described the progress of his transport up the Suez Canal as ' a revelation of Empire', as 'we found ourselves again steaming between company after company of Sepoys, then more Gurkhas' who cheered his men '("Heep, Heep, Hooray")' as they passed.[35] Many Australians had anticipated meeting Indians, though not here – the more pessimistic thought that novice dominion troops would never be exposed to battle, but would be given the job of garrisoning India; a task that went to British Territorials.

On arriving in Egypt the Indian brigades constituted some of the few professional soldiers in the theatre. Though a high proportion (perhaps two-thirds) of the Australians and New Zealanders had served in one military force or another before volunteering (albeit mostly citizen Militia), they had little opportunity of becoming trained in the months since joining. The bulk of the British troops in Egypt were Territorials – part-time soldiers, mobilised at the outbreak of war. The Indian troops, all regulars, many with long service and some with experience of war on the frontier, looked the part. Thomas Wilson, of a British field ambulance, recorded that while he found Port Said 'the most immoral place', he was impressed with its Indian defenders. 'They don't half look smart', he wrote in his diary. The Indians' exotic novelty led British and other empire soldiers to visit their camps. Thomas Wilson met some who spoke some English, and they invited him to have 'some of their little cakes … which they call "Rhottee" [*roti*]'.[36] It was symbolic of a relationship that would form between Indian and other soldiers of the empire, an association that would develop especially during the coming campaign on the Gallipoli peninsula.

---

35 Cutlack, (ed.), *War Letters of General Monash*, p. 14.
36 Diary, 9 April 1915, Thomas Wilson, 05/9/1, 13305, IWM.

3

'I came to the land of Egypt': defending the Canal, 1914-15

The *Teesta*, carrying the 1/6th Gurkhas, reached Suez on 16 November but could disembark only six days later, so congested were Egypt's ports, with troops arriving from India and Australasia. The Gurkhas disembarked at Suez on 22 November and were 'working on defences' by the 23rd – manual labour was often the sepoys' lot.[1] The 5th and 10th Gurkhas, though later part of the 29th Brigade on Gallipoli, were early in 1915 parts of the 28th and 22nd Indian Infantry Brigades respectively. The Indian Army moved units about between formations pragmatically; as will be apparent from the fate of the Punjabi battalions sent to Gallipoli.

'Away in the desert': Indian troops in Egypt

Indian troops lived in basic and uncomfortable desert camps, needing water delivered daily from the –surely ironically-named – Sweet Water Canal. Accustomed to spending long, monotonous months in isolated frontier posts, Indian troops expected few of the facilities that Australian, New Zealand and even British Territorial troops demanded, and few Indians other than those on duty were seen in Cairo or Alexandria. (However the mountaineering Charles Bruce, keen to climb anything, even something man-made, took a party of his 6th Gurkhas to the top of the Great Pyramid, keeping the exploit secret from its rivals of the 5th, though not secret enough, for on the way up they met a party from the 5th 'jeering at us in what they called a suitable manner'.[2]) But Indian troops mainly enjoyed the limited entertainment of Port Said where, Herbert Cox complained, his Indian troops seemed restive. He praised the neighbouring Patiala infantry, who 'gave no sort of trouble' ... which is more than could be said for our [14th] Sikhs and drink at Port Said'.[3] Safely away

---

1 War diary, 1/6th Gurkhas, November 1914, WO95/4432, NAUK.
2 Bruce, *Himalayan Wanderer*, p. 250.
3 Cox to Watson, 22 March 1915, History of Patiala State Forces, Part III, p. 99, Maharaja of Patiala collection.

Indians in Cairo – a curiosity to the locals as well as to empire troops.
(State Library of Victoria)

from its drinking shacks, they enjoyed football (the sand too soft for hockey, the 5th Gurkhas carrying off a bronze Sphinx trophy after defeating another Gurkha battalion in the final), catching eels and fishing in the canal. Apart from the consolations offered by gurudwaras and imams, they enjoyed only limited comforts distributed by regimental canteens. Egypt's winter climate suited Indian troops. While the troops remained healthy – a result of the Indian Army's medical officers' expertise in public health – their clothing and bedding became infested with lice. Rather than put up with the nuisance (which encouraged typhus) medical officers urged their military superiors to install disinfecting plants.

The Indian Army's senior officers knew that one of their men's long-standing grievances had been the adequacy of its pay, and service and wound pensions. Accordingly, soon after Indian troops arrived in France the Marquess of Crewe (Secretary of State for India) had sanctioned increases in wound and family pensions and through 1915 British and Indian officials continued to debate the need for and cost of increases in pay and allowances.

We know little about how Indian troops saw or described or thought of their time in Egypt. Their unit war diaries record only routine moves, and little of their men's lives. Unlike the Indians on the Western Front no censorship reports were made or have survived. Not until after Indian troops had been in Egypt for a month did it occur to someone in Simla to ask about what would soon be called 'field security'. 'Do any arrangements exist in your force for censoring letters from the front[?], Beauchamp Duff asked General Sir John Maxwell (the Commander in Chief in Egypt – or possibly their respective staffs), but no arrangements were made for a further month.[4] Sepoys could write home free of charge, and illiterates asked comrades write on their behalf. Indeed, Duff thought it 'advisable ... from a political point of view' that sepoys should 'occasionally write something more than the regulation postcard'. District officers in India had already picked up that 'absence of news from the front excites local comment'.[5] Because men often enlisted from the same villages one man's letter would be passed around an entire community, reassuring family, friends and neighbours: assuming the news were good. But such is the dearth of sources we simply do not know. This absence of evidence is particularly acute because as they arrived in Egypt British officers were deciding whether their Indian troops' beliefs and attitudes should affect which units should be committed to the war against the Ottoman empire.

Though a vital link in imperial communications, Egypt did not have a large British garrison. In 1914 it comprised just an infantry brigade, a cavalry regiment and batteries of horse and mountain artillery, and the army of the Khedive, organised along Ottoman lines and – bizarrely – carrying both the Egyptian and Ottoman flags. (Egypt remained an Ottoman province, though occupied by Britain for thirty years and in December declared a British protectorate.) By the end of 1914 the empire's forces met in Egypt – certainly the greatest gathering since South Africa (in which Indians did not serve – it was supposed to be a 'white man's war'; though no one told the Africans). The imperial force comprised troops from Britain (Territorials and regulars), the dominions of Australia and New Zealand, from India (both regulars and troops from the princely states), and of course from Egypt and the Sudan. While extolling their assembly as a token of imperial unity, the various contingents did not mingle much: even British Territorials and Australasians felt a tension because of the dominions' higher pay rates. Australians saw few Indians in the streets of Cairo. Mostly stationed on the canal (Ismailia was 80 miles to the north-east) they were visible in Port Said. Australians saw Sikhs and Gurkhas there as they passed through the canal (the former 'fine tall men', the Gurkhas 'very smart and soldierly').[6] It was these Indian troops who greeted John Treloar's ship, the *Orvieto*, on 30 November, calling out, 'Who are you?' They were Australians, the newcomers shouted back, 'going to Berlin'. 'Some of the Indians executed what seemed a cross between a cake-walk and a highland fling', yelling in 'a most weird, yet friendly way', Treloar recorded. He decided that they 'seemed real good fellows', their loyalty proved, he thought, because they held posts 'away in the desert in charge of a few white officers'.[7] Whether this loyalty could be taken for granted became increasingly uncertain.

---

4   Tel., 23 November 1914, Duff, to Maxwell, WWI/287/H, NAI.
5   Tel., 1 January 1915, Duff to Maxwell, WWI/289/H, War diary, NAI.
6   Diary, John Treloar, 1 December 1914, *An Anzac Diary*, p. 42.
7   Ibid., December/November 1914, p. 41.

'Why do you so much serve the English Nation?': sepoys' sensitivities

Ottoman Turkey's entry into the war (through astute German and inept British diplomacy on the side of the Central Powers) presented the Sircar with both fresh strategic challenges and with the management of an empire with sixty million Mohammedan subjects; more than any other. Now Britain was at war with the world's premier Islamic empire, and the home of the holy cities of Mecca and Jerusalem. Ottoman Turkey's Sultan, though politically powerless, was the spiritual leader of all Muslims. If Indian Muslims, and especially Muslim troops, were to declare for their religious rather than temporal rulers, the war effort and even the empire would be jeopardy. The dilemma left about a third of the army potentially liable to disaffection.[8]

Soon, Force E's headquarters reported that Musalman sepoys had made off, usually at night with their weapons and ammunition, walking from the canal defences eastward towards the Ottoman pickets in the Sinai desert. Five men of the 126th Baluchis deserted on 10 December, three of the 128th Pioneers on the 21st; four more Baluchis on the same night. When a patrol went out in search of them not only could it not find the fugitives, but one of the search party deserted too. Already Maxwell had drafted in British Egypt's Criminal Investigation Department to 'detect intrigues'. They suspected 'attempts by the Turks to tamper with the troops by selling Korans ... inciting to *Jehad*', but it is more likely that the troops acted out of apprehension that they might be asked to fire on their co-religionists.[9] Detectives soon found seditious papers in Urdu, Persian, Turkish and Arabic and urged, somewhat unrealistically, that Cairo's coffee shops be searched. In Egypt, British officials sought to allay sepoys' concern by inviting Sir Sultan Mahomed Shah Aga Khan, spiritual head of the Shi-ite Nizari Ismaili sect, to speak to Muslim troops who (Charles Bruce heard from officers of the Punjabis) 'rose to the occasion splendidly'.[10]

Cox's Musalman troops became more directly affected when four men of the 69th Punjabis deserted, possibly not to the Turks, but to visit Mecca. Captured, tried and convicted swiftly, three were executed and one sentenced to penal servitude for life. 'They took it perfectly calmly', one of their officers wrote.[11] Not only were two of Cox's four battalions partly Musalmans but he himself had commanded the 69th Punjabis. His diary betrays no mention of his fears: a sign of their profundity, perhaps. Doubts of the reliability of Punjabi Musalman companies circulated among British empire officers in Egypt even before the Dardanelles expeditionary force was formed. William Malone, the celebrated New Zealander commanding the Wellington

---

8 Tel 116, 10 October 1914, Adjutant-General to GOCs of divisions and brigades, WWI/286/H, NAI: *The Quarterly Indian Army List*, 1914.
9 Tel., 2 December 1914, Bingley to Duff, WWI/287/H, NAI.
10 Bruce, *Himalayan Wanderer*, p. 250.
11 Diary, 2 January 1915, Humphrey Gell, P158, 10048, IWM.

Battalion, recorded reports of the desertion of Punjabi soldiers and commented that they 'don't like fighting their co-religionists'.[12] But only 'getting on for twenty' sepoys actually deserted, and they mostly came from the far west and far north of the frontier provinces – Baluchis and Pathans.[13]

The response to the possibility of Muslim troops' unreliability demonstrated the Sircar's sensitivity to the fragility of its rule more broadly. Nor was the danger of the Indian Army's tenderness limited to Muslims. 'Indiscreet' articles misrepresenting Gurkhas' beliefs caused consternation in Simla.[14] Well-meaning but ill-informed British newspapers claimed that 'the jolly little Gurkhas' were 'given a dispensation [to] eat beef' were even more worrisome, and the India office arranged for the late Commander-in-Chief, India, Sir O'Moore Creagh, to refute such suggestions in the *Times*, lest such articles be 'used by ill-disposed persons in India to stir up sedition'. While it might seem unlikely that the *Daily Mirror* or *Town Topics* might find their way to camps in the canal defence zone, they certainly provoked a reaction in India, with Hindu newspapers in Calcutta asking Gurkha soldiers. 'Fie! Fie! Fie! … have your Gurkha people really begun to eat beef?' 'Why do you so much serve the English Nation who eat cow's meat'?[15] With an ineffective or non-existent censorship senior officers lacked surveillance of their troops' attitudes, reliant only on the reports of regimental officers, who were inclined to believe the best of their men.

While the reliability of Musalman soldiers might have been doubted, their Sikh comrades apparently had no compunction about prosecuting a war against Germany and its Ottoman ally. The 69th Punjabis' two Sikh companies had their own gurudwara and at a Sikh festival (probably Hola Mohalla, at which bellicose speeches would not be out of place) the regiment's Sikhs endorsed the declaration 'Down with the Germans & England's enemies and may the Sikhs have as large a share in doing it as anyone!'[16] This reassurance must have been passed to Cox, the 69th's former commanding officer and now its brigadier, and perhaps higher up the chain of command. The Indian troops reliability was even more important because the canal they defended had become the front line in the war with Ottoman empire.

' … or is the canal defending them?': the Canal Defence Force

The canal made Egypt one of the most critical points in the empire; indeed, the desire to control it had determined Britain's relationship with Egypt over the past half-century, and more (since the road between the Mediterranean and the Red

---

12 Diary, 2 February 1915, William Malone, PLC.
13 Kitchener Papers, PRO30/57/63, NAUK.
14 Foreign and Political Department, War – Secret, June 1915, Nos. 23-26, 'Articles in English newspapers regarding Muhammedan feeling …', NAI.
15 Foreign and Political Department, War A Secret, April 1915 No. 326, 'Publication of inaccurate and indiscreet remarks in English newspapers', NAI.
16 Diary, 7 March 1915, Humphrey Gell, P158, 10048, IWM,

Sea comprised part of the 'overland route' between Britain and India). British investors had partly funded the largely French-built and -run canal and the need to retain control over what swiftly became a vital link between Britain and its eastern empire in India, Asia and Australasia had brought successive British governments to intervene in Egypt's affairs since its opening in 1869. Britain's dominance over the nominally Ottoman province signified the decay of Ottoman power. The need to ensure the canal's security had brought involvement in the affairs of the eastern Mediterranean, the Sudan and Arabia. British Egypt's eastern border comprised the sandy and rocky wastes of the Sinai desert, and beyond it lay the domains of Ottoman Palestine.

From the outbreak of war with Turkey the canal's defenders were almost entirely Indian, including battalions that were to serve on Gallipoli. Six Indian brigades – trained, regular troops – were given the job of holding the line of the canal while the British Territorials and later Australians and New Zealanders, citizen soldiers and unused to active service, trained and prepared around Cairo. Maxwell, and General Alec Wilson, the Indian Army officer responsible for the Suez Canal Defence Force, organised them in three sections, from north to south from Port Said to El Ferdan; from El Ferdan to Derversoir, and from the Bitter Lakes to Suez, with a headquarters at Ismailia, mid-way along the canal's 100 mile length. The lakes and the inundation of large swathes of country in the north limited the vulnerable sectors to two lengths, especially in the central sector. A railway ran the length of the canal, enabling the defenders to move troops to meet threats or breakthroughs. The canal averaged 100 yards wide, making attackers wishing to cross it either seize the few bridges or ferries (at Ismailia, Kubri and Kantara) or transport pontoons across the desert from the Ottoman bases at Gaza and Beersheba. The great weakness of Wilson's force was artillery. Allowed no Indian artillery besides mountain batteries, Indian formations depended upon British field artillery. British and French warships moored in the canal supplemented the three batteries of Indian mountain artillery.

Alec Wilson adopted an essentially passive defence scheme, occupying strongpoints on the canal's eastern (or Ottoman) bank and sending patrols out to the east and along the canal. The obstacle of inundation, though opening the Salt Works Canal near Port Said, at the canal's northern outlet, threatened the integrity of the canal proper, and Gurkhas worked around the clock to stem the breach. The 6th stayed near Port Said for a month, its men building redoubts and defences when they were not patrolling into the desert to the east. The posts and redoubts were sited on the canal bank, on mounds of spoil excavated in its construction, looked out over a flat, sandy plain dotted with scanty bushes. They provided bases for company-sized detachments, protected by barbed wire, but between them, especially at night, little prevented intruders from reaching the canal.

The canal, the most vulnerable point in the empire, had effectively become Egypt's border. Critics of Maxwell's dispositions charged that he had used the canal as 'an obstacle in front of a fire trench', but the real obstacle (it seemed) was the 150 miles of

Life on the Canal Defences. Indian troops catching eels (top) and fishing.
(*Mullaly, Bugle and Kukri*)

desert between it and the nearest Ottoman concentrations, at Beersheba.[17] Troops of the two empires had first exchanged shots 20 miles east of Kantara on 20 November as Turkish cavalry and patrols of the Bikaner Camel Corps (sent by a Rajput maharaja) met in the desert of Sinai. In mid-December a patrol from the 69th Punjabis and the 6th Gurkhas, under Captains Christopher Birdwood and Jack Dallas encountered isolated Turkish scouts.

Herbert Cox assumed responsibility for the central, Kantara, sector. Cox's force included units he would command on Gallipoli – his own 29th Indian Infantry Brigade, Jacob's Battery and 108th Indian Field Ambulance – and detachments of

17 MacMunn & Falls, *Military Operations Egypt & Palestine*, Vol. I, p. 25.

the Imperial Service cavalry and the Camel Corps. Kantara was a vital point, where the north-south Egyptian State railway met a ferry, one of several crossing places. Captain Denis Ryan reflected Indian officers' misgivings over the defence scheme; that it implicated and perhaps imperiled the canal in its defence and quoted Kitchener's critique: 'are the troops defending the canal or is the canal defending them?'.[18] But there was surely little option – forward of the canal the open desert offered nowhere to anchor a defensive line, and the further east it might have been placed the more troops would have been needed to hold it.

Maxwell felt little fear of an Ottoman attack on either Egypt or the vital Canal. Characteristically under-estimating the tenacity and daring of their Ottoman opponents, British commanders deprecated the Turks' willingness or capacity to strike at the Canal. When an Egyptian noble asked General William Birdwood if he thought an attack likely, Birdwood replied that the difficulty of moving troops, guns and supplies from Palestine across the Sinai desert would render such a move unlikely. The Egyptian boldly disagreed, telling Birdwood that the Ottoman soldiers' hardihood made advance over the trackless and waterless desert possible. 'You are wrong,' he told Birdwood. 'You couldn't do it ... They will certainly come'.[19] And indeed they did.

Though pre-war intelligence reports estimated that the Turks would be hard-pressed to get a force of 5,000 across the almost trackless and practically waterless Sinai, up to 30,000 Ottoman troops and ten batteries of artillery were able to cross the desert. Sustained by columns of 5,000 camels carrying water (replenished by wells and soaks along the way) the force arrived within a day's march of the canal without being detected, even by the patrolling British and French hydroplanes. The Ottoman march confounded British assumptions that the Ottoman army, even under German command, could not accomplish the considerable logistical feat of mounting such a difficult operation. Alerted at last by air and camel patrols the canal's defenders prepared for attack late in January. The Ottoman central column, advancing from Beersheba towards Ismailia, was to make the main assault, supported by feints north and south toward Kantara and Suez respectively. Cox's 29th Indian Infantry Brigade faced the Ottoman feint launched toward Kantara.

'We held our own easily': the attacks on the Canal

Cox's brigade met the Ottoman incursions in small-scale actions in the week following their appearance out of the desert about five miles from the Kantara post. (Cox was momentarily embarrassed that on that day, 25 January, he had ordered a field exercise seven miles *west* of the canal, and had to hurry his troops back by the ferry.) By mid-afternoon the 14th Sikhs and a section of Jacob's Battery had arrived to reinforce the outpost line, though the Ottoman force seemed content to occupy a hill,

---

18   Ryan, Strahan & Jones, *Historical Record of the 6th Gurkha Rifles*, p. 69.
19   Birdwood, *Khaki and Gown*, p. 242.

Defending the Canal, 1914-15   61

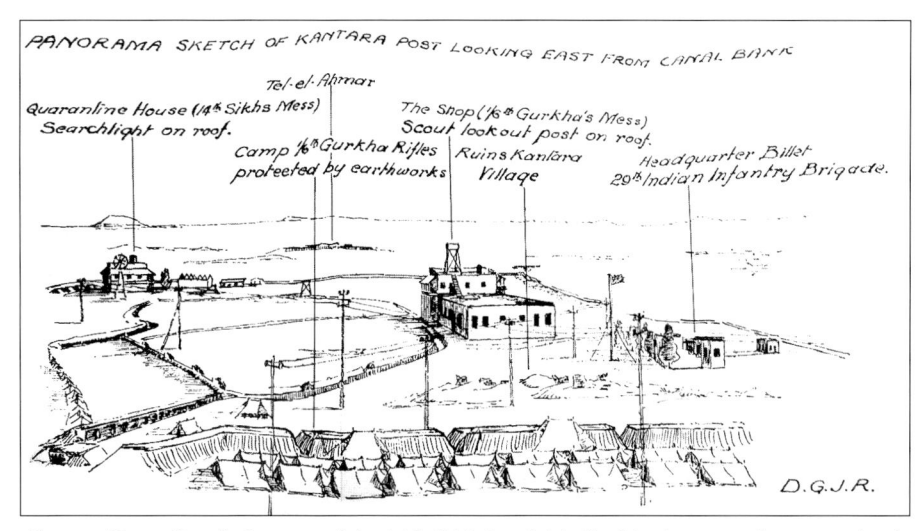

Captain Denis Ryan's drawing of the 14th Sikhs' and 6th Gurkhas' post on the eastern bank of the canal near Kantara. (*Historical Record of the 6th Gurkha Rifles*)

Sir William Birdwood's staff, photographed in Cairo. Among British and Australian officers, a New Zealander and a Canadian, the largest single group of officers were six of the Indian Army, including Charles Villiers-Stuart and Andrew Skeen. (AWM A01580)

'Position 70', giving Cox time to bring up his troops. The next day a force of Sikhs and 6th Gurkhas, supported by guns of Jacob's Battery, the Patiala Lancers, the Bikaner Camel Corps and 108th Field Ambulance, all commanded by Charles Bruce of the 6th Gurkhas, ventured out and occupied a hill ('Position 40') two miles from the Turks. Just as Bruce was about to mount an attack he received orders (presumably from Alec Wilson) to limit his action to observation. That afternoon the Indian force withdrew into the Kantara defences under the protection of the guns of the cruiser HMS *Swiftsure*, and were back behind the barbed wire by dusk. It was hardly the most glorious baptism of fire, but the important point about the brigade's experience was that its constituent units worked together. Later the 14th Sikhs supported the 89th Punjabis on the outpost line; the 1/6th Gurkhas and the 69th Punjabis went out together looking for Turkish stragglers; the mountain guns supported the infantry.

The encounters were not bloodless – the Gurkhas lost a man mortally wounded and four more evacuated wounded, as well as two machine-gun mules on 26 January – but the losses were minor given that a large Ottoman force lay beyond the outpost line. In the early hours of the 28th Turkish troops approached Number 5 Piquet, just 2,000 yards from the canal. Men of the 14th Sikhs repelled that incursion, losing a jemadar and a sepoy killed. For a further week the Ottoman force remained active, lurking in the desert and approaching the canal, even though it must have been obvious that they could do no serious damage. On 2 February Captain Christopher Birdwood took the 6th Gurkhas' scouts out to look for them, firing at a group of Turks at a thousand yards and driving them off before a sandstorm closed everything down and the patrols pulled back to the canal. The following day parties of Turks again approached the outpost line, this time held by the 89th Punjabis, but at dawn the guns of the *Swiftsure* opened on them and 'pursued them with fire' as the Gurkhas' war diary put it.[20] Later that day a hastily assembled column of double companies of the 89th Punjabis and 14th Sikhs, again with two mountain guns, went out, while the Gurkhas held the outpost line. The next day the war diaries reported 'enemy appear to have retired' and 'no enemy seen'.

The attacks at Kantara were actually merely feints for the main attack, near Ismailia and the Great Bitter Lake. The 2/10th Gurkhas, later to become part of the Gallipoli force, helped to defeat two attacks near the Serapeum East redoubt, north of the Great Bitter Lake. This action was the battalion's first, and saw one of its buglers, Joglal Rai, posthumously awarded an Indian Order of Merit for delivering messages while mortally wounded. The Turks, obstinate though unable to seriously damage the canal and its traffic, lurked in the desert making forays of little more than nuisance value. Closer to Ismailia the 5th Gurkhas continued to patrol eastwards to ensure that the Ottoman troops had been seen off. On 30-31 January a patrol under Subedar-Major Harkabir Thapa detected signs that Ottoman parties remained close by. Thapa ambushed a small party of five that had been creeping toward the canal with dynamite,

---

20 War diary, 1/6th Gurkhas, January-February 1915, WO95/4432, NAUK.

capturing one man. Further skirmishes confirmed that while Ottoman troops stubbornly remained out in the desert they could do little of any offensive value.

In the first days of February Indian patrols encountered a Turkish force of 3,000 infantry, artillery and cavalry four miles east of the Ismailia ferry. A fierce sandstorm, obscuring the sun, making hearing and sight impossible and jamming rifles, precluded any immediate response, though the defenders stood-to despite the storm. When it abated the Ottoman attackers (who must have suffered even more in the open) could not be seen. They made a weak attempt at the defences early the following morning, firing across the canal at the railway building opposite but easily driven off by the Gurkhas' fire from the El Ferdan post and by the shells of the cruiser HMS *Clio*. Covered by persistent but inaccurate fire by the Ottoman gunners (who had dragged their guns across the desert only to waste their ammunition) the infantry withdrew. All of the Ottoman attacks had been deterred or driven off. The Turks lost about a thousand men dead (killed by gunfire or drowned when their pontoons sank in the canal). Some 650 men were captured and an estimated 1,500 wounded endured a horrific journey back across the Sinai. The defenders lost 115 killed and wounded, most Indian sepoys.

Patrols and columns ranged out from the canal, including New Zealanders and Australians, sent (so a New Zealand battalion commander thought) to 'stiffen up' the Indians, though the inexperienced dominion troops gained valuable experience.[21] On 5 February a double company of the 5th Gurkhas, with a hundred New Zealanders, probed and occupied the Turks' positions east of El Ferdan, collecting evidence of the Turks' equipment and even of their state of mind. Curiously, despite their strength, the canal's defenders launched no general counter-attacks, and the Camel Corps and aeroplanes shadowed the retreating Turks only to establish that they were in retreat, losing an opportunity to harry and even destroy the disorganised (though perhaps not demoralised) attackers as they plodded eastwards. It was a sign of the determination that would help the Turks withstand the invasion of Gallipoli, and the lack of decisive command, even amateurism, that would produce so much suffering and result in defeat on the peninsula.

However impressive the Ottoman feat of marching across the sandy waste of Sinai had been, the attack when it came, as Gurkha officers agreed, 'never had a chance'.[22] While some resolute Ottoman engineers succeeded in launching into the canal the pontoons they had laboriously transported so far, the attackers met heavy fire at every point, and very few Turkish soldiers reached the western bank, and those who succeeded became prisoners or corpses. Worryingly, the interrogation of Ottoman prisoners disclosed that German and Turkish 'outside influence had been at work in connection with desertions in Egypt': possibly accurately.[23]

21 Diary, 26 January 1915, William Malone; Crawford, (ed.), *No Better Death*, p. 117.
22 Mullaly, *Bugle and Kukri*, p. 61.
23 Intelligence summary, 10 February 1915, WWI/290/H, NAI.

Meeting the Ottoman offensive, resembled the field days familiar to the Indian Army. Humphrey Gell of the 69th Punjabis described the action he had seen as 'a nice little scrap'. He thought that the Indian mountain batteries had 'fired very well', but recorded the belief in the Indian brigades' messes that Cox had been constrained from meeting the incursion as aggressively as he had wished.[24] In the time-honoured manner of the Indian Army, in which inter-generational tension and criticism warred with patronage, admiration and inspiration, some officers criticised their superiors' dispositions and decisions. Charles Bruce was disgusted that though possessing a superior mounted force (albeit one unused to the desert) 'not a cavalry soldier moved' in pursuit, and he loyally supported 'our most efficient brigadier' (Cox) whose proposals for 'local offensives ... were nipped in the bud'. Bruce attributed this prudence to 'the restraints on ordinary instructional manœuvres' of peacetime in persisting in war.[25] It also reflected Maxwell's caution in not wishing to see one of his pursuing columns cut off or even cut to pieces by Ottoman troops in the open desert.

For the moment it was enough to see the Ottomans driven off. The Turkish force, outnumbered something like four-to-one by the canal's defenders, never had a hope of making more than a demonstration. Cables despatched to Simla told the essence of the story: 'Canal Defences have been attacked ... on the whole, we held our own easily ... conduct of our troops was very good'.[26]

'A very trying time': Indians on the Canal

On 29 January traffic in the canal resumed. The Ottoman incursion had briefly disrupted shipping in the vital artery, but had failed to stop it or harm the waterway itself. When ships resumed their passage the Indian troops marveled at a procession of warships, merchant vessels and troopships passing their positions just a hundred yards away. The encounter moved men on both ships and shore, though only the Australians and New Zealanders, already inveterate diarists and correspondents, seem to have recorded the scene. Australian and New Zealand troops were also sent to some of the canal-side posts in groups of two or three platoons, supposedly to 'reinforce' Indian positions, but more probably to give the novice citizen soldiers experience in an actual front line, learning from its regular defenders more by osmosis and example than by explicit instruction. Gurkha troops (who never acknowledged or accepted that they were in any way inferior to European troops) especially relished this contact, and despite their mutual incomprehension enjoyed 'the happiest of relations' with their guests.[27] The reinforcement of the posts led to further fraternising between Indian and

---

24 Diary, 26 January 1915, Humphrey Gell, P158, 10048, IWM.
25 Bruce, *Himalayan Wanderer*, p. 249.
26 Tel., 5 February 1915, Maxwell to Duff, WWI/290/H, NAI.
27 Regimental Committee, *History of the 5th Royal Gurkha Rifles*, p. 210.

dominion troops, Gurkha officers noticing that 'each race obviously highly approving the qualities displayed by the other', despite the lack of a common language.[28]

Men of the various armies remained curious about each other. When in January a party of Gurkhas arrived at Mena to do a scouting course John Treloar decided that they were 'fine cheerful little fellows' who amused the Australians when they performed athletic exercises. He had been curious about how their very few British officers were able to command such men, assuming, as most Europeans did, that despite the martial races' fighting prowess they needed Europeans in command. He noticed that though their British subaltern returned to camp tired and hungry he declined refreshment for himself until he saw his men fed. 'Such treatment must win the loyalty of the troops', Treloar concluded.[29] The Indian Army's professionalism impressed the dominion troops even before they encountered them on Gallipoli.

Though the canal had been re-opened, its defenders stood-to for days after the attacks – not until 12 February were the Indian infantry at El Ferdan allowed to remove their boots at night. Ottoman troops remained in the Sinai desert, harassing the defenders even if unable to make more serious attacks. On 22 March, six weeks after the failure of the main attempt, a Turkish column of infantry, cavalry, machine-guns and artillery appeared out of the desert just two miles from El Kubri, on the canal, just seven miles north of Suez. Alerted by firing when an Indian patrol detected the incursion, the defenders stood-to and sent out parties to observe the Turks while the defenders assembled a column of Indian infantry (including four companies of the 5th Gurkhas) and cavalry, supported by Lancashire Territorial artillery. The column marched about nine miles through soft sand before locating the Turks. The two sides faced each other at a range of about a thousand yards over open desert. Under the cover of the Territorials' artillery fire the Indians advanced, the Turks prudently withdrawing. While the Indian cavalry (inexperienced states troops of the Hyderabad Lancers) fell away, the Indian infantry doggedly pursued the Turks across a waste of sandy dunes. After several hours the pursuers gave up, returning to the defences after a twenty-six-mile and 24-hour operation. Though the action demonstrated the value of disciplined Indian regulars, it also offered a reminder that Ottoman troops were a tough adversary, who again had evaded defeat.

Apart from detachments protecting an armoured train running on the canal-side railway, building or repairing defences and mounting a large column including British and Patiala cavalry on a patrol to Duiedar (in the desert ten miles east of Kantara on the sandy track to Katia oasis), the following month passed quietly. For days the war diaries bear the line 'nothing to report' or 'nil'. Though the entries are frustratingly uncommunicative, the reality for the Indians was a round of routine patrols and piquets, punctuated by hard labour endlessly shoveling sand out of trenches and revetting and wiring the redoubts built on the canal's eastern bank. All of the battalions

---

28   Ibid., p. 210.
29   Treloar, *An Anzac Diary*, pp. 80-81.

An artist's imagining, published in the *Illustrated London News*, depicting the Indian defence of the Suez Canal. (National Library of Australia)

that were to go to Gallipoli took their turns on the canal line. The 89th Punjabis, for instance, alternated between road-making, cleaning out sandy communication trenches, holding the posts and redoubts, and sending columns into the desert searching for further Turkish incursions and musketry training.

On 11 February Alec Wilson submitted his dispatch on the defence of the canal against the Ottoman incursion. Though not published until June 1916 his superior, John Maxwell read it. It seems likely that he noted that 'the bulk of the fighting' on the canal had fallen to the 22nd and 29th Indian Infantry Brigades, and its performance may well have persuaded him to select the Cox and the 29th for the expedition then forming to carry the war into the heart of the Ottoman empire.[30]

The clashes of late January had other consequences for Force 'E' and its units. After Maxwell's staff cabled Simla that the casualties after the 28 January clash at Kantara had been 'Killed, 14th Sikhs – 1 Jemadar, 1 sepoy. Wounded, 1/6th Gurkhas – 1 rifleman', Simla cabled back 'Please have names and regimental numbers of all casualties cabled to India as they occur'.[31] This marked the beginning of the dozens of detailed casualty telegrams eventually wired from Gallipoli to Egypt and on to India, to be filed by clerks in Army Headquarters in Simla and forwarded to the depots so that families could be advised. It was of course a manifestation of the Indian Army's obsession with detail, but also a reflection of the paternal desire of the regiments to ensure that their men were looked after.

It is notable that several of the units involved in the defence of the canal – including at least seven Punjabi battalions out of sixteen engaged – included Musalman troops, who performed perfectly well against their co-religionists.

The mainly Indian force on the Canal remained on the alert in their cheerless posts, redoubts and camps; conditions similar to those in the fortified camps they held

---

30 Supplement to the *London Gazette*, 21 June 1916, p. 6165.
31 Tel., 29 January 1915, Maxwell to Duff and reply, WWI/289/H, NAI.

Indians and other empire troops on the bank of the Suez Canal. (State Library of Victoria)

on the frontier. After an eventful but not uncongenial winter the warmer weather brought locusts and flies. George Swinley of the 14th Sikhs described how sandstorms increased in March, with days in April 'beastly ... impossible to go out at all'.[32] In late March a detachment of the 5th Gurkhas had to slog through soft sand fifteen miles in a violent sandstorm to prepare a landing ground for aeroplanes unable to make the distance back to their aerodromes west of the canal. If officers used to the discomforts of an Indian summer described the march as 'a very trying time' it can be regarded as very unpleasant indeed.[33]

Over the next three months the troops in the Canal Defences remained on alert against potential and even actual Turkish incursions. On 6 April a patrol of the 14th Sikhs killed a Turkish soldier actually on the canal bank, one of a party that placed a mine in the water (which Jemadar Narain Singh of the 14th Sikhs discovered). The 10th Gurkhas remained at Serapeum while the 5th moved to the more congenial location of Suez, though its camp was 'entirely devoid of shade and much exposed to wind and dust'.[34] In May the 5th returned to the canal, this time instructed to 'hut itself' – a common practice in the Indian Army, whose men were used to making bricks and thatching roofs. No sooner had the battalion begun building lines than it was ordered to return to Suez, this time to embark for the Dardanelles. By that time Lieutenant-Colonel John Parker's 7th Indian Mountain Artillery Brigade and Cox's 29th Indian Infantry Brigade had gone to war on Gallipoli as part of the Mediterranean Expeditionary Force.

32 Diary, George Swinley, March–April 1915, 7407-138, NAM.
33 Regimental Committee, *History of the 5th Royal Gurkha Rifles*, p. 216
34 Ibid.

4

'Behold O Master the mighty host': the Mediterranean Expeditionary Force

While John Maxwell and Alec Wilson's Canal Defence Force had met the ineffectual Ottoman offensive, in London decisions were made that would launch a major invasion of Ottoman Turkey that would involve many of the empire troops in Egypt. Decisions made by politicians in London and commanders in Egypt would result in about seven thousand Indian troops initially becoming a part of what came to be called the Mediterranean Expeditionary Force.

'With Constantinople as its objective': the idea of a Dardanelles campaign

In January 1915 the British War Council agreed to an operation against Ottoman Turkey that might relieve the pressure on its Russian ally in the Caucasus. While the Russian request was soon withdrawn, Winston Churchill, the First Lord of the Admiralty, seized on the idea of using British and French naval power to swiftly and economically capture Constantinople and defeat Turkey. Churchill persuaded the War Council to endorse his plan for an expedition to 'bombard and take the Gallipoli Peninsula, with Constantinople as its object': the germ of the entire lamentable venture.[1] It was to occupy the Gallipoli peninsula and the batteries on the eastern shore of the Dardanelles that had prevented the fleet from reaching the Sea of Marmara and Constantinople. This strategic objective percolated even to sepoys, who saw neither maps nor orders. Years after the war Indian veterans described how they had been a part of an expedition to capture 'Constantonia'.[2]

A combined naval attack on the Dardanelles in March failed and the option of an amphibious landing on the peninsula came to the fore. Kitchener (now Secretary of State for War) decided that it would be entrusted to Sir Ian Hamilton, one of

---

1   James, *Gallipoli*, p. 33.
2   Recollection of interview with Sikh Gallipoli veteran by Sqdn Ldr Rana Chhina, 3 March 2014.

the army's most promising generals. Hamilton was a sensible and justifiable choice to command the Dardanelles expedition. He had had campaign experience in India and South Africa, had witnessed modern war as an observer during the Russo-Japanese war, and had recently held senior commands in Britain. A protégé of both Lord Roberts (who had died in December 1914 after inspecting Indian troops in France) and Kitchener, Hamilton was an intelligent, cultured soldier, who lacked only the necessary ruthlessness to ensure success in such a command. His greatest asset, and perhaps his most fatal attribute, was his finely developed sense of loyalty, which had so helped him to rise to the rank of general. Hamilton owed his command to Churchill's influence. Hamilton's celebrated account of his interview with Kitchener (when he is supposed to have stood in deferential silence until his chief told him that he was to command the Dardanelles force and was given accepted a ridiculously small pile of maps, tourist guides and a handbook on his Ottoman enemy) seems to be bogus. Still, in a three-hour meeting on 12 March Hamilton failed to question his task or the 75,000 troops he was given to accomplish it – and Charles Callwell (who had inspected the Dardanelles in 1906 and recommended a force of 150,000 men) was present.[3] His loyalty and deference towards Kitchener arguably fatally wounded his chances of success. Humphrey Gell thought (after an inspection at Kantara on 5 April) he was 'a fine looking old man'. (He had actually just turned 62: Gell was 24.)

The preparation of the Dardanelles expedition has become legendary as an object lesson in how to plan to fail. From Hamilton's misguided decision to split his force, to the failures of intelligence, the muddle of the expedition's logistics and especially the debacle that the medical plans became, all explain, so clearly in hindsight, why the venture turned into one of the greatest fiascos in British military history. Underpinning its failure was the universal under-estimation of the Ottoman capacity for effective defence.

'An unknown destination': Indian units prepare for Gallipoli

In early March Herbert Cox believed that the 29th Indian Infantry Brigade would eventually follow the Meerut and Lahore divisions to France, where he thought the war would be decided over the northern summer of 1915. He told Humphrey Gell, the 69th Punjabis' signalling officer that 'there will be a certain amount of scrapping in [the] Dardanelles' but like many Cox and Gell agreed that they did not 'fancy [the] Turks will stick it long now'.[4] A month later advice from Indian Army officers who found themselves in the Royal Naval Division (formed of sailors and marines) passed on more pessimistic rumours. 'The warships have not made much progress in the

---

3   John Lee's sympathetic biography *A Soldier's Life* corrects Hamilton's misleading account of preparations for the campaign, but hardly exonerates Hamilton of responsibility for its failure.
4   Diary, 8 March 1915, Humphrey Gell, P158, 10048, IWM.

Dardanelles', they said, where the 'mines are as thick as herrings'. (In that many minesweepers were trawlers requisitioned by the Royal Navy, along with their crews, the fishing analogy was particularly apt.) Junior officers in the clubs and hotels of Cairo reached the same conclusion as senior officers in London: as Humphrey Gell wrote 'don't see how they can expect to get through without a land force too'.[5]

By then John Parker, the commander of the 7th Mountain Artillery Brigade had warned Arthur Fergusson to be ready for Kohat Battery to make 'a long march at a moment's notice', and a week later he received orders to move to Alexandria to embark for 'an unknown destination' as part of the Australian and New Zealand Army Corps.[6] After a couple of false starts (once being told to de-train after having loaded all 300 of the battery's mules), the battery arrived at Alexandria harbour and boarded the transport *Pera*, sharing the ship with a section of Captain Thomas Carey-Evans's 137 Combined Field Ambulance, the Indian medical unit allocated to the mountain artillery brigade. The *Pera* steamed for the Aegean island of Lemnos, where the force destined to invade the Gallipoli peninsula assembled in Mudros harbour.

While officers waited until their ships were out of sight of land to open sealed orders, their destination had become common gossip in Egypt and beyond. Fergusson recalled that John Bruce, his fellow battery commander, told him seven weeks before the landing on Gallipoli what he thought would occur – 'Naval Division land at Bulair, 29th Div at Helles, and we about half way between'.[7] Since this was a month before the operation's commander, Ian Hamilton, even arrived at Lemnos to began planning the invasion it is hard to see how Bruce knew, but the fact remains that the landings became an open secret in Cairo and the Mediterranean well before late April. Fergusson remained skeptical, thinking that the ship could turn north-east for a landing at Alexandretta, on Turkey's Levant coast, one of the several options under consideration, by bar-room gossip as well as staff officers in Cairo.

As they waited impatiently aboard the transports *Pera* and *Hessen*, the mountain gunners saw Mudros harbour gradually fill with a huge assemblage of ships, merchant and naval. Curiously, the mountain gunners (and, more importantly, their mules) were not put ashore to camp, as were some of the Australian and French troops. Keeping the animals fit in the confines of the ships challenged the brigade's drivers. Fergusson had his drivers lead the mules around the *Pera's* decks, making 'quite a good combined route march and hill parade around the whole deck'. But both animals and men lost condition while they waited for over a month. Sailors taught the men, none of whom had grown up near the sea, how to row, and they ran obstacle races around the ship to kill time and keep fit. The brigade's drivers accustomed the mules to the alarming business of landing by putting animals in slings daily.

---

5   Ibid., 3 April 1915.
6   'Gallipoli 1915', Arthur Fergusson, 3DRL3635, AWM.
7   Ibid.

Major-General Herbert Cox, commander of the 29th Indian Infantry Brigade in 1915. (*Mullaly, Bugle and Kukri*)

Punjabi Musalman troops meeting Australians in a railway truck in Egypt. Men of the two armies exhibited a strong curiosity about each other. (AWM PS0468)

In the meantime, the long wait in Mudros harbor saw the beginning of what became one of the most unexpected legacies of the campaign. Bored with hanging about, Australian and later New Zealand troops visited the *Pera* and *Hessen*, 'to look at the Indians'. Coming to inspect exotic, even legendary soldiers of the empire, the Australian and New Zealand visitors stayed to chat with the gunners. 'There commenced an entente which afterwards became most remarkable', Fergusson recalled.[8]

Language remained a barrier between Indian and other troops. The mountain gunners' British officers acted as intermediaries, but on the *Pera* the presence of an Australian gunner provided an interpreter outside the chain of command. A Gunner Meyer, Fergusson found, spoke fluent Urdu, the language of the mountain batteries' Punjabi Musalmans. In fact, 'Meyer' was 299 Gunner Cyril Mayer, a 31-year-old forest officer, the son of an Anglican missionary in Abbottabad. Fergusson tried to have him promoted and transferred to the mountain gunners, but was annoyed to find that the 14th Sikhs had already 'roped him in', but he seems to have spent time with the mountain artillery in the campaign's early months.[9] The story of Cyril Mayer (or Meyer or Maer, as he turned up in various records) represents yet another of the many rich strands of the relationship between Australia and India through Gallipoli. He had volunteered for the Australian Imperial Force (AIF) in August 1914. Having been born and grown up in India, Mayer was already an 'excellent linguist' and when his battery reached Lemnos he volunteered to act as an interpreter. He had been a member of the 1st Punjab Volunteers and had passed examinations in both Hindustani and Punjabi, facts that someone noted for later use. As Cyril Maer he also enters the story later.

Later in 1915 Birdwood told Hamilton that he had discovered a 'pucca' Gurkha as 'a full fledged Australian private'. Having migrated to Australia (and even more remarkably having been accepted into the AIF) he was 'now making himself most useful as an interpreter'.[10] Who this man was in a mystery – in accordance with Australia's obsession with keeping 'Australia for the White Man', non-Europeans were forbidden from joining the AIF. Only one volunteer for the AIF admitted having been born in Nepal (and he in 1917) and no man with any of the common Gurkha surnames can be found in any of the several digitised AIF sources.

'Worth his full weight in gold': Gurkhas on Gallipoli

If Punjabi Musalmans had temporarily fallen out of favour, Gurkhas remained the troops of choice among influential Indian Army officers. Ian Hamilton had seen

---

8   'Gallipoli 1915', Arthur Fergusson, 3DRL3635, AWM.
9   Ibid.
10 Letter, Birdwood to Hamilton, 21 August 1915, 7/1/16, Papers of Sir Ian Hamilton, LHCMA.

Gurkhas in action, in Afghanistan, Burma, Chitral and Tirah, and knew of his patron Lord Roberts's admiration. In late March, exactly a month before the planned invasion, he asked Kitchener, the dictatorial Secretary of State for War, to earmark a brigade of Gurkhas for the coming campaign. 'The scrubby hillsides on the southwest faces of the plateau', he thought (with an odd exactitude) 'are just the sort of terrain where these little fellows are at their brilliant best'. He knew that Egypt was 'stiff with troops' that could be spared, and urged that 'each little "Gurkh" might be worth his full weight in gold' in the coming campaign.[11] Hamilton's story was the closest he came to implicitly criticising his mentor.[12] Without actually saying so, the inarticulate Kitchener seems to have intended Hamilton to have more troops, but Hamilton, deferential to his chief, failed to take the hint. When he left Egypt for the Aegean early in April Hamilton asked Maxwell to 'jog K's elbow about the Gurkhas'. Maxwell, ambivalent over losing troops to what in his view remained, as the British official historian (and staff officer) Cyril Aspinall-Oglander put it, a 'subsidiary enterprise', failed to do so.[13]

But it is possible that the two developments – the suspicion of the Punjabis and the arrival of more Gurkhas – are connected. There is no direct evidence to suggest that Hamilton exploited concern over the Musalmans' reliability to gain in May what he had asked for, ineffectually, in March. The only evidence that supports the suggestion is that apparently no-one expressed any doubts over the loyalty of the Punjabi Musalman drivers and gunners of the mountain artillery brigade (which was about 50% Musalman) or the supply and transport units, which were 75% Musalman. They were earmarked for the Dardanelles at exactly the time when doubts about Musalmans were at their height. Certainly there was no other Indian artillery available in Egypt (and anyway all the batteries were 'mixed', as they said, including Sikhs and Punjabi Musalmans). But is it feasible that Hamilton, who openly professed his admiration for Gurkhas, deprecated the two Punjabi battalions and pressed for them to be replaced by Gurkhas? It seems plausible.

One reason for Hamilton and Maxwell preferring Gurkhas on Gallipoli was that they were supposed to be expert in mountain warfare, and the peninsula's hills resembled the frontier terrain that had trained and fought over. Charles Bruce, though fiercely loyal to his regiment and to the Gurkhas in general, acknowledged the challenge the Indian Army faced, especially in Europe but also in the war against Ottoman Turkey. Trained for and accustomed to fighting tribesmen on the frontier, they were to face 'modern war against modern enemies' – even the Ottoman army, backward compared to the Germans, was equipped and trained for a war of quick-firing, modern rifles, machine-guns and artillery. Indian troops, Bruce felt, were 'at that time quite incapable of realising what they had to face'. In this they were not

---

11 Mullaly, *Bugle and Kukri*, p. 65.
12 Regimental Committee, *History of the 5th Royal Gurkha Rifles*, p. xix.
13 Aspinall-Oglander, *Military Operations Gallipoli*, Vol. I, p. 124.

alone: the Australians and New Zealanders trained in Egypt for open warfare that lasted a matter of hours on Gallipoli before the trench stalemate confounded their expectations.

It was entirely explicable that Hamilton, who had served in India, should want Indian troops in his force. What is obscure is why he asked for and secured only one brigade, and then one impaired by the suspicion of disloyalty. The explanation is found in the correspondence between Simla, London and the Indian expeditionary forces, which discloses that within six months of the war's outbreak, India's army was stretched to meet the demands made upon it. Later it would send overseas even larger forces, especially to Mesopotamia, where eventually eight Indian divisions and many ancillary troops would fight. But in early 1915 one brigade was all that Hamilton could obtain.

The Indian force despatched to join the Mediterranean Expeditionary Force constituted one of several distinct overseas expeditionary forces sent from India in 1914. Force A, the largest, went to France, the infantry serving for a year from October 1914, its two cavalry divisions remaining for most of the war. Force B went to East Africa, suffering a reverse at Tanga in November 1914. Force C also served in East Africa, making an inconclusive contribution to the first British campaign in Tanganyika. Force D landed in Mesopotamia in November 1914, forming the core of the large (and largely Indian) army fighting the Ottomans there for the rest of the war. Force E, of which the Gallipoli units were at first a part, arrived in Egypt in October 1914. The Gallipoli force, a brigade of four (later five) battalions, two mountain artillery batteries and medical and supply and transport units, comprised the smallest of the Indian Army's forces.[14] For most of the Gallipoli campaign the Indian troops deployed to the Dardanelles were administered as part of Force E, but as we will see later became separate.

Sir John Maxwell, the General Officer Commanding in Egypt and Alec Wilson, the commander of the Canal Defences, supplied, administered, reported on and to an extent directed the Indian force provided to the Mediterranean Expeditionary Force. And, arguably, starved it of the troops Hamilton professed he needed. Maxwell, as has been well attested, proved to be lukewarm in his support for the Dardanelles force and released troops with what the historian Robert Rhodes James described as 'ill-grace and gloomy prognostication'.[15] (Ian Hamilton later complained bitterly that Maxwell was 'holding up a whole Army meant for me' on the basis of 'a Bogey Man called the Senoussi', the rebellious desert tribe in western Egypt.[16]) There is an argument that Maxwell's dilatory (at least) and obstructive (at worst) attitude to Hamilton's representations could have been critical to the success of the campaign,

---

14 There was a Force F, but not until 1918, when Indian cavalry sent from France arrived in Palestine: why the letter F remained unused for three years is a mystery.
15 James, *Gallipoli*, p. 84.
16 Hamilton, *Listening for the Drums*, p. 253.

though, it must be said, only if Hamilton had made different – and better – decisions about how the Indians were to have been used and – as with everything about Gallipoli – only if the fighting had turned out differently. Hamilton's criticism of Maxwell smacks of exculpation.

While the 'Indian' troops that served on Gallipoli came from a range of 'classes', as the Indian Army labeled its constituent ethnic, religious and regional groups, the infantry battalions were to overwhelmingly drawn from the Gurkhas – by the campaign's end including four of the Indian Army's twenty Gurkha battalions. At the campaign's outset, however, only one of the four battalions initially committed to the Dardanelles force were Gurkhas. Had Hamilton (who had served in India and knew their quality) pressed his view it is possible that a brigade of Indian infantry might have been present on 25 April, and that they might have included Gurkhas. Hamilton himself later asked 'why were there no Gurkhas on Gallipoli during that critical first twenty-four hours when empires hung in the balance?'[17] As the commander-in-chief of the invasion force, if he did not know then it was no use asking. As he admitted, Egypt was 'stiff' with Indian and Gurkha troops: an exaggeration, perhaps; but Egypt was under no direct threat, and after the repulse of the Ottoman advance on the canal they were available. (And, although there was no actual 'Gurkha brigade', the Indian Army pragmatically, and, for the historian, confusingly, often posted units between formations.) The answer seems to be simply that, as with many other aspects of the landing – maps, logistic and medical arrangements, reconnaissance and the necessary resolution among local commanders – no one seems to have decisively taken charge of what was needed and made sure it was done. Hamilton did not have an Indian brigade at the landings because he did not press Maxwell hard enough for one when he was assembling his force. Responsibility for this must lay with Hamilton, a man unequal to exercising the responsibility of high command in war: like most of us.

'Was ever a Commander given a more difficult task?': preparing for the campaign

As Hamilton arrived in the eastern Mediterranean what was at first called the Constantinople Expeditionary Force (later more prudently named the Mediterranean Expeditionary Force) assembled. By the time of the invasion, on 25 April 1915, it totaled some 75,000 troops, including a French corps, the British 29th Division, the Royal Naval Division and the Australian and New Zealand Army Corps, comprising Australasian troops commanded by a former Bengal lancer. General William Birdwood, had been Hardinge's Military Secretary, his representative at Army Headquarters at Simla. At Kitchener's behest Duff somewhat reluctantly released him and Birdwood gained a monthly salary of 4,500 rupees (or approximately four hundred times the pay of one of his sepoys). As Birdwood had read

---

17 Regimental Committee, *History of the 5th Royal Gurkha Rifles*, p. xix.

General Sir William Birdwood meeting Punjabi Musalman troops, probably members of the mountain batteries. Birdwood could speak to Indian troops in Hindustani or Urdu. (AWM C02159)

the closely argued minutes that Fenton Aylmer had submitted ineffectually to Beauchamp Duff in August 1914, he understood how brittle was the Indian Army, despite its size, experience and valour. A man as adept in committee rooms as on campaign, Birdwood assumed a command that was to bring him more regard than a failed operation might be expected to deliver and a boost to a career that saw him rise to become Commander-in-Chief in India.

While Birdwood's force was to include only some 650 Indian troops in the Gaba Tepe landings (the drivers, gunners and followers of the 7th Indian Mountain Artillery Brigade with its twelve 10-pounder guns), India influenced the conduct of the campaign at both the tactical level (in the actions of Indian units and their men) and at the level of operational command. Birdwood's staff, an Australian newspaper reported (with no concern in distant Kalgoorlie for operational security in the Aegean) 'has come from India with him'. He chose his staff from men he had known in India, including Brigadier-General Harold 'Hooky' Walker as his Chief of Staff, a British officer but with Indian experience. Lieutenant-Colonel Andrew Skeen of the 24th Punjabis was his GSO 1 (that is, his senior 'General Staff Officer'). Skeen seemed 'a very keen officer', a man with 'the appearance of a university professor of the young and athletic type', who had lectured for several years at the new Indian Army Staff College at Quetta and who was to exert a baleful influence on the campaign.[18] Major Charles Villiers-Stuart of the 56th Punjabi Rifles was chief intelligence officer, a man adventurous enough to fly over the peninsula ten days before the landings. One of his aides de camp was Lieutenant Brian Onslow, of Probyn's Horse ('quite a pretty boy' according to Edmund Bowler's letters).[19] These and others had had Indian service. They must have mused on and debated the challenge they faced; to land a force on what was known in the trade as a 'hostile shore', in the face of an alert and experienced army defending its own territory.

Hamilton's plan entailed splitting his force (arguably the single most critical failure of a campaign splattered with failures) to make two landings, one at Cape Helles and the other mid-way up its western shore, north of a fortified headland called Gaba Tepe. Birdwood's force's job was to advance across it to cut off the Turks opposing Hamilton's main landing, at the foot of the peninsula. To accomplish this Birdwood had a motley force. It comprised five brigades of Australian and New Zealand infantry, a brigade of the Royal Naval Division, with seven batteries of field artillery and the two Indian mountain batteries; about 25,000 men. 'Was ever a Commander given a more difficult task?', Charles Bruce asked in retrospect.[20]

Through March and April the invasion force assembled in a fleet of transports and warships in the harbour of Mudros, at the island of Lemnos, which had recently been seized by the Greeks from the Ottomans. The Indian infantry were not, however, among them. While warning orders reached the 29th Indian Infantry Brigade's units as early as 10 April, the battalions did not reach Port Said until 20 April, did not embark until 25 April and did not sail from Egypt until the next day. The most substantial Indian contribution to the first landings was the presence of a large supply and transport organisation, and it was better prepared than any other part of the army.

'Rather a stroke of luck': supply and transport preparations

Except for its size and cosmopolitan composition (and that it would land under fire) the Dardanelles expedition resembles the sort of force the Indian Army had been assembling for war for decades. It had sent forces to Burma, China and Abyssinia, and often on the north-west (and, indeed, the north-east) frontier. Comprising a mixture of British and Indian infantry, supported by modest artillery and a heterogeneous mixture of Indian engineering, supply and medical units, it was a familiar enough model. It even faced country, as Hamilton and Birdwood recognised, similar to the scrubby hills of Kohat or Waziristan; and hostile terrain at a distance from its bases. The Indian Army was operating on just such a basis even at the time, in Persia, Arabia and (less happily, it turned out) in Mesopotamia. Where it differed

18 Letter, Edmund Bowler, 18 March 1915, Bowler papers; Bean, *The Story of Anzac*, Vol. I, p. 123.
19 Ibid.
20 Bruce, *Himalayan Wanderer*, p. 252.

from the traditional 'Indian' model was that this was not a punitive expedition in what the pundit of *Small Wars*, General Charles Callwell, called 'remote regions peopled by half-civilized races'.[21] The Ottoman army, emerging experienced if not victorious from the Balkan wars, was a recognisably 'European' army, organised, equipped and trained on a German pattern. (British observers tended to under-rate the Ottoman army's capabilities and to over-estimate the influence of its German advisors, attributing its successes to their involvement.) What British planners did not recognise was how hard it would be to defeat Ottoman troops led by skillful and experienced commanders fighting in defence of their own country. In that respect, the Gallipoli expedition resembled a hybrid: a 'colonial' campaign in its environment but against a 'European' adversary.[22] Both the environment and the enemy would conspire to defeat the invasion.

India provided a substantial part of the expedition's supply services, drawn partly from units in France. The Anzac staff officers were delighted to hear days before the landing that they were to be supported by Indian mule troops – from their Indian experience they knew the value and capacity of the mule corps. The transport for an infantry force comprised heavy 'GS' wagons and limbers, unsuited for the rough tracks and road-less country they expected to use once they fought their way out of the beach-head. (They anticipated, of course, an advance through the hills of Thrace, for which the Indian experience and equipage would have been ideal.)

Both George Aylmer and Heber Alexander's mule corps had served in France over the autumn and winter of 1914-15, seeing hard service and wondering at the farms, customs and people they saw and met in Flanders. In March they were earmarked to go east. The Supply and Transport Corps, ordinarily organised in many small units, was used to improvisation, and by the time the corps embarked for the Dardanelles they included men of twenty-three different mule units. Common language, equipment and procedures, and a willingness to accept the command of its few British officers and warrant officers, allowed its improvised units to work well. Alexander had known from the time he reported to the docks at Marseilles that his unit was to go to the Dardanelles, though his men patiently embarked in the troopship *Ramazan* for another sea voyage to an unknown destination.

The *Ramazan*, a 3,500-ton merchant vessel owned by the Liverpool Shipping Company, left Alexandria for Lemnos carrying Alexander's mule corps and arrived at Mudros on 22 April to join the vast concourse of shipping assembling for the invasion. It included dozens of ships, from the Royal Navy's newest and most powerful battleship, HMS *Queen Elizabeth*, to tramp steamers like the *Ramazan*, as well as

---

21 Callwell, *Small Wars*, p 26.
22 I am grateful to Sir Hew Strachan, Chichele Professor of the History of War at Oxford, who presented a paper at the 'British Empire and the Great War' conference, Nanyang Technological University, February 2014, in which he argued that British commanders tackled the Tanga, Mesopotamian and Gallipoli campaigns as 'colonial' expeditions. I realised that Gallipoli at least ought to be regarded as a hybrid.

Lionel Lindsay's cartoon of his character 'Chunder Loo' as an Indian mountain gunner, one of his advertisements for Cobra boot polish in the Australian magazine the *Bulletin*. (National Library of Australia)

sea-plane, balloon and hospital ships; though too few of the latter. At Mudros Colonel Frederick Koe (the force's Director of Transport and Supply) had Alexander split his corps, sending three troops with 150 carts to serve with the 29th Division, the British formation mainly comprising regular battalions recalled mainly from garrison service in India, and the remainder to serve with the Australian and New Zealand Army Corps in the landing at Gaba Tepe. All confidently expected that the two parts of the expeditionary force would soon be reunited when the two corps of Hamilton's army joined somewhere around Maidos in a few days time – the troops took nothing but their immediate needs, expecting to be replenished, perhaps on the shores of the Dardanelles. (Alexander recalled that if they had not linked up in three days 'the campaign would have failed': as indeed it did.[23]) Alexander himself accompanied the troops detailed to support Birdwood's force. Heber Alexander met Birdwood aboard the *Minneswaska*, pleased to meet another Old Cliftonian, and equally glad to obtain a copy of the orders for the landing, now scheduled for 25 April.

23 Alexander, *On Two Fronts*, p. 142.

It was fortunate that the Indian Supply and Transport Corps units on Gallipoli were equipped for both cart and pack mule transport. Alexander described this as 'rather a stroke of luck': one of the few with which they were favoured.[24] Even so, they lacked water containers, either tanks or bags, a handicap in essentially waterless terrain, and a deficiency not rectified until August. Their service went largely unnoticed: the only mention of Indian muleteers in the first volume of Bean's *The Story of Anzac* is to include them in a list of units present. They are, however, central to the Indian experience and contribution to the campaign, and regardless of the outcome of the landings the entire invasion force had reason to see their presence as a stroke of luck.

Though the British organisation of the Dardanelles campaign is often criticised, rightly, for its inadequate medical planning, the involvement of an especially procured Indian Supply and Transport Corps demonstrated that Colonel Frederick Koe had anticipated the logistic needs of the coming campaign. (In its planning the landings were to herald an overland advance along the northern coast of the Sea of Marmara, a summer campaign in the hills of Thrace. The example of the Crimea, with its lack of requisitioned transport, may have spurred them to ensure that the invading force brought with it enough transport to meet its needs.) The Supply and Transport Corps therefore formed in France another four cart corps, each comprising ten troops, with each troop having sixty drivers, fifty carts and more than a hundred mules – a huge investment in logistics. Artificers (such as wheelwrights, saddlers and shoeing smiths) and other specialists, brought each corps strength to about 650 men. The organisation's only disadvantage was its paucity of British staff, though Alexander was fortunate to obtain the services of experienced conductors and in Ressaidar Hashmet Ali, Jemadar Wali Mahomed and clerk Mangat Rai equally experienced Indian subordinates.

The Supply and Transport units hint at relationships between the Indian Army's ethnic groups. Alexander tried to place men of the same 'caste' in the one troop, but the corps' NCOs and specialists came from various groups. As their names suggested, the jemadar and clerk were Musalman and Hindu respectively, but Alexander affirmed that Wali Mahomed and Mangat Rai were 'bosom friends'.[25] Virtually the only Sikhs in Alexander's unit were two, Chanda Singh and Bajinder Singh, who were to be badly wounded and killed respectively.

The four new cart corps were named the Indian Mule Cart Train, Mediterranean Expeditionary Force under Colonel Charles Beville. They embarked on their transports from Marseilles early in April and steamed for Egypt. Heber Alexander's corps travelled on the *Ramazan*, loading over 1,100 mules in a hectic six hours. Despite the hardships they had suffered through the winter Alexander and his men regretted leaving France but looked forward to the voyage, if not the coming campaign, with

24 Ibid., p. 141.
25 Ibid., p. 127.

Mountain gunners in 'mufti' (casual dress). The men come from the batteries' two main ethnic groups – Punjabi Musalman (left) and Sikh (right). (National Library of Australia)

Army Headquarters, Simla; today still used as offices by the Indian Army in Shimla. (Author)

'a pleasant feeling of anticipation'.[26] Except for caring for their animals, the muleteers were able to rest on the voyage, arriving at Alexandria on 11 April. It was the last rest they would get for months, if they survived.

Though the 29th Indian Infantry Brigade had not arrived, by the third week of April the plans and the initial invasion force were complete, and the landings were timed to begin just before dawn on Sunday, 25 April. Through the afternoon and evening of 24 April the battleships, cruisers, destroyers and the many transports weighed anchor and steamed out of Mudros harbour. The *Pera*, carrying the 21st Kohat Battery, happened to be among the first transports ordered to leave. Having been among the first to arrive, early in March, it was deep within the anchorage, and had to weave its way between transports and warships lying in the harbour. 'It was most thrilling', Fergusson remembered, as soldiers and sailors cheered each other as they passed. Looking back, he added that 'it was sad to think that for many of them it would be their last cheer'.[27] Heaving to in Purnea Bay, on the north coast of Lemnos, the *Pera* and other transports waited until midnight and steamed towards Gallipoli to join the invasion fleet assembling off the coast west of Gaba Tepe.

At Kubri, on the canal, Rifleman Dhanbir Gurung carefully stored the field kit of Major William Villiers-Stuart (Charles's brother), who, having been on leave in Britain in 1914, had been given a New Army battalion rather than serving with his beloved 5th Gurkhas. Dhanbir Gurung, Villiers-Stuart's batman, slipped into his kukri scabbard a 'touching little letter', in which he reported that the battalion would soon be going to Gallipoli, where he might be killed before seeing his Sahib again – as he was. He (or a literate man of his company) wrote that when Villiers-Stuart at last unpacked his kit 'you will get this and remember me, Sahib. If you too are killed, we will be once more together and so happy. Goodbye for now, Sahib.'[28]

---

26 Ibid., p. 131.
27 'Gallipoli 1915', Arthur Fergusson, 3DRL3635, AWM.
28 Gould, *Imperial Warriors*, p. 158.

5

'My friends and brothers dying': Anzac, April

Before dawn on 25 April Australian infantry landed north of Gaba Tepe, only to be held on the ridges a thousand yards inland from the shingly beach soon named Anzac Cove. The victims of their commanders' timidity, swift and relentless Ottoman counter-attacks penned them on the ridges they would hold but not break out of for the rest of the campaign. Around Cape Helles, twelve miles to the south, a British force landed soon after on beaches where they met determined resistance (and heavy casualties) and were paralyzed by a similar indecision as commanders had shown at Anzac. At neither landing did the troops reach their ostensible objectives. Ottoman willingness to trade lives for ground ensured that the two invading forces would fail, a fact that took eight months and the deaths of around 112,000 men before the campaign ended. Indian troops took part in the fighting at both Anzac and Cape Helles, but so distinct were the two theatres we will deal with their experiences and contribution in the two separately; first, Anzac.

'Very mixed up': the landing at Anzac

Aboard the transport *Pera*, Arthur Fergusson claimed that he woke at 4, roused by the sound 'the firing of big guns', though no firing was heard off Anzac until about 4.30, and no warships' guns fired until an hour later. Either way, he forced himself to lie in his cabin until about 6, when he 'could stick there no longer', and rose. By the time he came on deck dawn had broken and he saw 'a wonderful sight' off Anzac Cove, 'the whole sea full of ships with piquet boats towing barges, and every type of boat everywhere'. Every type, that is, except the lighters that the mountain gunners needed to carry ashore their mules. The landing went wrong from the start. Fergusson expected that John Bruce's Jacob's Battery would land about 6a.m. and that the boats of his 'tow' would come alongside the *Pera* at about 8a.m. In the event, Bruce's tows were two hours late and Fergusson's arrived only at 4p.m.; eight hours late.

Those on the decks of the transports looked eagerly at the ridges to the east. Officers had 'a splendid view of the proceedings' through their field glasses, though, as Fergusson recalled, 'things seemed very mixed up'. In contrast to the legend of the landing as propagated and still accepted in Australia, casualties were at first remarkably light. The commander of the 7th Mountain Artillery Brigade, Colonel John Parker, and two of his British officers, went ashore with the second wave, and their boat brought back only one man wounded on the beach. (Charles Bean, aged just 34, described Parker as 'an elderly Anglo-Indian officer; in fact he was little more than fifty.[1])

In the meantime, the transports withdrew out of range of Turkish shrapnel, which began to fall among them when Ottoman field artillery began firing around noon. 'The casualties began', Fergusson remembered, 'when Gaba Tepe battery woke up'. Ottoman guns emplaced on the headland fired at the transports, forcing them to withdraw and obliging the supporting warships to fire in return. The firing was not all in one direction, though. Escorted by a party of Tasmanians, the first of Jacob's Battery's six guns were action at the head of White's Valley by five minutes to noon. Its commander, Captain Horace Kirby went forward to find out from the Australian infantry where his fire could best be directed, and Bean recorded that they greeted word of the battery's arrival 'like a draught of cool water'. Overlooked by Ottoman observers on Battleship Hill, though, Jacob's Battery came under Turkish artillery fire, which from midday grew in intensity. Shrapnel bursting over the guns wounded Jemadar Dulla Khan and mortally wounded Captain Perceval Chapman. (He said he was 'only hit in the neck and could walk'. Evacuated to Egypt, he died a week later: his name is not on the Helles Memorial.[2]) In the meantime Gunner Sher Khan of Kohat Battery became the first Indian to die on Gallipoli, on 27 April. Soon a message would reach a family in a village near Rawalpindi, as telegrams and messages were going to towns and suburbs in Australia, New Zealand and Britain.) Kirby, wounded in the head, realised that his men could not remain and ordered the guns back, though the fire was so heavy that they had to be pulled out by hand. (Kirby was carried off to a hospital ship, from which he 'deserted' back to his men the next day.[3]) The mountain gunners' forward observation officers, notably Lieutenant John Thom, remained out on the ridges with the infantry, transmitting directions and requests for fire to the warships standing off the cove. Fergusson recorded his annoyance that 'the *Bacchante* and the *Triumph* were ... the only two ships that appeared to take any interest in ... observations from the shore'.[4]

The first shots fired by the mountain gunners had what Birdwood described as an 'electrifying effect' on the Anzac infantry.[5] The delay in Kohat's entering action was a sign of the failures of routine staff work that dogged the entire landing. Jacob's Battery was in action again by 5.45 p.m., and Kohat joined it ashore shortly after. If the mountain guns had not prevailed against the heavier weight of metal the Turks

---

1 Bean, *The Story of Anzac*, Vol. I, p. 393.
2 Walker, *To What End did They Die?*, p. 77.
3 Bean, *The Story of Anzac*, Vol. I, p. 395.
4 'Gallipoli 1915', Arthur Fergusson, 3DRL3635, AWM.
5 Birdwood, *Khaki and Gown*, p. 258.

deployed, they had at least heartened some of the invaders. Charles Bean overheard an exchange between two Australians. One complained that the Indian guns firing from what was soon named MacLagan's Ridge (after one of the irresolute Australian brigadiers whose dilatory orders had arguably scuppered the entire operation). He claimed that they drew Turkish shells upon them – Ottoman counter-battery fire was good; much better than the invaders had expected. The other Australian rebuked him: 'they're doing great work, those guns'.[6]

At last, about 4p.m. the laggard tow arrived and drivers and gunners loaded guns and animals, easily climbing down rope ladders in bare feet (something that European soldiers did not do). Choppy seas later in the day made the transfer hazardous – the *Pera's* captain said that he would not have attempted it in peacetime – and the troops and animals then had to sit in their lighters, bumping against the ship's side and feeling sick, in constant fear of being upset or damaged by the rough weather. At last, after two hours of this, Fergusson managed to hail a passing picket boat, which towed the lighters to the beach by about 6.30p.m. During the half-hour the tow took to reach the shore the lighters came under fire from Turkish artillery, still firing from Gaba Tepe despite the warships' efforts, and Fergusson 'felt more helpless than at any other time during the war'.[7] By the time Kohat Battery had unloaded dusk was falling, but the beach was by this time 'a shambles' with some of the several thousand Anzac dead and wounded the force has suffered in the course of the day. While the heavier Australian and New Zealand field batteries landed in the days following 25 April, space for battery positions (and the area they needed for ammunition limbers) became scarce in the gullies and steep hillsides. The mountain guns, though smaller and less powerful, were more nimble. As rain fell on 26 April mules carried four guns up the steep slope of Plugge's Plateau, overlooking the cove, as the core of an 'inner line', in case the precarious Anzac line on the second ridge should break. Two guns of each battery were to provide a final bastion. Other guns were sent forward to support the hard-pressed Anzac infantry, still trying to scratch and hold a rough line where the first day's fighting had left them, on the very edge of the crest of the second ridge, and on the broad expanse of the 400 Plateau, where the inevitable happened. In the confusion of units mingled in unfamiliar terrain the 4th Battalion made a sudden and erroneous advance. Arising from the sort of confused orders that had sent the Light Brigade to its death in the Crimea, the battalion moved forward on its own, drawing onto itself not only the fire of the astonished (and no doubt delighted) Turks, but also the fire of Kohat Battery. Gunner officers, observing movement in the scrub south of the Daisy Patch – more-or-less now the location of the Australian memorial at Lone Pine – fired on khaki-clad figures they believed to be Turkish. The Australians fired on their own lines and at the battery. Arthur Fergusson, suspecting a mistake was being made, called for his guns to cease fire.

6   Bean, *The Story of Anzac*, Vol. I, pp. 463-64.
7   'Gallipoli 1915', Arthur Fergusson, 3DRL3635, AWM.

Troops of the 1st Australian Division landing at Anzac Cove late on the morning of 25 April 1915. (AWM A01090)

Mountain gunners unloading their guns from mules at Anzac. (AWM P00046)

The beach at what became Anzac Cove with men of the 1st Australian Division forming up beside gunners of Jacob's Battery. (ATL PAColl-7581-84)

'A magnet for shells': Supply and Transport units

Like all Indian units the Supply and Transport corps had a small number of British officers and warrant officers, particularly important for liaising with ordnance staff at the dumps and depots on the beach. On 6 May Sub-Conductor Edgar Galway landed from the *Ramazan* (from where he had been sending supplies and fodder ashore). After spending a sleepless night (his first under fire), Galway was killed, again by shells fired virtually at random from the Gaba Tepe guns exploding over their mule lines. Sergeant Keith Little, who as clerk to the New Zealand staff officers at the beach supply dumps, saw a lot of the drivers. He recorded his admiration for them as 'most painstaking and patient in everything they do'.[8]

Three mule troops landed at Cape Helles from the *Ramazan*. Heber Alexander saw the aftermath of the landing at V Beach (Sedd-ul-Bahr) later on the morning of the 25th, with heaps of bodies lying about the gangways leading from the *River Clyde*, and corpses washing about in the sea beside the lighters that the attacking troops

8   Diary, 11 May 1915, Sgt Keith Little, 2003.409, QEIIAMM.

had attempted to get ashore against Turkish fire. Among the first Indian muleteers to land were Naik Narain Singh, who led a party to man-handle the first of 150 carts onto lighters and see them ashore, and Driver Bir Singh, a Dogra and one of Narain Singh's party. They drove mules and carts up onto a grassy bank above the beach near the fort of Sedd-ul-Bahr.

Having unloaded the three troops at Helles the *Ramazan* steamed for Gaba Tepe. Already it was clear that the optimistic plans composed in Mudros harbour had failed. Alexander realised that rather than being far inland, advancing on the Kilid Bahr plateau and the plain of Maidos, the Anzacs were penned in a shallow semi-circle of trenches on the crest of the ridges around Anzac Cove. Again the drivers wrestled mules and carts into two lighters lying alongside. One began to sink, so they pushed the mules over the lowered bow ramps and had them swim for the shore while the drivers (who could not swim) jumped for the other lighter. (Alexander's drivers were not quite the first Indians ashore, or even the first Indian Supply and Transport men ashore – some teams from the 33rd Mule Corps had gone ashore with the mountain artillery, probably carrying fodder for the batteries' mules.)

The muleteers worked for three days to clear the ship of animals, carts, forage and gear, working with little rest. One driver fell down a ladder into the hold, fracturing his thigh and having to be evacuated to the hospital ship *Devanha*. The muleteers collected supplies and ammunition from Australian supply and ordnance depots on the crowded beach and the *Ramazan* remained off Anzac for a time as the mule corps' depot ship, eventually driven off when the danger of submarines increased a month later. They came under the direction of the Australian Army Service Corps staff officer, Colonel Jeremy Marsh, who as a former Bengal lancer could speak Hindustani. He found the drivers' conduct 'admirable' and recommended some receive decorations.[9] Ressaidar Hashmet Ali, Lance-Naik Bahadur Shah and Driver Bir Singh received the Indian Order of Merit, and a hospital orderly Ganpat Rao the Indian Distinguished Conduct Medal. When the news arrived in the mule camp, just before the opening of the August offensive, there was 'great rejoicing', their officer remembered.[10]

Like the artillery, the Supply and Transport found Australians with whom they could communicate. Heber Alexander thought it 'remarkable how many among the Anzacs knew a little Hindustani'. Some had worked in India or even been born there, while others had lived in Fiji and had directed Indian indentured labourers. Men sought these 'interpreter billets' because they meant higher rank and pay, and a supposedly safer job, if such existed at Anzac. But Alexander found that of the Australians he obtained as interpreters one was killed the day he arrived, four or five were wounded and most of the rest were invalided sick. Alexander described how a Second Lieutenant, a 20-year-old 'merchant' from Terowie, South Australia, Hedley Cullen, was attached to the corps. Cullen 'knew no Hindustani at all', and was a

---

9   War diary, Indian Mule Cart Train, May 1915, 189, AWM 6.
10 Alexander, *On Two Fronts*, pp. 223-24.

novice at transport work, but he was conscientious and popular with the unit's Indian and British members.[11] Another, Driver Matthew Kirwan, a 34-year-old analytical chemist, left the 7th Australian supply company to become an interpreter on 3 May. Kirwan had worked with the Colonial Sugar Refining Company in Fiji, and his wife lived in Suva. He seemed to be 'a magnet for shells', and the superstitious muleteers preferred to avoid him. His luck held until at the end of August he was evacuated with a shell splinter in his back.

The Supply and Transport muleteers' call of 'Jhillo!' ['gee-up!'] became common around Helles, Anzac and later Suvla. The muleteers needed a sheltered place for their mule lines and found it in a gully below Walker's Ridge that soon became known, naturally enough, as Mule Gully. Drivers cut scrapes and dugouts into the surrounding slopes, which soon became a rabbit warren of increasingly elaborate bivouacs. They piled bales of fodder, bags of grain and boxes of food and stores in the gully's open mouth, hoping for protection from the explosions of Ottoman guns fired blind or off the map into the Anzac position. Heber Alexander described the effects of shelling by 'Beachy Bill' – one of the several Ottoman guns that fired into the Anzac position. As shells fell into the mule lines near Hell Spit (the southern headland defining Anzac Cove) Australians and New Zealanders untied mules from their head-ropes and led them away while Ressaidar Hashmet Ali led muleteers to carry the corps' precious gear to safety. Despite their efforts 89 mules were hit, and the NCO in charge of the picket and a driver, Bir Singh (possibly the same man who had been among the first Indian to land on the peninsula) wounded, along with several of the Australian helpers. Mule Gully became one of the most photographed spots at Anzac, a scene of noise and activity day and night. Though only 150 yards from the front-line trenches at the top of the spur above them, it was regarded as 'the safest place in the whole position'.[12] Here two New Zealand Army Service Corps officers ran the Indian distributing depot, sharing a dugout in the sandy cliff constructed by Alexander's surviving sub-conductor, Mr. Brown, with furniture made by one of the mule corps carpenters, Hashmet Ali (not the Ressaidar, of course). Unfortunately, individual Indians often appear only as names in the records.

'They stuck to us throughout': mountain gunners at Anzac

Fergusson was convinced that had his battery been landed ten hours earlier, as planned, the two mountain artillery batteries could have brought a cross-fire against the Turkish batteries firing at the Anzac infantry. This certainly 'would have helped our men a lot', he wrote, and speculating that 'they possibly would not have come back as they did' – that is, withdrew from the objectives the covering force had been

---

11 Alexander, *On Two Fronts*, p. 201.
12 Ibid., p. 172.

directed to seize. The mountain gunners' priority became to find gun positions from which they could support the invasion, the fate of which was still to be decided. One section went with a guide up the steep slopes of Plugge's Plateau, soon after relieved by a section of Jacob's Battery. The other four guns of Kohat Battery were at first placed near the mouth of Shrapnel Gully (near the later site of the cemetery), while two Jacob's guns were placed in the south of the Anzac line, on Bolton's Ridge.

Guides directed the rest of Kohat Battery to a spot on 'Queensland Ridge' (usually 'Point'; the southern slopes of MacLagan's Ridge), where the battery remained, under 'a tremendous fusillade all night and lots of bullets', keeping a sharp look-out in case the Australian and New Zealand infantry gave way. The next morning the gunners were awake before dawn and the battery commanders sought out Ewen Sinclair MacLagan, the commander of the 3rd Brigade, whose mistaken decisions on 25 April more than any other factor destroyed the Australians' hopes of making a successful landing. Arthur Fergusson found Maclagan on Braund's Hill (practically the centre of the Anzac line) and asked him where he wanted artillery support. Maclagan waved his arm vaguely in a semi-circle taking in the entire front line and said 'everywhere round there'. Fergusson pressed him for more specific targets and they agreed that the most danger came from Ottoman troops on what was even then called the Chessboard, a network of trenches high on the slopes of Baby 700, the height that dominated Shrapnel Valley.

This, Kohat Battery's first test, was not a success. A sweating subaltern soon returned from the firing position Fergusson had nominated, reporting that it was on a hill too steep for the mules to climb (weakened as they were after six weeks aboard ship) and that he could not get guns in action in less than four hours. Fergusson selected another, more accessible, position, and the guns were soon in action, after a while succeeding in shutting up the Turkish mountain guns firing from the Chessboard, including at Kohat Battery's guns. 'The Australians', Fergusson recorded somewhat ambiguously, 'were very polite about our assistance that day'.[13]

If Sinclair Maclagan was of little use in requesting support (he habitually told Fergusson simply to 'carry on'), the gunners and their Australian and New Zealand comrades developed a much warmer relationship. Participants and eye-witnesses give many examples of the close comradeship that grew between the Australians and the mountain gunners. Australian signalers were posted to the gunners' headquarters to maintain communications by telephone between the gun positions, battery headquarters and the infantry brigade and divisional headquarters. Three of the signalers (possibly named Sherer, Smith and Nye) liked the Indians so much that, Fergusson wrote, 'they stuck to us throughout'.

While men of the two armies liked each other, they were not blind to each other's shortcomings. Arthur Fergusson came to believe that one explanation for the Australians' failure to hold onto the gains they had made in the hours following the

---

13   'Gallipoli 1915', Arthur Fergusson, 3DRL3635, AWM.

An Australian gunner photographed what he called the '21st Indian Battery Guard', a sign of how the Indian mountain brigade maintained soldierly standards. (State Library of Victoria)

Indian gunners and Anzacs at one of the gunners' bivouacs at Anzac early in the campaign, evidence of the relationship between them. (AWM H00198)

first landing was that 'they were all out in little parties doing V.C. stunts'. When Australians (eager for the opinion of a regular soldier) asked him how they had performed, Fergusson had no compunction in telling them, 'and they mostly quite agreed with me', he wrote.[14]

'Don't shoot!' Indians in front?

Survivors' accounts of the landing at Anzac abound with a number of legends. Men told stories of the 'woman sniper' from the earliest days of the campaign, and many letters and diaries detail the presence of 'German officers' who called out orders to their enemies, supposedly appearing in the Anzac lines dressed in Australian uniforms to give men orders that placed them in peril. One of the most persistent stories is that German officers called out that the troops the Anzacs faced were not Ottoman but were 'Indians' or 'Gurkhas'. Many letters, diaries, memoirs and unit histories allude to false reports of Indian troops in front of the Australians and New Zealanders. Nothing illustrates the confusion prevailing at Anzac than the stories that Indian troops had been seen fighting there.

On the evening of 25 April the 16th Battalion's colonel, Harold Pope, was told by his adjutant (who got it from a sergeant) that Indian troops were fighting the Turks on the battalion's left flank – that is, on the slopes of Russell's Top. The sergeant and even the adjutant can be forgiven for not knowing that the Mediterranean Expeditionary Force included no Indian infantry, but Pope should have known. Still, he sent out to investigate a captain, William Elston, and Private Reginald Lushington, a former tea planter in Ceylon now settled in Western Australia. Lushington could speak Tamil and 'Pathan', and was expected to at least be able to make himself understood by troops who spoke Hindustani or Urdu. Elston and Lushington went out through the thick scrub in the darkness and Pope and his adjutant soon heard their voices 150 yards distant. They took their calls to be a request for another officer and Ronald McDonald, the adjutant, also went forward. He soon encountered a kneeling figure pointing a rifle at him. He said 'I'm an English sahib. I want burra sahib' [the 'big officer' – his commander] 'and other phrases in Hindustani'.[15] The man lowered his rifle but McDonald realised that he was among Turks. He escaped, but Elston and Lushington were taken prisoner, two of a handful of Australians captured at the landing. Private Phillip Harrison of the 16th Battalion described in a letter to his cousin in Western Australia how his platoon encountered 'a body of Turks' who had 'the D_____ cool cheek to pass themselves off as Indian Ghurkers' near what became known as Pope's Hill.[16] Lushington was 'a pal of mine', Harrison told his cousin. 'As

---

14 'Gallipoli 1915', Arthur Fergusson, 3DRL3635, AWM.
15 Bean, *The Story of Anzac*, Vol. I, p. 470; Lushington, *A Prisoner with the Turks*, p. 3.
16 Letter, Private Philip Harrison, 16th Battalion, PR91/005, AWM.

soon as we got the order to fire we let them have it'. Lushington would reappear in Indian Army records of the campaign.

Elston and Lushington's capture was only the most well documented occasion. The shout was also heard on German Officer's Ridge 'Don't shoot – Indian troops!' – Charles Bean does not make clear whether it was the Anzacs or Turks who called, but he attributes the error not to any ruse on the part of the Turks or their German advisers, but to 'the ordinary effects of battle strain'.[17] Bean records that elsewhere, on Baby 700, it was 'if you see men on the left … They're Indians'; likewise at Mortar Ridge, where it was 'Gurkhas on the left, don't shoot!'[18] Leslie Newton, author of an Australian battalion history, claimed that Turks deliberately called 'Don't fire, the Indians are advancing on the right'. They had, he wrote, 'good linguists, probably wearing similar uniforms, mingling in our ranks'.[19] The idea that Turkish or German officers infiltrated the invaders' lines spreading confusion has never been substantiated. It was, indeed, easy to confuse men of both sides. Soon after the landing Arthur Fergusson stopped a Royal Naval Division man firing at men who in the fading light of dusk 'looked very like Australians who had cut their hats into fancy shapes' (something 'very common … with them', he added) only to realise later that he had in fact seen his first Turkish troops. He realised later that their officer carried a sword (virtually no Anzac officers did) and the 'fancy shapes' were of course the Ottoman 'Enverei' soft helmet.

New Zealanders reported similar incidents. In a letter to his parents in Auckland John Atkins described hearing of German officers dressed in British uniforms (leading Turkish troops dressed as Indians), responding to challenges by saying 'don't shoot we're Indians'.[20] Along with bogus reports of spies and women snipers the story became 'one of the most persistent' of many rumours to circulate among troops at Anzac, and Bean devoted about nine pages to elaborating on them.[21] A small irony – which explains the Australians' seeming gullibility – was that many Anzac officers probably knew that Cox's Indian brigade had originally been destined to serve with Birdwood's Australian and New Zealand Army Corps. Birdwood, who did not know of its dilatory departure from Egypt, expected it to arrive on 27 April, and by 30 April was still expecting it, so poor were communications between the force's constituent formations and senior commanders. The troops at Anzac, so a New Zealand surgeon recorded, 'all wish the Gurkhas were with us'.[22]

17 Bean, *The Story of Anzac*, Vol. I, p. 470.
18 Ibid., Vol. I, pp. 308, xiv.
19 Newton, *The Story of the Twelfth*, p. 80.
20 Letter, 11 June 1915, John Atkins, Auckland Battalion, B1989.199, QEIIAMM.
21 Bean, *The Story of Anzac*, Vol. I, pp. xiii, 308, 439-43, 469-70.
22 Diary, 5 May 1915, Percival Fenwick, *Gallipoli Diary*, p. 17.

'Pifferpore': Indians established at Anzac

On 27 April, with the force ashore the two Indian mountain batteries were allotted for the time being to support the two Australasian divisions, Jacob's to Alexander Godley's New Zealand and Australian Division and Kohat to William Bridges's 1st Australian Division. While guns were distributed across the beach-head, most were used to help to hold the posts at the head of Monash Valley, the vital and vulnerable heights where an Ottoman breakthrough could swiftly result in the invaders' defeat.

Within days the mountain gunners had established a headquarters at what they soon christened 'Pifferpore' – after the Punjab Irregular Frontier Force – on a ridge near the mouth of Shrapnel Valley, 'the safest place in Anzac', or so Fergusson was told.[23] And so it proved, until after a week one of the Turkish guns known collectively as 'Beachy Bill' began firing and caught both men and mules, killing and wounding both. The battery headquarters and the mule lines shifted closer to the beach where the medical section had established a dressing station, and where it remained until the August offensive.

To make up for its losses at the landing (which left it short of two gun detachments) Jacob's Battery borrowed twenty men of the 3rd Australian Brigade's ammunition column (unable to operate as planned because it was unable to use wagons or limbers in the trackless country), who remained with it for over a month. In a reversal of traditional Indian artillery practice (which had seen 'native' gun lascars heaving cannon about for European gunners) the Australians assisted the few trained Indian gunners allotted to get the two guns back in action. They were sent up the steep track to Walker's Ridge, firing northward toward Turkish positions on the main range, around Baby 700.

In the first weeks of the campaign 'the O.P. [observation post] was very much worried by snipers', Fergusson recalled.[24] Snipers – or what men thought were snipers – inflicted a slow drain even on gunners in positions as far as hundreds of yards from the foremost trenches. Ottoman snipers remained a hazard, even in Shrapnel Valley, for months after the landing, though some of those killed by 'snipers' were killed by random shots. Kohat Battery's first casualties – Driver Havildar Saidullah wounded and Gunner Sher Singh, killed on 27 April while operating a telephone to one of the gun sections – were attributed to snipers.

The Indian gunners, regular soldiers and among the very few on Gallipoli who understood the requirements of mountain gunnery, were mostly free to select their own targets and methods. (General James McCay, commanding the 2nd Australian Brigade, whom Fergusson also asked for targets, like MacLagan 'did not know where he wanted fire and unhelpfully replied that 'all around was equally necessary', a response in accord with his reputation at the time and since.) The gunners' principal

---

23 'Gallipoli 1915', Arthur Fergusson, 3DRL3635, AWM.
24 Ibid.

problem was that the Anzac beach-head was both hemmed in by ridges and constituted a series of ridges, hills and gullies. This terrain offered serious challenges for weapons that essentially fired on a flat trajectory. Britain had no mountain howitzers, though artillery officers (especially those with experience of mountain warfare on the north-west frontier) had argued for years the need for one. In order to hit the foremost Turkish positions the mountain gunners were obliged to resort to novel improvisations. Cresswell Rawson proved to be especially inventive, at least five times taking a gun into the foremost line and mounting it at a steep angle on the Australian parapet, aiming at especially troublesome Turkish machine-gun positions. Usually firing in the early afternoon, when sentries might be assumed to be drowsy, and covered by infantry fire, the daring gunners had to dismantle their gun and decamp before retaliatory fire made their position untenable. Fergusson thought that it was unfair to ask men to risk such hazards, when a howitzer could have done the job without undue risk, but his battery fired up to nine times in this way, 'wonderfully lucky' to lose only one man.[25] (What the infantry, who remained exposed to the Turkish response, thought of this daring remains unrecorded.) Anzac infantry did, however, admire the mountain gunners' skill. Anzacs, virtually all of them citizen soldiers, acknowledged the mountain gunners' professionalism. John Treloar, a clerk at the Australian division's headquarters, noticed the 'precise machine-like motions' of the gunners' drill.[26]

Communication arrangements at Anzac between infantry and guns were often rudimentary, with appeals for support from front line positions having to go through higher headquarters, usually by precarious telephone lines and then back down the artillery command chain. Even then it was not always a simple matter to deliver shells onto targets often close to the Anzac front line, even for gunners with experience of firing in mountainous country. When during the Turkish attacks the Australian 1st Brigade troops at Lone Pine asked for shells to fall on the Turkish troops massing behind their front line, not only did the messages take many minutes to be transferred between the two divisional headquarters (because the only guns able to reach into Mule Gulley belonged to Jacob's Battery and came under the New Zealand and Australian Division. Then, in order to make the relatively short range John Thom had to use the lighter star-shell charges.

No Indian Army infantry served at Anzac until August, but it is compelling to wonder what might have happened had they been a part of Birdwood's force on 25 April. What if they and not the enthusiastic but partially trained 3rd Australian Brigade had landed first? What if regular Indian Army officers such as Cox, Palin or Bruce had been on the second ridge on the morning of the landing, trained and able to follow their orders, rather than the British-Australian brigadiers who, overwhelmed by the responsibility and stress of command, ordered their men to dig-in rather than press-on? Given the obduracy Cox displayed later in the campaign, carrying out

25 Ibid.
26 Treloar, *An Anzac Diary*, p. 173

unjustifiable plans regardless of cost, at Gully Ravine, Sari Bair and Hill 60, it is possible that had the 29th Brigade formed the 'covering force' the advance troops would have met the Turkish reserves much further east than did the untried Anzacs.

Ian Hamilton came to regret that he had not pressed harder for more Gurkhas to have been included in the Mediterranean Expeditionary Force, and sooner. Writing the foreword to the 5th Gurkhas' regimental history, he confided that 'the 5th Gurkhas should have landed with the Anzacs, whose headlong valour needed just that counterpoise ... afforded ... by a small reserve of regulars'. Moreover, the Gurkhas came with 'perfect discipline and an instinctive, inherited knowledge of woodcraft'. It might seem to be wishful thinking, but Hamilton felt that had the Gurkhas faced the Turks at Anzac on 25 April 1915 they could have 'worked round their flank or penetrated their line' – endorsing the classic Gurkha myth, to 'cut off their heads with their kukris almost before they knew they had lost them'.[27] That he did not reflected his weakness in failing to stand up to Kitchener and Maxwell. But the possibility of Indian infantry fighting at Anzac remains only one of the tantalizing might-have-beens of Gallipoli.

---

27 Regimental Committee, *History of the 5th Royal Gurkha Rifles*, pp. xviii-xix.

6

'Be not weary and faint hearted': Anzac, May

A week into the campaign optimism remained. General Alec Wilson (commanding the Canal Defences) asked for help from the Egyptian police to assist in 'searching the houses of political suspects when the Allies enter Constantinople'. One of the minor benefits of Turkey's anticipated defeat would be that the subversion of the Indian Army's Mohammedan troops would end.[1] The 29th Brigade's first operation order anticipated a rapid mobile war – it directed each battalion to prepare more than 90 mules to carry ammunition, food, water (and a mule for each battalion's officers' mess): clearly Cox and his superiors expected to break out of the beach-head and advance up the peninsula. Reports from Gallipoli would soon end any such optimistic plans.

'A pretty bad time': early May at Anzac

With Turkish counter-attacks dying down, Birdwood made the first attempt to break out of the Anzac perimeter, attacks that were as poorly co-ordinated as they were gallantly attempted. The mountain guns contributed to the supporting barrage. 'The attack was not a success', Fergusson admitted.[2] Just as the Turks had failed to break through against rapid-firing rifles supported by machine-guns and shrapnel, so the invaders learned the same lessons. 'Barrage' might be too grandiose a term for the weight of fire the little mountain guns could generate, though the heavier shells of the warships thickened it. Indeed, given that a single shell from the battleships standing offshore delivered a greater weight of steel than the entire battery, the artillery fire is best described as naval gun support complemented by the mountain guns and the batteries of field artillery scattered about Anzac in any available position.

As ever, the mobility of the mountain guns and their gunners' skill had them operating from the foremost Anzac lines against targets pointed out by infantry officers who developed a profound faith in the gunners' ability to help them. The Wellington

---

1   Tel., 3 May 1915, WWI/293/H, NAI.
2   'Gallipoli 1915', Arthur Fergusson, 3DRL3635, AWM.

Battalion's commander, William Malone, at first thought that the mountain guns would be 'bound to specially draw the Turks['] artillery fire', but later in May conceded that 'they have been doing good work'.[3] Rarely refusing requests exposed the mountain gunners to grave risks. 'We had a pretty bad time', Fergusson recorded, when his gunners tried to establish firing positions in full view of the Turks and within 'easy rifle range'. Only by using 'old Turk funk pits', possibly dating from the first day, were the gunners able to open fire.

Though the invading force fought a purely defensive battle between early May and early August, the mountain gunners needed to retain their mules, both to shift guns between positions and to deliver supplies of ammunition to the sections' positions. Nowhere at Anzac was free from the possibility of shells falling, whether aimed or at random, and the mule lines remained as vulnerable as their masters' dugouts and gun positions; more, since the animals could not hide except in the shelter of high banks in the walls of nullahs and gullies. Once, a shell burst over the mule lines, killing a battery's salutri (farrier) and wounding five drivers and four horses, with fourteen mules either killed outright or wounded so badly they had to be destroyed.

The daily program of fire from Beachy Bill and other heavy Turkish guns dictated movement between the gunners' sections and between the sections and the beach. Arthur Fergusson planned his route in touring his sections in accordance with the weight of shells falling around the area. (Believing as he did in the necessity of British officers to keep his guns in action, he assumed that only the presence of German gunners moving between Turkish batteries made them as effective as they were.) Bathing off the beach involved dashing out between bursts and getting under the protection of piers and lighters ready for the next salvo.

6 May saw a particularly bad bombardment of the Anzac rear area (if a location under a thousand yards from the front line may be called that). Early that afternoon several ranging shots fell on around Hell Spit, and then moved along the beach in fifty-yard lifts – these were directed shots, not random. Soon the shells reached the mule lines of the Indian Supply and Transport troops. Some of the drivers prudently fled, joining Anzacs in the lee of the piles of boxes of stores and rations along the beach. Others bravely stood by their animals, until officers shouted at them to lead the animals away – but southwards, into the busting shells. 'Great confusion prevailed', Bean wrote (who seems to have seen it himself) until Colonel William Lesslie, shouting in Hindustani, pointed to the drivers to lead the mules inland, into the gullies. Several Indian officers joined Lesslie and they directed the drivers and their animals toward cover. Even so, 34 mules were killed (or had to be put down), while of a shipment of 24 horses that had just been landed, fourteen died.

Ottoman artillery fire dominated the entire Anzac position and the lives of all of those in it, regardless of rank. On 17 May Birdwood's chief intelligence officer, Major

---

3   Diary, 1 May and 22 May, William Malone, Crawford, (ed.), *No Better Death*, pp. 171, 205.

Charles Villiers-Stuart died when a shell exploded while he sketched near Anzac Cove. An Australian sergeant recorded the circumstances of his death:

> Major Villiers-Stuart went out sketching this morning to one of our gun positions. He was sitting down on top of a hill ... and the shrapnel began to fly around. One shell burst just above him and one of the bullets went through the heart.[4]

Villiers-Stuart, who had served under Birdwood in command of the Kohat independent brigade five years before, was buried that evening, close to the shore in what became Beach Cemetery. Charles Bean wrote an unusually revealing account of his burial.[5] Acknowledging that novices to war had soon acquired an indifference to death and suffering surrounding them, he admitted that 'sometimes – for no reason that I can give –' death came as 'an unaccountable shock'. Bean, who lived near the corps headquarters dug-outs, had grown used to seeing Villiers-Stuart traversing the Anzac position with his maps and sketchpad, and was shocked to hear of him being struck by a shrapnel pellet from by a shell exploding two hundred yards away. Villiers-Stuart had been 'a British officer of the very best type, unassuming, quiet, considerate, and ... without ... fear'. Bean described how as the sunset faded over Imbros a small party stood at his graveside. They could hear the clink of the mules' harness and just make them out as dark shapes, with Indians leading them up the gullies. Overhead they heard the 'constant low sibilant hiss of bullets', the boom of warships' guns and in the distance rifle fire sounding (in a characteristic simile) 'like the crack of a cricket bat'. Bean ended with unusual sentiment, '... and there we leave him to the waves and the sea breezes amidst the little wooden crosses on that shrapnel swept point'. This, Birdwood decided, was 'a fitting tribute to a good soldier'.[6] Villiers-Stuart's grave is still there, in the beautiful, carefully tended Beach Cemetery, with its deserved inscription, 'A man greatly beloved'.

As a prominent and popular officer, Villiers-Stuart's death and burial attracted attention, noted in men's diaries and in reports published in newspapers as far away as Swan Hill in distant Victoria. More humble Indian Army soldiers attracted less notice; nor would they gain memorials as visible. Sikhs and Hindus among the mountain gunners and muleteers were to be cremated, and Anzac diaries record that they were. Musalmans were buried, with the religious injunction to be interred within the day coinciding with the military requirement to dispose of corpses in the increasing heat of the peninsula. Edmund Bowler, the New Zealand Anzac camp commandant selected a burial ground with one of the mountain batteries' officers on 7 May, though where that was – and what happened to the men interred in it – is unknown. Their

---

4 Diary, 17 May 1915, Sgt John McLennan, 5th Battalion, AIF, 1DRL454, AWM.
5 *Swan Hill Guardian and Lake Boga Advocate*, 9 August 1915, p. 4.
6 Birdwood, *Khaki and Gown*, p. 264.

graves were rarely marked, and few Musalman burials can be seen in the cemeteries of the peninsula today. The arrangements for cremation or burial were made within Indian units, the wood and oil for cremation provided by the Supply and Transport Corps, the entire business handled by the 'Indian' members: none of the British officers' memoirs, or even the official war diaries, make any reference to this aspect of life – or rather death – on Gallipoli.

Despite attempts to dispose of the dead, whether for religious or rational reasons, the sheer number of unburied dead lying about in the gullies and hillsides of Anzac (many unable to be reached, let alone interred) swiftly led to the massive infestation of flies that afflicted the entire area for the next seven months. The flies rapidly spread intestinal diseases, again, regardless of rank. Another of Birdwood's 'Piffer' officers, Henry Champion de Crespigny, also of the 56th Rifles, survived the campaign, partly because he was evacuated sick with the notorious dysentery that denuded Birdwood's force. (Birdwood acknowledged that while 'courage and grit' sustained de Crespigny, he lacked the 'strong internal works' that kept Birdwood from succumbing.[7]) Andrew Skeen was also evacuated sick, but unfortunately returned, as we will see.

'Every man deserved something': 19 May

Three weeks after the landing, the Ottomans sought to drive the invaders off the beach-head, launching a major offensive all along the Anzac line on 19 May. This, Arthur Fergusson recalled, became 'our worst day on the Peninsula'. For him the day began before dawn when he visited Centre Section, which was being badly shelled in preparation for the attack. He visited Rawson and Thom's positions, 'quite a lively trip', he wrote with deliberate understatement, moving in dashes from cover to cover up Shrapnel Valley and then down to Shell Green ('all living up to their names'), often taking a flying leap into trenches and landing among their occupants.

Beachy Bill had the range of Rawson's observation post on Bolton's Ridge 'to a foot', and Fergusson found Rawson with the hair singed off one side of his head and his Australian counterpart slightly wounded by a shell splinter. Fergusson gave them a spell to have breakfast and took over the post, though his arrival coincided with a lull in Turkish fire. Rawson had fired at a wagon he had spotted in the Turkish rear area – possibly carrying ammunition. He had his gunners place one of his guns on a parapet, fired and destroyed the wagon, while the Kohat Battery's Subedar, Mit Singh, fired at a 4-gun Turkish battery that had unlimbered 2,000 yards away and drove it off. 'Not a bad effort for a very old pattern Mountain Gun', Fergusson commented. This incident also illustrates the harmonious co-operation between Anzac and Indian gunners. Australian artillery officers and Indian 'native' officers shared an observation post. On 19 May the Australian Lieutenant Cyril Clowes is described by Bean as having 'assisted Subedar Mit Singh', presumably a recognition of Singh's greater

---

7   Ibid.

experience.[8] Guy Trenchard also shared an observation position with an Australian regular gunner, Major Owen Phillips, whom Fergusson called 'a real good gunner'. They worked together for months, often shelled, and losing men killed and wounded to Turkish fire, though targeted virtually at random. Only when a novice Australian gunner arrived just before the Suvla offensive to set up an observation post nearby was their position disclosed, and Trenchard and his signaller were briefly buried by a shell.

Fergusson then visited Thom's section, and found Thom with a bullet hole in his sun helmet. Thom had lost men, partly because his section was about forty yards from Rawson's, and had been hit by 'overs' directed at Rawson's guns. Thom's sector included Quinn's Post, where Anzac and Ottoman lines came closest. In fact 'no one could tell from his O.P. which was which'.[9] Thom had mostly fired at Turkish infantry massing between Quinn's Post and Pope's and between Pope's and Walker's Ridge. In both of these areas, in the vital and vulnerable northern sector of the Anzac line, the defenders' trenches were not continuous, and machine-gun fire from flanking positions and from the mountain guns helped to cut down the massed attacks the Turks made on them.

On 19 May Kohat Battery fired over 600 rounds – about a hundred rounds per piece, 'heavy going for such a slow firing gun', wrote Fergusson. Many of these rounds were carried up to the guns by the muleteers under heavy fire. Carey-Evans described the scene at battery headquarters, where the senior havildar sat at a telephone, taking orders from the gun positions. He would come to the entrance of the dug-out and call (as it might be) 'Three loads of ammunition for Right Section' and the next driver due to go out would start off without hesitation. Leading a mule up the ridges to the gun positions was a different proposition to their battery commander's zig-zag dashes between the sand-bag breastworks earlier in the day. 'A mule does not take cover when it hears a shell', Fergusson explained. Instead, mules would often freeze, braying and pulling in understandable fear. Its driver, unable to let of go the mule's halter, would stand with it, cajoling or cursing as suited his temperament. Fergusson was as proud of his drivers as of his gunners. 'Not a man jibbed and not a mule broke loose', he wrote in admiration of the drivers' work that day.

The gunners' work on 19 May resulted in the award of four decorations to Rawson's section alone. Characteristically, Fergusson saw the awards as going to 'the section' and not to the individuals honoured. One of the two Indian Orders of Merit went to Lance-Naik Karam Singh, who was passing orders from Rawson in the observation post to the gunners in the emplacement. Hit by shrapnel, Karam Singh continued to pass orders though wounded. A gunner found him leaning against the trench wall, covered in blood. 'Never mind about me', Singh said, 'I can carry on'. At last the Subedar, Mit Singh, himself wounded, heard about Karam Singh's wound and went to check on him. Still at his post, Karam Singh said *'Bilkul taqrah, Sahib'* – 'I am

---

8   Bean, *The Story of Anzac*, Vol. II, p. 157n.
9   'Gallipoli 1915', Arthur Fergusson, 3DRL3635, AWM.

Mountain gunners dragging a gun into position on Walker's Ridge. looking northward, toward Suvla Bay. (ATL 061508)

quite fit'. The citation to the Indian Order of Merit he was awarded made clear that 'he remained on duty until forcibly removed'. Eventually he was induced to go down to Carey-Evans's dressing station and was found to be 'rendered absolutely blind by a bullet which had passed behind his eyes'.[10] 'No one knows how long he carried on passing orders after he was hit', Fergusson wrote, intensely proud of his men. 'Every man deserved something for that day's work', he wrote.[11]

Charles Bean told Karam Singh's story in his *The Story of Anzac* to illustrate 'the magnificent spirit of the Indian artillerymen', even though he mis-rendered his name as Karm Singh – perhaps because he was told of his exploit rather than read of it. But witnesses (probably British officers of the Kohat Battery) gave Bean details. He heard that when a medical officer examined him he asked, 'Sahib, shall I have my sight?' The doctor (actually Carey-Evans), unwilling to disclose that this was impossible, answered 'Perhaps, after a time, with one eye'. Karam Singh was not deceived and answered 'It is nothing. Have I not eaten your salt and taken your bread?': a classic statement of the faithful ideal of the old Indian Army.[12]

10   Hypher, *Deeds of Valour*, p. 259.
11   'Gallipoli 1915', Arthur Fergusson, 3DRL3635, AWM.
12   Bean, *The Story of Anzac*, Vol. II, p. 158n.

Kohat Battery's guns of course became targets for Turkish counter-battery fire. Cresswell Rawson's gunners counted four direct hits from shell fragments on the gun shield and the marks of fifty shrapnel balls. One man of the section had been killed and seven taken to the dressing station wounded, but 'there were a good many other slight wounds unreported', a common theme among Indian units in this and other campaigns in the Great War.[13] Having been in action for nearly three weeks, Indian casualties merged into the confusion and muddle that had so marked the initial landings. Alec Wilson, the commander of the Canal Defences apologised on 19 May that he could not provide the details of casualties requested by Simla. It was, he replied, 'quite impossible to give full details regarding dates and nature of wounds', and he was 'using every endeavor to verify names and regimental numbers'.[14]

The fighting of 19 May resulted in the deaths of a man associated with the Indian story of the campaign. John Simpson Kirkpatrick, a legendary figure in Australia's Gallipoli story, was a stretcher-bearer with the 3rd Field Ambulance. A Geordie and formerly a merchant sailor, Simpson had jumped ship to spend four years on the tramp around Australia. In 1914 he had enlisted in Western Australia, seemingly hoping to get home to his family. Instead, he found himself on Gallipoli. Simpson's celebrity arose because instead of carrying casualties with a mate on a stretcher, he commandeered a donkey (possibly several) and used them to bring lightly wounded men down to the dressing stations at the beach. Well known around Anzac at the time, after his death on 19 May the legend of 'Simpson and the Donkey' grew and he became the most well known Australian in the campaign. A determined campaign to award him a retrospective Victoria Cross narrowly (but rightly) failed in 2013. Ironically, Simpson was not Australian, and though hailed as the embodiment of the Anzac qualities of courageous mateship in fact worked alone. In fact, if anything ostracized by his fellow field ambulance bearers, his closest friends in the three weeks in which he survived on Gallipoli were perhaps (apart from the donkeys) the gunners and especially the mule drivers of the mountain artillery. Simpson was known to live apart from his unit, and to eat with the mountain gunners. Indian gunners called him Murphy, 'because that is what he called all his donkeys', Arthur Fergusson recalled. Simpson survived just three weeks on the peninsula, and was killed by a stray machine-gun bullet on 19 May. The mountain gunners' drivers 'treasured his last donkey', and planned to present it to someone in authority in Australia together with 'short history of Simpson', but the donkey was stolen from the brigade's mule lines on Imbros and lost for ever.[15]

---

13   'Gallipoli 1915', Arthur Fergusson, 3DRL3635, AWM.
14   Wilson to Duff, 19 May 1915, 10472, General Staff Branch, Correspondence relating to the European Crisis, 1914, L/MIL/17/5/2461, OIOC, BL.
15   'Gallipoli 1915', Arthur Fergusson, 3DRL3635, AWM. In my 2011 novel for children, *Simpson's Donkey*, I used Fergusson's version of the fate of Simpson's donkey's fate as a point of departure to get the donkey to Egypt in order to continue its journey from Gallipoli to Palestine and back to Gallipoli. Fergusson wrote 'Mudros', but I believe that

Military medical officers of the Indian Medical Service had always been as interested in public health as in war surgery. While his Anzac counterparts were not indifferent to the problems of insanitary conditions, Carey-Evans was more used to dealing with the routine difficulties of keeping troops healthy in difficult climatic circumstances and in rugged terrain, and he offered valuable advice to them. Fergusson claimed that 'he taught the Australian Doctors how clean and sanitary trenches could be kept'. Australians may bridle at this, but it is true that Australian units' trenches were at first noticeably dirtier than those of other forces at Anzac.[16] Two 'priceless' hospital assistants supported Evans's efficient dressing station; Adjudhia Pershad and Daulat Singh.[17] It was as exposed to Turkish shelling as any spot in Shrapnel Valley. When shells fell in the vicinity the section's hospital assistants watched out. If they saw a man hit by shrapnel they would cry *Chello Bhai* and its stretcher bearers would dash out to carry the wounded man for treatment. Fergusson wrote that the Indian bearers did so, 'no matter how heavy the shelling'.

Carey-Evans's dressing station became something of a haven for Australians, another expression of the 'entente … most remarkable' that existed between the two forces. Australians, suffering from the stomach trouble that would soon become an epidemic of diarrhoea and dysentery, or simply fed up with the unvaried diet of bully beef and biscuit, sought relief at Evans's dugouts. 'Our men used to feed them on dhal and chapatties when their insides refused bully beef', Fergusson wrote.[18] Joseph Beeston, who commanded an Australian field ambulance, described his mess cook disguising bully with 'curry powder' obtained from nearby Indian cooks, pretending that he was serving curried goose: 'but it was bully beef all the time'.[19]

'Blazing away as good as ever': trench warfare and a truce

From mid-May Anzac engineers and infantry fatigue parties had carved out a road, enabling the Indian mule carts to carry supplies up Shrapnel Gulley to the Anzac front line, though only at night, because Ottoman snipers were able to fire into the valley until the New Zealanders finally suppressed them in June. Heber Alexander accompanied the first three convoys, setting out in the darkness on a rough track, with bullets fired either at random or on fixed lines zipping past drivers and mules. On reaching the track-head at the foot of the steep ridge on the crest of which was the Anzac front line, the carts had to be backed out, so constricted was flat ground.

---

he made the common mistake of confusing Mudros and the immediate base for the campaign, Lemnos.
16 Stanley, *Quinn's Post, Anzac, Gallipoli*, p 101.
17 Leigh's *The Punjab and the War* named nine sub-assistant surgeons or ward servants on Gallipoli who were variously decorated. Leigh was careful to name men from across the province and from all of its religious groups.
18 'Gallipoli 1915', Arthur Fergusson, 3DRL3635, AWM.
19 Beeston, *Five Months at Anzac*, p. 27.

Though the distance from beach to the track-head was less than a thousand yards, so difficult was the journey that the last convoy did not return to the beach until first light, and was shelled on the way back to the coast. The experiment led to more work by the sappers, digging passing places on the track to enable carts to come and go. Later in May more mule corps landed at Anzac, with two troops of the 9th Mule Corps, commanded by Bahwal Din and Ghulam Rasul, veterans of the Lahore Division in France, who worked to supply the New Zealand and Australian Division.

Lieutenant-Colonel William Lesslie, one of the 'Indian' officers of Birdwood's staff took charge of the unloading of supplies, the management of the depots by the wharfs and the dispatch of the mule cart convoys, his Indian experience useful in dealings between his Anzac and Indian troops. One of the persistent themes of the contemporary records – all written by British officers – is the number and gravity of casualties among British officers of Indian units. In its first four days on Gallipoli all of the officers of Kohat Battery became casualties in one way or another. ('Luckily all mildly', as Fergusson wrote, though their 'mild' injuries included, in Trenchard's case, being struck on the head by the driving band of a shell.) As was to occur often on Gallipoli (among both British officers and Indian officers and other ranks) men remained on duty rather than allow themselves to evacuated as wounded. Their conduct contradicted the condescending views of their own commanders. Lieutenant-General James Willcocks, the commander of the Indian Corps in France, believed that 'the Indian is simply not fit to lead his men against Europeans' because though brave and obedient 'if he has to think he fails'.[20] As this book demonstrates, the conduct of Indian and Gurkha officers on Gallipoli confounds this dismissive view.

Fear of the disease that would come of the thousands of corpses rotting in the spring sun induced the Turks to request a truce to attempt to bury them. Though British and Anzac officers were reluctant, the obvious sense of this led them to accept, and on 24 May men of both sides climbed out of their trenches to meet in no man's land to bury them. The truce enabled the mountain artillery officers to examine the terrain beyond the front line without risk, though only those detailed to bury the dead of the campaign's first month were supposedly allowed to visit the firing line. Even the burial of several thousand Turkish dead in no man's land left the foremost trenches exposed to stench and flies, and the mountain artillery officers (and presumably their men, though Fergusson did not say) became 'seedy'. Heber Alexander (whose drivers took advantage of the lull to water their animals in daylight) made straight for the trenches at Quinn's Post, to whose defenders his muleteers had been carrying supplies, where the opposing lines were closest – within bomb-throwing range. He watched lines of troops from both sides keep a wary watch in no-man's-land while burial parties hastily dug pits to hold the thousands of bodies.

---

20 Omissi, *The Sepoy and the Raj*, p. 161, quoting Jeffrey Greenhut, 'The Imperial Reserve: the Indian Corps on the Western Front', *Journal of Imperial and Commonwealth History*, Vol. 12, 1983.

Mangat Rai, Heber Alexander's clerk in his Supply and Transport unit at Anzac, to whom Alexander may have dedicated his book *On Two Fronts*. (Heber Alexander, *On Two Fronts*)

For the gunners the truce offered a rare break. In the disconcerting silence an Indian gunner caught a hare which varied their diet for the day.[21] Infantry units were able to be relieved periodically, but the gunners remained not only in their gun positions, exposed to shelling and sniping, but were also on call throughout the day. Fergusson arranged for his gunners to return to battery headquarters for occasional rest and to wash, but their officers, British and Indian, rarely got away, except for an occasional dip in the sea at the cove. Fergusson arranged for Rawson and Thom to be relived, he and the brigade adjutant, Lieutenant Herbert Kenyon, taking over their gun positions respectively. The battery headquarters 'looked after itself' under its Indian officers and non-commissioned officers, another sign that regardless of the rhetoric (and the sahibs' presence) capable Indians did their jobs.

The mountain guns were repeatedly called upon to fire at specific targets – in May, for example, to destroy Turkish observation and machine-gun positions on Lone Pine; to suppress Turkish sniper on Dead Man's Ridge; to destroy a Turkish emplacement threatening Quinn's Post. The mule-mounted pack guns gave the mountain batteries a welcome mobility. Raymond Baker, a New Zealand infantryman, recalled how 'whenever the guns were located by the enemy's shrapnel they simply dismounted, packed

21 Treloar, *An Anzac Diary*, p. 146.

on the mules, and in a few minutes [were] blazing away as good as ever in a new position'.[22] The gunners were called upon for tasks all over the Anzac position. When on 29-30 May a squadron of the Wellington Mounted Rifles was cut off in No. 3 Post, in the gullies north of Anzac, it was the mountain guns that were directed against the surrounding Turks while a relief force found a way through the tangled country and Turkish trenches to allow the survivors to fight their way out. The guns did not usually fire perpendicular to the Anzac front line, but often fired at an angle to the target, able to hit what their observers could see, or even fire directly at what gun-layers could see. Lieutenant Everard Whitting's gun high on the summit of Russell's Top, for example, invariably fired not at Baby 700 immediately opposite, but at Turkish trenches on the 400 Plateau, over a thousand yards more-or-less southward.

'If a man could die of fright': life at Anzac

The Indian gunners and muleteers shared the hardships and hazards of life at Anzac with the Anzacs and, indeed, with their Turkish adversaries. Except that none of them actually served in the front-line fire trenches, and therefore did not face bombs or shell-fire directed at the men holding the line at Quinn's Post, Lone Pine or Russell's Top, they faced much the same danger. The muleteers and the mountain batteries' drivers, routinely faced the risk of snipers, especially when using the track running up Monash valley, which Turkish snipers fired into for the campaign's first three months. Snipers also were able to hit men moving about the dumps on the beaches north and south of the cove. 'Brighton Beach was a bad place' Heber Alexander recalled – a nearby point earned the name of 'Casualty Corner'.[23]

Flies afflicted everyone, making sleep impossible in the daytime, a hardship for the muleteers who mostly worked after dark. They also made eating a torment, and though we have no accounts from Indian troops directly commenting on their lives, we can extrapolate from Australian accounts, by men used to flies. Men became physically tired, on duty for long hours, with observation post teams on the alert through the daylight hours, fighting off drowsiness through the warm spring days Signallers sat wearing heavy and uncomfortable head-phones, listening for calls from their counterparts in the observation posts and gun detachments waited at their guns ready for urgent calls from the infantry. The drivers' work usually began at dusk, when they were able to water and care for their mules, ready for ammunition and re-supply convoys. While the units' cooks, bhistis and sweepers took on their traditional domestic duties, every man had a job to do in constructing and maintaining the dugouts they shared on the hillsides, and both drivers and gunners could be called out at any time to shift guns and fire in emergencies. With the mountain batteries spread out all over the rugged Anzac position, keeping in touch with them imposed hardships on their

---

22 Typescript recollection by Raymond Baker, Baker, Canterbury Infantry Battalion, PLC.
23 Alexander, *On Two Fronts*, p. 195.

British and Indian officers. Fergusson 'wore out' three or four orderlies in as many weeks – they had to follow him. He eventually devised a half-time arrangement, using one in the mornings and one in the afternoons as he toured his batteries positions distributed across the steep ridges of Anzac.

Bathing was possible at Anzac Cove (where the water was not so clean) or on North Beach, where a couple of grounded barges protected bathers from shellfire or (early in the campaign) snipers. Neither beach was ever entirely safe from shellfire. Heber Alexander's orderly, Ajaib Shah, was wounded in the elbow while bathing. Water was also necessary for washing clothes. The mule corps' followers included a dhobi – a laundryman – called Lachman who washed clothes at the water's edge, singing as he worked. Lachman, 'a plucky little fellow', became a favourite among the muleteers. He was wounded twice, and learned to judge the safety of the beach, advising – actually forbidding – his officer (Alexander) from bathing when the danger was higher than usual. Later in the campaign Indian troops, who accorded a great importance to cleanliness for ritual purposes, built salt-water showers that enabled them to bathe without entering the sea.

Less usual dangers included the risk of accidents. Lance-Naik Mehdi Khan found an unexploded 8-inch shell in Mule Gully and carried it into Heber Alexander's nearby dugout, exclaiming '*Kaisa bara goli, sahib!*' [What a big shell, sir!][24] The celebrated fatalism of India's faiths must have helped men surmount the understandable fear that they could die in this place or suffer horrific wounds. His orderly, Ajaib Shah, remarked to him 'Sahib, if a man could die of fright, I should have been dead long ago'.[25]

Through these hardships the Indians maintained their accustomed resilience. The only time Fergusson thought that his men despondent was on 25 May, when the British battleship HMS *Triumph* was torpedoed and sank at about midday off Anzac Cove, an event witnessed by virtually every man with a view of the sea, including all of the Indian mountain gunners. Having been brought up to regard the Royal Navy as exceptional if not invincible, the loss of such a vessel within sight of Anzac affected morale across the force. 'They really thought we were going to lose the war for a bit', Fergusson recalled. A few days later, on 29 May, Jacob's Battery received its most severe blow when its commander, John Bruce, was killed. This left the battery in the hands of a few subalterns and Indian officers, all tired, spread around the Anzac position and all desperately over-worked. It seems that for a time its men lost heart.

Or so it seems. We actually know little about the thoughts and feelings of Indian soldiers on Gallipoli because, unlike the Indians on the Western Front, a very imperfect censorship was established over their correspondence. Arrangements for censorship remained unsatisfactory. In April, Johahir Singh, Base Postmaster, Ismailia, was appointed at a salary of £25 pounds per month as 'translator of Indian correspondence'

---

24 Alexander, *On Two Fronts*, p. 199.
25 Ibid., p. 197.

A benevolent Britannia doles out alms to Muslim widows in a poster seeking donations in Britain. It is a reminder of the needs of soldiers' widows. (Mary Evans Picture Library)

in the Chief Censor's office in Cairo. Maxwell reported that he was 'the only person he can obtain in Egypt knowing Persian, Gurmukhi, Urdu and Pushtu', and presumably English and Hindustani. The Marquess of Crewe asked the Viceroy whether he would 'not prefer what is done in France, viz., appointment of a British Censor who can read Indian letters?', but the answer seemed to be that no retired British Indian officers could be found in Egypt.[26] If the troops' mail was censored in India, no record of the censors' reports have survived.

'Those grand and game soldiers of India': Indians and Anzacs

Living and working in such proximity, mingling on tracks, at wells and on the beach, Indians and their Anzac comrades soon developed an acquaintance that sometimes grew into friendships. Sergeant Fred Aspinall, a signaller, recorded on 22 May how

26   Tel., 12 April 1915, WWI/293/H, NAI.

he made friends with Subedar-Major Paktar Singh of Kohat Battery. The two chatted at Aspinall's signal post in Monash Valley and Aspinall established that Paktar Singh hailed from Ludhiana.[27] The subedar wrote his name in Aspinall's notebook in Urdu; apparently the only handwriting by an Indian soldier on Gallipoli that has survived. Arthur Browett, a British-born South Australian school-teacher who had served in a field ambulance on Gallipoli, was evacuated to Britain after being wounded on 19 May. From hospital in Epsom he wrote to Austen Chamberlain, the new Secretary of State for India to praise the Indian bearers he had worked alongside at Anzac. He described the 'fine exhibition of the true empire spirit' around camp fires. While Australians gathered sticks, Indian gunners, drivers and bearers cooked 'chupattee cakes' for them. That the Australians then smeared jam on the chupatees did not diminish their regard. He praised 'those grand & game soldiers of India' and promised that despite the common prejudice Australians would 'extend an open hand of binding friendship … wherever we meet'.[28]

A New Zealander, George Donovan of the Wellington Battalion, made notes of useful conversational phrases in the back of his diary to help him converse with Indian gunners in Urdu:

> Rishman dicka "Do you see the enemy?"
> Salam "good day"[29]

Donovan's notes suggest not just the appeal of the exotic but also that he hoped to use his phrase book in other meetings with Indian troops, and perhaps did. Gunner Frank Cooper, a New Zealander, recalled the Indian gunners especially as 'the finest type of coloured men that it was possible to meet' – a condescending judgment of the time but sincerely intended. Detailed to deliver ammunition and stores from the ordnance depot on the beach to the mountain batteries' dumps, he came into close and repeated contact with officers and men. 'I was in a position to know the officers and NCOs intimately', he later wrote. He 'gradually picked up a certain amount [of Hindustani -] enough to yell at them to take cover when there was concentrated fire on the beach'. Cooper noticed that 'with their belief' – a fatalism he attributed to their various faiths – 'they will very seldom run away from shell fire'.[30]

The muleteers' camp lay off a track leading to the beach and they often hosted casual visitors, drawn either by curiosity about the Indians or reports of the Indians' generosity in serving snacks and tea. Many Anzac diaries and memoirs refer to men obtaining food from nearby Indian units as a relief from the monotonous (and, in the

---

27 Diary, Sgt Fred Aspinall, 1st Light Horse Signal Troop, 22 May 1915, PR88/96, AWM.
28 L/MIL/7/18921 (Collection 425/1673) 'Appreciation of assistance rendered to Australian Medical Corps by Indian ambulance men in Gallipoli' (Europeana.eu).
29 Diary, George Donovan, MS-Papers-2299, ATL.
30 Memoir, Frank Cooper, MS-Papers-1676-1, ATL,

An Indian follower cutting the hair of an Anzac; one of the ways Indians made money from their fellow soldiers at Anzac. (AWM C01139)

An Australian and a Hindu 'follower' (identifiable by his non-regulation clothing) photographed, perhaps while enjoying a chat at Anzac. (AWM C01544)

heat, sickening) diet of bully beef and hard biscuit. Frederick Senn, a New Zealand engineer, described in his 'Gallipoli recollections' how he ate 'a small windfall of rice scrounged from the Indian Mule Camp' to combat a bout of diarrhoea as the summer advanced.[31] The mule corps officers' mess cook, Kagan, produced 'stews and curries of quite extraordinary excellence' from tinned rations flavoured with spices from the muleteers' stocks.[32]

Australians also found themselves patients in Indian medical units. In the confusion that followed the landing wounded Australians were treated and evacuated willy-nilly, carried to hospitals in Egypt and Malta regardless of nationality. In this way 200 Australians arrived at No. 5 Indian General Hospital in Cairo a week after the landing. Taken in and treated, their arrival presented a supply problem, because European patients' diets differed from those provided to Indians. A hasty concord with the Australian authorities gave the wounded Australians food to which they were accustomed, with ice and mineral water, at a modest 8-20 piastres a day. The Australian Imperial Force's accountants and the Bombay Presidency Hospital, which engaged the victualing contractor, eventually worked out the bill to be paid by the Commonwealth government.[33]

While 'rizzat' – tangible reward; silver rupee coins – mattered to Indian troops, they also valued 'izzat' – honour; silver medals – as highly. The Indian Army had recognised its sepoys' service individually since the siege of Ghuznee in 1839, and had rewarded individual acts of bravery with the institution of the Indian Order of Merit and the Indian Distinguished Service Medal in 1837 and 1907 respectively. Sepoys were treated differently to European troops, however, in intangible ways as well as pay. Soon after Indian troops saw action in France, Army Headquarters in Simla sought to confirm the legitimacy of awards to followers ('non-combatants such as dooly-bearers, langris and drivers': about a third of all of those committed to Gallipoli). While careful to 'protect the integrity of the Order' it was Hardinge and Beauchamp Duff's desire to 'consider the claims of menials of a lower class'.[34]

Nor were the Indian members of the brigade overlooked. Indian other ranks' work on 29 May was recorded by Australian headquarters.[35] Subadar Jwala Singh of Jacob's, for example, received the Order of British India, 2nd Class, which entitled him to be known by the honorific 'Bahadur' – 'the brave one'. The Indian Order of Merit went to two other ranks of each battery, including the blinded Lance-Naik Karam Singh. Karam Singh was also later singled out for praise in the Punjab government's account of the province in the war. Driver Naik Nikka Singh received the Indian Distinguished Service Medal, a recognition of the drivers' steadfastness and tenacity

31 Frederick Senn, 'Gallipoli recollections', MS-Papers-1697, ATL.
32 Alexander, *On Two Fronts*, p. 175.
33 'Australians at No. 5 Indian General Hospital', 399/7, AWM 25.
34 Tel, 1 March 1915, Hardinge to Crewe, WWI/145/H, NAI.
35 1st Australian Division, Messages and signals on Gallipoli, 29 May 1915, AWM 38, 3 DRL6673, item 107, AWM.

in getting mule-loads of ammunition and other supplies to the battery positions regardless of Ottoman fire.

As the pleasant Aegean spring turned to an increasingly hot summer, the mountain gunners continued to fire in support of men who could now truly be called their comrades. As the dead of the terrible attacks of April and May rotted on the hillsides and in no man's land staff officers and commanders planned the campaign's next phase. After the failure of the 2 May attack at Anzac, Arthur Fergusson wrote, 'we settled down to trench warfare, hoping the Helles crowd would some day fight its way up to us'.[36] 'The Helles crowd', by May including the 29th Indian Infantry Brigade, had been fighting their own battle twelve miles south, at Cape Helles, but it was never going to fight its way to Anzac.

36 'Gallipoli 1915', Arthur Fergusson, 3DRL3635, AWM.

7

'When the smoke of the guns falls like a mist': Gurkha Bluff, May

When George Swinley arrived off Cape Helles in the *Dunluce Castle* on 30 April he and his Sikhs found it 'a grand sight to see all the ships in view'.[1] Charles Bruce's transport carrying the 6th Gurkhas steamed into the roadstead on the same 'glorious spring day' to see warships bombarding Achi Baba. Bruce was impressed by the 'glorious coloring and tranquility of the sea' and of the powerful assembly of ships, and hoped and expected to be a part of an army that would soon be in command of the peninsula and marching across Thrace to Constantinople and victory. But Swinley, Bruce and their men had been on the move, by train or ship, for the best part of a week and had not yet learned of the outcome of the landings made on 25 April. Their first impressions were deceptive: a week after the first landings the invaders were still short of the objectives set for the first day.

'A long-drawn out struggle must ensue': stalemate at Helles

The invasion had been, as Humphrey Gell recorded, 'a tough job and casualties heavy'.[2] In fact, although the landings had succeeded in putting a British-French force on the 'toe' of the peninsula, as at Anzac failures of leadership and co-ordination and decisive reactions a smaller Turkish force had held the invaders just a mile or two inland. An attempt to break out of the rapidly solidifying beach-head on 28 April had failed disastrously. Captain Clement Milward, a 53rd Sikhs officer attached to the headquarters of the 29th Division, recorded in disgust that 'the whole show was a toss-up' and foresaw that 'give the Turks time to breathe and a long-drawn out struggle must ensue': as it did.[3]

In the first days of May the Indians landed, gratefully after a voyage troubled by sea-sickness – three men of Rothney Battye's field ambulance fell into the sea,

---

1 Diary, 30 April 1915, George Swinley, 7407-138, NAM.
2 Diary, 25 April-9 July 1915, Humphrey Gell, P158, 10048, IWM.
3 Diary, 25 April 1915, Clement Milward, CAB45/259, NAUK.

including Battye (a fact he recorded in the unit's war diary). They camped in the open in the fields above the beach, listening to the fighting a mile-and-a-half away to the north. Cox's brigade was allotted to the far left or west of the British-French line at Helles, holding trenches that extended to the cliffs on the edge of the Aegean. The hills, scrubby and steep, were oddly familiar. Charles Bruce wrote that 'we found the terrain quite suitable', resembling the broken and arid hillsides familiar from both training and operations on the frontier.[4]

In the 69th Punjabis, Humphrey Gell also thought that the Helles force was 'a marvelous sight … more interesting than anything I've ever seen', thrilled to see the numbers of French, British, Indian, Australian and Senegalese troops. 'Things seem to be going well now', he wrote, looking towards the village of Krithia 'which it looks like we'll get shortly'.[5] Sepoy Nanak Singh of the 69th Punjabis remembered years later how 'the Turks were fierce soldiers'. He described how sepoys fell to snipers, whom the Punjabis could not locate. 'After many lives had been lost, we spotted … a Turk hiding behind the carcass of an animal', and they shot him.[6] Reginald Savory of the 14th Sikhs, perhaps noticing the fresh graves at Cape Helles thought 'there is some very hard fighting going on here'.[7] It soon became clear that simply being on Gallipoli was dangerous, and that nowhere in the Helles beach-head was safe from shellfire or snipers. In the Sikhs' first fortnight on the peninsula (in which they spent only two full days in the font line) they lost seventy-eight sepoys and three British officers, two of whom had been double-company commanders. Within a fortnight every one of the 108th Field Ambulance's tents was 'riddled' with shrapnel, and the operating table had been hit five times.[8] Savory decided to help his chances of surviving by growing a beard like his men but Palin ('a real autocrat' according to a regimental history) ordered him to shave it off minutes before going over the top at Helles.[9] At the same time it seems that Palin did not object to officers wearing turbans like their men: inconsistency being one of the privileges of autocracy, it seems.

At first unfamiliar – Aubrey Wiliams, the adjutant of the South Wales Borderers, had to reassure two nervous Sikh sentries he encountered in the dark that he was a 'friend', reminding them of hockey games their units had played in India.[10] The Indians became a notable part of the scene at Helles. Many British troops recorded their impressions of them, admiring them 'stalking forward in the dusk' after snipers and as at Anzac noticing how they 'work hard and silently' (though an artillery officer

---

4   Bruce, *Himalayan Wanderer*, p. 255.
5   Diary, 7 May 1915, Humphrey Gell, P158, 10048, IWM.
6   Communication from Dr Tajinderpal Singh, relaying his great-grandfather's recollection of Gallipoli, 2 May 2014.
7   Letter, 7 May 1915, Reginald Savory, 7603-93, NAM.
8   War diary, 108th Field Ambulance, May 1915, WO95/4272, NAUK.
9   Bamford, *The Sikh Regiment*, p. 31.
10 Memoir, Aubrey Williams, 88/56/1, 584, IWM.

116 Die In Battle, Do Not Despair

Sepoy Nanak Singh of the 89th
Punjabis, photographed later in life,
whose recollections of Gallipoli
are both rare and valuable.
(Dr Tajinderpal Singh, Perth)

Men of the 14th Sikhs arriving at Cape Helles, with Second Lieutenant Reginald Savory
conspicuous in his pith helmet in the centre of the lighter. (14th Sikhs Album)

heard them 'crooning').[11] British Territorials unused to Indians took an interest in Sikhs combing their hair, fascinated by their 'clam, quiet expression, almost child-like', but also with their ferocity ('I pity the wounded who fall into the hands of the Indians').[12] On the same day, another artillery subaltern was impressed at the enthusiasm of Punjabi or Sikh troops who when ordered to march toward the front line, 'as each company moved off … uttered a half prayer half cheer raising their right arm'.[13] Patrick Duff, a classically educated gunner, thought while watching Sikhs dress their long hair that in that place – across the straits from Troy – it puts you in mind of the Spartans before Thermopulae [sic].[14]

Cox's brigade had arrived on 1 May 'several vital days late', wrote historian Robert Rhodes James, possibly through Maxwell failing to ensure their prompt departure from Egypt.[15] After the war Hamilton tried to recruit Godley to support his contention that Maxwell had unjustifiably held the Indians back in Egypt, and that had they been available on 25 April the invaders' plan would have succeeded (not that Godley could have known – he was at Anzac).[16] But the original plan seemed to have involved using the Indians at Anzac; only when the Helles landings stalled was Cox's brigade diverted to the south.[17] As it arrived the invaders were making a further attempt to seize the village of Krithia and the commanding hill of Achi Baba that rose behind it. The first attempt had failed in the chaos of the landing. The Helles force had got ashore, albeit at the cost of about 3,800 casualties, but like the Anzac force it had got nowhere near its objectives for the first day. What can only be regarded as poor planning, bungled command, and unexpectedly decisive and determined Ottoman resistance had left the invasion force holding a line of trenches everywhere overlooked by Turkish artillery observers on the eminence of Achi Baba.

Major-General Aylmer Hunter-Weston, the commander of the 29th Division and from 24 May of 8th Corps, the British force at Helles, was able to call upon a force of Lancashire Territorials, British regulars, Australians and New Zealanders and sailors and marines of the Royal Naval Division, and to make what he hoped would be the final assault that would take the village of Krithia, leading to the capture of Achi Baba and its observation posts. The 29th Indian Brigade, allocated to the British 29th Division (which within a week had suffered so many casualties that its three brigades were merged into two) was to be held in reserve, in the scanty shelter of the Kereves Dere, a dry nullah in the centre of the allied line. (Here they briefly met Australian troops, about to attack.) The battle, a headlong rush towards

11 Diary, May 1915, Bartle Bradshaw, 06/33/1, 14940; Letter, May 1915, Patrick Duff, 91/10/1, 799, IWM.
12 Diary, 3 May 1915, Denis Buxton, 99/4/1, 797, IWM.
13 Diary, 3 May 1915, Angus McCracken, 01/45/1, 11617, IWM.
14 Letter, 27 May 1915, Patrick Duff, 91/10/1, 799, IWM.
15 James, *Gallipoli*, p. 148.
16 Travers, *Gallipoli 1915*, p. 291.
17 Steel & Hart, *Defeat at Gallipoli*, p. 146.

Turkish trenches unprotected by barbed wire, met lethal machine-guns, which cut down infantry attempting to move across open grassland. After three days the attack achieved an advance of less than 500 yards, at a cost of about 6,500 casualties, about a third of the number engaged. The Turks were so little pressed that their reserves were not even called forward. While Hunter-Weston recommended that the Indians be used to attack Achi Baba once Krithia had fallen, the attack never got close so they were fortunate not to be committed to a disastrous and futile venture, one of the two British brigades not ordered forward.

While not committed to battle, Helles immediately introduced the Sikhs and Punjabis to a new world of war. Though 'to our surprise not needed' in the attack, the next day a 'bomb dropped on camp [that] wounded 6 men bathing', as George Swinley recorded.[18] Charles Bruce observed that the Sikhs had 'a harder time' than his Gurkhas – being generally bigger men (more visible because of their tall turbans) they had to dig further to find security in depth. This was only the first of differences between the Indian units that became apparent during the campaign. But the two battalions camped together and sent men to perform the many fatigues necessary as they settled down for their first night on the peninsula. 'We worked side by side', Bruce wrote of the 14th Sikhs and his 6th Gurkhas.[19] Within days the hardships of the peninsula became all too apparent. Sepoy Nanak Singh of the 69th Punjabis recalled his rations – 'very bad, but we kept fighting on. I remember the dhal was off as it had gone sour and the roti had also gone hard.'[20]

'Brilliant little affair': Gurkha Bluff

Cox's brigade now took its turn in the trenches on Gully Spur, a long, narrow ridge lying between the Aegean coast and a deep, two-mile long nullah running parallel to the shore marked on Ottoman maps as the Saghir Deré but called by British empire troops the tautological-sounding Gully Ravine, from its precipitous walls. Here the Indians learned the ropes of trench warfare; not a kind of war they had encountered before: who had? Within a week Reginald Savory was telling his family that 'we are getting hardened to it now ... indifferent to shrapnel and bullets as the most experienced old veteran'. He asked for biscuits, potted meat, chocolate, Brand's Meat Lozenges (to make beef tea) and – curiously and hardly practically – 'a slab of bacon'.[21] Three weeks into the campaign it was possible to feel positive, though the conditions in the front line trenches surely tempered optimism. Savory passed on the hopeful rumour that 'the Turks are getting rather fed up', but confessed that 'judging

---

18   Diary, 3 and 4 May 1915, George Swinley, 7407-138, NAM.
19   Bruce, *Himalayan Wanderer*, p. 255.
20   Communication from Dr Tajinderpal Singh, relaying his great-grandfather's recollection of Gallipoli, 2 May 2014.
21   Letter, Reginald Savory, 7 May 1915, Savory Papers, 7603-93, NAM.

Charles Bruce's headquarters dug-outs on Gully Spur in May 1915, from the *Illustrated London News*. (*Illustrated London News*)

A clipping from the *Graphic* in September 1915, showing the Indians' rear area in Gully Ravine. It shows how broad and deep the gully was behind the front line. The tents (right) seem to house the 108th Indian Field Ambulance. (14th Sikhs album)

by the way they fight it hardly looks like it'. Rallying, he promised that 'when and if Constantinople is taken' he would collect 'a good bit of loot', but the qualification 'if' hung in the air like the stench of the rotting corpses around Gully Ravine.[22]

Within days of arriving, Cox's Gurkhas had demonstrated their value, exactly as foreseen. The 6th Gurkhas' scouts had discovered a ravine cutting inland that enabled them to bring up troops and ammunition out of sight of the defenders. Its assault on what became known as Gurkha Bluff called on the mountain-warfare skills of the Gurkhas: just as Ian Hamilton had hoped for when he begged Kitchener for a brigade of Gurkhas before the landings. Turkish troops on the bluff, a hundred feet above the water, were able to direct fire onto attacks at the extreme western end of the Helles line. They had defeated two attempts to take it by British regulars. The day after taking over the opposing lines Gurkhas reconnoitered the bluff, Captain Christopher Birdwood (General Birdwood's nephew) examining it from the sea, while Subedar Gambirsing Pun (soon to become the battalion's subedar-major) and Jemadar Nandalal Gurung scouted into the thick oak scrub. Within two days Charles Bruce (described by a fellow officer as 'a brilliant skirmisher') had himself examined the ground from a destroyer and secured permission to make another assault.[23]

Warships supported the attack, assisted by Birdwood who pointed out likely targets from the destroyer HMS *Talbot*. Bruce modestly described the attack as 'a very successful little action' that 'exactly suited the genius of the Gurkha'.[24] While the 89th Punjabis (or rather its Sikh, Brahman or Rajput companies) made a 'demonstration by fire' from its trenches at dusk on 12 May Gurkha companies assembled on the narrow, rocky beach shore the bluff. Crossing the mouth of a gully (later called Gurkha Ravine) covered by machine-guns they moved under the fire of naval guns and then began climbing the steep scrubby hillside. The swift and bold attack took the Turks by surprise, and the assaulting company reached the summit at about 8p.m. without opposition. Entrenching and calling for reinforcements, the entire Gurkha battalion then occupied the intervening ground, by daylight having established a huge coastal salient 500 yards long. Sikhs and later Inniskilling Fusiliers arrived to support a quite thinly held gain of some 700 yards of trenches, though amazingly the Turks made no counter-attacks. It gained about as much ground for the loss of 21 men killed and 92 wounded as had the three days of the second attack on Krithia, which had cost 6,500 casualties.

Hamilton, in his official despatch called the seizure of Gurkha Bluff 'a brilliant little affair'.[25] The feat of Bruce's men seems to bear out Hamilton's advocacy. He issued a general order naming the bluff for the Gurkhas' feat a week later. But it is worth recalling that while they were all regular soldiers, very few of the Gurkhas

---

22 Letter, Reginald Savory, 25 May 1915, Savory Papers, 7603-93, NAM.
23 Maxwell, *Villiers-Stuart on the Frontier*, p. 30.
24 Bruce, *Himalayan Wanderer*, p. 256.
25 Supplement to *London Gazette*, 20 September 1915, p. 9314.

Looking south from Gurkha Bluff. (Author)

Gurkha Bluff, depicted in the *Illustrated London News* in August, showing the rugged terrain across which Bruce's 1/6th Gurkhas attacked. (National Library of Australia)

who attacked on 12 May had much previous experience of war. The 6th Gurkhas' last active service had been in the Manipur campaign of 1891. Except for the day of long-range firing between Positions 40 and 70 near Kantara in January, in the attack on Gurkha Bluff virtually every man was facing action for the first time. That makes their achievement all the more remarkable.

'Foul and false whisper': the Musalmans withdrawn

Meanwhile the reliability of Musalman troops in France and Egypt continued to worry military and civil authorities. While about half of the Indian troops singled out for praise in the Turkish attacks on the canal had been Musalmans their reliability remained in doubt, though not among their officers or officers who knew them. Regimental officers never doubted their own men's loyalty but the army's senior commanders remained more sceptical. O'Moore Creagh remarked in his memoirs that 'it should always be remembered that the Indian, be he Musalman, Hindu, [or] Sikh ... regards his obligations to his co-religionists as having the first claim on him'.[26] But Charles Bruce, a younger, regimental, officer (though of Gurkha, not Musalman troops) wrote that 'it was wonderful ... to see how little the Mohammedan troops ... allowed their feelings for the Turk as co-religionists to interfere with their duty'.[27] In 1915, however, prudence won over confidence.

Late in April details of a letter written by a sepoy of the (almost entirely Muslim) Khyber Rifles at Landi Kotal on the Khyber Pass to a friend in the 27th Punjabis serving in Egypt reached Wilson in his headquarters at Ismailia. Again using a simple code, the sepoy asked his friend to advise him the number of 'trees [sepoys] from such and such a garden [units] were washed away by floods [deserted]'. Worryingly, 'letters containing similar enquiries have been received by men of the 69th Punjabis' – at that very moment approaching Gallipoli.[28] Through what a sympathetic observer described as 'a foul and false whisper' Hamilton decided not to risk leaving the Punjabis on Gallipoli.[29]

A Scottish member of the 29th Division on Gallipoli recorded that 'it was whispered in the trenches that the Mussulmans among them did not altogether like taking the lives of the Mussulman Turks' [sic], a suspicion that suggests that the decision to withdraw the Punjabis pandered to British officers' unease as much as reflecting the actual allegiance of the Musalman troops.[30] In the meantime, the four Muslim companies of the Punjabis worked as labourers, unloading stores on the beaches of Helles. (Ironically, the first man of the 89th Punjabis killed was a Musalman, Sepoy Fateh Din of Jhelum, on 4 May.) In that a quarter of the 29th Brigade's rifles were

---

26   Callwell, (ed.), *The Autobiography of General Sir O'Moore Creagh*, p. 246.
27   Bruce, *Himalayan Wanderer*, p. 252.
28   Tel. Wilson to Lake, 29 April 1915, L/MIL/17/5/2461, OIOC, BL.
29   Arthur, *Sir John Maxwell*, p. 181.
30   Mure, *With the Incomparable 29th*, p. 94.

Punjabi Musalmans, possibly of one of the Punjabi battalions withdrawn at the end of May, inspecting fragments of Turkish shrapnel in a posed photograph. (IWM Q013372)

idle, it was a waste of trained, regular troops, and perhaps an indictment of Cox's ability to advocate for his men. It is possible that Hamilton exaggerated the danger of the Muslim companies of the two Punjabi battalions. (He had inspected them in April, and the subject of their reliability must have been raised.) No men of the 89th Punjabis had actually deserted; no correspondence pointing to disloyalty in their ranks exists: both battalions later served well in both France and (against Ottoman Muslims) in Mesopotamia. It is probable that Hamilton used or allowed the suspicion of Muslim troops' reliability to obtain a brigade that by the end of May had become three-quarters Gurkha.

At last, on 14 May the officers of the 69th and 89th Punjabis received 'bad news tonight'. They would be withdrawn from Gallipoli and return to Egypt. Humphrey Gell was philosophical 'The reason is I suppose quite right from an outsider's point of view', but most of the Punjabis' officers thought it 'absurd' and 'feeble'. 'It's rotten luck on them', he wrote – 'them' rather than 'us' because Gell had been detailed to become the signals officer in Cox's headquarters.[31] (He succeeded Lieutenant Leopold Poynder, who returned to the 6th Gurkhas to take command of a company – the Gurkhas lost all of their British company commanders in their first three weeks.) It was indeed unfortunate for the two battalions: they were to go to the Western Front

---

31   Diary, 14 May 1915, Humphrey Gell, P158, 10048, IWM.

and were to suffer heavily at Neuve Chapelle, where the 69th lost 348 men out of 663. For the moment the 29th Brigade was to comprise just two battalions, the 14th Sikhs and 6th Gurkhas, but two more battalions had been summoned from Egypt.

The irony of the decision to send the Punjabis back to Egypt was that Indian troops, including many Musalman units and units including them, would form the bulk of the forces committed to fighting the Ottoman Turks in Mesopotamia, where few difficulties arose. For Indian troops on Gallipoli, the decision meant that the Punjabis would be replaced by two and in time three Gurkha battalions, decisively altering the composition of the 29th Brigade. By the end of the campaign it would comprise one Sikh and four Gurkha battalions, arguably making it the most least representative formation in the history of the Indian Army. The problem with the explanations offered – that Muslim troops were subject to subversive influences or were thought to be unreliable – is that neither seems to have actually been true. The desertion of a few Musalman sepoys might have seemed a worry, but in fact they formed no part of a wider pattern of disaffection or conspiracy. The author of a scholarly study of British-Indian intelligence in the war warns that 'British concern about pan-Islamism within India should not be exaggerated' and observes that the Government of India was probably less worried by Muslim support for Turkey in 1914 than it had been during the recent Balkan wars and that it 'soon died away'.[32] More importantly, Musalmans formed about half of the mountain artillery and most of the Supply and Transport troops: and no one questioned their reliability.

'Just like the photos': trench warfare on Gully Spur

For the rest of May the Indians shifted their front line forward stealthily, with working parties going out to dig new trenches in advance of the line, which they gradually occupied after a couple of nights, often without the Turks reacting. On 13 May the 14th Sikhs took over parts of the Gurkhas' gains on Gully Spur, joining men of the 89th Punjabis, who made local attacks to seize or secure sections of the Turkish line, their final action before they were ordered out. (The 89th lost ten men killed on Gallipoli, three on the day of their withdrawal.) The day cost the Sikhs nine killed and 24 wounded. With the captured trenches collapsed by the bombardment men moved about with inadequate head-cover, and Turkish snipers took advantage of their vulnerability. George Swinley, one of the Sikhs' majors and a member of an old Indian Army family, fell mortally wounded with a shot in the head. With the Punjabis' departure Cox's brigade was made up with two regular British battalions, the 1st Lancashire Fusiliers and 1st Inniskilling Fusiliers. The four battalions worked closely together defending and extending the Gurkha Bluff salient.

The policy of encroaching led to savage and costly fights. By 20 May the line had been moved closer to a trench dug by the King's Own Scottish Borderers (Herbert

---

32 Popplewell, *Intelligence and Imperial Defence*, pp. 179-80.

Cox's old regiment) when it landed on 25 April before withdrawing (one of the more regrettable debacles in the initial landings). A party from the 6th Gurkhas rushed and occupied it after dark on 20 May. This sparked a two-day struggle for possession of what was called KOSB Trench in which Inniskilling Fusiliers and Gurkhas fought hard to hold it, the Gurkhas at a cost of 30 dead or wounded. So choked with dead was KOSB Trench that it was filled in and another line dug. All along the new line the Indians and British battalions faced Turkish counter-attacks. On 22 May Captain Ralph Engledue led his company of the 14th Sikhs to occupy lines dug beyond the Indian front line the night before.[33] This time, the Turks reacted swiftly, launching a 'vigorous attack' against the Sikhs' flanking unit, the 2nd Royal Fusiliers. Engledue called up another Sikh company and in turn attacked the Turks in flank, driving them back and saving the position. Six years later, when both the Sikhs and the Fusiliers served together in the Khyber Pass, the Fusiliers' officers presented their counterparts with a silver grenade inscribed 'In Memory of Gallipoli 1915 ...'[34] The nightly business of digging stealthily and advancing to occupy new lines moved the British line closer to the Turks. By the month's end the two sides were on average about two hundred yards apart. The Indians sent out patrols nightly, dominating no man's land, with Gurkha officers especially enterprising.

Herbert Cox, whose brigade had done so well so soon, looked forward almost eagerly to further assaults. 'There is lots doing', he wrote in a hand-written account seemingly intended for his family, 'we hope to make another big push'. He was sure of his brigade, whose members were 'fit and quite ready for another scrap'. Despite the tenacious resistance the Ottoman infantry had offered since the landing Cox discounted their capacity. 'We have the upper hand of the Turks', he wrote, though he conceded that they were 'very good behind their trenches', mostly because of their 'German-placed machine-guns'.[35] Imbued with the martial race theory, Cox assumed that it operated across no man's land, but in fact the Ottoman resistance owed more to Turkish determination and willingness to die than to German advice.

For a fortnight no major attack occurred, though units holding the front line launched isolated local attacks, sapping forward at night and occupying new positions, often without the Turks' realising – the Indian battalions' scout sections patrolled up to the Turkish wire, dominating no man's land. This tactic, anticipating the 'peaceful penetration' of 1918, succeeded. Humphrey Gell noticed how they described minor actions to seize trenches as a 'bit of a scrap': 'a short time ago we should have called it a terrific battle'.[36]

---

33 Or Engledow, as he is listed in *The Quarterly Indian Army List*: he is 'Endledow' in both of the 14th Sikhs' histories and in the official records in the NAI. Presumably 'Engledue' was pronounced 'Engledow'.
34 Talbot, *The 14th (King George's Own Ferozepore) Sikhs*, p. 73.
35 Cox papers, 1DRL221, AWM.
36 Diary, 20 May 1915, Humphrey Gell, P158, 10048, IWM.

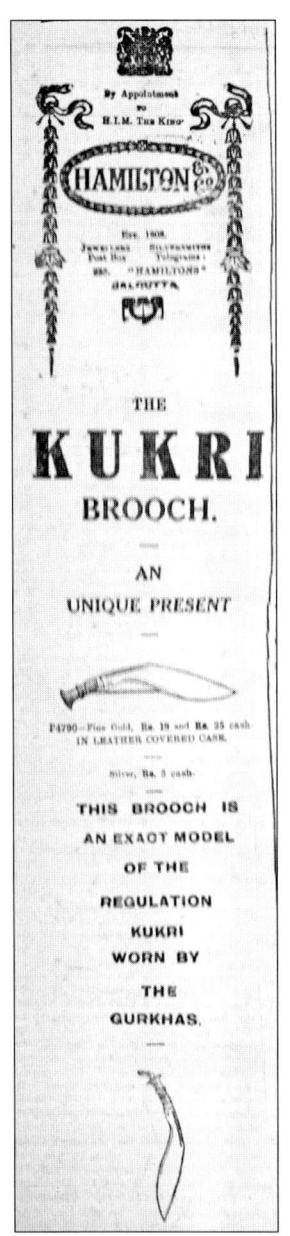

An advertisement for Gurkha 'sweetheart' brooches in the Allahabad *Pioneer* (a newspaper widely read across Bengal and the United Provinces), aimed at British officers' female relatives. (National Library of India)

The despatch of two further Gurkha battalions meant that Gurkhas now formed the bulk of the 'Indian' troops committed to the campaign. The two left Port Said at the end of May, the men of the 10th lustily cheering the 5th from the dockside. While the 5th mounted its two machine-guns on the stern of the transport *Annaberg* (useless against submarines, even on the surface) the transports reached Cape Helles, via the harbour of Lemnos, without incident. Both battalions disembarked at V Beach, Sedd-ul-Bahr, the 5th in the early hours of 3 June, using as a jetty the hulk of the collier *River Clyde*, run aground while landing British troops under fire on 25 April. Later that day the 10th landed, 734-strong. Arriving on the eve of another major attack, the battalions were directed to camp at Gully Beach, where a party of the 10th's men were immediately detailed to join an improvised workshop making 'jam-tin' bombs. They were to be plunged into battle almost immediately, the 5th serving alongside their long-standing rivals, the 6th.

Casualties came in major attacks, from unending bombardment and sniping, and in accidents. The 10th, which entered the trenches on 8 June, lost one of its few British officers within a week when one accidentally burned a hole in his hand when a Very flare pistol, a painful and disabling wound. (Ironically, it was to be hand wounds such as this – though inflicted deliberately – that would present such a challenge to the Gurkhas' discipline during the campaign.) The battalion lost a dozen men from shellfire and a dozen more to snipers before its men, unused to trench warfare, became accustomed to how to live in the front line. Not that the front line was necessarily any more dangerous: the 10th lost as many casualties (about fourteen killed or wounded) in its first spell in reserve as it had in its first tour in the line.

Members of his staff described Herbert Cox as 'extraordinary cheery and nice to us'. He toured his battalions' trenches daily, stopping for tea with their officers and chatting and chaffing their men in the approved hearty manner, in accordance with the Indian Army's cherished traditions, in which officers acknowledged and largely shared their men's discomfort and danger. (Officers ate better, but the risks of wounds were as great if not greater, and the stench of decaying bodies assailed them all.) In many ways Cox's first month on Gallipoli represented the pinnacle of his career. His brigade's achievements in seizing Gurkha Bluff and holding the line made it famous (though because of censorship not known by name) across the empire. Cox's popularity among his men rested on his personal bravery. The brigade war diary bears the line 'GOC visited f[ront] line' almost every day.[37] In June he was among a party bombed out of a front line trench, and he was beside his orderly officer, (Christopher Irvine of the 69th Punjabis) when Irvine was shot in the head, dying two hours later without regaining consciousness. Even the regrettable departure of the Punjabis did not dent Cox's confidence in his men's capacity. His brigade's trenches were regarded as models – and the pre-1914 Indian Army had little experience of trench warfare. Despite the importance of grenades (called bombs) in trench fighting the Indian troops remained untrained in their use until June. 'These bombs are horrid things', Herbert Cox told his family (having been in a trench into which they were hurled) 'the Gurkhas & Sikhs hate them … they have of course, never seen them before'.[38] While Gurkhas had helped to make bombs, and some Sikhs and Gurkhas learned how to use them, the oversight seems extraordinary, especially given how much Ottoman troops used them.

Most Indian troops had little idea of what they were to face in the trenches of Helles. But some of the 5th Gurkhas' men had at least an inkling. One of the many innovations that William Villiers-Stuart had introduced in the decade before the war had been to buy a packet of 144 stereoscope slides of the Russo-Japanese war, and periodically 'made the riflemen look at them and discuss them'. They depicted 'actual battlefields, effects of bombardments, misery of the wounded, and the dreadful state of the dead'. Kenneth Erskine later told Villiers-Stuart that while 'the horrid sights, sounds and odours of the battlefield were strange to the rest of the battalion', Villiers-Stuart's men 'were quite unmoved' and often said to Erskine 'It is just like the photos'.[39]

---

37 War diary, 29th Indian Infantry Brigade, June 1915, 186, AWM 6.
38 Cox papers, 1DRL221, AWM.
39 Maxwell, *Villiers-Stuart on the Frontier*, p. 192.

'When one was killed': casualties and casualty lists

The story of the chaotic medical arrangements for the landings at both Helles and Anzac, and the sufferings that followed for the wounded, has often been told. The man partly responsible for the failure to plan effectively was Major-General William Birrell, the Gallipoli force's Director of Medical Services at General Headquarters. Birrell wore the black velvet gorget tabs of the Indian Medical Service. The novelist Compton Mackenzie, who arrived at Hamilton's headquarters ship *Aragon* in May as an intelligence officer, recorded a conversation with Birrell that suggests his ineptitude. Birrell was astonished to learn that Mackenzie wrote books for a living. '"Extraordinary!" he ejaculated " … I may have bought a magazine occasionally … But never a book … How do you think of a book?"'[40] The exchange seems to reveal the paucity of imagination that explains Birrell's failure to anticipate that landings on such a hostile shore would cause massive losses. (The luxurious *Aragon*, explained a Rajputs officer assigned to a divisional headquarters, was 'a sort of Hotel Ship'.[41])

The casualty statistics are one thing; individual experience another. Arthur Behrend, a Lancashire Territorial officer, described the field ambulance in Gully Ravine in May

> … an open canvas shelter clinging to the side of the Gully … lit by oil lamps … inside we saw two British doctors bending over a table on which an Indian was lying. Beside them stood a statuesque Indian orderly holding a basin of dressings. Two bearers carrying a blanket-covered stretcher arrived from the firing line and placed it on the ground. A third British doctor came out of the shelter and knelt beside it. He lifted the blanket; the Gurkha beneath it was dead. He replaced the blanket and turned away; silently the bearers picked up an empty stretcher and marched back towards the firing line with dignified strides …[42]

'When one was killed', Joseph Beeston noticed of dead Indians on Gallipoli, 'he was wrapped up in a sheet and his comrades carried him shoulder-high to their cemetery, for they had a place set apart for their own dead'.[43] This was certainly so for Musalman troops, but Sikhs and Gurkhas were, according to their faiths, to be cremated. Just as the Indian Army took pains to meet the dietary laws of its constituent religions, so it observed their rules for the disposal of their bodies. Gallipoli's stunted bushes (much plundered for men's cooking fires) provided scant fuel for the number of cremation pyres needed. But evidence from elsewhere suggests that the Supply and Transport Corps provided firewood and oil to enable men to cremate their comrades fittingly.[44]

---

40 Mackenzie, *Gallipoli Memories*, pp. 66-67.
41 Letter, [June 1915?], Leonard Abbott, 14/15/1, 18517, IWM.
42 Behrend, *Make Me a Soldier*, p. 108. The scene may be depicted on p. 119 above.
43 Beeston, *Five Months at Anzac*, p. 32.
44 Tel., 21 October 1915, OC Commanding troops, Musquat to GCS, India, WWI/153/H, NAI.

Hindu drivers of the Supply and Transport corps cremating their dead later in the campaign on a specially constructed stone-built platform. (IWM Q013689)

The rituals governing cremation were exacting and various, depending upon the sect to which a family adhered and their piety, but sepoys accepted that the full ritual would be impossible to follow on service. They were consoled that a dead man's family would often cremate a grass effigy to ensure that the ritual would be observed.[45]

How did families know their sons' fates? A stream of casualty telegrams went from 3rd Echelon, Alexandria or 29th Brigade depot at Port Said to Army Headquarters, Simla, and back, with notifications and lists in one direction and queries in the other, often enquiring about the condition of individuals. On 12 May Army Headquarters wired 'Please report nature of wounds and progress Subedar Kulia Thapa, 1/6th Gurkhas'. This was partly the Indian Army's monumental obsession with detail – a telegram a few days later read 'please wire correct names of two non-commissioned officers whose regimental numbers are 1096 and 2687'. But those responsible for the Indian Army's administration knew that to lose control of detail meant losing control of the entire edifice of command.

45 Bingley, *Sikhs*, p. 105.

For a time the expectation of the orderly transmission of casualties could not be sustained in a campaign conducted thousands of miles from India and hundreds of miles from the force's Egyptian base. On 19 May Major-General Alec Wilson wired the Commander-in-Chief in Simla from Ismailia that it was 'quite impossible to give full details regarding dates and nature of wounds' though 'all details are being sent by telegram as soon as known and I am using every endeavour to verify names and regimental numbers'.[46] Despite the best efforts of officers, clerks and babus in headquarters on the peninsula and in Egypt, the system became strained. In May telegrams included phrases such as 'wounded degree unknown', 'not dated', and officers at all stages questioned and corrected details of unit attributions: 'no trace can be found of other native officers, 89th Punjabis … am endeavouring to trace them'.[47] Within weeks record offices in the Dardanelles, in Egypt and India became more organised. Soon, and throughout the campaign, details of individual wounds, including their nature and location were reported, at first in code then, more sensibly in clear; at first simply to 'Army Headquarters', later to the Central Casualty Bureau, India, established in October 1915.

Though seemingly merely routine paperwork of the kind the Indian Army generated in staggering quantities the casualty telegrams in themselves constitute an unwitting testimony to its inter-racial comradeship. One list of wounded men reported Captain Wandrill Churchill (of brigade headquarters) 'dangerously wounded' in the head by a shell fragment in a list between Sanaksing Chettri, a bhisti of the 10th Gurkhas, and Waras Ali, a lance-naik of the 1st Mule Corps. It is clear that casualty lists recorded only serious wounds, ones requiring evacuation. Both officers and other ranks seem to have ignored minor wounds – Reginald Savory, who had survived the Gully Ravine attack, mentioned 'a bit of a wound in the forehead' and a knuckle grazed by a shrapnel ball within a month, though Rothney Battye wanted to evacuate him ('but I refused, like an ass').[48] He warned his mother to be wary of mistaken reports in private letters that he had been wounded and to only trust official notifications. The advice was timely but, as it turned out, mistaken.

'Making themselves comfortable': Supply and Transport units at Helles

While the infantry filed into trenches on the far left of the allied line, the Supply and Transport Corps occupied designated spots on the bare hillsides overlooking the beaches at Cape Helles. Indian troops had always had a tradition of building their own lines, and in these bare, sunburned and windswept slopes they set about making themselves comfortable. A British supply officer, Captain John Gillam, noticed that the 'Punjabis' of the Indian supply units (though including more than just Punjabis)

---

46 Tel., 19 May 1915, WWI/429/H, NAI.
47 Ibid., 28 May 1915.
48 Letter, 8 June 1915, Diary, 5 June 1915, Savory Papers, 7603-93, NAM

built walls of mud and stone around their bivouacs, making shell-proof shelters and, it seems, mud-ovens too. They were, Gillam thought, 'much handier at making themselves comfortable than our white troops'.[49] These men, one of their officers, George Aylmer, thought, 'one of the most priceless gems of the Indian Army'. Mule drivers were, he told an audience in Rawalpindi later in the war, 'as brave as a Bengal tiger' but were burdened with the 'stigma' of being labeled 'followers'. Having served with drivers in France, Gallipoli and Mesopotamia, Aylmer said that 'once he possesses a cart and a pair of mules he becomes devoid of fear'.[50] In spite of the suspicion of the loyalty of Muslim soldiers, about three-quarter of the mule drivers on Gallipoli were Punjabi and Hindustani Musalmans.

The Supply and Transport men at Helles, mainly of No. 1 Corps, lived in what Heber Alexander described as a 'delightful camp' about a mile from the cape, in 'comparative comfort' – compared to Anzac, presumably. At Helles the more open country had allowed the invading force to spread out across the rolling fields, creating an impression that reminded Alexander of Salisbury Plain. Though the rear areas at Helles were shelled (obliging the mule corps officers to dig secure dugouts) they were at least safe from sniping. The mules, in open lines, suffered casualties from high explosive shells. During a second visit to Helles Alexander witnessed the bombardment of W Beach by 'Asiatic Annie', firing from across the mouth of the straits, supplemented by bombs dropped from 'Taubes' – aircraft, named after the German for 'dove'.

Gillam described the life of the Supply and Transport men whose mule carts delivered the ammunition and other supplies despatched from his dump between W and V beaches. He saw them making their evening meal, in May, before heat, flies and sickness had made open-air cooking a misery. He saw a man:

> ... making chupattee, a species of pancake, in broad, shallow metal bowls – I taste one and find it excellent. Other groups of these dark men are sitting outside their little tents smoking hookahs; all the men we meet salute punctiliously... The whole place is delightful and looks almost like a riverside picnic, only everything is very orderly ...[51]

The point about this account – and many like it – is that it is purely descriptive, and neither racist nor judgmental; if anything Gillam idealises the scene. But already in mid-May Reginald Savory had a case of 'mild dysentery' because 'the water tastes somewhat of dead Turks at times', though in general he was 'enjoying it all thoroughly & never felt better in my life'.[52] Wounds and deaths aside, Indian troops were arguably

---

49 Gillam, *Gallipoli Diary*, p. 79
50 Aylmer, 'Lecture delivered Deputy Assistant Director of Transport, ...', *Journal of the United Service Institution of India*, 1917, p. 297.
51 Gillam, *Gallipoli Diary*, p. 76.
52 Letter, 16 May 1915, Savory Papers, 7603-93, NAM.

Norman Wimbush's drawing of a 'langi' – a cook – delivering food to men of the 14th Sikhs in the regiment's front line trenches. (14th Sikhs album)

healthier than their British or dominion counterparts, not least because their food did not induce or exacerbate intestinal illness. Indian troops cooked chapatis, made of coarse atta flour, a variety of durum wheat, generally eaten with lentil dhal or porridge. Fresh vegetables or the buttermilk Sikhs relished could rarely be provided, but *gram*, made from chickpeas could be issued instead. Fresh goat meat was available, from flocks on Imbros and even on the peninsula, with animals killed by *jhatka* or decapitation. As a result, the 6th Gurkhas' medical officer reported his battalion's first case of dysentery (more serious than diarrhoea, which was prevalent) only on 14 June; six weeks after arriving. The Indian Army had long shaped its logistics to its troops' dietary requirements. Indian herdsmen grazed herds of goats in both areas. When the Lancashire Territorial Lieutenant Arthur Behrend first saw the confusion of Gully Ravine in May, he noticed goats among the headquarters, ambulances and dressing stations crowded into the gully.

Like Anzac and British troops, Indians took advantage of the opportunity to bathe in the sea. At Helles the Indian brigade's trenches abutted the Aegean (admittedly sometimes hard to reach at the base of steep cliffs), while the Supply and Transport lines were close to the jetties and beaches. John Gillam described the drivers he worked with at Helles as 'the most cleanly people on earth'. He watched 'groups of them, stripped except for a loin cloth, busy washing their shining, dusky bodies', oiling their bodies and combing and dressing their hair and beards.[53] A British yeomanry trooper admired the 'Johnnies' as 'very handsome fellows' who 'took an immense pride in their splendid black beards and long plaits of hair', who could be seen bathing by the shore.[54] The Indians persisted in sea bathing long after European troops gave up, often bathing at night to avoid shell-fire.

Like Gillam, we can only observe. Because virtually all the sources relating to the Indians' service come from their British officers the religious life of Indian soldiers remains opaque. Units with more than two or three companies of men of the same faith were entitled to appoint imams, gurus or priests and, as we have seen, British officers respected and (in the case of Sikh units) encouraged religious belief. However, clerics were paid less than private sepoys (Rs 8-10 a month), their pay presumably subsidised by their co-religionists. In accordance with the army's desire to sustain its Sikh sepoys' faith the sacred Granth was to be displayed in camp. It is unclear whether or how this was accomplished in the trenches on Gallipoli. It is clear that trench life made it difficult for Sikh soldiers. They ordinarily were expected to fold their turbans and comb their long, uncut hair twice a day, a routine presumably often impossible in the trenches; though such is our ignorance of the Indian other ranks' lives except for one drawing by an officer we actually know very little of how they fulfilled their obligations.

---

53   Gillam, *Gallipoli Diary*, p. 76.
54   McCustra, *Gallipoli Days and Nights*, p. 66.

8

'Death roams about with its mouth open': Gully Ravine, June

Hamilton planned a further push early in June; what became known as the Third battle of Krithia. On the left of the British line, the plan was for the Indian brigade to take part in a frontal assault on the Turkish line in and to the west of Gully Ravine, on a line of about 600 yards. To the Indians' right was the 88th Brigade (exhausted survivors of British regular battalions which had landed in April), with the rest of the 29th Division, the East Lancashire Territorials of the 42nd Division and the Royal Naval Division and then the French corps in order to the east. Hamilton repeated his error from the landings, attacking all along the line, nowhere strong, and allotted unrealistic objectives, requiring the attackers to take Turkish trenches a few hundred yards behind the Ottoman front-line: even if all were achieved, this was not to be the breakthrough that all hoped for.

'The day went badly': the 4 June attack

The 'Indian brigade' had two British battalions temporarily attached to it, and 1/6th Gurkhas and the 14th Sikhs, both reasonably fit and up to strength. The Sikhs had just received its first reinforcement draft, of two British officers and 49 men on 1 June. By this time, in a month of the peninsula it had lost 34 men killed and wounded, though only two British officers – Major George Swinley and Lieutenant Montague Spankie, both killed on 14 May. The battalion was to enter the attack with fifteen British officers, fourteen Indian officers and 514 men – 50 of whom remained as a trench garrison. The first wave of the attack comprised half the Gurkhas, half the Sikhs and half of the Lancashire Fusiliers, or what remained of them after the slaughter at Lancashire Landing on 25 April. They were to seize the first trench, J.10. The next wave, of half the Gurkhas, half the Royal Inniskilling Fusiliers and half the Sikhs, was to pass through and take J.11, and then move on to J.12 and J.13, the Indian brigade's ultimate objective, but no-one got anywhere near it and it plays no part in the story. The trench lines ended on the lip of Gully Ravine, a gash about seventy-five yards wide and forty to fifty feet deep, full of wire, trenches and obstacles and commanded by rifle pits and machine guns hidden from British observation.

Three Australians and a Sikh photographed in Egypt, published in the *Sydney Mail* with the caption 'Best of Chums'. The Australians on either side of the Sikh were killed in France in 1916. The Sikh's face is blurred, perhaps because he moved at the moment of exposure, but its indistinctness symbolises our knowledge of these men and their relations with other empire troops. (*Sydney Mail*)

The eastern or right-hand edge of the ravine was higher than the western or left side, allowing Turkish guns to fire into lines of attackers.

4 June dawned hot, and the bombardment began; though immediately some of the few guns allocated to the western sector were diverted elsewhere. A northerly wind blew the dust and smoke of the bombardment back towards the trenches in which the attacking troops crouched, the noise of field guns, the big 60-pounders and the naval guns, sounding to the novelist-turned-staff officer Compton Mackenzie 'like drums solemnly beaten' combining to make the heaviest bombardment yet in the campaign.[1] Hopeful of success, Mackenzie waited with other staff officers in a headquarters dugout near the cape, as messages arrived from the front a few thousand yards distant. Conforming to the classic image of the red-tabbed staff officer, they marked the results in coloured pencils on the maps before them – 'a redoubt gained, trench occupied, or at some point a check'. As it happened there were to be many checks that afternoon. A few hundred yards to the east Joe Murray of the Royal Naval Division described the day as 'hell let loose', with the sun shining 'pitilessly ... the air ... foul ... the stench was now sickening, and everywhere flies swarmed and maggots crawled – thousands of them from the dead bodies only inches below the soil'.[2]

1 Mackenzie, *Gallipoli Memories*, p. 113.
2 Murray, *Gallipoli 1915*, p. 93.

As the guns died at 11.20 troops, as ordered, cheered and raised their bayonetted rifles above the parapets. As expected, Turkish troops who might have moved back to avoid the shelling ran back to the front line, only to be hit by a brief resumption of the artillery fire. If it was an innovation it was the only one that day. At noon the first wave rose to attack the trenches. The vagaries of ground and fire immediately disrupted the attack. The Gurkhas found the Turkish wire before them untouched and virtually impenetrable, forced eventually to withdraw to their trenches. The Lancashire Fusiliers seemed to be cut down as they climbed over their parapet: their line too remained unchanged. The Sikhs, however, Humphrey Gell noted from Cox's brigade headquarters, 'were off to the second and dashing across the open 100 yards or so' to the nearest Turkish trenches.[3] The attack of 4 June was to be the 14th Sikhs' epic, and its nemesis.

To the watching staff officers, their binoculars trained on the open slopes beyond the front trenches, noon brought the end of the bombardment but no sign of the action they expected. This was an empty battlefield, in which men attacked from trench-to-trench, keeping prudently to dead ground as much as they could. The Sikhs attacked in and around Gully Ravine, their battle concealed from all but those within its stifling and dust-laden folds. They advanced in two waves, separated by fifteen minutes, most along the bed of the ravine, between the Gurkhas on the left and the 88th Brigade to the right. Their second wave was to pass through the first and attack the Turks' second line: leapfrogging, as British troops called it, though the Sikhs would not have recognised the word.

Compton Mackenzie, listening to the reports as they came into Hunter-Weston's headquarters, heard what happened. He described what he imagined as the messages arrived. 'The Sikhs … came into the full cross-fire of rifles and machine-guns as they moved over the exposed slope.' As the 4th Worcesters beside them overran four lines of Turkish trenches, the Sikhs fell in their hundreds in the bed of the gully. On the eastern side of the ravine Captain Ralph Engledue led his double-company beside the Worcesters and actually reached J.11, with several British sappers carrying jam-tin bombs in sandbags. By this time it had been reduced to Engledue, Jemadar Narain Sigh and about thirty men, with the British sappers killed or wounded. They hung on in the captured trench, throwing the unfamiliar bombs at Ottoman troops bombing their way along the trench. Engledue's party remained until the following morning. When he withdrew only twelve men returned. In the mess Engledue was regarded as 'the luckiest man alive': he had shaken three bullets out of his pagri.[4]

'Down in the ravine', Compton Mackenzie remembered, 'the day went badly for the Sikhs'.[5] Untroubled by the Gurkhas, stalled on the uncut wire further west, the Ottoman defenders were able to concentrate their fire on the hapless Sikhs, caught

3   Diary, 4 June 1915, Humphrey Gell, P158, 10048, IWM.
4   Ibid., 9 June 1915.
5   Mackenzie, *Gallipoli Memories*, p. 115.

between the impetus to press on and the uncut wire on the floor of the ravine. Some got 150 yards up the gully but were caught by 'a devastating machine gun fire'.[6] The Sikhs' losses were staggering. Of those who took part 15 British officers (including Captain Herajee Cursetjee, the battalion's Parsi medical officer), 13 Indian officers and 450 sepoys, no fewer than twelve British officers, eleven Indian and 371 sepoys were killed or wounded. The battalion suffered losses of 80 per cent, most within a few hours. (With Cursetjee wounded while attending British wounded and evacuated, the battalion's sub-assistant surgeon, Jemadar Bhagwan Singh took over until a new medical officer arrived, for which he was awarded the Indian Order of Merit.)

Witnesses described instances of outstanding courage. Lieutenant Murray Mathew, the Sikhs' machine-gun officer, hearing that one of his guns had been abandoned, led a party out to retrieve it. One after another men struggling to carry the heavy Maxim barrel fell hit and killed. Finally Mathew himself carried it until he too fell wounded in seven places. He died of his wounds a month later in Alexandria.

The attack up Gully Ravine disregarded one of the tenets of frontier warfare. Even the novice Reginald Savory admitted that to advance up a gully was 'a thing one has always learned should never be done, until all the ground commanding it is first seized'. Though newly-commissioned (he had arrived in India in 1914) he expressed his frustration with the way Hamilton, Hunter-Weston (and presumably his own brigade commander, Cox) were prosecuting the campaign. 'Our methods here seem to be based on a theory that all tactics are rot, and the only way to do anything is to rush forward bald-headed'.[7] Savory was able to reflect on the attack because he did not die of the wounds he suffered in a Turkish trench. Struck in the head by a bayonet, he had passed out. Groggily coming-to he realised that Turkish soldiers were resting on his body as they continued to fire on the Sikhs' second wave. After passing out again he staggered back to the Sikhs' front line, where Ude Singh, a former wrestler, picked him up and carried him back to the battalion's dressing station. But Savory was mistakenly posted as killed. His family in London received 200 letters of condolence. A week later the India Office 'very much regretted' that it had erred. This, Savory's father admitted with restraint was 'an unpleasant experience to go through'.[8]

In ugly hand-to-hand fighting Anatolians and Sikhs struggled in the warren of trenches– the Sikhs were three times forced out of one stretch of trench and three times they re-took it, each time leaving more bodies behind. With the loss of so many British officers, the example and leadership of Indian offices and NCOs counted most. Here, in the chaos of Gully Ravine comes a fragment of evidence suggesting how difficult it is to pronounce on whether the Sikhs' British officers were as revered as they assumed they were. In his tribute to his father's undoubtedly affectionate and long-lasting relationship with Reginald Savory, Harbans Singh Thandi inadvertently

---

6   War diary, 29th Indian Infantry Brigade, June 1915, 186, AWM 6.
7   Liddle, *Men of Gallipoli*, p. 177.
8   Telegrams and letters, Savory Papers, 7603-93, NAM.

implied that men of the 14th Sikhs on Gallipoli were indifferent to their officers' welfare. His father, Ude Singh, in recounting his experience in Gully Ravine on 4 June, described how when Ude Singh remarked that he had not seen Savory Sahib, several of his comrades replied 'Leave him to his fate'.[9]

Palin, Cursetjee and fewer than fifty men hung on in the cover of a few nullahs overnight, but the following morning the Turks bombed them out and the survivors retreated to their own line. Philip Palin had been struck by three bullets, saved by his having adopted a Sikh turban. Despite the Indian Army's competitive tribalism, even Gurkha officers conceded that the Sikhs had done all that could be expected of them. 'On that tragic day', Charles Bruce remembered, 'the behaviour of the 14th Sikhs was such as might form a pattern to any battalion in any army'.[10]

'Goodbye to my best friends': the Gurkhas and Gully Ravine

Charles Bruce's 6th Gurkhas attacked on the Sikhs' left, from the Gurkha Bluff salient against the Ottoman trenches on Gully Spur. Gerald Pepys, who seems to have written the brigade war diary, recorded that they went 'straight forward to the front' but could make no headway against the wire uncut despite the bombardment.[11] Captain Christopher Birdwood, the nephew of the commander of the Australian and New Zealand Army Corps, led his men across the cliff-face against the 'Mushroom Redoubt' at the seaward end of J.11 and got into part of it. Pressed on three sides by Turks bombing their way back into J.11, he and his men hung on, losing many men and himself wounded twice – once in the stomach. Unable to reinforce him, Bruce ordered Birdwood's company to retire and the survivors carried him out under heavy fire. He died on 7 June, of peritonitis. His fellow officers believed that he too would be recommended for Distinguished Service Order or even a Victoria Cross, but he missed out, receiving a mention-in-despatches (the DSO could not be awarded posthumously).

Bruce had felt no optimism before the attack, and his fears were realised. 'I don't think I ever had a more unpleasant task given to me', he wrote, recalling that he knew that 'I was saying goodbye to my best friends' – officers and men he had served with in the 6th Gurkhas. 'Naturally, he recalled bitterly, 'the attack was a complete failure'.[12] The 6th Gurkhas had lost 13 killed and 79 wounded. The eight recommendations Bruce made for men to receive the Indian Distinguished Service Medal offered him no consolation. Bruce's foreboding led him to order that the garrison of 64 he had to leave in the front line trenches should be 'young soldiers' – he had received a draft of 80 on the eve of the attack.

---

9   Thandi, *Down the Memory Lane*, p. 8.
10   Bruce, *Himalayan Wanderer*, p. 255.
11   War diary, 29th Indian Infantry Brigade, June 1915, 186, AWM 6.
12   Bruce, *Himalayan Wanderer*, p. 258.

Under pressure from Hunter-Weston's headquarters, Cox ordered the 5th Gurkhas to take the Mushroom Redoubt, the main Turkish position on the western flank. The 5th Gurkhas, whose men had spent their first night at Helles assembling jam-tin bombs on the beach, received orders to move up to the front line as the first waves of infantry went over the top; their first sight of the trenches of Gully Spur. They had expected to provide a reserve for the proposed advance on Krithia but as before no one got close to the village. Instead, the 5th was sent to attempt another assault on the Turkish J trenches – the objective that Bruce's 6th Gurkhas had wasted their lives trying to reach through the uncut barbed wire – this time against an enemy fully alert. Later in the afternoon orders arrived for them to pass through the foremost Indian units, moving along the beach and then up steep bluffs toward the Turkish line. Bruce pointed out the features of the utterly unfamiliar landscape and at 5 that afternoon, the 5th Gurkhas attacked. Three companies 'broke cover' (a phrase redolent of frontier war) and moved across the beach and up the slope, all under heavy fire. The battalion's commanding officer and second-in-command were both wounded (what Lieutenant-Colonel Guy Bolsragon was doing in the front line was never explained), moving up two knife-edged parallel spurs on a narrow frontage – only six yards, forcing men to bunch up as they ran towards the Turkish trenches. One officer drew and waved his sword, but no amount of gallantry could prevail against machine-gun fire and uncut wire. They reached the crest, holding on until nightfall, but having to withdraw, like the 6th unable to penetrate the uncut wire to break into let alone take the Turkish trenches. The regimental history describes the wounding and deaths of a succession of British and Gurkha officers, and with the loss of six officers killed and six wounded and 117 men killed or wounded in the battalion. The only bright spot in the entire episode was that Naik Dhansing Gurung, cut off and seized, evaded captivity by stripping off his kit and scrambling down the cliffs to dive into the sea, shot at by the Turks on the way. He swam down the coast and rejoined his battalion. (Where did he learn to swim? Presumably in Egypt on the canal.)

The Sikhs lost most heavily, but the Gurkhas also suffered heavy casualties, especially Birdwood's company in J.11. (Humphrey Gell heard that night that one company had been 'wiped out to a man').[13] June was the month of the heaviest losses for the Indians on Gallipoli, with 591 other ranks killed or died of wounds, the great majority in the 14th Sikhs in Gully Ravine on 4 June.[14] The days of agony had been wasted. As Compton Mackenzie wrote, 'Achi Baba was still before them, and eastward the sun was rising out of Asia'.[15] The attempt had arguably been doomed before the whistles blew. It had employed too few troops and insufficient firepower to expect to seize and hold any but odd pockets in the Turkish line. The defenders remained practically inviolable and the attackers remained well short of Krithia village let alone the slopes

13 Diary, 4 June 1915, Humphrey Gell, P158, 10048, IWM.
14 *Statistics of the Military Effort of the British Empire in the Great War*, p. 285.
15 Mackenzie, *Gallipoli Memories*, p. 117.

Gurkhas wounded in the hand: a reflection of the intensity of combat in the Gully Spur trenches. (ATL PA1-0-863-01-4)

of Achi Baba. An average gain of no more than 200-400 yards of ground had cost about 7,000 British and French casualties. Ian Hamilton mendaciously described it in his official dispatch as 'locally successful'.[16] This, Charles Bruce wrote, had been 'a very unpleasant day'.[17]

Bruce described an extraordinary coincidence that occurred in this attack. A havildar of the 5th Gurkhas left his pack in no man's land when he was carried away wounded. The pack include his notebook, listing men of his platoon and his name. The man was evacuated to India and, after convalescing, at length returned to his battalion, by that time fighting in Mesopotamia. In September 1917 the notebook was taken off a captured Turk by a man of another battalion in his brigade and returned to him.

The 'complete failure' of the Gully Ravine attack was even more shocking given the 'general feeling of optimism' among the Sikhs the night before.[18] Some Sikhs told Humphrey Gell that 'if they'd been supported more they could have got to Krithia',

---

16   Supplement to the *London Gazette*, 4 January 1916, p. 285.
17   Bruce, *Himalayan Wanderer*, p. 257.
18   Bamford, *The Sikh Regiment*, p. 33.

but they were deluded.[19] The casualty telegrams sent in the wake of the 4 June attack make grim reading; the words 'killed' and 'died of wounds', followed by great slabs of text interspersed with regimental numbers, and of course the name 'Singh'. The 14th Sikhs was wrecked for a time; not for ten days did it return to the front line, under Captain Ralph Engledue (Philip Palin was sent to command a brigade of Lancashire Territorials which had also suffered heavily). So weak was the battalion that its dump (where its men dropped their belongings and spare kit while in the line) was under the battalion's carpenter, armourer and boot-maker. The arrival of a draft of a hundred men enabled it to take on its share and as the brigade now included the 5th and 10th Gurkhas it was able to prepare for the next effort to gain Krithia and break through to victory. That prospect, seen through the heat haze and clouds of flies that lay over the trenches of Cape Helles like a miasma, seemed as remote as ever.

While historians can be sniffy about the veracity of the Indian Army handbooks and their authors' tendency to categorise and romaticise the sepoys' supposed characteristics, the Sikhs' actions in the attack do tend to bear out the generalisations the handbooks propagated. True to Arthur Bingley's handbook, the Sikhs in Gully Ravine had embodied 'his creed never to turn his back to his enemy'; they had been 'stubborn and earnest in action'; his qualities had been 'nowhere more conspicuous than in a … defeat'.[20] Losses in a unit the size of a battalion, especially one with barely a dozen British officers, hit the survivors hard. Reginald Savory, for a time as a lieutenant commanding the Sikhs ('or what little remains of it') confessed that he found it 'very depressing being such a small community, & one misses the others awfully'.[21] Shocked by the massive losses in such a short time in units in which all knew each other, some of the officers were bitter, even resentful. Humphrey Gell, distressed by the loss of men he had come to know well in the past month, claimed that 'if they had been supported more they could have got to Krithia'.[22] But even if they had, the capture of the summit of Achi Baba would have called for more attacks and further deaths. Gell's obsession with gaining minor steps of ground reflects how even senior officers on Gallipoli soon thought in terms of yards rather than miles, losing the strategic reason for the campaign for the tactical detail of seizing this trench or that, regardless of purpose.

'The loyalty of that martial race': Gully Ravine's effects in the Punjab

The north Indian monsoon of 1915 was unreliable – no rain would fall at all in August. The price of wheat, the Punjab's staple, was rising: the province's poor would soon face hardship. An unconventional British journalist in Bombay

---

19   Diary, 4 June 1915, Humphrey Gell, P158, 10048, IWM.
20   Bingley, *Sikhs*, p. 126.
21   Letter, 8 June 1915, Reginald Savory, 7603-93, NAM.
22   Diary, 4 June 1915, Humphrey Gell, P158, 10048, IWM.

considered that 'no country suffered economically more severely from the war than India', because its people ordinarily lived so precariously close to starvation.[23] What did India's country people know or think of the war? 'Many fantastic rumours … sprang up and died down like weeds', the Punjab's official chronicler conceded.[24] What effect would news of the slaughter in Gully Ravine have on the Punjab, and especially on Sikhs?

Sacrifice on such a scale demanded commensurate rhetoric. Ian Hamilton issued a communiqué, published widely in India, in which he praised the Sikhs' 'extreme gallantry'. 'The history of the Sikhs affords many instances of their value as soldiers', he wrote, 'but it may safely be asserted that nothing finer than the grim valour and steady discipline displayed by them on the 4th June has ever been done by soldiers of the Khalsa …'.[25] Curiously (for soldiers who served an imperial regime but no nation), Hamilton wrote that he hoped their conduct should 'make a record their nation should look back upon with pride for many generations'. Austen Chamberlain, Secretary of State for India, also later praised the Sikhs' 'glorious actions' in the House of Commons.[26]

In the Punjab, where Sikh recruitment had been noticeably depressed during 1914-15, largely through the influence and intimidation of the *Ghadr* movement, news of the Gully Ravine attack had an electrifying effect on Sikh sentiment. 'Recruitment has suddenly improved', Hardinge reported at the start of August.[27] Instead of finding the casualty lists depressing, with *Ghadr* unrest 'crushed', Sikh community leaders emphasised the heroism of the story.[28] Relying on translations of the reports of British journalists, Sikhs read of the 14th Sikhs' attack. Rather than focusing on the attack's futility and its cost, they hailed it as a 'glorious stand'. Michael O'Dwyer, the Punjab's lieutenant-governor (who devoted himself wholeheartedly, even unscrupulously, to stimulating recruiting in the province) quoted without attribution Compton Mackenzie's description of the action, though in a different spirit: 'no ground was given; no man turned his back; no man lingered on the way' He conjured a romantic description of the Sikhs' dead:

> On the slope beyond, the bodies of those tall and grave warriors, all face downwards, where they fell indomitably advancing, lay thickly among the aromatic scrub.[29]

---

23 Horniman, *Amritsar and Our Duty to India*, p. 17.
24 Leigh, *The Punjab and the War*, p. 25.
25 Talbot, *The 14th (King George's Own Ferozepore) Sikhs*, p. 82.
26 *Hansard*, 14 March 1917, p. 1140; Savory Papers, 7603-93, NAM.
27 Hardinge to Chamberlain, 6 August 1915; Leask, 'The Expansion of the Indian Army', p. 88.
28 O'Dwyer, *India as I Knew it*, p. 206.
29 O'Dwyer, 'India's Manpower in the War', *Army Quarterly*, Vol. 2, No. 2, July 1921, p. 262.

Such reports inspired rather than depressed recruiting among the Sikhs of the central and eastern Punjab, allowing them to respond to their critics 'now you see what stuff the Sikhs are made of'. In his memoirs (in which he defended his conduct after the Amritsar massacre of 1919) O'Dwyer reiterated that 'the annihilation of a gallant Sikh battalion' had been 'one of the most powerful factors in securing the loyalty of that martial race'.[30] Punjab government officials found that 'more interest was taken in minor events, which suggested some local connection' than in larger, more remote events, and the Sikh reaction to Gully Ravine supports that observation.[31] In Simla Sikh leaders convened a meeting in July recording their 'pleasure and pride [in] the heroic stand made by their brethren of the 14th Sikhs'.[32] More public demonstrations of loyalty would follow, to Ian Hamilton's satisfaction. 'After all', he wrote to Beauchamp Duff, 'we are fighting here for the British Raj … the sooner we can succeed the quicker things will quiet down there'.[33]

As reports spread of the 4 June attack and of 'generous rations and of the care given to the sick and wounded' enlistments rose, and by the war's end the Punjab contributed disproportionately to the Indian Army's expansion, especially from its Mohammedan majority. Of the 750,000 combatants raised, 350,000 came from the Punjab, 55,000 from Nepal and the whole of the rest of India the remainder. (Despite the concerns over pan-Islamism, it seemed that whether German or Ottoman instigated or homegrown it had 'little or no influence on Mohammedan recruiting': strengthening the suggestion that the worries over the Punjabi battalions' reliability had either been exaggerated or deliberately manipulated to secure Gurkha units.[34])

'Works easily and smoothly': treatment of Indian casualties

Cox's brigade had lost heavily over the campaign's first ten weeks – at least a thousand wounded; probably more – and the experience of wounds can be discerned through the force's medical records. Major Rothney Battye, commanding 108th Indian Field Ambulance, delivered a lecture to the 'Anzac Medical Association' in November. He described his unit's work since it landed at Helles with the first of the infantry on 1 May. It was unusual on Gallipoli, not just because it treated and evacuated only Indian casualties, but also because its bearers worked in the foremost fire trenches, as a field ambulance (responsible for stabilising and forwarding casualties) and as a casualty clearing station, performing major surgery and holding and caring for serious cases. The ship *Ajax* was earmarked for Indian casualties, staffed by members of 137th

---

30 O'Dwyer, *India as I Knew it*, p. 207.
31 Leigh, *The Punjab and the War*, p. 32.
32 *Khalsa Advocate*, 31 July 1915.
33 Letter, 8 September 1915, Ian Hamilton, 7/1/29, LHCMA.
34 O'Dwyer, 'India's Man-power in the War', *Army Quarterly*, Vol. 2, No. 2, July 1921, p. 263.

Indian medical orderlies, including men from at least three Indian communities, with Australian or British orderlies and a nurse, beside a third-class railway carriage used to transport wounded in Egypt. (AWM C00545)

Combined Field Ambulance, though other ships evacuated Indians also. A third of the bearers, mostly low caste Hindus, were killed or wounded during the campaign.

The broken country of Helles, the absence of roads (the track up Gully Ravine turned into a torrent after rain, and then into a muddy bog) and uncertain weather (gales prevented the evacuation of casualties) all presented difficulties, while the combination of growing heat and the plague of flies tormented wounded and medical staff and spread disease. (Despite the general squalor of Helles, the Indians' sanitation was 'nearly as perfect as it could be', thanks to the heroic work of Captain George Husband, the 69th Punjabis' medical officer, who remained as the Sanitation Officer throughout the entire campaign.[35]) Casualties arrived both in trickles each day – hit mainly in the head and upper body in the trenches – and in batches, when large numbers of badly wounded men overwhelmed the unit. With the beach hospitals only the first leg in the chain of evacuation, men died from shock, infection or haemorrhage, though the field ambulance's doctors rarely learned the fate of the men they saw carried aboard lighters and sweepers taking men on the long journey to Lemnos,

---

35   War diary, 108th Indian Field Ambulance, 1915, WO95/4272, NAUK.

Malta, Egypt or even Britain. The Indian Medical Service had recent experience of treating wounded on active service, though never in such numbers. When stretcher-bearers arrived at the dressing station medical officers asked three fundamental questions: is there much shock? Is there much pain? Are there signs of bleeding? They were able to question their patients directly, speaking the languages of the force – Urdu, Hindustani, Punjabi and Gurkhali.

Wounding brought shock – essentially a potentially fatal lowering of temperature and circulation. To combat this, orderlies applied direct heat, using rubber hot water bottles, and at busy times any bottle – officers' whiskey bottles or even employing used medicine bottles. Later in the campaign Battye experimented with heating large flat stones from the beach, and gave all except those suffering abdominal wounds hot tea. Practice naturally made the field ambulance's orderlies proficient, and Battye claimed that they could have a cannula introducing saline solution (to re-hydrate men often dehydrated even before they lost blood) within three minutes of a patient's arrival in his dressing station.

The field ambulance did not merely bandage wounds and forward casualties to hospital ships. Many wounded received treatment for days before they were fit to be evacuated. On 13 June, for example, an NCO of the 10th Gurkhas was admitted bleeding severely from a ragged shrapnel wound in his neck. Its surgeons attempted to tie the arteries but found that they had to widen the wound to tie them deeper, eventually packing it with gauze after removing a shrapnel ball near the man's vertebra, securing the dressing with a pair of forceps. The man's condition was 'very bad' – he had lost a great deal of blood – and he stayed for two-and-a-half days, with the dressing and forceps in place. They re-packed the wound, making sure that the sutures held, and sent him on to the hospital ship after six days.[36] Obviously it was easier to treat difficult cases in quiet periods than immediately after major attacks, but even at busy times the Indian doctors' experience saved men's lives. Battye described how a Sikh sepoy was admitted with what appeared to be a small wound in the shoulder blade. Not seeming serious, his wound was dressed and the medical officer turned to more urgent cases. Battye, reviewing the wounded two hours later, found the man sinking. Deciding that he was probably bleeding internally, he swiftly operated to tie the man's subclavian artery, which had been torn by the bullet. The next morning the man was well enough to evacuate. The Indian field ambulance's surprisingly low toll of men who died of wounds on Gallipoli (the War Office figures wrongly lists only four; the Indian casualty telegrams many more) testifies to its members' professionalism and skill.[37]

The medical history of the Gallipoli campaign has become a byword for poor planning, inefficiency and the sufferings of wounded and sick men. While mindful of the mismanagement at higher levels, the Indian field ambulance seems to have been

---

36 'Treatment of wounds prior to evacuation from the Gallipoli peninsula', 370/3, AWM 27.
37 *Statistics of the Military Effort of the British Empire in the Great War*, pp. 284-86.

both well equipped and run. Though operating in dugouts and tents it maintained a high standard of sterilization. Far from accepting front-line service as an excuse for dirt, Battye insisted on 'the avoidance of septic infection' in 'our ordinary dressing room routine'. Orderlies wore clean white coats (laundered by the unit's own dhobies) and the dressing station kept a Soyer stove of water boiling day and night. Medical officers and orderlies wore sterilised white coats and rubber gloves and orderlies placed sterilised towels around wounds being treated. He invented a metal cradle (a simple bar supported by two inverted V-shaped brackets) that could be used to support the legs of men fractured by bullets, or could shelter men with head or neck wounds. (In trench warfare head wounds were frequent, and the sight of them could unnerve the troops – Battye's cradle helped to shelter them from the sun and from what he called 'the public gaze'.) He admitted (in a talk to other medical officers at Anzac) that 'all this may seem [a] rather elaborate procedure' – perhaps a veiled criticism of less scrupulous practitioners – but argued that once the routine had been established 'it works easily and smoothly').[38]

'Absolutely as equals': in the trenches, late June

Hamilton himself inspected the Indian trenches ten days after the attack, seeing, and smelling, for himself the conditions in the front line, though he seems not to have acknowledged their endurance. The Indians' officers certainly submitted recommendations for awards. After the fight stories emerged on the exploits of individuals. At brigade headquarters Humphrey Gell heard of a Gurkha, who, lying wounded within fifteen yards of Ottoman trenches, was bombed and sniped at all day. The Turks called upon him to surrender but he refused: did he even understand the invitations? After dark he dragged another wounded comrade in, cutting a shallow communication trench as he went to protect them from Turkish fire. He then went back and brought in several more men. Humphrey Gell hoped that they would receive an 'immediate' Victoria Cross, but no Indian Army soldier received that decoration during the Gallipoli campaign.

But the aftermath of the attack also disclosed the other side of the medal. After retaking a trench in the days after the main attack the Sikhs found one of their men who had been 'mutilated' – the implication is castrated – but who died of 'shock' soon after.[39] Whether the Turks deliberately mutilated enemy wounded remains debatable. It is possible that the man suffered the effects of bomb fragments, or perhaps met a man maddened into committing an atrocity. Such actions were hardly one-sided. Nigel Woodyatt, a former Gurkha officer, heard a story of two Gurkhas on Gallipoli who, having cornered a Turk in a trench, 'took alternate charges at him with a fixed bayonet', deliberately missing him by an inch or two each time. Having

---

38 'Treatment of wounds prior to evacuation from the Gallipoli peninsula', 370/3, AWM 27.
39 Diary, 6 June 1915, Humphrey Gell, P158, 10048, IWM.

Indian troops bathing in the sea, probably at Cape Helles. (AWM C00805)

Sepoys of the 14th Sikhs in the trenches, 1915. (14th Sikhs album)

terrified the man, and amused themselves, they then reportedly 'took him away and fed him'.[40] Indian troops killed efficiently when ordered but could show compassion when circumstances allowed. At the end of the June-July fighting a Turkish soldier fell into an Indian trench, the only man of a wave of counter-attacking Ottoman soldiers to reach their enemies' trench. The Indians (it is not clear if they were Sikhs or Gurkhas) would not harm him, but gave him food and water and said 'he was the bravest man on the Peninsula'. He became a prisoner, one of some 500 men taken in the fighting. Grateful prisoners were an embarrassment to Cox. 'They come & seize my hand & kiss it', he complained.[41]

On 26 June the Turks dropped from an aeroplane leaflets (in Hindustani) urging Mohammedan Indians to desert. A French medical officer, 'Joe', sent a translation to his English wife.[42] Addressed to 'O Hindu, Mussulman and Sikh soldiers of India!' [sic], the leaflet asked them to 'think and reflect awhile': 'why have you come here?' It claimed that the Germans were gaining victories all over and mentioned a mutiny in Singapore (in February 1915, by Muslim Rajputs of the 5th Light Infantry) and the welcome accorded the Musalman sepoys who had deserted in Egypt. It reminded Muslims that 'our great Sultan, and Caliph of the Muslims, has ordered all Muhammedans to wage a religious war (Jehad) against the English'. Perhaps the most telling line was to point out that 'you know very well how here in the Dardanelles the English and French armies ... are all along being defeated by the army of the Turks'. Indians and sepoys were, the leaflet said, treated like 'dogs' by the British, who 'rob your country of its wealth'. The Ottomans called upon Indian soldiers to also 'take your revenge', or at least 'desert ... come to us'. 'We shall treat you as brothers', it promised. If it reached them, the leaflet naturally made no impression on the Sikhs and Gurkhas: there were few Musalman soldiers at Helles, with the exception of some of the Supply and Transport men (who like most of the rest were in any case illiterate).

Parties of men from the three Gurkha battalions went out at night, using the scrub-clothed hills and gullies to both gather intelligence about trenches and machine-guns and to unsettle their opponents and clashes between Gurkha patrols and Ottoman posts sometimes required gunfire support from the destroyers in the Aegean. All this prefigured a renewed attempt to break through and out of the Ottoman defences at the head of Gully Ravine. The scrubby hills and headlands of Gully Spur gave them (and perhaps especially the men of the 5th Gurkhas, known for 'greater experience in hill warfare', as an experienced Gurkha officer wrote) scope to bring their unique skills to the task.[43] The Gurkhas maintained their morale and their standards of discipline and efficiency in conditions that conspired to destroy both. Patrick Duff, a gunner subaltern, described to his family the 'rather picturesque' scene at evening stand-to

---

40 Woodyatt, *Under Ten Viceroys*, p. 181.
41 Cox papers, 1DRL221, AWM.
42 Anon, *Uncensored Letters from the Dardanelles*, pp. 144-46.
43 Woodyatt, *Under Ten Viceroys*, p. 175.

An 'Indian mule camp at Anzac', showing a muleteer at left donning his turban. Much of the domestic life of Indian soldiers remains obscure, revealed only in details of photographs. (*Sydney Mail*)

in a trench in mid-June: 'the evening sun on the sandbags, the rifles with fixed bayonets leaning against the wall & the little men crouching behind … ready to get up & shoot'. He found the Gurkhas 'simply topping and as jolly as can be, yammering away & laughing all the time … extraordinarily clean'.[44]

Late in June the South Wales Borderers lent to the Indian brigade a party of twenty Welsh miners, who dug trenches and underground galleries thrusting out beyond the front line. The miners had to work in the stench of corpses lying on and under the soil. Gurkhas and Sikhs may have wondered at white men being put to manual labour while they manned the trenches above, a sign that the war would challenge many conventions. Indeed, their service in Egypt and on Gallipoli must have brought to Indian soldiers many such unprecedented sights and experiences. As the many British and Anzac testimonies show, many met and even conversed with white men on terms

---

44 Letter, 11 June 1915, Patrick Duff, 91/10/1, 799, IWM.

of informality, familiarity and friendship undreamt of in cantonments in India (where few would have met British regular soldiers on such terms). Here on Gallipoli, in conditions of squalor, danger and discomfort, they were sharing hardships but also meeting, as a British officer recalled, 'absolutely as equals'; something that could only be regarded as revolutionary.[45] In another respect Indians and European troops found equality: in suffering and dying.

---

45 'Gallipoli 1915', Arthur Fergusson, 3DRL3635, AWM.

9

'The soldier must suffer': Gully Spur, June

'We started a big fight on 28th June', Herbert Cox wrote in early July, 'and have been at it more or less ever since'. This, the action of Gully Spur, suggested that the British commanders on the Cape Helles front could indeed learn from their mistakes, eventually. Analysis of the 4 June failure showed that Hamilton's force had too little artillery to support a general advance. Hamilton's intention was to capture the village of Krithia and the commanding height of Achi Baba overlooking it, one of the un-taken objectives on 25 April and the key to the defence of the southern peninsula. Its seizure was believed to make untenable the Ottoman batteries on the western shore of the Dardanelles, in turn the key to the passage of British and French warships through the strait.

'All over by lunch': the attack of 28 June

Ten months into the war, it had become clear that only by employing artillery fire in large quantities at precise targets would infantry be able to take and hold defended trenches. Ammunition at Helles was short (as it was throughout the British armies, in Europe and elsewhere until well into the war) but a third of the force's stock was allocated to the British force's renewed attack on the J trenches. The plan was simple. Following a bombardment heavy by the standards of 1915, the 87th Brigade (of four British regular battalions) would attack on the right while the Indians again attacked on the left. The plan called for the Indians to make a complicated advance, with the 10th seizing the closest trenches and the 5th and 6th passing through it to their objectives.

Cox's brigade again had responsibility for the western or left flank of the British line, holding a warren of trenches on Gully Spur and charged with taking Turkish trenches facing it, again, J.9 to J.13. The objective on 4 June, they were once again the objective later that month. The attack was to be launched by the 29th Division, including the 29th Indian Infantry Brigade. Once again the extreme left hand units (the 6th and 10th Gurkhas) would be advancing along the cliffs and the beach.

A follower (left) with a Gurkha rifleman, who displays his kukri, perhaps at the photographer's invitation. (ATL 077916)

The day again dawned hot and humid, calm and with a haze, with the dead of the 4 June attack still lying in the open between the two lines. The four Indian battalions gathered in the crowded communication trenches running off Gurkha Ravine, the 10th about to enter its first major attack. At 9 the artillery bombardment opened. As shells fell on the Turkish lines, raising thick yellow clouds of dust that hung in the heavy air the assaulting troops filed into the front line trenches as Turkish shells fell in retaliation. At 11 the whistles blew and the attackers, men from the Scottish border, Ulster and Wales, and from Nepal went over the top. The first assaults made headway, the British fusilier battalions gaining the Turkish front line and the 87th Brigade passing through them to reach J.12 and even J.13. The Indians' task was to pass through them and hold the J trenches, once again the scene of bitter fighting, especially J.13, the epicenter of the battle on Gully Spur.

Early in the afternoon Gurkha battalions, attacking over the scrub-covered bluff overlooking the sea, advanced in loose company formations, using the bushcraft that they had learned over years of training. Advancing northwards along the cliff-edge for nearly half a mile, the 10th's men scrambled to the summit of the knoll called Fusilier Bluff and then wheeled to the right, driving eastwards to seize the Turkish J trenches, still wreathed in dust. The 10th had gained its objective, under the protection of heavy artillery fire, with light losses and against little opposition. The 5th and 6th, as planned, followed, also wheeling right and they tumbled into Turkish trenches mainly held by dead and dazed Ottoman defenders. By late afternoon the J trenches were mostly in British hands. An Indian Army staff officer attached to the 29th Division headquarters, recorded what he had been told: 'the Gurkhas pushed right on, took the commanding knoll ... a splendid effort, all over by lunch'.[1]

It was not, of course, all over at all. The morning's attack had seized ground up to a thousand yards deep, a striking demonstration of the value of using a division of regulars. That afternoon, across the crest of Gully Spur British and Gurkha troops hastily began digging out the shattered Turkish trenches, sand-bagging and wiring, throwing out Ottoman dead and preparing to defend their gains from the inevitable counter-attack. Into the evening the Turks counter-attacked, repeatedly, with trenches changing hands amid bombing, bayonet charges and hand-to-hand fighting in the dusty, stinking ruins of what had been the Turkish front line. Writing from Harrogate on leave in 1929, Lieutenant-Colonel Hugh Lane, summarised his conversations since 1915. 'All survivors ... lay stress on the confused nature of the fighting'. So confused was Lane that he asked 'Were 2/10th there?'[2] The 5th Gurkhas history frankly admitted that even survivors of the fight had trouble giving a coherent account of the action, but vignettes of the fighting give a horrific impression for which detail is unnecessary.

The battle revolved around the Indians holding the junction between the newly-captured trenches (essentially running north-south) and J.13, intersecting it from the east. The Turks, plentifully equipped with bombs, repeatedly sought to push along J.13, hurling bombs from behind traverses, while Gurkhas tried to hold them with only rifles and what machine-guns they could drag up. The Gurkhas were given just 50 bombs per company (issued 'on indent', naturally), a pittance in the fight they faced.[3] The Turks, 'never appear to run out of bombs', Denis Ryan wrote. The entire battle occurred in summer heat, and with everyone, and particularly the wounded, suffering from thirst. As ever, leadership proved to be crucial, and again the 5th's commanding officer, Major Douglas 'Dod' Govan led parties into the hideous struggle, alongside British subalterns and his Gurkha officers. Govan was killed, Second Lieutenant Noel Cosby wounded several times but remaining on his feet.

It remains hard to penetrate the smoke and dust of the battle, now as then. On the afternoon of 28 June men of the 5th Gurkhas found themselves under fire from men of the Royal Munster Fusiliers when they entered J.13 from each end. Despite such errors, the Gurkha casualties were at first extraordinary light. The 10th lost two Gurkha officers and sixteen other ranks killed, and five British officers and 35 Gurkhas wounded. The regiment's langris and bhistis had carried rifle ammunition and bombs forward all day, and one of its followers died doing so. As the fighting died down they returned to their accustomed duties of providing the soldiers with food and

1   Diary, 28 June 1915, Clement Milward, CAB45/259, NAUK.
2   'Comments on Chapter IX' by Hugh Lane, War diary, 1/5th Gurkha Rifles, [filed with] August 1915, WO95/4432, NAUK.
3   Ryan, Strahan & Jones, *Historical Record of the 6th Gurkha Rifles*, p. 297.

drink. The 5th lost four out of six British officers and a hundred Gurkhas. Overall the Indians had gained a thousand yards, pushing the coastal salient further along, at a cost of 1750 casualties. Now they had to hold them.

'They held their trenches': the fight for the J trenches

Fighting continued into the night, with Ottoman troops making desperate and costly counter-attacks against the J trenches through the night and into the following day. The Gurkhas' machine-gun detachments carried their guns forward to fire into the flanks of attacks launched against the trenches of the adjoining brigades, and officers often conferred, moving their reserves to take over threatened sections of the line. While companies were withdrawn to rest, others would be called up to hold or re-take portions of the trenches, now smashed beyond recognition and offering little cover to their new defenders. In accordance with orders from General Headquarters officers led their men in counter-attacks immediately. 'It is the duty of troops … to recapture at once with the bayonet any portion of the front line trenches which may be temporarily lost'.[4] On the evening of 29 June Captain James Higgin led No. 4 Double Company in a bayonet charge to re-take part of J.12 which Turkish troops had seized. The Turks gave way, then came on again, bombing the Gurkhas out. Higgin and many of his men died in trenches now held by Turks. For days after his men indulged in a grim joke, pointing out a corpse and saying 'Higgin Sahib's boots'. Captain Michael Reaney, the 5th's medical officer, died when a shell struck his dressing station and blew off his head.

Holding parts of the ruined trenches, with Turks often a few feet away around traverses and corners, Gurkhas worked frantically to build barricades and bombing blocks, with both sides lobbing bombs over piles of sand-bags and baulks of timber. Subedar-Major Gambirsing Pun led men of A Company, standing at the bomb-stop and defending it alongside them. Bomb-throwing Turks pushed men of the 6th back towards the last two traverses of J.11A, which if lost would give them a crucial lodgment in the British line. Subedar Sahabir Thapa led men of D Company in holding the gap. The 6th's history (written by an officer who was present) described their actions:

> Man after man was shot down defending these last two traverses, and no sooner had one man been killed than another took his place …

Bombers of the 5th and 6th arrived and the danger passed.[5] Two buglers of the 10th, Ambare Gurung and Sriman Rai, distinguished themselves as bombers, gaining the Indian Distinguished Service Medal for their persistence and courage in holding on in these prolonged bombing duels, at any minute likely to receive appalling wounds

---

4   Force Order No. 6, War diary, GHQ, MEF, WO95/4264, NAUK.
5   Ryan, Strahan & Jones, *Historical Record of the 6th Gurkha Rifles*, p. 108.

from grenade fragments. The horrific state of the trenches, with dead and wounded men lying in the heat, can only be imagined. On 30 June Charles Bruce received his 'little present' – wounds in both legs – in the front line trenches after the seizure of Fusilier Bluff. He felt 'a shocking traitor' to be evacuated to the quiet of an Australian general hospital on Lemnos, but relieved to be away from the never-ending noise of the trenches and the unremitting strain of command.[6]

Turkish resistance continued for days. On 1 July there was 'more trouble in J.13', with both sides making furious attacks and counter-attacks. As long as the Gurkhas had bombs they could hold the Turkish counter-attacks at bay, able to bring up a machine-gun and keep the Turks off. That day a party of volunteers from the 5th and 6th followed bombers into J.13 and under fire erected barbed wire barricades to keep the Turks out. This, an officer reported 'ended the trouble with J.13'.[7] The supply of ammunition faltered and men resorted to using kukris and even picks and shovels in hideous fights. While the initial attack had succeeded in taking the trenches with relatively light losses, the days of hard fighting that followed saw all of the Gurkha battalions lose many more men. The 10th lost a further two Gurkha officers and 27 men killed and five Gurkha officers and 75 men wounded, with more men evacuated from dysentery that spread from filth and flies in the dirty, corpse-strewn trenches.

Though not committed to the initial assault, the 14th Sikhs had also suffered severely when it relieved the 6th Gurkhas in the trenches near the Nullah. (This, a gully running down into Gully Ravine proper, remained in Turkish hands, and allowed them to form up before attacking the newly won trench 150 yards away.) On the evening of 2 July, after a two-hour bombardment, the Turks attacked the Sikhs holding J.11A, a former Turkish communication trench, now the foremost front line. Thousands of Turks advanced, at their accustomed slow jog-trot, chanting 'Allah! Allah!', terrifying and seemingly unstoppable, only to run into rifle and machine-gun fire. The attackers fell in rows and piles within fifty yards of the Indian trench, their tenacity regarded by their enemies as 'great bravery'.[8] Later that evening the Turks renewed both the bombardment and the assault. As the Turks advanced over the bodies of their comrades Sikhs and Gurkhas apparently spontaneously rose from the support lines and ran toward the front line, sheltering behind the parados and firing over their comrades' heads into the attackers. Seven Sikhs were killed and thirty wounded in the fighting but the defenders estimated that the Turks (who 'never had a chance') lost at least 600 in the narrow stretch of no man's land.[9] After dark the lines of Turkish dead in no-man's-land seemingly crawling toward them caused nervous sentries to call out that the attack was being renewed.

---

6   Bruce, *Himalayan Wanderer*, p. 261.
7   War diary, 1/5th Gurkhas, July 1915, WO95/4472, NAUK.
8   Talbot, *The 14th (King George's Own Ferozepore) Sikhs*, p. 85.
9   War diary, 1/5th Gurkhas, July 1915, WO95/4472, NAUK.

But the Turkish counter-attacks continued, with bombing duels occurring when the old Turkish communication trenches intersected with the new front line. On 3 July a party of bombers from the Sikhs and the 5th and 6th Gurkhas under Captain Harold Wilmer (who had taken over command of the 14th and had been promoted to major, though he never learned of it) carried on a bombing attack at a barricade, making five attempts to break through to drive the Turks out of J.13. Wilmer was another of the battalion commanders who felt it necessary to lead from the foremost trenches, an Indian Army tradition. A fellow officer wrote to explain that 'the men were tried [sic] and shaken by losses and heavy shelling, and his example was just what they wanted to … keep them together … that they held their trenches and repulsed the attack was due to Captain Wilmer'.[10] Cox wrote to Wilmer's widow, Vi, telling her how he had died 'directing the fire of our men in the front trench', encouraging men 'shaken' by shelling and 'a strong attack'. Wounded in the head, he had his wound bandaged and returned to the fire trench, only to be killed. 'We were all very fond of him' – Wilmer had served on Cox's staff – 'I feel I have lost a valued friend'.[11] It was the high point of the advance at Helles: the Turks retained control of J.13 for the rest of the campaign.

The Turks, however, persisted. British officers admired the Turks' courage in repeatedly making such murderous assaults. In the early hours of 5 July sentries heard murmuring and noises that suggested an impending assault. Out of the pre-dawn gloom came another massive attack, to be met by a heavy fire from Gurkhas and Sikhs. The 6th Gurkhas estimated that on its stretch of a front a few hundred yards long some 1,400 bodies lay; the 5th thought 2,000 bodies. With their lines on the coast, the Gurkhas could call upon the support of the torpedo-boat destroyer standing off in the Aegean. Captain Denis Ryan, the 6th's adjutant, recalled how he was able to call upon naval gunfire by signalling with his electric torch, and watched, presumably half-horrified, half relieved as the ship swung its searchlight onto the lines of Turks emerging from their trenches as the ship's shells burst within the beam. The Sikhs' casualties included six killed, including Harold Wilmer and Subedar Dhiyan Singh, and 24 wounded. The Sikhs for the time being ceased to exist as a separate unit, with only one British and one Indian officer and 117 men attached to the 10th Gurkhas' ration strength.

'Fresh lustre to British arms': aftermath of Gully Spur

Cox was proud of what his brigade had achieved. 'We took 5 lines of Turkish trenches on [the] 28th and have killed about 3,000 [of] them (& I suppose wounded another 4,000 or more)' he wrote.[12] While it gained ground at the head of Gully Ravine, the action of Gully Spur also caused further grievous losses among Cox's battalions.

---

10   *Pioneer*, 11 October 1915, p. 4.
11   Letter, Herbert Cox to Vi Wilmer, July 1915, courtesy of Anto O'Brien.
12   Cox papers, 1DRL221, AWM.

Hamilton and senior officers in Egypt and India debated how the Sikhs especially could be restored to efficiency. The options included reinforcing it with men Hamilton called a 'foreign element' – the 14th was a 'class regiment': all of its men were Jat Sikhs. He wondered whether Dogras would mix well with them, but deplored transfers of Oudh Rajputs or Brahmans. Maxwell urged Duff to send 'young recruits … who have fired [a] recruits' [musketry] course'.[13] But all knew that sufficient recruits – the battalion was 443 Indian other ranks under-strength – could not be obtained for months. Ian Hamilton urged Beauchamp Duff to draft recruits with only six weeks training, on the grounds that trench warfare 'did not demand much training'. Men merely had to

> shoot anyone coming against him … or … once in a fortnight perhaps, to dash out … with his bayonet fixed and run forty or fifty yards.[14]

For all his ineffectual demeanour toward Kitchener, in this Hamilton disclosed an indifference toward his men's sacrifice, the results of which became apparent in the front line.

Another result of the 28 June attack was to disclose the fate of the Sikhs killed in the disastrous 4 June attack. Advancing British troops found the rotting corpses of Sikhs lying in piles. The losses among the Gurkhas' British officers were, as ever, grievous. In the 10th, Colonel Francis Sutton was eventually forced to leave the front line after he was wounded in the head, and after four days of this the battalion had three British officers, the most senior a lieutenant. The Sikhs, now at half strength, remained short of the British officers all considered vital and was left as brigade reserve. Even so, it suffered critical losses. On 29 June a shell burst over its officers, seriously wounding Ralph Engledue and slightly wounding Reginald Savory: his second wound. With Philip Palin detached again, to a Scottish Territorial brigade, Savory, still a second lieutenant, briefly assumed command of the 14th Sikhs.

Hamilton's attackers suffered some 4,000 casualties, the Turks over 10,000. Festering, fly-blown corpses choked Gully Ravine, and later in the campaign, scattered by shellfire and scavenging dogs, their bones formed drifts of white visible for decades. For the time being the hideous losses suffered by both sides precluded further offensive action. Anxious to make sense of the sacrifices the fight had entailed and conscious of the 5th's reputation, Colonel Lane assured the official historian that 'it can perhaps be claimed … that they did good work in extending the gains on the left to Fusilier Bluff', and in repelling Turkish counter-attacks. Even before the newly-captured trench line was secured Ian Hamilton praised the 29th Division (including the 29th Brigade) for having 'added fresh lustre to British arms' – characteristically archaic phraseology – but the rhetorical flourish of his

13   Tel., 17 June 1915, Maxwell to Duff, WWI/294/H, NAI.
14   Letter, 23 June 1915, Ian Hamilton, 7/1/29, LHCMA.

general orders did not conceal that the 28 June attack had also failed. The British front line at Cape Helles had reached its furthest extent, but it never gained the village of Krithia and from the summit of Achi Baba Ottoman artillery observers continued to direct fire into the British lines. The 29th Indian Infantry Brigade left over 500 of its men in the tortured soil of Gully Spur, but from July its battle on Gallipoli would be elsewhere.

The 28 June attack had also involved the mountain gunners at Anzac. As a diversion troops at Anzac mounted several feint attacks intended to divert Turkish attention and reserves from the major effort at Helles. Like the main attack in the south these diversionary attacks were utter failures in that they did not deter the Turks from recognising and meeting the Helles assaults. The southern guns of Kohat Battery fired during an attack by the (dismounted) 5th and 7th Light Horse on the so-called Balkan Gun Pits, also supported by Anzac artillery and a destroyer (which fired on the attackers in error). The attack was costly (the light horsemen lost 30 killed and a hundred wounded) for no gain. Further north the next day a great storm swept over the peninsula. The Turks, thinking that the Anzacs might renew their attacks under its cover, opened fire all along their line, a commotion coinciding with a planned demonstration by fire from the Australian line. A hurricane of shooting erupted from both lines of trenches, all to no purpose. Star shells fired by the Indian batteries set alight the scrub on Lone Pine, the flames and smoke adding to the confusion for both sides.

Indian newspapers re-printed Ellis Ashmead-Bartlett's exaggerated account of the fighting at the end of June. The *Civil and Military Gazette*, published in Lahore, the centre of the Sikh contribution to the Indian Army, reported that British (and Indian) troops 'successfully advanced on 28 June for about a mile': 'about' in this case meaning actually about five hundred yards; in places.[15] But as well as misleading propaganda, the reports also reflected something of the reality of the experience of fighting on Gallipoli. It described the millions of flies infesting the trenches around Gully Ravine, and the 'awful stench' that men lived with. But it optimistically (and surely misleadingly) claimed that stretcher bearers had left 'not one' wounded man in no-man's-land.[16]

The fighting at the end of June rightly led to more decorations being awarded.[17] Having seen for himself the dust, stench and blood of the trenches of Gully Ravine, Hamilton cabled Simla to report that 'last night Indian Brigade again greatly distinguished itself'. He went on to advise that the King had granted him discretion to confer British decorations – the Distinguished Service Order and Military Cross for officers, the Distinguished Conduct Medal for other ranks. He asked for similar

15 *Civil and Military Gazette*, 12 August 1915.
16 Ibid.
17 Hypher, *Deeds of Valour*, p. 258-59.

Stretcher-bearers evacuating a man pose for a photograph. These men are of the Army Bearer Corps, who were generally Hindus from Ganges valley. (14th Sikhs album)

powers to be devolved from the Indian government for the Indian Order of Merit and the Indian Distinguished Service Medal, and a fortnight later received permission.[18]

Following the British tradition of awarding decorations sparingly, Hamilton did not award many medals, but ensured that some of the Indians' most outstanding deeds would be recognised; provided that they had been witnessed by the brigade's few British officers. Accordingly, Subedar Sahabir Thapa of the 6th Gurkhas received the Indian Order of Merit for 'special bravery' in meeting the Turkish counter-attacks on the night of 28-29 June. Though his post had run out of bombs, Sahabir Thapa held off a 'heavy attack', leading a charge that regained ground earlier lost. Vicious bomb-fights in the J trenches figured in several citations. Jemadar Bajirdhoj Rai of the 10th Gurkhas 'led bombing parties covering orderly retirements when bombs were exhausted'. A Turkish bomb struck Bajirdhoj Rai on the shoulder, which he retrieved and threw back. Many of the citations for awards gained in 1915 (regardless of nationality) are sketchy. The citation for the Indian Order of Merit awarded to Jemadar

18 Tel., 1 July 1915, Hamilton to Duff, Tel., 20 July 1915, Chamberlain to Hardinge, WWI/295/H, NAI.

Dalbahdar Thapa of the 6th merely recognised his 'consistent gallantry on many occasions' and that he had distinguished himself 'as a leader'.

While the theme of reckless and exemplary bravery runs through the Gurkha and Sikh citations for the June fighting, the citations recognise leadership as well as gallantry. Subadar Dhanjit Gharti of the 5th and Subedar Dhanraj Gurung of the 6th both received the Indian Order of Merit not just for 'conspicuous gallantry' – the Indian Army's traditional virtue – but for exhibiting it 'in command of a double company'. The significance of this remains largely unappreciated. The 'Indianisation' of India's Army was twenty years off. No Indian officer had commanded a company alone in action since the Mutiny. But here, in the shambles of Gully Ravine and the slopes around it, Gurkha officers, their British superiors dead or wounded, took command of their companies in some of the most trying fighting their units had ever seen. At the time experienced India hands simply denied the facts of what had occurred. O'Moore Creagh, displaying the paternalism that marked his affection for the army, wrote that 'on some occasions

> ... when the British officers have all been killed, higher duties have fallen temporarily on Indian officers, who have ... done it very well; but ... Indian military history proves that Indian leaders have ever been inferior to Europeans.[19]

Indian and Gurkha officers on Gallipoli proved this to be false, and the example of the 29th Indian Infantry Brigade in the Gully Spur battle deserves to be better known in an army insufficiently aware of its history before 1947.

'Perfect nonsense – madness!': judgment on Helles

Over ten weeks the invaders had launched four major assaults on the Helles front, seeking to take the approaches to the objectives they had failed to seize at the landings – when light Ottoman resistance would have allowed them to have done so, had their commanders been more resolute. Once the Turks held the slopes of Achi Baba and the increasingly strong lines running across the peninsula it seemed impossible for the attackers to penetrate or break through, at least using the tactics they had employed. Though successive attacks had pushed the invaders' front line further north – and nowhere as far as in the Indian brigade's sector – it had become clear by the end of June that no cost they were willing to pay would bring victory.

The 29th Indian Infantry Brigade had made valiant and costly contributions to the fighting at Helles, in the capture of Gurkha Bluff and the attacks on 4 and 28 June. Charles Bruce, realistic as ever, admitted that the attempts to break the Turks' line had been 'to a large extent abortive'. He explained the failure by pointing to the dearth of artillery support at Helles, condemning the artillery available on 4 June

---

19 Creagh, *Indian Studies*, p. 274.

as 'entirely and absolutely ludicrous'.[20] By contrast, Turkish artillery had become the main danger to the troops occupying the dusty trenches. An analysis of the casualty lists telegraphed from Egypt to Simla shows that among the Indian wounded in the brigade's final weeks at Helles almost half were evacuated with shrapnel wounds, and a further fifth were wounded by bombs, though the percentage varied depending on how much time a battalion had spent in positions close enough for bomb-throwing.[21] The lists, giving concise descriptions, suggest the horror with which the field ambulances' bearers, orderlies and doctors grappled:

   4630, Sepoy Santa Singh, 14th Sikhs, dangerously wounded bomb, neck and shoulder
   3118, Rifleman Kirpe Rai, 2/10th Gurkha Rifles, severely wounded bomb, both hands
   4539, Rifleman Tulbir Pun, 1/5th Gurkha Rifles, slight gunshot wound, left thumb
   255, Rifleman Karbir Thapa, 2/10th Gurkha Rifles, severely wounded shrapnel, right shoulder

No one was able to enumerate the causes of deaths in action, though many died of shock, blood loss or infection – all five of the 10th's dead in the 22 July list were listed as 'died of wounds'. About a third of men wounded suffered gunshot wounds, and here a pattern seemed to emerge, suggesting not just the inherent danger of the firing line but also the effects of weeks of front-line service on men's minds. The field ambulance clerks generally recorded where men had been hit, and their ledgers show that wounds to the hands, and especially the left hand, appeared disproportionately – over four (left) to one (right) overall. For two battalions, the 6th and 10th, wounds in the hands were a small proportion – a quarter (10th) or a seventh (6th). For both the 14th Sikhs and the 5th, however, wounds to the hands amounted to half of their gunshot wound casualties. It is possible that the discrepancies were the result of different rifle drills (as ever a matter of regimental rather than army-wide training). If men of one battalion were trained to stand to fire from a trench then being exposed for twice as long as another (even a matter of seconds) then more would be hit in the left hand, the one exposed to fire. In the 14th Sikhs a group of half a dozen men, with hand wounds (especially to 'left thumb') must have alerted those reading the lists. At Brighton Indian hospital at the same time Colonel Sir Bruce Seton established that a minute proportion of wounds – about six in a thousand – were self-inflicted among sepoys in France.[22] Despite the qualifications, it is clear that Gurkhas and Sikhs sought a way out through mutilation. (And not just sepoys. It will be recalled that Captain Henry

---

20 Bruce, *Himalayan Wanderer*, p. 256.
21 Tel. 22 July 1915, Wilson to Duff, WWI/343/H, NAI.
22 'An analysis of 1000 wounds and injuries received in action', 1915 L/MIL/L/7/5/2401, BL.

Weekes of the 10th Gurkhas painfully burned his left hand with a Verey flare pistol soon after arriving on Gallipoli. This was 'considered by most people to be a "self-inflicted wound"' on the part of 'a first class swine', William Villiers-Stuart judged, recording mess gossip. Weekes spent the rest of the war as a staff officer in India.[23]) While the rate of deliberate self-wounding might be lower than the figures might suggest, it would seem that some men who had had enough shot themselves to escape: and who could blame them? Rothney Battye was disturbed to find in May two men of the 2/10th with wounds to their fingers and thumbs, obviously self-inflicted. He advised Francis Sutton to charge them, and was furious when Sutton declined and Cox backed him. Battye felt that he had to take 'a strong line' against self-mutilation, lest the 'rot spreads'.[24]

From the heights of Anzac Heber Alexander could see the dust of shells bursting over Gully Spur, but he like all knew that no progress was being made against it. 'The show was hanging fire', he wrote, '… our prospects did not look too bright'. All he and the entire Anzac force could do was to 'sit tight, strengthening our positions and waiting till strong reinforcements could be sent from home'.[25] The Turks now made few serious attacks at Helles. Reginald Savory thought them 'demoralised', the few attacks they made 'half-hearted' and costly. He described them 'doddering along like a lot of old men' – Ottoman infantry attacked at a slow, rhythmic pace, chanting. He thought he could detect each man 'thinking to himself "I know I am going to be hit & I wonder when & where it will be"'. But his sympathy did not prevent him from taking up a rifle and 'potting them over'.[26]

Hamilton seems to have learned – too late – that his plans for the Krithia attacks had been flawed. 'To attack all along the line is perfect nonsense – madness!' he wrote to Kitchener on 2 July: while the corpses of Krithia rotted in the sun.[27] There the four battalions of the 29th Indian Infantry Brigade remained in the trenches of Gully Spur into July. On 5 July, however, word came of the brigade's withdrawal from the peninsula. The decision was not just prompted by the battalions' losses or by their need for a well-deserved rest, but from the fear that casualties among their British officers had been so severe that to leave them in the line would risk some units having no officers at all. On 2 July, days before the first men were withdrawn, Maxwell cabled Simla to report that 'an urgent telegram has been received from Sir Ian Hamilton to say that Cox's Brigade has scarcely any [British] officers left'. Maxwell explained that he had sent from Egypt every Gurkhali speaking officer he had and, though already 'reduced to the minimum for safety', was taking one officer from each of his twelve Indian battalions, to send more.[28] (Shared language was crucial to the relationship

23 Gould, *Imperial Warriors*, pp. 162-63.
24 War diary, May 1915, 108th Indian Field Ambulance, WO95/4272, NAUK.
25 Alexander, *On Two Fronts*, p. 181.
26 Letters 3 July & 8 July 1915, Savory Papers, 7603-93, NAM.
27 Travers, *Gallipoli 1915*, p. 105.
28 Tel., 2 July 1915, Maxwell to Duff, WWI/295/H, NAI.

between sepoys and their British officers. When Lieutenant William Moran of the 10th Gurkhas was mortally wounded in the head on Gully Spur on 28 June he lost the ability to speak English but somehow retained his ability to speak Gurkhali before he died in Malta a week later. Sadly, no one else present spoke both.)

'Accustomed to dealing with Indians': replenishing officers

We can imagine the dismay in Simla when cable cypher staff deciphered telegram M-79 on 9 June. It listed no fewer than eleven British and eleven Indian officers of the 14th Sikhs lost in the 4 June attack. That two reported dead (Lieutenant Reginald Savory and Captain Reginald Wreford) turned out to have been only wounded offered little consolation. Nor was the dismay only because of the loss of so many officers, many of them known to those working in Army Headquarters in Simla that summer. That the entire command structure, British and Indian, of one of the finest Sikh battalions had been destroyed in one day boded ill not just for that unit's cohesion and effectiveness, but offered a portent of the fragility of the Indian Army's effectiveness in the war. In offices and messes at Simla British officers, even as they mourned men they had known, must have discussed how the losses of British officers could possibly be replaced, and when. Already British officers had been posted from units with similar class composition. (Officers needed to speak their men's language, and among the 14th Sikhs' dead were two officers drafted from Punjabi regiments, which also comprised Sikhs.) But how was the entire officer cadre of a battalion to be replaced when the unit was on Gallipoli and its depot was at Multan? The mountain artillery likewise suffered a steady drain of British officers, with only two fit officers with each battery by mid-July. One solution to the need for British officers was to post men from the Indian Army Reserve of Officers, and particularly from the Ceylon Planters' Rifle Corps. On the very day of the 14th Sikhs' sacrifice on the wire in Gully Ravine Maxwell urged Simla to send reinforcements to Egypt in anticipation of even heavier losses on Gallipoli, asking for drafts totaling 20 per cent of the Gallipoli force's strength and, as he later testified 'I was asked for and sent every … Gurkha or Hindustani-speaking officer that could be spared'.[29] So much for Maxwell's supposed obstruction.

The smallest unit in Birdwood's corps, the 150-odd men of the Planters' Rifles had been given the job of protecting Birdwood's corps headquarters. As most had been in commercial pursuits, and even, as Birdwood recalled, 'all very keen and mostly well educated', they now were seen as potential officers for Indian troops, even though Ceylon, a Crown colony, was not part of the Indian empire. Though usually proficient in Tamil or Singhalese, few of them spoke Indian languages, and especially of the north, whence most of the army was recruited, though they were, as Birdwood put it,

---

29 Statement by Lt-Gen J.G. Maxwell to the Dardanelles Commission, 1 December 1916, 102, AWM 51

'accustomed to dealing with Indians'.[30] The Ceylon volunteers were, he reported, 'practically all public school boys', though few had more than a smattering of Hindustani, the lingua franca of the Indian Army.[31] Beauchamp Duff agreed that they offered a chance 'too good to let slip by' and within a week Birdwood and Maxwell had selected 60 of them (twice as many as the number who volunteered) to whom to offer commissions in the Indian Army. The first men of the Planters' Rifles to serve with Indian battalions arrived in January, when three joined the 6th Gurkhas at Kantara.

Alec Wilson saw that 'their position *vis a vis* the [regular] Indian Officers is rather a difficult one'. Many were 'of a certain age', some of whom had previous service, and being commissioned as second lieutenants often placed them awkwardly under younger officers of less life experience but greater seniority.[32] Anxious not to see the Indian battalions in Egypt further denuded of officers for Gallipoli, Wilson improvised 'a regular system of instruction' for often untrained reserve officers sent from India (covering routine administration, drill, musketry, machine gun and signalling, and 'Hindustani' for those from other than India's Hindi-speaking heartland). Maxwell reported success, with most of 'a suitable class [who] readily adapt themselves to the social life of a regiment', though in this they often needed help.[33] Hardinge acknowledge that reserve officers, unlike many regulars, had 'no private means', and recommended that they be granted a daily allowance of a rupee or two a day to enable to meet mess expenses – because even on active service officers had to find and pay for their own food, and employ cooks as 'private followers' to prepare it.[34]

But the expedient of turning Ceylon planters into subalterns sufficed only for junior officers. To fight effectively an Indian battalion needed experienced, professional lieutenants, captains and majors, the men whose reckless leadership in the trenches of Gully Spur had created the dearth. The immediate response to the problem was to withdraw the brigade from the peninsula.

'Part of their contract': casualties and casualty lists

Wounds were only one of the medical effects on Force G's men. As numerous were cases of sickness that resulted in almost as many men being evacuated. Sickness debilitated the Dardanelles Army, and by the height of the summer virtually all of its members suffered from endemic intestinal diseases spread by the millions of flies feeding and breeding on the thousands of unburied corpses. Scurvy was 'pretty bad', Fergusson conceded, partly because 'GHQ refused to give them a [dried] milk ration'

30   Birdwood, *Khaki and Gown*, p. 244.
31   Tel., 3 January 1915, Birdwood to Duff, WWI/289/H, NAI.
32   Letter, [nd] September 1915, Wilson to Military Secretary to Duff, WWI/151/H, NAI.
33   Ibid.
34   Tel., 25 September 1915, Hardinge to Chamberlain, WWI/151/H, NAI.

Sikh, Punjabi Musalman and Hindu wounded on a hospital ship carrying them to Malta, relieved to be away from the peninsula. The man on the right has been wounded in the hand: a common occurrence among Indian troops on Gallipoli. (*Sydney Mail*)

for months and, like other troops on the peninsula, the Indians suffered from the lack of fresh or indeed tinned vegetables. The Indian mountain batteries' sick rates were remarkably low, averaging (across the campaign) 5.5 per cent for the brigade as a whole and only 3.6 per cent for Kohat Battery. Fergusson argued that some of the reinforcements sent later in the campaign 'ought never to have been sent'; a judgment arguing for the fitness of the units' original members and Carey-Evans's care of them. Experienced in public health as much as war medicine, as word of the conditions on the peninsula reached India medical staff asked 'in view of the possibilities of cholera in the Dardanelles', whether vaccine was needed.[35]

Prolonged service on Gallipoli tested men's resilience. Some thrived – Arthur Tillard met Birdwood when he arrived (in September) and was surprised to find that he 'hasn't changed a bit & is wonderfully young looking'. He went about in shirt sleeves (as indeed, photographs confirm) and 'the Australians love him'.[36] Others fared badly. Herbert Cox, in his mid-50s, began to doubt his ability to meet the challenges of the campaign. Asthmatic (but a heavy smoker) and suffering from frequent digestive trouble (flies tainted headquarters' rations as much as front line food), he had written to Walter Braithwaite, Hamilton's chief of staff, admitting 'I was not fit to

---

35 Tel., 29 June 1915, Duff to Maxwell, WWI/294/H, NAI.
36 Diary, 8 September 1915, Arthur Tillard, GM.

lead a Gurkha B[riga]de on hills'.³⁷ (On the same day Rothney Battye examined him, diagnosed 'chronic bronchial asthma' 'not fit for hard physical work': on the eve of the coming offensive.³⁸ But Cox was not alone in feeling worn out. The war diary of the 5th Gurkhas records in the weeks after the August fighting how a 'continual stream of men going to hospital with slight fever and dysentery' sapped the battalion's strength. Active service weakened men's health individually as well as weakening the battalion collectively.³⁹ British officers, even younger men, suffered from the strain. Two reinforcement officers who joined the 10th Gurkhas on Imbros in July were evacuated on the day they arrived at Anzac suffering from colitis and water on the knee respectively.

Sick men generally went no further back than Lemnos or Egypt, but men disabled by wounds were returned home for treatment or discharge. By mid-year the first Indian wounded from Gallipoli were returning to India, where they, their families, and the families of those killed faced an uncertain future. A Nepalese official, appalled by the disfigured and disabled men he visited in military hospitals in India in 1915 asked 'how could life linger in such desperate souls?'⁴⁰ Wound and injury pensions provided for the families of men killed and gave disabled men pensions on a scale ranging from partial incapacitation through incapacitated but not requiring an attendant to men who needed care for life. A lance-havildar with a partially disabling wound would receive Rs13/8/6 per month – about a quarter of his military pay.⁴¹ In an unprecedented boon, the Viceroy also directed that wounded sepoys receive a bonus of a hundred rupees, ten times their monthly pay, and 'they returned to their villages as millionaires': an exaggeration by a man who was a millionaire, in rupees at least.⁴² Some remained for a time in Bombay for industrial or craft training through Queen Mary's School for Indian Soldiers.

Casualty notifications continued to go from Simla to the regimental depots so unit officers could advise families, for Gurkha units often by sending runners into the hills of Nepal. Before doing so the depot record *dufters* [offices] checked names, numbers and family details, sometimes finding errors. The difficulties of telegraphic communication and Gurkha names and numbers necessitated corrections. A telegram on 16 June, sent from the 1/6th Depot at Abbottabad to the Adjutant-General in Simla read 'name of 343 is Hembahadur Rana not Ranbahadur Rana number of Bebesur Gurung is 733 not 833 number of Girman Thapa is 4935 not 4933'.⁴³

Astonishingly, perhaps, Indians sent overseas to fight the empire's war were not lost to their families. Battalion and regimental depots helped families, whether in

---

37   Diary, 26 July 1915, Herbert Cox, 1DRL221, AWM.
38   War diary, July 1915, 108th Field Ambulance, WO95/4272, NAUK.
39   War diary, 1/5th Gurkhas, August 1915, WO95/4472, NAUK.
40   Gould, *Imperial Warriors*, p. 198.
41   Tel., 8 October 1915, Hardinge to GG, South Africa, WWI/333/H, NAI.
42   Hardinge, *My Indian Years 1910-1916*, p. 109.
43   Tel., 16 June 1915, OC, 1/6th Gurkha Depot to Adjutant-General, India, WWI/430/H, NAI.

Orderlies and bearers at the Surgical Dressing Room of 108 Indian Field Ambulance later in the campaign, a photograph preserved in its war diary. (National Archives, UK)

Ferozepore district or in the remote hills of Nepal, to keep in contact with their sons and husbands. When the record office of Force 'A', in France, overwhelmed with casualty notifications, proposed that their frequency and detail be reduced, Army Headquarters in Delhi objected, pointing out that sepoys' 'relatives want fresh positive information which they now get' – and often within a week.[44] Every year 'hundreds' of members of soldiers' families, called 'chittiwallas', visited the Gurkha depot at Gorruckpur 'to communicate with their relatives in Gurkha battalions' (from where officers would send telegrams – chittis – to the battalions), and the war intensified that phenomenon.[45] It is clear from the correspondence quoted by telegrams from depots that relatives learned within weeks of their loved ones being killed or wounded, including the location, nature and severity of those wounds. The ready provision of news did not necessarily allay relatives' fears: news from the depots was invariably bad.

44 Tel, 8 June 1915, War Office to Duff, WWI/148/H, NAI.
45 'British Gurkha recruiting in Nepal: Notes on Gurkha recruitment, 1914', p. 5, GM.

A ward of the Lady Hardinge War Hospital in Bombay, where Indian wounded from Gallipoli would be treated through 1915. (*Illustrated London News*)

One representative case is instructive. In July, the 1/6th's depot at Abbottabad enquired about the death of 4010 Rifleman Duble Gurung, who had been killed in action just over a month before, in the 4 June assault on Gully Spur. The depot commandant wrote concerned that new of this man's death had not been conveyed to the man's family. Before he could, he asked for confirmation so that 'if found correct' he could pass 'the usual message of sympathy for the family of the deceased'.[46] The message might well travel for days – Duble Gurung's family lived in the village of Lamjung, a two-day walk north-west of the little town of Gorkha in central Nepal. It seems possible – as we will see – that they never learned of his death. But his family could have learned the worst in a time comparable to the 'notifications' that went from the trenches on Gallipoli to suburban homes in, say, Australia or Britain. Depot staff also took on responsibilities extending beyond the mere transmission of casualty advice. In July the depot staff at Abbottabad asked for confirmation of whether 4802 Apai Gurung had died as a rifleman or a naik: 'The information is desired in order to make out the claim for his family pension'. (He had in fact been promoted to temporary naik, meaning the difference of a few rupees a month.[47])

As ever in India, a few rupees could make all the difference. Hardinge vigorously put the case for a substantial increase in the field allowances paid to Indian troops, arguing that 'the twenty-five per cent increase should apply to the forces operating in the Dardanelles'. This would be 'regarded by them as part of their contract', a revealing admission that fundamentally the Indian Army was a mercenary force. For all its members' loyalty and capacity to endure, their material interests needed to be observed.[48] While bureaucrats in London and Simla wrangled over paying higher allowances to sepoys, in July free rations for Indian Army officers and their servants – and their horses and ponies – was not only approved, but back-dated to the war's outbreak.[49] On Gallipoli, their men were 'played out & worn to shreds'.[50]

46 Memo, 8 July 1915, OC Depot, 1/6th Gurkha Rifles to Adjutant-General, Simla, WWI/342/H, NAI.
47 Memo, 24 July 1915, OC Depot, Abbottabad to Adjutant-General, and reply, WWI/343/H, NAI.
48 Tel., 2 July 1915, Hardinge to Chamberlain, WWI/295/H, NAI.
49 Letter, 30 July 1915, Army Department to Maxwell, WWI/295/H, NAI.
50 Diary, c. 28 June 1915, Humphrey Gell, P158, 10048, IWM.

10

'When my body was weak and despaired': summer on Gallipoli

At Anzac the mountain batteries and supply and transport units served into the summer. The war correspondent Henry Nevinson wrote that 'the Indians stood the climate far better than the British or Australians'. He thought this attributable to their being vegetarians (as some were), 'habituated to the sun', 'protected by their colour', and resistant to diseases that felled white men.[1] (Or rather, white men burned by the Summer sun: John Treloar observed in June that many Australians had turned 'as black as our Indian comrades'.[2])

'Hanging around chatting to our fellows': summer life at Anzac

In the summer the day began before dawn. Men could bathe early – back for chota hazri (breakfast) just as the first Turkish shells arrived. The battery commanders would inspect their mules as they finished their night's work. The mules (and their drivers) worked through the night carrying stores, ammunition and water to the gun positions, and for neighbouring Australian troops (a further example of the close relationship between men of the two forces). Through the day battery commanders would tour their gun positions and visit the supply dumps on the beach. In the evening Fergusson at least would visit John Parker at brigade or Charles Cunliffe-Owen, the senior gunner at the nearby corps headquarters 'to pick up the latest news', reaching his bed, he recalled without irony or exaggeration 'quite pleasantly tired'.

At Anzac as well as at Helles, casualties among its few British officers remained one of the Indian Army's crucial weaknesses. From the outset it became clear that shortages among British officers would throw much of the burden of routine administration on Indian officers: even before the invasion of Gallipoli the ammunition column supporting the 7th Mountain Artillery Brigade had neither British nor Indian officers. As an expedient the Brigade's havildar-major was hastily commissioned as

---

1   Nevinson, *The Dardanelles Campaign*, p. 357.
2   Treloar, *An Anzac Diary*, p. 159 [26 June].

A muleteer of one of the Supply and Transport companies in a deep sap – possibly the now vanished 'Great Sap' – at Anzac. (ATL 077970)

a jemadar. Despite the belief that 'native officers' could not be relied upon one was entrusted with the responsibility of supplying the brigade with ammunition. While Indian officers were perfectly competent in both running their units and, in the case of the mountain gunners, maintaining and firing their guns, the only officers fully capable of communicating with other units and headquarters were British. When on 26 May both Rawson and Thom had been wounded 'we were a bit up a tree', Fergusson remembered. He reclaimed Guy Trenchard from the New Zealand howitzer battery to which he had been lent, and borrowed an Australian gunner from the 3rd Field Artillery Brigade. Captain Arthur Jopp, a 'permanent' artillery officer, knew no Hindustani (and presumably had no experience of mountain gunnery), but both he and his Indian gunners shared the English words of command used by both forces. Fergusson advised Jopp to 'stick absolutely to the drill book and he would be right', and so it proved. By the third day he was firing at unregistered targets within ten yards of the Anzac front line.

Into a burning summer the entente between the mountain gunners and the Anzacs remained, as Arthur Fergusson wrote, 'simply perfect'. 'They were always hanging around chatting to our fellows', he recalled, 'though how they communicated was a marvel'. The Australians (and the New Zealanders of the New Zealand and Australian Division) actually became something of 'a nuisance at times'. Infantrymen with time on their hands and a taste for dhal and chapatties would loiter about the gun positions, disclosing their locations to Turkish observers. At one time the battery commanders had to post armed sentries to prevent thoughtless Anzacs giving the game away. John Treloar commented that 'the camaraderie between these little fellows and our Australians was, I believe, grand'.[3]

As well as sharing food Indian troops and followers exhibited aspects of the culture of their homeland. An Otago infantryman, George Cloughley, described how later in the campaign New Zealanders would 'gather in little bunches and sing and yarn by the hour' – presumably in the 'rest' areas by the shore. Nearby (probably in Mule Gully), 'the Indians used to hold concerts on their own and make a most unearthly noise'.[4] This music could have been produced by men from half-a-dozen regions of northern India: all producing 'unearthly noise' to unaccustomed ears. Indians were highly visible, as well as audible, at Anzac, their mules and guns figuring in many Anzacs' photographs, diaries and letters. The mountain gunners established a shell fuzing depot on the crowded beach of Anzac Cove. Fergusson described it as 'exactly like a bunnia's [a merchant's] shop in an Indian bazaar'.[5]

The Indians' mules continued to carry supplies not just for their own positions, but for the Anzac defenders generally. This brought Indian muleteers into close contact with large numbers of Australian and New Zealand volunteer soldiers. Surprisingly, only once did Fergusson have one of his men complain of ill-treatment, and that was by a man who had drunk too much rum and who supposedly 'got six months for it'. He had seen his men, whom he knew to have been out all night, take Australians back up the hills toward the front line, and saw his unit's followers carry water and other supplies up the hills from the cove on their own initiative. Cordiality in such conditions might be surprising. Even more surprising is that the Australians even accepted orders from Indian NCOs, 'probably better than their own'. This may be attributable to the individual authority of Indian NCOs, who were generally much older, sometimes twice the age, of Australian volunteers (who averaged in the mid-twenties) and perhaps to the respect the Indian Army enjoyed throughout the empire.

Fergusson told the story of Lance-Naik Satar Mohammed to illustrate his account of the good relations between men of the two forces. He had been detailed to look after a well (or possibly a soak) near Pifferpore. The mountain gunners were on a strict ration, but Satar Mohammed was told that he could distribute any surplus water

---

3   Treloar, *An Anzac Diary*, p. 170 [7 August].
4   David Cloughley, (ed.), 'The Riverton Boys', p. 22.
5   'Gallipoli 1915', Arthur Fergusson, 3DRL3635, AWM.

to thirsty Australians. Naturally word spread and queues formed long before Satar Mohammed decided that the well could be used each day. The well was within sight of Turkish snipers, and Satar Mohammed had the waiting Australians queue under cover in a communication trench while he operated a pump and supplied his own unit's water carriers (presumably himself working in view of Turkish observers). He would tell the waiting men to stay in cover, check the well's depth and summon men up in ones and twos when he judged that sufficient water justified him filling a can. When he decided that the well had been pumped dry for the day he unshipped his pump and ended the encounter with a brisk 'Goodnait'; one of his few words of English. This, Fergusson reported, continued twice a day for three months, with never a complaint from the waiting Australians or a man trying to jump the queue. 'And yet people say the Australians have no discipline', Fergusson ended.[6] Satar Mohammed's achievement was not just in getting Australians to accept the necessity to queue (not easy still), but that they accepted the orders of a man they saw as 'coloured' is astounding in the era of White Australia. Satar Mohammed's age and standing as a regular soldier perhaps swayed them.

The story of Satar Mohammed also underlines how vital water was on Gallipoli in summer. A 10th Gurkha officer recalled that his most pressing memory of Anzac was of 'a continuous and abiding thirst'.[7] Except for wells dug and captured, practically every drop of water was brought from Egypt or Malta and had to be carried to the track-heads by Indian mules (from there men carried it up the steep slopes to the foremost trenches). Hamilton, though an inept general was not unsympathetic, noticed that at Anzac when the Indian mule convoys arrived carrying "pakhals" of water 'men would rush up to them in swarms just to lick the moisture that had been exuded through the canvas bags'.[8] On the less steep tracks on the southern sectors carts were used; in the north pack mules. As the summer advanced some of the wells ran dry, increasing the pressure on both men and beasts. Shortages of water and heavy losses among the muleteers imposed a limit on the number of animals able to work at Anzac. By the time of the August offensive the Anzac and new Suvla sector required 3,700 mules, most of them Indian.

Experience dictated that no more than 600 mules could be watered at Anzac, even though wells sunk above North Beach supplemented the water brought from Egypt. As the summer advanced it became clear that the well was giving out and the 'water expert' at corps headquarters warned that the mules would soon have to be watered only once a day. (Not only would this shortage distress the animals, but it would in time reduce the amount of stores they could carry to the line.) Fergusson cannily extracted an undertaking from corps headquarters that if he found water he could use it himself. Havildar-Major Paktar Singh of Kohat Battery swiftly found a likely spot

---

6   Ibid.
7   'Operations at Anzac in August 1915', 2/10th Gurkhas Digest of Service, GM.
8   Supplement to *London Gazette*, 6 January 1916, p. 298.

Indian stretcher-bearers carrying wounded down from the firing line during the summer of 1915. (AWM P01116-055)

and in one morning dug a well able to support 200 animals twice a day. (The discovery doubtless chagrined the water expert, but the well lasted until November.)

With the guns on call throughout the daylight hours, the batteries' signallers (who included Australians) worked under continual strain, a problem exacerbated by the guns being spread around three positions, all of which needed signallers to man telephones and repair wires vulnerable to shellfire and other hazards. The signallers were often obliged to stand 24-hour shifts, sleeping with their telephone receivers at their ears, while Kohat Battery's mess orderly, Piyara Singh, took over operating the headquarters telephone between meals. Breaks in the lines, whether from enemy fire or from being broken when men or animals stepped on them, had to be repaired immediately. Only one of Kohat Battery's linesmen, Narain Singh, survived the war. On Gallipoli he several times returned to the battery headquarters bearing a 'chit' (a note) from Australian officers who had seen him repairing lines under heavy fire. Narain Singh received an Indian Distinguished Service Medal for this sustained devotion to duty.

One of the mysteries of Anzac is that it appeared that the Turks were firing into Anzac shells that appeared to have been made in India. At first this suggested to the Anzac infantry incompetence on the gunners' part (and indeed the infantry did report 'drop-shorts'). One day Australians showed the gunners a shell that had just hit their trench, the markings on which showed that it had been manufactured at the Cossipore gun foundry, near Calcutta, and filled at the magazine at Rawalpindi. Their officer realised that though an Indian shell, it must have been fired from outside the Anzac line. The 'scoop' of the impact point proved to trained gunners that the shell could not have come from a gun in the Anzac area, though the Australians remained unconvinced. Enquiries to the British mountain batteries at Cape Helles disclosed that no guns had been lost, and the shells remained a mystery until New Zealand gunners revealed that the shells came from Indian mountain guns and ammunition sold off by New Zealand to Turkey long before the war.

'Showing signs of wear': mountain gunners in summer

Birdwood's force had been penned into the shallow Anzac beach-head since the night of the 25 April landing. After the failure of both the Ottoman attempts to drive the invaders into the sea and the invaders' attempts to break out of the beach-head, Anzac settled into a stalemate. Both sides attempted minor attacks and raids – the Turks on Quinn's Post at the end of May and the New Zealanders from Quinn's Post in June – but neither saw any prospect of decisive action. Anzac artillery officers had worked out the positions from which they could best support the infantry holding the trenches and posts, calculations involving considerations of where guns could be carried, what targets they could reach from them, and what the Turks could see and fire at in retaliation. Anzac's terrain left few suitable sites, but the mountain guns' size, and especially their mobility, gave them a valuable flexibility, even though they fired a shell (10-pounds) only about half the weight of the standard field gun (18-pounds).

While some Indian guns were moved about, others had very particular tasks. Two guns of Jacob's Battery were sited high up Russell's Top, virtually in the Anzac front line. Another, emplaced on Bolton's Ridge (which ran down to the sea as both the southern-most extension of the Sari Bair ('Yellow Ridge') Range and the end of the Anzac line) was positioned to fire on the Turkish guns sited near Gaba Tepe. A Turkish gun there had to be run out of its cover to fire, and so close was the watch maintained by Indian gunners that the mere 'appearance of the arm or shoulder of a Turk' became the signal for the gun to fire.[9] Throughout June the mountain gunners fired, at targets of opportunity and as part of the increasingly complex programs devised to support the various raids mounted from the Anzac line in attempts to unsettle the Turks (all both futile and costly).

The Anzac battle also moved underground, turning the firm sandy soil of the ridges into the battlefield. By June engineer officers and sweating infantry working parties had driven a network of saps and tunnels under Courtney's and Steele's Posts, and someone had the idea of using them to open embrasures in the hillside to fire at Turkish guns emplaced on Mortar Ridge, 400 yards away. One of these tunnels was large enough for gunners to drag along it and assemble a mountain gun of Thom's section of Kohat Battery, and in late June he was to fire from it.

9   Bean, *Gallipoli Mission*, p. 262.

Thom's section performed a 'spectacular job' on 21 June when the Indian gunners were asked to suppress two Turkish mountain guns emplaced at German Officer's Trench and firing on Quinn's Post, the most vulnerable part of the Anzac line at the very head of Monash Valley, where the opposing trenches were only ten or twenty yards apart at the narrowest. Fergusson and Thom had a tunnel dug in the steep wall of the rear of the post (where sappers and infantry labourers had dug a network of trenches, terraces and tunnels). Unfortunately the gunport was poorly concealed, and the Turks detected the sacking covering it and deduced that it was no mere observation post. As soon as they saw movement they fired. Before gun-layer Naik Jan Mahomed fired his first round a Turkish shell exploded in Thom's observation post and knocked him over. Thom 'gallantly unmasked his piece', as Bean quaintly put it, and the Kohat gun opened fire.[10] Thom groggily told Jan Mahomed, to keep firing at the Turkish emplacement. He continued regardless of the fire of two guns in reply, and got off another 17 or 21 rounds before Thom came around. Jan Mahomed received an Indian Order of Merit for his conduct, which praised him for 'distinguished service', working in a 'cramped underground emplacement', the walls of which collapsed after being hit by Turkish shells. 'In spite of clouds of dust and the extreme difficulties of the position' Mahomed fired seventeen rounds 'straight into the enemy's gunpots [sic]', seemingly destroying the two Turkish guns.[11] Fergusson was proud of such feats by his gunners. The Australians, he claimed, said that 'they could never have stopped in Quinn's Post if it had not been for them'.

Even so, the Turkish guns returned to action soon after, and were never effectively suppressed. The incident points not just to the extraordinary initiative, energy, bravery and technical skill the Indian gunners displayed (which even Turkish officers acknowledged, speaking to Bean in 1919), but also the appalling futility of the trench warfare of the spring and summer.

Heber Alexander found the Anzac infantry 'enthusiastic in their praise of the gunners', whose guns 'proved just as invaluable as in Indian frontier warfare'. They appreciated the mountain gunners bringing their weapons into the foremost trenches, singling out Everard Whitting of Jacob's Battery 'who finished off numerous troublesome machine-guns'.[12] The gunners found that their frontier experience translated readily to the demanding new environment of Anzac. They were accustomed to improvise. Later, exhibiting the ingenuity characteristic of Gallipoli, the mountain gunners attempted to turn their guns into howitzers by reducing the size of their charges and calculating their own range tables (because they were firing at targets closer than the official tables envisaged as possible). Indeed, technical problems plagued the mountain batteries, even though they had been using the 10-pounder

---

10 Bean, *The Story of Anzac*, Vol. II, p.71n.
11 Hypher, *Deeds of Valour*, p. 259. His name is rendered Muhammad in the citation to his Indian Order of Merit
12 Alexander, *On Two Fronts*, p. 184.

guns in action since the Tirah expedition of 1897, without being addressed, including in action on the North-West Frontier. Fergusson claimed that his shrapnel shells broke up prematurely. This the gunner officers rightly regarded as a 'disgrace'. Cables between ordnance officers in Egypt and India confirmed Fergusson's criticism. Their tests found that shrapnel shells did not shatter on detonation as intended. The shrapnel pellets clumped together, the resin acting as glue. About one shell in thirteen burst defectively. In a classic illustration of the bureaucratic inertia that afflicted the army, ordnance staff in India replied that no action will be taken … as the defect … is inherent in the design'.[13] Ferguson found that boiling them helped the problem, softening the resin holding the shrapnel balls together.

Nor were British officers alone in feeling frustrated at their equipment. The amount of firing eroded the vents in the guns' breech blocks. (Firing generated corrosive gases at high pressure within the breech blocks, and repeated use caused leaks that reduced the guns' effectiveness and accuracy.) Though they sent damaged blocks to ordnance artificers based at Mudros, the deficiencies of the over-worked guns became obvious to the batteries' Indian gunners. One evening while Fergusson and his medical officer, Thomas Carey-Evans, were at dinner, one of his gunners ('a very keen, fire-eating Lance Naik' named Prem Singh) burst in on them. He

> … chucked a breech block on the table and said what being broadly translated was "What the devil is the use of supplying things like this, the other gun is getting off many more rounds than us because all our breech blocks are bad.[14]

The mountain artillery fired so many rounds in the defence of Anzac that just under a month after the landing Hamilton's artillery staff cabled the War Office to report that its guns were 'showing signs of wear', and learned to their alarm that no replacements could be obtained from Britain, but needed to be found in India.[15] By mid-June many of the mountain guns needed 'urgent repair', needing to be sent to Britain, as soon as replacements could be found.[16]

As the only group of regular artillery officers at Anzac, the young Indian mountain artillery officers trained their Australian counterparts as well as doing their own jobs. Lieutenant Cresswell Rawson taught two Australian gunner officers how to run a battery observation post, operating a joint post. The post's observers looked out not only at the Turkish lines to the east, but also toward the batteries placed on the headland of Gaba Tepe, virtually to the right-rear of the Anzac position. Its guns, collectively known as 'Beachy Bill', fired into the Anzac lines seemingly with

---

13   Memo, 10 March 1915, Assistant Director, Ordnance Stores, 11th Indian Division to Director of Ordnance Stores, India, and reply, 20 April 1915, WWI/292/H, NAI.
14   'Gallipoli 1915', Arthur Fergusson, 3DRL3635, AWM.
15   Tel., 3 May 1915, War Office to Duff, WWI/293/H, NAI.
16   Tel, 11 June 1915, Duff to Maxwell, WWI/294/H, NAI.

impunity. Rawson's immediate and persistent retaliation forced the Turks to leave their emplacements on Gaba Tepe, though they re-located them, and the Beachy Bill guns were never knocked out. Casualties in the mountain artillery's officers compelled Fergusson to reclaim Trenchard and the experiment lapsed.

At Anzac the Turks continued their unavailing attempts to subvert Indian troops. Late in July Turkish leaflets circulated on Gallipoli bearing a photograph of Indian soldiers and 'exhorting all Mohammedans to come in and surrender'.[17] Frank Cooper, a New Zealand gunner, recorded the words of a propaganda leaflet in Hindustani, or possibly Urdu, picked up in the trenches:

> 'Oh! Soldiers of Hindustan! The English are those who have conquered your country and made you their slaves. Why have you come here? Why are you losing your valuable lives?'[18]

It is unlikely that the gunners or the muleteers at Anzac read much less heeded these leaflets. But the Ottoman leaflet's questions – why had they come to Gallipoli; why were they losing their lives? – remained relevant, to invading soldiers regardless of race or army.

Having forced the mountain gunners off their unduly exposed position at Pifferpore, Turkish artillery fire continued to cause casualties and narrowly missed Fergusson himself. One morning just as his bearer Hussain Khan brought Fergusson his breakfast porridge a shell burst at the entrance to the gunners' officers' mess. Fergusson looked down to find 'a plateful of porridge and blood', and that Khan and the medical officer's orderly had been wounded.[19] Like the infantry at Helles, the mountain gunners at Anzac felt the strain of continual action, though without relief.

'A rest cure on some island': Imbros, July

The ordeal that the 29th Indian Brigade had suffered at Helles through May and June was about to end at last. 'I am told the brigade is first for a rest cure on some island', Herbert Cox recorded in an account of the fighting written for his family. It came not a moment too soon: 'we have been 60 days in the front line without relief', he wrote.[20] Between 5 and 9 July the Indian battalions handed over their lines to British battalions and marched down Gully Ravine for the last time, generally making for Gurkha Beach and trawlers to take them away. They left behind reminders: trenches named after them – Gurkha Mule Trench and Sikh Street. After being ten weeks continuously in the front line (for the Sikhs and the 5th Gurkhas) the brigade could

---

17 Diary, 16 July 1915, John McLennan, 1DRL454, AWM.
18 Memoir, Frank Cooper, MS-Papers-1676-1, ATL.
19 'Gallipoli 1915', Arthur Fergusson, 3DRL3635, AWM.
20 Cox papers, 1DRL221, AWM.

at last be sent to what the war diaries described as an 'unknown destination' to rest and re-build. It turned out to be the island of Imbros, visible from their lines, 12 miles away. Men lived in tents in a field near the coast, able to sleep and bathe and, as importantly, 'safely live above ground and walk about in the open'.[21] Philip Palin, writing to Vi Wilmer, Harold's widow, from Imbros, described how 'one feels so free … not having to dodge bullets and shells and being able to live decently above ground instead of having to grovel in dug-outs and trenches'.[22] After sleeping and eating well the Gurkhas played football, between companies and battalions, but also with some of the British New Army battalions assembling on the island, a reminder of the camaraderie they shared with other British soldiers of the empire. Once out of the line many men succumbed to – or admitted that they had – dysentery. Intestinal disease had spread easily in the trenches – 36 of the 45 men of the 10th evacuated from Helles had been diagnosed with dysentery.

The Indians' officers, who thought they were to return to Helles, remained astonishingly optimistic, at least to outsiders. An Australian sapper, Charles King, met a couple of Gurkha officers while looking for beer in a village, probably Kephalos, near the 10th Gurkhas' camp. They told King that 'they would have Achi Baba next assault and the whole Peninsula by 10th August'. King, who had been at Anzac since the landing, merely added 'We hope so'.[23] We do not know what Indian other ranks felt about the deepening debacle of the campaign, but some British officers' feelings are plain. On the voyage from Madras Cecil Allanson spoke to Major Rudolph Hogg, an Indian cavalryman serving with the Royal Flying Corps, who said that 'if Winston [Churchill] was to put his foot on the Peninsula … he would be scragged alive'. Someone, Hogg said, 'is terribly to blame, and the Army thinks it is Winston'.[24] Reginald Savory, who had been wounded and mistakenly posted as killed, was downcast. He wrote that 'we don't want to go back'; the first sign that the Sikhs' losses erode even his relentless optimism.[25] (Savory's father had written to the Sikh's commanding officer to enquire about the circumstances of his son's death and to obtain his effects. Savory, by this time himself temporarily commanding the battalion, took pleasure in replying to the black-edged letter with a formal reply assuring him that he was alive.)

The rest enabled the troops to repair or possibly replenish worn out uniforms, weapons and kit. By mid-year Indian troops became increasingly shabby. (A fragment of an interrogation report of a 6th Gurkha rifleman, 'Guel Bahadur' captured around 4 June described 'all the Indian troops were in terrible condition'.[26]) Within a week of arriving on the peninsula the brigade war diary complained that the cloth

21 Talbot, *The 14th (King George's Own Ferozepore) Sikhs*, p. 88.
22 Letter, 23 July 1915, Herbert Cox to Vi Wilmer, courtesy of Anto O'Brien.
23 Diary, 18 July 1915, Charles King, courtesy of Terry King.
24 Diary, Allanson, *Copy of the personal diary kept in the field*, p. 11.
25 Letter, 17 July 1915, Reginald Savory, 7603-93, NAM.
26 Tetik, Demirtaş & Demirtaş, *Çanakkale Muharebeleri'nin Esirleri* [*Prisoners of War at the Canakkale Battles*], Vol. I, p. 55.

Gurkhas and Anzacs mixing, possibly on the island of Imbros during the Indian troops' rest there during the summer of 1915. (AWM P08678)

supplied for breeches 'were of bad material & quickly wore out'.[27] A defensive response for the Quartermaster General's staff in Simla asserted that liberal supplies had been despatched to Egypt (whence supplies went to Gallipoli), but conceded that stocks had been based on 'the assumption of active military operation[s] on the North-West Frontier' – that is short low intensity operations, not a protracted, distant, major war.[28] Photographs suggest that on Imbros some infantry at least received new tunics and breeches.

Already Gurkha battalions were receiving drafts from the Assam Military Police, and arrived on Gallipoli dressed in motley clothing. A system under which regimental tailors or 'durzies' made up uniforms from cloth obtained by the unit could not cope at a distance from wholesalers in the bazaars in northern India. Not only uniforms (hats, coats, shorts, socks and boots) but also accoutrements (such as water bottles and haversacks) were of 'regimental' manufacture, unable to be replaced or even repaired on service. Though well trained and highly cohesive as units, Indian units looked surprisingly scruffy. Cecil Allanson, who had been restive as the Military Secretary to

27 War diary, 29th Indian Infantry Brigade, May 1915, WO95/4432, NAUK.
28 Letter, 6 August 1915, Quartermaster General, India to Wilson, Egypt, WWI/296/H, NAI.

the Governor of Madras, arrived on Gallipoli in August and, seeing the state of the troops, immediately condemned the Indian Army's lack of bandobast – organisation.

During the brigade's rest on Imbros the Indian troops in the Mediterranean Expeditionary Force, previously part of Force E in Egypt, formally became 'Force G'.[29] As the volumes of cables demonstrate, Army Headquarters in Simla took a close interest in the Indian force in the Dardanelles. Beauchamp Duff asked Maxwell that 'if at any time heavy casualties take place an intermediate return should be cabled'. This, he explained would 'enable me to keep more closely in touch' with the force's reinforcement needs.[30] While all telegrams ostensibly went in the name of 'Commander-in-Chief, India', it is significant that Duff wrote 'me', and not 'my headquarters' or 'my staff'. The most frequent telegrams sent from Imbros to Simla and beyond concerned casualties. His interest did not, however, stop Maxwell telegraphing Duff to ask 'What is Force "G" please?' – a sign of the lack of communication between Egypt, Simla and the Dardanelles that explains some of the administrative confusion and bad feeling that afflicted the two forces' relationships.[31] Cecil Allanson found when he spoke to Maxwell's staff after arriving in Egypt that 'there seemed to be a good deal of "cross-pulling"' between the staff in Maxwell's and Wilson's headquarters, Simla and Imbros.[32]

Recognising the need to reward exceptional conduct by Indian troops more swiftly than the telegraph trail from battalion headquarters, through Cox's headquarters to General Headquarters and on to Simla via Maxwell's offices in Egypt, late in July Beauchamp Duff delegated to Ian Hamilton 'power to confer limited number of Indian Orders of Merit and Indian Distinguished Service Medals on Indian troops at your discretion'. (He left 'limited' undefined, but suggested a ratio of one to two or three.)[33] As part of Hamilton's obligations to his former colleagues in Simla, he visited Imbros and inspected the Indians, complimenting its men on their part in the Helles fighting. The battalions soon returned to a regime of training rather than rest, with parades (that is, drill and weapon training), instruction in bomb-fighting (at last) and night exercises in preparation for their inevitable return to battle. Just as the lack of British officers had prompted the brigade's withdrawal to Imbros, so during July replacement officers arrived, from Indian units in Egypt and the Indian Reserve of Officers. They included Major Cecil Allanson to take command of the 6th, though he did not speak Gurkhali. Their diverse origins underpinned the brigade's dearth. The ten officers came from ten different regiments, some of whom also could not speak their new battalion's language. Geoffrey Tomes and John Le Marchand went to the 6th Gurkhas without speaking a word of Gurkhali. Lieutenant Douglas 'Rob'

---

29 Tel., 19 July 1915, Chamberlain to Hardinge, WWI/295/H, NAI.
30 Tel., 7 July 1915, Duff to Maxwell, WWI/295/H, NAI.
31 Chhina, 'Their mercenary calling', p. 245.
32 Allanson, *Copy of the personal diary kept in the field*, p. 6.
33 Tel. 25 July 1915, Duff to GOC, MEF, WWI/149/H, NAI.

Indian troops, possibly Gurkhas, bathing using improvised showers, possibly on Imbros during the brigade's rest in July 1915. (AWM H00758)

Shewen, posted from the 27th Punjabis to the 10th Gurkhas, depended upon his subedar, Pharsalhoj Rai, the only man in his company who could speak Urdu.

When Ian Hamilton inspected the Indians he found them 'cheerful and much recovered'.[34] But what did they did actually feel about the ordeal they had just left behind? The words of the Gurkha verses collected by officers who served in other theatres suggest that their men did ponder, talk about and even comment on what they had seen, done and survived. That Gurkha verses include lines such as 'my friends and brothers dying – shall any count them?' and 'Carrying my friend and brother my body has been wetted with drops of his blood' strongly suggests that they did indeed

---

34 Hamilton, *Gallipoli Diary*, Vol. II, p. 15.

talk about what they had faced at Helles, and surely would again.[35] As they sat around camp fires, resting at last, away from the stink of the trenches of Gully Spur, it seems that, like unlettered people, they talked, perhaps in that way coming to terms with an experience that, like their British and dominion comrades, none could have imagined a year before.

At the other end of the chain of command, their brigadier, Herbert Cox, was dealing with what he had seen and done in his own way. He mused in his diary

> isn't it sad to stand as I have, in trenches & see brave men lying out there, & one cannot get at them even to bury them it's terrible & makes one hate war & those who made this one.[36]

On the day on which he made this entry, 24 July, Cox was resting with his men, on Imbros, far from the corpse-littered no man's land at Helles. Was he describing a nightmare, or writing down a disturbing memory in the hope of shaking it? Either way, he could not have been alone. Indeed, officers' letters in the summer are little more than mortuary lists. A letter from Francis Sutton of the 10th is typical:

> Atkinson Higgin Russell killed, Clarke Moran Scott Campbell Firth and myself … wounded… Tejganje Hansrup Barkhbahadur Rajman killed and Dhandhoj Ajitia Sukhman wounded Motilal hospital …[37]

'Equal to our own Indian troops': Patiala reinforcements

By July even Beauchamp Duff had accepted that 'our Indian reserve system has proved a thorough failure'.[38] Anxious to restore to efficiency one of his few regular brigades, Ian Hamilton embraced a suggestion from Herbert Cox to circumvent the problem that reinforcements were months away, and would mainly comprise inexperienced wartime recruits. Knowing that the Maharaja of Patiala's Rajendra Infantry was already in Egypt, Cox lobbied Hamilton, who asked Maxwell to release a double company (a quarter of the battalion) to reinforce the Sikhs on Gallipoli.[39] Both knew, as Maxwell had reported to Simla, that the Patialas had caused 'no friction, no trouble' in Egypt.[40] But Maxwell demurred, asking for Dogras (mainly Hindus from the hills of northern India) or Rajputs (also mainly Hindus, from Rajputana) to compensate him for the loss of trained Sikhs. Hamilton would 'gladly have accepted' a double company of Dogras or Rajputs for the 14th Sikhs, but with his Indian service

---

35   Lowe, 'Gurkhas remember France and Palestine', *The Kukri*, No. 41, May 1989, p. 139.
36   Diary, 24 July 1915, Herbert Cox, 1DRL221, AWM.
37   Letter, 5 July 1915, Francis Sutton, 2/10th Gurkhas Digest of Service, GM.
38   Letter, 11 August 1915, Beauchamp Duff, 7/1/29, LHCMA.
39   Tel., 1 July 1915, WWI/295/H, NAI.
40   History of Patiala State Forces, Part III, p. 91, Maharaja of Patiala collection.

he understood that it would be impractical to quickly alter the composition of a 'class regiment', a jealously guarded privilege, a fact that Wilson's headquarters in Ismailia confirmed. Beauchamp Duff conceded that 'to attach Imperial Service Troops' to Cox's brigade 'would be possible'; but it would also require political negotiation in India.[41]

Patiala, in the south-eastern Punjab, close to the 14th Sikhs' heartland around Ferozepore, had for almost a century been one of the most loyal princely states. Patiala had stood with the beleaguered British in 1857, its rulers recognised and rewarded since, though the number of guns accorded to Patiala in the strict pecking order of salutes remained an irritant on both sides, with the maharaja arguing that it justified more than the seventeen stipulated. Patiala became one of the first to offer troops for imperial service, in the 1880s. Its ruler since 1900, Bhupinder Singh, was seen as 'a man of great ability, strength of character and enterprise, a lover of dogs and horses and an important Freemason'.[42] Bhupinder Singh was and has remained a figure of fascination, the subject of scurrilous and mostly exaggerated stories, though still one of the most colourful of the princes through his extravagance and indulgence.

Most states' forces were justifiably regarded as (and indeed deliberately kept) inferior to the Indian Army, in training, weapons, experience and (so British officers thought) leadership. But among the 29 little armies those of several states were singled out as 'absolutely equal to our own Indian troops'; and they included the cavalry and infantry regiments of Patiala. British officers thought the absence of British officers (except as advisers) a failing, and among themselves derided its pretensions. A patronising guffaw can practically be heard in the proceedings of the 1912 enquiry into the Army in India when the committee learned that Patiala's little army had three major-generals, one appointed 'as a matter of fact', the Inspector General of Imperial Service Troops condescendingly let slip, because 'he ... was the best polo player in India'. But Gurbaksh Singh, its actual commander, was 'a really good man ... the only [Indian] I know who can take men out on manœvres and move them about as well as our own Generals'.[43]

Patalia's battalion was a happy choice. The state recruited many men from Ferozepore, the home district of the 14th Sikhs, and they too were Jat Sikhs, the sons of farmers in the province's flat green fields of sugar, wheat and corn. They shared a language, a faith, home villages and often enough friends and even relations.

Maxwell's unease was only part of the sensitivity. The Patialas, though part of the Army of Occupation in Egypt, belonged to the Maharaja, and his permission was needed before a man could be drafted. Still, while the Foreign and Political Department and the Government of India's agent in Patiala went to trouble to advise and consult

---

41 Tel., 2 July 1915, Duff to Maxwell, WWI/295/H, NAI.
42 MacMunn, *The Indian States and Princes*, p. 211.
43 Proceedings of the Army in India Committee, 1912, Vol. II, Minutes of Evidence, pp. 78-80.

Sikh officers, almost certainly of the Patiala Infantry–and probably Major Harban Singh on the left. (IWM Q013665)

the Maharaja, it is apparent that asking his permission was a formality. Hamilton raised the idea of drawing on the Patiala in Egypt on 1 July and on 7 July Maxwell cabled Simla that 'to reinforce 14th Sikhs I am sending … one Double Company of Patiala Imperial Service Infantry with their native officers'.[44] The Patialas, attached as a fifth double company, arrived on Imbros on 12 July, suggesting that they were despatched with unusual celerity.

Rather than being pleased that his troops would go to Gallipoli, Maharaja Bhupinder Singh told the Sircar's agent that he felt 'disappointed', fearing that as reinforcements the Patialas' identity would be lost. The Government of India's Foreign and Political Department reassured His Highness that Patiala's double company's identity would be preserved, that casualties would be reported as belonging to the Patialas and not the 14th Sikhs, and he would be sent occasional reports of its doings. The agent emphasised that 'he had the honour of being the only ruler who had troops in the Dardanelles'.[45] As Rana Chhina has recently observed, Patiala was actually not the only state with troops on Gallipoli. Supply and Transport units from Indore, Bharatpur and Gwalior served

---

44 Tel., 7 July 1915, Maxwell to Duff, WWI/295/H, NAI.
45 Foreign and Political Department, Deposit Internal August 1915, No. 7, 'Despatch of a double company of Patiala Imperial Service Infantry as reinforcements to the 14th Sikhs at Dardanelles', NAI.

there as well, though in fact few seemed to be aware of Patiala's or the other states' forces contribution at the time or since.[46] The detachment from the Bharatpur Imperial State Transport Corps (a small princely state in Rajputana) also 'did magnificent work' according to one of their officers as part of George Aylmer's unit.[47] As state forces they and the Indore mule corps had not only British officers and warrant officers but also like the Patialas Indian commissioned officers.

The Maharaja of Patiala was among few Indians to be regularly informed of the troops' doings on Gallipoli. Reginald Savory condemned the postal arrangements for Indian troops as 'a damned scandal', decrying 'the whole bally show' because it was run by 'a babu', the Anglo-Indian word for 'clerk' that signified Bengali inefficiency and corruption.[48] He was of course especially annoyed at inefficient postal arrangements because his parents in London had been told that he had been killed. Sahib-like, he blamed that on 'some damned silly babu' as well.[49]

Most of the Indian troops Anzacs met were necessarily gunners, drivers and riflemen who knew little English. Raymond Baker, however, a Canterbury infantryman, recorded an encounter with an Indian of a very different stamp. While resting on Imbros in July he met Gurkhas, whom he called 'Johnny'. One ushered him into a tent where he met two 'bushy-whiskered Indians of evidently high rank' – or at least of higher rank than Baker, a private. One spoke English without a trace of an accent, quizzing him on his experiences on the peninsula and apologising that he did not make himself clear.[50] It seems probable that Baker met an officer of the Patiala Infantry drafted to the Sikhs, who arrived on Lemnos in July and who would have been curious about the peninsula. It would seem that John Hargrave, the observant British field ambulance sergeant also saw this officer. At Suvla he recorded seeing 'one of the most picturesque sights I ever saw', an Indian officer riding a white horse 'with a long flowing mane, and a tail which swept in a splendid curve'. The officer, who wore a khaki turban 'with a long end floating behind' rode in 'the proper military style'. Against the blue of the Aegean 'it made a magnificent picture, worthy of the *Thousand-and-One Nights*'.[51] Could this have been anyone but Major Harban Singh of the Patialas?

'Ever ready to sacrifice': propaganda in the Punjab

As a regular, volunteer army serving an unrepresentative colonial state, it might seem that the Indian Army had no need to generate popular support – that its members fought for reasons other than patriotism, and owing allegiance to the regiment rather

---

46   Chhina, 'Their mercenary calling', p. 244, fn. 49.
47   Letter, 12 November 1915, W.B.S. Deverell, 04/37/1, 13093, IWM.
48   Letter, 31 May 1915, Reginald Savory, 7603-93, NAM.
49   Ibid., 3 July 1915.
50   Raymond Baker, 'Four months at Anzac', MS-Papers-1560, ATL.
51   Hargrave, *At Suvla Bay*, pp. 136-37.

than to the state, they lacked the need for the mobilisation of popular sentiment that was so much a part of the war effort of European nation-states. In fact, the Government of India needed to harness Indian support to create a network of recruiting agents among the more 'martial' groups, and indeed, groups previously thought insufficiently martial. With the expansion of Sikh recruiting after Gully Ravine the Sikhs of the Punjab became noteworthy supporters.

In July and August 1915 several thousand people – mostly men – gathered at the Golden Temple in Amritsar. The July meeting praised the 14th Sikhs' conduct and its 'bravery and heroic deeds', 'to express feelings of satisfaction at the recent heroic deeds of the 14th Sikhs'. The meeting expressed sympathy for the regiment's 'martyrs' and declared its trust that 'the Sikhs would always continue to fight for the Government as bravely as ever'. At Ferozepore a month after the attack a meeting at the Sikh Girls' School affirmed its admiration for the 'devoted loyalty and unsurpassed gallantry' of the 14th Sikhs.[52] In Rawalpindi a Sikh meeting marked the war's first anniversary with hymns and prayers, and a sermon emphasising the need for 'every Sikh to place everything … at the disposal of the benign British government which has shown so many favours to the Khalsa'. Speakers linked 'the old Sikhs' – the Khalsa that had fought so valiantly against the British – with the conduct of the 14th Sikhs on Gallipoli'.[53] The meetings ended with shouts of *'Sat Sri Akal!'* (Victory to the faithful!)

Punjabis offered more practical support too. Individuals and organisations, both Indian and British, collected 'comforts' to be sent to troops serving overseas. Much of this complemented official supplies, such as the 500 pounds of raisins or 530 pounds of sugar sent from Amritsar in the first week of August. It also included comforts such as socks, cigarettes or soap indistinguishable from parcels sent from virtually all combatant countries (though including betel nut; over 900 pounds donated in early August). But the goods donated in the Punjab also included items specific to Sikh troops, such as 200 combs and 750 yards of phibti cloth, for sepoys' pagris.[54] Individual donations could be substantial. Later in August Harpal Singh of Faridkot (in Ferozepore District) gave 600 combs, two tins of mustard oil and two bags of ritha nuts specifically for the 14th Sikhs.[55] At the other end of Punjabi society the Maharaja Bhupinder Singh donated a quantity of iron kirpans [knives] and 792 maunds of sweets to mark the King-Emperor's birthday in 1915.[56] (Presumably not all this boon was destined for his contingent: this amounted to some 65,000 pounds of sweets.)

English-language newspapers became part of the propaganda campaign that the Government of India mounted or assisted. The provincial government welcomed and promulgated news of Punjabi soldiers being mentioned in despatches or decorated,

---

52   *Khalsa Advocate*, 14 August 1915.
53   *Civil and Military Gazette*, 15 August 1915.
54   Ibid., 14 August 1915.
55   Ibid., 27 August 1915.
56   Anon, *Patiala and the Great War*, p. 67.

mentioning their home districts to encourage villagers to see that they too had a stake in this war. So it was put about the Havildar Gurdit Singh and Naik Nikka Singh of Kohat Battery, mentioned in Ian Hamilton's first despatches from the Dardanelles, hailed from Jullunder and Nabha respectively. Decorated Punjabi soldiers were especially celebrated, such as mountain gunner Fazl Ilahi of Jhelum, who extinguished a fire in an exploding ammunition dump.[57]

Ian Hamilton asked Beauchamp Duff to ensure that stories about the Sikhs' heroism in Gully Ravine appeared in Indian newspapers, and editors readily complied. The *Civil and Military Gazette* published private letters sent from Gallipoli, including one from an Australian artillery officer, presumably to friends in India. His description of Gallipoli ('the climate is delightful') and his opinion that he doubted any army was ever better fed, equipped or clothed, suggests undetected sarcasm at least, though the newspaper's readers might have been reassured.[58]

In mid-August the *Civil and Military Gazette* published a letter from Ajat Singh, presumably a relative of a member of the 14th Sikhs. Headed 'Sikh chivalry and German brutality', Ajat Singh's letter described an incident he had obtained from a friend in the regiment, an example of the kinds of stories that men were circulating in the Punjab. After 'a fierce action' on Gallipoli in July wounded Sikh soldiers saw a wounded European officer lying nearby; not of his regiment. They crawled over and asked 'Sahib, pani?' – would he want a drink of water? The European officer was not, it appeared, British, but was a 'wily German'. He took the pani bottle and, now revived, drew his pistol and shot them. A Sikh officer nearby said to a comrade: 'Khalsaji, I have only a few moments to live. I have a few hundred rupees with me now, the sum may well serve some of you to redeem his land; let him who may hear me come and take it away'. The German shot the officer in the head too and took the money from him. 'Reader, that is true Germany', the letter-writer thought, and urged 'let every Indian read and tell it to his children and friends: let the vernacular press circulate it through the length and breadth of the land'.[59] The story sounds highly implausible: are we to believe not only that German officers were involved in front line fighting on the peninsula, but were wounded, behaved so abominably *and* spoke Punjabi? That it was published in several newspapers suggests it was a crude propaganda story.

Did Indian soldiers' families know of their being killed or wounded, and if so, when? English language newspapers published details of casualties, but both of British and Indian officers and men. In this way newspaper readers in the Punjab learned that Captain John Daniell (of the 14th Sikhs), Jemadar Ram Singh and Subedar Mit Singh of the mountain artillery had been wounded (Mit Singh for the second time). The regiments' efficient local networks, in which local officers maintained personal

---

57 Leigh, *The Punjab and the War*, p. 217.
58 *Civil and Military Gazette*, 19 August 1915.
59 *Khalsa Advocate*, 21 August 1915.

A mule camp of the Supply and Transport Corps, which made such an important contribution to the maintenance of the British empire force on Gallipoli. (AWM J02706)

relationships with the villages and their officials, ensured that families learned of their sons' being wounded or killed, and were advised on how to apply for pensions.

The Government of India was naturally eager to publish details of the honours bestowed on officers and men from Indian units serving overseas, including on Gallipoli. In August awards made to British officers of Gurkha battalions and the mountain artillery appeared publicly: to Captain Denis Ryan (6th Gurkhas) for his 'daring reconnaissance' at Krithia on 13 May, and to Captain John Thom of Kohat Battery for his 'exceptional and gallant conduct'.[60] In this way friends, former comrades and acquaintances across north-west India learned of their achievements; though they might just as well expect to read in subsequent issues of their deaths. English language newspapers publicised the deeds of 'native' soldiers also. In this way the deeds of men like Subedar Gambirsing Pun became known and admired.

Throughout the expressions of sympathy and support runs the strong message that men owed a duty to volunteer for the war. The Maharaja of Patiala took a robust view of his subjects' obligations, both in life and in death. Those who enlisted in his forces would, he later told potential recruits, 'secure for themselves a life long happiness'. Should the idea of being killed 'trouble the heart of a weak minded person':

> He should at once chase this unmanly idea away by remembering that hundreds of thousands of our people have met their death of plague, cholera and other terrible diseases ... Can anyone say that death on a field of battle is worse [than] death by horrible diseases'?[61]

On a more positive note, the Maharaja had printed (in Punjabi) 3270 copies of a booklet telling the story of a man named Bir Singh – perhaps the mule driver who landed first on Gallipoli, but it is a very common name.

The Great War came at a time when dramatic events were accelerating another of the successive crises in the governance of British India that were within a lifetime to transform it from the premier possession of the empire into the first of the independent nations that a second world war would spawn. One of the architects of that transformation, Jawaharlal Nehru, wrote that 'the World War absorbed our attention' – a great struggle between the world's imperial powers could not but be riveting for those who sought to redefine their relationship to imperial authority. But Nehru also admitted that actually the war was 'far off and did not affect our lives much'.[62] Indeed, the Indian Army had very little to do with the British-educated barrister in Allahabad, far from the army's main centres of recruiting.

On Gallipoli, shelling continued throughout the summer, and as we have seen took men of all ranks. Once, when Ian Hamilton visited the mule camp (as an officer with

60 *Civil and Military Gazette*, 28 August 1915.
61 History of Patiala State Forces, Part III, pp. 46-47, Maharaja of Patiala collection.
62 Nehru, *An Autobiography*, p. 31.

Three subedars who served with the 14th Sikhs on Gallipoli, from left to right, Subedar Major Sham Singh, Subedar Kishan Singh (transferred from the Burma Military Police) and Subedar Bhagat Singh of the Patiala Infantry. The Indian units' efficiency and everyday management largely depended upon men such as these. (14th Sikhs album)

extensive Indian service he particularly visited Indian units) a shell burst seemingly in the middle of the gaggle of staff officers as he stepped ashore at the nearby wharf, though they emerged from the cloud of dust unscathed. Death came randomly. Heber Alexander described a lance-naik who marched into the corps office one morning to be told that he had secured promotion to naik. He saluted and turned about. As he left the dugout a stray bullet hit him in the chest and killed him. In August he would be joined by many hundreds of others.

11

'May I die fighting in the thick of battle': Sari Bair, August

In the final days of the battalions' rest on Imbros orders arrived that directed them to break camp for yet another 'unknown destination'. They were sure it would mean a return to the peninsula: but where? 'There are big things afoot of which we know nothing', Humphrey Gell wrote.[1] His fellow officers, and soon after the officers' mess servants, and soon after that the battalion as a whole, would have learned that their orders were to involve 'breaking out of Anzac and the seizing of the Sari Bair Range', the massif dominating the north of the peninsula.[2] The 29th Indian Infantry Brigade was no longer attached to the British 29th Division, but came under the orders of William Birdwood's Australian and New Zealand Army Corps as part of General Alexander Godley's New Zealand and Australian Division. Its officers were positive: 'we are all expecting great things', Allanson wrote.[3]

'Ideal country for Gurkhas': the Anzac plan

The continuing stalemate impelled hopeful commanders and staffs to propose a dramatic attempt to break out of the Anzac beach-head, seeking to cut the peninsula, or at least gain the high ground that dominated the ground north of Anzac. Staff officers proposed that the 29th Indian Brigade would take a leading role: it would at last serve in the Anzac sector, as Hamilton had originally envisaged. As one of the Mediterranean Expeditionary Force's four regular brigades (with the three of the 29th Division) Cox's brigade could be relied upon – its training in mountain warfare would be useful in the terrain over which it was to be ordered to advance. Planning the renewed effort involved an immensely complex series of orders, not just co-ordinating the movement of troops on Gallipoli, but the transport of several fresh divisions from Britain. Clement Milward, now a major and at General Headquarters, recorded that

---

1   Diary, 25 July 1915, Humphrey Gell, P158, 10048, IWM.
2   War diary, 2/10th Gurkhas, August 1915, WO95/4472, NAUK.
3   Diary, Cecil Allanson, 4 August 1915, Allanson papers, 6602-33-4, NAM.

it entailed 'strenuous days spent in the office tent, among the dust and flies and oaths and tempers, working out the last details of this great landing ...'[4]

The break-out was to be made by mounting an offensive over the rugged country north of Anzac, the Sari Bair range (pronounced in Turkish 'sarry by-eer', but usually rendered by English speakers then and now as rhyming with 'hair). Capturing and holding the heights would not in itself ensure victory, but would merely be the preliminary to a further advance to seize the neck of the peninsula and gain the objectives which the April landing had failed to approach. The Anzac plan was largely worked out by a forceful lieutenant-colonel, Andrew Skeen, an officer of the 56th Punjabi Rifles and later the author of the Indian Army's final major mountain warfare text, *Passing it on*. Skeen and other Indian Army officers on Birdwood's staff knew the value of troops experienced in mountain warfare. As his staff developed the various plans for breaking out of what they thought of as Anzac's open flank, he reiterated his requests for Gurkhas especially. Anzac was 'an ideal country for Gurkhas', he wrote at the end of May, and asked for it to be sent to Anzac when it had 'completed its present work'.[5]

At least Ian Hamilton would have more troops for the renewed effort. His plan for what became the August offensive relied upon the arrival of fresh British divisions of the New Army and Territorial Army (the 10th, 11th and 13th of the former and the 53rd and 54th of the latter). But the assault on Sari Bair was to be made by Cox's Indians (actually more than three-quarters Gurkha) but also John Monash's 4th Australian Brigade and Francis Johnston's New Zealand Brigade, which were arguably the weakest brigades of any available. Why he allotted to the offensive troops in such a condition is unclear. At least the attacks would not be made all along the Anzac line, as they had been at Krithia, but would be made only on the Sari Bair range (seemingly the Turks' weak point), with diversionary attacks at both Helles and Anzac. Historian Tim Travers described the plan as ambitious but feasible, 'obviously a winner'; not so obviously perhaps.[6]

The offensive had several subsidiary components: a night attack on the main range and a landing at Suvla Bay directed at creating a base for later operations, which in turn necessitated occupying the vital high ground north of Anzac. The renewed offensive's intention was ambitious: to 'hold the line Quinn's Post-cross roads near Scrubby Knoll-Chunuk Bair-Koja Cemin Tepe' – the aim was to gain a huge swathe of ground, which might eventually enable the invading force to at last break out.[7] Possession of Chunuk Bair (pronounced, though probably not by the British empire troops at the time, as 'djonk by-eer'), was the key to the ambitious objective. The offensive coincided with the first anniversary of the war's outbreak. The reflective Cecil Allanson,

---

4   Diary, 4 August 1915, Clement Milward, CAB45/259, NAUK.
5   Bean, *The Story of Anzac*, Vol. II, p. 189.
6   Travers, *Gallipoli 1915*, p. 116.
7   War diary, 40th Brigade, 13th Division, August 1915, WO95/4303, NAUK.

who often seems to have been unusually troubled by what his profession entailed, pondered the challenge he faced. He did not expect to survive, confessed in his diary that he felt the burden of responsibility and wrote farewell letters to his family. Then he walked over the gullies of Anzac inspecting the 'rabbit holes' where his men would be billeted while they waited for the order to advance.[8]

Most of the Indian battalions landed at Anzac from trawlers on 5 August. In an ominous foretaste Turkish shells fell while the Sikhs and Patialas were disembarking and half the battalion, and 108th Field Ambulance, hauled off to land after dark. Those obliged to remain at sea spent and uncomfortable day, 'tossed about like corks' – especially unpleasant for land-bound men.[9] Those ashore moved to bivouacs around Reserve Gully. There they squatted all day, under orders not to move lest Turkish artillery observers detect the unusual movement and bombard their bivouacs. (Routine shellfire fell on the congested gullies anyway and hit 20 men in the 6th Gurkhas alone.) They crowded into hot terraces and dugouts, waiting for dusk. Allanson wrote on that afternoon that 'one's heart could not help bleeding for what I knew they must go through'. (No officer recorded what he explained to his men before the offensive: did they know what they were expected to do and why? No one now can say.)

Their quartermasters meet the Supply and Transport officers, Indian and British, and NCOs they would rely on for the next five months, trying to obtain enough water to cook the rations they would take with them and fill their water bottles. For the duration of the offensive the mule cart troops that had supplied the Australian brigades on the southern flank of Anzac were cut down, to supply the Australian, British, Indian and New Zealand infantry attacking on Anzac's left or northern flank. With Anzac's supply services ordinarily stretched by the shortage of mules (ruled by the availability of water) the muleteers were, Heber Alexander wrote, 'done to a turn … for the fortnight preceding the [reinforcements'] landing they got practically no rest'.[10] The mule corps needed all the experienced personnel it could muster. Just before the opening of the offensive Ressaidar Hashmet Ali, who had been invalided to Egypt and listed to be invalided to India, persuaded a Supply and Transport officer there that his sahib (Alexander) needed him, and he arrived back at Anzac in time to take on heavy responsibilities. While (contrary to other reports) the Mule Train war diary shows that animals were allocated to carry food, water and ammunition up the deres, the organisation seemed to fail. Allanson described it as 'shocking and lets regiments down most awfully'.[11]

Carrying two hundred rounds of rifle ammunition per man and entrenching tools, water and rations, the attackers were heavily burdened, and not just with weight. Indian troops laboured under leather kit that, though known to hamper their movements,

---

8 Diary, Cecil Allanson, 4, 5 August 1915, Davies, *Allanson of the 6th*, p. 38.
9 Talbot, *The 14th (King George's Own Ferozepore) Sikhs*, p. 89.
10 Alexander, *On Two Fronts*, p. 222.
11 Letter, Cecil Allanson, 6 August 1915, Davies, *Allanson of the 6th*, p. 39.

remained in service. 'It was a very bad system for hill work', wrote an officer, 'it pressed heavily on the chest and dragged on the waist'.[12] By August many belts were frayed and dried out, cutting into men's shoulders. The water bottle and haversack hung awkwardly and took time to adjust, an almost impossible task in a hurry or in the dark. The leather bandolier over the shoulder held too few rounds, but often burst open, spilling its cartridges. Men stuffed ammunition into their haversacks, tainting both their food and the bullets. Between the bandolier's weight on their chest and the unwieldy entrenching tool bobbing on their backs, men had trouble breathing, especially when slogging uphill.[13] Each man wore white calico arm-bands to help to distinguish friend from foe in the battle to come.

As the Gurkhas landed Turkish artillery observers spotted the movement and shelled the jetties, giving them what Joseph Beeston (whose field ambulance tents were nearby) called a 'cordial welcome'. He thought that they were 'at first rather scared, but were soon reassured'. The initial impression did not persist. 'We were to see a good deal of these little chaps, and to appreciate their fighting qualities', he wrote.[14] In the days before the opening of the offensive the Supply and Transport units worked particularly hard and lost heavily. Forced to move in daylight, one convoy lost two drivers killed and six men (including an interpreter) wounded when bombs fell off a mule and exploded.

'A mad looking country': terrain and preparations

Herbert Cox and his battalion commanders and the brigade staff had reconnoitered by warship and Cox went ashore to trek up the steep ridges to positions on the extreme left flank of Anzac. He described on his return as 'a mad looking country', reminding him of the terrain around Rawalpindi.[15] Gurkha officers puzzled over maps in which there seemed 'no reason why the hills should go where they do'.[16] They tried to discern where Ottoman troops might be and what routes could lead them through the gullies and onto the crest of the main range. Cox met Alexander Godley, the prickly British commander of the New Zealand and Australian Division, Richard Shaw (the commander of the newly-arrived British 13th Division), and the bold New Zealand mounted riflemen who had scouted the approaches to Chunuk Bair, Arthur Bauchop and Philip Overton. On 4 August, two days before the scheduled opening of the offensive, he met John Monash, the Australian citizen colonel commanding the 4th Brigade, whose men had held Quinn's Post, the critical position in the Anzac line, but who were now to attempt a strenuous night march up

12   Maxwell, *Villiers-Stuart on the Frontier*, p. 161.
13   Memo, 29 Nov 1915, WWI/154/H, NAI.
14   Beeston, *Five Months at Anzac*, p. 49.
15   Diary, 3 August 1915, Herbert Cox, 1DRL221, AWM; Evidence to the Dardanelles Commission by Maj-Gen Herbert Cox, 36th Day, 25 January 1917, p. 681, 103, AWM 51.
16   'Operations at Anzac in August 1915', 2/10th Gurkhas Digest of Service, GM.

rugged hills. On 5 August Birdwood, Godley, Cox and the other brigadiers, held a 'pow-wow' outside the dugout Cox's headquarters briefly occupied before the offensive began. All seemed confident, despite the magnitude of the task and the formidable terrain they faced.

Birdwood's Anzac force would attempt to seize the crest of the Sari Bair ridge as the first stage in a projected break-out from the beach-head, while a British force landing at Suvla Bay would gain a base for later operations. Hamilton wrote, in his official dispatch, that 'I meant to try and win through to Maidos' – on the Dardanelles.[17] The first stage depended on the seizure of the Sari Bair range running inland north-eastwards from Anzac, and in this Cox's Indian brigade would play a central part. 'We were to go for the big hill', Allanson explained soon after.[18]

The rugged terrain which made the attackers' approach march so confused likewise affects its narration. The Sari Bair range ran north-eastwards from Anzac, increasing in height with each successive pinnacle – Chunuk Bair, Hill Q, and the height of Hill 971. A tangle of gullies and spurs ran down to the sea from this range, each dry gully known as a dere: from north to south, Asmak Dere, Aghyl Dere (the large gully that British Indian officers called 'the main nullah'), Chailak Dere and Sazli Beit Dere. The country was virtually uninhabited, but a farm – known as The Farm – lay above the head of Aghyl Dere, and there were occasional stone-walled sheep pens and small fields. The whole country was covered with thick, prickly scrub, often too dense to penetrate, and the featureless, tangled gullies made navigation difficult, while movement in the summer heat in the airless, dusty gullies soon exhausted men and animals (as then, still). The Ottoman defenders at first had few troops on the heights – a few companies – but as the threat developed they were able to rush reserves to the crest.

Even to troops used to campaigning (or at least training) in the hills and scrub of the north-west frontier, the advance on Sari Bair presented challenges. Herbert Cox summed it up when he described the country as 'a tangled mass of hills, cliffs and ravines & very difficult even for Gurkhas'.[19] Reginald Savory described the range as 'very high country covered in dense scrub in places sometimes six feet high'. This was 'perfect for defence but damned hard for the attackers', and, he conceded, he and his Sikhs were 'none of us very hard after three months of enforced inactivity in the trenches'.[20] When slogging uphill he found that they had to stop to recover their breath; and all suffered from more or less endemic diarrhoea: and the Indians were the most rested of the troops in the assaulting columns and explicitly denied that they were in ill-health.

The diversionary attacks at Helles and Anzac began on 6 August. At Helles, British troops (including the long-suffering 29th Division) made a series of 'holding' attacks

17 Supplement to *London Gazette*, 6 January 1916, p. 286.
18 Diary, August 1915, Cecil Allanson, Allanson papers, 6602-22, NAM.
19 Diary, 11 August 1915, Herbert Cox, 1DRL221, AWM.
20 Liddle, *Men of Gallipoli*, p. 205.

in an attempt to distract the Ottoman reserves, which even at the time seemed unlikely to have succeeded. The futile attacks, dignified as the battle of Krithia Vineyard, costing about 4,000 British and 7,000 Turkish casualties. The main feint at Anzac, at Lone Pine, also began on the afternoon of the 6th. Two Australian brigades became embroiled in horrific, pointless and costly fight for a warren of trenches in which perhaps 5,000 Turks and 2,000 Australians became casualties. Neither attack altered Ottoman dispositions. Minor Australian feints at Anzac, at German Officer's Trench, Quinn's Post and the Nek, were of even less use.

'A feeling of panic and doubt': the night advance of 6-7 August

At dusk on 6 August, with the sound of battle coming from the feint attack at Lone Pine to the south, the Indians emerged from the bivouacs, dugouts and shelters in which they had waited all day and marched down to the narrow coastal plain to form up in the columns in which they would enter the second phase of their service on Gallipoli. Accompanying Cox's 'Left Assaulting Column' were four guns of Kohat Battery ('our old friends', the 5th Gurkhas recalled from the Canal Defences), escorted by a double company of Sikhs; still being nursed by Cox.[21] The Right Assaulting Column comprised the New Zealand Infantry Brigade and four guns of Jacob's Battery. The Left Assaulting Column would march 'in echelon'; that is, with the Australians on the left and the Indians slightly inland. To complicate matters, two 'supporting' columns also moved out, the Left and Right Covering Columns which were to secure the country through which the main columns passed and their left flank, around the low hill of Demakjelik Bair. In fact there was too little room on the congested coastal plain for such a force to move freely, only the first of the errors made in planning the offensive. Cox's column was to turn right and move up a gully, the Aghyl Dere, the right to march up Chailak Dere and the nearby Sazli Beit Dere, with both to move up and take the main Sari Bair range, for the time being virtually free of Turkish defenders. The plan began to break down from the first hours, when the columns took much longer to move out of the Anzac perimeter than expected.

Not until 11 o'clock did Cox's column move off, and it was after one before the head of the column got much beyond the Anzac outposts. In absolute darkness (the moon was in its last quarter), with officers conferring in whispers, men enduring unexplained delays and hasty shuffles, the columns concertinaed forward, soon losing both their route and the timings so precisely specified by staff officers. Allanson described 'a feeling of panic and doubt in the air'.[22] Above them searchlight beams and shells from warships off-shore stabbed at the heights above them. In the dark officers lost

---

21 Regimental Committee, *History of the 5th Royal Gurkha Rifles*, p. 249.
22 Diary, Cecil Allanson, 6 August 1915, Davies, *Allanson of the 6th*, p. 41. Obviously this entry must have been revised afterwards: Allanson could hardly have written it on the night of the 6-7th August.

direction and dawn disclosed that despite both reconnaissance and guides the leaders had blundered. Despite the protests of Gerald Pepys, Cox's brigade major, the New Zealand scout officer, Overton, had allowed himself to be persuaded and misled by local Greek guide pointing out a supposed short-cut through a pass known as Taylor's Gap. The entire column turned east prematurely, taking a gully that narrowed as they climbed. The route soon required sappers to hack away brush and the short-cut cost time and cohesion. As the column snaked into the Aghyl Dere units and sub-units took different routes. The next day the 5th's adjutant described in its war diary the reasons for the confusion: 'on account of [the] rapidity of [the] advance and bad country close touch was lost'.[23]

Soon, the leading files of the 5th's leading files ran into Turkish pickets just as night turned to daylight. What time was that, the official historian wanted to know. In 1931 Colonel Hugh Lane, now back at Abbottabad with the 5th Gurkhas, could not give a time, but he was able to quote his Subedar-Major, Harkabir Gurung, who remembered that 'it was just light enough to see the short hairs on the back of his hand when the Turks opened fire'.[24] It is not an exact chronology; but it is clear enough. The 5th deployed, formed into loose lines and charged up the slopes between the two forks of the Aghyl Dere, just as they had trained in the hills of the frontier. They drove in the Turkish pickets but lost 'a number of casualties' (from the start wounded men were left in the thick scrub), including two British officers killed and one wounded. As at Helles, leadership incurred a heavy cost.

By dawn units were straggling along in single file, looking for some sign of where they were and where they were supposed to be. A double company of the 5th (under Lieutenant Noel Cosby, who had taken such a prominent part in the 28 June fighting on Gully Spur) became detached, leading the companies of the 10th astray down the south fork of the Aghyl Dere and up towards Rhododendron Ridge. It was to fight a separate battle to the rest of the battalion. Navigational problems – the difficulty of finding the way in unfamiliar, rugged terrain in utter darkness – then took a hand. Hugh Lane, who around 1930 contacted surviving officers to trace the route of the two companies of the 10th and the company of the 6th which led them astray, described the 'lack of direction at the nullah junction' – the fork of the Aghyl Dere; or one of them.[25] This reflected poorly on Godley and Cox's staff work.

In daylight Gurkhas were seen to move off the main path, returning to wipe their bloody kukris on bushes, identifying and clearing out snipers. The main body of the 5th continued to climb, their officers attempting to follow orders as imprecise as they were seemingly detailed, using maps that were vague at best. Cox's orders for the initial advance directed them to march north, turn right at the exit of Aghyl Dere 'as

---

23 War diary, 1/5th Gurkhas, August 1915, WO95/4472, NAUK.
24 Letter, Hugh Lane, 27 July 1931, War diary, 1/5th Gurkhas, August 1915, 95/4432, NAUK.
25 Ibid.

far as the Eastern fork' and then to follow 'the branch leading from West for about 800 yards until the long spur which meets the track at point 92zl is met'.[26] Even if the maps had been accurate orienteering of this kind in such confused and unfamiliar country left the leading companies' commanders disoriented and their men thirsty and exhausted even before they encountered the Turks.

'No sign of the main column': 7 August

As the sun rose hotly over the range officers looked about and tried to relate what they could see to where they understood they should be. The lost company of the 5th and the two companies of the 10th linked up with the New Zealanders of the right assaulting column on the northern and western slopes of Chunuk Bair. Allanson's 6th found itself 500 yards west-north-west of Hill Q – more or less where it should have been – Captain Jack Dallas's scouting ahead of the main body helped its navigation. The other three companies of the 5th lay astride a branch of the Aghyl Dere. 'Somewhere behind them', Colonel Lane concluded, 'were the remaining two companies of the 2/10th Gurkhas'. Lacking contacts in the 14th Sikhs, he was unable to say where they were, at the time or later. In fact the 14th Sikhs were also more or less where they should have been, on the brigade's left, near Monash's Australians, waiting while the companies that had spent the uncomfortable day at sea and the company detached to protect the mountain guns hurried up. The Australians were also wildly off-track, 'somewhere to the north of Aghyl Dere'. As the far left wing of the assault, but also by far the sickest of all the units involved, the Australians were in no condition to continue the advance over the roughest terrain any Australian troops faced in the war.

The Gurkhas' officers, skilled in mountain warfare, understood their predicament in terms of the frontier. Lieutenant-Colonel Richard Firth, commanding the 5th, understood just how dire was his situation:

> The route was not piquetted, both his flanks were exposed, there was no sign of the main column nor yet of the rest of his own column, the scrub was full of Turks, he had lost three British officers ..., and casualties among the rank and file were mounting ...[27]

Some of the also 5th got within a few hundred yards of Hill Q, but were driven off by machine-gun fire so severe that 'further advance must have spelt annihilation'.[28]

Many officers had no idea of where they were. 'Fighting all day', wrote Herbert Cox in his diary, though exactly who they fought, why and with what effect is as obscure

---

26 War diary, 1/5th Gurkhas, August 1915, WO95/4432, NAUK
27 Ibid.
28 Regimental Committee, *History of the 5th Royal Gurkha Rifles*, p. 253.

now as it was then.[29] Cox, with no headquarters besides a scrape in the side of a gully, commanded the Left Assaulting Column, comprising eight battalions – his own four and four of the 4th Australian Brigade, under its commander, the ambitious John Monash, unhappy at being under the more senior Cox; or indeed anyone. Cox kept up with his troops, so close to the action that he was wounded twice, hit in the foot by a spent bullet on 7 August and in the right knee on the 8th. 'Now v. lame', he wrote in his diary.[30] (Cecil Allanson expressed his skepticism: he claimed that the first time 'a bullet cut his gaiter' and the second merely 'skimmed' him.[31]) But a sick man in his fifties, exhausted by the night march and the hot, airless, dusty days in the deres, Cox and his small staff struggled to keep control of a large, disparate force, practically uncontrollable in rugged, unfamiliar terrain. Cox remained nearly a thousand feet below the crest, unsure of what was concealed by the gullies and scrub of Sari Bair.

Allanson, with the 6th Gurkhas, found his way blocked by a deep precipice and Cox allowed him to 'swing off to the south and make straight for the hill'. His scouts practically reached the crest, but he received orders to halt to protect the New Army battalions moving out from Anzac. 'I was very upset at being told to stop', he told the Dardanelles Commission. Had he been allowed to continue, he thought, he would have seized the crest while it lay practically undefended.

The disarray into which the columns fell within hours of crossing their start lines diminished the offensive's parlous chances of success. While the Turks had barely two companies on the crest of Sari Bair on the morning of 7 August, as the hours passed the defensive force grew. What might have been claimed by a battalion on that day could not be taken by a division or more two days later. Monash's Australians failed, but were so debilitated they should never have been given the task. The 14th Sikhs was detached to support the attack Monash's 4th Brigade should have made about 11a.m., but the Australians did not move, partly from the 'excessive fatigue of the men' (which was indeed no excuse). This immobility reportedly dismayed the Sikhs, who had not encountered Australians before. They had been told, and accepted, that the Australians were invincible. The tired men they found dozing in the scanty shade of the gullies above the Aghyl Dere, their breeches stained with diarrhoea, were not what they had expected.

Meanwhile, the three Gurkha battalions were even more scattered, their companies all over the gullies of the Aghyl Dere, and far below the main range. The battalions trying to work their way towards Hill Q, their nominal objective, found themselves fighting Turks in thick scrub, often falling to snipers they could not see let alone kill. Men died lonely deaths – a survivor recalled how 'often it must have happened that a man fell to a sniper's bullet, and that his comrades only a yard or two away, knew

---

29 Diary, 7 August 1915, Herbert Cox, 1DRL221, AWM.
30 Ibid., 8 August 1915.
31 Letter, undated, Davies, *Allanson of the 6th*, p. 66.

Patiala sepoys wounded in the August offensive recuperating in hospital in Egypt.
(*Patiala and the Great War*)

nothing of it'.[32] Many of the men posted 'missing' at day's end must have bled to death or perished of dehydration; eventually. Among them was Rifleman Dhanbir Gurung, who had left a note for his sahib in Villiers-Stuart's kukri-scabbard.

Noel Cosby's companies wandered to the south-east towards the New Zealanders advancing on Rhododendron Ridge. Cosby saw men in slouch hats ahead of them. Thinking they were Gurkhas they moved toward them, but found them to be New Zealanders. Though hundreds of yards distant from their intended location, they (and Francis Sutton's 10th Gurkhas, who followed them) joined the New Zealanders in attacking through a cornfield towards what they thought was Hill Q but was actually far south-west of it, though they came under fire from a Turkish machine-gun on Hill Q. Using a false crest as cover (another sign of their frontier experience) they raced down the far slope, sheltering behind the rough stone wall and a stone hut. Cosby lost touch with both the 10th and the New Zealanders, sheltering as explosions burst around them – he thought naval shells. Thirsty in the hot sun, they hung on all day, 'hopes of support waning', Cosby reported. Towards dusk, noticing Turks trying to cut them off, they slipped away, in a drill Cosby's men knew well – 'the movement conformed to the accepted tenets of hill warfare'.[33] Carrying their wounded (yet another practice of the unforgiving frontier) they withdrew to the west, down a ravine they supposed would take them towards the Aghyl Dere.

32 Regimental Committee, *History of the 5th Royal Gurkha Rifles*, p. 252.
33 Ibid., p. 255

Officers of the 10th had quite a different recollection. Lieutenant Rob Shewen of the 10th claimed that Cosby's men in front of him refused to move. 'Get on', said Sutton. He claimed to have led his men around them and joined the New Zealanders.[34] Shewen's company was pinned down near the Farm and its Subedar, Pharsalhoj Rai, was carried out wounded in the leg on the 9th. 'I lost my best Gurkha Subedar', Shewen recalled. He was still learning Gurkhali from him, and Shewen recommended Rai for the Indian Order of Merit; presumably not just for his language skills.[35] Exactly what occurred on the slopes of Sari Bair can surely now not be established, but it offers a reminder that even troops as highly trained and well led as the 5th Gurkhas can refuse to go forward. The 10th certainly saw action – it had lost 166 men, including 38 killed; exactly a quarter of its starting strength. Only next morning did Noel Cosby find the rest of the 5th. Though the battalion had barely made contact with the main Turkish force on Sari Bair the 5th had lost 265 men, including 65 killed.

British empire units largely wasted 7 August thrashing around in the scrub-covered gullies while Ottoman commanders rushed units toward the crest of the range. While the mountain artillery at Anzac had contributed to the bombardment of the Turks on Sari Bair, neither Monash nor Cox, nor indeed their brigades, had performed well on 7 August. The confusion on Sari Bair marks the nadir of the Indians' fortunes on Gallipoli. The judgment of the British official history is harsh but just. Cox's 29th Indian Infantry Brigade was 'widely scattered', having 'lost all cohesion'.[36] The battle was not quite lost, but fresh Turkish reserves were arriving, able to fire at the attackers from above and their flanks, while Gurkhas, Sikhs, Britons, Australians and New Zealanders struggled to move forward, without co-ordination and with increasingly heavy losses. The following day would see a final chance for victory.

'Fresh attack on ridge failed': 8 August

The upper slopes of Sari Bair challenged even troops experienced in fieldcraft. Men hauled themselves up by grabbling roots and bushes, gasping for breath in the heat, often under fire from Turks on adjacent hills. Their determination impressed those who had not encountered them before. On the slopes of Sari Bair Allanson met a Warwickshire Territorial lieutenant named Slim, better known to history as Field Marshal William Slim, the victor of the Burma campaign in the Second World War. Slim had found some lost Gurkhas and brought them to join Allanson, with whom he shared a 'dirty envelope of raisins' shortly before he was badly wounded. His encounter with Allanson and his men profoundly impressed the young officer. Surviving the

---

34 [Douglas Shewen], 'Notes' [on the official history's account of the August offensive], c. 1925', 2/10th Gurkhas Digest of Service, GM.
35 'Pharsaldhoj Rai IOM', *The Bugle and Kukri*, 2011, p. 92.
36 Aspinall-Oglander, *Military Operations Gallipoli*, Vol. II, p. 208.

war, Slim not only joined the Indian Army as a regular but joined the 6th Gurkhas, so much had the men he saw on Sari Bair captivated him.[37]

Cox's diary entries during the terrible fight for Chunk Bair are sparse and ambiguous. On 9 August he writes 'Fresh attack on ridge failed, tho' 6th G's might have stayed there'. His records lag behind the action. 'Footing on Chunuk Bair … 6th lost very heavily'; though the 'footing', as we will see, lasted just a few minutes.[38] Characteristically, as the magnitude of the failure became apparent, Cox did not reflect or repine, but concentrated on what he had to do as a commander to at least hold what his force had secured, fashioning a line even though overlooked by Ottoman artillery observers and often snipers. (Even Cox noted that men could not gather in groups of more than three for fear of attracting the attention of Turkish snipers in the hills above them.)

Messages between his scattered battalions and Cox's headquarters took hours to travel by runner – or perhaps scrambler – up and down the gullies, and were often out of date by the time they arrived, if at all. Word that the offensive was failing did not reach commanders and their staff officers, a sign that they had little control of the battle once the troops stepped off. The Indian Army officer Major Clement Milward, at General Headquarters, heard on 7 August that 'the New Zealanders and Cox's Indian Brigade had done well'. He heard that Cox's men had seized 'a ridge directly under the top', and that the 6th Gurkhas and the New Zealanders had 'actually got to the [crest] … They could actually see across [to the Narrows in the distance]'.[39] It was untrue. On the evening of the 7th Cox had received orders (from Godley's headquarters, whose staff had as vague an idea of the reality as did General Headquarters) to resume the assault, and to assume command over the entire, unwieldy force. Though the eight battalions available to him were scattered all over the slopes of the Sari Bair range, Cox also distributed orders to commanders of the improvised columns in the hope that they could concentrate and co-ordinate their attacks by the early hours of 8 August. In that the column commanders were mostly battalion or brigade commanders who had experience of action in the mountains of the north-west frontier, his presumption was perhaps realistic, but no amount of front-line experience could have pushed tired and often sick troops over such rugged country and thick scrub.

Not even men with Indian experience ('we fought as on manoevres in India', Cecil Allanson remarked, describing how his men moved forward along the crests, 'which we always do in frontier fighting'.[40]) were able to marshal and direct their scattered and tired units on 8 August. Number 1 Column, under Francis Sutton of the 10th,

37 Lewin, *The Standardbearer*, p. 23.
38 Diary, 10 August 1915, Herbert Cox, 1DRL221, AWM.
39 Diary, 7 August 1915, Major Clement Milward, CAB45/259, NAUK.
40 Undated report, probably 10 August 1915, Davies, *Allanson of the 6th*, p. 57; Evidence before the Dardanelles Commission of Lt-Col Cecil Allanson, 32nd Day, 18 January 1917, p. 616, 103, AWM 51.

was to attack the northern slopes of Chunuk Bair. It lost a further 40 men, for no gain. Number 3 Column, under Philip Palin, comprised the 14th Sikhs and, at last Richard Firth's 5th Gurkhas, but the two became separated, a reminder of how tangled was the country. (The 5th Gurkhas' war diary records a curious entry on this day. Men of A Company reported seeing a 'Turkish general on a white horse' ahead of them. They must have shot him, and described taking from his body 'a sword of gold, heavily jewelled', but were obliged to drop it or otherwise give it up. Who was this 'general'?[41]) Orders for the day's attack reached Palin's forward companies only 45 minutes before the 4.15 a.m. start. Both battalions immediately ran into heavy Turkish resistance and by 8.30 both the Indians and the flanking 4th Australian Brigade had returned to their start line. While the Sikhs had suffered some casualties on the offensive's first day, 8 August became the day they, and especially the Patiala double company, suffered most. Thirteen Patialas were killed that day and 57 wounded (almost exactly half the battalion's casualties on Gallipoli), including Major Harban Singh, the Patialas' senior officer. Soon after, the commander of the Imperial Service Brigade in which the Patialas served in Egypt again wrote to Patiala asking Colonel Gurbaksh Singh [sic] to publish in the state force's general orders a congratulatory order. He was certain that it would 'bring honour and glory' to the 'good name of the Sikh brotherhood, to … the regiment and to … Imperial Service troops'.[42]

Despite their forebodings on Imbros men and officers displayed their accustomed courage. Reginald Savory was to gain a Military Cross for recklessly carrying up ammunition under fire and Palin's orderly, Lance-Naik Hazara Singh the Indian Order of Merit for taking messages under fire. To the Sikhs it was a familiar story, with the northern wing of the Sikhs most heavily involved reduced to only 69 effectives by the day's end, with two British officers killed and two wounded; and all for nothing. It seems that on 8 August the last real chance of reaching and taking the Sari Bair range passed.

'The fortune of war was against us': Allanson on Sari Bair

The only column that seemed able to act on Cox's orders was Number 2 (Allanson's 6th Gurkhas and men of two or three New Army battalions). Though it 'never really operated as a column at all', as a survivor recalled, two of its units made the most dramatic attempt of the entire offensive.[43] Allanson pushed his men on and up, on the night of 8-9 August digging in about a hundred feet below the southern crest of Hill Q, with men of the 6th South Lancashires and the 9th Warwickshires and a few North Staffords doggedly following them up the steep slope. The Gurkhas' achievement seems in keeping with the traditions and training of a unit used to moun-

---

41 War diary, 1/5th Gurkhas, August 1915, WO95/4432, NAUK.
42 History of Patiala State Forces, Part III, p. 100, Maharaja of Patiala collection.
43 Mullaly, *Bugle and Kukri*, p. 93.

A company of the 14th Sikhs or the Patialas beside a barbed wire cage holding captured Turks. The soldiers wear the white armbands issued to those taking part in the August offensive. (ATL 077922)

tain warfare under an Indian sun. That men of Kitchener battalions from cold, wet, flat counties in their first action should be able to join them seems astounding. The contrast should remind us that, contrary to the proponents of the martial races theory, proficiency in war was nothing to do with racial predisposition, but had everything to do with training, motivation and leadership. (And, indeed, with failures of leadership. It is clear that the New Army battalions had more men on the slopes of Sari Bair than their commanders allowed to go in support of Allanson and his few Gurkhas. But the British troops were exhausted and no one should be surprised that they could not struggle further up the precipitous slopes.)

A century on, what happened on Hill Q soon after dawn on 9 August continues to fascinate. It is illusory to think that the British empire troops on and about Sari Bair could possibly have taken and held the crest of the range – that chance passed the day before. The attraction of the climactic attack is that it was so clearly doomed. It belongs to that familiar genre of heroic failure in British imperial military history – Balaklava, Cawnpore, Isandlwana, Maiwand, Spion Kop; the landings at V Beach and Lancashire Landing and the charge at the Nek elsewhere on Gallipoli. We know that the heroism was wasted and that the deaths were futile, but we cannot look away. We have a detailed account by Cecil Allanson himself, but otherwise such a dearth of sources from anyone else, that accounts of what happened – and especially who said what happened – cannot but be contentious.

Major Cecil Allanson, who commanded the 1/6th Gurkhas in the climactic assault on Sari Bair, and whose life was marked forever after by the ordeal. (Gurkha Museum, Winchester)

Looking from Hill Q, the scene of Allanson's attack, eastwards toward the Dardanelles, early one August morning. (Author)

Cox had ordered Allanson to make an attempt on the crest, telling him that five battalions would be following. In fact, under the cover of a furious and accurate bombardment timed to stop at 5.15 a.m. on the 9th, Allanson's Gurkhas and the Englishmen climbed the final, almost vertical slope and breasted the crest between Hill Q and the summit of Chunuk Bair, a few hundred yards north-west of where the New Zealanders fought for the crest. The defending Turks had been driven back by the bombardment and the attackers gained the crest without impediment. They drove its shocked defenders down the eastern slopes of the ridge. Allanson's descriptions of the fighting (and he gave several, differing in detail) suggest the savagery of the hand-to-hand struggle, which he recalled continued for ten minutes, though no one can be sure. In the fighting Allanson was wounded by a bayonet in the thigh, Lieutenant John Le Marchand; killed (either shot or bayonetted in Allanson's two versions). 'I felt a very proud man', Allanson wrote, for below him was a panorama that few British empire soldiers had seen since 25 April. Looking beyond the shambles of the Turkish trenches on the summit they could have seen, five or six miles distant, the dull silver streak of the Dardanelles, the possession of which supposedly justified the deaths of thousands of men from Anatolia, Britain, Australasia, and India. For a few minutes victory – albeit a limited, qualified, tactical victory – seemed possible. The moment is represented as the literal and symbolic high point of the campaign, and has attracted the appropriate rhetoric: 'the fortune of war was against us', wrote Hamilton, as if the outcome had nothing to do with him.[44] The rhetoric is deceptive. Despite the drama of the glimpse of the Narrows, the reality was that the Turks were much closer and in greater strength than any of the troops who should have been following, and would surely have pushed Allanson's men off the crest with the counter-attack they did in fact mount.

Allanson's men were not to keep their gains. As they began to move down the eastern slope, pursuing the Turkish defenders shells began to fall on the summit. Allanson remembered a Gurkha being hit full in the face and killed instantly. 'The place was a mass of blood and limbs and screams', and they pulled back to the crest in understandable 'panic'.[45] Looking down to the Dardanelles he saw for the last time the straits the invaders were never to seize, but also Ottoman reserves massing below the crest. Ottoman officers, seeing the advance falter, rallied their men and led them back up the slope. Limping from his wound, Allanson led his few survivors back down the precipitous slope and back to the scrapes where the attackers had spent the night. But his men achieved something that only Malone's Wellingtons also managed in the entire campaign, and the vision of what might have followed continues to haunt those who ponder what Gallipoli was and what it might have been.

The question of whose guns shelled Allanson and the attackers off the crest of Sari Bair has been debated for nearly a century. At the time the consensus ashore was that the guns were naval, from a destroyer or a monitor: Allanson thought so. But the flat trajectory of naval guns would not allow shells to strike the reverse slope. The guns must have been howitzers, therefore probably fired by New Zealand gunners.[46] Indeed, Tim Travers found that Anzac howitzer batteries were programmed to fire on the reverse slopes of Sari Bair, though Allanson (or Cox) did not know it.[47] In yet another confirmation that (as Gallipoli survivor Joe Murray famously put it) the invaders were beaten by their own commanders, a fire-plan he did not know about destroyed Allanson's slim chance of seizing Sari Bair at the moment he seemed to have achieved it.

Herbert Cox later told Allanson, in the hearing of his staff, that he would recommend him for a Victoria Cross. Cox recorded on 11 August that he had recommended Allanson '& will get it I think'.[48] It did not eventuate (like the several other VCs that Indian troops did not gain on Gallipoli). Allanson, exhausted, wounded and deeply distressed that his battalion had been destroyed to no purpose, gave Cox a frank account of the debacle on Sari Bair before agreeing to go to a dressing station. Was his criticism frank enough to frighten Cox into seeing that Allanson was liable to reveal

---

44 Supplement to *London Gazette*, 6 January 1916, p. 296.
45 Undated report, possibly 10 August 1915, Davies, *Allanson of the 6th*, p. 60.
46 The only question is raised by Edward Phipson's description of the Gurkha wounded stained bright yellow, by Lyddite: did the field artillery's shell do this? Is this controversy resolved?
47 Travers, *Gallipoli 1915*, p. 171, fn. 35.
48 Diary, 11 August 1915, Herbert Cox, 1DRL221, AWM.

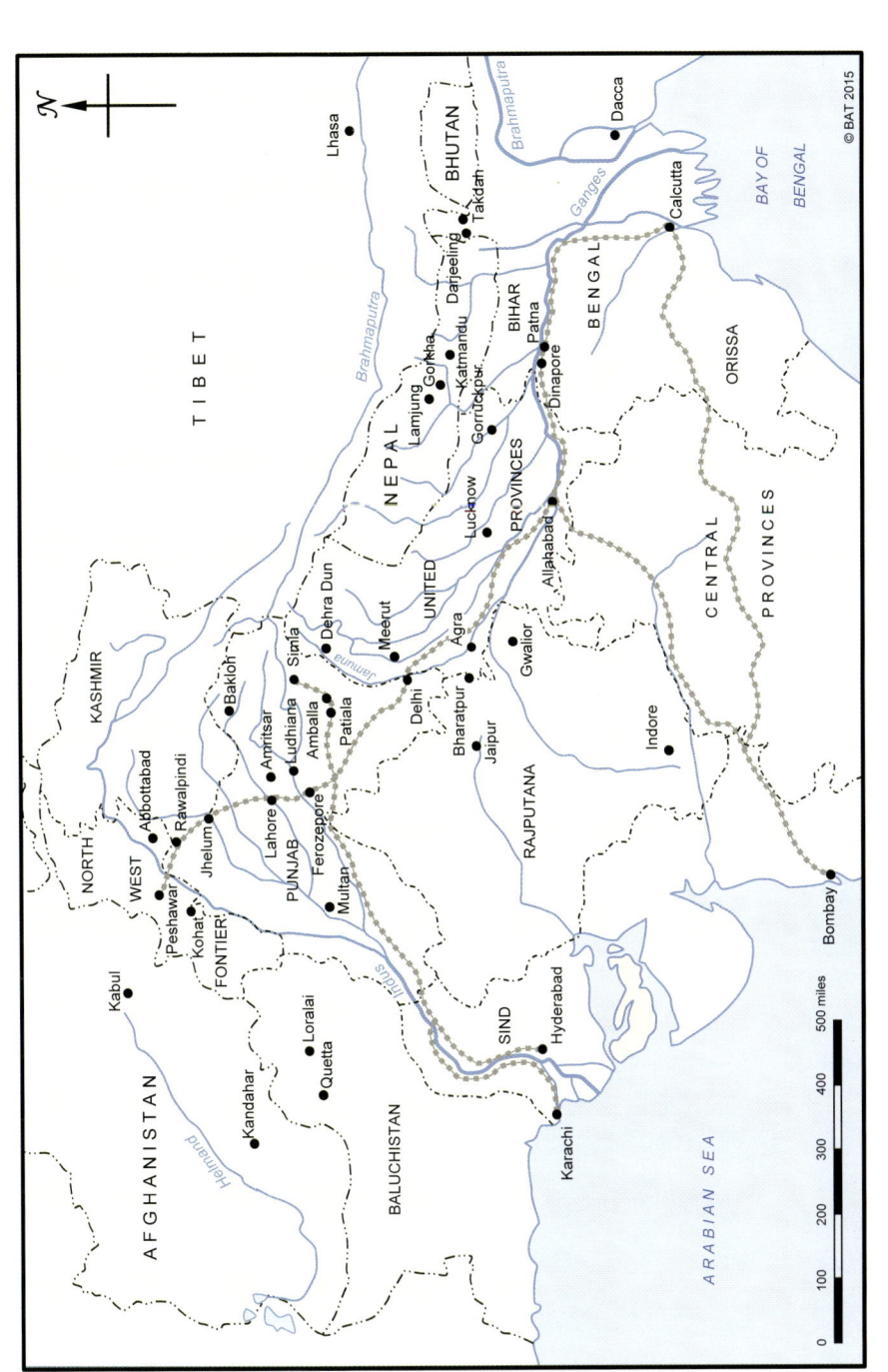

Map 1 Northern India, 1914

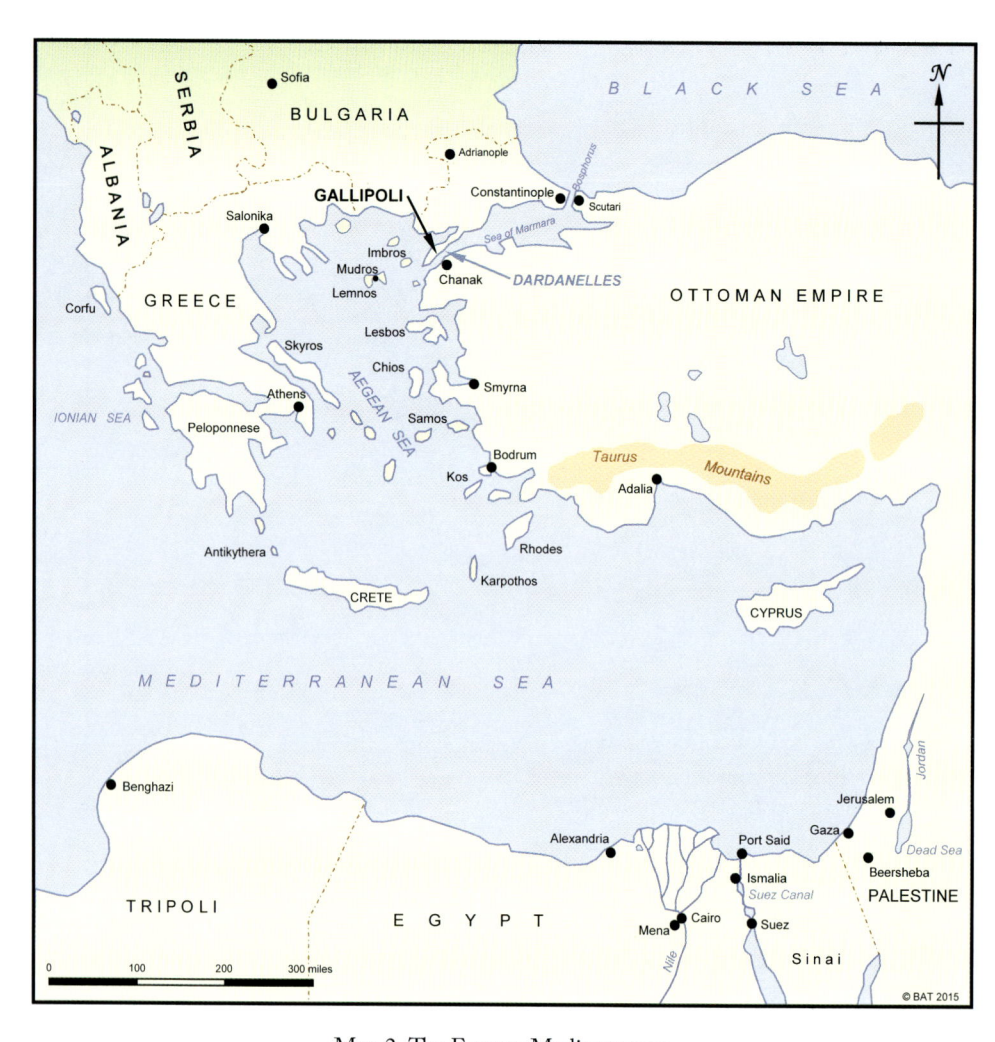

Map 2 The Eastern Mediterranean

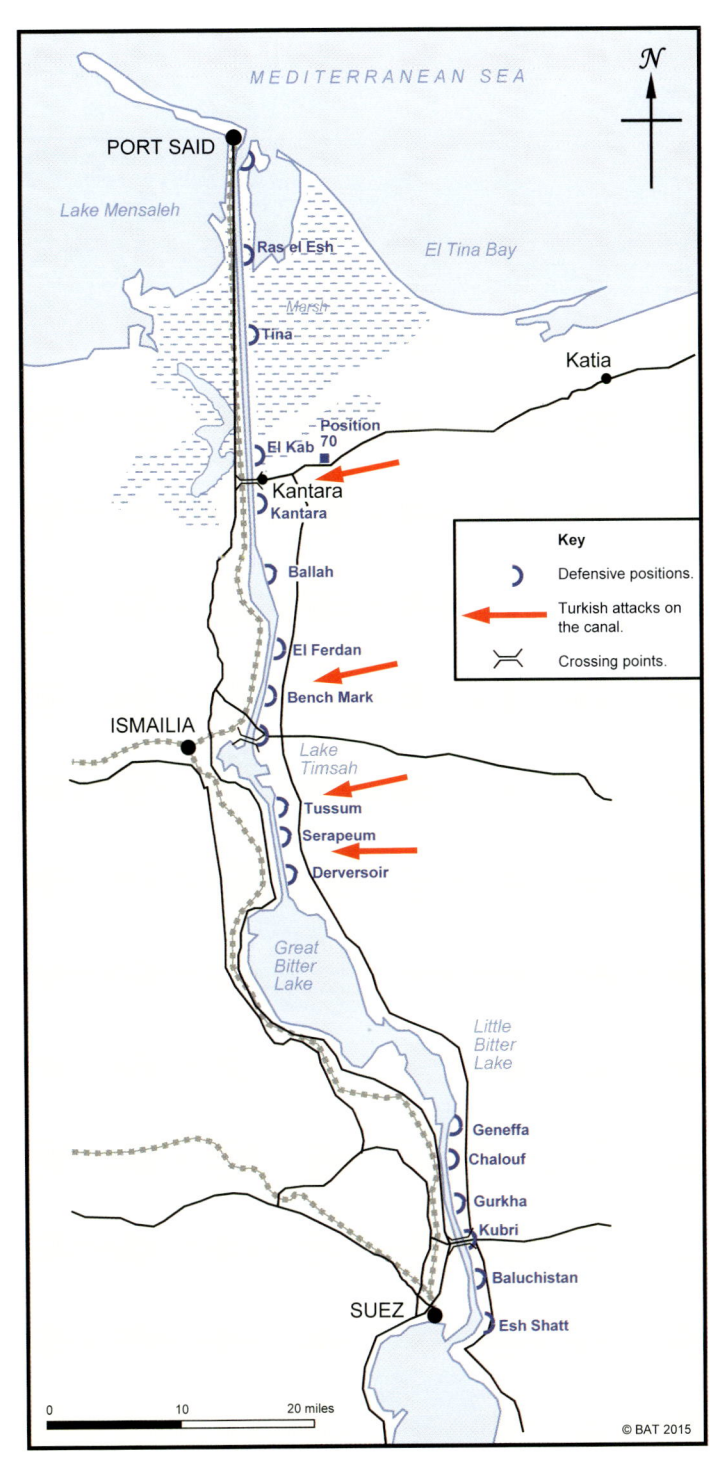

Map 3 Suez Canal defences, 1914-15

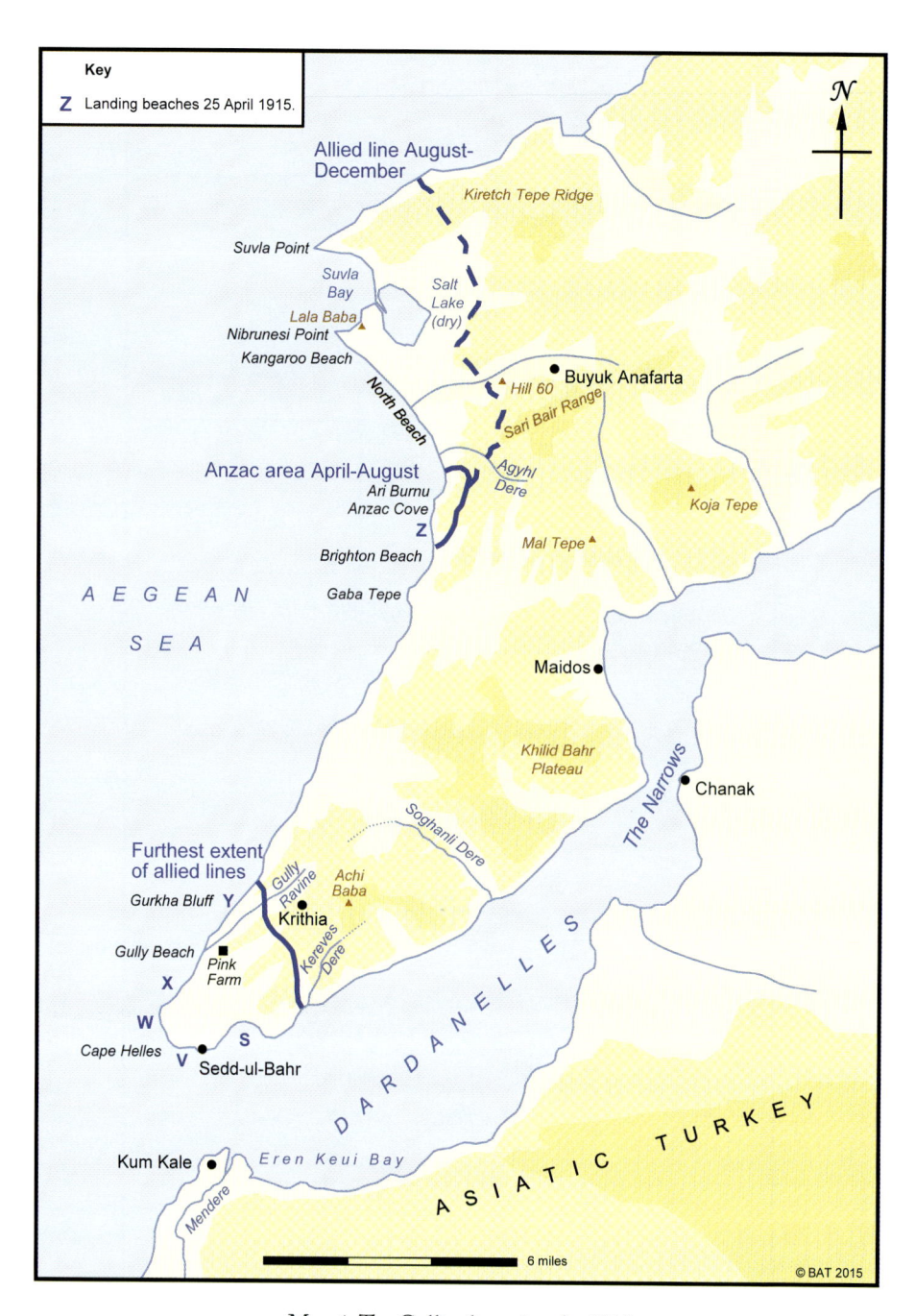

Map 4 The Gallipoli peninsula, 1915

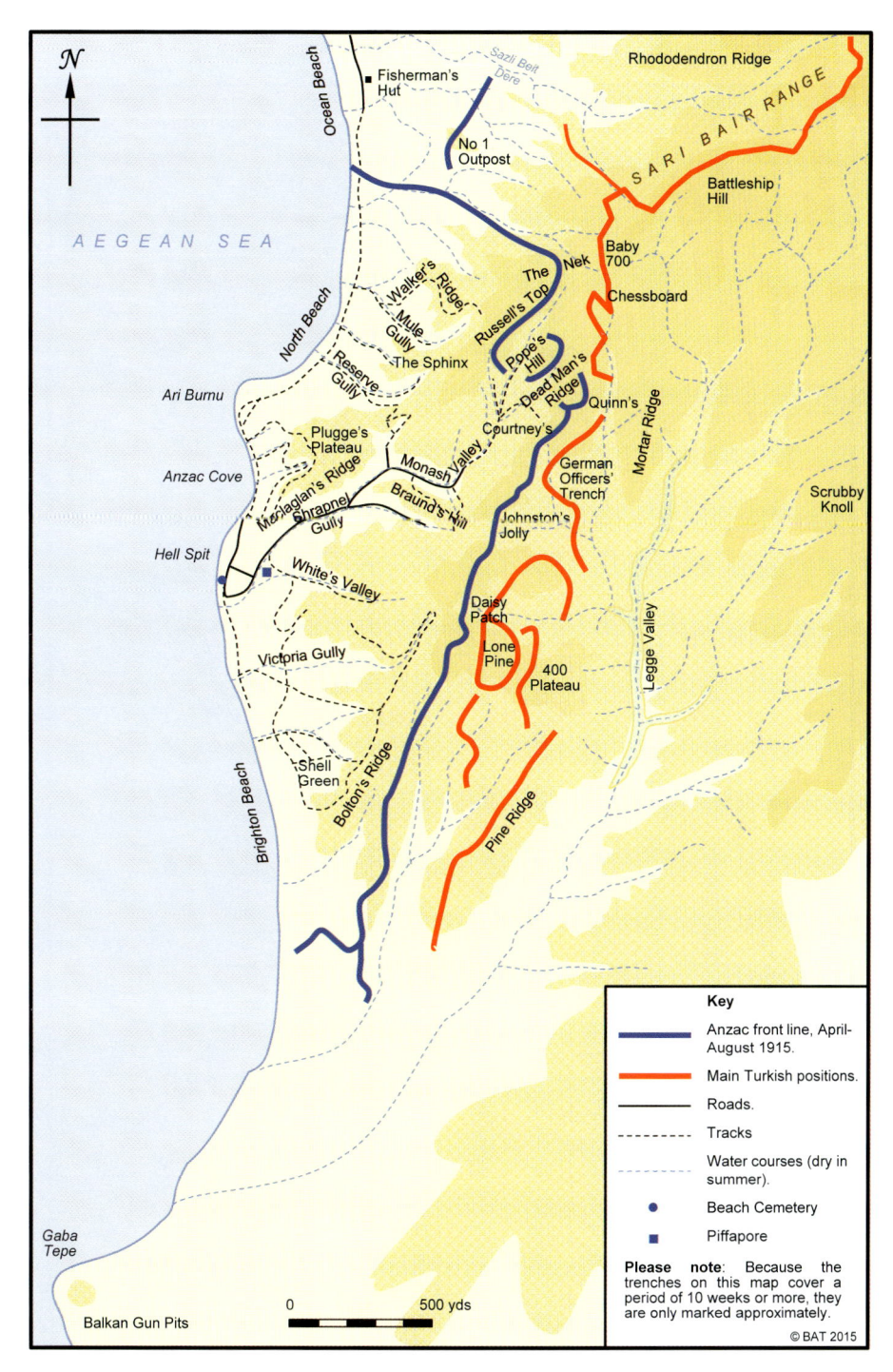

Map 5 Anzac area, 1915

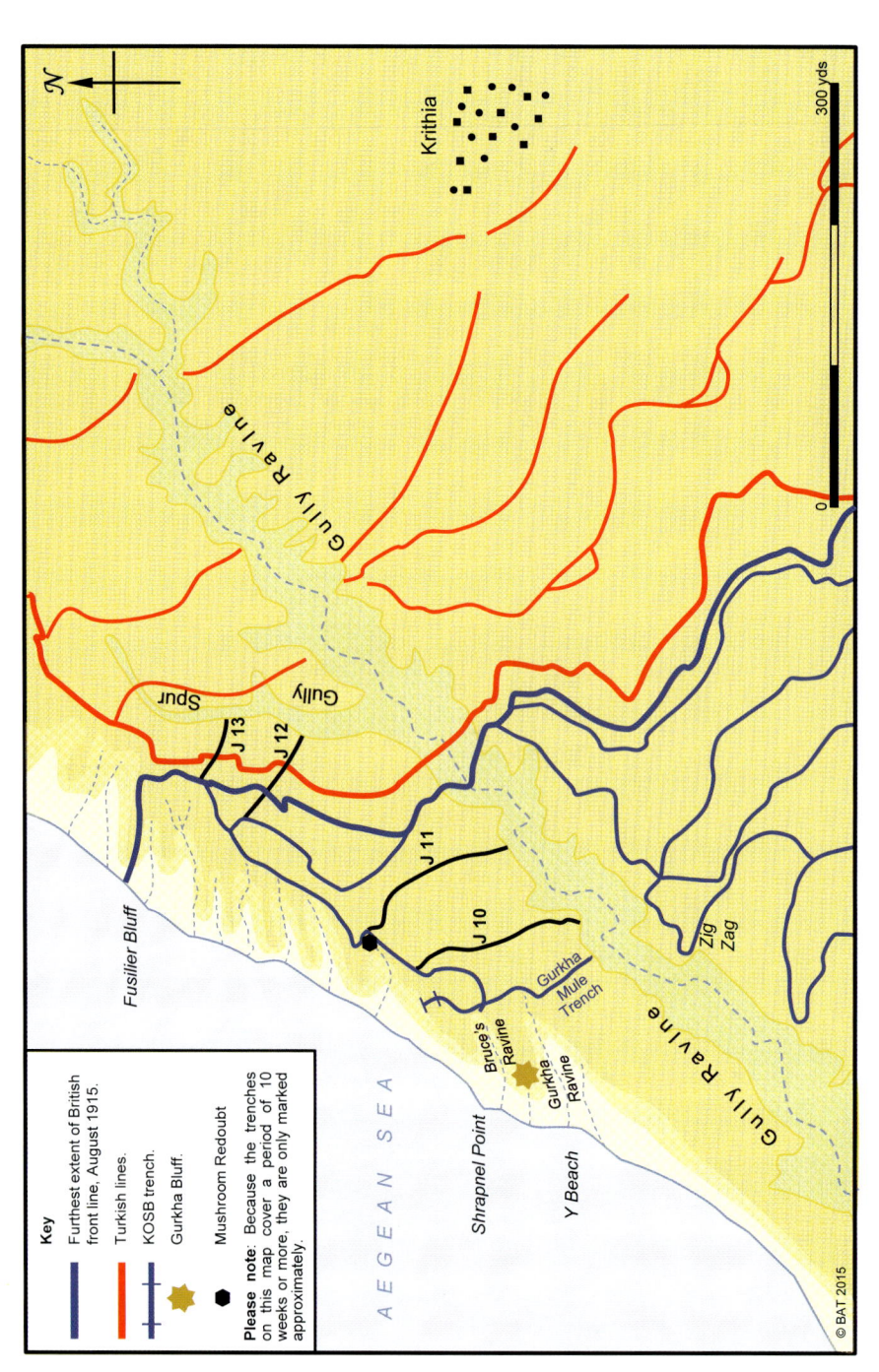

Map 6 Gully Ravine, 1915

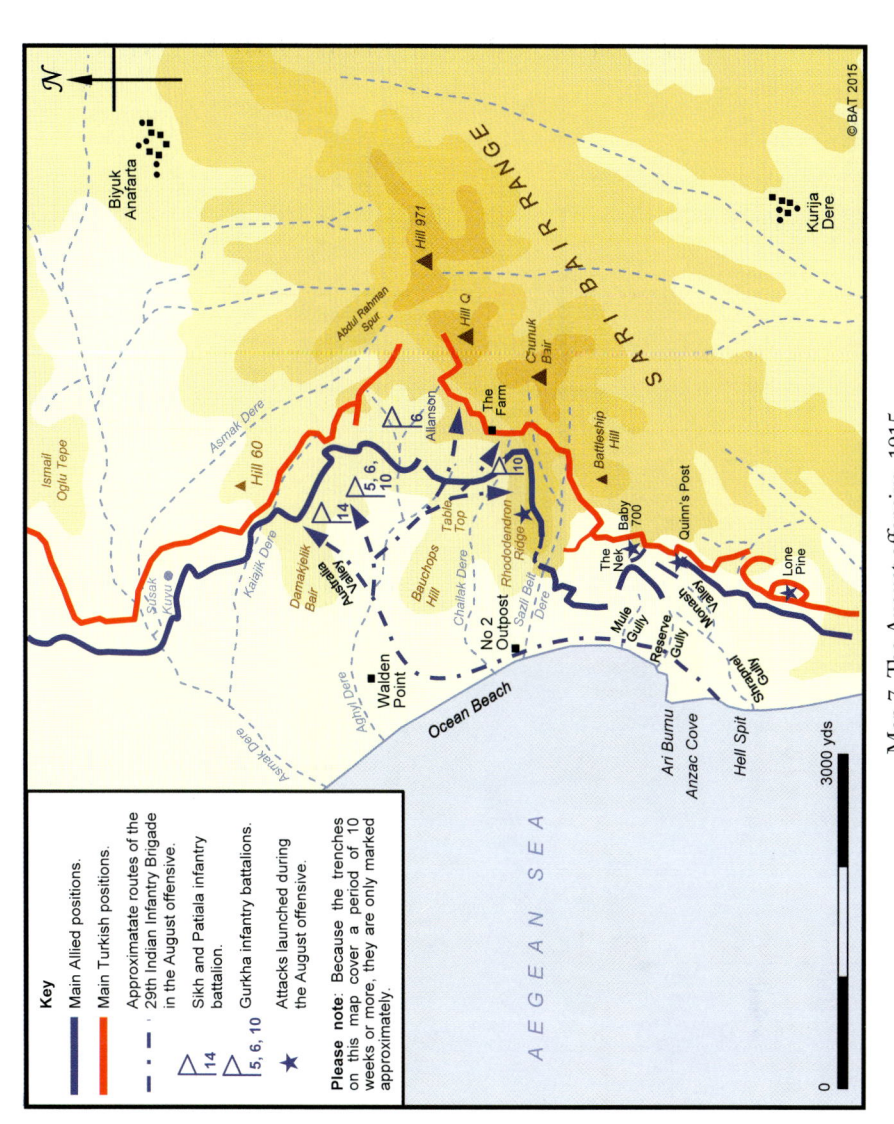

Map 7 The August offensive, 1915

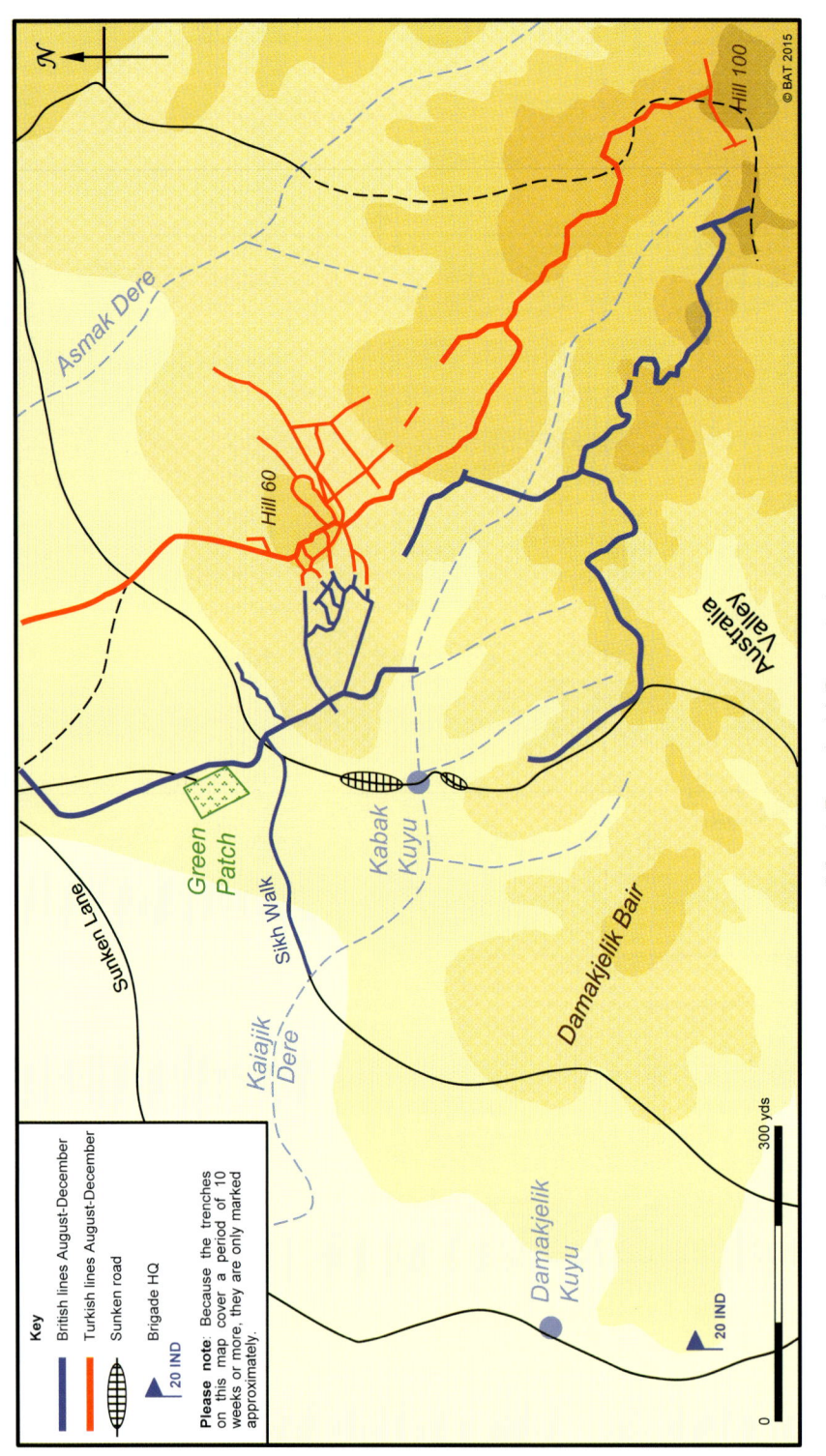

Map 8 Damakjelik Bair, 1915

Men of the 2/10th Gurkhas on Sari Bair ridge during the August offensive, one of the very few photographs of Indians in action on Gallipoli. (14th Sikhs album)

uncomfortable truths? The Victoria Cross was not awarded, though who killed the recommendation is unclear. Birdwood, Godley and Cox saw Allanson as excitable and unreliable: the opposite of Villiers-Stuart's ideal of a British officer being 'very sound'. In hearings before the Dardanelles Commission in January 1917 he revealed that the trauma he had experienced on Sari Bair affected him as much as ever. He read from is diary ('the place was a mass of blood and limbs and screams') and seemed unbalanced in his insistence that he had taken the crest but lost it because he was not supported.[49] Allanson was a man who could not conceal his feelings (he knew he had annoyed Godley by telling him frankly that the assault on Sari Bair had been botched), but that did not make him unreliable. (Hamilton also described as 'excitable' Major-General Granville Edgerton. After his 52nd Division had been so badly battered at Helles, until rebuked Edgerton introduced his units to Hamilton as 'the remains of the …'.[50]) Hamilton, Birdwood, Godley and Cox could be relied upon not to reveal the truth, if it were inauspicious or incriminating. Hamilton, for example, deprecated the release of documents through the Dardanelles Commission which would 'show up Lord K. with altogether too bright a searchlight beam'.[51]

---

49 Evidence before the Dardanelles Commission of Lt-Col Cecil Allanson, 32nd Day, 18 January 1917, pp. 616-17, 103, AWM 51.
50 James, *Gallipoli*, p. 231.
51 Hamilton, *Listening for the Drums*, p. 254.

Despite the bogus exultation of Hamilton's despatch – 'they *were* our own fellows – the topmost summit was ours!' – the occupation of Sari Bair proved to be temporary.[52] British empire troops could nowhere stay upon the crest-line. Further south, Trenchard's guns of the Kohat Battery had fired in support of the New Zealanders attacking up Chunuk Bair, where William Malone and his Wellington Battalion (and men of the New Army 7th Gloucesters and 8th Welch) had managed to get onto the crest of Chunuk Bair at daylight on the 8th. The Wellingtons and the Kitchener men (the latter facing battle for the first time, in the unaccustomed heat) had held on all day against Turkish shell- and machine-gun fire, and against repeated assaults by columns of infantry who approached close enough to hurl bombs (of which the Wellingtons had none). Malone had encouraged his men by urging them to 'hang on – the Gurkhas are coming', as two Turkish regiments (that is, brigades) attacked.[53] (The Turks were of the 9th Division, which had faced the Indian brigade at Gully Ravine two months before.) After dusk the Wellingtons and their British comrades were withdrawn, the Wellingtons with fewer than 70 men unwounded of the 760 who had climbed the ridge that morning, with Malone lying dead among his men. Despite his encouragement the Gurkhas were not coming, and never would. The seizure of Chunuk Bair had not been a 'presage of victory', and by the time Hamilton wrote those words he knew it.[54]

Allanson's account of the assault on Sari Bair, privately published in 1919 and later ably interpreted by Harry Davies, remains as some of the most vivid but also the most problematic of the documents describing and explaining the failure of the offensive. More than any single source, his account of the dramatic minutes on the crest, when men from flat, industrial Lancashire and mountainous rural Nepal together took and then lost the crest, evokes the pathos of the opportunity so nearly won and absolutely lost. Written by a man tormented by the loss of his friends and men, traumatised by an ordeal as harrowing as any on Gallipoli and under the strain of being disbelieved and denied by his erstwhile superiors, his version of those August days remains contentious. Allanson believed that responsibility for the failure lay on Brigadier-General Anthony Baldwin and his Kitchener battalions: 'if he had come up we should have won'.[55] But like all Gallipoli's 'ifs', the gap between plan and execution yawned wide.

---

52   Supplement to *London Gazette*, 6 January 1916, p. 295.
53   Bean, *The Story of Anzac*, Vol. II, pp. 676-79.
54   Supplement to *London Gazette*, 6 January 1916, p. 295.
55   Evidence before the Dardanelles Commission of Lt-Col Cecil Allanson, 32nd Day, 18 January 1917, p. 618, 103, AWM 51.

The Narrows, seen from Sari Bair soon after the war; the view seen by Allanson and his men on the morning of 9 August. (*The 5th Royal Gurkha Rifles*)

'Under very trying conditions': the offensive ends

While Allanson's men were on Sari Bair the 10th Gurkhas, with other men of the 9th Warwickshires and the Maoris, had climbed the steep hillside toward Chunuk Bair at 5 a.m. on 9 August from trenches in front of the Farm. They reached a line about sixty yards below the summit and could make no further progress, enfiladed by Turkish machine-guns on Hill Q to the north and assailed by 'friendly' naval gunfire. While naval gunfire has been absolved of the blame for shelling Allanson and the attackers on the crest of Sari Bair on 8 August, on 9 August the four Kohat guns fired in support of the bombardment directed on the crest of the range but the 10th's men were shelled out of their positions (this time actually by the battleship HMS *Bacchante*, whose observers mistook them for Turks). The 10th's war diary recorded that 'when within 30 yards from the ridge it [the battalion] came under fire of naval guns and the advance was brought to a standstill'.[56] As on Hill Q, the Turks counter-attacked and drove the 10th down the slope, back to the trenches they had left to struggle uphill at dawn. The 10th lost another fifty men, and another thirty

---

56 War diary, 2/10th Gurkhas, August 1915, WO95/4472, NAUK.

when they withdrew at midday to conform to the line coalescing below the ridge.[57] Allanson admitted in a message to Cox that 'a good many of the troops went rather far down the gully': even Gurkhas have limits.[58] By the time the gunfire ended and Brigadier Anthony Baldwin's exhausted men straggled out of the scrub of the Aghyl Dere Turkish counter-attacks were flooding over the crest, pushing the hapless New Army men back down the slopes toward the Farm in disorder.

Alexander Godley, Cox's superior, decided that the failure to take Sari Bair at dawn on the 9th effectively ended the attempt. He ordered Cox to pull his brigades back to a line between the Farm and Demakjelik Bair – the danger now not mere failure, but defeat. Cox again re-organised his dwindling force. Though a brigadier usually responsible for four battalions, he was now directing his own brigade, 4th Australian Brigade and two battalions of the 39th Brigade – ten battalions, albeit battalions diminished and scattered by hard fighting in appalling country. The New Army units had no chance in the most difficult terrain, in unaccustomed and debilitating heat and against an enemy more skillful, determined and, by this time, more numerous. Baldwin's New Army battalions became lost, only at the Farm when they should have been below the crest. And as the bearer parties struggled to bring men down from the deres – if they found them, and alive, the wounded reached the dressing stations and piers, Noel Tattersall, a British doctor, described the day after 9 August as '24 hours of Hell', treating up to 800 British, Australian, New Zealand and Indian wounded lying in rows in the sun and tormented by flies but 'wonderfully patient'.[59]

At Anzac death continued to visit men not in the front line. On 9 August the Indian mule corps lost one of its most popular and efficient officers when Hedley Cullen, was carried off wounded. He had celebrated his 21st birthday the evening before with the mule corps' officers, who drank his health. The next day he was shot in the stomach and, while bullets zipped overhead, was carried down to the pier by No. 2 Outpost, where lay among hundreds awaiting treatment and evacuation. He died of his wounds on the hospital ship *Dongala* the day after.

By the 9th all of the 6th Gurkhas' British officers had been killed or wounded. (Captain Geoffrey Tomes, an officer of the 53rd Sikhs posted to the battalion though he could not speak Gurkhali was killed within half an hour of arriving to replace Allanson.) Only the battalion's medical officer, Captain Edward Phipson remained, who stripped off his Red Cross brassard and sent his 'salaam' to Subedar-Major Gambirsing Pun.[60] Together they commanded the 6th on the slopes of Hill Q. Unable to speak or read English, Pun needed the doctor's help in understanding messages (which came by hand, the telephones lines being cut). Eventually he received orders to withdraw down the slope to the Demakjelik Bair, a hill a mile away down

---

57 Ibid.
58 War diary, 29th Indian Infantry Brigade, August 1915, 187, AWM.
59 Diary, 8-9 August 1915, Norman Tattersall, 98/24/1, 7878, IWM.
60 Memoir, Edward Phipson, 76/175/A, 21088, IWM.

the tangled deres, and in the face of a gathering Turkish advance. Pun had his men destroy anything they could not carry away, throwing away ammunition and rifle bolts and even cutting up belts to deny them to the enemy. Carrying their wounded out, as they had trained on the frontier, the 6th's survivors reached the Demakjelik Bair on the late afternoon of the 10th, its last act of the offensive. Gambirsing Pun received the Military Cross – introduced only in 1915 and still an unusual decoration for Indian officers – for 'conspicuous gallantry'. (He had already received the Indian Order of Merit for his 'splendid example' in the attack on 28 June.) His MC citation, though couched in the restrained prose typical of the genre, reveals the reality: he 'set a splendid example of bravery under very trying conditions', during the attack and 'throughout the hand-to-hand fighting which followed', showing himself to be 'a leader of remarkable merit and undaunted courage'.[61]

Cecil Allanson almost certainly submitted the recommendation that became the basis of the citation. The Indian Army seems to have been extraordinarily dilatory in awarding Military Crosses. Gambirsing Pun's was the only one awarded on Gallipoli, and only two were awarded in 1916, 5 in 1917 but 43 in 1918. The proportion suggests that many actions in 1915 that might have merited recognition went unrecognised. By then many of the Indian Army's most daring and reckless spirits were dead. It seems not to have occurred to anyone that what he had done in the absence of British officers could be done alongside them.[62] But British officers continued to believed that Gurkhas 'won't get out of the trench unless white officers are there', and as the Turks had begun sniping them, 'the regiment goes phut'.[63]

On 10 August the Ottomans launched what Hamilton called, in his curiously antique manner, a 'grand attack'. Turkish counter-attacks 'simply overwhelmed' the Kitchener divisions' scattered and often leaderless battalions. The counter-attacks continued on the fourth day of the fight, with an entirely fresh Ottoman division sent against the exhausted units clinging to the slopes of Chunuk Bair. The disjointed advances of the various columns stopped in the tangle of gullies, with Brigadier-General Baldwin himself dying in the fighting around the Farm. The 5th Gurkhas, which had been held in reserve on the 9th, met the Turkish counter-attacks on the 10th, using its machine-guns, which 'did great execution'.[64] The 10th and the 6th (or rather their surviving men) held a rough line across the upper reaches of the Aghyl Dere, with a mixture of parts of units from three divisions on their flanks. The Gurkhas 'dug all night till dawn' creating fresh trenches – with the collapse of the offensive now on the defensive – and 'buried numerous Australian dead'.[65]

61   Hypher, *Deeds of Valour*, p. 190.
62   Ryan, Strahan & Jones, *Historical Record of the 6th Gurkha Rifles*, p. 122.
63   War diary, 29th Indian Infantry Brigade, August 1915, 187, AWM 6.
64   War diary, 1/5th Gurkhas, August 1915, WO95/4432, NAUK.
65   War diary, 2/10th Gurkhas, August 1915, WO95/4472, NAUK.

On that day, the mountain guns again tried to stop the great Turkish counter-attack that drove the Gurkhas, Australians and New Zealanders off the crest, though the toll of the previous four months virtually continuous operations began to be apparent. At one point the vent problems left only one of Kohat Battery's guns in action, though the battery fired 685 rounds that day. Thom fired at concentrations of Turkish troops, also doing 'great execution' by firing at a gully they called 'Thom's Fork', though the name did not make it to any official map. The batteries' gunners, drivers and signallers had by this time spent four days in continuous action. The three signallers working from the Centre section had kept the wires open day and night, never missing an opportunity to alert the gunners.

'A too ambitious scheme': judgment on the August offensive

The four-days of fighting had cost the Indian brigade severely. The 10th had lost six officers killed (2 British and 4 Gurkha) and 83 men killed, with 280 wounded (including seven officers); 40% of the men who had embarked at Imbros less than a week before. The 14th Sikhs (and the Patialas) had on 11 August just 223 sepoys, half of its strength at the outset. The sufferings of the wounded in the summer fighting on Gallipoli became legendary. Many lay for days in the blazing sun, without water, tormented by clouds of flies. Stretcher-bearers of all of the armies involved – British, Australian, New Zealand and Indian – worked for days to find and carry in the wounded. They scoured the wide expanse of scrub, often the target of snipers, finding wounded men – but often corpses – in the thick scrub. For all of the heroic conduct in the battle, the rewards offered remained astoundingly niggardly. (Brian Mullaly, author of the 10th Gurkhas' history, attributed the dearth of recognition to the 'gravely mistaken belief … that deeds of gallantry in battle were part of a soldier's duty and should not receive special award'.[66] Allanson was outraged to learn that officers who had been killed in the offensive had all been 'struck out' of honours recommendations.[67]) Accordingly, the 10th saw only one gallantry award for the entire battle, an Indian Distinguished Service Medal to Rifleman Harkasing Thapa, for his tenacity in finding and succouring wounded. Astonishingly, given the Sikhs' sacrifice, Ian Hamilton's final list of recommendations for awards included only one member of the 14th Sikhs – Philip Palin, its commanding officer. The 1/5th Gurkhas received 14, the 1/6th 8, the 2/10th 9: the affront seems pointed.[68]

The mountain gunners' part in the bold but misguided attack up the Sari Bair ridge is often overlooked in general accounts of the dramatic but tragic story of the August offensive. Fergusson gave three reasons for its failure: 'a long night march

---

66 Mullaly, *Bugle and Kukri*, p. 100.
67 Typescript notes, Allanson Papers, 6602-22, NAM.
68 'List of officers, NCOs & men …', Ian Hamilton, 7/7/13, LHCMA.

and an attack in extremely difficult country and practically un-reconnoitred'.[69] Accompanying the columns were eight guns, two from each of the batteries. Kohat Battery supported the Right Attacking Column and Jacob's the Left. The Jacob's guns went to Rhododendron Ridge, where they supported the New Zealanders but had little opportunity to influence the fight. Kohat's guns, under Thom, Rawson and Tyler, became the only guns to cover the doomed attack on Sari Bair. Fergusson, reflecting the reports of his subalterns, talked darkly of 'want of bandobast' at the very outset.

The offensive had failed, at a cost of some 12,000 British empire casualties, with more at Helles, and many more on the Ottoman side. Nearly a thousand of those casualties were Indians. Charles Bean loyally thought the cost 'not excessive when the nature of the fighting is considered', but when measured against the offensive's intention – to capture the high ground above Anzac and Suvla and perhaps lead to a break-out – it was surely excessive. Indeed, the offensive had cost the equivalent of the entire garrison of what was now called 'old Anzac'.[70] It was clear to those who had seen the confusion in the deres on the western slopes of Sari Bair what had happened. An anonymous officer of the 5th Gurkhas dispassionately analysed what had gone wrong:

> The Indian Brigade failure was in no way due to sickness or fatigue, but solely to the dislocation caused by the breakdown of a too ambitious scheme.[71]

This is as direct a criticism as could be recorded in a war diary – a document routinely seen by the staff of higher formations – an indictment of the planning of Andrew Skeen and the staff officers in Hamilton and Birdwood's headquarters; the men who conceived of the assault on Sari Bair and who must be blamed for its failure. When he learned of Skeen's plan – from Skeen himself – Cecil Allanson asked himself 'what one would have done to a subaltern at a promotion examination who made any such proposition'?[72] Hamilton admitted in his official dispatch that 'No General on peace manœuvres would ask troops so break-neck an enterprise'.[73] Writing fifteen years later Kenneth Erskine (now a lieutenant-colonel and advisor to the Punjab states' forces, including Patiala's) laid the blame without compunction: 'not a single officer had ever seen the country over which the night march and attack was to take place'.[74] The entire enterprise, the author of the latest and most detailed study decided, was 'as good as doomed from the start'.[75] It was clear even to Ian Hamilton as he drafted his valedictory despatch that the entire scheme had been unduly, disastrously ambitious.

---

69 'Gallipoli 1915', Arthur Fergusson, 3DRL3635, AWM.
70 Bean, *The Story of Anzac*, Vol. II, p. 725.
71 War diary, 1/5th Gurkhas, August 1915, WO95/4432, NAUK.
72 Allanson, *Copy of the personal diary kept in the field*, p. 24.
73 Supplement to *London Gazette*, 6 January 1916, p. 293.
74 Letter, Kenneth Erskine to Cyril Aspinall-Oglander 18 April 1931, War diary, 1/5th Gurkhas, [filed with] August 1915, WO95/4432, NAUK.
75 Rhys Crawley, *Climax on Gallipoli*, p. 378.

'Our aims had not been fully attained', he conceded, 'and the help we had hoped for from Suvla had not been forthcoming'.[76] Hamilton's mildness, one of his admirable qualities as a man, had been a tragic flaw in a senior commander. In a private letter to Beauchamp Duff, he blamed his failure not on his own flawed plans and irresolute command, but on 'the huge unleavened mass of raw troops' who had suffered and died on the slopes of Krithia, Anzac and Sari Bair, unforgivably.[77]

76 Supplement to *London Gazette*, 6 January 1916, pp. 294-95.
77 Letter, 8 September 1915, Ian Hamilton, 7/1/29, LHCMA.

12

'Considering your duty as a warrior': Hill 60, August

After four days and nights of intense fighting the exhausted Indian battalions at last handed over their positions to the New Army units and stumbled down the Aghyl Dere to positions around Demakjelik Bair, north of Anzac. For the rest of the campaign their war would revolve around an area of about a square mile, alternating between front line trenches and cheerless reserve dugouts. There was no real rest. The Gurkhas and Sikhs immediately began entrenching, digging a line of trenches running more-or-less east-west across Demakjelik Bair that could serve as a block should the Turks break through the new line in the hills. The digging imposed a terrible burden on units that had lost half or more of their strength in the offensive. Towering above them, a thousand feet high, was the Sari Bair range: 'a most awe inspiring spectacle', Allanson wrote to Tomes's widow, Harriet.[1]

'The narrow front we hold': the Hill 60 line

The 10th Gurkhas' war diary records that 'during the day two parties [of 90 men] … after digging all the previous night were employed in digging fresh communication trenches'.[2] ('We were all pretty worn out', Cecil Allanson recorded, rejoining the 6th barely a week after being evacuated wounded.[3]) For the rest of the campaign the Indian infantry would be concentrated on a group of bare scrubby hills plagued by incessant rifle, machine-gun and artillery fire, a routine alternating between trenches and dugouts and a few violent actions. 'I can only speak for the narrow front we hold', Allanson wrote.[4] Both sides occupied new trench lines snaking over the spurs and gullies hundreds of yards apart, the victorious Turks overlooking British empire lines. Though the offensive had died down the front line remained dangerous – the Turks

---

1   Allanson to Harriet Tomes, 1915, Allanson Papers, 6602-22, NAM.
2   War diary, 2/10th Gurkhas, August 1915, WO95/4472, NAUK.
3   Notes c. 14 August 1915, Davies, *Allanson of the 6th*, p. 66.
4   Ibid., 1 September 1915, p. 75.

Sikh sepoys in the front line at Demakjelik Bair with a bomb catapult, a sign of how close Ottoman and Indian trenches were. (14th Sikhs album)

sent snipers into the open country around Demakjelik Bair. The 5th Gurkhas claimed to have killed 20-30 Turkish snipers on 10 August alone: too few. On 14 August Lieutenant Duncan Lloyd was killed while accompanying Cox in a tour of the 6th Gurkhas' piquet line. (Note, not just the front line, the piquet line; Cox's courage is unquestioned: a brigadier had no place inspecting his brigade's piquet line.)

The Gurkhas' traditional strengths in patrol work became useful, and patrols went out to dominate the rugged country. On 14 August Captain Arthur Dawes led out a patrol of men of the 10th Gurkhas, one of two to go out that day. (Why a captain, one of only several of the battalion's British officers, should be out patrolling is not clear from the battalion's war diary or history: again, the inclination of British officers to risk their lives recurs in the records.) Dawes's men 'got into trouble near the Kaiajik Dere' (the deep valley north of Demakjelik Bair): nature of trouble unspecified.[5] All but Dawes was killed or wounded, but he met Kamansing Limbu, the 10th's Scout Naik, who had got to know the area – he had captured five Turks a few days before. Kamansing had also lost all three of his men to a sniper but rather than return, the two decided to continue to search for Ottoman positions, working their way closer to Hill 60. Though seen and fired at, they not only remained out but Dawes decided to

5   Mullaly, *Bugle and Kukri*, p. 102.

Anzac and Gurkha snipers. The dress of the two demonstrates their very different attitudes toward smartness. As regulars, the Gurkhas, despite serving in the front line, wear their uniform and kit correctly: the Australians or New Zealanders adopt a more casual approach. (AWM A05612)

climb a tree to gain better observation. This foolhardy act saw Dawes shot in both legs. Kamansing began to carry Dawes but attracted more shots. He and Dawes agreed to leave Dawes in cover, to return to the Gurkha lines and return.

When Kamansing returned to the dere with another patrol Dawes was gone: captured. (Kamansing, though recommended for a gallantry award, received no decoration.) Dawes died as a prisoner of war in Constantinople in June 1917 and today lies in Haidar Pasha war cemetery overlooking the Bosphorus. Months after the landing, in a telegram from Simla (presumably instigated by relatives in India) seeking details of his fate, came a report of another man captured, on 25 April: 'Private Reginald Lushington unofficially reported prisoner by Turkish Red Crescent'.[6] His mother, Mary, was for a while alarmed that her son's allowance stopped – suggesting that he was dead, but it was only a bureaucratic hiccup.[7]

6   Tel., 9 July 1915, Duff to Wilson, Egypt, and reply, WWI/342/H, NAI.
7   507, Pte Reginald Lushington, B2455, NAA.

A man of the 29th Indian Infantry Brigade in the front line near Hill 60 in August, one of the few photographs taken on Indians under fire on Gallipoli. Though in the 14th Sikhs' album, and standing beside Sikhs, the man does not seem to be a Sikh. (14th Sikhs album)

As well as Dawes's capture the week of patrol clashes cost the 10th no fewer than seven killed and eleven wounded. Other officers escaped death or capture by luck. Gunner Cyril Mayer (or Meyer), whose Urdu had been so useful to Arthur Fergusson at Anzac, secured a transfer to the 14th Sikhs on 26 July. Mayer – or Maer as he now wished to be known – was found to possess 'professional knowledge very much above the average I[ndian] A[rmy] R[eserve of] Officer' and he joined the Sikhs as a second lieutenant.[8] In time Maer would become the brigade machine-gun officer, though he suffered from the autocratic Philip Palin. On a date unclear, Palin ordered Maer to clear a sand-bag barricade in a sunken road (presumably on the track leading to the village of Buyuk Anafarta) behind which Turkish snipers were known to lurk. Palin had meant Maer to go out at night and destroy the barricade but he did so with two men in daylight. This was debated in the Sikhs' mess dug-out as either 'one of the coolest pieces of cold-blooded gallantry known' or 'a gross breach of discipline'. Palin took the later view, shouting at Maer 'You bloody fool! … What the devil do you mean by doing it by day?' Maer, lucky that the barricade

---

8   299 Gunner Cyril Mayer, B2455, NAA.

Demakjelik Bair, looking eastwards to roughly the site of the Indian brigade headquarters in 1915. (Author)

was not manned, felt too shocked to salute and merely replied 'Sorry, sir'.[9] Later in August more Indian troops would face death and wounds in the attacks on the nearby Hill 60.

'In the main successful': the 21 August attacks

Hill 60, standing, as the name suggests, sixty feet above sea level is today known as the name (and location) of a Commonwealth War Graves Commission cemetery off the main road running between Anzac and Suvla. The few visitors who drive along the rutted and often boggy track find a large cemetery, laid out on an impressive circular plan and holding 788 graves, including 712 unknowns. The name perplexes: the site seems rather flat. It is more-or-less on the site of Hill 60, but the creation of the garden cemetery has filled in the network of trenches and flattened and beautified the hill, obscuring its tactical significance. It was the scene of some of the most horrific trench-fighting of the campaign though, judging by the headstones, not one of them

---

9   Bamford, *The Sikh Battalion*, p. 41.

The second contingent of Patiala Sikhs to serve on Gallipoli undergoing kit inspection before departure from Egypt, September 1915. (Patiala album)

were members of the Indian Army. Yet Hill 60 claimed some 100 Indian lives; and many others besides.

While the August offensive had failed and the British War Council deprecated Ian Hamilton's requests to reopen the breakout by sending more troops to the Dardanelles, Hamilton ordered further attacks north of Anzac, on Turkish lines at Hill 60, part of a larger series of attacks on the Suvla front. The offensive had ended untidily. The Turks overlooked the 'new' Anzac trench lines extending north to Suvla, especially around the entrance to the Kaiajik Dere and Hill 60. Whoever held Hill 60 commanded the coastal plain or the Turkish-held valley to the east. The hill might have been seized for nothing early in the offensive; but now Ottoman troops held it in force and it had to be fought for. Tragically, Hamilton decided to mount these attacks using troops who had already seen serious attacks and heavy losses, including the 29th Indian Brigade. Though presented as a way of winning the garrison of Anzac 'elbow room' and gaining them access to water wells, the attacks were to cost the lives of thousands of troops, Ottoman and British empire, to little purpose.

The British 9th Corps, holding the Suvla line, was detailed to attack locally dominant hills to the north, while the Anzac Corps was ordered to devise attacks on Hill 60 and to seize the wells Susak Kuyu and Kabak Kuyu. Herbert Cox, the senior brigadier on the spot, was given the job of planning the Anzac attacks (the attack straddled the boundary between the 9th Corps and Anzac Corps, in itself a recipe for failure). He chose to make them using a patchwork of units drawn from several divisions. The opening attack, on 21 August, involved 400 New Zealand Mounted Riflemen

A folded print of a blurred photograph of no man's land looking toward Hill 60 in the late summer of 1915, showing the bare ground over which British empire troops attacked. (14th Sikhs album)

(dismounted, obviously), 350 men of two battalions of the 4th Australian Brigade, men of the 18th Battalion of another Australian brigade, 330 Hampshire New Army men, the 5th Connaught Rangers of the newly arrived 10th (Irish) Division, the 4th South Wales Borderers (of the 13th Division) and the three Gurkha battalions of his own brigade. The 14th Sikhs, despite receiving drafts from several Sikh regiments and the Burma Military Police (recruited in the Punjab) was too depleted even to be considered. The scratch force from half a dozen countries was necessary because no individual component amounted to more than a weak battalion – the Australians, of four battalions, totalled only 350 men, almost all suffering from exhaustion, battle fatigue and dysentery. Using so many units from so many formations practically ensured that it would fail amid confusion and miscommunication: as it did. Why he accepted such a force (which, working through so many headquarters must have been harder to co-ordinate and control) is unknown. Cox had acquiesced before, and by late August he was sick and tired.

The Hill 60 attacks have largely been ignored – the battlefield is confusing and today hard to find or reach, less visited than any of the Gallipoli battlefields except the remote slopes north of Suvla. Lacking the scenic drama of so many sites on Gallipoli, it is hard today to grasp the terrain, which like much of Anzac has changed beyond recognition. The attacks failed, though unspectacularly, unlike, say, at Krithia or the Nek. And yet in the forces involved, Hill 60 offers a reminder that Gallipoli truly was an imperial campaign. The troops involved came from almost every element of the Mediterranean Expeditionary Force: they fought, failed, suffered and died together.

The Indian brigade's starting position was on the plain below and to the north-west of Demakjelik Bair, the link between the British 9th Corps and the Anzac troops – literally the left hand men of the entire Anzac position. Even holding the trenches cost casualties. The 14th Sikhs and the 6th Gurkhas held the line while the 5th and 10th joined in the attack, making for the well of Susak Kuyu. The Sikhs suffered 30 casualties on 21 and 22 August, including seven Patialas killed.

Cecil Allanson thought that the attack should have been made at night and was dismayed at the lightness of the preliminary bombardment. He noticed of his men that 'every face was strained and drawn': so much for the relentlessly cheerful Gurkha.[10] The attack was, the 5th Gurkhas' war diary recorded, 'in the main successful'.[11] The Gurkhas attacked together, with the 10th on the left, the 5th on the right and the 6th in support. Though struck by rifle and machine-gun fire as soon as they left their trenches (because the bombardment stopped prematurely, as soon as they went over the top), the Gurkhas pressed on and reached their objectives. The 10th took the wells while the 5th took an area called 'Green Patch Farm', on the track to the village of Buyuk Anafarta. Officers later described the attack from within. Survivors told Hugh Lane how 'it was made over open ground exposed to enfilade fire from the wells and from Hill 60 itself'. Almost immediately the 5th's leading company lost its two British officers, killed and wounded. The acting adjutant, Lieutenant Harry Cummins, hearing this immediately went forward to lead the foremost men on. He too was killed 'as were all the men with him'. Only by seeking the shelter of a sunken road (still visible today) was Captain Henry Molloy able to make contact with the Connaught Rangers, and two more British officers fell wounded that day.[12] Bean subscribed to the view that 'the Gurkhas depended almost entirely upon the leadership of their white officers', and he thought that losses among them explained the hold up. Since the 'white' units engaged also made no headway against Mauser bullets and Krupp shells, the explanation probably lies elsewhere.

Early the following morning – evidently before dawn – Allanson ordered the 6th Gurkhas' remaining double company forward to the new line. As they prepared to leave Turkish shells fell on the trench. Only one man was hit, but it was Subedar-Major Gambirsing Pun, who had commanded the battalion on Sari Bair. Pun fell wounded in the head by shrapnel. Though 'nearly senseless', he told his orderly to fetch Allanson, who described his shock at seeing Pun wounded. Pun called to Allanson

> 'Sahib, what will you do without me? What will the regiment do? I do not mind death – what is that! But you want me, and the regiment wants me, and I cannot be spared.'

Pun took Allanson's hand and Allanson told him to 'be of good cheer', reassuring him that they would carry on to the end. Pun 'would not be comforted', but was carried off to Edward Phipson's dressing station and Rothney Battye's field ambulance. The incident prompted further reflection from Allanson: 'war is horrible and

---

10 Diary, 21 August 1915, Davies, *Allanson of the 6th*, p. 68.
11 War diary, 1/5th Gurkhas, August 1915, WO95/4472, NAUK.
12 Letter, Hugh Lane, in War diary, 1/5th Gurkhas, August 1915, WO95/4472, NAUK.

loathsome', he wrote, redeemed only by witnessing a man willing to live by for others, 'making one's life a willing sacrifice'.[13]

Elsewhere on 21 August the dismounted yeomanry regiments of the British 2nd Mounted Division had advanced from the coast across the shining white surface of the salt lake (foolishly; in full view of Turkish gunners, and they paid the price accordingly). Indian mule teams followed carrying their ammunition. A yeomanry medical officer admired how the muleteers shared the danger and 'showed the greatest contempt for the enemy's fire'.[14] The New Army flanking units on the right, in the Suvla sector, could make no headway and the Gurkhas found their northern (or left) flank open to Ottoman fire. On the Australian front the weak 4th Brigade units lost heavily as they emerged, and their wounded faced the horror that the scrub, tinder-dry in summer, caught fire, scorching men helpless before the flames. In the end the 10th took the well of Susak Kuyu and the Connaught Rangers some trenches on the lower slopes of Hill 60. In retrospect it might have been better if they had failed. The partial success encouraged Cox, and above him Godley and Birdwood to order the effort be resumed.

The 10th held a position almost half-a-mile ahead of the line, exposed to the rear and subject to Ottoman fire from ahead and the left. (Cox's staff seemed unaware of their success and the British official history recorded that they too had failed. Only careful scrutiny by the Australian official historian's account and the testimony of other Gurkha battalions' officers later established the facts.) The 10th had again achieved is objective with light loss: only eleven other ranks killed, though 63 wounded, plus two British and three Gurkha officers. The mortal wounding of the battalion's officers' mess cook, Bahadur Thapa, represented a grievous loss. And again the niggardly award of medals failed to recognise the battalion's achievement. It was significant that Jemadar Nar Bahadur Rai received the 2nd Class Indian Order of Merit, a sign that far from needing British officers, the Gurkhas' willingness to go forward under fire owed much to the Gurkha officers' example and encouragement.

On the evening of the 21st the 10th Gurkhas held the line around the well at Susak Kuyu, with a motley assembly of units straggling southwards along the old Turkish lines; in order the Connaught Rangers, the 10th Light Horse, the 5th Gurkhas, the New Zealand Mounted Rifles and the Australians of the 4th Brigade. A hundred men of the 14th Sikhs were sent forward to help hold the Gurkhas' line, in time to meet a crowd of 300 Turks in no man's land 'making a beastly noise' – were they attacking or were they coming over to surrender?[15] The Sikhs fired on them anyway, taking a dozen or more captive. In the new trench lines the Gurkhas and Sikhs (like the European troops) immediately went to work to strengthening and deepening the trenches. The 5th Gurkhas' war diary noted that though they were tired 'the men were constantly

---

13 Diary, 22 August 1915, Davies, *Allanson of the 6th*, p. 69.
14 Teichman, *The Diary of a Yeomanry M.O.*, p. 28.
15 Diary, 23 August 1915, Humphrey Gell, P158, 10048, IWM.

on fatigue & burying the dead'.[16] Though occupying trenches often just yards from the hill's Ottoman defenders' trenches, both sides used artillery. On 22 August the 10th Gurkhas recorded that they were shelled by both British and Ottoman artillery at different times, and losing six killed and 15 wounded 'all by British shell fire'.[17]

Demonstrating yet again the value of their mobility, one of Fergusson's mountain guns had been carried into the old Australian forward trenches and was firing into the Turkish defenders of Hill 60, who nevertheless hung on. The Gurkhas entrenched on the days following, their exposed position unclear to British artillery, which again mistakenly shelled their trenches, killing three and wounding another fifteen. A week later, after further Irish and Australian attacks, in which they and the Turks fought with rifles, bayonets and bombs in a filthy shambles, the Turks regained some of the trenches they had lost. Late in August Cox launched a further series of attacks (which the Indians mainly supported) and regained part of the Hill. There the carnage stopped. The 5th Gurkhas relieved the Connaughts and the 6th then took over. Early in September the Sikhs took over the line, then the newly-arrived 1/4th Gurkhas. They took their turn in a maze of trenches and machine-gun posts. After gaining possession of part of the shell-torn and festering trenches on the hill – the Turks always held its low summit – the line settled down to what a 5th Gurkha officer called 'the routine of trench warfare, with its long spells of drudgery, punctuated by moments of intense excitement'.[18]

'400 more acres of Turkish territory': judgment on Hill 60

Hill 60, though a significant tactical feature, was hardly worth the death of the Gurkhas' mess cook, let along hundreds of others. It is arguable that attempting to take it cost many more lives than not taking it would have. Herbert Cox thought that both of the attacks the Indians made on Hill 60 had been successful, even though 'a much more difficult and complicated job' than he had expected. The task proved difficult in every way. Co-ordinating infantry and artillery, with the primitive communications available, remained hard. Attacking – in this case against Turkish infantry determined to hold their ground and armed with machine-guns and bombs – was always difficult. Even if the attackers could take the position they had to hold it. 'keeping them is the difficulty', Cox admitted. 'I never reckon a position as really gained till we have held it for three nights'. But even if they were to seize and hold the Turkish trenches on the smoking, dusty knoll, the point of their sacrifice remained obscure. Again the contending armies fought over minor tactical features, possession of which made no difference to the outcome of the campaign. Cox, like all officers, found that he had to order men to perform deeds that would almost certainly result in

---

16 War diary, 1/5th Gurkhas, August 1915, WO95/4472, NAUK.
17 War diary, 2/10th Gurkhas, August 1915, WO95/4472, NAUK.
18 Regimental Committee, *History of the 5th Royal Gurkha Rifles*, p. 265.

some being killed or wounded. In a rare moment of introspection around the time his men were attacking Hill 60 he admitted that 'one has to harden one's heart sometimes when one sends them into these assaults & knows half will be knocked out even if the show comes off well'.[19] Seemingly easy phrases like 'knocked out', mask Cox's feelings – he often visited the front line.

Cox was proud of his brigade's part in the Hill 60 attacks. His typescript diary includes a clipping from a bulletin issued by Anzac headquarters a week later, describing 'the attack on Knoll 60', in which 'the capture of the hill was entrusted to Major-General Cox'. It announced that 'the position has been consolidated, and a good view now obtained over the valley to the North'. It admitted that the attacks had cost a thousand British empire casualties, but claimed that they had inflicted 5,000 Ottoman casualties. The admission that the three days of fighting in an area little larger than a football pitch had 'gained 400 more acres of Turkish territory' must have dismayed those wondering if they were to make the next attempt. Nevertheless, Cox retained his officers' respect ('seems a very good chap & is I believe a good soldier', wrote Arthur Tillard).[20] Through August and into September the Indians around Hill 60 held trench lines in an area 'strewn with bodies' – of Gurkhas, Australians, New Zealanders and Connaught Rangers – and Turks, of course. Allanson described 'the smell, another of the minor horrors of war' as 'appalling, the sights revolting'.[21]

The assaults on Hill 60 produced an incongruously small number of gallantry awards compared to the effort the attackers made. Two jemadars, one from each of the two Gurkha battalions involved, received Indian Orders of Merit for their 'gallantry and devotion to duty' on 21 August. Jemadar Nandlal Gurung of the 6th Gurkhas was commended for his actions on that day when he 'recklessly exposed himself to encourage his men to advance over a plain under a heavy shrapnel and rifle fire. He insisted on remaining in the trenches though badly shaken by a shell burst. Jemadar Nar Bahadur Rai of the 10th 'encouraged his men to advance under a heavy shrapnel and machine gun-fire.[22] In both cases Indian officers were praised for encouraging their men to go forward: a sign that after four months of almost continuous action even the devoted men of the old Indian Army were losing their resolve in the face of such hardship and losses.

Later in the fight for Hill 60 the mountain gunners were included in planning, though not very well. Arthur Fergusson, back off the sick list from a septic foot, arrived at the Number 2 Outpost position to learn that an attack was to be made against Hill 60, though no one seems to have thought to advise the mountain guns – an extraordinary lapse by officers who by this time were experienced, though also exhausted. Fergusson and his gunner 'chipped in as best we could', though not as well as they

19 Cox, papers, 1DRL221, AWM.
20 Diary, 8 September 1915, Arthur Tillard, GM.
21 Diary, 23 August 1915, Davies, *Allanson of the 6th*, p. 70.
22 Hypher, *Deeds of Valour*, p. 289.

might have had the guns been included in the planning of the attack. Later, Herbert Cox told Fergusson to select a position from which his guns could fire directly at Hill 60. Knowing the value of plunging fire – that is, shells that arrive from above the target, he selected a position 600 yards from the objective. Cox then told Fergusson that his position would not do and that he wanted the mountain guns 'here', pointing to a spot on the map. 'Here', Fergusson thought, would not suit, but having been told to dig in he had his men dig emplacements overnight. Sure enough, at dawn it became clear that the position Cox had specified did not give the guns direct fire at Hill 60, and at least one of them needed to be shifted. After what Fergusson described as 'some fairly dangerous reconnoitring', they found a better site, though one exposed to Turkish snipers 450 yards away. By this time Kohat Battery was operating in six separate detachments when it was short of everything from trained signallers to British officers – it had only three officers to cover the six separate positions. The mountain gunners concentrated at trying to impede the movement of Turkish reinforcements. He described, in a gruesome passage, how he succeeded in breaking down part of the Turkish parapet and could see the heads men moving toward the fight. He continued to fire on the spot, and soon could see down to their knees 'presumably because they were walking over their dead'. Fergusson told Gerald Pepys that if his gun had been able to fire twenty rather than just two rounds a minute he 'could have stopped the Turks altogether and our men would have had the whole knoll'.[23] But Humphrey Gell's judgment seems soundest: 'a terrific big show for a very small hill'.[24]

Though the summer offensive had failed, officers who had borne the brunt of the campaign were recognised. At the end of August the *London Gazette* carried notifications that British officers had been awarded decorations – Rawson and Thom of the Kohat Battery received DSOs (somewhat unusual in going to men who had been promoted to captain only during the campaign), while Frederick Rossiter and Everard Whitting of Jacob's Battery received the Military Cross, joining Kirby, whose MC had been gazetted in July. Though he had been given to understand that he was to be recommended for the Victoria Cross, Allanson heard no more. When Hamilton visited the 29th Brigade just before his departure in October he said nothing about the 6th Gurkhas' feat of reaching the crest of Sari Bair (perhaps embarrassed that he had again made a plan that failed at such cost). Allanson later learned that Godley and Birdwood had endorsed Cox's recommendation but that Hamilton had not. Despite having invented the modern system of honours for outstanding conduct in battle, the British armies remained niggardly in recognising acts of courage, leadership or self-sacrifice. In fact, Allanson received the Distinguished Service Order; no mean decoration, but not what he deserved and, indeed, had been led to believe he would receive. Sensing his unreliability, perhaps – his devotion to telling the truth rather than a convenient fiction – may explain the curious outcome.

---

23 War diary, 29th Indian Infantry Brigade, August 1915, 187, AWM 6.
24 Diary, 29 August 1915, Humphrey Gell, P158, 10048, IWM.

Norman Wimbush's drawings of men of the 14th Sikhs firing a periscope rifle (left) and of a sniping team operating (with a British officer observing and a sepoy firing) from the trenches at Demakjelik Bair. (14th Sikhs album)

'Common language': Indians and empire troops

The fighting around Hill 60 brought into contact Australian and British troops who had had little experience of Indians. Their comments reinforce the impressions we have already seen. With units from four armies joining the attacks on Hill 60, men had ample opportunity to observe and judge each others' efforts. The New Zealander George Cloughley described in a letter home how 'the Ghurkas [sic] and Maoris done good work'. Cloughley was one of many who persevered in talking to Gurkhas, and his description suggests how the two understood each other:

> A Ghurka [sic] was explaining the advance to me, his knees ... scratched by the rough ground and scrub ... he mimicked them sneaking up a hill on their stomachs ... said "Pur-r-r machine gun" and ducked his little black head, then made me imagine Turks running like hares and yelling "Allah Allah" or surrendering and begging for mercy.[25]

Cloughley noticed wounds in some Gurkhas' left hands: 'through seizing the Turks' bayonet[s] to use the terrible kukri'. He was not alone in admiring the Gurkhas' willingness to attack aggressively. 'One of the most impressive sights' he saw was 'a wounded N.Zer with his arm round a wounded Ghurka walking down a Gully ... the

25 Cloughley, (ed.), 'The Riverton Boys', p. 25

N.Zer with his arm round "Johnny's" short bullock neck and Johnny's arm [around] the N.Zer's back'.

George King, a train guard from the Hunter Valley in New South Wales, serving in the 19th Battalion, described his first encounter with the trenches at Hill 60 that Gurkhas and British troops had just taken from the Turks: 'very dirty and narrow and all round dead men are lying in all stages of decomposition and the smell is horrible ... We went to work ... widening and deepening communication trench leading into Ghurkhas [sic] firing line'.[26] It was not just George's first impression of Gurkhas, but the first exposure to war for the newly-arrived men of the 2nd Australian Division. He later, heard that the Turks had counter-attacked but had been repulsed by Gurkhas and British troops. This prompted George to record his impressions of Indian troops since he had arrived on the peninsula. 'Nothing too good can be said about them,' he wrote. 'They are a fine, sturdy, strongly built lot of men ... and are very brave, their religion being that if they die on the battlefield, they will surely go to Heaven'. The Sikhs,' he thought 'another Indian tribe', were 'more of a mixed lot' – meaning that they included some tall men – and 'quieter, although they are also very brave'. Both demonstrated 'a great respect for the Australian and New Zealand boys', and the Gurkhas 'do their best to talk to us, but very few of them speak English'.[27]

Sometimes men needed no words. The shared ordeal of the fight for Hill 60 can be seen in the recollection of a man from Christchurch, New Zealand. Many years after he had been wounded at Hill 60, Justin Westenra, formerly of the Otago Mounted Rifles, described his arrival aboard a hospital ship. He lay alongside 'a little Gurkha', both on mattresses. 'I looked at mine and he looked at his and we both grinned' at the unaccustomed luxury. 'We couldn't speak a common language', Mr Westenra recalled, 'but we were so pleased'.[28] Westenra and the anonymous Gurkha sank back to enjoy 'beautiful peace and blissfulness' of a hospital ship. For their comrades, the fighting at Hill 60 continued.

The intensity of both the fighting at Hill 60 and the bonds that formed under fire between Australians and Gurkhas can be glimpsed from a paragraph published in an Australian periodical. An Australian captain, Ross Harwood of the 16th Battalion, wrote his wife in Sydney to explain that he had been slightly wounded in the face. His wife at first read her husband's letter as a 'splinter of Gurkha's lead', which made no sense to her. Harwood later explained. He had taken charge of a group of Gurkhas who had lost their officer. Coming under fire, one of them had 'sprung in front of him' to protect him and had been hit. A fragment of bone from

---

26 Diary, 1 September 1915, George King, <http://users.bigpond.net.au/rhearne/gallipolli5.htm>
27 Diary, 4 and 5 October 1915, ibid.
28 Interview, Justin Westenra, PLC.

Three men of the Patiala Rajindra Infantry who may have served on Gallipoli, showing the sepoys' uniform and kit. As Sikhs they wear the sacred 'kara', or metal ring, on the turban. (Patiala album)

the unknown Gurkha's *head* had pierced Harwood's face. The doctor who cut it out was keeping it 'as a curio'.[29]

'Number doctors in Egypt ample': the wounded after the August offensive

'The hospital arrangements were bad', Cecil Allanson flatly wrote, possibly while he lay on a stretcher in a dressing station, though he admitted a few lines on that 'the Indian Brigade hospital arrangements were really jolly good'.[30] Rothney Battye, with characteristic energy, developed a large hospital site on the slope of Chailik Dere, adding and strengthening his tented and sand-bagged wards. But even the optimistic Heber Alexander admitted that the wounded of the offensive lay in hundreds in the summer sun, tormented by flies and thirst, where they 'suffered terribly from exposure and neglect' because the medical units could not cope with the influx.[31]

In the course of the campaign at least 4,000 Indian troops were wounded. Joseph Beeston, whose 4th Field Ambulance supported the attack on Chunuk Bair, saw that Sikhs and Gurkhas 'all seemed to think that it was part of the game; patience loomed large among their virtues'.[32] The more 'lightly' wounded remained with their units, relying on rest to return them to health. Most of the others were carried, down the gullies to the dressing stations and to the jetties and wharfs where tenders and lighters would take them to the hospital ships and transports lying offshore. Virtually all of Gallipoli's wounded were probably also sick as well. Diarrhoea claimed practically every man through the fly-blown summer.

All wounded men experienced similar sensations – of physical pain, of course, but also the relief of knowing that they had escaped the ordeal of the front line. For Indian troops the experience was overlain with contrasting emotions – the anxiety of leaving the security of the comrades among which they lived, but also for some the excitement of seeing more of the world beyond India and its army. Indian casualties were carried and treated aboard hospital ships and medical transports virtually indistinguishably to their British or Anzac counterparts. While they might be handled by Indian orderlies sometimes able to speak their language, they experienced little undue discrimination – indeed, in that special ration scales were laid down for them, they received the Indian Army's customary administrative solicitude.

Many wounded found the swift transition from the front overwhelmingly – when he was sent aboard a hospital transport in July John Gillam noticed among the wounded 'a few Punjabis', who 'sit apart philosophically and say nothing' – perhaps intimidated by the novelty of being looked after by white orderlies or even nurses

---

29 *Bulletin*, 9 December 1915, p. 14.
30 Undated report, possibly written 10 August 1915, Davies, *Allanson of the 6th*, pp. 57-58.
31 Alexander, *On Two Fronts*, p. 230.
32 Beeston, *Five Months at Anzac*, p. 56.

– but perhaps simply exhausted by months of arduous service and now wounds.[33] Conditions in Indian hospitals remained notably more Spartan than in British, Australian and New Zealand establishments. In peacetime the condition of Indian native hospitals had been poor: the outspoken Charles Bruce condemned them as 'a real scandal'. European military hospitals, whose patients' welfare depended upon 'comforts' donated by civilian charities at home, principally the Red Cross. Indian military hospitals had less abundant facilities (lacking even basic furniture besides charpoys, for instance) and generally without the support of charities supplying, for example, soap or towels. While European hospital patients received special 'hospital blues' (partly to ensure that they could be identified and controlled) Indians were obliged to wear civilian clothes, something which men evacuated from the peninsula clad only in filthy and blood-stained uniforms could not usually count on. (It explains why the few photographs of Indian wounded from Gallipoli show them looking like ragamuffins, dependent upon the charity of British civilians in Egypt.) Later in August No. 5 Indian General Hospital expanded to 700 beds – the equivalent of a battalion on service – and it was only one of two Indian hospitals in Egypt, with other Indian casualties sent to Malta.

Indian wounded, like their Anzac and British comrades, faced protracted treatment and convalescence. When visiting Alexandria late in the summer Heber Alexander visited wounded muleteers in an Indian hospital. He found some 'disabled for life', including Ajaib Shah, with his elbow shattered, his arm useless.[34] They would be pensioned, living in poverty on a tiny allowance. Others – those less severely wounded – were judged able to return to the front after convalescence, not always willingly. This contravened the Indian soldier's traditional implicit contract, a grievance expressed by many of the wounded whose letters from British hospitals the censors intercepted.[35] 'Only those who have lost a leg or an arm or an eye will see the Punjab again', a Musalman soldier told his family from Europe.[36]

One wounded Indian facing such a future was Chanda Singh, a Sikh muleteer. While serving as orderly to one of the Indian medical officers in 108th Field Ambulance he had lit what he thought was a lamp – a friend had taken it from the trenches. It was actually a bomb – both had wicks. Chanda Singh's error led to him losing his left hand and part of his lower jaw. Heber Alexander visited him aboard the hospital ship *Sicilia* and spoke to him. Despite his wounds, Chanda Singh was able to converse, and told Alexander how having seen his sahib he could now die content. The hospital ship's medical officers had little hope that he would survive the journey to Egypt, and Alexander never learned if he survived. (As no 'Chanda Singh' appears

33 Gillam, *Gallipoli Diary*, p. 103.
34 Alexander, *On Two Fronts*, p. 242.
35 Omissi, *The Sepoy and the Raj*, p. 118
36 Ibid.

on the Commonwealth War Graves Commission's lists of dead, he may have survived only to face poverty.)

Even before the massive casualties of the August offensive the evacuation of Indian wounded from the peninsula to Egypt and back to India became strained. Staff officers in India complained to Egypt of 'conditions of over-crowding and insanitation' on ships arriving in Bombay (claims which Maxwell's staff investigated and refuted).[37] Indian wounded usually followed a common route; back to Alexandria either direct or via the general hospitals on Lemnos, though a few reached Britain, either by accident or because their wounds demanded more sophisticated treatment. One who arrived by accident was Havildar Chandra Singh Rana of the 6th Gurkhas, wounded by a bomb and picked up unconscious on a stretcher at Anzac. Mistaken for a Maori, he was sent aboard a hospital ship leaving for Britain. By the time he recovered consciousness he could not be returned and, unable to communicate with anyone aboard, apparently spent a lonely time in a hospital in Hampshire until hospital authorities contacted Charles Bruce, who enterprisingly appropriated him as an informal orderly. If medical arrangements remained inadequate medical staff officers did not necessarily accept all the assistance available. In response to an offer from a 'lady doctor', Miss R.E. Glanville, Maxwell cabled brusquely 'Do not want lady doctors number doctors in Egypt ample'.[38]

Meanwhile, Indian Army medical units received and treated casualties from Gallipoli. Vyner Jones, another railwayman from New South Wales who had been badly wounded on the peninsula soon after the landing, had been admitted to a hospital in a former hotel in Alexandria taken over by the Indian Medical Service. He told his father that it was 'a "bonza" [very good] place'. Vyner described its doctors and orderlies (all Indians) as having 'plenty of skill'. (They needed it: Vyner had suffered a compound fracture of his right leg.) He wrote that 'they say all Indians are very gentle in their ways' and he thought himself 'lucky being in such hands'.[39] Other observers found the experience of working with Indian medical orderlies frustrating. Rita Lyons, an Australian nurse from western Queensland nursing on the hospital ship *Guildford Castle* (and one of the few Australian nurses to work with Indians in 1915), wrote home that 'they do get on one's nerves – always stand at attention and salute if you look at them'. Indian orderlies, imbued with the superiority of white men and especially women, found it hard to accept that nurses were to work. Rita complained that they 'won't let you carry a dish', but conceded that at nursing 'they are good though'.[40]

37 Tel., 30 July 1915, Duff to Maxwell, and reply, WWI/295/H, NAI.
38 Tel., 31 July 1915, Maxwell to Duff, WWI/296/H, NAI.
39 Letter, 16 May 1915, Pte Vyner Jones, 1st Battalion, AIF, PR360, AWM.
40 *Western Champion and Commercial Advertiser*, 23 October 1915.

Leslie Hore's water-colour, of 'Mule Gully'. (State Library of New South Wales)

'With his face to the foe': the stress of battle

In 1915 the Indian Army faced serious stresses. 'The frontier', Sir Charles Lucas opined in *The Empire at War*, 'is always unsteady'.[41] 1915, Hardinge recalled, became the year of the largest military operations on the north-west frontier since 1897, when it had blazed. By the end of 1914 the Indian Army had 100,000 men – nearly two-thirds of its fighting strength, on active service outside India. Campaigns in East Africa, Mesopotamia, south-west Arabia, Persia and Gallipoli, not to mention the costly fighting in Flanders, were not the Indian Army's only commitments. Intelligence summaries prepared weekly at Army Headquarters show that the frontier was rarely quiet. As the August offensive on Gallipoli failed, on the north-west frontier 4,000 'Hindustani fanatics' occupied the Ambeyla Pass. A mullah raised his standard at Shabkadr 'and Mohmand tribesmen were becoming very excited'. A week later Buner tribesmen fired at cavalry patrols, a lashkar (force) 15,000-strong was reported gathering in Swat and reports arrived that in the Upper Swat valley 'all the tribes have agreed to fight'. At the month's end 24 Afridis of the 19th Punjabis deserted and made for Afghanistan, while eight men of the Zhob Militia were caught attempting to desert – one of them had received a letter advising that 'the Turks were marching

41   Lucas, *The Empire at War*, Vol. V, p. 182.

on India'.⁴² Meeting these threats consumed all of one and part of another division. While Force G was not the army's largest commitment, it was part of the greatest crisis the Indian Army had seen since 1857.

After the battles the bureaucracy continued. As in June, the ferocity and confusion of the fighting precluded orderly record-keeping. Many casualties in the August offensive are recorded simply as 'killed' or 'wounded'. As a report noted: 'all above casualties probably occurred between 6th and 10th August but definite information not yet to hand'. Herbert Cox simply recorded in his diary that in a week of fighting from 6 August his brigade had lost a thousand men. Casualty lists begin to note men wounded 'second occasion'. A Kohat Battery list of seven men wounded in August included three who had already been wounded in April or May. These men included Subedar Mit Singh of the Kohat battery, Rifleman Padambir Thapa (wounded on 13 May and killed on 5 July) and Captain Jack Dallas of the 6th, severely wounded in the taking of Gurkha Bluff and mortally wounded in the head in August. He died in Egypt a month later without regaining consciousness. Buried at Chatby cemetery, Alexandria, he is one of the almost a hundred Indian Gallipoli dead not explicitly commemorated on the peninsula.

The lists of casualties transmitted to Simla often included details of the location and severity of men's wounds, and they again include many references to wounds in the hands: more than mere happenstance would allow. It seems that men drafted from other regiments and Patiala men were particularly susceptible to inflict a wound to escape the peninsula. In a list of 36 Patiala casualties in August no fewer than eleven were wounded in the left hand or wrist, or the right index ('trigger') finger. Others bore wounds on the left foot or knee. In the same list there are no wounds in the left hand in the 14th Sikhs whom they served alongside. Birdwood's qualified comment to Hamilton ('they are doing all right – the remnants of them that is') reveals how precarious even sympathetic commanders recognised was their morale.⁴³

The enquiries prompted by the casualty telegrams were not simply motivated by comradely or paternal concern. As depot staff looked through a mid-July return, they like the historian could not help notice the number of wounds to sepoys' hands. 'Will you kindly let me know if the man's statement is correct …'?, he asked guardedly.⁴⁴ The officer commanding the 45th Sikhs' depot at Multan wrote to check Sepoy Hukam Singh's statement about his wound. Hukam Singh (one of the men drafted to the 14th from another Sikh regiment) was one of a large group of Indian wounded sent to hospitals in Malta; perhaps the man holding his bandaged hand in the photograph showing smiling Sikh wounded there, evidently and understandably relieved to be out of the trenches. (The reply came back 'Hukam Singh Shrapnel wound left hand 14 May' – his wound could not possibly have been self-inflicted: but that officers felt

---

42   Intelligence summaries, August 1915, WWI/150/H, NAI.
43   Letter, 8 September 1915, Ian Hamilton, 7/1/29, LHCMA.
44   Tel., 17 July 1915, and reply, OC 45th Sikhs to Adjutant-General, WWI/342/H, NAI.

obliged to ask suggested flaws in the resilience of their hard-pressed men.)[45] Officers must have investigated other suspected cases. This evidence is neither conclusive nor uncontested.[46] Besides the confidence in the Sikhs expressed by their British officers, the entire rhetoric of the Sikh faith professed an explicit resilience to the hardships of war. The battalion's gurus quoted the great Sikh gurus' many pronouncements urging the Khalsa to endure:

> Who loseth his life with his face to the foe
> For all the drops of blood that fall from his body
> So many years shall he enjoy the company of his God.[47]

Indeed, it is incontrovertible that the great majority of Indian troops endured conditions on Gallipoli as bad as, or worse than, those facing soldiers of other armies. Perhaps the most concise explanation of 'what carried many Indian men through the struggle' was offered by De Witt Ellinwood, who offered 'a kind of religious fatalism combined with a sense of pride' in their units.[48]

The attacks on Hill 60 were the last offensive operations the Indians mounted on Gallipoli. Though the campaign had exactly four more months to run. The Indians, except for some of the Supply and Transport men now serving together, endured a miserable autumn in the trenches of Demakjelik Bair.

45 Tel., 17 July 1915, OC, Depot, 45th Sikhs to Adjutant-General, India, WWI/342/H, NAI.
46 I am grateful to participants at the conference 'India and the Great War', held at the United Service Institution of India in March 2014, especially Harry Fecitt, who demonstrated the difference various weapon drills could make in the trenches.
47 History of Patiala State Forces, Part III, p. 70, Maharaja of Patiala collection.
48 Ellinwood & Pradhan, *India and World War I*, p. 184.

13

'Shall we live to return to India?' Demakjelik Bair, September-October

The failure of the August offensive, on which so much hope had been pinned, depressed men holding the dangerous, dirty and disease-ridden trenches around Demakjelik Bair, in the foothills of the Sari Bair range. When Arthur Tillard reached Lemnos at the end of August, he was told that 'there wasn't a chance of breaking through'.[1] Though victory had eluded the invaders, months of suffering remained, though a greatly reduced intensity of fighting, before the campaign would end. (Indeed, the August offensive began only 103 days into the 239 days the campaign lasted.) Through the autumn more Indian troops would be serving on the peninsula than ever. While the August offensive ended in exhaustion in the second week of August, the consequences of extending the Anzac position and landing a large British force around Suvla Bay continued to demand of the Indians further sacrifices around Hill 60, 'most unpleasant spot in the line'.[2]

'So different from France': arrival of 1/4th Gurkhas

In August the War Office (possibly at Hamilton's request) raised with Maxwell the possibility of sending from Egypt to Gallipoli the 28th Indian Brigade, or at least the 51st and 54th Sikhs (also Jat Sikh 'class regiments'). Maxwell 'for once put his own toes in the ground', as his sympathetic biographer described it, arguing that he could spare no more trained troops, and there the matter rested.[3] Instead, a further battalion of Gurkhas was to be sent from France. The 1/4th Gurkhas, which had been the very first Indian unit to embark in 1914, had fought at Neuve Chapelle, Ypres and Festubert, losing 250 dead. Made up by reinforcements to 990 strong, they at least had a holiday of a kind aboard its transport (again, the *Teesta*) from Marseilles, arrived at Anzac on 7 September and took over a section of trenches a week later.

---

1   Diary, 30 August 1915, Arthur Tillard, GM.
2   Humphrey Gell Papers, P158, 10048, IWM.
3   Arthur, *Sir John Maxwell*, p. 191

Coming from the Western Front, Lieutenant-Colonel Hugh Bateman-Champain's 1/4th officers found their situation 'unsatisfactory' – their trenches were overlooked by the Turks, artillery support was even more niggardly than in Flanders and many of the Indian troops were recruits, not fully trained. They were dismayed to find that 'they were constantly under fire, and could get no real rest at all' (in France billets could be out of artillery range) and 'food was bad and drinking water scarce'.[4] Arthur Tillard complained he could not get equipment he expected (such as telephones) and damned the Gallipoli force as 'a rotten run show & so different from France'.[5] The newcomers spent three weeks in the line without relief, working to improve the trenches, which they found 'much below the standard of those in France'.[6] The old hands, Humphrey Gell wrote, 'get rather tired of it'.[7] As newcomers the 4th Gurkhas' war diary described reactions to conditions that most Indian troops had become used to. A month after arrival the 4th's war diary noted that a mild form of dysentery was 'becoming very prevalent' – all of its British officers suffered from it, and every week men were evacuated sick; more than were wounded.[8] (Influenced by their Western Front experience the 4th also reported that they thought that the Turks were preparing to use poison gas – they were not.)

Reinforcement drafts reached the battalions, but all observers described them critically. Cecil Allanson thought drafts to the 6th 'chiefly little recruit boys of only seven months service' who could not understand army Hindustani.[9] Fenton Aylmer's forebodings in 1914 proved to be well-founded. The heavy losses in France could not easily be replenished, and the casualties on Gallipoli merely added to the crisis faced by Sikh and Gurkha recruiters and depot staff. Despite intensive recruiting from the war's outbreak by the time Indian troops landed on Gallipoli the depots were full of young soldiers, although 'coming on' under their drill havildars, as the Commander-in-Chief advised the War Office.[10] Frank Coen described them as 'mere boys'.[11]

It is hard to establish what either newcomers or veterans thought about the trenches around Demakjelik Bair. Censorship records for forces E and G may have existed and were destroyed after their usefulness passed; or they might never have existed. In November the Army of Occupation in Egypt acquired the services of Khan Sahib Fazl Rahman Khan, of the North-West Frontier Province Police, who had been 'entrusted with the conduct of many delicate enquiries of a confidential nature, demanding loyalty, tact and discretion'.[12] How else but by reading men's letters would

---

4   Macdonell & Macaulay, *A History of the 4th Prince of Wales's Own Gurkha Rifles*, p. 273.
5   Diary, 14 October 1915, Arthur Tillard, GM
6   Macdonell & Macaulay, *A History of the 4th Prince of Wales's Own Gurkha Rifles*, p. 274.
7   Diary, 2 October 1915, Humphrey Gell, P158, 10048, IWM.
8   War diary, 1/4th Gurkha Rifles, October 1915, WO95/4472, NAUK.
9   Diary, c. 14 September-4 October 1915, Davies, *Allanson of the 6th*, p. 77.
10   Tel., 10 May 1915, C-in-C, I to War Office, WWI/147/H, NAI.
11   Letter, Frank Coen, [late August 1915], 1DRL203, AWM.
12   Letter, 24 November 1915, Bingley to Duff, WWI/335/H, NAI.

Alec Wilson at Ismailia have been able to report that Supply and Transport men felt that they should have been paid and pensioned equitably with fighting troops, since they had shared the dangers and hardship with them (not least for seven months on Gallipoli)?[13]

But if the Indians on Gallipoli were lightly censored, they were even more scantily seen in British press and book propaganda. 'Indian' troops appeared at times in correspondents' reports. Ellis Ashmead-Bartlett's despatches were published in English language newspapers in British India, though not in the princely states or in the vernacular, though the book of his despatches refers only vaguely to 'the gallant Indian Brigade'.[14] In his *Gallipoli*, published in 1917, John Masefield mentioned 'Gurkhas' twice (once in a panegyric for Allanson and the lost vision of the Narrows on 8 August) but other 'Indians' but once.[15] After the high points of the pointless heroism of Gully Ravine and the gallant failure on Sari Bair the Indians virtually disappear from newspaper reports except as local colour.

However further news did at last arrive about the very few Indians (Gurkhas) captured on Gallipoli. In July Rifleman Kulbahadur Gurung of the 6th was reported wounded in Gul Khane Hospital in Constantinople while in October Subedar Premsing Thapa of the 4th, previously reported missing, also turned up on a Turkish list. Kulbahadur Gurung survived captivity and apparently dictated an account of his three-and-a-half years as a prisoner in which he described working alongside Australians, Italians and French internees. He was 'received with extraordinary sympathy everywhere', a friendly general who read his narrative wrote.[16] Thanks to the diligence of Ottoman officers in interrogating prisoners of war and recording the testimony and the work of Turkish scholars in transcribing and publishing their statements, we have in Kulbahadur Gurung's statement a unique document: the longest and most detailed account by an Indian soldier in his own words.

Kulbahadur Gurung was a Hindu, a 28-year-old Rifleman who had served for nine years, was expecting to become a naik in 1916 and looked forward to becoming a havildar after twelve years service. He had been married for four years and had a child, presumably living either at the depot at Abbottabad or with his family in Nepal – his village's name was too badly mutilated in translation. His account reveals what Gurkha soldiers knew and felt, but also the limits of their ken. Kulbahadur said he could 'get by' on his pay, even though 'we even pay for our uniforms'. He described how his huge convoy left Karachi and 'made their way among the battleships'. In the ships were 'English, Muslim and Gurkha soldiers', and he described the 'Sheiks' – Sikhs – as 'semi idol worshippers'. The English, however, 'favor Gurkhas', perhaps because (he thought) 'Gurkhas are better soldiers than the Sheiks'. Kulbahadur could

---

13 Memo, 15 November 1915, Wilson to Duff, WWI/335/H, NAI.
14 Ashmead-Bartlett, *Ashmead-Bartlett's Despatches from the Dardanelles*, p. 138.
15 Masefield, *Gallipoli*, pp. 126, 150-51.
16 Woodyatt, *Under Ten Viceroys*, p. 180.

The country around Demakjelik Bair in 2014. (Author)

A Gurkha machine-gun in the front line at Demakjelik Bair. At right is a periscope wrapped in hessian and an improvised gong, used as an alarm against attack. (14th Sikhs album)

read and write Hindustani but either knew little of the force to which he belonged or gave deliberately misleading answers. He said that 'there are 3 Gurkha regiments, 3 English regiments and 2 Sheik regiments, and 8 artillery companies', which resembles the Indian infantry on Gallipoli. He thought that he had been fighting 'on an island near Çanakkale' [Chanak in 1915]: 'we heard that we were going to fight against the Turks only on the ship after our departure from Port Said', but as a member of a mercenary force, 'it was all the same with us'. He had evidently heard a garbled account of the reluctance of Musalman sepoys to fight the Ottomans because he reported that 'when the Indian troops … learned that they were to fight against the Turks they revolted'. The British, he heard, 'executed their leaders by shooting and sent all the Muslim soldiers to France'. Kulbahadur Gurung's statement exemplifies many themes evident in this book: the Gurkhas' pride in their prowess, their wonder at being a part of a great imperial adventure, the limited horizons within which they lived, their ignorance of greater issues and the way even literate Indian soldiers could become a prey to hearsay.[17]

'Difficult to keep alive here': supply and transport at Suvla

The expansion of Anzac area and the creation of Suvla intensified the logistical difficulties with which the Supply and Transport Corps had been grappling since the landing in April. While the fresh British divisions had their own Army Service Corps units and arrangements, the allocation of the 29th Indian Infantry Brigade to the Demakjelik sector brought changes to the system Frederick Koe and the Indian Army officers had devised. Seeking flexibility and reliability, the Indian mule corps were organised in four groups. 'A' comprised the first-line pack mules, able to take ammunition, water and stores up to the communication trenches. Its men and mules remained at No. 2 Outpost and the Sazli Beit Dere. 'B', the base mule transport, remained at the old camp in Mule Gully, responsible for up to 500 animals. 'C' was the small cart group that worked the big dumps at Anzac Cove, and 'D' handled the cart convoys supporting the 1st Australian Division (soon joined by a 2nd) in the southern sectors of the Anzac line. With more water available from new wells, by the autumn nearly 2,000 mules were at work in the Anzac-Suvla area. Even so, the main road from Mule Gully to No. 2 Outpost remained under intermittent Turkish machine-gun fire, and men and mules continued to be killed and wounded. Mule drivers piled up boxes and bags on the right or inland side of the cart and were allowed to travel as fast as they

---

17 Tetik, Demirtaş & Demirtaş, *Çanakkale Muharebeleri'nin Esirleri* [*Prisoners of War at the Çanakkale Battles*], Vol. I, p. 52. The 1/6th Gurkhas' history states that Kulbahadur Gurung had been captured after he became lost at the evacuation of Gallipoli in December.

Leslie Hore's depiction of Mule Gully. (State Library of New South Wales)

Looking down Mule Gully today. (Author)

could, though on journeys south they usually had no protection. Between August and November over a thousand mules were killed or wounded.[18]

Turkish shellfire fell across the Suvla area – a British yeomanry medical officer described the line of dead mules that marked the mule convoy route from the ordnance depots across the salt lake. Heber Alexander recalled how mule drivers would arrive breathless at Mule Gully, calling to him *'Bachgia, sahib!'* ('I've escaped, sir!').[19] One of George Aylmer's drivers once drily said to him at Anzac 'Sahib, it is very difficult to keep alive here'.[20] Further awards recognised the muleteers' steadfastness. Jemadar Hashmat Ali of the 1st Corps and Naik Bahadur Shah and Driver Bir Singh of the 9th received the Indian Order of Merit. More importantly, perhaps, the muleteers attracted widespread admiration for their endurance under fire. Joseph Beeston (mistaking them for Sikhs) described them as 'a brave body of men'. They moved at a trot in convoys of fifteen to twenty mules, with animals hitched in threes, their drivers walking beside the trios. A mule hit by shrapnel would be unhitched, his boxes rolled off and the column proceeded: 'nothing stopped them'. Likewise with the men – a wounded man would be left beside the track to await stretcher bearers, but, in accordance with Indian custom, a bhisti would soon appear bearing a water bottle.[21]

John Hargrave's verse 'Jhill-o, Johnnie' captured the sensation of the Indian mule columns that went out 'across the bed of the Salt Lake every night from the Supply Depot at Kangaroo Beach to the firing-line':

> With creaking of and jingle of harness and pack;-
>   "Jhill-o! Johnnie, Jhill-o!"
> Where the moonlight's white and the shadows are black,
> They are climbing the winding and rocky mule track;-
>   "Jhill-o! Johnnie, Jhill-o!"[22]

While at Anzac the main danger to mule trains had been machine-guns and snipers as well as artillery fire, at Suvla the threat was shell-fire. One day a 5.9 shell hit the mule lines and killed and wounded 111 mules and fifteen men. George Aylmer claimed that the loss was sufficiently notable that a report was sent to the War Office, the only time that the Supply and Transport Corps, usually taken for granted, was mentioned in despatches. It was notable but not unique: soon after in three days mule lines near Lala Baba Hill lost 225 animals out of 350 in three days. Aylmer calculated that the Supply and Transport units on Gallipoli lost a thousand men killed, wounded

---

18 War diary, Headquarters, Mule Cart Corps, August-November 1915, WO95/4358, NAUK.
19 Alexander, *On Two Fronts*, pp. 231-32.
20 Aylmer, 'Lecture delivered Deputy Assistant Director of Transport, …', *Journal of the United Service Institution of India*, 1917, p. 303.
21 Beeston, *Five Months at Anzac*, p. 33.
22 Hargrave, *At Suvla Bay*, p. 131.

Two Indians (one Hindu, the other Musalman) pause for a snapshot with a group of Australian service corps men, suggesting the informal relationships between the two.
(AWM C01174)

and sick. 'There were very, very few sick', he claimed, though with about 112 killed the muleteers' losses were actually probably evenly divided between sick and wounded.[23]

John Hargrave was not the only European soldier to transmute his observations of the Indian muleteers into art. Lieutenant Norman Wimbush, a Reserve officer who served with the 14th Sikhs later in the campaign, also drew scenes of trench life. And among the visitors to the Supply and Transport officers' dugouts in Mule Valley was Captain Leslie Hore of the 8th Australian Light Horse, whose brother-in-law Heber Alexander had known on leave in Tasmania before the war. Hore was, as Alexander wrote, 'a clever artist', and his 'Sketches at Gallipoli' are among the State Library of New South Wales's Gallipoli treasures. They depict life in and behind the front line, including Indians in half-a-dozen water-colours, ubiquitous in the landscape of Anzac. Hore depicted muleteers 'having a pot' [shooting] from the trenches on Walker's Ridge in June, officers taking tea brought by turbaned bearers and Gurkhas stoically enduring the shelling of their lines in November.[24]

---

23 Aylmer, 'Lecture delivered Deputy Assistant Director of Transport, …', *Journal of the United Service Institution of India*, 1917, pp. 304-05.
24 'Sketches at Gallipoli, 1915', PXE 702, SLNSW.

A Punjabi Musalman herds sheep imported from Egypt to provide halal meat for the mountain artillery's members. (AWM C01614)

Punjabi Musalman muleteers in a camp near Demakjelik Bair face the rigors of the approaching winter. (AWM H16578)

Most of the Indians in Hore's water-colours were men of the Indian Supply and Transport trains that served on Gallipoli with their 2,000 two-wheeled AT carts, the most common vehicle on the peninsula and the mainstay of supply arrangements for the entire force. Mule troops served about sixty battalions, each using up to 30 carts. British supply officers, used to their heavier 'limbers', found the Indian carts 'most ingenious', and better suited to the rough tracks they faced. Each was drawn by two animals, 'small mules, not larger than ponies', and again, smaller than the big American mules used by their British counterparts. 'Lord! How they work', wrote John Gillam admiringly, 'they can pull almost anything, and they are so surefooted and the little carts so evenly balanced they can go about anywhere'.[25]

Though partially sheltered by the gullies in which they stood and by barricades of sandbags, the mules remained vulnerable to the steady shelling, by increasingly heavy artillery the Turks brought up. Early in September a six-inch shell hit over a hundred mules and a Supply and Transport officer had to make his way around a scene of carnage shooting animals too badly wounded to survive. This, a fellow officer noted with considerable understatement, was 'a most unpleasant performance before breakfast'. Disposing of so many carcasses in the late summer heat presented the train's drivers and the surviving mules with a massive and pressing problem, and they carted the dead beasts to the beach, loaded them onto a lighter and pushed them overboard offshore. The whole disgusting business must have taken the best part of a day.[26] The dead animals were often towed out to sea rather than buried. Many washed ashore again. Their hoofs, showing above the surface, were at times 'mistaken for the periscope of a hostile submarine', a British officer recalled.[27]

British and Anzac observers noticed that muleteers and drivers cared for their beasts. John Gillam, who as a transport officer knew good animal husbandry when he saw it, wrote that 'they are well looked after … these little mules – the drivers have had the care of them for years, perhaps – and their training is perfect. They [the mules] look as fat as butter, and their coats shine like satin'.[28] Their drivers' skill was mentioned in many memoirs. They would 'talk to their charges and soothe them down' using 'cooing, coaxing and persuasive' sounds.[29] The animals needed soothing. Though the new base at Suvla gave the invading force a much larger area in which to spread out, the danger of shellfire remained. Heber Alexander visited the detachment camped on and below cliffs above the beach at Lala Baba, between Anzac and Suvla. Though less congested than in Mule Gully at Anzac, the lines remained vulnerable, and once an 8-inch shell burst in the lines. Sixty mules were killed or had to be put down and another 55 were wounded – the entire mule complement of a mule corps.

25 Gillam, *Gallipoli Diary*, pp. 76-77.
26 Letter, 6 September 1915, W.B.S. Deverell, 04/37/1, 13093, IWM.
27 Reid, *Gallipoli 1915*, p. 127.
28 Gillam, *Gallipoli Diary*, p. 77.
29 Beeston, *Five Months at Anzac*, p. 34.

Because the men were not tending their animals at the time none of the drivers was harmed. The Musalmans among the Supply and Transport units were notably devout. 'They never neglected their prayers', John Hargrave noticed, 'even under heavy shell fire'.[30] The danger surely encouraged piety.

By September Hamilton felt moved to record his appreciation for what the Supply and Transport units had achieved throughout the campaign. He sent a telegram to Beauchamp Duff describing its services and commenting on how its men – overwhelmingly 'followers' – had been received by the dominion troops in his force. The muleteers had worked without ceasing since April 'under trying and difficult conditions owing to constant shell fire'. He noted 'the excellent work which every one of this detachment has performed, thereby adding greatly to the efficiency and comfort of the fighting troops'. He especially noted how his Anzac troops 'get on capitally with the Indian rank and file and are genuinely fond of them. In no campaign that I have yet served in have I seen [Indians] so well treated, so well fed, or so happy.'[31]

'We have reached the limit of our ability': the strains of reinforcing Gallipoli

The relationship between the Indian Army's British officers and their men remained practically feudal. When Charles Bruce of the 6th Gurkhas was wounded and evacuated he was accompanied by his Gurkha servant, who was allowed to sleep on the deck beside Bruce's bed. 'If his master stirred in his sleep, he sat up, watching him intently'.[32] Cox wrote that he would miss Bruce 'as he was splendid with the Gurkhas & always cheerful and ready' – much like his men, which perhaps explains his attraction.[33] Dennis Jones, an Anglican padre with the 87th Brigade (which served beside the Indians at Helles and at Suvla) described visiting the Indian field ambulance tents one night. He recalled the soft yellow light thrown by the oil lamps, with officers' followers sitting on their haunches 'crooning a weird hymn and stroking their "sahib's" head in sympathy'.[34]

The Gurkhas' British officers, always too few for the work to be done, became wretchedly weak and sickly, partly because their formerly ample messes became scantier. A letter from an officer (probably of the 4th Gurkhas) to the Allahabad *Pioneer* described their monotonous diet in September – salt bacon for breakfast and bully beef for dinner, with hard biscuits, rice and jam their 'entire and unvaried diet'. He compared it unfavourably to the fare available in France, observing that while the fighting there was more severe, the hardship of life on Gallipoli was 'five times as bad'.[35] (Though it depended who you knew: because the British warrant officers of

---

30 Hargrave, *At Suvla Bay*, p. 130.
31 Letter, 27 September 1915, Hamilton to Duff, WWI/333/H, NAI.
32 Gillam, *Gallipoli Diary*, p. 105.
33 Cox papers, 1DRL221, AWM.
34 Jones, *The Diary of a Padre at Suvla Bay*, p. 48.
35 *Pioneer*, 2 October 1915, p. 8.

Leslie Hore's depiction of 'tea on the terrace', in which turbaned bearers serve tea to Supply and Transport and visiting light horse officers. (State Library of New South Wales)

Supply and Transport mule trains were supposed to be qualified bakers, the headquarters beside the mule camp at Suvla enjoyed 'rolls and buns' made in their clay ovens.[36])

Their men's rations – and for the Indian Army comprising very particular requirements – were more basic but not necessarily unpleasant or inadequate. Rothney Battye wrote that while fresh vegetables and meat had sometimes been unobtainable, the Indians on Gallipoli had been 'better catered for, probably, than any similar Field Force before'.[37] Flies were drawn by officers' jam rather than men's dhal, and they suffered as much as or more than their men from the endemic diarrhoea. By the middle of September Herbert Cox was feeling 'very seedy … very weak' with what he called the 'trots', and soon after he was evacuated sick, recuperating in Malta.[38] Philip Palin of the 14th Sikhs assumed command from the month's end and remained into

---

36   Aylmer, 'Lecture delivered Deputy Assistant Director of Transport, …', *Journal of the United Service Institution of India*, 1917, p. 306.
37   Letter, Rothney Battye, 15 December 1915, Statement [by H.F.P. Percival] to the Dardanelles Commission, p. 102, AWM 51.
38   Diary, 14, 19 September 1915, Herbert Cox, 1DRL221, AWM.

1916. Palin, an experienced commander with a knack of getting the best out of Indian troops, remained 'marvellously cheery and full of buck' even when the cold at night seemed to herald a grim winter in the trenches.[39] Palin's sepoys ate better, or at least more appropriately, than their British officers. Indian troops had distinct and diverse dietary requirements – atta (flour), lentils, ginger, chilies, turmeric, rice, barley and gram (chickpeas), all in quantities (bags of 2½ maunds – about 100 pounds) specific to India. Men's rations were not just a matter of nutrition (indeed, the standard rations were heavy on protein and carbohydrate and reliance on them led to scurvy). All of the army's constituent faiths made binding stipulations of what was and was not acceptable, and meeting their demands imposed difficulties on active service. The British Resident in Katmandu, Colonel John Manners-Smith, achieved a useful concession at the war's outset by securing a dispensation to allow Gurkhas on field service to 'eat without scruple the flesh of long tailed sheep'.[40] As critics of the army's observance of religious dietary rules emphasised, 'when meat is used by either Hindus, Sikhs or Musulmans it is the flesh of goats killed either by the men themselves or by camp followers of their caste … for two former by "jatka" [rules] and for the latter by "halal"'.[41] Accordingly, Indian troops on Gallipoli, unlike their British or dominion comrades, were to eat fresh meat – either sheep or goat.

The burden on the few British officers was unremitting. In the 6th Gurkhas, Allanson never had more than five British officers, distributing the duties of adjutant, quartermaster, machine-gun, signalling and double-company commanders between them and himself. The strain told. Denis Ryan, who had served on the peninsula since the attack on Gurkha Bluff and been evacuated sick and returned, became 'a bundle of nerves' by November, when he was evacuated again (on the same day that Edward Phipson left, with dysentery).[42] Gurkha and Indian officers suffered especially in an army that unduly respected age. 'The idea that a rifleman was as good at forty as he was at twenty was a great mistake', William Villiers-Stuart recalled. 'At forty he was a cunning old dodger'.[43] Allanson, though revering Gambirsing Pun's devotion, thought that many older Indian officers were 'wash-outs', upset by the challenges of war, observing with characteristic candour that they could 'very rarely meet the change of conditions in an emergency'.[44] When Villiers-Stuart took over the 5th Gurkhas in

---

39 Letter, 7 December 1915, Savory Papers, 7603-93, NAM.
40 Circular, 1914, Foreign and Political Department, Internal – B, May 1915, Nos 1214-1220, 'Steps taken by the Nepal Durbar to protect the interests of the Gurkha soldiers … Religious prohibition against Gurkhas on active service eating tinned mutton', NAI.
41 Foreign and Political Department, War Secret, April 1915 No. 326, 'Publication of inaccurate and indiscreet remarks in English newspapers', NAI.
42 Letter, 3 November 1915, Davies, *Allanson of the 6th*, p. 89
43 Maxwell, *Villiers-Stuart on the Frontier*, p. 181
44 Diary, c. 14 September-4 October 1915, Davies, *Allanson of the 6th*, p. 81.

Sikhs presenting their rifles for inspection in the trenches at Demakjelik Bair. The disciplined maintenance of their weapons, part of the regular army's routine, was one explanation for the Indian brigade's endurance. (14th Sikhs album)

Egypt in 1916 he found 'many useless' Gurkha officers and NCOs 'who had of necessity been promoted in the field to replace casualties'.[45]

The autumn brought no more attacks, but the tedious, uncomfortable and still dangerous trench life familiar to millions of men on both sides from the Caucasus to the North Sea. Herbert Winn, who arrived in the 5th Gurkhas' trenches in a chilly, rainy night in September, described the battalion as 'enjoying a fairly slack time', though 'bullets & shrapnel whiz over our heads occasionally'.[46] But Winn misled his family that 'there is nothing to do but lie about'. He described his men as doing 'a bit of work' – the fatigues inescapable to trench warfare, such as extending and repairing communication trenches in the sector, created barely a month before. One of his men's fatigues entailed digging Winn a dugout for him and his orderly.

45 Maxwell, *Villiers-Stuart goes to War*, p. 177.
46 Letter, 1 October 1915, Herbert Winn, 97/18/12, 6508, IWM.

By the autumn there was as much need for men with shovels as with rifles. The brigade's new trenches in the line between the old Anzac and Suvla positions, needed constant work to develop and strengthen them, creating positions in which men could live as well as fight – no one was under the illusion that their home was temporary, to be left behind in a great advance. When Arthur Tillard toured them in early September (a month after their creation) he found them still too narrow and shallow, lacking dugouts, and the scrapes men had dug in the trench walls were likely to collapse once the autumn rain came. In some places men constructed individual dugouts all over the hillsides, lending their bivouacs an improvised and untidy appearance that irritated regular officers.

Accordingly, and despite the presence of over 3,000 Indian Supply and Transport drivers and followers on Gallipoli, the demand for disciplined military labour grew. Gangs of Greek and Egyptian civilian labourers proved unwilling to work under fire on the peninsula and inefficient on Imbros, and soldiers could not be spared. Austen Chamberlain suggested that India could provide a 'semi-military organisation', a corps of 'Coolies from the Punjab' – labourers under military direction of the kind that had been used to build roads in the tribal areas of the frontier. Kitchener urged Hardinge to 'do everything possible to comply … the matter is urgent'.[47] In fact, while the military authorities in the Punjab began to recruit a corps of labourers, by the time it left India the campaign had ended and the labourers never reached the Dardanelles. A year of active service had also used up the Indian Army's supply of specialists: in October the Director of Medical Services in India advised his counterpart in Egypt that reserves of assistant surgeons (many of whom were Indian) was 'almost exhausted'.[48]

As ever, finding reinforcements remained a challenge. While drafting Patialas had solved the Sikhs' immediate needs in time for the August offensive, even sending a further double company late in September did not replace their losses. Large drafts of ethnically compatible Sikhs arrived in September from the 87th Punjabis and 200 men from the Burma Military Police, though like all reinforcements they retained their own uniforms and badges; visibly different to men of their new units. The 14th Sikhs was reorganised in October into four double companies, but only one wholly comprised Ferozepore men. One double company comprised Patiala men, but Patialas were mixed with Sikhs, which technically breached the understanding reached with the maharaja in July.

By late August Lord Hardinge's military staff admitted to the Secretary of State for India, Austen Chamberlain, that 'we have reached the limit of our ability to provide experienced officers for Indian Expeditionary Forces "B", "D", "E" or "G".[49] Shortages

---

47 Tel., 1 September 1915, Chamberlain to Hardinge, WWI/151/H, NAI.
48 Tel., 13 October 1915, Director, Medical Services in India to Principal Director, Medical Services, Alexandria, WWI/152/H, NAI.
49 Tel., 26 August 1915, Hardinge to Chamberlain, WWI/150/H, NAI.

of effective British officers continued to plague units built on a dependence on Europeans. Every battalion had only one or two regular officers (the 14th Sikhs' only regular early in September was its medical officer, while among the Gurkha battalions at times only the acting CO was a regular.) Though few reserve officers reached the peninsula before Charles Bruce was wounded on 30 June he wrote that most had been 'intimately experienced in the handling of native troops'.[50] Reserve officers spanned the spectrum from effective to useless but regardless of aptitude or effort if they could not communicate with their men (and with Indian officers) they could not contribute. Tillard's diary is full of complaints about his reserve officers – 'had to speak severely to [Herbert] Winn for not having his men out at work' – (Winn had perhaps given his family an unfortunately true idea of his energy).[51] The young, inexperienced officers had to learn quickly and cope under the strain of leadership. One Tillard thought 'capable' early in September had by late October become 'very jumpy', who had 'always got some excuse for letting his men do as little as possible'. A 'telling off' – the young officer was not long out of school – had the desired effect, but Tillard wondered what he was to do if he could not trust his British officers.[52]

Both officers and men worked strenuously – it was ten nights before Tillard was able to wear pajamas at night. The battalions took their turn in the lines at Hill 60, where the gains of the August attacks had left the invaders' and defenders' lines just a few yards apart, with the Turks generally holding the higher ground. Just as at Quinn's Post, both sides resorted to bombing and mining. Once again Welshmen, though in this case not miners (members of the Welsh Horse, mainly farmers from the Welsh hills) arrived to lead the digging of tunnels and galleries (one sap called Ton-y-Pandy (more usually Tonypandy); Pandy a name once common among sepoys as well as a village in Glamorgan). The Gurkhas worked with them, hill-men together. The Welshmen also took to chapaties, which they found a convenient food in the mine galleries. Allanson noticed the Welshmen's 'exceptional kindness … to our men, with whom they willingly shared everything they had'.[53]

Relations between Indian battalions remained at times uneasy. Arthur Tillard, a newcomer (almost immediately posted to take command of the 5th Gurkhas), recorded his dissatisfaction with the Sikhs' working parties. He thought their productivity 'too disgraceful for words … I don't believe they did a stroke of work all night', blaming their officers for failing to keep their men at work.[54] A report by Major Edward Earle of the 14th Sikhs of an incident in South Wales Borderers Gully on 22 August suggests that losses and privation had begun to sap the Sikhs' capacity to continue to endure. The Sikhs were in reserve, supporting the 5th Gurkhas in the forward line, who were

50   Bruce, *Himalayan Wanderer*, p. 263.
51   Diary, 23 September 1915, Arthur Tillard, GM.
52   Ibid., 23, 27, 28 October 1915.
53   Diary, 24 November 1915, Davies, *Allanson of the 6th*, p. 94
54   Diary, 7 October 1915, Arthur Tisdall, GM

holding off a local Turkish attack. Reginald Savory and Earle ran forward to see if the Sikhs were needed. Thomas Kirkwood passed the word that they needed ammunition from the nearby dump. Earle called for men to help but 'being somewhat shaken' they were reluctant. Savory picked up a box and carried it up. With Savory showing the way four Sikhs followed. They merited praise for 'going up splendidly', but the incident was a worrying sign that the Indians' resilience, tested for four months, may have been weakening.[55]

'Poor chaps … all gone': the loss of the *Ramazan*

Later in the summer, after a fortnight's sick leave in Egypt, supply officer John Gillam returned to the peninsula in the transport *Anglo-Egyptian*, accompanied by a draft of Sikhs and Gurkhas and their British officers. As the ship left Alexandria harbour the Sikhs and Gurkhas gave what Gillam called their 'war-cries', comparing them to the Maori *haka*, and suggesting that reinforcement drafts remained enthusiastic about the prospect of seeing active service.[56] The troops formed submarine guards as the ship entered 'the danger zone for submarines' in the Greek islands. Gillam thought that the Gurkhas enjoyed watching for submarines 'with orders to fire when one comes into sight'. They would 'appreciate the fun if one came along, so that they could show off their marksmanship'.[57] The story of the *Ramazan* suggests that their insouciance was misplaced.

The Commonwealth War Graves Commission's data base shows that the Indians' single most costly day on the peninsula was not in June or August, but on 19 September: why?[58] The answer reveals the largely untold story of the single worst loss the Indian Army suffered during the Gallipoli campaign, the sinking of the transport *Ramazan*. With losses mounting, especially after the August offensive, the 29th Indian brigade needed further drafts. By autumn the Indian Army's improvised reinforcement system had managed to find men in the depots of the Gurkha and Sikh regiments who were able to serve alongside the Gallipoli units without unduly disturbing either their dietary supply system or the communal identity on which their military efficiency depended. To make good the August losses drafts assembled in Egypt and on 15 September left Alexandria harbour aboard the transport *Ramazan* – the ship that had brought Alexander's mule corps to Gallipoli. Like all transports destined for Gallipoli the *Ramazan* was unarmed and unescorted, despite the presence of enemy submarines in the Aegean. Lieutenant Neville Irwin of the 10th Gurkhas, the senior British officer aboard, described the *Ramazan* as 'a rotten old cat'.[59] As Heber Alexander had

55 Report by Maj E. Earle, 23 August 1915, 7603-93-12, NAM.
56 Gillam, *Gallipoli Diary*, p. 169.
57 Ibid., p. 170
58 The Commonwealth War Graves Commission's data base gives Indian deaths on those dates as: 4 June: 207, 28 June: 47, 8 August 46.
59 Letter, Neville Irwin, 11 October 1915, 2/10th Digest of Service, GM.

found in April, it could make no more than eight knots, and alone: in 1915 no British ships steamed in convoy.

U-35 was one of the most successful U-boats in the war (it sank over half a million tons of Allied shipping between March 1915 and March 1918). Under the command of *Kapitan-Leutnant* Waldemar Kophamel it sailed from the Austrian naval base of Pola, in Croatia. Kophamel found the *Ramazan* 55 nautical miles off the Greek island of Antikythira, between the north-western point of Crete and the Greek mainland. Why the ship did not take a more direct route between Egypt and Lemnos is unclear, but it had encountered unseasonably rough weather on the previous two days and may have been seeking a more sheltered route. At dawn on 19 September Kophamel's submarine surfaced and fired at the transport, smashing some of its boats. Neville Irwin described in a letter to his parents how he heard firing, raced from his cabin and on opening the door found 'a poor fellow with his head half blown off' lying on the deck. Running to the hold to get men on deck, he felt the submarine 'plunking shell after shell' into the ship – the shells were not warning shots. While the *Ramazan* slowly ploughed on, its steering gear smashed, Kophamel continued to fire. Lieutenant Donald Campbell, a reinforcement officer destined for the 10th Gurkhas, described how the shelling killed and wounded 'crowds of fellows'. Irwin added 'and some poor chaps fearfully wounded'.

Irwin realised that his men's best chance would be to get into the water and be picked up by the few remaining boats than to try to load the boats on their davits under fire. He 'begged and implored' the men (who were at least wearing life jackets) to jump into the water, but they would not: this was only their second sea-voyage. The submarine would take them prisoner they replied. With the men refusing to leave and the British officers convinced that the ship would be sunk, one of the officers said 'I am going overboard' and Irwin and a few sepoys followed, to be collected by boats, presumably launched by the crew. Campbell was slightly wounded in the leg but survived having to jump into the sea when a shell hit his boat.[60] 'Those who stayed, poor chaps, are all gone'. Irwin said that then began 'a terrible experience, the worst strain I have ever had', of watching the *Ramazan* sink by the bows, 'going down with crowds of men hanging on to her'. The submarine cruised past the survivors but did nothing further.

The sea was still rough, and one of the five ship's boats capsized, drowning Second Lieutenant Michael Unger of the 14th Sikhs. Then for the whole day and into the night (fortunately moonlit) the men in the overcrowded boats tried to row and sail, making very sow progress and fearing that they would be dashed against the rocks of Antikythira. The islanders gave the survivors black bread and red wine ('they scarcely had enough to feed themselves') and put them in cow-sheds, later feeding them stewed goat and more red wine ('quite good but very strong'). What the Sikhs and Gurkhas made of this unfamiliar food is, as ever, unknown. After a week 'a la Robinson

---

60 Letter, Donald Campbell, 1 October 1915, 2/10th Gurkhas Digest of Service, GM.

Crusoe', as Campbell described it, the survivors were taken by a Greek warship to Athens, where the British consul was 'awfully good to us'. Campbell, a reserve officer, casually mentioned amputating the leg of a sepoy on Antikythira ('the flies had got at it').[61] Eventually they reached Malta and, after hospital treatment, Egypt.

Of the nearly 400 Indian troops aboard only between 75 and 93 were saved, though 28 of the ship's crew of 29 survived. The figures given in various sources cannot be reconciled, but at least 80 men of the 14th Sikhs and 173 of the 10th Gurkhas also died in the attack. It is possible that confusion or disorder aggravated the death toll: Alexander described the *Ramazan's* crew as 'unruly and careless' – they certainly seem to have got off the ship first.[62] The disproportionate loss among the Indians is easily explained. Having been raised in the mountains of Nepal and on the plains of the Punjab, few Indian soldiers could have been expected to be able to swim.

The *Ramazan* was one of several transports sunk while carrying troops to Gallipoli, part of a renewed German submarine campaign in the eastern Mediterranean, which saw eighteen vessels attacked or sunk in under two weeks from late September, including several troop transports.[63] A month before the torpedoing of the big Canadian-owned troopship *Royal Edward* had cost the lives of almost a thousand out of the 1,500 aboard, and a fortnight before the troopship *Southland* had been torpedoed, though both the ship and all but 24 Australians had been saved. A month later Kophamel's U-35 sank the steamer *Maquette*, killing 169 of the 650 on board, including ten New Zealand nurses. The *Ramazan's* loss was therefore the second greatest loss in the campaign, though it remains the least known. The losses of the *Maquette* and *Southland* were widely publicised at the time (in popular art works urging retribution, for example) and the *Royal Edward's* dead are explicitly mentioned and individually distinguished on the Cape Helles memorial: though not the *Ramazan's*.

The *Ramazan's* dead suggests both the extent to which losses on Gallipoli demanded replacement after the losses of August. The 10th Gurkhas, which had suffered severely on Chunuk Bair and Hill 60, would have received enough men to replace an entire double company. (Most of them came from the 10th's other battalion, still in India.) The dead included a large group of Sikhs of the Burma Military Police and the 14th Sikhs (and one man each of the Assam Military Police, the 15th and 45th Sikhs). They included four men of the mountain artillery, whether reinforcements arriving afresh or men returning to their batteries after convalescing in Egypt. No fewer than 43 men of the Supply and Transport Corps died, as well as individuals from the Indore and Gwalior transport corps, sent to Egypt at the behest of their princely rulers.

The *Ramazan* dead were reported 'killed in action' in a long casualty list dated 28 October 1915 but detailed accounts of the sinking reached headquarters in Egypt

---

61 Ibid.
62 Alexander, *On Two Fronts*, p. 135.
63 Smith, *World War 1 at Sea – British Merchant and Fishing Vessels Lost and Damaged* <http://www.naval-history.net/WW1NavyBritishBVLSMN1507.htm>

months later, to be transmitted to Simla by post. The reports (presumably collated by interviewing survivors) refer tantalizingly to the praiseworthy conduct of 546 Pay Havildar Mohammed Baksh of Kohat Battery, descriptions of whose conduct were 'placed at the top of the pile'; but not transcribed in the record preserved at Simla.[64] No fewer than 294 Indians are recorded in the War Graves Commission's list as having died on 19 September. On that day no serious fighting occurred on Gallipoli.

'Hullo Johnny': Indian and empire troops at campaign's end

With the arrival at Anzac of the 29th Indian Infantry Brigade from August, the great bulk of the Indian force on Gallipoli was at Anzac, and many Anzacs saw and met Indian troops. Their letters, diaries and memoirs repeatedly refer to encounters with Indian troops. Magazine stories and illustrations ensured that the Anzacs already knew of Sikhs and Gurkhas, and they recognized them in the flesh. Sergeant Archie Barwick, a Tasmanian-born surveyor in the 1st Battalion, kept one of the war's most observant and candid diaries. He described Gurkhas as 'very good little soldiers'. 'They are rarely more than 5 feet high', he wrote, 'and very much resemble Chinamen … I think they belong to Nepal', he wrote, a little uncertainly. The Gurkhas' kukris fascinated European soldiers, and they exerted a mystique – many believed that they could not be unsheathed without drawing blood. Barwick recorded one of the jokes doing the rounds of the Anzac lines:

> A Gurkha and a Turk … met face to face one day during battle. The Turk fired and missed the Gurkha and the latter threw his kukri at him. The old Turk said "missed that time Johnny". "You shake your head and see," said the little warrior …

The 'shaking head' story recurs in Anzac letters, diaries and memoirs. Archie Barwick said that he didn't vouch that the story was true, but he did believe that the Gurkhas were 'great ones for snipping their heads off', and had heard that a wounded Gurkha evacuated on a hospital ship held a haversack containing a Turk's head: one of many unsubstantiated rumours.[65] Walter Morrice, a light horse officer, recorded a popular story, of two Indian mule drivers who, enraged that one of their 'mates' was sniped, disappeared for two days and returned with the sniper's head.[66] A Scots Territorial passed on a story told to him by a wounded officer of a Gurkha climbing down a tree, wiping the blade of his kukri 'with tender care' while head of a Turkish

---

64 Letter, 24 January 1916, GOC E Force to Duff, WWI/337/H, NAI.
65 Diary, Archie Barwick, MLMSS 1493/Box 1, item 1, p. 42, ML.
66 Memoir, Walter Morrice, 1DRL513, AWM.

sniper lay dripping, caught between two branches. 'The Indian climbs like a monkey', he affirmed, 'and will follow his prey anywhere'.[67]

The Sikhs likewise impressed Australians with their toughness. An Australian who had served alongside Sikhs in the attack on Chunuk Bair returned with a similar story. 'On me off-side', he said, 'was one of them Indian Silks [sic]'. A piece of shrapnel nearly severed one of his hands. 'Without stoppin' he screwed the paw off and threw it away'.[68] If not literally true, if it was believed it suggests the Sikhs' formidable reputation. The New Zealander Frank Cooper also recalled a story he had been told while working in an ordnance depot on the beach. An Indian driver, he heard, had been sniped at while returning from the front line with his mules. Seeing the flash of the sniper's rifle, he handed his mule to a passing Australian, unsheathed his knife and 'in a few moments returned with the sniper's head and a collection of Australian identity discs which the Turk had in his possession'.[69]

Barwick also encountered 'a good many Sikhs', describing them as 'fine big men' and noting that they dressed their uncut hair in turbans. He was 'on good terms with them and often paid their camp a visit', and must even have offered them something – cigarettes or food, perhaps – because he wrote that they 'will take nothing from you as it is against their religion'. But the Sikhs offered food to Barwick, and he accepted. 'Many's the taste of their curry, jam and chupputties I have had'.[70] The Sikhs, lacking the kukri, attracted less mystique, though unscrupulous newspapers made stories up regardless – Reginald Savory denounced to his mother reports in the *Daily Graphic* about Sikhs 'crawling on their stomachs, with knives in their mouths, tracking snipers'. He told her that this was 'all rot'.[71] These stories speak of the regard Anzacs had for the fighting prowess of their Indian comrades; Gurkha, Sikh and Musalman.

The Indians' officers were apprehensive at their men working so closely with Australians. 'We at first thought that the Anzacs might ill treat our drivers as they don't care much for the native in their own country', wrote George Aylmer. They were agreeably surprised to find that 'tremendous camaraderie between them', echoing the observations made by Indian Army officers such as Arthur Fergusson at Anzac. George Aylmer recalled that when one of his Naiks, Mohamed Din, went into hospital the commanding officer of an Australian unit wrote to Aylmer to say that he hoped that Din would return to his unit, where he was an honorary member of its corporals' mess. Why did the Anzacs not treat Indians on Gallipoli as they would have in Australia? Aylmer wrote simply that 'I put it down to the fact that "Johnny" was as brave as the Anzacs themselves'.[72] What did Indians think of the Australians they

---

67 Mure, *With the Incomparable 29th*, p. 93.
68 *Bulletin*, 2 March 1916, p. 11.
69 Memoir, Frank Cooper, MS-Papers-1676-1, ATL.
70 Diary, Archie Barwick, MLMSS 1493/Box 1, item 1, p. 43, ML.
71 Letter, 11 June 1915, Reginald Savory, 7603-93, NAM.
72 Aylmer, 'Lecture delivered Deputy Assistant Director of Transport, …', *Journal of the United Service Institution of India*, 1917, pp. 304-05.

Norman Wimbush's drawing of Sikhs, Anzacs and Gurkhas mixing in the trenches. In the centre an Anzac (with a curiously Asian cast of face) inspects a Gurkha's kukri. (14th Sikhs album)

met? Almost nothing is known from their own mouths, though when in the 1970s Indian Great War veterans were asked about how they got on with white soldiers 'the most enthusiastic comments were about the Australians who apparently treated them heartily and with a spirit of equal comradeship'.[73]

Indian troops formed their own shrewd judgments of their comrades. One described the different characters of three of the armies on the peninsula under shell-fire:

> "British Tommy," said he, "Turk shell, Tommy says 'Ah!' Turk shell, Indian say 'Oosh!' Australian say 'Where the hell did that come from?'[74]

Heber Alexander described relations between both Indian and Anzac combatant troops and his mule drivers as 'cordial in the extreme'. He contrasted this with the 'slightly contemptuous attitude' that Supply and Transport men had often struck

---

73 Ellinwood & Pradhan, *India and World War I*, p. 197.
74 Beeston, *Five Months at Anzac*, p. 33.

from Indian fighting units.[75] The shared hardships of service on the peninsula transformed the 'drabi' – the follower – in the sepoys' eyes. But encounters with Anzacs might also have had a coercive aspect. Nigel Woodyatt, a Gurkha officer, described meeting a group of Gurkhas arriving at the depot at Abbottabad 'after a long absence in Gallipoli'. Woodyatt chatted with them, noticing that 'there wasn't a uniform button amongst them'. He asked why, and heard men explain something he could not understand about '*Asstrely*' and '*sufner*'. A 'very intelligent NCO' explained that they meant 'Australians had taken them all as souvenirs' – perhaps regardless of whether the Gurkha needed them or not.[76]

As Australian reinforcements arrived, they too made the acquaintance of the exotic Indians, and by this time several months of contact with dominion soldiers have given many Indians a greater knowledge of English and a confidence to use it. An Australian stretcher-bearer, Private Septimus Elmore, who arrived with a 2nd Division field ambulance in September, described a conversation with a lance-naik. Having mixed with Anzacs for several months, the Indian could conduct a rudimentary conversation, and Elmore must have asked him his name and how to write it. The man explained that he was a Punjabi Musalman and traced out the letters of his name, 'commencing at the right & writing backwards', spelling out the name that Elmore thought was 'Nahdar'.[77] The meeting sounds trivial, but it reflects how men of the two forces did more than smile and nod, but exchanged names and personal details. An Indian who spoke to Frank Coen ('we had many opportunities of conversing with them. Some of them speak English freely – all understand it') said to him, '"Australian very good. Me Australian!" meaning he coupled himself or would like to be regarded as an Australian'. Spoken by 'a coloured man' in Australia at the time, this would have earned a rebuke or a belting. On Gallipoli, Coen told his mother, 'I am proud to say such magnificent soldiers have the highest admiration of Australians'.[78]

With large numbers of Indian troops serving in the trenches at Cape Helles and on the Anzac/Suvla boundary, British troops too had ample opportunities to observe and meet Indians, and their greater familiarity with white troops emboldened some. A Scots Territorial officer lost in the tracks behind the Helles front line, asked a couple of 'Pathas' – meaning 'Pathans', but probably Musalman drivers of the Supply and Transport corps, where his brigade headquarters might be. One interrupted him with 'No talk Englishe. Talk Hindustani'.[79] As with the Anzacs, it is clear that they did talk. John Hargrave, a British field ambulance sergeant at Suvla, recorded his attempts to conduct a conversation with a Punjabi muleteer when his mule column halted nearby. He opened with a name an Indian might recognise: 'Rabindranarth

---

75 Alexander, *On Two Fronts*, p. 247.
76 Woodyatt, *Under Ten Viceroys*, p. 182.
77 Diary, 1 October 1915, Septimus Elmore, MS1825, AWM.
78 Letter, [late August 1915], Frank Coen, 1 DRL 203, AWM.
79 Mure, *With the Incomparable 29th*, p. 128.

Tagore'. The man shook his head, saying 'No, sergeant'. Hargrave uselessly tried 'Buddha' and 'Ganga' (a word he recalled from reading Kipling's *Kim*) but the man responded to 'Mahomet'. 'Yes – me, Mahommedie,' he said proudly', confirming that after the war he wanted to 'go Mokka', explaining that 'Kashmir my house'. The man (evidently a Kashmiri Musalman) had enough language and confidence to essay a question of his own – 'you go Indee, sergeant?' – before his convoy moved on.[80] With little language in common Indian and white troops relied upon gestures – the sharing of food or cigarettes – and upon simple and necessarily visual humour. John Hargrave recorded how when Indian drivers moved his field ambulance from the salt lake to Lala Baba, they were 'much amused and interested' at the unit's sergeant clerk, who at 6-foot-8-inches towered over the Indians, most shorter than the Britons. As they were pointing at him, Hargrave gestured to the tall sergeant and the sky and said 'Himalayas, Johnnie!' The Indians laughed and called the man by this nickname as long as they worked with the medical unit.[81]

British and Anzac troops called Indians 'Johnny' universally. Indeed, Frank Coen told his mother, 'They call us Johnny and they answer to the same name. "Hullo Johnny" is our mutual greeting'.[82] John Hargraves's verse 'Jill-o, Johnny', while intended to praise the muleteers and drivers, also reflected ignorance and misunderstandings common to white soldiers:

> By the blessings of Allah he's more than one wife; -
>   "Jhill-o! Johnnie, Jhill-o!"
> He's forbidden the wine which encourages strife,
> But you don't like the look of his dangerous knife;-
>   "Jhill-o! Johnnie, Jhill-o!"
>
> The picturesque whallah is dusky and spare;
>   "Jhill-o! Johnnie, Jhill-o!"
> A turban he wears with magnificent air,
> But he chucks down his pack when it's time for his prayer;-
>   "Jhill-o! Johnnie, Jhillo!"
>
> When his moment arrives he'll be dropped in a hole;-
>   "Jhill-o! Johnnie, Jhill-o!"
> 'Tis Kismet, he says, and beyond his control;
> But the dear little houris will comfort his soul;-
>   "Jhill-o! Johnnie, Jhill-o!"[83]

---

80 Hargrave, *At Suvla Bay*, pp. 127-28.
81 Ibid., pp. 130-31
82 Letter, Frank Coen, [late August 1915], 1 DRL 203, AWM.
83 Hargrave, *At Suvla Bay*, p. 132.

British observers supposed that Indians exhibited a particular stoicism. John Hargrave (a field ambulance man, accustomed to seeing wounded men) recalled seeing a Supply and Transport man sitting on a rock smoking a cigarette, his left leg having been blown off by shrapnel. The man sat stoically, the only sign of his suffering the 'great tears' rolling down his cheeks. 'He said no word. Not a groan or a cry of pain'.[84]

'Devilish hard to keep up a smile': autumn begins

With the extension of the lines to the Anzac/Suvla boundary the focus of the Indian effort shifted northwards. Mountain artillery guns shifted out of what became known as the 'old Anzac' area and the infantry took up trenches around Hill 60 and Demakjelik Bair, where in some places the lines were just 15 yards apart. Accordingly, the supply and transport and medical camps shifted northward as well. British troops working in the seaside dumps around the salt lake became accustomed to seeing Indians. 'Near Kangaroo Beach' (the camp of the Australian naval 'bridging train'), one recalled, 'was the camp of the Indians, and here you could see the dusky ones praying on prayer mats and cooking rice and "chupatties"'.[85] While the warm weather lasted men continued to bathe. An officer of the newly-arrived 1/4th Gurkhas found it 'amusing to see the British and Gurkha officers and men hurrying ashore and scampering for cover in a state of nature' when the Turks directed their artillery at the shore.[86] (Indians retained the modesty of a loin-cloth: officers described their men as outraged by Europeans bathing naked.)

As well as reinforcements wounded men returned to their battalions after an all-too short convalescence and often resenting that they had to return. Allanson did not welcome returned wounded, because they 'as a rule never have the dash they once had'. He spent much time in the trenches, talking to his men, encouraging them. 'I love and admire them', he wrote, lamenting that they were giving their lives in a campaign in which he himself had ceased to regard as worthwhile[87]

During the autumn, with five battalions to co-ordinate and a stable front line, 29th Brigade staff devised a more-or-less regular system of reliefs in which groups of two double companies rotated through the front line trenches. This gave men spells of about a week in the line and out of it; but out of the line they had to perform fatigues, including digging and strengthening trenches, saps, roads and latrine pits and disposing of dead mules. In the front line battalions sent out patrols and wiring parties; the trench routine familiar on every front. While the Turks fired artillery and catapult-propelled bombs, the most common summaries in the war diaries are 'everything quiet'. Every few days an incident is recorded – a Turk trying to surrender (and being

---

84 Hargrave, *At Suvla Bay*, pp. 129-30.
85 Ibid., p. 98.
86 Macdonell & Macaulay, *A History of the 4th Prince of Wales's Own Gurkha Rifles*, p. 275.
87 Diary, 25 August 1915; c. 10-17 November 1915, Davies, *Allanson of the 6th*, pp. 72, 91.

shot by wary sentries), a machine-gun being turned on Turkish work parties when the sound of brush-cutting or digging carried to the Indian lines; sudden bombardments, in which men were wounded or buried; bursts of Turkish firing prompted by the noise of British empire troops cheering. Though stable the lines were also nervy and dangerous: Allanson noticed how after shelling 'all the faces are white and scared … it is devilish hard to keep up a smile with high explosive flying around'.[88] The 10th Gurkhas' war diary records day by day through September no major action – the 'narrative' of the diary reads simply 'in trenches at Susak Kuyu' – but a stream of losses of one, two or three killed or wounded every day.[89] The troops in the foothills came under pressure to push their lines forward, closing the distance to the Turks until in some places they were only twenty yards away – well within bombing distance. The Turks, who were always up-hill, simply held on, bombarding the British lines often.

In poor health after what had often been months on the peninsula on monotonous rations, many wounded took months for their wounds to heal, with infection a constant and recurrent risk. The average number awaiting evacuation during the winter each month was 1,500.[90] By Christmas over 1,800 invalids would await passage to India, almost all wounded and sick sepoys from Gallipoli, a sign of the severity of Indian casualties in the campaign. Medical and naval staffs arranged a program of sailings for the hospital ships *Loyalty*, *Syria*, *Madras* and *Sicilia* between December 1915 and April 1916 to at last clear the backlog. Cables from Egypt informed Indian medical authorities of the departure of a series of hospital ships as the wounded on the August offensive and the campaign's final months slowly recovered and became fit enough to be transported home. An Australian reinforcement recalled passing one of the Indian hospital ships as his transport entered the Red Sea later in 1915, and he and his comrades cheered the bandaged Indians they could see on its decks (though with a sober edge: 'we must be getting near to the war').[91] The hospital ships also carried 'cot cases' – men too severely wounded to return to service – and a small group of men labeled 'insane', each guarded by a handful of armed sepoys under a havildar.

As the weather worsened and troops fell prey to illness the medical units saw the third of the periods of crisis they experienced. By early November the two Indian hospitals in Egypt were seeking additional payments from the 'Imperial Relief Fund' of £200 each, while 108th Field Ambulance, on Gallipoli, sought £50 'urgently required'.[92] Most of their new patients suffered from illness (especially respiratory complaints) and related conditions. Staff officers at General Headquarters had little idea of the severity of the coming winter – staff officers writing from Tenedos early in November advised Simla that 'poshteens' – warm fur coats, made and worn on the

---

88   Diary, c. 14 September-4 October 1915, Davies, *Allanson of the 6th*, p. 76.
89   War diary, 2/10th Gurkhas, August 1915, WO95/4472, NAUK.
90   Tel., 19 November 1915, Maxwell to Duff, WWI/334/H, NAI (my emphasis).
91   Colman, *There and Back with a Dinkum*, p. 50.
92   Tel., 3 November 1915, Maxwell to Duff, WWI/334/H, NAI.

north-west frontier – would not be needed.[93] They were wrong. Despite heroic efforts and some success, India's supply system could still not meet the demand for equipment and supplies. In November Simla advised Egypt that its requisitions for tents could not be completed for two months: the needs of units on Gallipoli remained unfulfilled. Officers coped – Cecil Allanson even had to send privately to India to buy tiffin cans to keep his men's food hot – or their men went without.

The Indians' ordeal would soon be over, but it would become unendurable before the end came.

---

93 Tel., 4 November 1915, Monro to Duff, WWI/334/H, NAI.

14

'The sea wind blew away the hates': evacuation, October-December

Ottoman shellfire remained a danger at Anzac and in the rear areas of Suvla until the end. On 22 November Lieutenant Charles Smyth and Cecil Allanson were walking at Anzac, having visited the ordnance stores looking for warm clothing, when a shell burst in front of them. A shrapnel ball had pierced Smyth's greatcoat, another Allanson's hand, but the blast had wounded an Australian and a Sikh, and killed two mules; a toll evocative of the Indians' part in the campaign. Ten days later Allanson was caught by another shell at the entrance to his dug-out and evacuated with blindness that turned out to be temporary, but for him Gallipoli was over. For those left behind the ordeal was almost over.

'Too sickening': the strain of trench warfare continues

In mid-October the weather turned: 'very much colder' on 12 October, the 4th Gurkhas noted. With water still scarce and tainted, dysentery cases increased, and flies survived in warm spells into November.[1] Arthur Tillard thought 'we are in for a bad time soon', dreading the coming winter and fearing that run-down men in such conditions would develop pneumonia.[2] At the end of October the mountain artillery headquarters clerks totted up the campaign's cost for its two batteries. Their losses had been surprisingly even. Kohat Battery had lost eleven men killed and 131 wounded, Jacob's twelve killed and 132 wounded.[3] With the onset of autumn the mountain guns were re-organised for what would become the campaign's final phase. The strain of trench warfare continued, with effects on men's morale. In November Rothney Battye again recorded a 1/5th Gurkha who had cut off his thumb with his kukri.[4] Soon after

---

1 War diary, 1/4th Gurkhas, October 1915, WO95/4472, NAUK.
2 Diary, 17 October 1915, Arthur Tillard, GM.
3 War diary, 7th Indian Mountain Brigade, October 1915, WO95/4289, NAUK.
4 War Diary, 108th Field Ambulance, November 1915, WO95/4272, NAUK.

'corrigenda' to earlier lists casualty lists mention two Sikhs, stating 'both of these casualties were due to self-inflicted wounds'.[5]

Through the exclusive composition of its units the Indian Army had encouraged comparison and competition, as a senior officer observed, fostering 'the vanity of the Gurkha at the expense of the Sikh' and vice versa.[6] The two responded differently to the demands of the campaign. Humphrey Gell, who as brigade signals officer saw much of both, wrote without affectation of 'the little Gurkha and the brawny Sikh'.[7] Sikhs, who were taller (and wore large turbans), dug deeper trenches, which, Gurkha officers complained, their men could not even see out of, let alone fire from. The two also responded differently to the hardships of the campaign, and especially to the losses they suffered. The disastrous casualties at Helles severely affected the Sikhs' resilience. Hamilton discussed in a letter to General Sir Beauchamp Duff, Commander-in-Chief in India the performance of the two. He described the Sikhs as 'depressed' and the Gurkhas as 'cheerful'. After inspecting the 110th Indian Field Ambulance at Mudros he found it 'hard to get a smile out of the solemn old Sikh'.[8] Certainly as the weather worsened the Sikhs appear to have lost heart, at least in Arthur Tillard's eyes. He complained repeatedly of Sikh working parties as 'too disgraceful for words … it is too sickening the way those Sikhs refuse to work'.[9] On the other hand, the 14th Sikhs appeared to suffer fewer casualties from frostbite, with only 40 cases by the first week of December, less than half of the Gurkhas' rate, possibly because their regimental clothing supplies held up, or because they were able to keep the men's feet dry. Lieutenant Arthur Behrend saw men of each kind face a flooded washway. He watched a 'Punjabi' alone attempt to cross the torrent but give up, 'forlorn and defeated', but then saw two Gurkhas cross, clasping hands, reaching the further bank 'drenched but grinning'. They were followed by an Indian mule-cart convoy, whose drivers plunged into the stream at the gallop, 'a vision of mighty splashes and water swirling at the sides of the lurching carts'.[10] The point is not to endorse easy stereotypes, but to reflect that 'Indian' troops manifested a range of behaviours and reactions.

Australian accounts of the campaign repeatedly praise the mountain gunners' help. The war diary of the 11th Battalion (by this time in the northern sector of Anzac) recorded that on 22 September the Indians fired six shots before changing position, their gunners and drivers 'well trained and quick', and that "Jacko" 'did not get a return shell in until the Indians had been gone 20 minutes'. By then the gun detachments were in action elsewhere.[11] The batteries maintained more positions than they

5 Memo, 30 December 1915, Wilson, to Duff, WWI/348/H, NAI.
6 Gould, *Imperial Warriors*, p, 123, quoting General Sir Willcocks, *With the Indians in France*, pp. 82-87.
7 Diary, 17 June 1915, Humphrey Gell, P158, 10048, IWM.
8 Letter, 8 September 1915, Ian Hamilton7/1/29, LHCMA.
9 Diary, 7 October 1915, Arthur Tillard, GM.
10 Behrend, *Make Me a Soldier*, pp. 106-07.
11 Belford, *Legs Eleven*, p. 157.

A badly wounded Supply and Transport driver, his leg torn off by shrapnel, awaiting stretcher-bearers, a depiction by John Hargrave of the stoicism shown by many Indian soldiers. (John Hargrave, *At Suvla Bay*)

INDIAN WITH LEG BLOWN OFF SMOKING & WAITING FOR STRETCHER PARTY

Gurkhas, cold, sick and fed-up but resigned, in the trenches at Demakjelik Bair later in the campaign. (14th Sikhs album)

had guns, and moved between them to avoid retaliatory fire from Ottoman batteries which became both more numerous and effective as the campaign continued. Still, the tensions of the weary weeks of cold weather are suggested by a line in the war diary of the 2nd Australian Division: 'held inquiry into reported striking of Indian Driver by an Officer'.[12] The second division had not shared the hardships of the campaign as had the first four brigades to land.

'When all others failed': frostbite

By late November everyone was miserable: cold, run-down, fed-up, and suffering the effects of prolonged dehydration (though the weather was colder the water supply barely improved). November's weather was mainly mild: in some ways the month was the most peaceable and least costly of the campaign, with both sides exhausted and ill (though scurvy, night-blindness and jaundice among run-down men joined fly-borne dysentery). Up to late October nearly 5500 patients were admitted to an 'Indian clearing hospital', almost equally divided between wounds (2863) and sickness (2624).[13] At the month's end the weather broke. On 26 November a bitter wind blew out of the north-east, bringing sleet as the sky darkened. In the evening came torrents of rain 'more violent than any of our army had ever seen', the writer John Masefield recorded (though had he spoken to men familiar with the Indian monsoon?)[14] Floods of brown water carrying debris and even drowned Turks swept down gullies and the newly-dug trenches, pouring into dug-outs, soaking everyone (on both sides) and turning tracks and camps into bogs. As if this was not enough, it then froze.

The storms brought (as a friend wrote to George MacMunn, exponent of the martial races theory and now a staff officer on Imbros) 'immense rain, – trenches flooded … a good many drowned'. Men shivered in the ruins of tented hospitals blown down by the storm, wrapped in wet blankets.[15] The 14th Sikhs could not cook for four days, leaving men with only dry (but presumably soggy) biscuits. For once quartermasters acted promptly and compassionately, breaking open dumps and issuing dry clothing willy-nilly, without waiting for requisitions.

The blizzard that followed the storm killed over two hundred men from exposure: the 14th Sikhs' headquarters telephone orderly was found frozen to death in his dug-out. As the snow fell the temperature dropped and the first frost-bite casualties reached the field ambulances. ('Freezing hard … tracks now much better', an optimistic British Gurkha officer recorded on 28 November.[16]) Major Battye's bearers, who themselves were suffering from cold and exposure, drew praise for their devotion

---

12 War diary, 2nd Australian Division, 15 November 1915, WO95/4346, NAUK.
13 War diary, 108th Indian Field Ambulance, December 1915, WO95/4272, NAUK.
14 Masefield, *Gallipoli*, p. 169.
15 Letter to George MacMunn, [early December 1915], MS21, MacMunn Papers, Folder 2, Special Collections, ADFA.
16 War diary, 1/5th Gurkhas, November 1915, WO95/4472, NAUK.

'Crippled on Gallipoli': William Villiers-Stuart's annotation to a photograph of one of his beloved 1/5th Gurkhas. (Gurkha Museum, Winchester)

to duty in carrying hundreds of men with frost-bitten feet. The number of sick admitted to 9th Corps medical units in the days before had averaged about 250. By 30 November the figure was over 300, and of them 99 were suffering from frost-bite, and on the following day the number treated for frost-bite alone reached 244.[17] The 10th reported 477 cases of frostbite, including eleven Gurkha officers; three quarters of the strength of the battalion of 628; 350 of them on one night.[18] The battalion's war diary suggests a reason for this extraordinary loss. An unknown officer wrote:

> a [double company] under Brigade orders lay out at night for two nights on Connaught Ridge [a spur of Demakjelik Bair] in rain and snow & frost without shelter.

With the freezing rain the men in the trenches were 'knee deep in mud'.[19]

What had gone wrong? An account by Captain Charles Smyth of a neighbouring unit, the 6th, gives one officers' perspective – one surprisingly bitter, and even more so when it was published in a regimental history, and only ten years after 1915.[20] Smyth (an officer of the 1st Brahmans who could not speak Gurkhali) was ordered on 26 November to take over from a British battalion in trenches on the right sector of Hill 60. He went ahead of his men to examine the line he was to take over. 'Words fail me', he wrote, surveying the warren of waterlogged, muddy trenches he faced, parts of which had been blown in and left unrepaired, meaning that he had 'to make a circuit of about fifty yards actually to travel five yards straight'. He complained to Philip Palin (pointing out that a British battalion had allowed the trenches to fall into such disrepair) and was allowed to defer the relief until the next morning. In the meantime, though, Palin directed Smyth to take his men to bivouac on Connaught Ridge. His men sat exposed to the rain – 'a real tropical downpour' – for hours. As the weather became colder he had them stand and walk about in the open behind the trenches, risking stray bullets but forbidding them from sleeping for fear that they would freeze to death. At dawn they took over the trenches (the British battalion having cleared off), which they found flooded, deeper than the Gurkhas were tall. They did what they could to make the trenches habitable, the Gurkhas winning Smyth's regard by their cheerfulness. When it froze, so severely that men's hats froze to their heads, and the men, their feet sodden after two days of standing in waterlogged trenches, suffered from frost bite. By the morning of the 30th Smyth found that most of his men were afflicted. His own orderly, Hastabir Pun, who had followed him about and remained

---

17 DDMS reports on sickness, IX Corps, November-December 1915, MS21, MacMunn Papers, Folder 2, Special Collections, ADFA.
18 Mullaly, *Bugle and Kukri*, p. 108.
19 War diary, 2/10th Gurkhas, November 1915, WO95/4472, NAUK.
20 Ryan, Strahan & Jones, *Historical Record of the 6th Gurkha Rifles*, pp. 133-36.

'cheerful and keen', at last revealed that both of his feet were black from frostbite. Over a hundred of the 6th were evacuated.

Losses from the cold were not, however, uniform. Thanks to the excellence of their bathing and drying arrangements, the mountain gunners suffered no casualties at all. The Sikhs, which happened to be out of the line, also fared well. The 4th Gurkhas, with its experience of a French winter behind it, suffered only 6% of the brigade's frost-bite casualties, a rate attributable to the prudence of its quartermaster in obtaining extra clothing and outsize boots (to accommodate extra socks) for his men. Just as they had developed a rapport during the campaign, frost-bite casualties among both Indians and Australians in the trenches around Demakjelik Bair increased at the same rate, virtually doubling as the frost reached into dugouts and fire-steps, chilling men huddling under blankets and shuffling boots in attempts to keep warm. Ian Hamilton's former aide de camp, touring the trenches, encountered Gurkhas suffering from frost-bite. He described to Hamilton, his uncle, how he had 'met numbers of the little chaps limping along the saps carrying their boots' – that is, walking through freezing slush bare-footed, making their way painfully to the dressing stations.[21] (The Turks, who were often dressed in threadbare cotton uniforms, suffered as severely as their enemies. When some were so cold they got out of their trenches and walked about to keep warm, Reginald Savory cold-bloodedly admitted to his mother that 'we shot as many as possible', adding 'poor devils'.[22])

Indian regulars might have been inured to hardship, but the danger and privations of trench service told on even the most dedicated troops. Wartime volunteers (some practically pressed men) reacted badly. Officers found more cases of self-inflicted wounds. One of the 5th Gurkhas' men was found with two of his fingers blown off. 'I'm sorry to say it looks … as if he did it himself', Tillard wrote, hoping that 'he will suffer the full penalty', though the charge of 'self-inflicted-wound' failed due to lack of evidence.[23] Three weeks later Tillard had to ask his Gurkha officers to watch for more cases. Kenneth Erskine loyally disagreed. He affirmed that the 5th

> held their pride in work and discipline all through the Gallipoli and Mesopotamian fighting, … not only always the best, but were looked on by the Brigade as something quite exceptionally sound and reliable, when all others failed to some extent under the terrific losses they had to bear.[24]

21 Letter, 6 December 1915, A.M. McGrigor, P399, 9984, IWM.
22 Letter, 7 December 1915, 7603-93, NAM.
23 Diary, 30 September-1 October 1915, Arthur Tillard, GM.
24 Maxwell, *Villiers-Stuart on the Frontier*, p. 188.

Frost-bitten Gurkhas and other Indian troops awaiting evacuation from behind the line at Demakjelik Bair, December 1915. (AWM C02448)

Norman Wimbush's drawing of men carrying supplies to the 14th Sikhs' flooded front line trenches early in December. (14th Sikhs album)

'The long continued life': mountain gunners in winter

Now (since 21 September) commanding the mountain artillery at Anzac, Arthur Fergusson decided that he needed to make his brigade comfortable. He had his Indian officers ensure that their men's dugouts were waterproof, and urged his officers to make the Right Section headquarters a model for all units at Anzac: Birdwood agreed. The Indian gunners collected discarded Turkish clothing (presumably stripped off the dead on Sari Bair and Hill 60 or taken from their discarded kit). They set Phumman Singh 'a real bad hat but priceless at that sort of thing' to become the 'chief acquirer of stolen goods and chattels' and with his officers' concurrence he gathered enough for two greatcoats and four blankets per man. (Turkish greatcoats could not be worn outside the gunners' lines, for obvious reasons, but the clothing ensured that the men were warm. Inventive senior NCOs, notably the brigade Havildar-Major Amar Singh, made bathing and drying rooms in tunnels, heated by a British Soyer boiler, which dispensed hot water, and every man was directed to bathe weekly. The inability to bathe, such an important part of the religions of India, imposed a severe burden on Indian troops throughout the campaign, and they relished the chance now, despite the weather. One freezing day Fergusson passed a crowd of his men queuing for the bathing tunnel. He asked if they had been ordered to in spite of the cold. They told him that they were bathing on their own initiative and would not miss their weekly bath.

While the mountain gunners could be expected to be handy with tools, both Sikhs and Gurkhas displayed a flair for technical work. Havildar Buddria Shanti led a fatigue party of the 5th Gurkhas in a light rail-laying gang and an officer observed how 'they soon fell into the work'. They called to each other to share the tools – 'Jeem Kerow' – a crow bar – and 'Yshpanner' – a spanner.[25] Indian gunners even rigged up what was mysteriously described as a 'Serbian Barrel', which enabled them to disinfect their clothes every three weeks, presumably using steam, probably fueled by wood obtained from the mule corps.[26]

Arthur Fergusson saw that Jacob's Battery 'wanted a lot of bucking up'. It had not only lost its battery commander, John Bruce, early in the campaign, but also all of its pre-war regular officers and many of its Indian officers. It was now losing men sick in much larger numbers than its sister battery. Fergusson had been able to command Kohat Battery as firmly as he had partly because Parker had imposed a light hand from brigade headquarters. Despite Fergusson's care in looking after his men's welfare, 'the old stagers also began to suffer from the long continued life' in the observation posts and gun pits. In October, with very little action in the trenches, Fergusson secured permission to at last send half of his brigade at a time over to rest on Imbros. (As with Simpson's donkey, he wrote 'Mudros' in his memoir, but it was actually Imbros.) The

---

25 Letter, 25 October 1915, Herbert Winn, 97/18/1, IWM.
26 'Gallipoli 1915', Arthur Fergusson, 3DRL3635, AWM.

first contingent left on 24 October, exactly six months after the landing. No less than half of the brigade (267 men) had served continuously on the peninsula, but only half as many other ranks in Jacob's compared to Kohat's suggests how ruinous Jacob's sick rates must have been.[27] It is possible that some of the Jacob's men evacuated sick from the peninsula took advantage of the corruption endemic to even the Indian Army. The going rate for evacuation from Lemnos to India was apparently ten rupees – effectively a month's pay – and it is possible that some demoralised men took advantage of the option.

Even though active operations practically ceased with the onset of autumn, the need to maintain the more extensive trenches that had been created after the expansion of the Anzac area after the August offensive meant that if anything labour demands increased. This imposed a greater burden on men weakened by a grueling campaign. Again, the responsibility of encouraging men to do what was necessary fell on the units' Indian officers. On 9 November Nar Bahadur Rai of the 10th, who had won the Indian Order of Merit for his leadership in the attacks on Hill 60, now a Subedar, got out of his trench to encourage his men to repair a loophole, and was wounded as a result. The following day Lance-Naik Naharsing Gurung of the 6th Gurkhas risked his life to hurl a bomb over the parados, saving four men from wounds or death: his 'great bravery' gained him an Indian Order of Merit.

Further (and higher) honours and awards also arrived that autumn. Birdwood (an Indian Army officer) had become a Knight Commander of the Order of St Michael and St George in June, and in October was promoted to Lieutenant-General. (Given that Gallipoli became the graveyard of several generals' reputations (Hamilton, Hunter-Weston, Stopford) Birdwood arguably gained most from the campaign, going on to command the First Anzac Corps for the following two years, and in 1918 taking command of the Fifth Army. In October 1915 Herbert Cox, now sick in hospital, joined Birdwood as a KCMG. John Parker, whose 7th Mountain Artillery Brigade had made such a sustained contribution to the defence of Anzac, became a Companion of the same order in October, and became senior gunner of a British division at Suvla.

By the winter the force holding the trenches snaking over the ridges north from Anzac to Suvla had truly become an empire army. In addition to Indians and the Australians and New Zealanders who had formed the mainstay of the invasion force, it now comprised a majority of British (including Irish, Scots and Welsh) troops, but also a Newfoundland battalion, which reinforced the reduced 29th Division, and a Maori battalion. (Birdwood, seeing a dark-skinned man on a stretcher, addressed him heartily in Gurkhali. The man said 'A Gurkha? No, sir, I am a Maori!'[28]) But by the campaign's end the single Indian brigade, even when augmented by an extra battalion, had become a tiny proportion of what had been re-named the Dardanelles Army.

27 Ibid.
28 Birdwood, *Khaki and Gown*, p. 286.

As Christmas approached staff officers established how many of Force G's men were smokers, in anticipation that gift tins would be distributed in the name of Princess Mary, the King and Queen's only daughter. The figures disclosed that 1199 Indian soldiers out of 6,966 were non-smokers – most of them Sikhs whose religion forbade tobacco. (In the event there was a muddle and the gift tins turned up full of cigarettes anyway.)[29]

'Does a man want to go to heaven?': evacuation

Ian Hamilton's replacement by General Sir Charles Monro in October heralded the beginning of the end. Kitchener, who visited the peninsula in November, agreed that the campaign could not succeed and needed to be closed down. Early in December the War Council decided to risk evacuation and staff officers devised plans to get away without it becoming a bloodbath.

'We began to train the Turks to be evacuated', Fergusson wrote. The Anzac and Suvla forces imposed a program in which all guns were at times prohibited from firing, to accustom the Turks to long periods of silence. During these 'silent stunts' Fergusson took advantage of the quiet, despite the cold, to revisit his old Anzac haunts (the brigade was now largely in the Suvla sector, firing in support of the British 54th Division). In this period it was heartening to the Indians that 'many Australians … came over to see their old pals of the early days' – the more so when the visits entailed treks of several miles along muddy trenches in weather that would have tried fit men, let alone men who had suffered the privations of the peninsula.

Staff officers planned for the final evacuation, set for the night of 19-20 December. Just as the Supply and Transport units had worked to land and distribute stores and ammunition during the campaign, so mule convoys now carried valuable goods to the jetties. On the night of 15 December an anonymous Australian diarist recorded his account of meeting mules of the Kohat Battery making for wharves north of the cove. He 'at once thought – "My goodness, if the Turks don't see all this … they must be blind"', but then realised how quiet the mules were. 'They had big loads', he wrote, 'but … they made no sound at all as they walked except for the slight jingle of a chain now and then …' Charles Bean noted (having often chatted to Indian officers) that the gun mules had been trained to be silent – making them especially valuable. He saw them loaded aboard a lighter along with several (Anzac) guns and the battery's baggage. He doubted whether the Turks could see more than 'a black serpentine streak' even in the moonlight, or any noise at more than 200 yards, and concluded (as did Bean) that the Turks could not have concluded that the beach-head was being 'lightened', as the phrase used at Anzac put it.[30]

---

29 Table, Tel. 10 November 1915, WWI/334/H, NAI.
30 Bean, *The Story of Anzac*, Vol. II, pp. 866-67.

The impending evacuation also coincided with the end of another saga. London and Delhi (by this time Army Headquarters had made its annual cold weather migration from Simla) still wrangled over who should be rewarded for the exertions Indian troops had made and the terrible conditions they had endured. Hardinge argued for a more liberal distribution, not least because to deny it to units transferred from eligible areas (west of Suez) to areas where it was not paid could provoke what he called 'grave, and we think just, discontent'.[31] The Indian Army had seen several protests in 1915 and with images of 1857 in mind Indian officers wanted no undue cause for protest. Days before the final evacuation officials settled arrangements for payments to Indian troops serving in Europe and the Mediterranean, agreeing that Indian wounded sent to Malta and Egypt should also receive allowances, 'so long as they form part of the Mediterranean Expeditionary Force' – (which was about to cease to exist: did a bureaucratic trap lie concealed in that qualification?)[32] On the very day of the final evacuation of Anzac and Suvla the argument was finally settled. From their next pay day sepoys received a monthly bonus of upwards of 3 rupees, with naiks receiving 6, havildars 7 and subedars 30, an increase of roughly a third of their pre-war pay. The increase, coming after many years of sepoys feeling that their pay had been eroded by increasing prices, coincided with further wartime inflation.[33]

The Indian brigade joined the evacuation on 12 December when 1,300 men (including men of the neighbouring British yeomanry) were taken off. The 14th Sikhs (one of the units that had lost most and served longest on Gallipoli) left first. Relieved by the 4th Gurkhas on 14 December, its men filed down to the beach and boarded just two lighters, to be towed out and taken to Lemnos. During the campaign the Sikhs had lost 28 British officers killed or wounded (including every officer who had landed on 1 May, though Reginald Savory remained with his battalion until the end), 18 Indian officers and 344 sepoys dead and 840 wounded. Another 380 men had been invalided sick. The 10th Gurkhas left on 14 December. The 4th, relatively fresh and having lost fewest men (only thirteen dead in three months) provided one of the final parties, of six officers and 45 men (a large number for so few men, but the need for control was critical).

Carey-Evans's medical section left on 15 December, when the first of the mountain guns went. The brigade headquarters stretcher-bearer-cum-cook Rangasammy also left, worried for Fergusson Sahib's welfare once he was gone. The next day six more went, with all the mules except eight. Skeleton detachments served the remaining guns, living in dug-outs in the almost deserted gullies. They stockpiled large quantities of shells– 300 for each gun – in case the Turks should realise that their adversaries were slipping away and attack, but in the end they fired only 400 rounds in the final week and some 800 rounds had to be tossed into pits filled with sea water.

---

31 Tel., 15 December 1915, Hardinge to Chamberlain, WWI/153/H, NAI.
32 Tel., 13 December 1915, Chamberlain to Hardinge, WWI/335/H, NAI.
33 Tel., 20 December, Chamberlain to Hardinge, WWI/154/H, NAI.

Some of the Indian troops had remained on the peninsula from the first days to the evacuation. Heber Alexander praised the endurance of Mangat Rai, the mule corps's clerk, as 'truly remarkable'.[34] The Australian gunner-cum-interpreter-cum-officer, Cecil Maer had also spent eight months on the peninsula from the arrival of his Australian battery just after the landing to the evacuation of the Sikhs a few days before the force's final departure. After up to eight months on the peninsula (for men of the mountain artillery and the mule corps) the Indians were as exhausted as any. While still performing their duties in the trenches, gun positions and mule lines with the dedication expected of the Indian Army, they were relieved to learn of the coming evacuation. No senior commanders took Indian soldiers into their confidence. While some may have deduced that evacuation was happening no one told them until the last days. Some felt disappointment as well. South Indian muleteers misheard their destination as 'Madras' rather than Mudros, and when an officer queried their wish to return to India, one replied 'Does a man want to go to heaven?'.[35]

The last Indians to die on the peninsula were Dirgasing Gurung of the 1/5th Gurkhas and Amaldhoj Rai of the 2/10th. Gurung was killed by flying clods of earth when a Turkish mine exploded under the 5th's front line. Twenty men suffered severe shock, one after being buried for 45 minutes: 'a very unpleasant morning', Noel Cosby recorded.[36] That night, on the principle of last on last off, the 4th Gurkhas left a party of 400 men to be withdrawn on the final night, the final days becoming 'a severe trial of the nerves' of men unsettled by inhabiting trenches, now largely deserted that formerly held thousands of men and animals. (The 4th were in fact regarded as the right-hand unit of the British 9th Corps; their neighbours the 5th and 6th the extreme left-hand units of the Australian and New Zealand Army Corps.) On the last night the Supply and Transport Corps drivers were sent out 'for the purpose of squealing only', the noise of their ungreased wheels persuading the Turks that regular convoys were running as usual.[37] Presumably these mules were among those shot in their stalls to prevent them from falling into Turkish hands the next morning.[38]

Not all of the artillery's precious mules were destroyed, however. For a time it seemed that the remaining eight gun mules might be slaughtered in the final minutes, once the guns had been loaded aboard lighters. But Fergusson again lobbied Birdwood (by now commanding the Dardanelles Army) and had the order rescinded. Fergusson saw Birdwood on the last day, 19 December, and thanked him. They agreed that destroying trained gun mules would have been a criminal waste. On the final evening, after Fergusson had watched his four remaining guns carried down to the piers by his eight remaining mules, he had dinner with the staff of the New Zealand and

34 Alexander, *On Two Fronts*, p. 246.
35 Nevinson, *The Dardanelles Campaign*, p. 393.
36 Diary, 19 December 1915, Noel Crosby, 08/94/1, IWM.
37 Aylmer, 'Lecture delivered Deputy Assistant Director of Transport …', *Journal of the United Service Institution of India*, 1917, p. 306.
38 Chhina, 'Their mercenary calling', p. 239.

Australian Division, with whom he had been messing since Rangasammy's departure. Fergusson 'began to buck' – to boast – about having been on the peninsula from the very first day to the final. A New Zealand sapper produced a corporal who had also arrived on the first day, but who was listed to leave on one of the last boats, due to leave at 2 a.m.

In the end, Fergusson wrote, 'the actual finish was just like going to Waterloo to catch the last train'. He found his few remaining men in a nullah including three British officers (Campbell, Rawson and Armstrong), Subedars Hem Singh and Chanda and Jemadar Puran Singh. Fergusson led them to the pier, where they boarded a lighter and by the time they were being towed toward the transport Fergusson was fast asleep. The 7th Indian Mountain Brigade had served at Anzac for 238 days, in action almost without pause. The two batteries had suffered 24 killed and 278 wounded (effectively the equivalent of an battery's establishment), and 62 mules wounded and 212 killed. It seems that the mountain guns did not fire on only three days of the 238 they spent on the peninsula: on the truce of 24 May and on the two days of the 'silent stunts' in December.

Early that evening the first of the final 600 men slipped quietly away in the winter darkness. They were followed at intervals by groups who marched as quietly as they could (wearing boots muffled with socks) toward the evacuation piers. (The 6th Gurkhas went down Sikh Walk, others down Tillard Sap.) That left a handful of men in the front line trenches – about 80 of the 5th and 50 of the 6th – to make the noise that Turkish sentries would expect to hear. It was a bitterly cold and dark night, haze fortunately obscuring the full moon. At about 1a.m. they set the 'drip rifles' that would buy the final parties time to get away even if the Turks suspected something was up, and they embarked at the wharves at the mouth of the Asmak Dere at the dead of night. Everyone agreed that the evacuation had been 'admirably done & was a perfectly wonderful piece of work' that 'went like clockwork', as Herbert Winn told his family.[39] 'We all had a glorious nights sleep last night', Arthur Tillard scrawled in his diary on 21 December.[40] The artillery brigade's only losses were an officer's shaving kit and a gunner's bedding. Sultan Ali, Kohat Battery's Pay Havildar, managed to get all of the brigade's gear away by virtually camping on the piers and sending small consignments with many lighters and launches as they left. The evacuation had succeeded brilliantly, at virtually no cost, a final, ironic triumph.

The staff officers supervising the evacuation feared that the orderly withdrawal they planned could turn into a bloody debacle. George MacMunn, responsible for the logistics at Dardanelles Army headquarters, warned that the medical units should plan for ten thousand 'unexpected wounded' – something of a paradox, but he meant

---

39 Letter, 23 December 1915, Herbert Winn, 97/18/1, IWM.
40 Tillard diary, 21 December 1915, GM.

for them to be prepared for heavy casualties, warning that a thousand wounded might need to be abandoned as the last parties fought their way to the beaches.[41]

Did the Turks know the evacuation was happening? George Aylmer heard 'fairy tales … that we paid the Turks to let us go', and described the allegations as 'absolute bunkum!' But did they know something was afoot and let it proceed? The war diaries of the Indian battalions in the line in the final days of the campaign suggest an unusual degree of activity. In contrast to the 'everything quiet' that appears so often through October and November, in the last week of the occupation of Anzac the war diaries record outbreaks of sniping, bombing and shelling, and a 'good deal of Machine-Gun and rifle fire': 'Turks very active', reads the 5th Gurkhas' diary on the 17th.[42] On the final day a Turkish mine exploded under the 5th Gurkhas (wounding thirteen Gurkhas) and the Turks had fired a heavier bombardment on the Hill 60 lines (held by the 4th and 5th Gurkhas) than they had for weeks previously: did they realise that something was afoot? Humphrey Gell thought that the Turks knew of the evacuation but were content to let the invaders go: 'of course they may think "All right if the blighters are going … let them go … it's what we've been trying to make em do since April".[43] Whether the worn down Ottoman troops would have obeyed orders to storm the enemy's trenches seems to have been a point their commanders did not test. Two days before the final evacuation leaflets were supposedly dropped on the Indian lines 'telling the Indians that they were being abandoned only to have their throats cut on the peninsula'.[44] Writing from hospital in Britain, Cecil Allanson acerbically observed that 'our real success was due to the inertia of the Turk'.[45] The evacuation of Cape Helles, where Supply and Transport trains remained until January 1916, proceeded as smoothly, further suggesting that Ottoman commanders knew of the impending evacuation and allowed it to proceed.

Ironically, in the light of the 69th and 89th Punjabis' withdrawal from Gallipoli for fear that their Musalman companies would not fight their co-religionists, some senior officers deprecated the option of evacuation because of the effects of defeat on Britain's Muslim subjects. Birdwood, in whose corps the 29th Brigade had served, counseled against evacuation for fear of the reaction of the Muslim world. General Sir Charles Monro, Hamilton's successor, argued that Musalman soldiers had fought their co-religionists over the frontier and that far from expressing reluctance at shooting Turks, 'their conversation led one rather to believe that they enjoyed doing these things'.[46] Not that Monro, a British officer who had served in the second Afghan war as a subaltern, understood such conversations.

---

41 'Tentative outline of withdrawal of wounded', December 1915, MS21, MacMunn Papers, Folder 2, Special Collections, ADFA.
42 War diary, 1/5th Gurkhas, December 1915, WO95/4472, NAUK.
43 Diary, 15 December 1915, Humphrey Gell, P158, 10048, IWM.
44 Nevinson, *The Dardanelles Campaign*, p. 370.
45 Letter, 27 January 1916, Davies, *Allanson of the 6th*, p. 99.
46 Barrow, *The Life of General Sir Charles Carmichael Monro*, p. 74.

'The most mismanaged show on earth': judgment on Gallipoli

The idea of capturing Constantinople, knocking Turkey out of the war and bringing aid to Russia seems as beguiling a century on as it seemed to some of the War Council in the war's first (northern) winter. The vision was destroyed by hasty planning, bad command decisions and sheer bad luck: if the battleships had not run onto a row of mines on 18 April; if Hamilton had not split his force on 25 April; if only the Australian brigadiers had pushed on; if only, if only … Among this list of 'if only' is the dates of arrival of troops at Helles. The Indian brigade arrived just too late for the first, 28 April, attack on Krithia. Later in the campaign, the drama of Allanson reaching the crest of Sari Bair, with the water of the Narrows winking sarcastically in the distance, though in reality illusory, remains the greatest of Gallipoli's might-have-beens.

And yet it was all for naught. Herbert Cox himself, in a forthright statement to the Dardanelles Commission in 1916 condemned the entire operation. By then a major-general (having commanded an Australian division on the Somme and about to go to the India Office as Military Secretary) he was blunt. 'The landings at Helles and Anzac were too far apart to be able to assist one another … it was never likely that the taking of Achi Baba … would open the Dardanelles … it was hopeless from the first that real progress would ever be made from Helles'.[47] The 1,600 Indian dead and 4,000 wounded of Gallipoli truly died for no purpose. The campaign was lost by the time Cox's brigade landed at Helles on 30 April; perhaps by the time the mountain guns landed at Anzac on 25 April. The terrible casualty lists of Gully Ravine, Gully Spur, Sari Bair and Hill 60 did not bring, and never could have brought, victory. A century on, Gallipoli remains compelling because it is a tragedy, a seemingly inevitable tragedy once several portentous decisions had been taken. Cecil Allanson was of course absolutely correct in predicting in 1915 that 'when everything comes out, this Dardanelles show will prove to have been the most mismanaged show on earth'.[48] It was – and responsibility for that mismanagement lies at least partly with senior British officers of the Indian Army. Its regimental officers and men, however, performed their part in accordance with its traditions as a professional, trained force.

Service on Gallipoli certainly confirmed and perhaps the enhanced the reputation of the 6th Gurkhas, and it became regarded as the outstanding Indian unit of the campaign. The 14th Sikhs also attracted admiration and sympathy for its travails, especially at Gully Ravine. The 1/5th and 2/10th received less attention, in their officers' eyes undeservedly. Rob Shewen's summary (written in the 1920s) of the 2/10th's of its part in the August offensive ended on a carping note:

---

47 Statement by Maj-Gen H.V. Cox to the Dardanelles Commission, 9 December 1916, 102, AWM 51.
48 Allanson, *Copy of the personal diary kept in the field*, p. 33.

One of the piers at Anzac from which the Indians left the peninsula. (14th Sikhs album)

The 1/6 G.R. undoubtedly did most magnificently throughout the battle but they certainly got a better "write up" than the 2/10 G.R. on the 10th Aug. for doing precisely the same work – no more, no less.[49]

Collectively, Indian troops had made an arguably greater contribution to the campaign man-for-man than any other single formation; or at least as great as the British 29th Division and some of the Anzac formations. They had made three attacks at Helles, at least one of which could justifiably be regarded as the single most tactically effective of the campaign, and had taken part in the climactic attack of the entire campaign, the failed assault on the summit of Chunuk Bair. The mountain artillery, which by December numbered seventeen guns (more than the batteries' establishments, with twelve at Anzac and five at Suvla) had served throughout the entire campaign at Anzac, firing a total of some 19,000 rounds over eight months.[50]

In the light of Hamilton's pleas for a 'Gurkha Brigade' in March, and his apparent machinations to swap the Punjabis for more Gurkhas (and the arrival of a further Gurkha battalion in September) it is notable that Hamilton came to attach to the Gurkhas one explanation for the failure of his campaign. At Christmas 1918 Hamilton had his secretary send a card to the 6th Gurkhas. On it his secretary passed on Hamilton's 'most cherished conviction that if he had been given more Gurkhas at the Dardanelles he would never have been held up by the Turks'.[51] Perhaps; but Hamilton was not 'held up' by the Turks, he was defeated. There is no saying that the consequence of more Gurkhas on Gallipoli would not have been merely more Gurkha names on the Helles Memorial.

49 [Douglas Shewen], 'Notes on [the official history's account of the August offensive], c. 1925', 2/10th Gurkhas Digest of Service, GM.
50 War diary, 7th Indian Mountain Brigade, April 1915-January 1916, WO95/4289, NAUK.
51 Ryan, Strahan & Jones, *Historical Record of the 6th Gurkha Rifles*, p. 144.

If despite all their suffering and sacrifice the Indian Army's combatant units made no decisive contribution to the victory that eluded the entire Mediterranean Expeditionary Force, can it be said that Indian troops made a notable contribution to the campaign? It can. When Ian Hamilton, in his typically chatty way, asked a British yeomanry officer what had impressed him most at Suvla, he did not mention the Australians, the Connaught Rangers or even the 'incomparable' 29th Division. He simply replied 'the Indian Mule driver and the stretcher bearer'.[52] The mule drivers, the largest single component of the Indian Army on Gallipoli, were ubiquitous and invaluable. Without them operations at Helles, Anzac and Suvla could not have continued. They did not go over the top in the futile and sacrificial assaults of Gully Ravine, Gully Spur, Sari Bair or Hill 60, but every day they loaded their mules and AT carts and jogged beside them up the tracks, risking wounds and death from snipers, machine-guns and shell-fire.

---

52 Aylmer, 'Lecture delivered Deputy Assistant Director of Transport …', *Journal of the United Service Institution of India*, 1917, p. 306.

15

'He is here today; he will be here hereafter': remembering Gallipoli

As Indian units settled down in tented camps on bare, windswept Lemnos (though free of the danger of shells and snipers) or approached Alexandria on the transports that carried them south, a Christmas message arrived from the King-Emperor. King George V sent all ranks of his armies 'a heartfelt Christmas greeting and our good wishes for the New Year', expressing 'confidence that their devotion, their valour and their self-sacrifice will under God's guidance lead to victory and an honourable peace'.[1] Did they bother to translate this message (a Christmas message making little sense to Hindu, Sikh or Musalman soldiers)? Or was the discrepancy between its hearty optimism and their withdrawal and even defeat all too apparent? Gallipoli must have imposed a physical and mental strain on Indian troops, though there is little record of it. After Gallipoli William Villiers-Stuart found his beloved 5th Gurkhas 'very subdued', and his orderly (who greeted him by throwing his arms about him, laughing and crying) said of the battalion's dead how 'they longed for you to come before they died'.[2] Another officer of the 5th wrote of the 'conscious effort' he made in Egypt 'to combat the reaction following the previous stress', but exactly how that 'reaction' manifest is unknown.[3]

'This shall be my gratification': after Gallipoli

Just as Force G had scooped up reinforcements from a dozen units, so with its return to Egypt the process was reversed. Drafts left to return men to their parent units, now everywhere from France to Egypt and Mesopotamia. (Some Indian units evacuated from Gallipoli were even sent to Salonika – 137 Combined Field Ambulance, and some mule corps, including those from Bharatpur and Indore.) In mid-January the 14th Sikh's Patiala men finally rejoined the Rajindra Infantry, still on the canal.

---

1 Tel., 23 December 1915, Chamberlain to Hardinge, WWI/335/H, NAI.
2 Maxwell, *Villiers-Stuart goes to War*, p. 175.
3 Regimental Committee, *History of the 5th Royal Gurkha Rifles*, p. 274.

Men of the 14th Sikhs unpacking at Suez after the evacuation of the peninsula. (14th Sikhs album)

Drafts were still of course embarking from Bombay and Karachi for Force G units – over 850 rank and file in December, excluding 1,000 followers, most men of the labour corps, now destined for the slowly developing debacle that was Mesopotamia. The return to Egypt broke relationships that had been created through the strain of the campaign. Arthur Fergusson found that he had 'the greatest difficulty' in persuading Sherer, Smith and Nye, his Australian signallers, to leave the mountain gunners and return to their units.[4]

For the battalions of 29th Brigade, 'it remained, then, to go and fight elsewhere', a 5th Gurkha officer recalled.[5] The brigade became part of the reconstituted 10th Indian Division, serving on the canal, as it had a year before. Pragmatically, Force E's headquarters re-distributed the units of 29th Brigade. By January the 14th Sikhs was listed in the location statements as being 'at base' – staff officers' jargon for ready to be sent somewhere else. In May 1916 it and the 10th Gurkhas embarked for Bushire, on the Persian coast, safeguarding the approaches to western India. In 1918, like the bulk of the Indian Army, it went to Mesopotamia, where the 5th and 6th Gurkhas, and the 7th Mountain Artillery Brigade, were already serving. The Patialas served on in Egypt, Sinai and Palestine, meeting the Maharaja himself when he visited Jerusalem in 1918.

To Australians or Britons, who for at least three generations have been taught to regard war as abhorrent; at best an evil necessity, it is hard to comprehend the attitude toward war common among the men whose stories this book tells. Gurkhas, Sikhs

4   'Gallipoli 1915', Arthur Fergusson, 3DRL3635, AWM.
5   Regimental Committee, *History of the 5th Royal Gurkha Rifles*, p. 273.

and Punjabis, both Hindu and Musalman, did not regard war as evil. Rather, they saw in it the fulfillment of noble aspirations, of manly attributes and destiny of a kind that in European societies could not long survive the carnage of the trenches. But to societies that saw war as a test and fulfillment of faith felt no unease at its pursuit. At a gathering on the third anniversary of the war's outbreak, in 1917, the Maharaja Bhupinder Singh quoted the Tenth Guru venerated by Sikhs, the Guru Gobind Singh Sahib. His prayer was

> Only grant the desire of my heart
> To die fighting with arms
> In the thick of battle. This shall
>   Be my gratification …[6]

Patiala's (and indeed Punjab's) support for the war intensified after 1915. Maharaja Bhupinder Singh's recruiters used the Patiala contingent's contribution on Gallipoli to urge more of his subjects to volunteer. He reminded recruiting rallies that they had 'heard of the conspicuous gallantry displayed by the 14th Sikhs at Gallipoli', asking 'is this not good testimony of the deeds of the valiant Khalsa'.[7] The Maharaja reminded his subjects that 'the Punjab tops the list of all the Provinces of India in the recruitment of combatants for the front, and Patiala holds similar honour amongst the Indian States'.[8] By the war's end Patiala had indeed contributed over 28,000 men, including 1,300 non-combatant followers, more than any district of British India: four times more than any other princely state.[9]

The individuals whose stories have been told in this book met diverse fates. Some prospered. Herbert Cox went on to command an Australian division (through Birdwood's patronage; an established Indian Army custom), and in 1917 became Secretary to the Government of India's Military Department – the most influential Indian soldier besides the Commander-in-Chief. Sir William Birdwood retained an association with both India and Australia. He toured Australia to rapturous welcome after the war and in 1925 became Commander-in-Chief of the Indian Army. P.P. Hypher, whose *Deeds of Valour Performed by Indian Officers and Soldiers* recorded many of the acts of gallantry performed by Indian troops on Gallipoli, dedicated his book to Birdwood: significantly, not to the men whose deeds it recorded. Others fared less well. Charles Bruce became a general but gained greater fame in leading the failed Everest expedition of 1922 and the expedition in 1924 when George Mallory and Andrew Irvine almost certainly reached the summit. Arthur Tillard retired in 1921, worn out by Flanders, Gallipoli, Mesopotamia and the frontier. Cecil Allanson,

---

6   Anon, *Patiala and the Great War*, p. 19.
7   Ibid., p. 15
8   History of Patiala State Forces, Part III, p. 76, Maharaja of Patiala collection.
9   Leigh, *The Punjab and the War*, p. 86.

recovering from blindness but still oppressed by the trauma of Sari Bair ('an everlasting torment', he told Harriet Tomes; to John Le Marchand's mother he confessed that he had not expected to survive) read some of the most graphic passages of his diary to the Dardanelles Commission, one of its few candid witnesses (though Herbert Cox was another) whose pain is evident a century on.[10]

Indian survivors entertained and perhaps attained more modest ambitions; if they survived the arduous Mesopotamian campaign, to which virtually all the Gallipoli units were committed. If they survived the war and wounds the fortunate enjoyed promotion and the pensions for which they endured so much. But Tulbir Gurung, the 6th Gurkas' champion khud-runner, was wounded on Gallipoli – in the leg. He never ran again. Though among the least well paid troops in the British empire force, the Supply and Transport followers gained a greater reputation. Heber Alexander wanted his muleteers' 'reward for his behaviour during the Great European War' to be merely 'a fuller recognition and more sympathetic treatment' in an army which regarded them merely as 'followers'.[11]

While after the war the Indian Army belatedly recognised sepoys' longstanding grievances and increased its pension rates, men disabled on Gallipoli and the families of those killed received pensions of a few rupees a month. Sepoys wives were already, as 'An Englishwoman' noticed just before Indians in Egypt saw action for the first time, 'a veiled womanhood whose voice we cannot hear and whose burden we cannot lighten'.[12] Later in the war the Indian Army increased its pensions, but in the war's first years many disabled sepoys or widows could expect little more than a life of beggary. The most fortunate were the Patialas, who thanks to Maharaja Bhupinder Singh's erratic generosity received comparatively ample pensions and gratuities. Its sepoys who served on Gallipoli and survived the war received a bonus of three months pay and six months paid leave.[13] Surprisingly, perhaps, among those who suffered financially after being wounded were British officers, who immediately lost the field and other allowances they depended on. 'We all lose heavily when wounded', wrote Cecil Allanson to his brother.[14] The Indian Army's promotion regulations characteristically were unduly inflexible to cope with the number and impact of the casualties in a major war, though representations to the India Office seemed not to assist the many British officers wounded on Gallipoli and affected by the Indian Army's financial bureaucracy.

The combination of the exigencies of war and the Indian Army's bureaucracy affected some wounded men. In 1916 the 6th Gurkhas learned that no one had maintained their individual service records since July 1915, and it took until November

10 Allanson Papers, 6602-22, NAM; Letter, 12 August 1915, Cecil Allanson, Donlea Papers, LHCMA.
11 Alexander, *On Two Fronts*, p. 248.
12 *The Spectator*, 23 January 1915.
13 History of Patiala State Forces, Part III, p. 141, Maharaja of Patiala collection.
14 Letter, 8 March 1916, Davies, *Allanson of the 6th*, p. 102.

1916 to sort out the mess. 'The result of this spelt hardship in the case of many men', Denis Ryan recorded with understated anger. He described the plight of a man who had lost a leg on Gallipoli and who was invalided out without his full settlement. Before he was carried home through the hills sympathetic depot officers estimated and gave him his payout.[15] What happened to Sikhs and Gurkhas who returned from war disabled? When Lord Hardinge visited the hospital patronised by Lady Willingdon (wife of Bombay's governor) which she had tricked out largely in mauve fabric, where many Gallipoli wounded were treated, he agreed to buy 'cork legs' for amputees. (He was aggrieved to learn that so precious did men consider them, at £20 apiece, that they regarded them as 'a sort of heirloom' and declined to wear them.)[16] One such man was perhaps the muleteer whom John Hargrave saw sitting smoking after losing his leg to shrapnel.

But the consequences of wounds lasted or became apparent years later. Subedar-Major Gambirsing Pun, for example, who fell wounded in the head with the 6th Gurkhas at Hill 60, evidently suffered permanent brain or nerve damage. Seemingly recovered from his wound he served with the battalion in Mesopotamia, but three and a half years later became paralysed and was discharged as an invalid. As a senior Gurkha officer, decorated and respected, he would have had a relatively large pension, but he must have been looked after by his family for the rest of his life. Captain Godfrey Tomes's widow, Harriet, asked after his welfare of Pun, who had served with her husband. Cecil Allanson assured her that he had 'everything that can be done for him, financially', indeed, in a village in Nepal, 'more than he wants'.[17] What of disabled men with more modest means ? We do not know.

'He died for freedom and honour': India's dead

The Indian dead of Gallipoli largely remain on the peninsula. As the Guru Nanak wrote: 'He is here today; he will be here hereafter'.[18] The first British war graves detachments arrived about a fortnight of the armistice with Turkey, camped at Maidos, which a few of the 6th Gurkhas had glimpsed but which none would reach. Soon including Australian, New Zealand and Indian Army officers, the detachment's parties went to work, identifying and labelling the cemeteries at Anzac, Helles and Suvla, searching the hillsides for remains and graves. Living in tents and leaky, bug-ridden buildings, the soldiers and the gangs of Greek and Turkish labourers they directed began work in wintry weather. Not all the remains they discovered could or should have been interred. In February 1919 an officer of the 2/4th Gurkhas (a battalion that had not served on Gallipoli) went with a team to Anzac to 'carry out

15 Ryan, Strahan & Jones, *Historical Record of the 6th Gurkha Rifles*, pp. 151-52.
16 Hardinge, *My Indian Years 1910-1916*, p. 109.
17 Allanson Papers, 6602-22, NAM.
18 *Hymns of the Guru Nanak*.

Rifleman Chandrabin Rana, 1/6th Gurkhas, who, as William Villiers-Stuart annotated in his album, 'did not return from Gallipoli'. (Gurkha Museum, Winchester)

religious rites in connection with Indian burials', suggesting that Hindu or Sikh holy men accompanied him.[19] It is clear that they exhumed at least one 'graveyard [that] contains only Indians'.[20] Photographs taken at the time reveal they cremated identifiable Gurkha and presumably Sikh remains – by this time only bones. In this way at least some of the Indian dead of Gallipoli were treated with the respect in death that had been impossible to show in 1915.

19   War diary, Graves Registration Unit (Gallipoli), 1918-19, WO95/4954, NAUK.
20   Letter, 17 October 1919, Allanson Papers, 6602-22, NAM.

The 'British' officers of the 14th Sikhs (including the MO, Herajee Cursetjee, at left), photographed at Peshawur in 1914. The annotations record that all but four of them died in the war, eight of them on Gallipoli in 1915. (14th Sikhs album)

The Great War was to cost the lives of some 60,000 members of the Indian Army, in Europe, the Middle East, Africa and south-western Asia. At the beginning of the war's final year the India Office sought advice from senior representatives of the main religious communities to which the army's members belonged. Lord Islington, the Parliamentary Under Secretary of State for India, convened a meeting at the India Office in March 1918, explaining (belatedly, perhaps) that the government recognised the need to treat India's war dead in accordance with its religious observances. Senior Indian lawyers and community leaders represented Muslim and Hindu interests respectively. They explained Muslim rules governing interment, stressing that graves should be left undisturbed, and that cremation was expected for 'Hindoos, Sikhs and Gurkhas'. Both wanted the dead of their faiths to be commemorated by the erection of temples or mosques in the larger war cemeteries, with the names of the dead recorded on large panels. The Imperial War Graves Commission acknowledged the need to incorporate Mohammedan and Hindu elements in designing its cemeteries, and indeed one of its principal architects was Sir Edwin Lutyens, who was already designing the official buildings of British India's capital, New Delhi. The Commission also drew on advice from Indian Army officers, notably 'General Cox' – Herbert Cox, who had commanded the 29th Indian Infantry Brigade on Gallipoli.

Reflecting the respect for custom characteristic of British India, the Commission adopted a respectful policy for the treatment of Indian soldiers' remains. Mohammedan graves 'should be left undisturbed ... except where there was the slightest apprehension of the grave being removed', a qualification which permitted their 'consolidation' into larger cemeteries. 'Hindoo', Sikh and Gurkha remains should, if they had been buried, be exhumed and cremated and then 'taken out to sea to be scattered on the water by Hindoo soldiers, under a Hindoo officer', or taken back to India to be scattered in an acceptable way. The policy seemed clear, though Herbert Cox's advice recognised that the reality on the ground was not necessarily so neat:

> In the case where Hindoos and Moslems are mixed up together, and unidentified, [probably the case on Gallipoli], a decision should be made as to which shall be ignored.[21]

Reports of 'Indian troops' sent to Gallipoli in 1920 to 'bury' remains at sea suggest that the policy was carried out.[22] Cox also deplored the erection is most cemeteries of the Cross of Sacrifice. Perhaps thinking it resembled structures seen on shooting ranges, he decried it as 'a sort of target that you shoot at'.[23]

The disposal of the Indian brigade's dead concerned all of its members, though in different ways and for different reasons. For its British officers the question of the location of men's graves mattered. Cecil Allanson wrote at the war's end how he was 'very seriously distressed about the Gallipoli graves'. He assured Harriet, widow of Captain Geoffrey Tomes (who had died with the 6th Gurkhas on 10 August), that Tomes had been buried, on the slopes of Sari Bair, and that he remembered exactly where. Allanson feared 'interference' by the Turks in the three years since, and indeed Geoffrey Tomes's grave could not be found, even though 'its location was brazen on my memory', Allanson wrote.[24] Tomes had been buried literally on the battlefield, in a shallow grave 'under fire within 50 or 60 yards of the enemy & ... on practically the highest point we ever reached'. His grave (and John Le Marchand's, nearby) lay on steep slopes and may have been washed away by later rain storms.

---

21 'Policy for Hindoos including (Sikhs & Gurkhas)', 909/5, CWGC.
22 *Ashburton Guardian* (NZ), 2 November 1920, p. 5.
23 Longworth, *The Unending Vigil*, p. 48.
24 Allanson Papers, 6602-22-3, NAM.

Several Indian units remembered Gallipoli especially. Until Partition Kohat Battery's officers sent a telegram of greeting to Australia every Anzac Day, to recall the shared hardships of Anzac. The 6th Gurkhas marked 'Gallipoli Day' on 4 June, the 10th on 7 August. Becoming part of the Brigade of Gurkhas in the British Army after 1947, it came to regard Sari Bair as one of its most important regimental anniversaries. In 1981 the regiment commissioned Terence Cuneo, an artist with a reputation for large commemorative battle pieces, to paint *Sari Bair*, depicting Allanson and his men coming over the crest of the ridge. Painted in the artist's 70s it is not his finest work, though it might be thought appropriately gory – in the foreground a Gurkha bayonets a Turk through his chest. Today it hangs in the splendid Gurkha Museum, Winchester, home to much of the British Gurkha regiments' heritage. The continuing significance of Gallipoli in Gurkha collective memory is seen in that while the Royal Gurkha Rifles now only has two battalions and six rifle companies, two of those companies are named Gallipoli and Sari Bair, an extraordinary share of a regiment with literally dozens of significant actions to choose to remember in that way.

Sepoys' wives had expected little but hardship from the war. 'Write my name among the widows', a Punjabi folk song put it.[25] The families of Indian soldiers who died overseas received a portrait of Queen Mary, the Queen-Empress, and what the Lieutenant-Governor, Michael O'Dwyer described as a 'beautiful message of sympathy' translated into the relevant vernacular. This gesture he thought 'a source of great comfort', and noticed that later in the war parents and widows brought their portraits to display at recruiting durbars.[26] Around September 1919 (four years after Gallipoli) the families of all the empire's dead, regardless of race, were presented with a large bronze medallion in the name of the King bearing (in English) the inscription 'HE DIED FOR FREEDOM AND HONOUR', and accompanied by a facsimile letter from the Viceroy:

> The King-Emperor commands me to assure you of the true sympathy of his Imperial Majesty and the Queen Empress in your sorrow.

Neither the slightly misjudged words of the medallion – what 'freedom' did Indians enjoy? – nor the austere comfort of the message could be read by any bereaved family. The medallions, in their large dark grey cardboard cases were sent to the depots to be forwarded to the families of dead sepoys. Some could not be despatched for lack of details of next-of-kin. By an extraordinary coincidence, one illustrated in the 6th Gurkha's booklet about its regimental 'chattels' refers to Duble Gurung, the rifleman

---

25 Punjabi 'tappa', cited in the *Empire, Faith and War* exhibition, School of Oriental and African Studies, 2014
26 O'Dwyer, 'India's Man-power in the War', *Army Quarterly*, Vol. 2, No. 2, July 1921, p. 260.

about whom the depot enquired in July 1915.[27] It seems that his family in Lamjung never did learn of his fate. The 6th at least kept the medallions in the officers' mess as paperweights. Though prosaically used to hold down newspapers blown by punkahs or fans, they each bore the name of a dead Gurkha. Medallions still held by the Royal Gurkha Rifles almost certainly belong to Gurkhas killed on Gallipoli.

'Quite undefeated': Indian veterans of Gallipoli

The war affected India as a whole profoundly – in 1917 the British government announced that India would move toward dominion status, and the nationalist movement emerged from the war with a more robust approach to its demands. But how did their war service affect the survivors of Gallipoli? It is difficult to find them amid the million sepoys who served, but some signs can be traced.

If in 1914 sepoys had manifest what a correspondent described to Hardinge as a 'simple soldierly devotion', the war exposed them to new experiences, of travel, different countries and encounters with foreigners, as well as to horrific slaughter.[28] While the Indian Army respected (and even entrenched) its men's religious scruples, military service introduced recruits to new ideas, of time-discipline, sanitation, literacy, vaccination and efficiency. (And even diet – sepoys acquired new tastes, for meat and tea, and for different clothes, such as suits and pullovers.) Their encounters with other Indians may have engendered respect between communities (Indian veterans interviewed in the 1970s spoke often of regarding men of other 'classes' as 'like brothers'.[29])

On leaving the army, the survivors of Gallipoli and the Great War returned either to their home villages or (in the Punjab) to settle in new plots in fertile but bare canal colony blocks. They might meet fellow veterans from their villages or districts, especially on pension pay-days (if they had qualified for a service pension, which wartime recruits generally did not), but otherwise would rarely have seen their former comrades, and did not form the ex-service associations which became such an important part of the remembering of British or dominion soldiers. But occasionally former comrades would meet. George MacMunn happened to be at Amballa, the main cantonment in the eastern Punjab, in March 1930, when veterans of the Indian mountain batteries gathered for a reunion. Over several days some 230 Indian officers and 1,300 pensioners, many with wartime service, gathered to meet each other and some British officers, in the presence of the Commander-in-Chief, General Sir Phillip Chetwode. MacMunn (always inclined to the sentimental and an ardent

---

27 6th Gurkha Rifles, *An Abridged History of the 6th QEO Gurkha Rifles Regimental Trust Property*, p. 55.
28 'Mr Steel' to Lord Hardinge, 14 October 1914, quoted in, 'The Indian Soldier, the Indian Army and Change', in Ellinwood & Pradhan, *India and World War I*, p. 178.
29 Ellinwood & Pradhan, *India and World War I*, p. 189.

Sikh veterans of Gallipoli with Reginald Savory in 1945.
(Bamford, *1st King George's Own Battalion*)

propagandist for the martial races theory) described this as 'a scene of romance and fidelity beyond description', and recounted affecting scenes as old gunners and drivers reminisced about or even greeted their old sahibs, enjoying an open-air cinema show and posing for many photographs, proudly wearing the medals they had earned as soldiers of the Sircar. Among the officers they remembered was Arthur Fergusson of Kohat Battery – 'Percussion Sahib' as they called him, 'the most famed among them'. MacMunn celebrated the gunners' demonstration of affection and loyalty because he, like the old solders, was conscious that India was changing. Forgetting that Gandhi and Congress had supported the war in 1914, the pensioners averred that if only the King would say the word they would march on Delhi to clear out what they called the 'Gandhi-Shandis' and the 'babu-shabu' whom they thought were behind nationalist agitation.[30]

In 1945 the British charity St Dunstan's reported on its work in India. Its 'outpost' in Dehra Dun was training seventy Indian servicemen, most blinded in the Second World War, then in its final months. But among the younger men was a 'spritely old Sikh', Karam Singh, who had been blinded as a Lance-Naik in Kohat Battery on 19 May. St Dunstan's reported that as well receiving the Indian Order of Merit, he had been granted twenty-five acres in a Punjab irrigation colony, since transformed

---

30 George MacMunn, 'The Reunion of Veterans', unidentified article, Vol. XL, No. 3, MS21, MacMunn Papers, Folder 7, ADFA Special Collections.

Patiala veterans (including men who served on Gallipoli) greeting the Prince of Wales in Patiala in 1922, with His Highness Bupinder Singh mounted on the left. (Patiala album)

by water to rich crop-land shaded by trees. He heard about St Dunstan's and wrote to be admitted, though by this time aged sixty. 'He arrived in a cheerful mood, with spotless turban above his snowy, flowing beard, and quite unwearied by three days in grilling heat in overcrowded trains'. At Dehra Dun, 'quite undefeated', he began a program of learning weaving, music and even braille.[31] Others were marked more darkly. Cecil Allanson, one of the campaign's most reflective and candid officers, was deeply affected by what he had seen and done on Gallipoli. He felt embarrassed at becoming prominent in accounts by John Masefield and Henry Nevinson, and dwelt on what he had done and not done. 'Every minute of that time is always with me', he wrote, and reproached himself for having survived 'presumably because I took less risks' – this from a man who had been bayonetted on the crest of Sari Bair.[32]

As pensioners who had served the Sirdar in war these men's loyalty is understandable, but it may not be the only consequence of service in the Great War. Lance-Naik Khela Singh, who had served with the Patiala infantry – and therefore may have served on Gallipoli – reflected in 1972 how before seeing overseas service 'we

---

31 *St Dunstan's Review*, July 1945, p. 5.
32 Allanson Papers, 66-2-22-3, NAM.

remained satisfied with the existing circumstances'.[33] After the war 'when we saw various peoples and got their views', he said, 'we started protesting against the inequalities and disparities which the British had created between the white and the black'. In this way the experience of war contributed to the momentous changes that India would face in the decades after the Great War.

'In memory of gallant warriors': war memorials

The war cut a swathe through an entire generation of the Indian Army, both Indians and British. Charles Bruce remembered that of the party of his regiment who went mountaineering in Ladakh in the summer of 1914 both his European companion and all of the Gurkhas who accompanied them became 'victims of the war'.[34] Remembering the dead of Gallipoli – or at least their British officers – naturally began in 1915. As word spread of the severity of the losses the 14th Sikhs had suffered at Gully Ravine on 4 June, families organised a memorial service, held in London at St Luke's Redcliffe Square in Chelsea on 26 August. At first a memorial service for Lieutenant Dick Meade, who had been killed trying to bring in his wounded adjutant, Lieutenant Leonard Cremen (who also died of his wounds), it became a service for the thirteen British officers the regiment had lost on Gallipoli. Meade's old tutor spoke about him and the British and Indian officers, and 440 men the Sikhs had lost to a congregation including grieving families and the Secretary of State for India, Austen Chamberlain. Holy Trinity, Eltham, south London, gradually became a sort of shrine to Gallipoli generally. Regiments erected memorials, though without permanent homes they were not always visible. The 14th Sikhs' officers mounted a bronze plaque in the Anglican church in Ferozepore cantonment, where it remains, uncared for and largely (I suppose) unknown. The 10th Gurkhas placed a roll of honour in All Saints, Maymyo, Burma, recovering the plaques after the church was looted by the Japanese in 1942. With Partition and the loss of congregations from cantonment churches the 5th Gurkhas shifted its plaques from St Luke's, Abbottabad, to St Luke's, Chelsea. Until 2000 it preserved collective and individual memorials naming all of its British officers who died on Gallipoli, the memorials now held by the National Army Museum.

Indian soldiers are not entirely forgotten – a stained glass window in the Indian Army Memorial Room at the Royal Military Academy, Sandhurst, depicts Gurkhas on Sari Bair – but they are not generally commemorated individually. To an extent this reflects Hindu and even Muslim cultural practices – the sites of Hindu and Sikh cremations are rarely marked individually, and Muslim graves do not often bear names. Accordingly, while the India Gate in New Delhi became from 1931 the memorial to the dead of undivided India (actually more than the 13,300 named on it),

---

33 Pradhan, 'The Sikh soldier in the First World War', in Ellinwood & Pradhan, *India and World War I*, p. 224.
34 Bruce, *Himalayan Wanderer*, p. 243.

'In Memory of Gallant Warriors' – the war memorial erected at Patiala by the Maharajah Bupinder Singh, one of the few such war memorials in India, depicting the Patiala Rajendra Infantry on Sari Bair and listing the names of men of the regiment who died on Gallipoli. (Author)

India has very few counterparts to the local war memorials of the kind so common in Britain, Australia or New Zealand. Though during the war British officials compiled 'complete lists of the honoured dead', it seems that no local memorials were built.[35] The exception to that rule is seen in Patiala, no longer a princely state but a large, prosperous industrial city in the Punjab.

In a park near the present Maharaja's New Moti Bagh Palace is a memorial obelisk, carved in pink sandstone, set on vivid pink stone steps and flanked by tanks as reminders of some of the more recent of India's wars. It bears bas reliefs depicting the Patialas' exploits, including Gallipoli and the inscription 'IN MEMORY OF GALLANT WARRIORS'. The steps bear the names of Patiala's war dead. Except for the pinkness, it could be a war memorial in suburban Melbourne or provincial New Zealand. It appears to be the only such memorial in the sub-continent.

Herbert Cox wanted to erect a memorial on Gallipoli and British Gurkha officers discussed building a memorial on Hill Q. By the war's end with battalions serving far from Gallipoli, not to mention the 'very considerable sum of money' involved, the idea lapsed.[36] Commemoration on Gallipoli would become the responsibility of governments rather than the unit and formation associations that erected so many memorials on the Western Front. Like their British, Australian and New Zealander counterparts, the Indian regiments that served on Gallipoli did not erect memorials on the peninsula; that was left to national governments and the imperial agency of the Imperial War Graves Commission, which in the mid-1920s completed the Helles Memorial to the Missing, a great pylon at the foot of the peninsula designed by Sir John Burnet, surrounded by panels bearing 20,000 names, over 1,500 of them Indian.

But one Indian regiment did build a Gallipoli memorial; the 14th Sikhs, which lost more men in battle on the peninsula than any other. Twenty years on, one of Cox's former staff captains, becoming commander of the Ferozepore Brigade Area, felt able at last to carry out Cox's desire to build a memorial. Collecting donations from serving and retired officers, Sikh community leaders and the Maharaja of Patiala (still Bhupinder Singh), he collected enough to build a hospital on land donated by the Rajah of Faridkot an extension to the Ferozepore Cantonment Hospital. The building, intended to treat the wives of Indian soldiers, was explicitly in memory of men and officers of the 14th Sikhs and the Patiala infantry who died on Gallipoli. The hospital was opened in February 1937 before military and civilian dignitaries and officials, and over three hundred military pensioners, some of whom had served on Gallipoli. Five Gallipoli survivors of the 14th Sikhs who were still serving, now dignified and respected subedars and a havildar, stood proudly to attention beside a commemorative tablet. A sweeper, named Channi, who had been on Gallipoli and considered that he had as much right as anyone to be present, simply sat down on the ground before it. The brigadier spoke, and officers of the Ferozepore Cantonment Board, and a poet

---

35 Leigh, *The Punjab and the War*, p. 105.
36 Allanson Papers, 6602-22-3, NAM.

who recited verses in Punjabi extolling the bravery of the 14th Sikhs – the sacrifices of Gully Ravine and Sari Bair were not forgotten in Ferozepore. Reginald Savory, another survivor, now a lieutenant-colonel, unveiled the tablet as buglers sounded the Reveille. The pensioners did justice to a meal provided by a local merchant, singing a song as they enjoyed the unaccustomed attention and entertainment. Thus did the Sikhs of Ferozepore remember.

As this and MacMunn's report suggests, British officers and their former soldiers reputedly enjoyed a respectful relationship after their service. In 1936, for instance, the Indian officers of what was now the 1st Sikhs (though still King George's Own) wrote to Vi, Harold Wilmer's widow, sending their felicitations to the Wilmers' daughter, Kitty, on the occasion of her wedding. These men had not seen any of the Wilmers for over twenty years.[37] The evidence is not abundant, though the well documented, long-standing and undoubtedly affectionate relationship between Reginald Savory and some of his former sepoys testifies that at its best a recognition of shared service could produce long-lasting comradeship. In 1945 Savory (now a lieutenant-general) attended a reunion in Dehra Dun, photographed with a dozen former comrades. He wrote in 1968, when he visited India again after more than twenty years, how 'deeply touched' he was that Bhola Singh, a lance-naik on Gallipoli, should have visited him.[38] He had invited Ude Singh into his office even when Adjutant-General of the Indian Army, and during the crisis over partition. After Savory's retirement Savory wrote often to Singh and then, after his death in 1947, corresponded with his son, Harbans Singh Thande, exchanging gifts and visiting his family when he returned to India in 1968. Lady Savory must have known how her husband valued his relationship with the family of the man he felt had saved his life – when he died in 1980 she sent a telegram to inform Harbans Singh Thandi of his passing, on the very morning of his death.[39]

'Wholly unidentified': Gallipoli's cemeteries and memorials

Today thousands of visitors travel annually to the Gallipoli peninsula, from Australia and New Zealand, from Britain, and (overwhelmingly) from Turkey. It is easy for all of them to overlook the Indian contribution to the Gallipoli campaign. While it is possible to see Gurkha and Sikh soldiers' names on the panels on the great memorial to the missing at Cape Helles (which records the names of all of those who died in the campaign but who have no known grave) their inclusion in the single main memorial to the missing breaks the connection between the dead and the places where they fought: and, unfortunately, many Australasian visitors do not venture so far from Anzac, nor is the presence of 'Indian' names readily intelligible.

---

37 Letter, Jaswant Singh to Mrs. Wilmer, 1936, courtesy of Anto O'Brien.
38 Sikh Regiment, *Presentation of the Regimental Colours to the Sikh Regiment*, p. 10.
39 Thandi, *Down the Memory Lane*, p. 15.

Because of the different burial customs of the forces that fought on Gallipoli, the casual visitor to the peninsula would gain a quite misleading impression of the composition of the forces involved from its cemeteries. For example, the remains of some 798 British and Dominion soldiers lie in the cemetery at Hill 60. Seventy-six of their graves can be named. Not one of the identified dead is an Indian soldier. While some of the 699 bodies that were 'wholly unidentified' may have been Gurkhas, Hindu burial practices make it impossible for the cemeteries to contain any identified Indian bodies.[40] The Indian Army's part in the campaign is therefore almost invisible. While British officers' graves can be seen in several cemeteries, notably Pink Farm, the closest cemetery to Gully Ravine, the graves of their men are hard to find. There are, for example, no Indian graves at all in the cemeteries at Pink Farm or Chunuk Bair, even though they were among the Indians' most costly actions.

Memorials and cemeteries now dictate much of how visitors understand the campaign. Before about 1980 the only reminders in the landscape were the memorials and cemeteries created by the Imperial (later Commonwealth) War Graves Commission. From about 1980 with the Turkish discovery of Gallipoli and the creation of memorials and faux cemeteries, it became possible to 'read' the campaign through the stone memorials and burial grounds located at its critical junctures – the Turkish Corporal Seyit memorial, Lancashire Landing cemetery at Helles, the Australian memorial at Lone Pine, the string of cemeteries along the Anzac line, the huge Turkish 57th Regiment memorial, the New Zealand memorial and the statue of Mustapha Kemal Atatürk on the summit of Chunuk Bair. Visitors imbibe the story of Gallipoli from these edifices. But where among them are the Indians? The landscape of much of the peninsula has changed, by re-afforestation and cultivation: Gully Ravine is heavily overgrown; Hill 60 has disappeared. Only in the gullies and slopes of Sari Bair can we sense 1915.

British journalist Mihir Bose noticed on the 90th anniversary of the campaign that 'the Indian dead have no names'.[41] He found, of course, that Gallipoli's cemeteries contain almost no Indian dead. Apart from several Indians (evenly distributed among the Indian force's constituent communities) the cemeteries naturally and rightly hold no identifiable Indian dead. At Anzac, for example, Chunuk Bair cemetery holds 668 unidentified remains, but among the ten identified bodies is that of Havildar Punahang Limbu of the 10th Gurkhas, who died on 10 August 1915. Beach Cemetery at Anzac holds the remains of three men of the 22nd Mule Corps, who died on Gallipoli in November 1918, when it was re-occupied. (One of their headstones is inscribed 'Om Bhagwati' – 'God, I salute you'.)

---

40 Imperial War Graves Commission, *The War Graves of the British Empire ... Hill 60 Cemetery*, p. 10.
41 Bose, 'Why were the heroic Gurkhas forgotten?', *Daily Telegraph*, 23 April 2005, Research files Ops/137, GM.

The Commonwealth War Graves Commission memorial at Cape Helles, which commemorates 1500 Indian Army troops among 20,000 British Empire soldiers who died on Gallipoli but who have no known grave. (Author)

But the vast majority of Indian dead were not buried. The result is that 'Indian' dead are virtually invisible in the cemeteries of the peninsula, and therefore are unnoticed by visitors who gravitate to cemeteries and memorials. Contrary to Mihir Bose's observation, Indian dead actually *are* named – on 37 of the panels surrounding the great obelisk of the 'British' memorial to the missing at Cape Helles. The dead of the Indian Army who have no known grave – which includes those whose bodies were not recovered and those who were cremated – are recorded, unit by unit, in order of rank, named individually, including non-combatant 'followers'. But to find them a visitor needs to know that they are recorded on the Helles Memorial, and has to search it carefully among the 21,000 names to find the 1,516 Indians (including over thirty British officers).

While Indians are almost invisible in Commonwealth commemoration on the peninsula (and in Turkish museums and displays), 'one Indian soldier' is in fact a part of an eclectic, not to say kitsch, sculpture in a park adjacent to the *feribot* terminal in Eceabat (Maidos in 1915). Prof. Tankut Öktem's towering *Ataturk in Anafartalar*, erected in 2008, includes figures of Ottoman and enemy soldiers emerging from a plinth including the local hero-gunner Corporal Seyit, 'the Mother of War' (lamenting her loss) and, of course, the ubiquitous figure of Mustafa Kemal.

'Their place in history': India's Gallipoli history

While the Indian Army had a long tradition of commissioning 'staff histories' of its overseas and frontier campaigns, its Great War histories became subsumed into the massive official history headed by Sir James Edmonds (noticeably cool toward the Indian Army) and written by authors working under the Historical Committee of the Committee of Imperial Defence. While Cyril Aspinall-Oglander (who had served as a staff officer in Hamilton's headquarters) wrote lyrically and poignantly about episodes of the campaign, his two volumes sat securely in the 'general staff tradition'. Its focus was on the decisions of commanders and the movements and actions of units; usually no smaller than battalions. Unlike the more democratic Australian and New Zealand histories, whose smaller forces and egalitarian ethos inclined their authors to mention small units and individuals, both officers and men, the British official histories rarely mentions anyone besides formation commanders, and certainly no Indians. The official histories' documentation was likewise severely official, notably formation and unit war diaries, though they often failed to clearly record exactly what had happened. (As we have seen, with casualties among British officers so heavy, rarely could time or attention be spared for detailed daily chronicles.) Official historians necessarily checked details with surviving British officers. For the August battle especially, so confused were the official records that the officers' recollections written fifteen years later were filed with the war diaries.

When in 1947 what had been the Indian Army was dismembered, to be distributed to the successor states of India and Pakistan, the units that had served together on Gallipoli became parts of two armies which within months found themselves at war, the first of several conflicts and a state of perpetual belligerence. The 14th Sikhs went to India; the mountain artillery batteries to Pakistan. When the Gurkha regiments were divided the 4th and 5th went to India (as Gorkhas), the 6th and 10th to Britain. As a result, the latter battalions, though now subsumed into the composite Royal Gurkha Rifles, have a somewhat more accessible history to western researchers. But hardly anyone has taken much interest in the Indian contribution to Gallipoli besides Rana Chhina and myself. Thanks to his initiative in creating an Indian program of research and commemoration in response to the centenary of the Great War, there seems to be a better chance than at any time since 1915 that the Indian story of Gallipoli will be known in India, and elsewhere.

As even casual tourists realise when visiting its temples, forts, palaces and tombs, the past is important in India: but not all of India's pasts are important to all Indians. Despite the prominence of India Gate at the heart of New Delhi, symbolically, the names on it are almost all unintelligible, either unable to be read (because visitors are forbidden from approaching it) or incomprehensible (because they are unexplained). India's experience of the Great War has largely been forgotten. As I found when I met serving and former officers of some of the Indian units which served on Gallipoli, India's army values its Great War history. But that history is known essentially at the unit or operational level, with the significant exception of the exploits of some officers

'He died for freedom and honour' – Rifleman Duble Gurung's medallion, preserved in the 2/10th (and later Royal Gurkha Rifles) officers' mess after his family in Nepal could not be traced. (Gurkha Museum, Pokhara)

and some decorated soldiers. The experience of individual sepoys, gunners, drivers and followers is certainly little known, and presumably little valued, at least publicly. Conversely, some families know and cherish the part played in a great global drama by great-grandfathers (and presumably great-great-uncles) in a war fought a century ago. Partly because of India's traditions of family privacy, and partly because no one has ever asked, these stories remain largely obscure. Ultimately, the Indian Army on Gallipoli served a 'Master' whose rule would last barely another thirty years, and the independent India that supplanted the British Sircar had little interest in battles in the cause of empire. As Rana Chhina observed:

> The lack of a political identity in 1915 thus served to rob Indian soldiers not just of an acknowledgment of their role, or of a commemoration of their sacrifice, but also of their place in history.[42]

The research for this book, mostly conducted at a distance of thousands of kilometres, and in a language few Indian soldiers spoke or wrote, has uncovered a few of these stories; enough to suggest that more might be found, if only someone equipped for the task were to try; and soon. Family stories have a fragile half-life, and the passing of generations makes their survival more perilous. Who knows what evidence has been lost in the upheaval that afflicted the Punjab especially in 1947 or to climate, natural disaster or the turbulence of migration. The effort is worth making: as the Gurkhas sang in 1915: die in battle; do not despair.

---

42 Chhina, 'Their mercenary calling', p. 233.

Appendix I

Force G: Indian Units with Mediterranean Force[1]

7th Indian Mountain Artillery Brigade
    Headquarters
    21st (Kohat) Mountain Battery
    26th (Jacob's) Mountain Battery
    Mountain Artillery Section, Divisional Ammunition Column

29th Indian Infantry Brigade
    Headquarters
    14th (King George's Own Ferozepore) Sikhs
    1st Rajindra Patiala Imperial Services Infantry (attached 14th Sikhs)
    1/4th Gurkha Rifles
    1/5th Gurkha Rifles (Frontier Force)
    1/6th Gurkha Rifles
    2/10th Gurkha Rifles[2]

Medical units
    108th Indian Field Ambulance (with 29th Indian Infantry Brigade)
    110th Indian Field Ambulance (with Convalescent Depot) (Clearing Hospital)
    C Section (Indian) 137th Combined Field Ambulance (with Indian Mountain Artillery Brigade)
    C Section (British) 137th Combined Field Ambulance

---

1   At the height of the Indian commitment to the Gallipoli campaign, from September 1915
2   The list of units in the 29th Indian Infantry Brigade on the panels at the Helles Memorial includes the '1/10th Gurkha Rifles'. This is incorrect. Men were transferred from the 1/10th to the 2/10th, as were members of other battalions, but the 1/10th as a unit did not serve on Gallipoli.

Supply and Transport Corps
> 1st, 2nd, 9th, 11th, 15th, 28th, 31st, 32nd Mule Corps
> Detachments from following Mule Corps: 3rd, 6th, 7th, 8th, 10th, 12th, 14th, 18th, 19th, 20th, 21st, 22nd, 23rd, 24th, 26th, 27th, 29th, 33rd, 34th, 35th, 36th, and 37th, also from Bharatpur, Gwalior and Indore Imperial Service Transport Corps

Appendix II

Regiments of the Indian Army represented on Gallipoli

Because many of the Indian troops who served on Gallipoli had been drafted to units serving there, many units are represented on the Helles Memorial to the Missing. Note that this list is somewhat misleading in that in many cases units were represented by small numbers of men transferred, or even individual officers and men. Those which served as complete units are in bold.

    Indian Army Reserve of Officers
    Royal Artillery
    21st (Kohat) Mountain Battery
    23rd (Peshawur) Mountain Battery
    26th (Jacob's) Mountain Battery
    27th Mountain Battery
    28th Mountain Battery

Infantry
    2nd Queen Victoria's Own Rajput Light Infantry
    4th Prince Albert Victor's Rajputs
    14th (King George's Own Ferozepore) Sikhs
    15th Ludhiana Sikhs
    33rd Punjabis
    36th Sikhs
    45th Rattray's Sikhs
    51st Sikhs (Frontier Force)
    53rd Sikhs (Frontier Force)
    54th Sikhs (Frontier Force)
    56th Punjabi Rifles (Frontier Force)
    66th Punjabis
    69th Punjabis
    87th Punjabis
    89th Punjabis

90th Punjabis
92nd Punjabis
93rd Burma Infantry
110th (Mahratta) Light Infantry
122nd Rajputana Infantry
128th Pioneers
2nd King Edward's Own Gurkha Rifles (The Sirmoor Rifles)
1/4th Gurkha Rifles
1/5th Gurkha Rifles (Frontier Force)
1/6th Gurkha Rifles
2/10th Gurkha Rifles
Assam Military Police
Burma Military Police

State Forces
1st Patiala Rajindra Infantry

Supply and Transport Corps
    Mule Corps
    Bharatpur Transport Corps
    Gwalior Transport Corps
    Indore Transport Corps

Indian Medical Department
    Army Bearer Corps

Appendix III

Sources of chapter titles

Introduction: 'A song of the War will I make': Gurkha verse
Chapter 1 'To slay the enemy was the Master's order': Gurkha verse
Chapter 2 'O my lover, thou wilt leave me': Gurkha verse
Chapter 3 'I came to the land of Egypt': Gurkha verse
Chapter 4 'Behold O Master the mighty host': *Bhagavad Gita*, Part I
Chapter 5 'My friends and brothers dying': Gurkha verse
Chapter 6 'Be not weary and faint hearted': *Q'ran* 47:35
Chapter 7 'When the smoke of the guns falls like a mist': Gurkha verse
Chapter 8 'Death roams about with its mouth open' *Hymns of Guru Tegh Bahadur*
Chapter 9 'The soldier must suffer': *Bhagavad Gita* 2:37
Chapter 10 'When my body was weak and despaired': Gurkha verse
Chapter 11 'May I die fighting in the thick of battle': vow of Guru Gobind Singh
Chapter 12 'Considering your duty as a warrior': *Bhagavad Gita* 2:31
Chapter 13 'Shall we live to return to India?': Gurkha verse
Chapter 14 'The sea wind blew away the hates': Gurkha verse
Chapter 15: 'He is here today; he will be here hereafter': *Hymns of the Guru Nanak*

Appendix IV

Indians on Gallipoli today

Thousands of British and Australasian visitors to Turkey go to Gallipoli, and it has become a destination for many more Turks, all seeking in the peninsula's memorials, cemeteries and sites a connection with the various histories to which it represents. Very few visitors have specifically sought out the Indian Army's part in the campaign though, as this book seeks to show, the 'Indian' experience of Gallipoli is of enduring interest.

Travelling to Gallipoli is relatively easy, since the peninsula is a four-hour drive from Istanbul airport, and there are several grades of accommodation on the peninsula and in nearby Çanakkale. While it is all too easy to be sold a package tour from Istanbul or in Çanakkale, travelling independently to and around Gallipoli is so easy and rewarding that I would encourage it. Few Turkish guides will do more than offer a 'standard' tour, or know much about the Indian experience.

While most available guide books are either aimed at British or Australian visitors interested in a cemetery crawl, or at specialist military historians, they will be helpful, even if not dealing in detail with Indian sites.[1] The best guide of all, Phil Taylor and Pam Cupper's *Gallipoli: A Battlefield Guide*, has unfortunately been out of print for a decade, but is worth obtaining second-hand if possible. It is still valuable, despite appearing before the present boom in Turkish commemoration and visitation. (It is worth obtaining the excellent guide map, available from the new 'Çanakkale Epic Promotion Centre' – the re-vamp of the tired old museum at Gaba Tepe. In navigating around the peninsula it is worth acquiring a familiarity with the Turkish words appearing on the recent proliferation of signs.) No guidebooks, however, deal specifically with the Indian part in the campaign. The customary visitors' approach

---

1   Other guidebooks include Toni and Valmai Holt's *Major and Mrs.Holt's Battlefield Guide to Gallipoli*, Ian McGibbon's *Gallipoli: a Guide to New Zealand Battlefields and Memorials*, Mat McLachlan's *Gallipoli: the Battlefield Guide*, Steve Newman's *Gallipoli Then and Now*, Glen Wahlert's *Exploring Gallipoli: an Australian Army Battlefield Guide*.

to Gallipoli, essentially navigating from cemetery to cemetery, will not work for the Indian experience.

As will be clear from this book, Indian troops were involved in fighting at Anzac throughout the campaign, around Gully Ravine from May to July, in the August offensive on the Sari Bair range and around Hill 60 from August. While it is perfectly feasible to visit all these sites, the current management of the 'Gallipoli Peninsula Battlefield Park' actually militates against visitors being able to see all the sites they desire. The construction of roads, culverts, drains, new Turkish memorials and the Anzac ceremonial site, the banning of grazing animals at Anzac, the planting of trees and the failure to conduct controlled burning means that the landscape has profoundly changed, making much of the country impassable. Visitors are largely obliged to follow a fixed one-way route around the battlefield and heading off the roads and into the scrub is very difficult. It is now virtually impossible to reach the site of 'Pifferpore' (a hundred yards from the main coast road, near Shrapnel Valley cemetery) or to follow the mule trains' route up Shrapnel Gully and Monash Valley or to walk into Mule Gully, as was possible a few years ago. While several cemeteries contain 'Indian' graves (mainly of British officers) at Anzac visitors can mostly look at but not reach the mountain artillery's gun sites.

Elsewhere the problem of accessibility is not so severe. From Cape Helles (where a visit to the memorial is an essential starting point) the western road leading to Alcitepe (Krithia in 1915) offers several points of entry to Gully Ravine and Gully Spur. Stephen Chambers's *Gully Ravine* is the essential guide to this area. It is possible (depending on the season) to walk much of Gully Ravine, taking care in the gully, which is a water course in spring. Gurkha Bluff can be reached by an easy half-hour walk across the fields from the Turkish Nur Yamut memorial, located on a sealed road 2.5 kilometres west of Alcitepe, though no trace exists of any trenches, except for vestiges of Gurkha Mule Trench. It is possible, but not advised, to walk along the shore from the mouth of Gully Ravine. The shoreline is rocky and a twisted ankle here could be disastrous. Walking alone off the track anywhere on the peninsula is not recommended. The common-sense rules of bush-walking apply: walk with a companion, let your accommodation know your expected time of return; take compass, maps and enough water.

Particular prudence is recommended if attempting to follow the Indian routes in the advance on Sari Bair. Again, Stephen Chambers's *Anzac: Sari Bair* is an essential guide. But beware! Commanders and guides in August 1915 became confused in the tangle of ridges and valleys. Visitors today can at least use the big Turkish flags flying at various landmarks (especially at Chunuk Bair) as reference points. It may be wise to explore the lower slopes of the route on foot (or in a four-wheel drive if you can obtain one) and then drive to Chunuk Bair and explore the culmination of the assault on foot from the road leading through the Chunuk Bair cemetery to the 'saddle' of Hill Q (about where the sign indicates 'Besim Sirte'). Again, plantations of pine and thick scrub largely block the view over the crest (and it is dangerous to try to reach the location from which Allanson's men made their final assault, on a near-vertical hillside) but you can see the view of the Dardanelles Allanson had to the east.

The area around Hill 60, Demakjelik Bair and Kaiajik Dere can be reached along the rough track running off the main Anzac-Suvla road. This area is also much changed, with thick scrub, trees and olive groves turning what were bare hillsides into an even more confusing tangle of slopes and gullies, in which the tactical logic of Hill 60 and the commanding position of Demakjelik Bair is obscured. As with other areas, there is little trace of the network of trenches the Indians occupied, but the fixed features are the 'sunken road' – a farm lane – where Henry Molloy was killed on 21 August, the well of Susuk Kuyu and the cemetery of Hill 60, which is actually to the south of the summit of the hill. Its location can be seen behind the cemetery, occupied by a virtually impenetrable thicket.

For advice on how to go about planning and conducting battlefield research, consult my own *A Stout Pair of Boots: a Guide to Exploring Australia's Battlefields*. Though mainly relating to Australian battlefields, the techniques and approaches discussed are widely applicable.

Appendix V

Strengths, reinforcements and losses

There has long been misplaced certainty over the number of Indians who served on Gallipoli. The Government of India's summary *India's contribution to the Great War* gives the figure of 4,428 men sent 'to Gallipoli'.[1] This actually appears to be the number of men who embarked from Indian ports intended for Gallipoli in 1915. It does not appear to count those sent to Gallipoli from Egypt (that is, the initial deployment) or those sent from France (the Indian Mule Cart Train and the 1/4th Gurkhas). The War Office's *Statistics of the Military Effort of the British Empire During the Great War* gives contradictory figures within its covers. On one page it records the 'number [of Indian troops] sent on service overseas from India' up to the war's end, and for Gallipoli gives the figure of 90 Indian officers and warrant officers, 3041 other ranks and 1819 non-combatants; a total of 4,950 (which excludes British personnel).[2] On other pages, however, the total of Indian casualties on Gallipoli, including dead and wounded, comes to over 6,300, a total that appears not to include the men who died when the *Ramazan* was sunk, nor Indians evacuated sick, who do not seem to have been tallied by any one. The official figures therefore appear to grossly understate the actual number of Indians who served on Gallipoli in total. In 2013 Rana Chhina gave the size of the expeditionary force as 'barely 5000 men' – which in terms of its size at any one time seems accurate.[3]

The aggregate, however, must be greater. The Indian Army's notorious bureaucracy works to history's advantage, provided the records are preserved and can be consulted; not something we can take for granted. Virtually every day in every unit havildars checked their rolls and submitted returns to the adjutant, for transfer to brigade headquarters and, inexorably, to be collated and in time periodically sent on to Simla; the basis of the returns preserved in the war diaries. With men being killed and evacuated wounded and sick and reinforcement and convalescent drafts arriving, Force

---

1 *India's Contribution to the Great War*, pp. 96-97
2 *Statistics of the Military Effort of the British Empire During the Great War*, p. 777
3 Chhina, 'Their mercenary calling', p 233

G's strength fluctuated daily. This makes establishing how many Indians served on Gallipoli almost impossible to establish definitively. However, by adding the numbers killed and wounded to strength returns late in the campaign we can reach a provisional figure.

To do this we need a 'base' figure; that is, the number of Indian Army troops serving on the peninsula at as late a stage in the campaign as possible. Adding to this the number killed or those evacuated sick or wounded should give a more realistic total figure. A return dated 7 December, though apparently omitting about 170 Indian medical personnel, gives a total just on 10,000 Indian Army troops present on Gallipoli on or about 5 December:[4]

	BO	IO	BOR	IOR	F
Mountain artillery	9	7	-	647	42
Supply & Transport	14	12	32	223	3462
Medical units	12	10	17	[omitted]	261
14th Sikhs	12	16	-	729	41
Patiala Infantry	2	4	-	182	18
1/4th Gurhas	10	20	-	651	40
1/5th Gurkhas	8	19	-	637	39
1/6th Gurkhas	12	7	-	727	47
2/10th Gurkhas	12	21	-	1019	47
Totals	91	116	49	4815	3997
Grand Total					9068

While some further drafts arrived after 7 December (for example, 110 men for the 2-10th on 10 December) and adding the missing Indian other ranks in the medical units (who appear on every other return) we can presume that this represented as many men as were serving on Gallipoli when the evacuation began in mid-December: say 10,000.

A return dated late October gives the number of men recorded as killed or evacuated wounded to 20 October (including the Punjabi battalions withdrawn in May). It shows the following losses:

4   Tel. 7 December 1915, WWI/335/H, NAI

	Killed or Died of wounds	Wounded
Mountain artillery	38	312
Supply & Transport	40	294
Medical units	12	54
14th Sikhs	283	742
Patiala Infantry	[Apparently included in 14th Sikhs]	
69th Punjabis	4	26
89th Punjabis	12	101
1/4th Gurkhas	6	24
1/5th Gurkhas	185	489
1/6th Gurkhas	146	555
2/10th Gurkhas	174	540
Totals	900	3137[5]

The figure for dead is, of course, at least 715 fewer than the Commonwealth War Graves Commission figures (1,516 commemorated on the peninsula) to which we must add the 70-odd who died of wounds in Malta or Egypt. Adding the strength on the peninsula in early December (almost exactly 10,000) to this lower figure for dead, (say 1550) and the total for wounded (3137) gives a total of at least 14,687 Indians who served on Gallipoli. While a number of men were wounded twice, and therefore must have returned to the peninsula at least once, the number cannot affect the figures unduly, especially since the total of 'Indians evacuated sick' seems not to have been tallied by anyone. Other sources give higher figures for Gallipoli dead. The War Office compendium *Statistics of the Military effort of the British Empire during the Great War* gives a seemingly exact figure: 33 Indian officers, 1692 other ranks, including 101 men 'missing' and 127 followers, a total of 1,852 (though we know that at least three were captured).[6] But pages 284-86 of the same volume list 'approximate' month-by-month casualty figures for each component of the force. The figure for 'Indian Native' troops totals 2,893 dead. That figure cannot include the *Ramazan* dead, because the total deaths for September 1915 is only 68. If the higher figures for dead are included then the total number of Indians who served on Gallipoli reaches up to 16,000. I have preferred the Commonwealth War Graves Commission figures because the figure represents actual names and dates.

We can triangulate these calculations, as it were, by comparing them with other known and reliable figures. The 14th Sikhs' accounting, for example, shows that just over 2104 sepoys passed through that battalion's ranks alone in the course of the campaign.[7] As the Indian force comprised a brigade of five battalions, plus the

---

5   Tel. 5 December 1915, WWI/154/H, NAI
6   *Statistics of the Military effort of the British Empire during the Great War, 1914-1920*, p. 778
7   Talbot, *The 14th (King George's Own Ferozepore) Sikhs*, p. 100

artillery and the more numerous supply and transport corps (which suffered fewer casualties) then the figure of as many as 16,000 seems perfectly justified.

Ironically, for all the Indian Army's concern for record-keeping, it remains impossible to reach a definitive figure for either Indian strengths or losses on Gallipoli. Still, it is clear that the total of Indian troops who served on Gallipoli must be at least twice and possibly three times that previously accepted.

Appendix VI

Indian Army dead of the Gallipoli campaign

As Appendix IV shows, the available Indian Army casualty figures for Gallipoli vary quite considerably. The basis of the following list is the list of some 1,516 names on the Helles Memorial (a digital copy of which was kindly provided by the Commonwealth War Graves Commission and which forms the basis of this list). In addition to the Helles Memorial list at least 73 other members of the Indian Army are buried or commemorated in cemeteries at Anzac, Suvla or Helles, in Malta and Egypt and on Lemnos. The Commission's figure includes the dead of the *Ramazan*, and British Indian officers, including officers of Indian regiments serving with British units.[1]

It is presently impossible to devise a definitive list of the Indian dead of Gallipoli for those who died of wounds inflicted on the peninsula but not on the peninsula. While it is possible to be reasonably certain of some members of infantry or artillery units who died of wounds in Egypt and Malta, it is almost impossible to identify men of Supply and Transport or medical units, or to identify men serving on attachment with units on Gallipoli. Sorting out the confusion is possible, but only by laborious cross-checking of casualty lists against memorial records, and that proved to be impracticable in the time available for this book. Further research is needed. A few anomalies and questions remain, notably about the several individuals buried on the peninsula despite Hindu and Sikh practices. Of the hundreds of Musalman dead (who were of course rightly buried), only a handful lie in named graves, even in cemeteries within British empire lines. The explanation for this seems to be that in accordance with Muslim custom the graves were not marked, or not marked in ways that made them identifiable to British war grave parties from 1918. The list of dead assumes that men are commemorated on the Helles memorial, unless otherwise specified.

---

1 At least nine Indian Army officers were to die serving with seven British, mostly New Army battalions on Gallipoli. They give the list of Indian Army regiments on the Helles memorial its variety, including as they did officers from the 51st Sikhs, 75th Carnatic Infantry, 93rd Burma Infantry, the 120th Rajputana and the 22nd, 25th and 66th Punjabis. It is poignant that Captain Wynyard Brown of the 1/5th Gurkhas died with the West Yorks on 4 June, several hundred yards east of where his battalion was on Gully Spur.

ABDUL AZIZ KHAN, Follower, Lucknow/829, S&T Corps, 19 Sep 1915

ABDUL HAMAD, Follower, 831, S&T Corps, 19 Sep 1915

ABDUL HAMAD, Dvr 1359, Mule Corps, 19 Sep 1915

ABDUL KARIM, Dvr 1202, Mule Corps, 13 Oct 1915, of Karkhana, Secunderabad, Madras

ABDUL LATIF, Dvr 1057, Mule Corps, 21 Dec 1915, of Moholla Chapperbandan, Ambala, Punjab

ABDULLAH, Dvr 2061, Mule Corps, 2 Jan 1916 (Lancashire Landing Cemetery, Helles)

ABDULLAH, Sepoy 4269, 14th Sikhs, 15 Sep 1915, of Kotli Loharan Laindi Sialkote, Punjab

ABDULLAH, Follower, 830, S&T Corps, 19 Sep 1915

ABDULLAH KHAN, Dvr 408, 26th Jacob's Battery, 30 Nov 1915

ABDUR RAHIM, Dvr 501, Mule Corps, 17 Aug 1915, of Karkhana, Secunderabad, Madras

ABDUR RAHMAN, Dvr 1345, Mule Corps, 17 Dec 1915, of Galadir, Mardan, Peshawar, NWF Province

ABIR THAPA, Rfmn 72, 1/5th GR, 3 Sep 1915

ABIR THAPA, Rfmn 77, 1/5th GR, 3 Sep 1915, of Deolghare, Dailekh, Nepal

ACHHAR SINGH, Dvr 858, Mule Corps, 28 Dec 1915, of Musa Singh Hayat, Shadra, Lahore, Punjab

ADALSUR PUN, Rfmn 591, 1/6th GR, 10 Jul 1915, of Sewla, Baglung, 4000, Parvat, Nepal

ADAMSING RANA, Rfmn 607, 1/6th G, 18 Nov 1915, of Lafh, Piuthan, Nepal

AGAMSING RAI, Rfmn 2697, 2/10th GR, 28 Jun 1915, of Majhuwa, Rawakhola, Okhaldunga, Nepal

AGANSING LIMBU, Rfmn 1188, 2/10th GR, 19 Sep 1915, of Hangpang, No.5, District, Dhankuta, Nepal

AHMAD ALI, Dvr 765, Mule Corps, 5 Aug 1915

AIBIRIA PUN, Rfmn 480, 1/6th GR, 28 Jun 1915, of Shina, Parvat, Palpa, Nepal (Pieta Cemetery, Ma)

AJAIB SINGH, Sepoy 4517, 14th Sikhs, 14 May 1915, of Boparal, Ludhiana, Punjab (Skew Bridge Cemetery)

AIJANSING RAI, L/Nk 431, 2/10th GR, 7 Aug 1915, of Salatem, Khotang, Bhojpore, Nepal

AIMAN THAPA, Rfmn 956, 2/10th GR, 28 Jun 1915, of Pheyakote, Gulmi, Palpa, Nepal

AIMANSING RANA, Bugler, 130, 1/5th GR, 7 Aug 1915, of Thaprek, No.3 West, Tanhu, Nepal

AINSWORTH, Capt. Henry Lawrence, 2/10th GR, 30 Dec 1915, of Rochdale, Lancashire, England (Chatby Cemetery, Egypt)

AITABIR LIMBU, Rfmn 1162, 2/10th GR, 19 Sep 1915, of Thumithap, Mewakhola Dhankuta, Nepal

AITABIR THAPA, Rfmn 130, 1/6th GR, 4 Jun 1915, of Banguthok, Palpa, Nepal

AITASING GURUNG, Rfmn 513, 1/6th GR, 3 Jul 1915, of Malang, No.2 West, Lamjung, Nepal

AITLAL LAMA, Rfmn 4247, 1/6th GR, 24 May 1915, of Lakhinpore, Assam, Bengal

AJIRMAN RAI, Rfmn 1086, 2/10th GR, 19 Sep 1915, of Gairi, Solo, Okhaldunga, Nepal

AJMER SINGH, Sepoy 4204, 14th Sikhs, 4 Jun 1915, of Begalehra, Moga, Ferozepore, Punjab

AKHU, Dvr 1501, Mule Corps, 30 Aug 1915, of Gora, Abbottabad, Hazara, Punjab

ALA SINGH, Sepoy 2380, BMP att 14th Sikhs, 9 Sep 1915, of Manochahal, Taran Taran, Amritsar, Punjab

ALA SINGH, Sepoy 4420, 14th Sikhs, 2 Jul 1915, of Gholia Kalan, Moga, Ferozepore, Punjab

ALAF DIN, Dvr 2034, Mule Corps, 25 May 1915, of Banda Pir Khan, Abbottabad, Punjab

ALI GAUHAR, Dvr 717, 21st Kohat Battery, 27 Oct 1915, of Wahala, Pinddadan Khan, Jhelum, Punjab

ALI KHAN, Dvr 1610, Mule Corps, 13 Aug 1915, of Panyan, Hanpore, Hazara, Punjab

ALLAH DAD, Dvr 1344, Mule Corps, 5 Jul 1915, of Sodawar, Gujarkhan, Rawalpindi, Punjab

ALLAH DIN, Sepoy 2384, 89th Punjabis, 14 May 1915, of Moza Tur, Jhelum, Punjab

ALLA DITTA, Dvr 1527, Mule Corps, 20 Nov 1918 (Ari Burnu Cemetery, Anzac)

ALLAH DITTA, Dvr 2153, Mule Corps, 4 Aug 1915, of Takal, Gujarkhan, Rawalpindi, Punjab

AMALDHOJ RAI, Rfmn 2526, 2/10th GR, 19 Dec 1915, of Solu, No.3 East, Nepal

AMALDHAJ RAI, Rfmn 955, 2/10th GR, 7 Jul 1915, of Sasarkha, Rawadumri, Okhaldunga, Nepal

AMAR DAT, Bearer 4616, ABC, 108th Field Amb, 19 Jun 1915, of Jayjaydi, Pauri, Garhwal, United Provinces

AMAR GURUNG, Rfmn 256, 2/10th GR, 10 Aug 1915, of Sarang, Bandipore, Nepal

AMAR SINGH, Havildar 54, Patiala Infantry, 10 Aug 1915, of Jlunda, Barnala, Patiala, Punjab (Heliopolis (Port Tewfik) Memorial), Egypt)

AMAR SINGH, L/Nk 1442, BMP att 14th Sikhs, 19 Sep 1915, of Mahalkhurd, Barnala, Patiala, Punjab

AMAR SINGH, Sepoy 1605, BMP att 14th Sikhs, 19 Sep 1915, of Garrihan Singh, Gujranwala, Punjab

AMAR SINGH, Sepoy 3498, 54th Sikhs att 14th Sikhs, 4 Sep 1915, of Kanjla, Dhuri, Patiala State, Punjab

AMARBAHADUR THAPA, Rfmn 4736, 1/5th GR, 7 Aug 1915, of Kumaldanra, Palpa, Parvat, Nepal

AMARDHAJ LIMBU, Rfmn 708, 2/10th GR, 1 Jul 1915, of Tinglabo, Mewakhola, Dhankuta, Nepal

AMARSING GURUNG, Rfmn 863, 1/6th GR, 13 May 1915, of Gun Pokhra, No.2 West, Lamjung, Nepal

AMARSING PUN, Rfmn 4171, 1/5th GR, 26 Dec 1915, of Nawakote, Palpa, Parvat, Nepal

AMARSING THAPA, Sub. Maj. 1/5th GR, 7 Aug 1915, of Ratikola, Duluk, Nepal

AMARSING THAPA, Rfmn 1204, 1/6th GR, 13 Aug 1915, of Nagar Danra, Palpa, Nepal

AMARSING THAPA, Rfmn 4997, 1/6th GR, 8 Aug 1915, of Naya Sunra, Bandipore, Tanhu, Nepal

AMBARSING RAI, Rfmn 307, 2/10th GR, 7 Aug 1915, of Khare, Tamarkhola, Dhankuta, Nepal

AMIR ALI, Dvr 1177, Mule Corps, 5 Oct 1915, of Nuthal, Jhelum, Punjab

AMIR BAKSH, Follower, Jhansi/12, S&T Corps, 19 Sep 1915, of Orcha Gate, Jhansi, United Provinces

AMIR KHAN, Dvr 1121, Mule Corps, 24 Dec 1915, of Shinkhna, Mamwa, Abbottabad, Punjab

AMRIK SINGH, Sepoy 4058, 14th Sikhs, 4 Jun 1915, of Mum, Barnala, Patiala, Punjab

AMRIK SINGH, Sepoy 4143, 14th Sikhs, 8 May 1915, of Dosanjh, Moga, Ferozepore, Punjab

AMRIT RAI, Rfmn 187, AMP att 2/10th GR, 28 Jun 1915

ANANDABAHADUR LIMBU, Rfmn 2416, 2/10th GR, 30 Jun 1915, of Nagi, Chaubisia, Dhankuta, Nepal

ANANDAHANG LIMBU, Jem. 2/10th GR, 7 Aug 1915, of Santakre, Mewakhola, Dhankuta, Nepal

ANIMARDAN RAI, Rfmn 219, 2/10th GR, 4 Sep 1915, of Tekanpore, Okhaldhunga, Nepal

ANOKH SINGH, Sepoy 2801, 14th Sikhs, 4 Jun 1915, of Rajeana, Moga, Ferozepore, Punjab

APAI GURUNG, Naik 4802, 1/6th GR, 1 Jul 1915, of Khairekote, No.4 West, Bhirkot, Nepal

ARJAN SINGH, Sepoy 358, 45th Rattray's Sikhs att 14th Sikhs, 4 Jun 1915, of Bhango Wani, Gurdaspore, Punjab

ARJAN SINGH, Sepoy 635, Patiala Infantry, att 14th Sikhs, 8 Aug 1915, of Kishangarth, Barnala, Patiala, Punjab

ARJAN SINGH, Sepoy 730, Patiala Infantry att 14th Sikhs, 16 Oct 1915, of Kheri, Xajpura, Patiala, Punjab

ARJAN SINGH, L/Nk 3680, 14th Sikhs, 5 Jun 1915, of Jodh Pore, Malaud, Ludhiana, Punjab

ARJAN SINGH, Sepoy 4202, 14th Sikhs, 4 Jun 1915, of Dhaleke, Moga, Ferozepore, Punjab

ARJAN SINGH, Sepoy 4256, 14th Sikhs, 9 Aug 1915, of Balloh, Dhanaula, Nabha, Punjab

ARJAN SINGH, Sepoy 4463, 14th Sikhs, 4 Jun 1915, of Jodh Chak No. 76, Lyallpore, Punjab

ARJUN RAI, Rfmn 457, 2/10th GR, 27 Jun 1915, of Ankhisala, Chethar, Dhankuta, Nepal

ARJUN SINGH, Naik 2643, 14th Sikhs, 4 Jun 1915, of Kelpore, Ludhiana, Punjab

ARJUN SINGH, Naik 3034, 14th Sikhs, 4 Jun 1915, of Jhandooke, Sangrur, Punjab

ASAPATRA RAI, Rfmn 979, 2/10th GR, 10 Aug 1915, of Ambote, Rawadumre, Okhaldhunga, Nepal

ASBIR GURUNG, Rfmn 4820, 1/6th GR, 10 Aug 1915, of Kumlang, No.2 West, Farinda, Nepal

ASBIR LIMBU, Rfmn 1826, 2/10th GR, 30 Jun 1915, of Pokri, Chhatar, Dhankuta, Nepal

ASBIR LIMBU, Naik 1796, 2/10th GR, 25 Jul 1915, of Phedap, Dhankuta, Nepal (Heliopolis (Port Tewfik) Memorial, Egypt and on Helles Memorial as Aspar Limbu)

ASJIT RAI, Rfmn 2728, 2/10th GR, 3 Dec 1915, of Thepang, Panthar, Dhankuta, Nepal

ASRAJ LIMBU, Rfmn 3548, 2/10th GR, 19 Sep 1915, Gumansing Limbu, of Yansingok, Yangrup, Dhankuta, Nepal

ASRAM RAI, Rfmn 3070, 2/10th GR, 19 Sep 1915, of Pakribas, Chainpore, Dhankuta, Nepal

ATAR SINGH, Sepoy 1879, BMP att 14th Sikhs, 19 Sep 1915, of Chachowali, Kathunangal, Amritsar, Punjab

ATARSING THAPA, Rfmn 595, 2/10th GR, 30 Jun 1915, of Mobuwala, Dehra Dun, United Provinces

ATKINSON, Capt. William, 2/10th GR, 29 Jun 1915 (Twelve Trees Copse Cemetery, Helles)

ATMA SINGH, Sepoy 445, Patiala Infantry att 14th Sikhs, 8 Aug 1915, of Bhagrana, Bassi, Patiala, Punjab

ATMA SINGH, Sepoy 3338, 14th Sikhs, 14 May 1915, of Balbehra, Patiala, Punjab

ATTARSING THAPA, Rfmn 1054, 1/6th GR, 5 Jul 1915, of Batela, Bakloh, Punjab

AZIM KHAN, Follower, Bombay/132, S&T Corps, 19 Sep 1915, of Shahpur, Shahpur, Belgaum, Bombay

BABESAR GURUNG, Rfmn 926, 1/6th GR, 30 Sep 1915

BABU SINGH, Sepoy 883, BM att 14th Sikhs, 30 Aug 1915, of Padori, Adampore, Jullundur, Punjab

BACHAN SINGH, Sepoy 1277, BMP att 14th Sikhs, 19 Sep 1915, of Soorewala, Mukhtsar, Ferozepore, Punjab

BACHAN SINGH, Sepoy 2786, 14th Sikhs, 4 Jun 1915, of Bajewala, Bhikhi, Patiala, Punjab

BACHAN SINGH, Sepoy 4339, 14th Sikhs, 14 Jun 1915, of Raman Was, Sangrur, Punjab

BACHAN SINGH, Sepoy 4341, 14th Sikhs, 4 Jun 1915, of Dosanjh, Moga, Ferozepore, Punjab

BACHINT SINGH, Follower, 14th Sikhs, 27 Nov 1915

BADAN SINGH, Naik 466, 69th Punjabis, 5 May 1915, of Jhanjowal, Garhshankar, Hoshiarpore, Punjab

BADAN SINGH, Sepoy 4243, 14th Sikhs, 4 Jun 1915, of Bhalur, Moga, Ferozepore, Punjab

BAGA SINGH, Havildar 2839, 14th Sikhs, 23 May 1915, of Mandhir, Moga, Ferozepore, Punjab

BAGA SINGH, Sepoy 3997, 14th Sikhs, 23 May 1915, of Dosanjh, Moga, Ferozepore, Punjab

BAGA SINGH, Sepoy 4751, 14th Sikhs, 19 Sep 1915, of Farwahi, Barnala, Patiala, Punjab

BAGDHAN RAI, Rfmn 3564, 2/10th GR, 19 Aug 1915, of Batase, Chainpore, Dhankuta, Nepal

BAGGA, Dvr 1239, 27th Mountain Battery att 26th Jacob's Battery, 14 Aug 1915, of Siralian, Bhimbar, Mirpore, Jammu and Kashmir, State

BAGGA KHAN, Follower, ABC, 108th Field Amb, 11 Jul 1915

BAGH ALI, Dvr 1245, 26th Jacob's Battery, 11 Aug 1915, of Nala Musalmanan, Kahta, Rawalpindi, Punjab

BAGH ALI SHAH, Dvr 1571, Mule Corps, 24 Oct 1915, of Mial, Pind Dadan Khan, Jhelum, Punjab

BAGSING LAMA, Rfmn 3115, 2/10th GR, 19 Sep 1915, of Chitre, Bijulakote, No.3 East, Nepal

BAGTABIR RAI, Rfmn 1129, 2/10th GR, 19 Sep 1915, of Yubu, Cheme, Okhaldhunga, Nepal

BAHADAR LIMBU, Rfmn 577, 2/10th GR, 28 Jun 1915, of Mewakhola, Dhankuta, Nepal (Heliopolis (Port Tewfik) Memorial, Egypt)

BAHADUR ALE, Rfmn 2506, 1/5th GR, 7 Aug 1915, of Rangbang, Rangbang, Sataun, Nepal

BAHADUR ALE, Rfmn 3781, 1/5th GR, 22 Aug 1915, of Hajikote, Kothar, Rising, Nepal

BAHADUR GURUNG, Rfmn 172, 1/6th GR, 7 Aug 1915, of Kapalchora, No.3 West, Tanhu, Nepal

BAHADUR GURUNG, Naik 429, 1/6th GR, 12 Oct 1915, of Bhujung, Lamjung, No.2 West, Nepal

BAHADUR GURUNG, Rfmn 936, 2/10th GR, 21 Aug 1915, of Pakribas, Chethar, Dhankuta, Nepal

BAHADUR GURUNG, Rfmn 967, 1/6th GR, 9 Jul 1915, of Thaprakh, No.3 West, Tanhu, Nepal

BAHADUR GURUNG, Rfmn 2737, 1/5th GR, 7 Aug 1915, of Aththar, Burakote, Bhirkote, Nepal

BAHADUR GURUNG, Rfmn 4620, 1/5th GR, 2 Jul 1915, of Arebale, No.3 West, Tanhu, Nepal

BAHADUR KHAN, Dvr 609, 21st Kohat Battery, 26 Jun 1915, of Vag, Pind Dadan Khan, Jhelum, Punjab

BAHADUR LIMBU, Rfmn 1116, 2/10th GR, 19 Sep 1915, of Orokma, Mewakhola, Dhankuta, Nepal

BAHADUR RAI, Rfmn 1098, 2/10th GR, 19 Sep 1915, of Dingding, Chainpore, Dhankuta, Nepal

BAHADUR RANA, Rfmn 444, 1/6th GR, 28 Jun 1915, of Sore, No.2 West, Gurkha, Nepal

BAHADUR RANA, Rfmn 640, 1/6th GR, 9 Aug 1915, of Rangram, No.4 West, Bhirkote, Nepal

BAHADUR RANA, Rfmn 4915, 1/6th GR, 28 Jun 1915, of Garandi, No.4 West, Gairhung, Nepal

BAHADUR RANA, Rfmn 4982, 1/5th GR, 6 Sep 1915, of Kapasi, Garhung, No.5 West, Nepal

BAHADUR THAPA, Rfmn 4400, 1/6th GR, 30 Jun 1915, of Naya Gaun, No.3 West, Tanhu, Nepal

BAHADUR THAPA, Rfmn 4857, 1/6th GR, 30 Jun 1915, of Kirani, Palpa, Gulmi, Nepal

BAHADUR THAPA, Follower, 2/10th GR, 16 Sep 1915

BAHADURSING THAPA, Bugler, 72, 2/10th GR, 8 Sep 1915, of Samalbung, Ilam, Nepal

BAHAL SINGH, Sepoy 4561, 14th Sikhs, 4 Jun 1915, of Jaimal Singh Wala, Barnala, Patiala, Punjab, (Name wrongly shown as Bal Singh)

BAJAHANG LIMBU, Havildar 1725, 2/10th GR, 9 Aug 1915, of Jitpore, Ilam, Nepal

BAJINDAR SINGH, L/Nk 782, Mule Corps, 24 Jul 1915, of Majair Oona, Hoshiarpore, Punjab

BAJIRAM THAPA, Rfmn 4725, 1/5th GR, 5 Sep 1915, of Syarma, Piuthan, Nepal

BAKHSI SINGH, Sepoy 4383, 14th Sikhs, 14 May 1915, of Jaito, Nabha, Punjab

BAKHTAWA SINGH, Bearer 4529, ABC, 108th Field Amb, 13 May 1915, of Gaddri, Pauri, Garhwal, United Provinces

BALA SINGH, L/Nk 1550, 14th Sikhs, 19 Sep 1915, of Begewal, Kathunangal, Amritsar, Punjab

BALANE RAI, Rfmn 420, 2/10th GR, 28 Jun 1915, of Helua, Sabhayauttar, Dhankuta, Nepal

BALANEKI RAI, Rfmn 2316, 2/10th GR, 7 Dec 1915, of Dongma, Bhojpore, Bhojpore, Nepal

BALARAM LIMBU, Rfmn 3577, 2/10th GR, 19 Sep 1915, of Tangkhua, Chhatar, Dhankuta, Nepal

BALARAM PUN, Rfmn 2076, 1/5th GR, 22 Aug 1915, of Manua, Piuthan, Nepal

BALASING GURUNG, Naik 396, 1/6th GR, 7 Aug 1915, of Bowandanra, No.4 West, Bhirkote, Nepal

BALASING GURUNG, Rfmn 4912, 1/5th GR, 24 Jun 1915, of Jilriadung, Nawakote, No.4 West, Nepal

BALASING THAPA, Naik 816, 1/6th GR, 28 Jun 1915, of Chandrakote, No.5 West, Satun, Nepal

BALBAHADUR GURUNG, Rfmn 187, 1/6th GR, 4 Jun 1915, of Chamarekote, Palpa, Gulmi, Nepal

BALBAHADUR RAI, Rfmn 1085, 2/10th GR, 19 Sep 1915, of Bairag, Dhankuta, Nepal

BALBAHADUR RAI, Rfmn 3100, 2/10th GR, 29 Jun 1915, of Dilpa, Siktel, No.4 East, Nepal

BALBAHADUR RAI, Rfmn 3501, 2/10th GR, 19 Sep 1915, of Luring, Gangtok, Sikkim, Nepal

BALBIR GHARTI, Rfmn 4372, 1/6th GR, 13 Oct 1915

BALBIR RANA, Havildar 42, 1/6th GR, 9 Aug 1915, of Durgh, No.4 West, Bhirkote, Nepal

BALBIR THAPA, Rfmn 703, 1/6th GR, 8 Aug 1915, of Gopalchap, Palpa, Nepal

BALBIR THAPA, Rfmn 745, 1/6th GR, 21 Aug 1915, of Punakharka, Sallyana, Nepal

BALBIR THAPA, Naik 2945, 1/4th GR, 17 Dec 1915, of Nandi, Palpa, Nepal

BALDHAR THAPA, Naik 4696, 1/6th GR, 8 Aug 1915, of Patel Dunra, Palpa, Argha, Nepal

BALDHOJ LIMBU, Rfmn 2765, 2/10th GR, 19 Sep 1915, of Kasua, Chainpore, Dhankuta, Nepal

BALE ROKA, Rfmn 4791, 1/5th GR, 7 Aug 1915, of Ryansi, Palpa, Parvat, Nepal

BALIMAN RAI, Rfmn 3122, 2/10th GR, 10 Aug 1915, of Kunku, Chisankhu, No.3 East, Nepal

BALIRAM LIMBU, Rfmn 342, 2/10th GR, 2 Jul 1915, of Minglumba, Mewakhola, Dhankuta, Nepal

BALIWANTE LIMBU, L/Nk 1908, 2/10th GR, 9 Sep 1915, of Kurungbang, Panthar, Dhankuta, Nepal

BALMAN RAI, Rfmn 582, 2/10th GR, 30 Jun 1915, of Pirgaon, Dhankuta, Nepal

BALSING RAI, Rfmn 2940, 2/10th GR, 9 Aug 1915, of Rippa, Chisankhu, Okhaldhunga, Nepal

BANTA SINGH, Rfmn 1642, 14th Sikhs, 19 Sep 1915, of Viring, Jullundur, Punjab

BARA SINGH, Sepoy 3313, 14th Sikhs, 22 May 1915, of Burgari, Faridkote, Ferozepore, Punjab (Name wrongly shown as Bur Singh)

BARA SINGH, Sepoy 3920, 14th Sikhs, 4 Jun 1915, of Gharkhan Samrala, Ludhiana, Punjab

BARA SINGH, Sepoy 4747, 14th Sikhs, 19 Sep 1915, of Dablan, Nabha, Punjab

BARA SINGH, Sepoy 4844, 14th Sikhs, 19 Sep 1915, of Malla, Jagraon, Ludhiana, Punjab

BARKHABADUR RAI, Jem. 2/10th GR, 28 Jun 1915, of Birgaon, Dhankuta, Nepal

BARYAM SINGH, Naik 3608, 14th Sikhs, 6 Jun 1915, of Sandaur, Malerkotla, Ludhiana, Punjab

BASANT SINGH, Sepoy 3752, 14th Sikhs, 15 May 1915, of Laungowal, Sunam, Patiala, Punjab

BASANT SINGH, Havildar 2985, 54th Sikhs att 14th Sikhs, 6 Dec 1915, of Bachhowana, Fattehabad, Hissar, Punjab

BASANT SINGH, Sepoy 4743, 14th Sikhs, 19 Sep 1915, of Bhanra, Patiala, Punjab

BATTYE, Maj. Hedley, 1/5th GR, 4 Jun 1915

BAZ ALI, Dvr Mule Corps, 24 Nov 1915

BECHAR DAN, Follower, Poona/1796, S&T Corps, 26 Nov 1915, of Sampura, Kamraj, Nowsari, Bombay

BEDDY, Lt Rafe, 1/5th GR, 4 Jun 1915, of Budleigh Salterton, Devon, England (Pink Farm Cemetery, Helles)

BEDI, Bearer 6086, ABC, 137 Field Ambulance, 10 Aug 1915, of Koilaha, SuLtanpur, United Provinces (Heliopolis (Port Tewfik) Memorial, Egypt)

BEDNATH LIMBU, Rfmn 958, 2/10th GR, 28 Jun 1915, of Tumbayong, Mewakhola, Dhankuta, Nepal

BELA SINGH, Gnr 2816, 26th Jacob's Battery, 28 Aug 1915, of Desarpore, Jullundur, Punjab

BESHAR THAPA, Rfmn 2590, 1/5th GR, 10 Nov 1915, of Pakhrichhap, No.4 West, Polo Nawakote, Nepal

BHABESAR THAPA, Havildar 3997, 1/5th GR, 7 Aug 1915, of Kulma, No.4 West, Nawakote, Nepal

BHADARBIR THAPA, Rfmn 3973, 1/5th GR, 4 Jun 1915, of Garhunkote, No.4 West, Bhirkote, Nepal

BHADAR THAPA, Rfmn, 1/6th GR, 24 Aug 1915, of Purngaon, Palpa, Nepal (Heliopolis (Port Tewfik) Memorial, Egypt and on Helles Memorial as Bhadrabir Thapa of Purano Gaon)

BHAG SINGH, Havildar 3036, 14th Sikhs, 4 Jun 1915, of Kalakh, Ludhiana, Punjab

BHAG SINGH, Sepoy 3607, 14th Sikhs, 2 Jul 1915, of Kotha, Barnala, Patiala, Punjab

BHAG SINGH, Sepoy 4068, 14th Sikhs, 4 Jun 1915, of Jodhpore, Ludhiana, Punjab, (Name wrongly shown as Bhan Singh)

BHAG SINGH, Sepoy 4311, 14th Sikhs, 6 May 1915, of Ghudda, Bhatinda, Patiala, Punjab

BHAG SINGH, Sepoy 4575, 14th Sikhs, 4 Jun 1915, of Breta, Mansa, Patiala, Punjab

BHAGALIMAN RAI, Rfmn 886, 2/10th GR, 30 Jun 1915, of Budop, Panchthar, Dhankuta, Nepal

Appendix VI 321

BHAGAT SINGH, L/Nk 541, 14th Sikhs, 19 Sep 1915, of Chuk, Lyallpore, Punjab

BHAGAT SINGH, Dvr 795, 26th Jacob's Battery, 10 Aug 1915, of Lalian, Jullundur, Punjab

BHAGAT SINGH, Rfmn 3280, 14th Sikhs, 29 Nov 1915, of Hassowal, Raikote, Ludhiana, Punjab

BHAGAT SINGH, Sepoy 3690, 14th Sikhs, 31 May 1915, of Narangwal, Ludhiana, Punjab

BHAGATABIR THAPA, Rfmn 2527, 1/5th GR, 6 Aug 1915, of Beholibas, Payung, No.4 West, Nepal

BHAGATBIR RAI, Naik 2019, 2/10th GR, 7 Aug 1915, of Lamaphok, Chainpore, Dhankuta, Nepal

BHAGATBIR RANA, Rfmn 264, 1/6th GR, 11 May 1915, of Surpani, Gurkha, Nepal

BHAGATBIR THAPA, Rfmn 4696, 1/5th GR, 21 Aug 1915, of Panikatere, Palpa, Parvat, Nepal

BHAGATBIR THAPA, Rfmn 4903, 1/5th GR, 1 Sep 1915, of Kunhu, Tanhu, No.3 West, Nepal

BHAGATBIR THAPA, Rfmn 4913, 1/6th GR, 30 Aug 1915, of Ranghane, Palpa, Parvat, Nepal

BHAGIMAN RAI, Rfmn 3202, 2/10th GR, 19 Sep 1915, of Damku Irawadumre, Okhaldhunga, Nepal

BHAGTE GHARTI, Rfmn 481, 1/6th GR, 2 Jul 1915, of Tunapani, Sallyana, Nepal

BHAGTE SUNWAR, Rfmn 1151, 2/10th GR, 19 Sep 1915, of Som, Darjeeling, Bengal

BHAGTWALA, Follower, ABC, Hospital Field Amb, 13 May 1915

BHAGWAN SINGH, Sepoy 4315, 14th Sikhs, 4 Jun 1915, of Dhandoli Chhoti, Dhode, Patiala, Punjab

BHAGWAN SINGH, Sepoy 4485, 14th Sikhs, 23 May 1915, of Bhodi Pura, Phul, Nabha, Punjab

BHAGWANDAS GHARTI, Rfmn 4680, 1/5th GR, 28 Jun 1915, of Sarah, Kangra, Punjab

BHAGWANTE LIMBU, Rfmn 2659, 2/10th GR, 21 Aug 1915, of Suhrawa, Taplejung, Dhankuta, Nepal

BHAIMANE RAI, Rfmn 3272, 2/10th GR, 19 Sep 1915, of Sondel, Rawadomre, Okhaldunga, Nepal

BHAJAN SINGH, Rfmn 1764, 14th Sikhs, 19 Sep 1915, of Jodhpore, Sahna, Ludhiana, Punjab

BHAJAN SINGH, Sepoy 4081, 14th Sikhs, 4 Jun 1915, of Mirjeke, Ferozepore, Punjab

BHAKTABAHADUR LIMBU, Rfmn 2646, 2/10th GR, 19 Sep 1915, of Kumaru, Phedap, Dhankuta, Nepal

BHAKTAMAN SUNWAR, Rfmn 3355, 2/10th GR, 21 Aug 1915, of Base, Solu, No.3 East, Nepal

BHALAMAN RAI, Rfmn 812, 2/10th GR, 18 Aug 1915, of Sondel, Rawadomre, Okhaldhunga, Nepal

BHAN SINGH, Rfmn 1603, 14th Sikhs, 19 Sep 1915, of Tharoo, Taran Taran, Amritsar, Punjab

BHAN SINGH, Sepoy 4757, 14th Sikhs, 19 Sep 1915, of Khudi, Barnala, Patiala, Punjab

BHANGA SINGH, Naik 3121, 14th Sikhs, 4 Jun 1915, of Ukandwala, Dhanaula, Nabha, Punjab, (Name wrongly shown as Baga Singh)

BHANU THAPA, Rfmn 388, 1/6th GR, 30 Jun 1915, of Bhujgiri, No.3 West, Rising, Nepal

BHARAT THAPA, Rfmn 1166, 1/6th GR, 1 Jul 1915, of Sorhalang, Bandipore, Tanhu, Nepal

BHARTASING RAI, Naik 2186, 2/10th GR, 29 Jun 1915, of Kolbote, Charkhola, Ilam, Nepal

BHAWAN SINGH, Bearer 4623, ABC, 108th Field Amb, 14 Aug 1915, of Melgaon, Pauri, Garhwal, United Provinces

BHAWANSING RANA, Rfmn 4622, 1/5th GR, 28 Jun 1915, of Kunokote, Palpa, Nepal

BHIMBAHADUR RAI, Rfmn 1147, 2/10th GR, 19 Sep 1915, of Nirang, Siktel, Bhojpore, Nepal

BHIM BAHADUR THAPA, Rfmn 1/5th GR, 20 Aug 1915, (Pieta Cemetery, Malta)

BHIMBAHADUR THAPA, Rfmn 295, 1/5th GR, 21 Aug 1915, of Yamni, Tanhu, No.3 West, Nepal

BHIMBAHADURTHAPA, Havildar 121, 1/6th GR, 13 May 1915, of Gonathora, No.3 West, Tanhu, Nepal

BHIMDAHADUR THAPA, Rfmn 4894, 1/5th GR, 20 Aug 1915, of Padmi, Gulmi, Palpa, Nepal

BHIMSING THAPA, Rfmn 641, 1/6th GR, 6 Sep 1915, of Ghundrang, No.3 West, Tanhu, Nepal

BHOJBAHADUR RAI, Rfmn 3191, 2/10th GR, 19 Sep 1915, of Parpe, Chainpore, Dhankuta, Nepal

BHOJMAN RAI, Rfmn 3349, 2/10th GR, 19 Sep 1915, of Punekhu, Talawa, No.3 East, Nepal

BHOLA SINGH, Naik 2946, 14th Sikhs, 4 Jun 1915, of Jarg, Pail, Patiala, Punjab

BHOTABIR LIMBU, Rfmn 3579, 2/10th GR, 19 Sep 1915, of Sanglep, Phedap, Dhankuta, Nepal

BHOWANSING RANA, Naik 473, 1/6th GR, 7 Aug 1915, of Tarle, No.4 West, Bhirkote, Nepal

BHOWRAJ LIMBU, Havildar 2638, 2/10th GR, 19 Sep 1915, of Angsingbe, Yangrup, Dhankuta, Nepal

BHUDBIR GHARTI, Rfmn 592, 1/6th GR, 13 May 1915, of Berabari, No.3 West, Tanhu, Nepal

BHUDIMAN RAI, Rfmn 579, 2/10th GR, 19 Sep 1915, of Palisampang, Bhojpore, Nepal

BHUJIBAL THAPA, Rfmn 4394, 1/5th GR, 11 Aug 1915, of Bakham, Palpa, Nepal

BHULBIR THAPA, L/Nk 4280, 1/5th GR, 13 Jun 1915, of Keroli, Palpa, Nepal

BHUP SINGH, Sepoy 3970, 14th Sikhs, 4 Jun 1915, of Bainra, Dhuri, Patiala, Punjab

BIDEHI, Bearer 6086, ABC, 137th Field Amb, 7 Aug 1915, of Koilaha, SuLtanpore, Oudh

BIDEHI, Bearer 6986, ABC, 137th Field Amb, 19 May 1915

BIDHI CHAND, Bearer 4515, ABC, 108th Field Amb, 13 May 1915, of Papargaon, Mohamadabad, Farukhabad, United Provinces

BIDHIMAN LAMA, Rfmn 1077, 2/10th GR, 19 Sep 1915, of Rangbang, Phedap, Dhankuta, Nepal

BIKRAMSING RAI, Rfmn 1067, 2/10th GR, 7 Aug 1915, of Dipsan, Siktel, Bhojpore, Nepal

BILLU, Dvr 1327, Mule Corps, 19 Aug 1915, Fazal Khan, Bagh, Poonch, Punjab

BIMAN RAI, Rfmn 1093, 2/10th GR, 19 Sep 1915, of Tangdam, Chainpore, Dhankuta, Nepal

BINDHOJ GURUNG, Rfmn 927, 1/6th GR, 28 Jun 1915, of Maling, No.2 West, Lamjung, Nepal

BIRDWOOD, Capt. Christopher, 1/6th GR, 7 Jun 1915, of Bexhill-on-Sea, Sussex, England (Pink Farm Cemetery, Helles)

BIR SINGH, Jem. 14th Sikhs, 4 Jun 1915, of Isewal, Ludhiana, Punjab

BIR SINGH, L/Nk 784, 14th Sikhs, 19 Sep 1915, Maija Singh, of Nurpore, Khatra, Lahore, Punjab

BIR SINGH, Gnr 1376, 26th Jacob's Battery, 12 Aug 1915, of Kassoana, Zira, Ferozepore, Punjab

BIR SINGH, Havildar 2689, 14th Sikhs, 4 Jun 1915, of Lehra, Moga, Ferozepore, Punjab

BIR SINGH, Sepoy 2937, 14th Sikhs, 4 Jun 1915, of Biroke, Bhikhi, Patiala, Punjab

BIR SINGH, Sepoy 4012, 14th Sikhs, 28 May 1915, of Tibba, Dhuri, Patiala, Punjab

BIR SINGH, Sepoy 4663, 14th Sikhs, 2 Jul 1915, of Barampore, Ropar, Ambala, Punjab

BIRBAHADUR LIMBU, Rfmn 3259, 2/10th GR, 12 Aug 1915, of Hathikharka, Chhatar, Dhankuta, Nepal

BIRBAHADUR RAI, Rfmn 2747, 2/10th GR, 10 Aug 1915, of Malgaun, Dhankuta, Nepal

BIRBAL BURA, Rfmn 4848, 1/6th GR, 1 Jul 1915, of Gama, Piuthan, Nepal

BIRBAL LIMBU, Rfmn 605, 2/10th GR, 1 Jul 1915, of Mahbu, Charkhola, Ilam, Nepal

BIRBAL THAPA, Havildar 3854, 1/5th GR, 30 Aug 1915, of Gaya, Bahakote, Pallo Nawakote, Nepal

BIRBHAN BURA, Rfmn 38, 1/5th GR, 28 Jun 1915, of Bhalkote, Palpa, 4000, Patvat, Nepal

BIRDHOJ LIMBU, Rfmn 161, 2/10th GR, 31 Jul 1915, of Tembhe, Mewakhola, Dhankuta Nepal

BIRDHOJ RAI, Rfmn 1114, 2/10th GR, 19 Sep 1915, of Magdi, Pawa, Dhankuta, Nepal

BIRDHOJ RAI, Naik 2566, 2/10th GR, 29 Jun 1915, of Kole, Panthar, Dhankuta, Nepal

BIRDHOJ RAI, Rfmn 2623, 2/10th GR, 29 Jun 1915, of Birgaun, Panthar Dhankuta, Nepal

BIRDHOJ RAI, Rfmn 3360, 2/10th GR, 9 Aug 1915, of Gairigaun, Solu, No.3 East, Nepal

BIRDHOJ SUNWAR, Rfmn 3080, 2/10th GR, 19 Sep 1915, of Buji, Ramechhap, No.3 East, Nepal

BIRHARKA RAI, Rfmn 778, 2/10th GR, 29 Jun 1915, of Sarsepore, Chisankhu, Okhaldhunga, Nepal

BIRJAMAN RAI, Rfmn 2549, 2/10th GR, 30 Jun 1915, of Majhuwa, Charkhol, Ilam, Nepal

BIRKBAHADUR LIMBU, Rfmn 2529, 2/10th GR, 7 Aug 1915, of Kongwa, Yangrup, Dhankuta, Nepal

BIRKBECK, Lt Edward, 128th Pioneers, 7 Aug 1915

BIRKHABADUR LIMBU, Naik 3134, 2/10th GR, 19 Sep 1915, of Lingbang, Phedap, Dhankuta, Nepal

BIRKHASING LIMBU, Rfmn 697, 2/10th GR, 29 Jun 1915, of Lingdep, Mewakhola, Dhankuta, Nepal

BIRKHASING THAPA, Rfmn 674, 1/6th GR, 10 Aug 1915, of Dugung, Bandipore, Rising, Nepal

BIRKHE PUN, Rfmn 1022, 1/6th GR, 25 Oct 1915

BIRKHSING THAPA, Rfmn 3793, 1/5th GR, 8 Aug 1915, of Koldanra, Palpa, Nepal

BIRLAL RAI, Rfmn 1071, 2/10th GR, 7 Aug 1915, of Tumaphuk, Dasmajhwa, Dhankuta, Nepal

BIRTHASING GURUNG, Rfmn 978, 1/6th GR, 3 Jul 1915, of Golma No.4 West, Nawakote, Nepal

BIRU LAMA, Rfmn 1164, 2/10th GR, 19 Sep 1915, of Jhaku, Khotang, Charikote, Nepal

BISHN SINGH, Havildar 188, 14th Sikhs, 19 Sep 1915, of Wanian Wala, Gujranwala, Punjab

BISHN SINGH, L/Nk 1020, 14th Sikhs, 19 Sep 1915, of Chappe, Sherpore, Patiala, Punjab

BISHN SINGH, Sepoy 4014, 14th Sikhs, 3 Jul 1915, of Attar Singh Wala, Dhanaula, Nabha, Punjab

BISHN SINGH, Sepoy 4046, 14th Sikhs, 4 Jun 1915, of Sawajpura, Dhanaula, Nabha, Punjab

BISHN SINGH, Sepoy 4577, 14th Sikhs, 25 May 1915, of Mangewal, Maloh, Nabha, Punjab

BISHN SINGH, Follower, 14th Sikhs, 19 Sep 1915

BISHNBAHADUR RANA, Havildar 4927, 1/6th GR, 28 Jun 1915, of Kainas, Palpa, Gulmi, Nepal

BISHNU RANA, Rfmn 4655, 1/6th GR, 8 Sep 1915, of Gorkhali Chap, Bandipore, Tanhu, Nepal

BISHNU THAPA, Rfmn 1195, 1/6th GR, 3 Sep 1915, of Dhami, Balteri, Doti, Nepal

BISTARSING LIMBU, Rfmn 519, 2/10th GR, 2 Jul 1915, of Changia, Mewakhola, Dhankuta, Nepal

BOJINDRA GURUNG, Bugler, 4855, 1/6th GR, 13 May 1915, of Churibas, Bandipore, Tanhu, Nepal

BOLANSING LIMBU, Rfmn 3239, 2/10th GR, 31 Aug 1915, of Thurpu, Yangrup, Dhankuta, Nepal

BOMBAHADUR RAI, Rfmn 3509, 2/10th GR, 19 Sep 1915, of Baspani, No.3 East, Okhaldhunga, Nepal

BORAH, Bearer 6545, ABC, 108th Field Amb, 9 Aug 1915, of Kothabundy, Boandi, Kotah, Rajputana

BOSTAN, Dvr 1247, Mule Corps, 18 Dec 1915, of Nassur, Kahuta, Rawalpindi, Punjab

BOSTAN, Dvr 2104, Mule Corps, 18 Dec 1915, of Mirkuligalun, Jhelum, Punjab (Turkish Military Cemetery, Malta)

BRIJ LAL, Bearer 4265, ABC, 108th Field Amb, 17 Jun 1915, of Rainpore, Phagwara, Jullundur, Punjab

BROWN, Capt, Wynyard Keith, 1/5th GR att 9th Bn, West Yorkshire Regiment, 4 Jun 1915, of Yateley, Hants

BUDH SINGH, Rfmn 1504, 14th Sikhs, 19 Sep 1915, of Jikhapal, Sanam, Patiala, Punjab

BUDH SINGH, Naik 3274, 14th Sikhs, 4 Jun 1915, of Talwandi, Bhatinda, Patiala, Punjab

BUDH SINGH, Sepoy 4556, 14th Sikhs, 21 Jun 1915, of Malkana, Bhatinda, Patiala, Punjab

BUDHA SINGH, L/Nk 1168, 89th Punjabis, 13 May 1915, of Jalal Usma, Amritsar, Punjab

BUDHIBAL GURUNG, Rfmn 45, 1/6th GR, 25 Oct 1915, of Kumlang, No.2 West, Lamjung, Nepal

BUDHIBAL GURUNG, Rfmn 4193, 1/5th GR, 4 Jun 1915, of Naiji, No.2 West, Lamjung, Nepal

BUDHIBAL GURUNG, Rfmn 4962, 1/5th GR, 4 Jun 1915, of Jaspore, Dhor, No.3 West, Nepal

BUDHIBAL THAPA, Rfmn 4694, 1/5th GR, 7 Apr 1916, of Bhakonde, Palpa, Nepal

BUDHIBAL THAPA, Rfmn 4809, 1/5th GR, 5 Jun 1915, of Jebre Dunga, No.4 West, Purunkote, Nepal

BUDHIBAT GURUNG, Rfmn 4850, 1/6th GR, 30 Aug 1915, of Mankali Bang, Piuthan, Piuthan, Nepal

BUDHIMAN GURUNG, Havildar 529, 2/10th GR, 21 Aug 1915, of Kanglabong, Chethar, Dhankuta, Nepal

BUDHIMAN GURUNG, Rfmn 2578, 2/10th GR, 7 Aug 1915, of Jamuna, Ilam, Nepal

BUDHIMAN GURUNG, L/Nk 4408, 1/5th GR, 7 Aug 1915, of Cherjung, No.3 West, Kaski, Nepal

BUDHIMAN LIMBU, Rfmn 2722, 2/10th GR, 30 Jun 1915, of Mawa, Panthar, Dhankuta, Nepal

BUDHIMAN RAI, Rfmn 3591, 2/10th GR, 19 Sep 1915, of Chhapgaun, Hatuwa, Bhojpore, Nepal

BUDHIRAM BURA, Rfmn 4301, 1/5th GR, 8 Aug 1915, of Taman, Palpa, Parvat, Nepal

BUDHU, L/Nk 1261, Mule Corps, 4 Jan 1916, of Jermiah, Chakkadgarh, Gurdaspore, Punjab

BUDHU SINGH, Follower, 14th Sikhs, 14 Jul 1915

BUGHA SINGH, Havildar 2508, 14th Sikhs, 5 Jun 1915, of Sandoha, Bhatinda, Patiala, Punjab, (Name wrongly shown as Bogh Singh)

BUR SINGH, Sepoy 1602, 14th Sikhs, 19 Sep 1915, of Dadupura, Kathunangal, Amritsar, Punjab

BUR SINGH, Sepoy 1625, 14th Sikhs, 19 Sep 1915, of Bhagthari, Dehranank, Gurdaspore, Punjab

BURHAN ALI, Dvr 1575, 26th Jacob's Battery, 19 Sep 1915, of Nala Musalmanan, Kahuta, Rawalpindi, Punjab

CAMPBELL, Lt George, 2/10th GR, 7 Aug 1915

CHABILAL ALE, Rfmn 392, 1/6th GR, 7 Aug 1915, of Banjghari, No.3 West, Rising, Nepal

CHABILAL GURUNG, Rfmn 4062, 1/5th GR, 28 Jun 1915, of Deorali, Bachha, Payung, Nepal

CHABILAL LIMBU, Rfmn 557, 2/10th GR, 7 Aug 1915, of Purjan, Phedap, Dhankuta, Nepal

CHABILAL SARKI, Rfmn 2256, 2/10th GR, 15 Jul 1915, of Hathuwa, Hathuwa, No.4 East, Nepal

CHAINCHAL SINGH, Sepoy 4216, 14th Sikhs, 4 Jun 1915, of Panjgarain, Malerkotlaa, Ludhiana, Punjab

CHAKRABAHADUR RAI, Rfmn 3520, 2/10th GR, 19 Sep 1915, of Bosikhora, Hathuwa, Bhojpore, Nepal

CHALIA PUN, Rfmn 4688, 1/5th GR, 7 Aug 1915, of Thabang, Palpa, Parvat, Nepal

CHAMPASING GURUNG, Rfmn 1487, 1/6th GR, 21 Nov 1915

CHANAN, Dvr 746, Mule Corps, 15 Jul 1915, of Musania, Jullundur, Hoshiarpore, Punjab

CHANAN SINGH, Sepoy 1246, 14th Sikhs, 19 Sep 1915, of Paranah, Khalra, Lahore, Punjab

CHANAN SINGH, Sepoy 3819, 14th Sikhs, 4 Jun 1915, of Dhidari, Ludhiana, Punjab

CHANAN SINGH, Sepoy 4067, 14th Sikhs, 23 May 1915, of Rumi, Jagraon, Ludhiana, Punjab

CHANAN SINGH, Sepoy 4116, 14th Sikhs, 19 Sep 1915, of Ladbanjara, Dhode, Patiala, Punjab

CHANAN SINGH, Sepoy 4366, 14th Sikhs, 4 Jun 1915, of Roda, Moga, Ferozepore, Punjab

CHANAN SINGH, Sepoy 4391, 14th Sikhs, 4 Jun 1915, of Diyalpura, Sangrur, Punjab

CHANDA SINGH, Sepoy 290, Patiala Infantry att 14th Sikhs, 8 Aug 1915, of Sanaur, Patiala, Punjab

CHANDA SINGH, Sepoy 363, Patiala Infantry att 14th Sikhs, 22 Aug 1915, of Ballar, Sunam, Patiala, Punjab

CHANDA SINGH, Sepoy 4154, 14th Sikhs, 4 Jun 1915, of Bahadarpore, Phul, Nabha, Punjab

CHANDARBIR THAPA, Havildar 4045, 1/5th GR, 10 Aug 1915, of Dabhangkote, No.4 West, Bhirkote, Nepal

CHANDARSING GURUNG, Rfmn 4277, 1/5th GR, 4 Jun 1915, of Ramja, No.3 West, Kaski, Nepal

CHANDRABAHADUR RAI, Rfmn 1165, 2/10th GR, 19 Sep 1915, of Dowa, Bhojpore, Nepal

CHANDRABIR RAI, Rfmn 1110, 2/10th GR, 19 Sep 1915, of Birgaon, Dhankuta, Nepal

CHANDRABIR RAI, Rfmn 1156, 2/10th GR, 19 Sep 1915, of Tekhutang, Gangtok, Sikkim

CHANDRABIR THAPA, Rfmn 635, 1/6th GR, 4 Jun 1915, of Kafle, Palpa, Gulmi, Nepal

CHANDRABIR THAPA, Rfmn 1420, 1/6th GR, 7 Aug 1915, of Musikote, Palpa, Nepal

CHANDRAMAN RAI, Rfmn 1094, 2/10th GR, 19 Sep 1915, of Dingding, Chainpore, Dhankuta, Nepal

CHANDRASING GURUNG, Rfmn 548, 1/6th GR, 8 Aug 1915, of Dhapu, No.4 West, Bhirkote, Nepal

CHANDRASING GURUNG, Rfmn 4678, 1/6th GR, 6 Aug 1915, of Simle, Parewadanra, Lamjung, Nepal

CHANKABIR LAMA, Rfmn 2838, 2/10th GR, 29 Jun 1915, of Humangdin, Chhatar, Dhankuta, Nepal

CHARBAHADUR LIMBU, L/Nk 2392, 2/10th GR, 7 Aug 1915, of Megsorang, Mewakhola, Dhankuta, Nepal

CHATAR GURUNG, Rfmn 820, 1/6th GR, 5 Jul 1915, of Balakote, No.5 West, Payung, Nepal

CHATAR SINGH, Sepoy 4546, 14th Sikhs, 4 Jun 1915, of Kanech, Ludhiana, Punjab

CHATARSING GURUNG, Rfmn 3760, 1/5th GR, 29 Jun 1915, of Balakote, Dheruakote, Payung, Nepal

CHATARSING LIMBU, Rfmn 478, 2/10th GR, 1915, Gangasing Limbu, of Thembe, Mewakhola, Dhankuta, Nepal

CHATURDHOJ RAI, Rfmn 286, 2/10th GR, 7 Aug 1915

CHATURE LIMBU, Rfmn 30, 2/10th GR, 22 Aug 1915, of Lingdep, Mewakhola, Dhankuta, Nepal

CHATURE THAPA, Rfmn 2850, 1/4th GR, 10 Nov 1915, of Bajarkote, No.3 West, Tanhu, Nepal

CHATURMAN RAI, Rfmn 1154, 2/10th GR, 19 Sep 1915, of Solo, Majuwa, Okhaldhunga, Nepal

CHHAJU SINGH, L/Nk 1360, 26th Jacob's Battery, 27 Sep 1915, of Salodi Singhandi, Samrala, Ludhiana, Punjab

CHHOTA SINGH, Sepoy 546, Patiala Infantry att 14th Sikhs, 16 Oct 1915, of Allo Arakh, Bhawanigarh, Sunam, Patiala, Punjab

CHINNASWAMI, Follower, 754, Mule Corps, 27 Sep 1915, of Yellagooda Palium Shooley, Bangalore, Mysore, Madras

CHINTABIR THAPA, Rfmn 4177, 1/5th GR, 7 Aug 1915, of Gyaja, Palpa, Nepal

CHIRAN THAPA, L/Nk 459, 1/6th GR, 3 Jul 1915, of Bhirkote, No.3 West, Tanhu, Nepal

CHIRMAN THAPA, Havildar 1983, 2/10th GR, 19 Sep 1915, of Muriabar, Chaubina, Phankuta, Nepal

CHUNA, Follower, 2/10th GR, 28 Jun 1915, Chabba, of Sisambag, Fatehgarh, Pharakabad, United Provinces, (Name wrongly shown as China)

COWASJI, Follower, S&T Corps, 19 Sep 1915, of Satara Sadar Bazar, Satara, Bombay

CREMEN, Lt Leonard Francis, 14th Sikhs, 4 Jun 1915, of Bury, Lancashire, England (Pink Farm Cemetery, Helles)

CUMMINS, Lt Harry Jackson, 1/5th GR, 21 Aug 1915, of Glanmire, Co, Cork, Ireland

DADARAJ GHALE, Rfmn 1156, 1/6th GR, 9 Dec 1915, of Ganpokhra, No.2 West, Lamjung, Nepal

DADBIR GURUNG, Rfmn 737, 1/6th GR, 16 May 1915, of Dartta, No.2 West, Lamjung, Nepal

DADRAJ GURUNG, Rfmn 659, 1/6th GR, 4 Jul 1915, of Langarkote, No.2 West, Lamjung, Nepal

DADRAT GURUNG, Rfmn 659, 1/6th GR, 2 Aug 1915, of Langekot, Lamjung, Nepal (Pieta Cemetery, Malta)

DALBADUR RANA, Rfmn 398, 2/10th GR, 20 Sep 1915, (Heliopolis (Port Tewfik) Memorial, Egypt)
DAL BIR RANA, Sub. 3516, 1/6th GR, 27 Jul 1915 (Pieta Cemetery, Malta)
DALLAS, Capt. Jack, 1/6th GR, 12 Sep 1915 (Alexandria (Chatby) Cemetery, Egypt)
DAL SINGH, Sepoy 721, 45th Rattray's Sikhs att 14th Sikhs, 4 Jun 1915, of Thanewala, Bhatinda, Patiala, Punjab
DALBAHADUR GURUNG, L/Nk 4128, 1/5th GR, 4 Jun 1915, of Sapongdi, No.4 West, Bhirkote, Nepal
DALBAHADUR GURUNG, Rfmn 4971, 1/5th GR, 2 Jul 1915, of Chanote, No.4 West, Parvat, Nepal
DALBAHADUR LIMBU, L/Nk 3143, 2/10th GR, 17 Aug 1915, of Suwachi, Panthar, Dhankuta, Nepal
DALBAHADUR RAI, Rfmn 1128, 2/10th GR, 19 Sep 1915, of Suwachi, Panthar, Dhankuta, Nepal
DALBAHADUR RANA, Rfmn 398, 2/10th GR, 20 Sep 1915
DALBAHADUR RANA, Rfmn 4952, 1/5th GR, 2 Jul 1915, of Gurkha, Gurkha, No.2 West, Nepal
DALBAHADUR THAPA, Rfmn 4420, 1/5th GR, 7 Aug 1915, of Biolibas, No.5 West, Payung, Nepal
DALBIR RANA, Sub. 1/6th GR, 21 Jul 1915
DALBIR RANA, Rfmn 1048, 1/6th GR, 30 Jun 1915, of Labang, Palpa, Parvat, Nepal
DALBIR RANA, Rfmn 1266, 1/6th GR, 21 Aug 1915, of Lekhane, Palpa, 4000, Parvat, Nepal
DALBIR THAPA, Naik 4147, 1/5th GR, 4 Jun 1915, of Galdu, Palpa, Nepal
DALIP SINGH, Sepoy 3032, 4th Prince Albert Victor's Rajputs att Indian Field Amb, 9 Jul 1915, of Kasan, Gurgaon, Punjab
DALIP SINGH, Sepoy 4230, 14th Sikhs, 5 Jun 1915, of Khiala, Bhatmda, Patiala, Punjab
DALIP SINGH, Sepoy 4318, 14th Sikhs, 14 May 1915, of Jodhpore, Ludhiana, Punjab
DALIP SINGH, Sepoy 4328, 36th Sikhs att 14th Sikhs, 9 Aug 1915, of Gondpore, Garhshanker, Hoshiarpore, Punjab
DALLU GURUNG, Rfmn 13, 1/6th GR, 6 Sep 1915, of Dandasura, No.4 West, Bhirkote, Nepal, (Name wrongly shown Dalbar Gurung)
DALLU THAPA, Rfmn 4432, 1/6th GR, 29 Jun 1915, of Basantpore, Bandipore, Tanhu, Nepal
DALMAN RAI, Bugler, 11, 2/10th GR, 7 Aug 1915, of Kolbote, Charkhola, Ilam, Nepal
DALMAN THAPA, Rfmn 4829, 1/5th GR, 7 Aug 1915, of Thantap, No.4 West, Parvat, Nepal
DALMARDAN RAI, Rfmn 1182, 2/10th GR, 19 Sep 1915, of Damdi, Okhaldhunga, Nepal
DALSING ALE, Rfmn 996, 1/6th GR, 3 Jul 1915, of Rangoon, Bandipore, Tanhu, Nepal
DALSING THAPA, Rfmn 381, 1/6th GR, 13 May 1915, of Bihargarh, Palpa, Nepal
DALSUR ALE, Rfmn 4934, 1/5th GR, 7 Aug 1915, of Danrulak, No.4 West, Nawakote, Nepal
DALSUR PUN, L/Nk 4700, 1/6th GR, 16 Aug 1915, of Luka, Khalanga, Piuthan, Nepal
DALSUR RANA, Rfmn 394, 1/6th GR, 4 Jun 1915, of Basantpore, No.3 West, Tanhu, Nepal
DALU THAPA, Rfmn 47, 1/5th GR, 29 Aug 1915, of Gyaptung, No.5 West, Payung, Nepal
DAMARSING GURUNG, Rfmn 4391, 1/5th GR, 7 Aug 1915, of Thaprek, No.3 West, Tanhu, Nepal
DAMARSING GURUNG, Rfmn 4986, 1/5th GR, 5 Jun 1915, of Ratanpore, No.3 West, Tanhu, Nepal
DAMARSING PUN, Rfmn 4859, 1/5th GR, 5 Jun 1915, of Owakhet, Palpa, Parvat, Nepal
DAMBARSING LIMBU, Naik 2437, 2/10th GR, 19 Sep 1915, of Lungja, Mewakhola, Dhankuta, Nepal
DAMBARSING RAI, Naik 2772, 2/10th GR, 19 Sep 1915, of Lungja, Mewakhola, Dhankuta, Nepal
DAMBIR THAPA, Naik 4892, 1/6th GR, 30 Jun 1915, of Okhaldunga, Palpa, Nepal
DAN SINGH, Sepoy 1515, 14th Sikhs, 19 Sep 1915, of Kishanpura, Balwali, Sangner, Punjab
DAN SINGH, Sepoy 4376, 14th Sikhs, 2 Jul 1915, of Sukhanwala, Faridkote, Punjab
DANBAHADUR LIMBU, Bugler, 394, 2/10th GR, 23 Jul 1915, of Salambo, Amchok, Bhojpore, Nepal

DARANDHOJ RAI, Rfmn 707, 2/10th GR, 30 Jun 1915, of Saplaku, Yangrup, Dhankuta, Nepal

DASAUNDA SINGH, Sepoy 245, Patiala Infantry, att 14th Sikhs, 8 Aug 1915, of Kasiana, Amargarh, Sunam, Patiala, Punjab

DASAUNDA SINGH, Sepoy 3437, 14th Sikhs, 4 Jun 1915, of Chime, Sunam, Patiala, Punjab

DASAUNDA SINGH, Sepoy 4177, 14th Sikhs, 4 Jun 1915, of Kalsian, Phul, Nabha, Punjab

DATAHANG LIMBU, L/Nk 2870, 2/10th GR, 19 Sep 1915, of Sunthokra, Mewakhola, Dhankuta, Nepal

DAULAT SINGH, Sepoy 767, 14th Sikhs, 25 Nov 1915, of Kalalmajra, Ludhiana, Punjab

DAULATMAN RAI, Rfmn 3532, 2/10th GR, 19 Sep 1915, of Santhakra, Mewakhola, Dhankuta, Nepal

DAYA SINGH, Sepoy 2253, 14th Sikhs, 4 Jun 1915, of Sikandarpura, Malerkotla, Ludhiana, Punjab

DAYA SINGH, Havildar 2380, 14th Sikhs, 26 Jun 1915, of Madnipore, Pail, Patiala, Punjab, (Name wrongly shown as Dhiya Singh)

DEBISING THAPA, Naik 111, 1/6th GR, 28 Jun 1915, of Darsing-Danra, Palpa, Nepal

DEORAJ GURUNG, Rfmn 120, 1/6th GR, 6 Sep 1915, of Gairathok, No.3 West, Tanhu, Nepal

DESA SINGH, Dvr 1583, 26th Jacob's Battery, 17 Aug 1915, of Raipore, Bhulath, Kapurthala, Punjab

DESBIR RAI, Rfmn 1157, 2/10th GR, 19 Sep 1915, of Oyenang, Siktel, Bhojpore, Nepal

DE VOEUX, Lt Harold Charles, Indian Army att 8th Bn, Royal Munster Fusiliers, 11 Jun 1916, of Kensington, London, England (Lancashire Landing Cemetery, Helles)

DEWA SINGH, Havildar 41, Patiala Infantry, att 14th Sikhs, 22 Aug 1915, of Ahnon, Malerkotla, Punjab

DEWA SINGH, Sepoy 1573, 14th Sikhs, 19 Sep 1915, of Gajal, Gandasinghwala, Lahore, Punjab

DEWA SINGH, Naik 2579, 14th Sikhs, 4 Jun 1915, of Malah, Jagraon, Ludhiana, Punjab

DEWA SINGH, Sepoy 4336, 14th Sikhs, 7 Oct 1915, of Nawi Talwandi, Jagraon, Ludhiana, Punjab

DEWANSING GURUNG, Rfmn 4303, 2nd GR att 1/4th GR, 6 Oct 1915, of Kasikuna, Sarangkote, Kaski, No.3 West, Nepal

DHALBAHADUR RANA, Rfmn 398, 2/10th GR, 20 Sep 1915 (Heliopolis (Port Tewfik) Memorial, Egypt)

DHAMPAL LIMBU, Rfmn 1068, 2/10th GR, 17 Jan 1916, of Sokaba, Yangrup, Dhankuta, Nepal

DHANA SINGH, Sepoy 4162, 14th Sikhs, 4 Jun 1915, of Daudhar, Moga, Ferozepore, Punjab

DHANBAHADUR GURUNG, Rfmn 156, 1/6th GR, 29 May 1915, of Panchagaon, No.3 West, Kaski, Nepal

DHANBAHADUR GURUNG, Rfmn 672, 2/10th GR, 29 Jun 1915, of Pakribaswa, Dhankuta, Dhankuta, Nepal

DHANBAHADUR LIMBU, Rfmn 394, 2/10th GR, 23 Oct 1915, of Mehakhola, Dhankuta, Nepal (Heliopolis (Port Tewfik) Memorial, Egypt)

DHANBAHADUR LIMBU, Rfmn 323, 2/10th GR, 10 Aug 1915, of Tamrang, Mewakhola, Dhankuta, Nepal

DHANBAHADUR LIMBU, Rfmn 662, 2/10th GR, 2 Jul 1915, of Yektan, Panchthar, Dhankuta, Nepal

DHANBAHADUR LIMBU, Rfmn 923, 2/10th GR, 10 Aug 1915

DHANBAHADUR RAI, Rfmn 966, 2/10th GR, 29 Jun 1915, of Maidane, Chainpore, Dhankuta, Nepal

DHANBAHADUR RAI, Rfmn 3584, 2/10th GR, 19 Sep 1915, of Dilpa, Siktel, Bhojpore, Nepal

DHANBIR GURUNG, Rfmn 43475, 1/5th GR, 7 Aug 1915, of Bachok, No.2 West, Lamjung, Nepal

DHANBIR GURUNG, L/Nk 4385, 1/5th GR, 1 Sep 1915, of Dhor, Palpa, Gulmi, Nepal

DHANBIR THAPA, Sub. 1/6th GR, 22 May 1915, of Dairene, Palpa, Nepal

DHANBIR THAPA, Havildar 4626, 1/6th GR, 8 Aug 1915, of Narju, No.3 West, Rising, Nepal

DHANBIR GURUNG, Rfmn 12, 1/6th GR, 30 Sep 1915, of Bhoktiyani, No.2 West, Gurkha, Nepal

DHANBOJ LIMBU, Rfmn 239, 2/10th GR, 29 Jun 1915, of Bhadanre, Panchthar, Dhankuta, Nepal

DHANHAJUR RAI, Rfmn 2925, 2/10th GR, 17 Jul 1915, of Watung, Dhankuta, Nepal

DHANHARKE RAI, Rfmn 190, 2/10th GR, 7 Aug 1915, of Chaunka, Bhojpore, No.4 East, Nepal

DHANIA GURUNG, Rfmn 4262, 1/5th GR, 28 Jun 1915, of Melang, No.2 West, Nepal (Heliopolis (Port Tewfik) Memorial, Egypt)

DHANIRAM BHURA, Rfmn 4805, 1/5th GR, 7 Aug 1915, of Barakot, Palpa, Nepal (Heliopolis (Port Tewfik) Memorial, Egypt)

DHANLAL BURA, Rfmn 4882, 1/5th GR, 10 Aug 1915, of Baglung, Palpa, Parvat, Nepal

DHANMAN RAI, Rfmn 3137, 2/10th GR, 15 Aug 1915, of Dehang, Khelang, No.3 East, Nepal

DHANNA SINGH, Sepoy 834, 14th Sikhs, 22 Aug 1915, of Sohawi, Pasrur, Sialkote, Punjab

DHANPAL LIMBU, Rfmn 1068, 2/10th GR, 17 Jan 1916, of Yangrup, Dhankuta, Nepal (Heliopolis (Port Tewfik) Memorial, Egypt)

DHANRAJ GURUNG, Follower, 1/6th GR, 29 Nov 1915, of Murao, No.5 West, Satun, Nepal

DHANRAJ LIMBU, Rfmn 449, 2/10th GR, 7 Aug 1915, of Mewakhola, Dhankuta, Nepal

DHANRAJ MAL, Rfmn 4713, 1/5th GR, 8 Aug 1915, of Longku, No.3 West, Payung, Nepal

DHANSING GURUNG, Havildar 317, 1/6th GR, 28 Jun 1915, of Nurak, Palpa, Khanchi, Nepal

DHANSING PUN, Rfmn 441, 1/6th GR, 22 May 1915, of Nisi, Palpa, Parvat, Nepal

DHANSING RANA, Naik 3984, 1/5th GR, 25 Jul 1915, of Chindi-Kharak, Payung, Payung, Nepal

DHARAMDHOJ RAI, Rfmn 1145, 2/10th GR, 19 Sep 1915, of Binpa, Khamthing, Okaldhunga, Nepal

DHARAMRAJ THAPA, Rfmn 4933, 1/5th GR, 7 Aug 1915, of Orasti, No.4 West, Nawakote, Nepal

DHARME KAMI, Rfmn 2626, 2/10th GR, 11 Sep 1915, of Nowyang, Menglung, Dhankuta, Nepal

DHARMRAJ GURUNG, Rfmn 1081, 1/6th GR, 22 May 1915

DHIRAJ BURA, Rfmn 4412, 1/5th GR, 29 Jun 1915, of Thaman, Palpa, Parvat, Nepal

DHIYAN SINGH, Sub. 14th Sikhs, 5 Jul 1915, of Badowal, Ludhiana, Punjab, (Rank wrongly shown as Jem.)

DHOJBIR RAI, Rfmn 2631, 2/10th GR, 19 Sep 1915, of Katta, Udaipore, Okhaldhunga, Nepal

DHOJE LIMBU, Rfmn 1198, 2/10th GR, 19 Sep 1915, of Tofrek, Tamarkhola, Dhankuta, Nepal

DIGPAL RAI, Rfmn 857, 2/10th GR, 7 Aug 1915, of Sangpang, Dingla, Bhojpore, Nepal

DILAPSING GURUNG, Havildar 4632, 1/6th GR, 8 Aug 1915, of Khaller, Palpa, Isma, Nepal

DILARAM THAPA, Rfmn 2299, 1/5th GR, 9 Aug 1915, of Sodhu, Palpa, Khachi, Nepal

DILBAHADUR GURUNG, Rfmn 4972, 1/5th GR, 30 Jun 1915, of Dangsing, No.4 West, 8000, Parvat, Nepal

DILBAHADUR RAI, Rfmn 2486, 2/10th GR, 29 Jun 1915, of Phulbari, Hathuwa, No.4 East, Nepal

DILBAHADUR RANA, Rfmn 668, 2/10th GR, 7 Aug 1915, of Chingre, Waldiapatti, Almora, United Provinces

DILBAHADUR THAPA, Bugler, 122, 1/5th GR, 21 Aug 1915, of Disingkote, No.4 West, Bhirkote, Nepal

DIMANAND LIMBU, Rfmn 677, 2/10th GR, 28 Jun 1915, of Hatikarka, Chethar, Dhankuta, Nepal

DIRGASING GURUNG, Rfmn 2504, 1/5th GR, 19 Dec 1915, of Hille, Payung, No.5 West, Nepal

DIWANSING GURUNG, Rfmn 923, 1/6th GR, 8 Aug 1915, of Padli, Pokhra, Kaski, Nepal

DIWANSING RANA, Rfmn 1060, 1/6th GR, 7 Aug 1915

DIYAL SINGH, Sepoy 4332, 14th Sikhs, 4 Jun 1915, of Ubawal, Sunam, Patiala, Punjab

DOJE LAMA, Rfmn 639, 2/10th GR, 31 Aug 1915

DOOLA, Dvr 1932, Mule Corps, 3 Oct 1915, of Khariot, Jhelum, Punjab

DUBLE GURUNG, Rfmn 4010, 1/6th GR, 4 Jun 1915, of Pacha, No.2 West, Lamjung, Nepal

DUD GURUNG, Rfmn 4723, 1/5th GR, 30 Jun 1915, of Ghanpokhra, No.2 West, Lamjung, Nepal

DULLAH KHAN, Dvr 1576, 26th Jacob's Battery, 6 May 1915, of Nala Musalmanan, Kahuta, Rawalpindi, Punjab

DUMAN SINGH, Sepoy 3620, 14th Sikhs, 5 Jun 1915, of Landa, Malerkotla, Ludhiana, Punjab

DURGBIR THAPA, Rfmn 4695, 1/5th GR, 30 Jun 1915, of Palisunra, Palpa, Parvat, Nepal

DURGE THAPA, Rfmn 2847, 1/5th GR, 17 Nov 1915, of Charghale, Palpa, Nepal

FARMAN ALI, L/Nk 2198, Mule Corps, 30 Dec 1915, of Kukra, Gujar Khan, Rawalpindi, Punjab

FATEH CHAND KANNA, Follower, Jhansi/6, S&T Corps, 19 Sep 1915, of Chandausi, Bilari, Muradbad, United Provinces

FATEH DIN, Sepoy 2185, 89th Punjabis, 4 May 1915, of Jhelum, Punjab

FATEH SINGH, Naik 3482, 14th Sikhs, 4 Jun 1915, of Bakhtgarh, Ludhiana, Punjab

FATTEH, Bearer 2291, ABC, 108th Field Amb, 15 Jun 1915

FAZAL DAD, Dvr 2008, Mule Corps, 12 Aug 1915, of Nar, Rawalpindi, Punjab

FLETCHER, Second Lieutenant, Amiraux Silver, IARO, 7 Aug 1915, of East Dereham, Norfolk, England (7th Field Ambulance Cemetery, Anzac)

FOWLE, Lt Louis Richard, 14th Sikhs, 4 Jun 1915, of Summer Cove, Kinsale, Co, Cork, Ireland

FRASER, Maj. D'Arcy Mackenzie, 75th Carnatic Infantry att 6th Bn, Lincolnshire Regiment, 7 Aug 1915, of Weston, Fermoy, Co. Cork, Ireland (Green Hill Cemetery, Suvla)

FUTTAH, Dvr 1053, Mule Corps, 30 Jun 1915, of Gandian, Hanpore, Hazara, Punjab

GAGARE LIMBU, L/Nk 2389, 2/10th GR, 13 Sep 1915, of Change, Mewakhola, Dhankuta, Nepal

GAHIL SINGH, Havildar 1863, 36th Sikhs att 14th Sikhs, 9 Aug 1915, of Dander, Moga, Ferozepore, Punjab

GAIL SINGH, Sepoy 5824, 14th Sikhs, 19 Sep 1915, of Ranika, Ajnala, Amritsar, Punjab

GAJADHAR JIDIAPH, Bearer 4578, ABC, 108th Field Amb, 19 Jun 1915, of Ganjawa, Ulrota, Gonda, United Provinces

GAJAN SINGH, Sepoy 4227, 14th Sikhs, 4 Jun 1915, of Lehra Mahabat, Moga, Ferozepore, Punjab

GAJAN SINGH, Sepoy 4756, 14th Sikhs, 19 Sep 1915, of Kanech, Pail, Patiala, Punjab

GAJANSING THAPA, Rfmn 734, 1/6th GR, 5 Jul 1915, of Boyan, No.3 West, Tanhu, Nepal

GAJARSING THAPA, Sub. 1/5th GR, 7 Nov 1915, of Kangram, Bahakote, Nawakote, Nepal

GAJBIR RAI, Rfmn 960, 2/10th GR, 29 Jun 1915, of Thimthimbo, Yangrup, Dhankuta, Nepal

GAJDHAR GURUNG, L/Nk 44165, 1/5th GR, 7 Aug 1915, of Bagidhara, No.3 West, Tanhu, Nepal

GAJJAN SINGH, Dvr 843, 26th Jacob's Battery, 31 Dec 1915, of Dehla, Bhikhi, Patiala State, Punjab

GAJJAN SINGH, Sepoy 691, Patiala Infantry, 5 Sep 1915, of Gadaya, Dhuri, Patiala, Punjab (Heliopolis (Port Tewfik) Memorial, Egypt)

GALWAY, Sub-Cond. Edgar, S&T Corps, 7 May 1915 (Beach Cemetery, Anzac)

GAMANDHOJ LIMBU, L/Nk 1993, 2/10th GR, 17 Aug 1915, of Morahang, Dhankuta, Nepal

GAMARSING GURUNG, Rfmn 4511, 1/5th GR, 21 Aug 1915, of Payangchor, Dailekh, Nepal

GAMARSING GURUNG, Rfmn 4770, 1/5th GR, 5 Jun 1915, of Lamdanra, No.4 West, Bhirkote, Nepal

GAMARSING THAPA, Rfmn 4624, 1/5th GR, 22 Aug 1915, of Thurimdi, No.5 West, Garhung, Nepal

GAMBA THAPA, Havildar 4713, 1/6th GR, 10 Aug 1915, of Kharagaon, Gulmi, Palpa, Nepal

GAMBARSING GURUNG, Rfmn 1291, 1/6th GR, 21 Aug 1915, of Halale, No.5 West, Satung, Nepal

GAMBIR THAPA, Havildar 4049, 1/5th GR, 8 Aug 1915, of Mabangkote, Nawakote, Bhirkote, Nepal

GAMBIRSING GURUNG, Havildar 4444, 1/6th GR, 2 May 1915, of Bharsa, Palpa, Gulmi, Nepal

GAMIDHOJ RAI, Rfmn 946, 2/10th GR, 21 Jun 1915, of Damtala, Rawakhola, Okhaldhunga, Nepal

GANDA SINGH, Sepoy 1510, 14th Sikhs, 19 Sep 1915, of Jikhapal, Sanam, Patiala, Punjab

GANDA SINGH, Sepoy 4171, 14th Sikhs, 19 Sep 1915, of Lehra Mahabat, Moga, Ferozepore, Punjab

GANGA DIN, Bearer 4566, ABC, 108th Field Amb, 5 Jun 1915

GANGA RAM, Artisan, 686, Gwalior Transport Corps, 19 Sep 1915, of Gird, Gwalior, Central Provinces, (Name wrongly shown as Ganda Ram)

GANGA SINGH, Sepoy 2411, 89th Punjabis, 2 Jun 1915, of Sakhiri, Taran Taran, Amritsar, Punjab

GANGA SINGH, Sepoy 4613, 14th Sikhs, 21 Jan 1916, of Khudi, Barnala, Patiala, Punjab (Heliopolis (Port Tewfik) Memorial, Egypt)

GANGA SINGH, Sepoy 3780, 14th Sikhs, 15 Jul 1915, of Jangran, Kharar, Ambala, Punjab

GANGA SINGH, Sepoy 3884, 14th Sikhs, 25 May 1915, of Ghanauli, Ropar, Ambala, Punjab

GANGA SINGH, Sepoy 4186, 14th Sikhs, 4 Jun 1915, of Alipore, Malerkotla, Ludhiana, Punjab

GANGABIR PUN, Rfmn 3846, 1/5th GR, 7 Aug 1915, of Narchan, Mallajee, Parvat, Nepal

GANGASING THAPA, Rfmn 837, 1/6th GR, 9 Aug 1915, of Arehali, No.3 West, Rising, Nepal

GANJAMAN RAI, Rfmn 931, 2/10th GR, 19 Sep 1915, of Nembang, Ilam, Nepal

GANJAMAN RAI, Rfmn 3282, 2/10th GR, 19 Sep 1915, of Salabo, Amchok, Bhojpore, Nepal

GANJAMAN RAI, Rfmn 3543, 2/10th GR, 19 Sep 1915, of Chachalung, Okhaldhunga, Nepal

GANJASING GURUNG, Rfmn 4856, 1/5th GR, 21 Aug 1915, of Ratanpore, No.3 West, Tanhu, Nepal

GARJMANIBURA, Rfmn 3766, 1/5th GR, 4 Jun 1915, of Jaman, Palpa, Parvat, Nepal

GAYAN SINGH, Bearer 4582, ABC, 108th Field Amb, 11 Jul 1915, of Andersheon, Pauri, Garhwal, United Provinces

GHAMAJIT RAI, Rfmn 2729, 2/10th GR, 29 Jun 1915, of Gaudani, Bangdel, Okhaldhunga, Nepal

GHARIB, Follower, 2156, Mule Corps, 7 Apr 1915

GHIBA KHAN, Dvr 991, Mule Corps, 15 Jan 1916, of Tikal Kalan, Kahuta, Rawalpindi, Punjab

GHICHAR SINGH, Sepoy 4732, 14th Sikhs, 19 Sep 1915, of Kambarwal, Bassi, Karnal, Punjab

GHULAM HUSAIN, Dvr 1955, Mule Corps, 8 Oct 1915

GHULAM MUHAMMAD, Dvr 854, Mule Corps, 29 Sep 1915, of Dhak Khuda Bakhsh, Jhelum, Punjab

GHULAM MUHAMMAD, Dvr 1729, 26th Jacob's Battery, 10 July 1915, of Padrar, Khusab, Shahour, Punjab (Heliopolis (Port Tewfik) Memorial, Egypt)

GHULAM MUHAMMAD, Bearer 6840, ABC, 108th Field Amb, 11 Jul 1915

GOBINDIA PUN, Jem. 1/5th GR, 28 Jun 1915, of Danga, Sallyana, Nepal

GOKULSING THAPA, Rfmn 4992, 1/5th GR, 28 Jun 1915, of Mohere, No.4 West, Bherkote, Nepal

GOPILAL GHALE, Rfmn 424, 1/6th GR, 4 Jun 1915, of Barapore, No.2 West, Gurkha, Nepal

GORE LIMBU, Jem. 2/10th GR, 9 Aug 1915, of Lingdep, Mewakhola, Dhankuta, Nepal

GORE RANA, Rfmn 1090, 2/10th GR, 19 Sep 1915, of Gogal, Alampore, Ramechhap, No.2 East, Nepal

GORE THAPA, L/Nk 1904, 2/10th GR, 4 Nov 1915, of Amsarung, Palpa, Nepal

GORIA RANA, Rfmn 100, 1/6th GR, 7 Nov 1915, of Lampge, No.3 West, Tanhu, Nepal

GOVAN, Maj. Douglas Moncrieff, 1/5th GR, 28 Jun 1915
GOVINDSWAMI, Dvr 849, Mule Corps, 27 Nov 1915
GREENE, Lt Henry, 92nd Punjabis, att 1/6th GR, 21 Aug 1915, of Clontarf, Dublin
GUJAR, Follower, 26th Jacob's Battery, 12 Jun 1915
GUJAR SINGH, Sepoy 1612, 14th Sikhs, 19 Sep 1915, of Batorla, Bhadson, Nabha, Punjab
GUJAR SINGH, Sepoy 3994, 14th Sikhs, 4 Jun 1915, of Ramanwas, Sangrur, Punjab
GUJAR SINGH, Sepoy 4459, 14th Sikhs, 5 Jul 1915, of Lilowal, Sunam, Patiala, Punjab
GUL SAMAD, Dvr 1304, Mule Corps, 21 Aug 1915
GUL ZAMAN, Dvr 1581, Mule Corps, 30 Aug 1915, of Gajl, Abbottabad, Hazara, Punjab
GULJARA SINGH, Naik 3213, 14th Sikhs, 4 Jun 1915, of Bawrai, Malerkotla, Ludhiana, Punjab
GULJARA SINGH, Naik 3411, 14th Sikhs, 7 Aug 1915, of Dakhe, Ludhiana, Punjab
GUMAN THAPA, Naik 2472, 2/10th GR, 7 Aug 1915, of Wamgsurung, Tansin, Nepal
GUMANDHOJ LIMBU, L/Nk 1993, 2/10th GR, 17 Aug 1915, of Phedap, Dhankuta, Nepal (Heliopolis (Port Tewfik) Memorial, Egypt)
GURBAKHSH SINGH, Sepoy 4127, 14th Sikhs, 4 Jun 1915, of Bhaiki Bhasaur, Dhuri,
GURBAKHSH SINGH, Sepoy 4307, 14th Sikhs, 15 May 1915, of Patarsi Bari, Sirhind, Patiala, Punjab Patiala, Punjab
GURDIT SINGH, Sepoy 630, Patiala Infantry att 14th Sikhs, 28 Aug 1915, of Gujran, Bhawanigarh, Sunam, Patiala, Punjab
GURDIT SINGH, Sepoy 1341, 14th Sikhs, 19 Sep 1915, of Khothala, Pajjgran, Malerkotla, Punjab
GURDIT SINGH, Sepoy 3597, 14th Sikhs, 4 Jun 1915, of Khokh, Maloh, Nabha, Punjab
GURDIT SINGH, Sepoy 3840, 14th Sikhs, 14 May 1915, of Sadhupore, Panjgraian, Malerkotla, Punjab

GURMUKH SINGH, Sepoy 3664, 14th Sikhs, 2 Jul 1915, of Gurditpura, Dhuri, Patiala, Punjab
GURMUKH SINGH, Sepoy 4153, 14th Sikhs, 4 Jun 1915, of Jangpore, Jagraon, Ludhiana, Punjab
HAIKAMSING RAI, Rfmn 3537, 2/10th GR, 19 Sep 1915, of Dilpa, Siktel, Rhojpore, Nepal
HAJI KHAN, Gnr 604, 21st Kohat Battery, 20 May 1915, of Pind, Rawalpindi, Punjab
HAMIR SINGH, Sepoy 4372, 14th Sikhs, 4 Jun 1915, of Gurusar, Muktsar, Ferozepore, Punjab
HANGDOJ LIMBU, Rfmn 492, 2/10th GR, 28 Aug 1915, of Ningalia, Panchthar, Dhankuta, Nepal
HANSARUP LIMBU, Sub. 2/10th GR, 28 Jun 1915, of Barbote, Ilam, Nepal
HARAKBIR GHARTI, Rfmn 4697, 1/5th GR, 2 Jul 1915, of Naya-Gaon, Palpa, Parvat, Nepal
HARAKBIR GURUNG, Rfmn 36, 1/5th GR, 21 Aug 1915, of Bachha, No.5 West, Payung, Nepal
HARAKJIT GURUNG, Rfmn 4957, 1/5th GR, 25 Oct 1915, of Lamdanra, No.4 West, Bherkote, Nepal
HARIMARDAN RAI, Rfmn 219, 2/10th GR, 4 Sep 1915, of Tekanpur, No.3 East, Nepal (Heliopolis (Port Tewfik) Memorial, Egypt)
HARDIT SINGH, Havildar 2538, 14th Sikhs, 4 Jun 1915, of Kalis, Barnala, Patiala, Punjab
HARDIT SINGH, Sepoy 3344, 14th Sikhs, 5 Jul 1915, of Karar Wala, Dhanaula, Nabha, Punjab
HARDIT SINGH, Sepoy 3732, 14th Sikhs, 4 Jun 1915, of Jakhepal, Sunam, Patiala, Punjab
HARI LAL RAI, L/Nk 109, 2/10th GR, 7 Aug 1915, of Sangpang, Dingla, Bhojpore, Nepal
HARI SINGH, Sepoy 4762, 14th Sikhs, 19 Sep 1915, of Ghandawana, Ludhiana, Punjab
HARILAL THAPA, Naik 4723, 1/6th GR, 4 Jun 1915, of Ambeli, Palpa, Nepal
HARIPERSHAD PUN, Rfmn 529, 1/6th GR, 10 Aug 1915, of Tinkuna, No.4 West, Parvat, Nepal

HARKA GURUNG, Rfmn 1153, 1/6th GR, 29 Nov 1915, of Salui, Palpa, 4000, Parvat, Nepal

HARKABAHADUR LIMBU, Rfmn 163, 2/10th GR, 29 Sep 1915, of Tembhe, Mewakhola, Dhankuta, Nepal

HARKABAHADUR LIMBU, Rfmn 690, 2/10th GR, 19 Sep 1915, of Maidane, Chainpore, Dhankuta, Nepal

HARKABAHADUR LIMBU, Rfmn 843, 2/10th GR, 7 Aug 1915, of Sakrapa, Chaubisya, Dhankuta, Nepal

HARKABAHADUR LIMBU, Rfmn 3130, 2/10th GR, 9 Aug 1915, of Adipore, Chaubisya, Dhankuta, Nepal

HARKABAHADUR RAI, Rfmn 230, 2/10th GR, 30 Aug 1915, of Khokhu, Khalsa, Dhankuta, Nepal

HARKABAHADUR RAI, Rfmn 1109, 2/10th GR, 19 Sep 1915, of Birgaon, Dhankuta, Nepal

HARKABIR GARTI, Rfmn 4697, 1/5th GR, 7 Aug 1915, of Nyagaon, Palpa, Nepal (Heliopolis (Port Tewfik) Memorial, Egypt)

HARKABIR RAI, Rfmn 1069, 2/10th GR, 19 Sep 1915, of Pewang, Dhankuta, Nepal

HARKABIR THAPA, Rfmn 1013, 1/6th GR, 7 Jun 1915, of Sekhan, No.4 West, Bhirkote, Nepal

HARKABIR THAPA, Havildar 2082, 2/10th GR, 19 Sep 1915, of Malbanse, Ilam, Ilamdanda, Nepal

HARKABIRTHAPA, Rfmn 303, 1/6th GR, 13 May 1915, of Narjung, Kothar, Rising, Nepal

HARKADHOJ RAI, Bugler, 954, 2/10th GR, 4 Jul 1915, of Chituwakhaka, Panchthar, Dhankuta, Nepal

HARKAJANG LIMBU, Havildar 1718, 2/10th GR, 22 Aug 1915, of Sinjang, Phedap, Dhankuta, Nepal

HARKAJANG RAI, Havildar 2387, 2/10th GR, 7 Aug 1915, of Tauka, Chaubisya, Dhankuta, Nepal

HARKAJANG RAI, Rfmn 3353, 2/10th GR, 22 Dec 1915, of Budhe, Chaubisya, Dhankuta, Nepal

HARKAJIT LIMBU, Colour Havildar 1529, 2/10th GR, 19 Sep 1915, of Libong, Mewakhola, Dhankuta, Nepal

HARKBAHADUR LIMBU, Bugler, 36, 2/10th GR, 9 Aug 1915, of Jimjecwa, Panchthar, Dhankuta, Nepal

HARKBIR BURA, Rfmn 1226, 1/6th GR, 21 Aug 1915

HARKE LIMBU, Rfmn 962, 2/10th GR, 30 Jun 1915, of Amjo, Charkhola, Ilam, Nepal

HARKJAS LIMBU, Rfmn 17, 2/10th GR, 10 Aug 1915, of Siawa, Panchthar, Dhankuta, Nepal

HARNAM SINGH, Sepoy 794, Patiala Infantry att 14th Sikhs, 8 Oct 1915, of Lalru, Rajpura, Bassi, Patiala, Punjab

HARNAM SINGH, Sepoy 821, 14th Sikhs, 9 Sep 1915, of Dhurkote, Dehlon, Ludhiana, Punjab

HARNAM SINGH, Sepoy 1836, 14th Sikhs, 19 Sep 1915, of Sadhanwali, Derababananak, Gurdaspore, Punjab

HARNAM SINGH, Sepoy 2276, 14th Sikhs, 22 Aug 1915, of Ghaninke, Fatehgarh, Gurdaspore, Punjab

HARNAM SINGH, Sepoy 2293, 90th Punjabis, 11 May 1915, of Dipharwala, Gurdaspore, Punjab

HARNAM SINGH, Sepoy 2900, 14th Sikhs, 4 Jun 1915, of Dhaula, Dhanaula, Nabha, Punjab

HARNAM SINGH, Sepoy 3378, 14th Sikhs, 4 Jun 1915, of Jitwal Chhota, Malerkotla, Ludhiana, Punjab

HARNAM SINGH, Sepoy 3476, 14th Sikhs, 9 May 1915, of Chhapar, Ludhiana, Punjab

HARNAM SINGH, Sepoy 3498, 14th Sikhs, 4 Jun 1915, of Chau, Ludhiana, Punjab

HARNAM SINGH, Sepoy 3815, 14th Sikhs, 4 Jun 1915, of Lohakhera, Sunam, Patiala, Punjab

HARNAM SINGH, Sepoy 4015, 14th Sikhs, 4 Jun 1915, of Jassi Bagwali, Bhatinda, Patiala, Punjab

HARNAM SINGH, Sepoy 4102, 14th Sikhs, 20 May 1915, of Dalewali, Bhikhi, Patiala, Punjab

HARNAM SINGH, Bugler, 4441, 14th Sikhs, 19 Sep 1915, of Khiali, Ludhiana, Punjab

HARNAM SINGH, Sepoy 4678, 14th Sikhs, 7 Aug 1915, of Khadiale, Sangrur, Punjab

HARNAM SINGH, Sepoy 4764, 14th Sikhs, 19 Sep 1915, of Sandaur, Ludhiana, Punjab

HARNAM SINGH, Follower, Patiala Infantry, att 14th Sikhs, 23 Oct 1915, of Badauchhi, Bassi, Patiala, Punjab

HARPADHAN LIMBU, Rfmn 531, 2/10th GR, 26 Jun 1915, of Nigalia, Panchthar, Dhankuta, Nepal

HARRISON, Maj. Richard Scorer Molyneux, 51st Sikhs att 7th Bn, Royal Dublin Fusiliers, 16 Aug 1915, of Tettenhall, Wolverhampton

HASLUCK, Second Lt Sidney Vandyke, IARO, att 14th Sikhs, 4 Jun 1915, of Salisbury, WiLtshire, England

HASMAT KHAN, L/Nk 1272, Mule Corps, 11 Nov 1915

HASTA BIR, Havildar 4902, 1/6th GR, 13 May 1915, of Bechha, No.4 West, Payung, Nepal

HASTABAHADUR RAI, Rfmn 698, 2/10th GR, 7 Aug 1915, of Halesi, Rawadumre, Okhaldhunga, Nepal

HASTABAHADUR RAI, Rfmn 3371, 2/10th GR, 19 Sep 1915, of Basa, Chisankhu, No.3 East, Nepal

HASTAMAN RAI, Rfmn 1096, 2/10th GR, 19 Sep 1915, of Diding, Chainpore, Dhankuta, Nepal

HASTBIR GHARTI, Rfmn 4508, 1/6th GR, 10 Aug 1915, of Bhewkote, Palpa, 4000, Parvat, Nepal

HASTBIR GURUNG, Rfmn 177, 1/6th GR, 5 Dec 1915, of Deorali, No.4 West, Payung, Nepal

HASTBIR THAPA, Rfmn 4745, 1/5th GR, 7 Aug 1915, of Sakri-Bang, Piuthan, Nepal

HAYAT MUHAMMAD, Dvr (Vet, Asst), 552, Mule Corps, 19 Sep 1915, of Nangiran, Rawalpindi, Punjab

HAY-WEBB, Capt, Allan, 1/5th GR, 23 Aug 1915, of Mooktapore, Bihar, India, and Broadclyst, Devon

HAZARA SINGH, Sepoy 3528, 14th Sikhs, 2 Jul 1915, of Talwandi Majuki, Barnala, Patiala, Punjab

HAZARSING GURUNG, Rfmn 2129, 2nd GR att 1/4th GR, 12 Oct 1915, of Lamagaon, No.3 West, Dhor, Nepal

HEMBAHADUR RAI, Rfmn 1142, 2/10th GR, 19 Sep 1915, of Bardu, Phikal, Ilam, Nepal

HEMLAL GURUNG, Rfmn 1100, 1/6th GR, 10 Aug 1915, of Bacha, No.5 West, Payung, Nepal

HEMLIA RANA, Rfmn 4418, 1/5th GR, 7 Aug 1915, of Mohari, No.4 West, Bherkote, Nepal

HIGAHANG LIMBU, Havildar 2120, 2/10th GR, 30 Jun 1915, of Parwadin, Chhatar, Dhankuta, Nepal

HIGGIN, Capt, James Lawrence, 2/10th GR, 29 or 30 Jun 1915, of Summerland, British Columbia, Canada

HIRA LAL, Follower, Mhow/405, S&T Corps, 19 Sep 1915

HIRA SINGH, Sepoy 3801, 14th Sikhs, 4 Jun 1915, of Akandwala, Dhanaula, Nabha, Punjab

HIRACHAND THAKUR, Havildar 1942, 2/10th GR, 9 Aug 1915, of Baskote, Siliguri, Nepal

HIRALAL GURUNG, Rfmn 1052, 1/6th GR, 30 Jun 1915, of Samjah, No.2 West, Lamjung, Nepal

HIRASING THAPA, Rfmn 1145, 1/6th GR, 24 Aug 1915, of Kundhar, Palpa, Nepal

HORE, Capt, William Barras, IARO, 120th Rajputana Infantry att 9th Bn, West Yorkshire Regiment, 7 Aug 1915

HORNSBY, Second Lt G.W., IARO att 14th Sikhs, 4 Jun 1915

HOSHIARSING DAMAI, Rfmn 4669, 1/5th GR, 28 Jun 1915, of Chukhuwala, Dehra Dun, United Provinces

HUNTER, Second Lieutenant, Eric HamiLton, 1/5th GR, 7 Aug 1915, of Overcott, Dawlish, Devon, England (7th Field Ambulance Cemetery, Anzac)

HUSAIN KHAN, Dvr 506, Mule Corps, 19 Sep 1915, of Jhathi, Abbottabad, Hazara, Punjab

HUSAIN SHAH, Dvr 1416, Mule Corps, 19 Sep 1915

HUSSAIN KHAN, Dvr 669, 26 Nov 1918 (Ari Burnu Cemetery, Anzac)

IDAH, Bearer 4563, ABC, 108th Field Amb, 19 Jun 1915, of Mozad, Raya, Sialkote, Punjab

IKHIA THAPA, Rfmn 4911, 1/5th GR, 7 Aug 1915, of Thabang, Palpa, Parvat, Nepal

IMAM DIN, L/Nk 547, Mule Corps, 19 Sep 1915

IMAN DIN, Dvr 1508, Mule Corps, 20 Nov 1918 (Ari Burnu Cemetery, Anzac)

INDAR SINGH, Sepoy 591, Patiala Infantry, att 14th Sikhs, 8 Aug 1915, of Mulepore, Rajpura, Bassi, Patiala, Punjab

INDAR SINGH, Sepoy 1105, 15th Ludhiana Sikhs att 14th Sikhs, 23 Aug 1915, of Majara, Phillaur, Jullundur, Punjab

INDAR SINGH, L/Nk 1389, 14th Sikhs, 19 Sep 1915, of Udat Bhagatram, Boha, Patiala, Punjab

INDAR SINGH, Havildar 2516, 14th Sikhs, 4 Jun 1915, of Pattoke, Moga, Ferozepore, Punjab

INDAR SINGH, Sepoy 2772, 14th Sikhs, 4 Jun 1915, of Khai, Moga, Ferozepore, Punjab

INDAR SINGH, Sepoy 4304, 14th Sikhs, 15 Jun 1915, of Karmgarh, Barnala, Patiala, Punjab

INDAR SINGH, Sepoy 4344, 14th Sikhs, 4 Jun 1915, of Dosanjh, Moga, Ferozepore, Punjab

INDAR SINGH, Sepoy 4430, 14th Sikhs, 4 Jun 1915, of Phul, Dhanaula, Nabha, Punjab

INDARSING CHETTRI, Rfmn 426, 2/10th GR, 30 Jun 1915, of Bangoli, Gopipore-Dehra, Kangra, Punjab

INDRABAHADUR GURUNG, Rfmn 3404, 2/10th GR, 19 Sep 1915, of Pakribas, Sabhayautar, Dhankuta, Nepal

INDRABAHADUR LIMBU, Rfmn 3507, 2/10th GR, 19 Sep 1915, of Chinim, Mewakhola, Dhankuta, Nepal

INDRABIR RAI, Havildar 1399, 2/10th GR, 16 Dec 1915, of Puamajna, Ilam, Nepal

INDRADHOJ LIMBU, Rfmn 3581, 2/10th GR, 19 Sep 1915, of Birmanganj, Chaubis, Dhankuta, Nepal

INDRAMAN RAI, Rfmn 3522, 2/10th GR, 19 Sep 1915, of Kuksi, Chainpore, Dhankuta, Nepal

INDRASING GURUNG, Havildar 493, 1/6th GR, 10 Aug 1915, of Dara, No.4 West, Satun, Nepal

IRKHARAM PUN, Rfmn 4704, 1/5th GR, 30 Jun 1915, of Jabang, Palpa, Parvat, Nepal

IRVINE, Lt Christopher, 25th Punjabis att 89th Punjabis, 28 Jun 1915, of London, England (Pink Farm Cemetery, Helles)

ISARSING RAI, Naik 2910, 2/10th GR, 12 Aug 1915, of Chhutgaun, Chainpore, Dhankuta Nepal

ISTAMAN RAI, Rfmn 3395, 2/10th GR, 19 Sep 1915, of Sasarka, Rawadumre, No.3 East, Nepal

JABARSING THAPA, Rfmn 1907, 2/10th GR, 15 Dec 1915

JACQUES, Lt -Col, Francis, 14th Sikhs, 4 Jun 1915, of San Diego, California, USA

JAG MOHAN, Bearer 8634, ABC, 137th Field Amb, 30 Dec 1915, of Ochowrie, Maharajganj, Raebareily, United Provinces

JAGAT SINGH, Sepoy 1166, 14th Sikhs, 19 Sep 1915, of Nurpore, Khalra, Lahore, Punjab

JAGAT SINGH, Naik 3584, 14th Sikhs, 4 Jun 1915, of Dhaula, Dhanaula, Nabha, Punjab

JAGAT SINGH, Sepoy 3784, 14th Sikhs, 22 Jun 1915, of Sodhewala, Maloh, Nabha, Punjab

JAGAT SINGH, Sepoy 4118, 14th Sikhs, 1 Feb 1916, of Sukrullapore, Kharar, Ambala, Punjab

JAGAT SINGH, Sepoy 4571, 14th Sikhs, 4 Jun 1915, of Didarpore, Rupar, Ambala, Punjab

JAGAT SINGH, Sepoy 4834, 14th Sikhs, 19 Sep 1915, of Ubewal, Sunam, Patiala, Punjab

JAGATSING DAMAI, Havildar 4201, 1/4th GR, 23 Nov 1915, of Dehradun, United Provinces

JAGATSING LAMA, Rfmn 1136, 2/10th GR, 19 Sep 1915, of Liste, Chautara, No.1 East, Nepal

JAGBAHADUR LIMBU, Rfmn 3188, 2/10th GR, 25 Aug 1915, of Hathikharka, Tamarkhola, Dhankuta, Nepal

JAGBIR BURA, Rfmn 124, 1/5th GR, 26 Aug 1915, of Machi, Dailekh, Nepal

JAGBIR GURUNG, Rfmn 4322, 1/5th GR, 4 Jun 1915, of Kapre, No.3 West, Tanhu, Nepal

JAGBIR PUN, Rfmn 4173, 1/5th GR, 7 Aug 1915, of Chinman-Goan, Palpa, Parvat, Nepal

JAGIA GHARTI, Rfmn 798, 1/6th GR, 13 May 1915, of Dhanibor, Piuthan, Nepal

JAHAJIT RAI, Rfmn 1123, 2/10th GR, 19 Sep 1915, of Tamring, Chainpore, Dhankuta, Nepal

Appendix VI 335

JAHAN DAD, Sepoy 2576, 89th Punjabis, 14 May 1915, of Jatal, Gujar Khan, Rawalpindi, Punjab

JAHAN KHAN, Dvr 1175, 26th Jacob's Battery, 1 Jul 1915, of Kakhari Murid, Gujar Khan, Rawalpindi, Punjab

JAHANA, Gnr 681, 21st Kohat Battery, 27 Aug 1915, of Karsal, Chakwal, Jhelum, Punjab

JAHANDAD, Dvr 1244, Mule Corps, 2 Sep 1915, of Akhunki Bandi, Hanpore, Hazara, Punjab

JAHANSING RAI, Naik 13, 2/10th GR, 10 Aug 1915, of Ripa, Chisankhu, Okhaldhunga, Nepal

JAHARSING THAPA, Rfmn 1907, AMP att 1/4th GR, 15 Dec 1915, of Gairigaon, Aijal, Lushai Hills

JAHERSING THAPA, Rfmn 92, 1/6th GR, 9 Aug 1915, of Jakodi, Palpa, Palpa, Nepal

JAI RAM, Follower, 1/6th GR, 9 Dec 1915, of Nawagu, Rahiwa, Rahiwa, Punjab

JAIBAHADUR RAI, Rfmn 2669, 2/10th GR, 7 Aug 1915, of Nare, Chhathar, Dhankuta, Nepal

JAIBAHADUR RAI, Rfmn 3583, 2/10th GR, 19 Sep 1915, of Khamare, Bhojpore, Nepal

JAIBAHADUR THAPA, Rfmn 740, 1/6th GR, 23 May 1915, of Mnhor, No.3 West, Bhirkote, Nepal

JAIKAKNA LIMBU, Rfmn 3571, 2/10th GR, 19 Sep 1915, of Songopo, Phedap, Dhankuta, Nepal

JAIMAL SINGH, Sub. Patiala Infantry att 14th Sikhs, 8 Aug 1915, of Rajpura, Kajpura, Bassi, Patiala, Punjab

JAIMAL SINGH, L/Nk 1401, 14th Sikhs, 19 Sep 1915, of Dair Mandin, Bagan Wala, Ambala, Punjab

JAIMAN RAI, Bugler, 185, 2/10th GR, 30 Jun 1915, of Dilpa, Siktel, Bhojpore, Nepal

JAIMUKHI RAI, Rfmn 747, 2/10th GR, 7 Aug 1915, of Dari, Rawadumre, Okhaldhunga, Nepal

JAINE RAI, Rfmn 3582, 2/10th GR, 19 Sep 1915, of Kaspakhalu, Menglung, Dhankuta, Nepal

JAIRAJ RAI, Rfmn 825, AMP att 2/10th GR, 30 Dec 1915

JAIRAM GURUNG, Rfmn 437, 2/10th GR, 13 Aug 1915, of Bhagsu, Kangra, Punjab

JAMAN LAL, Follower, Jhansi/9, S&T Corps, 19 Sep 1915, of Kairawa, Muzzaffarnagar, United Provinces

JAMAN RAI, Rfmn 895, 2/10th GR, 7 Aug 1915, of Bagsila, Rawadumre, Okhaldhunga, Nepal

JAMANSING GURUNG, Rfmn 1717, 1/5th GR, 28 Oct 1915, of Gukhiap, No.4 West, Bhirkote, Nepal

JAMANSING THAPA, Naik 3893, 1/5th GR, 7 Aug 1915, of Mujakote, No.3 West, Rising, Nepal

JAMIT SINGH, L/Nk 4267, 14th Sikhs, 19 Sep 1915, of Gholia Kalan Moga, Ferozepore, Punjab

JANCHBIR LIMBU, Rfmn 3661, 2/10th GR, 19 Sep 1915, of Phedap, Panthar, Dhallkuta, Nepal

JANGBIR BURA, Rfmn 4933, 1/6th GR, 29 Jun 1915, of Sebbung, Piuthan, Palpa, Nepal

JANGBIR THAPA, Havildar 577, 1/6th GR, 6 Jun 1915, of Dungaigari, Piuthan, Nepal

JANGBIR THAPA, Rfmn 1201, 1/6th GR, 22 Aug 1915, of Rahu, No.4 West, Bhirkote, Nepal

JANGBIR THAPA, Rfmn 4153, 1/5th GR, 4 Jun 1915, of Chibung, Palpa, Nepal

JANGDHOJ, Rfmn 2874, 2/10th GR, 19 Sep 1915, of Hathuwa, Chhatar, Dhankuta, Nepal

JANGDHOJ RAI, Rfmn 545, 2/10th GR, 2 Jul 1915, of Gormari, Okhaldhunga, No.3 East, Nepal

JANGDHOJ RAI, Rfmn 3101, 2/10th GR, 22 Aug 1915, of Songdel, Rawadumre, Dhankuta, Nepal

JANGI SARKI, Rfmn 2693, 1/5th GR, 20 Jul 1915, of Chapakote, Gaerlung, No.5 West, Nepal

JANGIR SINGH, Sepoy 4174, 14th Sikhs, 4 Jun 1915, of Tungwali, Moga, Ferozepore, Punjab

JANGMAN RAI, Havildar 1603, 2/10th GR, 30 Jun 1915, of Majtala, Dhankuta, Nepal

JANGRA GURUNG, Havildar 1181, 2/10th GR, 29 Jun 1915, of Sankajung, Ilam, Nepal (Heliopolis (Port Tewfik) Memorial, Egypt)

JANGRA SARKI, Rfmn 2695, 1/5th GR, 20 July 1915, of Mewabari, No. 3 West, Nepal (Heliopolis (Port Tewfik) Memorial, Egypt)

JASASING LIMBU, Rfmn 450, 2/10th GR, 6 Aug 1915, of Wasum, Panchthar, Dhankuta, Nepal

JASBAHADUR GURUNG, Rfmn 3685, 1/5th GR, 5 Jul 1915, of Ratanpore Galekhan, Tanhu, Nepal

JASBAHADUR GURUNG, Havildar 3938, 1/5th GR, 7 Aug 1915, of Makunpore, No.3 West, Tanhu, Nepal

JASBAHADUR LIMBU, Rfmn 491, AMP att 2/10th GR, 19 Sep 1915

JASBIR ALE, Rfmn 3873, 1/5th GR, 21 Aug 1915, of Chaur, No.2 West, Lamjung, Nepal

JASBIR GHARTI, Rfmn 4945, 1/6th GR, 30 Jun 1915, of Solagarhi, Sallyana, Nepal

JASBIR GURUNG, Rfmn 2576, 2/10th GR, 3 Nov 1915, of Pakri, Yangrup, Dhankuta, Nepal

JASBIR RANA, Bugler, 1057, 1/6th GR, 1 Jul 1915, of Jaskana, Palpa, Nepal

JASDHOJ LIMBU, L/Nk 591, 2/10th GR, 7 Aug 1915, of Pungling, Tamarkhola, Dhankuta, Nepal

JASPAL RAI, Rfmn 3560, 2/10th GR, 19 Sep 1915, of Sumlikha, Khotang, Bhojpore, Nepal

JASRATH LIMBU, L/Nk 2510, 2/10th GR, 9 Aug 1915, of Dingla, Mewakhola, Dhankuta, Nepal

JASSA SINGH, Sepoy 1212, 14th Sikhs, 19 Sep 1915, of Bal, Kathunangal, Amritsar, Punjab

JASWANT SINGH, Drum Maj. 14th Sikhs, 19 Sep 1915, of Lopoke, Ajnala, Amritsar, Punjab

JAWAHIR SINGH, Sepoy 4461, 14th Sikhs, 4 Jun 1915, of Mango, Maloh, Nabha, Punjab

JAWAHIR SINGH, Sepoy 1185, 14th Sikhs, 19 Sep 1915, of Khatrakhurd, Ajnala, Amritsar, Punjab

JAWALA, Follower, ABC, 108th Field Amb, 13 May 1915

JAWALA SINGH, Sepoy 4278, 14th Sikhs, 4 Jun 1915, of Mallesri, Moga, Ferozepore, Punjab

JAWALA SINGH, Sepoy 4529, 14th Sikhs, 4 Jun 1915, of Chuga, Zira, Ferozepore, Punjab

JAWALSING GURUNG, Rfmn 81, 1/6th GR, 10 Sep 1915, of Hangnbir, No.3 West, Kaski, Nepal

JAWAND SINGH, Sepoy 1622, 14th Sikhs, 19 Sep 1915, of Kotsewian, Lahorimal, Amritsar, Punjab

JAYA, Dvr 1853, Mule Corps, 9 Dec 1915

JENNINGS, Maj. Jack, 66th Punjabis att 6th Bn, Royal Dublin Fusiliers, 10 Aug 1915, of London, England

JETBAHADUR RAI, Naik 2589, 2/10th GR, 30 Jun 1915, of Chaibari, Chainpore, Dhankuta, Nepal

JETRAJ RAI, Rfmn 2866, 2/10th GR, 2 Jul 1915, of Charku, Chisankhu, Okhaldhunga, Nepal

JHAGARSING RAI, Rfmn 3142, 2/10th GR, 10 Aug 1915, of Dingla, Soran, Dhankuta, Nepal

JHANDA SINGH, Sepoy 1595, 14th Sikhs, 19 Sep 1915, of Gunuwal, Guruka Jandiyala, Amritsar, Punjab

JHANDA SINGH, Sepoy 4213, 14th Sikhs, 4 Jun 1915, of Dan Singh Wala, Dhanaula, Nabha, Punjab

JHANDA SINGH, Sepoy 4456, 14th Sikhs, 15 May 1915, of Husnar, Muktsar, Ferozepore, Punjab

JHURI, Follower, S&T Corps, of Dinapur, Bihar, 19 Sep 1915

JIRMAN RAI, Rfmn 580, 2/10th GR, 10 Aug 1915, of Birgaon, Dhankuta, Nepal

JITABIR PUN, Rfmn 4944, 1/5th GR, 7 Aug 1915, of Basagha, Palpa, 4000, Parvat, Nepal

JITBAHADLTR LAMA, Rfmn 3103, 2/10th GR, 19 Sep 1915, of Sorakpo, Chaubisya, Dhankuta, Nepal

JITBAHADUR GURUNG, Rfmn 32, 1/5th GR, 30 Jun 1915, of Lakhanbast, No.3 West, Tanhu, Nepal

JITBAHADUR GURUNG, Rfmn 4918, 1/5th GR, 30 Jun 1915, of Baochak, No.2 West, Lamjung, Nepal

JITBAHADUR GURUNG, Follower, ABC, 137th Field Amb, 30 Dec 1915

JITBAHADUR GURUNG, Rfmn 3752, 1/5th GR, 8 Aug 1915, of Boksing, No.5 West, Nepal (Heliopolis (Port Tewfik) Memorial, Egypt)

JITBAHADUR THAPA, Havildar 470, 1/6th GR, 4 Aug 1915, of Arkolathok, No.3 West, Rising, Nepal (Pieta Cemetery, Malta)

JITBAHADUR RAI, Havildar 101, 2/10th GR, 7 Aug 1915, of Sangpang, Dingla, Bhojpore, Nepal

JITBAHADUR RAI, Rfmn 744, 2/10th GR, 27 Aug 1915, of Dorpa, Sanamajhuwa, Bhojpore, Nepal

JITBAHADUR RAI, Rfmn 1161, 2/10th GR, 19 Sep 1915, of Mukli, Chisankhu, Okhaldhunga, Nepal

JITBAHADUR RAI, Bugler, 2226, 2/10th GR, 11 Jul 1915, of Dunglacho, Dingla, No.4 East, Nepal

JITBIR PUN, Rfmn 4944, 1/5th GR, 7 Aug 1915, of Besaga, Palpa, Nepal (Heliopolis (Port Tewfik) Memorial, Egypt)

JITHARKA RAI, Rfmn 3316, 2/10th GR, 19 Sep 1915, of Necha, Chisankhu, No.3 East, Nepal

JITMAN ALE, Rfmn 2236, AMP att 1/4th GR, 7 Oct 1915

JITMAN ALE, Rfmn 4229, 1/5th GR, 7 Aug 1915, of Dumkote, No.3 West, Garhung, Nepal

JITMAN LAMA, Rfmn 2569, 2/10th GR, 19 Sep 1915, of Rawakhola, Rawadumre, No.3 East, Nepal

JITMAN RAI, Rfmn 3457, 2/10th GR, 7 Aug 1915, of Punku, No.3 East, Nepal (Heliopolis (Port Tewfik) Memorial, Egypt)

JITMAN RAI, Rfmn 225, 2/10th GR, 28 Jun 1915, of Tekanpore, Okhaldhunga, Nepal

JITMAN RAI, Rfmn 299, 2/10th GR, 9 Jul 1915, of Lungtung, Bhojpore, Nepal

JITMAN RANA, Rfmn 4080, 1/5th GR, 1 Jul 1915, of Gyansing-Chap, Palpa, Palpa, Nepal

JITMAN THAPA, Rfmn 4837, 1/5th GR, 28 March 1915, of Hirting, No.3 East, Leyanllyang, Nepal
Rfmn 4837, 1/5th GR, 28 Jun 1915, of Hirting, No.2 East, Nepal (Heliopolis (Port Tewfik) Memorial, Egypt)

JIWAN, Bearer 4280, ABC, 108th Field Amb, 10 Aug 1915, of Natain, Jhelum, Punjab

JIWAN KHAN, Dvr 1369, 26th Jacob's Battery, 12 Jun 1915, of Domeli, Jhelum, Punjab

JIWAN SINGH, Gnr 739, 28th Mountain Battery, 9 Dec 1915, of Kishengarh, Bhiki, Patiala, Punjab

JIWAN SINGH, Sepoy 3558, 14th Sikhs, 19 Sep 1915, of Changali, Dhode, Patiala, Punjab

JIWAN SINGH, Sepoy 3872, 14th Sikhs, 12 Jun 1915, of Mansa Bari, Bhikhi, Patiala, Punjab

JIWAN SINGH, Sepoy 3999, 14th Sikhs, 22 Aug 1915, of Baurhai Kalan, Malerkotla, Ludhiana, Punjab

JODHAN THAPA, Rfmn 97, 1/6th GR, 13 May 1915, of Malbaga, Palpa, Palpa, Nepal

JOKHA RAM GURUNG, Rfmn 4701, 1/6th GR, 28 Jun 1915, of Libang, Pluthana, Nepal (Heliopolis (Port Tewfik) Memorial, Egypt)

JOKHIA BURA, Rfmn 323, 1/6th GR, 10 Aug 1915, of Lamchora, Palpa, Parvat, Nepal

JOKHIA GHARTI, Rfmn 1006, 1/6th GR, 4 Jun 1915, of Polassi, Piuthan, Nepal

JUDHBIR GURUNG, Colour Havildar 1490, 1/5th GR, 28 Aug 1915, of Baseri, No.1 West, Sallyana, Nepal

JUDHBIR THAPA, Rfmn 4488, 1/5th GR, 27 Aug 1915, of Batasar, Palpa, Nepal

JUMA KHAN, Dvr 517, Mule Corps, 16 Aug 1915, of Sherpore, SuLtanpore, Jullundur, Punjab

JUMPARSAD GURUNG, Rfmn 4811, 1/4th GR, 22 Nov 1915, of Parvat, Nepal, (Name wrongly shown as Ramparsad Gurung)

JUTHIA GURUNG, Sub. 1/5th GR, 4 Jun 1915, of Darakarka, Satung, Nepal, Nepal

KABIT RAI, Rfmn 3539, 2/10th GR, 19 Sep 1915, of Santha, Yangrup, Dhankuta, Nepal

KABUL SINGH, Sepoy 4492, 14th Sikhs, 15 May 1915, of Rani Majra, Kharar, Ambala, Punjab

KADIR BAKSH, Gnr 1235, 26th Jacob's Battery, 19 Sep 1915, of Sang, Gujar Khan, Rawalpindi, Punjab

KAHARSING THAPA, Rfmn 4030, 1/5th GR, 8 Aug 1915, of Balask, Palpa, Nepal

KAKA SINGH, Dvr 867, 21st Kohat Battery, 1 Aug 1915, of Hateka, Gujrat, Gujrat, Punjab

KAKA SINGH, Sepoy 4400, 14th Sikhs, 4 Jun 1915, of Chhinewal, Barnala, Patiala, Punjab

KAKSING GHARTI, Rfmn 2606, 1/5th GR, 6 Aug 1915, of Tham, Palpa, Nepal

KAKU SINGH, Sepoy 3399, 14th Sikhs, 14 May 1915, of Gill, Sangrur, Punjab

KAKU SINGH, Sepoy 4199, 14th Sikhs, 12 Sep 1915, of Danewala, Bhatinda, Patiala, Punjab

KALA GURUNG, Havildar 3960, 1/6th GR, 13 May 1915, of Malagiri, No.4 West, Bhirkote, Nepal

KALA SINGH, Sepoy 1605, 14th Sikhs, 19 Sep 1915, of Pandoni Ransinghdi, Taran Taran, Amritsar, Punjab

KALA SINGH, Havildar 2555, 14th Sikhs, 4 Jun 1915, of Ladda, Amargarh, Patiala, Punjab

KALA SINGH, Sepoy 3359, 14th Sikhs, 4 Jun 1915, of Dakhe, Ludhiana, Punjab

KALA SINGH, Sepoy 4173, 14th Sikhs, 4 Jun 1915, of Dosanjh, Moga, Ferozepore, Punjab

KALAHAN RAI, Rfmn 779, 2/10th GR, 15 Jun 1915, of Ratmate, Chisankhu, Okhaldhunga, Nepal

KALLU, Bearer 6460, ABC, 137th Fld Amb, 8 Aug 1915, of Janspore, Jelalabad, Shahjahanpore, United Provinces

KALU GURUNG, Rfmn 1138, 1/6th GR, 21 Aug 1915, Birsing Gurung, of Bijuli, Piuthan, Nepal

KALU THAPA, Rfmn 551, 1/6th GR, 16 Nov 1915, of Mirkote, No.2 West, Gorkha, Nepal

KALUMAN RAI, L/Nk 2610, 2/10th GR, 30 Jun 1915, of Tilote, Darangna, Dhankuta, Nepal

KALUMAN RAI, Rfmn 3514, 2/10th GR, 19 Sep 1915, of Khana, Siktel, Bhojpore, Nepal

KALUSING LIMBU, Rfmn 3022, 2/10th GR, 4 Jun 1915, of Naugoun, Chabisia, Dhankuta, Nepal

KAMANSING GURUNG, Rfmn 4716, 1/5th GR, 12 Oct 1915, of Bainsi-Gaunra, No.5 West, Satung, Nepal

KAMANSING PUN, Rfmn 4174, 1/5th GR, 8 Aug 1915, of Chinman-Gaon, Palpa, Nepal

KAMANSING THAPA, Rfmn 4743, 1/6th GR, 30 Jun 1915, of Chundrian, No.5 West, Tanhu, Nepal

KAMANSING THAPA, Follower, 1/5th GR, 21 Aug 1915

KAMI GHALE, Rfmn 2712, 1/4th GR, 10 Dec 1915, of Galegaon, No.2 West, Lamjung, Nepal

KANCHALAL RAI, Rfmn 1075, 2/10th GR, 19 Sep 1915, of Mardin, Chaubisya, Dhankuta Nepal

KANSHIRAN THAPA, Bugler, 1059, 1/6th GR, 4 Jun 1915, of Siridanra, Palpa, Palpal

KANSMAN SUNWAR, Rfmn 57, 2/10th GR, 7 Aug 1915, of Kichi, Okhaldhunga, Nepal

KANU LIMBU, Rfmn 2709, 2/10th GR, 30 Aug 1915, of Tinglabu, Mewakhola, Dhankuta, Nepal

KAPILAL LIMBU, Rfmn 636, 2/10th GR, 28 Jun 1915, of Chongipung, Mewakhola, Dhankuta, Nepal

KAPUR SINGH, Sepoy 4526, 14th Sikhs, 19 Sep 1915, of Bhani Sahib, Ludhiana, Punjab

KARAGBAHADUR THAPA, Rfmn 4862, 1/5th GR, 10 Aug 1915, of Payang, No.5 West, Nepal (Heliopolis (Port Tewfik) Memorial, Egypt)

KHARAK SING THAPA, Rfmn 1214, 1/6th GR, 18 Aug 1915 (Pieta Cemetery, Malta)

KARANSING GURUNG, Havildar 3862, 1/5th GR, 28 Jun 1915, of Lamdara No.4 West, Bhirkote Nepal

KARBIR GURUNG, Rfmn 3931, 1/5th GR, 10 Aug 1915, of Kilong, Kaski, Nepal

KARBIR LIMBU, Rfmn 3505, 2/10th GR, 19 Sep 1915

KARBIR RAI, Naik 4049, 1/4th GR, 24 Oct 1915, of Phikal, Maipur, Ilam, Nepal

KARBIR RANA, Rfmn 193, 1/6th GR, 7 Aug 1915, of Dabankani, Palpa, Gulmi, Nepal

KARBIR SANWAR, Rfmn 1178, 1/6th GR, 7 Aug 1915, of Rasualu, Ramechap, No.2 West, Nepal

KARBIR THAPA, Jem. 1/5th GR, 7 Aug 1915, of Kalku, Nawakote, Nepal, Nepal

KARBIR THAPA, Rfmn 255, 2/10th GR, 19 Sep 1915, of Dehlunga, Tansing, Nepal

KARIM HAIDAR, Dvr 1698, Mule Corps, 26 Aug 1915, of Phuttan Ali, Kahuta, Rawalpindi, Punjab

KARKU GURUNG, Rfmn 4642, 1/5th GR, 8 Aug 1915, of Jerinas, No.2 West, Gurkha, Nepal

KARM DAD, Dvr 2157, Mule Corps, 15 Dec 1915, of Panjera, Kotli, Mirpore, Kashmr

KARM SINGH, Follower, 187, S&T Corps, 19 Sep 1915

KARM SINGH, Havildar 2173, 14th Sikhs, 5 Jul 1915, of Gagha Sunam, Patiala, Punjab
KARM SINGH, Sepoy 2666, 14th Sikhs, 28 Nov 1915, of Chhina, Dhoriwal, Gurdaspore, Punjab
KARM SINGH, Sepoy 3687, 14th Sikhs, 4 Jun 1915, of Bath, Bassi, Patiala, Punjab
KARNABAHADUR LIMBU, Rfmn 731, 2/10th GR, 7 Aug 1915, of Pheding, Panchthar Dhankuta, Nepal
KARNABAHADUR RAI, Rfmn 884, 2/10th GR, 10 Aug 1915, of Dara, Dhankuta, Dhankuta, Nepal
KARNABAHADUR RAI, Rfmn 1207, 2/10th GR, 19 Sep 1915, of Makhiya, Yangrup, Dhankuta, Nepal
KARNABAHADUR RAI, Rfmn 3245, 2/10th GR, 19 Sep 1915, of Sursipa, Chisankhu, Okhaldhunga, Nepal
KARNASING LIMBU, Rfmn 1186, 2/10th GR, 19 Sep 1915, of Yanguom, Panchthar, Dhankuta, Nepal
KARNE THAPA, Rfmn 841, 1/6th GR, 28 Jun 1915, of Namchi, No.4 West, Nawakote, Nepal
KARTAR SINGH, Sepoy 879, 45th Rattray's Sikhs att 14th Sikhs, 4 Jun 1915, of Purian, Batala, Gurdaspore, Punjab
KARTAR SINGH, Sepoy 4478, 14th Sikhs, 4 Jun 1915, of Lande, Moga, Ferozepore, Punjab
KARTAR SINGH, Sepoy 4746, 14th Sikhs, 19 Sep 1915, of Rangian, Dhuri, Patiala, Punjab
KASIBAR GURUNG, Rfmn 4320, 1/5th GR, 2 Jul 1915, of Bhajung, No.2 West, Lamjung, Nepal
KASUR GURUNG, Rfmn 926, 1/6th GR, 17 Sep 1915, of Arkosing, No.2 West, Lamjung, Nepal
KEHR SINGH, Sepoy 409, Patiala Infantry att 14th Sikhs, 8 Aug 1915, of Kurar, Dhuri, Bassi, Patiala, Punjab
KEHR SINGH, Havildar 2634, 14th Sikhs, 4 Jun 1915, of Jahangir, Dhuri, Patiala, Punjab
KEHR SINGH, Naik 2933, 14th Sikhs, 4 Jun 1915, of Bassian, Jagraon, Ludhiana, Punjab
KEHR SINGH, Sepoy 3791, 14th Sikhs, 2 Jul 1915, of Mangewal, Dhuri, Patiala, Punjab

KEHR SINGH, Sepoy 3975, 14th Sikhs, 4 Jun 1915, of Patto, Moga, Ferozepore, Punjab
KEHR SINGH, Sepoy 4008, 14th Sikhs, 6 May 1915, of Khanaura, Tohana, Hissar, Punjab
KEHR SINGH, Drummer, 4419, 14th Sikhs, 5 Jun 1915, of Boparai, Jagraon, Ludhiana, Punjab
KEHR SINGH, Sepoy 4464, 14th Sikhs, 4 Jun 1915, of Rorike, Dhanaula, Nabha, Punjab
KEHR SINGH, Sepoy 4536, 14th Sikhs, 4 Jun 1915, of Phul, Dhanaula, Nabha, Punjab
KEHR SINGH, Sepoy 4552, 14th Sikhs, 4 Jun 1915, of Dakha, Ludhiana, Punjab
KEHR SINGH, Sepoy 4563, 14th Sikhs, 4 Jun 1915, of Bassian, Jagraon, Ludhiana, Punjab
KEHRSING ALE, Rfmn 1088, 1/6th GR, 3 Jul 1915, of Binikote, No.2 West, Tanhu, Nepal
KEHRSING BURA, Rfmn 782, 1/6th GR, 16 Nov 1915, of Sigure, Piuthan, Nepal
KEHRSING GHARTI, Rfmn 483, 1/6th GR, 2 May 1915
KESAR RANA, Rfmn 4746, 1/5th GR, 7 Aug 1915, of Kaldara, No.3 West, Ghiring, Nepal
KESAR SINGH, Sepoy 145, 45th Rattray's Sikhs att 14th Sikhs, 4 Jun 1915, of Satarpore, Pasrur, Sialkote, Punjab
KESARAM GURUNG, Rfmn 599, 1/6th GR, 16 Nov 1915, of Taun, No.3 West, Kaski, Nepal
KESBIR GURUNG, Rfmn 4997, 1/5th GR, 21 Aug 1915, of Singdi, No.2 West, Lamjung, Nepal
KESBIR RANA, Rfmn 1275, 1/ 6th GR, 8 Aug 1915, of Satiyati, Palpa, Nepal
KHAGE RANA, Rfmn 609, 1/6th GR, 8 Jun 1915, of Suran, No.4 West, Bhirkote, Nepal
KHAIR MUHAMMAD, Dvr 1800, Mule Corps, 18 May 1915
KHAIRUDDIN, Follower, S&T Corps, 19 Sep 1915
KHAMBASING GURUNG, Rfmn 1121, 2/10th GR, 19 Sep 1915, of Kalingo, Athrai, Dhankuta, Nepal
KHARAKBAHADUR GURUNG, Rfmn 2888, 1/5th GR, 7 Aug 1915, of Sanja, Tanhu, No.3 West, Nepal

KHARAKSING THAPA, Havildar 3729, 1/5th GR, 28 Jun 1915, of Dangsi, Sirkote, Garhung, Nepal

KHARAKSING THAPA, Rfmn 4531, 1/5th GR, 20 Aug 1915, of Sattentti, Palpa, Gulmi, Nepal

KHARJUNG GURUNG, Rfmn 1097, 1/6th GR, 13 May 1915, of Tambu, No.2 West, Lamjung, Nepal

KHARKABAHADUR LIMBU, Rfmn 3007, 2/10th GR, 19 Sep 1915, of Paireni, Chainpore, Dhankuta, Nepal

KHARKABAHADUR THAPA, Rfmn 208, 2/10th GR, 9 Jun 1915, of Madah, Palpa, Gulmi, Nepal

KHARKABIR THAPA, Rfmn 4786, 2/10th GR, 9 Jan 1916, of Harkpore, Tanhu, No.3 West, Nepal

KHARKAMAN RAI, Rfmn 138, 2/10th GR, 11 Nov 1915, of Yankala, Siktel, Bhojpore, Nepal

KHARKASING RANA, Rfmn 241, 1/6th GR, 9 Aug 1915, of Kairekote, No.5 West, Gaerung, Nepal

KHARKBAHADUR THAPA, Rfmn 1072, 1/6th GR, 10 Aug 1915, of Abu, No.3 West, Tanhu, Nepal

KHARKBAHADUR THAPA, Rfmn 4690, 1/5th GR, 4 Jun 1915, of Japundanra, No.4 West, Bhirkote, Nepal

KHARKBAHADUR THAPA, Rfmn 4862, 1/5th GR, 2 Jul 1915, of Payung, No.5 West, Payung, Nepal

KHARKBIR THAPA, Rfmn 3689, 1/5th GR, 5 Jun 1915, of Umsekote, Kahun, Rising, Nepal

KHARKSING ALE, Rfmn 1199, 2/10th GR, 19 Sep 1915, of Kharpu, Rawakhola, Okhaldhunga, Nepal

KHARKSING GURUNG, Rfmn 13, 1/5th GR, 8 Aug 1915, of Marchikote, No.3 West, Kaski, Nepal

KHARKSING GURUNG, Rfmn 1085, 1/6th GR, 28 Jun 1915, of Deoragaon, No.2 West, Lamjung, Nepal

KHARKSING PUN, Rfmn 65, 1/6th GR, 19 May 1915, of Tangas, Palpa, Gulmi, Nepal

KHARKSING RAI, Rfmn 2547, 1/6th GR, 14 Aug 1915

KHARKSING RANA, Rfmn 1186, 1/6th GR, 12 Aug 1915, of Chanchil, No.3 West, Bandipore, Nepal

KHARKSING THAPA, Rfmn 645, 1/6th GR, 7 Jun 1915, of Kasiyani, Palpa, Nepal

KHARKSING THAPA, Rfmn 1214, 1/6th GR, 8 Aug 1915, of Sundara, Sallyana, Nepal

KHARKSING THAPA, Rfmn 4837, 1/6th GR, 2 Jul 1915, of Musikote, Palpa, Nepal

KHARU GURUNG, Rfmn 3778, 1/5th GR, 2 Jul 1915, of Naya-Gaon, Ragis-thal, Lamjung, Nepal

KHATANSING GURUNG, L/Nk 4442, 1/5th GR, 21 Aug 1915, of Bhomdi, No.3 West, Kaski, Nepal

KHAZAN SINGH, Drummer, 4576, 14th Sikhs, 4 Jun 1915, of Deol, Kohmarhi, Rawalpindi, Punjab

KHAZAN SINGH, Sepoy 4656, 14th Sikhs, 5 Jul 1915, of Rahurian Wali, Sarsa, Hissar, Punjab

KHEMSING RANA, Rfmn 1102, 1/6th GR, 9 Aug 1915, of Patandara, Argha, Palpa, Nepal

KHETBAHADUR GURUNG, Rfmn 1089, 1/6th GR, 9 Jul 1915, of Arkha, Palpa, 4000, Parvat, Nepal

KHUDA BAKSH, Jem. 26th Jacob's Battery, 7 May 1915, of Dhok Malak Mauza Khau, Jhelum, Punjab

KHUDA BAKSH, Dvr 760, Mule Corps, 30 Aug 1915, of Dingi, Jhelum, Punjab

KHURE, Follower, Bareilly/3, S&T Corps, 19 Oct 1915

KHUSHALI, Bearer 6471, ABC, 137th Field Amb, 18 May 1915, of Faridpore, Faridpore, Bareilly, United Provinces

KHUSHIYA SINGH, Sepoy 4633, 14th Sikhs, 19 Sep 1915, of Munak Kalan, Dasuha, Hoshiarpore, Punjab

KIRPA SINGH, Gnr 1565, 26th Jacob's Battery, 26 May 1915, of Mallu Pota, Nawan Shahar, Jullundur, Punjab

KIRPADAN RAI, Rfmn 1762, AMP att 2/10th GR, 16 Dec 1915, of Angtep, Bhojpore, Khekamacha, Nepal

KIRPADHOJ RAI, Rfmn 783, 2/10th GR, 23 Jul 1915, of Chichinga, Halesi, Okhaldhunga, Nepal

KIRPADHOJ RAI, Rfmn 3035, 2/10th GR, 13 Aug 1915, of Kerabari, Rawadumre, Okhaldhunga, Nepal

KIRPAL SINGH, Sub. 14th Sikhs, 4 Jun 1915, of Pakho, Malaud, Ludhiana, Punjab

KIRPAL SINGH, Sepoy 359, Patiala Infantry att 14th Sikhs, 9 Aug 1915, of Gehal, Barnala, Barnala, Patiala, Punjab

KISHAN SINGH, Sepoy 419, Patiala Infantry att 14th Sikhs, 22 Aug 1915, of Kumbara, Khar, Ambala, Punjab

KISHAPAL RAI, Rfmn 488, 2/10th GR, 15 Aug 1915, of Sangpang, Dingla, Bhojpore, Nepal

KISHN SINGH, Jem. 14th Sikhs, 19 Sep 1915, of Galimehar Singh, Dhupia, Gujranwala, Punjab

KISHN SINGH, Sepoy 1759, 69th Punjabis, 5 May 1915, of Laroya, Jullundur, Punjab

KISHN SINGH, Havildar 2775, 14th Sikhs, 1 Jul 1915, of Jalal Diwal, Barnala, Patiala, Punjab

KISHN SINGH, Sepoy 3442, 54th Sikhs att 14th Sikhs, 29 Jun 1915, of Gago Buha, Tarntaran, Amritsar, Punjab

KISHN SINGH, Sepoy 3659, 14th Sikhs, 4 Jun 1915, of Tajpur, Ludhiana, Punjab

KISHN SINGH, Naik 3719, 14th Sikhs, 2 Jul 1915, of Ramanwas, Sangrur, Punjab

KISHN SINGH, Sepoy 4179, 14th Sikhs, 4 Jun 1915, of Dosanjh, Moga, Ferozepore, Punjab

KISHNABAHADUR LIMBU, L/Nk 2776, 2/10th GR, 30 Jun 1915, of Tamrang, Mewakhola, Dhankuta, Nepal

KISHNBAHADUR GURUNG, Rfmn 546, 1/6th GR, 22 Aug 1915, of Waigha, No.4 West, Haerhung, Nepal

KISHNBAHADUR GURUNG, Rfmn 2719, 1/5th GR, 22 Aug 1915, of Jhargaon, Gurkha, No.2 West, Nepal

KISNABIR THAPA, Naik 203, 2/10th GR, 7 Aug 1915, of Bengna, Chaubisya, Dhankuta, Nepal

KRISHNABAHADUR LIMBU, Havildar 2176, 2/10th GR, 7 Aug 1915, of Thechumba, Yangrup, Dhankuta, Nepal

KRISHNADHOJ THAPA, Rfmn 1139, 2/10th GR, 19 Sep 1915, of Alampore, Nepal

KRISHNAMAN RAI, Rfmn 3527, 2/10th GR, 19 Sep 1915, of Khowa, Bhojpore, No.4 East, Nepal

KULBAHADUR THAPA, Havildar 4599, 1/6th GR, 22 May 1915, of Ramche, No.3 West, Tanhu, Nepal

KULMAN THAPA, Rfmn 1044, 1/6th GR, 22 May 1915

KUMANSING GURUNG, Rfmn 4876, 1/6th GR, 25 Aug 1915, of Chandra, No.4 West, Satun, Nepal

KUNDA SINGH, Sepoy 3074, 14th Sikhs, 14 May 1915 (Name wrongly shown as Kanaiya Singh)

KUNDA SINGH, Sepoy 4198, 14th Sikhs, 4 Jun 1915, of Chalanwala, Bhikhi, Patiala, Punjab

KUNDA SINGH, Sepoy 4250, 14th Sikhs, 31 May 1915, of Jhakhar Wala, Faridkote, Ferozepore, Punjab

KUNDA SINGH, Sepoy 4435, 14th Sikhs, 4 Jun 1915, of Jodhpore, Ludhiana, Punjab

LABH SINGH, Sepoy 1173, BMP att 14th Sikhs,19 Sep 1915, of Dhanoe, Gharinda, Amritsar, Punjab

LACHHIRAM CHETTRI, Rfmn 384, 2/10th GR, 19 Sep 1915, of Malgaon, Almora, United Provinces

LACHHMAN GURUNG, Havildar 1131, 2/10th GR, 7 Aug 1915, of Sikimba, Phedap, Dhankuta, Nepal

LACHHMAN GURUNG, Rfmn 4616, 1/5th GR, 8 Aug 1915, of Dansing, Palpa, Parvat, Nepal

LACHHMAN LIMBU, Colour Havildar 1788, 2/10th GR, 30 Jun 1915, of Banchore, Chhathar, Dhankuta, Nepal

LACHHMAN LIMBU, Rfmn 3528, 2/10th GR, 19 Sep 1915, of Gidange, Chaubisya, Dhankuta, Nepal

LACHHMAN LIMBU, Rfmn 3536, 2/10th GR, 19 Sep 1915, of Parwadin, Chhathar, Dhankuta, Nepal

LACHHMAN RAI, Rfmn 3513, 2/10th GR, 19 Sep 1915, of Husbo, Siktel, Bhojpore, Nepal

LACHHMAN THAPA, Rfmn 916, 1/6th GR, 18 Jul 1915, of Manlaqa, Palpa, Nepal

LACHIA PUN, Naik 296, 1/6th GR, 22 May 1915, of Lilam, Piuthan, Nepal

LAHARMAN RAI, Rfmn 1048, 2/10th GR, 29 Jun 1915, of Birigun, Dhankuta, Nepal

LAKHA SINGH, Sepoy 1488, 14th Sikhs, 19 Sep 1915, of Masorawal, Dhilwan, Kapurthala, Punjab

LAKHBHAJ LIMBU, Havildar 2357, 2/10th GR, 21 Aug 1915, of Kuwapok, Chhathar, Dhankuta, Nepal

LAKHBIR LIMBU, Naik 15, 2/10th GR, 21 Aug 1915, of Hatikarkharka, Chethar, Dhankuta, Nepal

LALBAHADUR GURUNG, Rfmn 949, 2/10th GR, 15 Aug 1915, of Madi, Dhankuta, Nepal (Heliopolis (Port Tewfik) Memorial, Egypt)

LALHOJ RAI, Rfmn 906, 2/10th GR, 25 Aug 1915, of Necha, No.3 East, Nepal (Heliopolis (Port Tewfik) Memorial, Egypt)

LAL KHAN, Dvr 1387, 26th Jacob's Battery, 19 Sep 1915, of Mehra Khurd, Rawalpindi, Punjab

LAL SINGH, Sub. Maj. 14th Sikhs, 4 Jun 1915, of Baibal, Faridkote, Ferozepore, Punjab

LAL SINGH, Sepoy 429, 45th Rattray's Sikhs att 14th Sikhs, 19 Sep 1915, of Lale Nangal, Batala, Gurdaspore, Punjab

LAL SINGH, Sepoy 3820, 14th Sikhs, 4 Jun 1915, of Thakarwal, Ludhiana, Punjab

LAL SINGH, Sepoy 4504, 14th Sikhs, 26 May 1915, of Bajewala, Bhatinda, Patiala, Punjab

LAL SING THAPA, Rfmn 4899, 1/4th GR, 23 Dec 1915, of Kangkrum, Palpa, Nepal (Pieta Cemetery, Malta)

LALBAHADUR, Bugler, 949, 2/10th GR, 15 Aug 1915, of Madi, Chainpore, Dhankuta, Nepal

LALBAHADUR GURUNG, Rfmn 20, 1/5th GR, 5 Jun 1915, of Lamdanra, No.4 West, Bhirkote, Nepal

LALBAHADUR GURUNG, Rfmn 3546, 2/10th GR, 19 Sep 1915, of Pakhribas, Dailekh, Nepal

LALBAHADUR RAI, Rfmn 1144, 2/10th GR, 19 Sep 1915, of Deosa, Rawakhola, Okhaldhunga, Nepal

LALBAHADUR RANA, Rfmn 1121, 1/6th GR, 22 Oct 1915, of Baskote, Palpa, 4000, Parvat, Nepal

LALBAHADUR SUNWAR, Rfmn 1102, 2/10th GR, 19 Sep 1915, of Sije, Likukhola, Okhaldhunga, Nepal

LALBAHADUR THAPA, Rfmn 851, 1/6th GR, 4 Jul 1915, of Mohonedanra, No.4 West, Bhirkote, Nepal

LALBIR BURA, Rfmn 4607, 1/5th GR, 7 Aug 1915, of Assare, Palpa, Parvat, Nepal

LALBIR LIMBU, Rfmn 365, 2/10th GR, 3 Jul 1915, of Sampunga, Chekung, Sikkim

LALBIR RAI, Havildar 2021, 2/10th GR, 28 Jun 1915, of Dholmukha, Yangrup, Dhankuta, Nepal

LALBIR RAI, Rfmn 3155, 2/10th GR, 19 Sep 1915, of Likhkharka, Chisankhu, No.3 East, Nepal

LALBIR THAPA, Rfmn 27, 1/6th GR, 7 Aug 1915

LALBIR THAPA, Rfmn 4922, 1/5th GR, 29 Jun 1915, Amarsing Thapa, of Thiangrang, Palpa, Nepal

LALBIR THAPA, Rfmn 4923, 1/6th GR, 10 Dec 1915, of Sirukharka, Palpa, Parvat, Nepal

LALDHOJ RAI, Rfmn 906, 2/10th GR, 18 Aug 1915, of Necha, Chisankhu, Okhaldhunga, Nepal

LALSING GURING, Rfmn 173, 1/6th GR, 29 Oct 1915, of Purchok, No.3 West, Lamjung, Nepal

LALSING GURUNG, Rfmn 4185, 1/5th GR, 7 Jan 1916, of Langdi, Palpa, Parvat, Nepal

LALSING MAL, Naik 42605, 1/5th GR, 21 Aug 1915, of Dhanour, Champawati Almora, United Provinces

LALSING THAPA, Rfmn 3230, 1/4th GR, 23 Dec 1915, of Kangkrum, Palpa, Nepal

LE MARCHAND, Lt John, 56th Punjabi Rifles att 1/6th GR, 9 Aug 1915

LEHNA SINGH, Sepoy 3485, 14th Sikhs, 4 Jun 1915, of Bassian Jagraon, Ludhiana, Punjab

LILAMANJ RAI, Rfmn 865, 2/10th GR, 19 Sep 1915, of Sale, Rawadumre, Okhaldhunga, Nepal

LILARAM GURUNG, Sub. 1/6th GR, 4 Jun 1915, of Amile, Palpa, Parvat, Nepal

LILE RANA, L/Nk 4334, 1/5th GR, 7 Aug 1915, of Lokari, Palpa, Nepal

LLOYD, Lt Duncan Ian Bowen, 1/5th GR, 14 Aug 1915, of Maesycrugiau, Carmarthenshire, Wales

LOWRY, Second Lt William Augine Harper, IARO att 14th Sikhs, 4 Jun 1915, of Bournemouth, Hants, England

MACLEAN, Capt, Alastair, 33rd Punjabis, 8 Aug 1915

MADAN SINGH, Bugler, 4442, 14th Sikhs, 19 Sep 1915, of Mahori, Dhanaula, Nabha, Punjab

MADHANSING GURUNG, Rfmn 427, 2/10th GR, 7 Aug 1915, of Jakhan, Dehra Dun, United Provinces

MADHIA, Dvr 806, Mule Corps, 16 Dec 1915, of Karkhana, Karkhana, Secunderabad, Madras

MAGBAHADUR RAI, Havildar 2243, 2/10th GR, 28 Jun 1915, of Chunghang, Khalsa, Dhankuta, Nepal

MAGHAR SINGH, Sepoy 3495, 54th Sikhs att 14th Sikhs, 9 Aug 1915, of Larian, Raya, Sialkote, Punjab

MAHABIR LAMA, Rfmn 1152, 2/10th GR, 19 Sep 1915, of Kalikhola, Kalimpong, Darjeeling, Bengal

MAHABIR LIMBU, Naik 2673, 2/10th GR, 19 Sep 1915, of Dingla, Dhankuta, Nepal

MAHABIR THAPA, Rfmn 372, 1/6th GR, 30 Jun 1915, of Wangsurang, Tansen, Palpa, Nepal

MAHAKMAN RAI, Rfmn 2824, 2/10th GR, 19 Sep 1915, Bhojpore, Nepal

MAHALAL LIMBU, Rfmn 2534, 2/10th GR, 28 Jun 1915, of Singbong, Mewakhola, Dhankuta, Nepal

MAHASER LIMBU, Rfmn 2888, 2/10th GR, 19 Sep 1915, of Tinglabo, Mewakhola, Dhankuta, Nepal

MAHASING RANA, Rfmn 107, 1/6th GR, 21 Aug 1915, of Tirabas, Palpa, Nepal

MAHDO ALE, Rfmn 735, 1/6th GR, 11 Aug 1915, of Boyan, No.3 West, Tanhu, Nepal

MAHENDRADHOJ LIMBU, Rfmn 1610, 2/10th GR, 19 Sep 1915, of Tauka, Chhathar, Dhankuta, Nepal

MAHENDRASING LIMBU, Rfmn 2932, 2/10th GR, 7 Aug 1915, of Kurungba, Panthar, Dhankuta, Nepal

MAIDANE LIMBU, Rfmn 3572, 2/10th GR, 19 Sep 1915, of Songaupo, Phedap, Dhankuta, Nepal

MAIHMA SINGH, Sepoy 3315, 14th Sikhs, 19 Sep 1915, of Hironbadi, Bhikhi, Patiala, Punjab

MAITAHANG LIMBU, Havildar 2299, 2/10th GR, 19 Sep 1915, of Mandria, Ilamdanda, Ilam, Nepal

MAKANBIR RAI, Rfmn 3105, 2/10th GR, 24 Aug 1915, of Arkholi, Chisankhu, No.3 East, Nepal

MAKHANSING LIMBU, Jem. 2/10th GR, 29 Jun 1915, of Lingkep, Tambarkhola, Dhankuta, Nepal

MAKHARDHOJ LIMBU, Rfmn 2126, 2/10th GR, 19 Sep 1915, of Sunghongpe, Newakhola, Dhankuta, Nepal

MAKRAN SINGH, Bearer 6461, ABC, 137th Field Amb, 14 May 1915, of Khudilpore, Jelalabad, Shahjahanpore, United Provinces

MAL SINGH, Sepoy 4496, 14th Sikhs, 23 May 1915, of Bharowal, Jagraon, Ludhiana, Punjab

MALIA GHARTI, Rfmn 3722, 1/5th GR, 22 Aug 1915, of Lugham, Parvat, Nepal

MANBAHADUR ALE, Rfmn 781, 1/6th GR, 8 Aug 1915, of Sipadal, Bhatgaon, Nepal, Nepal

MANBAHADUR GURUNG, Rfmn 542, 1/6th GR, 29 May 1915, of Rauri, No.2 West, Lamjung, Nepal

MANBAHADUR GURUNG, Rfmn 635, 1/6th GR, 1 Oct 1915

MANBAHADUR GURUNG, Rfmn 2720, 1/5th GR, 7 Aug 1915, of Lamsore, Lamjung, No.2 West, Nepal

MANBAHADUR GURUNG, Rfmn 4632, 1/5th GR, 4 Jun 1915, of Daram, No.5 West, Satung, Nepal

MANBAHADUR GURUNG, Rfmn 4801, 1/5th GR, 2 Jul 1915, of Deorali, No.5 West, Payung, Nepal

MANBAHADUR GURUNG, Rfmn 4899, 1/6th GR, 8 Aug 1915, of Kunirdhan, No.4 West, Bhirkote, Nepal

MANBAHADUR KHARKI, Havildar 1944, 2/10th GR, 21 Aug 1915, of Adikhola, Nuwakote, Pokhra, Nepal

MANBAHADUR LIMBU, Rfmn 3043, 2/10th GR, 19 Sep 1915, of Nandari, Chainpore, Dhankuta, Nepal

MANBAHADUR NEWAR, Rfmn 3482, 2/10th GR, 19 Sep 1915

MANBAHADUR RAI, Rfmn 832, 2/10th GR, 19 Sep 1915, of Audrung, Dhankuta, Nepal

MANBAHADUR RANA, Rfmn 1263, 1/6th GR, 8 Dec 1915

MANBAHADUR THAPA, Rfmn 137, 1/6th GR, 22 Aug 1915

MANBAHADUR THAPA, Rfmn 469, 1/6th GR, 13 May 1915, of Arkholathok, No.3 West, Rising, Nepal

MANBIR GURUNG, Rfmn 214, 1/6th GR, 30 Jun 1915, of Gharu, Parvat, Baglung, Nepal

MANBIR GURUNG, Rfmn 4967, 1/6th GR, 4 Jun 1915, of Pokhrichok, No.2 West, Lamjung, Nepal

MANBIR LIMBU, Rfmn 1036, 2/10th GR, 19 Sep 1915, of Phedap, Dhankuta, Nepal

MANBIR MAL, Rfmn 4740, 1/5th GR, 4 Jun 1915, of Khari-Gairah, Dailek, Nayabasti, Nepal

MANBIR RAI, Rfmn 193, 2/10th GR, 29 Jun 1915, of Chaunka, Bhojpore, Nepal

MANDHOJ GURUNG, Rfmn 176, 1/5th GR, 7 Aug 1915, of Milim, No.2 West, Gurkha, Nepal

MANDHOJ GURUNG, Rfmn 846, 1/6th GR, 11 Aug 1915, of Tulsara, No.2 West, Lamjung, Nepal

MANDHOJ GURUNG, Rfmn 2943, 1/5th GR, 28 Oct 1915, of Tulajang, No.2 West, Gurkha, Nepal

MANDHOJ LIMBU, Rfmn 2982, 2/10th GR, 19 Sep 1915, of Nandari, Chainpore, Dhankuta, Nepal

MANDHOJ RAI, Rfmn 971, 2/10th GR, 19 Sep 1915, of Majagaon, Rawadumri, Okhaldhunga, Nepal

MANDHOJ RAI, Rfmn 1184, 2/10th GR, 19 Sep 1915, of Binpa, Okhaldhunga, Nepal

MANDHOJ RAI, Rfmn 2501, 2/10th GR, 2 Nov 1915, of Chauka, Hathuwa, No.4 East, Nepal

MANDHOJ RAI, Rfmn 3330, 2/10th GR, 7 Aug 1915, of Witcha, Dingla, No.4 East, Nepal

MANDHOL LIMBU, Rfmn 2407, 2/10th GR, 19 Sep 1915, of Kuretar, Mewakhola, Dhankuta, Nepal

MANGAL SINGH, Sepoy 504, Patiala Infantry att 14th Sikhs, 22 Aug 1915, of Charachon, Bhawanigarh, Sunam, Patiala, Punjab

MANGAL SINGH, Gnr 584, 21st Kohat Battery, 26 Jun 1915, of Khadial, Kaital, Karnal, Punjab

MANGAL SINGH, Havildar 2532, 14th Sikhs, 22 May 1915, of Janaud, Ludhiana, Punjab

MANGAL SINGH, Sepoy 2641, 14th Sikhs, 4 Jun 1915, of Baner, Sunarn, Patiala, Punjab

MANGAL SINGH, Sepoy 3181, 14th Sikhs, 4 Jun 1915, of Doler, Malerkotla, Ludhiana, Punjab

MANGAL SINGH, Naik 3559, 14th Sikhs, 11 Jun 1915, of Ghandu, Dhode, Patiala, Punjab

MANGAL SINGH, Sepoy 3726, 14th Sikhs, 4 Jun 1915, of Pashahpore, Dhuri, Patiala, Punjab

MANGAL SINGH, Sepoy 4001, 14th Sikhs, 4 Jun 1915, of Bhagta, Faridkote, Ferozepore, Punjab

MANGAL SINGH, Sepoy 4597, 14th Sikhs, 22 Aug 1915, of Baloh, Dhanaula, Nabha, Punjab

MANGALSING GURUNG, Rfmn 485, 1/6th GR, 2 Dec 1915, of Mahor, No.4 West, 4000, Parvat, Nepal

MANGALSING GURUNG, Rfmn 835, 1/6th GR, 29 May 1915, of Surung, No.2 West, Lamjung, Nepal

MANGALSING LAMA, Rfmn 900, 2/10th GR, 7 Aug 1915, of Pakhiung, Gangtok, Sikkim, Nepal

MANGLIA THAPA, Rfmn 4127, 1/6th GR, 8 Aug 1915, of Chisopani, Palpa, Palpa, Nepal

MANGRU, Follower, Patiala Infantry, 7 Jan 1916, of Jhall, Dhuri, Patiala, Punjab (Heliopolis (Port Tewfik) Memorial, Egypt)

MANIHANG RAI, Rfmn 2905, 2/10th GR, 6 Jun 1915, of Chentang, Halesi, Bhojpore, Nepal

MANINHARKA THAPA, Havildar 247, 1/6th GR, 4 Jun 1915, of Mahthar, No.3 West, Tanhu, Nepal

MANIRAJ GURUNG, Naik 318, 1/6th GR, 8 Aug 1915, of Lamdang, No 3, West, Kaski, Nepal

MANIRAJ RAI, L/Nk 2681, 2/10th GR, 28 Jun 1915, of Sangbe, Charkhola, Ilam, Nepal

MANIRAJ SUNWAR, Rfmn 1204, 2/10th GR, 19 Sep 1915, of Sabralu, No.2 East, Ramechhap, Nepal

MANIRAM THAPA, Bugler, 129, 1/5th GR, 30 Jun 1915, of Tamdaura, No.3 West, Dhor, Nepal

MANRUP LIMBU, Jem. 2/10th GR, 10 Aug 1915, of Pedung, Kalimpong, Darjeeling, Bengal

MANSARAM GURUNG, Rfmn 687, 1/6th GR, 16 Nov 1915, of Andherikhola, Pokhra, Kaski, Nepal

MANSING GHARTI, Rfmn 4890, 1/6th GR, 28 Jun 1915, of Simalkuna, Sallyana, Nepal

MANSING RANA, Rfmn 4192, 1/4th GR, 10 Dec 1915, of Namrikote Danra, Piuthan, Nepal

Appendix VI

MANSING THAPA, Rfmn 347, 2/10th GR, 14 Aug 1915, of Kotera, Almora, United Provinces

MANSON, Second Lt Charles, IARO att 1/4th GR, 4 Dec 1915

MANSURE LIMBU, Rfmn 570, 2/10th GR, 7 Aug 1915, of Chongwa, Athrai, Dhankuta, Nepal

MANTARE LIMBU, Rfmn 3700, 2/10th GR, 19 Sep 1915, of Thepang, Panthar, Dhankuta, Nepal

MARDBIR THAPA, Rfmn 3673, 1/5th GR, 29 Jun 1915, of Katiakote, Khyakin, Bhirkote, Nepal

MASTERS, Lt George E, 89th Punjabis att 14th Sikhs, 4 Jun 1915

MATAMBIR RAI, Rfmn 3424, 2/10th GR, 22 Dec 1915, of Pathake, Rawadumre, No.3 East, Nepal

MATBARSING RANA, Rfmn 4520, 1/5th GR, 5 Jun 1915, of Orasti, No.4 West, Nawakote, Nepal

MATHAR GURUNG, Rfmn 4522, 1/6th GR, 30 Jun 1915, of Knaledi, Palpa, Gulmi, Nepal

MATTANSING GURUNG, Rfmn 652, 1/6th GR, 20 Jun 1915, of Landi, Palpa, Parvat, Nepal

MAWAG, Dvr 2193, Mule Corps, 20 Jul 1915, of Doongi, Gujarkhan, Rawalpindi, Punjab

McRAE, Capt, Archibald William, 14th Sikhs, 4 Jun 1915, of Robertsbridge, Sussex, England

MEADE, Lt Richard, 14th Sikhs, 4 Jun 1915 (Pink Farm Cemetery)

MEGH SINGH, Follower, 14th Sikhs, 19 Sep 1915

MEHR AHMAD, L/Nk 857, Mule Corps, 12 Aug 1915, of Badra Khan, Attock, Hazara, Punjab

MEHR SINGH, Sepoy 3024, 14th Sikhs, 4 Jun 1915, of Mansa Chhota, Sangrur, Punjab

MEHR SINGH, Sepoy 3400, 54th Sikhs att 14th Sikhs, 3 Jul 1915, of Shankar, Nakodar, Jullundur, Punjab

MEHR SINGH, Sepoy 4262, 14th Sikhs, 4 Jun 1915, of Pakka, Faridkote, Ferozepore, Punjab

MEHR SINGH, Sepoy 4738, 14th Sikhs, 19 Sep 1915, of Ladda, Dhuri, Patiala, Punjab

MEHRSING BURA, Rfmn 1119, 1/6th GR, 4 Jun 1915, of Nigalpani, Palpa, 4000, Parvat, Nepal

MIR DAD, L/Nk 2273, 89th Punjabis, 14 May 1915, of Khingar Khurd, Rawalpindi, Punjab

MIRA, Naik 962, Mule Corps, 4 Aug 1915

MIT SINGH, Sepoy 4239, 14th Sikhs, 4 Jun 1915, of Bangi Mirje Wali, Bhatinda, Patiala, Punjab

MIT SINGH, Drummer, 4424, 14th Sikhs, 4 Jun 1915, of Dakha, Ludhiana, Punjab

MOBIDHAN RAI, Rfmn 1132, 2/10th GR, 19 Sep 1915, of Mamatem, Rawakhola, Okhaldhunga, Nepal

MOHAN SINGH, Gnr 438, 23rd Peshawar Mountain Battery, 9 Oct 1915, of Sohel Tanda, Akhnur, Tammu State, Punjab

MOHANSING THAPA, Rfmn 1007, 1/6th GR, 2 Jun 1915, of Kusi, No.4 West, Bhirkote, Nepal

MONEY, Maj. Noel, 22nd Punjabis att 5th Bn, Connaught Rangers, 6 Sep 1915 (Pieta Cemetery, Malta)

MORAN, Lt William Paul, 2/10th GR, 8 Jul 1915 (Addolorata Cemetery, Malta)

MORARI, Follower, S&T Corps, 19 Sep 1915

MOSHANG LIMBU, Rfmn 290, 2/10th GR, 22 Jun 1915, of Chityok, Yangrup, Dhankuta, Nepal

MOTILAL RAI, Rfmn 2535, 2/10th GR, 23 Aug 1915, of Sangpang, No.4 East, No.4 East, Nepal

MOTIRAM BURA, L/Nk 578, 1/6th GR, 10 Aug 1915, of Khora, Palpa, Parvat, Nepal

MUHAMMAD ABDULLAH, Dvr 1325, Mule Corps, 19 Sep 1915, of Karkhana, Secunderabad, Madras

MUHAMMAD ALAM, L/Nk 410, Mule Corps, 30 Nov 1915, of Sarli, Palangi, Poonch, Punjab (Rank wrongly shown as Dvr)

MUHAMMAD ALAM, Naik 441, 21st Kohat Battery, 20 May 1915, of Banal, Kahuta, Rawalpindi, Punjab (Rank wrongly shown as Gnr)

MUHAMMAD ALI, Dvr 1662, Mule Corps, 15 Nov 1915, of Karal, Murree, Rawalpindi, Punjab

MUHAMMAD FAZL KHAN, Havildar 257, 21st Kohat Battery, 7 May 1915, of

Hiranda Mohra, Kahuta, Rawalpindi, Punjab (Rank wrongly shown as Salutri)
MUHAMMAD HUSAIN, L/Nk 837, Mule Corps, 2 Sep 1915, of Mana, Chakwal, Jhelum, Punjab
MUHAMMAD KHAN, Dvr 1325, Mule Corps, 3 Jan 1916
MUHAMMAD NUR, Dvr 1347, Mule Corps, 6 Jan 1916, of Kharderpore, Rawalpindi, Punjab
MUHAMMAD SADIQ, Dvr 1614, Mule Corps, 31 Dec 1915, of Sidhir, Narrashera, Gujrat, Punjab
MUKANDH SINGH, Sepoy 1505, 14th Sikhs, 19 Sep 1915, of Jikhapal, Sunam, Patiala, Punjab
MUKARAB KHAN, L/Nk 557, Mule Corps, 30 Apr 1915, of Mukyal, Pindigape, Rawalpindi, Punjab
MULA SINGH, Dvr 120, Indore Transport Corps, 23 Sep 1915, of Barkheda, Alampore, Mehidpore, Central India
MULA SINGH, Sepoy 1596, 14th Sikhs, 19 Sep 1915, of Bhitewash, Ajnala, Amritsar, Punjab
MUNASWAMI, L/Nk 919, Mule Corps, 19 Sep 1915, of Karkhana, Secunderabad, Madras
MUNISWAMI, Follower, 1322, Mule Corps, 18 Jul 1915
MUNSHA SINGH, L/Nk 1238, 14th Sikhs, 19 Sep 1915, of Salempore, Morinda, Ambala, Punjab
MUNSHA SINGH, Sepoy 4261, 14th Sikhs, 4 Jun 1915, of Gholia Kalan, Moga, Ferozepore, Punjab
MUNSHI SINGH, Sepoy 717, Patiala Infantry att 14th Sikhs, 8 Aug 1915, of Dakala, Bhawanigarh, Sunam, Patiala, Punjab
MURLI RAM, Dvr 998, Mule Corps, 20 Jan 1916
NADIR KHAN, Dvr 1371, Mule Corps, 28 Jul 1915, of Taleyana, Chakwal, Jhelum, Punjab
NAGINDA SINGH, Sepoy 4407, 14th Sikhs, 23 May 1915, of Maihma Singh Wala, Ludhiana, Punjab
NAHIR SINGH, Sepoy 3648, 14th Sikhs, 4 Jun 1915, of Kasaiwara, Bhatinda, Patiala, Punjab
NAHIR SINGH, Sepoy 4417, 14th Sikhs, 3 Jun 1915, of Jodh Chak No, 76, Lyallpore, Punjab

NAIKE LIMBU, Bugler, 361, 2/10th GR, 30 Jun 1915, of Libang, Mewakhola, Dhankuta, Nepal
NAIKSING LIMBU, Rfmn 3529, 2/10th GR, 19 Sep 1915, of Gidange, Chaubisya, Dhankuta, Nepal
NAINBAHADUR GURUNG, Rfmn 4782, 1/5th GR, 7 Aug 1915, of Tamleh, No.4 West, Parvat, Nepal
NAINSING THAPA, Naik 4581, 1/6th GR, 13 May 1915, of Sukikote, Palpa, Nepal
NAKARSING GURUNG, Rfmn 4186, 1/4th GR, 6 Dec 1915, of Paka Pani, Palpa, Parvat, Nepal
NAND SINGH, L/Nk 1077, 14th Sikhs, 19 Sep 1915, of Mannan, Batala, Gurdaspore, Punjab
NAND SINGH, Naik 2962, 14th Sikhs, 4 Jun 1915, of Kalsian, Dhanaula, Nabha, Punjab
NAND SINGH, Sepoy 3934, 14th Sikhs, 4 Jun 1915, of Kube, Pail, Patiala, Punjab
NAND SINGH, Sepoy 4040, 14th Sikhs, 4 Jun 1915, of Kalian, Nathana, Ferozepore, Punjab
NAND SINGH, Sepoy 4534, 14th Sikhs, 12 Jun 1915, of Sadikpore, Kharar, Ambala, Punjab
NANDABIR RANA, Rfmn 200, 1/6th GR, 3 Jul 1915, of Chitre, No.4 West, S, Nawakote, Nepal
NANDABIR THAPA, Rfmn 1106, 1/6th GR, 22 May 1915, of Rochin, Palpa, Parvat, Nepal
NANDABIR THAPA, Rfmn 2838, 1/5th GR, 20 Aug 1915, of Dharam Patti, No.5 West, Payung, Nepal
NANDALHO KAMI, Rfmn 56, 2/10th GR, 19 Sep 1915, of Menglung, Phedap, Dhankuta, Nepal
NANDLAL LIMBU, Rfmn 3531, 2/10th GR, 19 Sep 1915, of Gidange Chaubisya, Dhankuta, Nepal
NANDLAL RAI, Rfmn 3512, 2/10th GR, 19 Sep 1915, of Siktel, Bhojpore, Nepal
NANDLAL THAPA, Rfmn 1261, 1/6th GR, 23 Oct 1915, of Bharse, Palpa, Gulmi, Nepal
NANDLAL THAPA, Rfmn 4984, 1/6th GR, 30 Jun 1915, of Waigha, No.4 West, Gaerhung, Nepal
NANGDALEL LIMBU, Rfmn 477, 2/10th GR, 7 Aug 1915, of Hastapore, Yangrup, Dhankuta, Nepal

NANGHA, Sepoy 2411, 122nd Rajputana Infantry, att 108th Indian Infantry, 11 Sep 1915, of Nahardo, Ghosla, Jaipore, Rajputana

NANU, Follower, 10, S&T Corps, 19 Sep 1915, of Lahera, Esanagar, Bundelkhand, Central India

NARAIN DAT, Bearer 2626, ABC, 108th Field Amb, 20 Jun 1915

NARAIN SINGH, Follower, 264, S&T Corps, 19 Sep 1915

NARAIN SINGH, Sepoy 2045, 14th Sikhs, 31 Dec 1915, of Moon, Padhaur, Patiala, Punjab

NARAIN SINGH, Naik 3149, 14th Sikhs, 4 Jun 1915, of Khudi, Barnala, Patiala, Punjab

NARAIN SINGH, Sepoy 3962, 14th Sikhs, 4 Jun 1915, of Tungaheri, Ludhiana, Punjab

NARAIN SINGH, L/Nk 4839, 14th Sikhs, 19 Sep 1915, of Bhatian, Ludhiana, Punjab

NARAINSING RANA, Rfmn 4398, 1/5th GR, 28 Jun 1915, of Lankhuri, Palpa, Nepal

NARANJAN SINGH, Sepoy 4189, 14th Sikhs, 21 May 1915, of Kajlean Da Majra, Kharar, Ambala, Punjab

NARANJAN SINGH, Sepoy 4266, 14th Sikhs, 4 Jun 1915, of Gholia Kalan, Moga, Ferozepore, Punjab

NARAYAN SINGH, Sepoy 4354, 14th Sikhs, 13 May 1915, of Alamgir, Ludhiana, Punjab

NARBAHADUR BURA, Rfmn 2657, 1/5th GR, 15 Dec 1915, of Pampokar, Gulmi, Palpa, Nepal

NARBAHADUR CHETTRI, Rfmn 661, 2/10th GR, 30 Jun 1915, of Turuk, Manjitar, Darjeeling, Bengal

NARBAHADUR GURUNG, Havildar 285, 1/6th GR, 10 Aug 1915, of Gallong, No.3 West, Kaski, Nepal

NARBAHADUR GURUNG, Rfmn 920, 1/6th GR, 2 Dec 1915, of Subran, No.2 West, Lamjung, Nepal

NARBAHADUR GURUNG, Rfmn 1028, 1/6th GR, 7 Aug 1915, of Bardhani, Palpa, Parvat, Nepal

NARBAHADUR GURUNG, Rfmn 1154, 1/6th GR, 23 Aug 1915, of Bharang, No.2 West, Lamjung, Nepal

NARBAHADUR GURUNG, Rfmn 5110, 2/10th GR, 3 Dec 1915, of Sanari, Patap, No, 1 East, Nepal

NARBAHADUR LIMBU, Rfmn 654, 2/10th GR, 14 Aug 1915, of Dumrise, Yangrup, Dhankuta, Nepal

NARBAHADUR LIMBU, Rfmn 1213, 2/10th GR, 19 Sep 1915, of Hamrok, Yangrup, Dhankuta, Nepal

NARBAHADUR RAI, Rfmn 902, 2/10th GR, 30 Jun 1915, of Sangpang, Dingla, Bhojpore, Nepal

NARBAHADUR RAI, Rfmn 3469, 2/10th GR, 19 Sep 1915, of Patika, Rawadumre, No.3 East, Nepal

NARBAHADUR THAPA, Rfmn 1193, 2/10th GR, 19 Sep 1915, of Pornagwikha, Pokra, Bilari, Nepal

NARBHAKTE RAI, Rfmn 904, 2/10th GR, 30 Aug 1915, of Namphok, Gangtok, Sikkim (Name wrongly shown as Narbhoj Rai)

NARBIR GURUNG, Rfmn 3069, 1/4th GR, 5 Nov 1915, of Dum Dumi, Harpun, Kaski, Nepal

NARBIR GURUNG, Naik 4803, 1/6th GR, 15 Jun 1915, of Ranisur, No.4 West, Bhirkote, Nepal

NARBIR LIMBU, Rfmn 276, 2/10th GR, 30 Aug 1915, of Perwaden, Chethar, Dhankuta, Nepal

NARBIR SAHI, Rfmn 1208, 1/6th GR, 3 Dec 1915, Palpa, Nepal

NARBIR THAPA, Rfmn 4843, 1/5th GR, 7 Aug 1915, of Rohu, No.4 West, Bhirkote, Nepal

NARCHINDRA GURUNG, Rfmn 357, 1/6th GR, 28 Jun 1915, of Chere, No.5 West, Gearhung, Nepal

NARDHOJ GURUNG, Rfmn 4776, 1/5th GR, 7 Aug 1915, of Naram, No.3 West, Nepal (Heliopolis (Port Tewfik) Memorial, Egypt)

NARE PUN, Havildar 3852, 1/5th GR, 30 Jun 1915, of Pagdhar, Palpa, Parvat, Nepal

NARJANG GURUNG, L/Nk 4742, 1/5th GR, 21 Aug 1915, of Tegren, No.2 West, Lamjung, Nepal

NARJIT GURUNG, Rfmn 997, 1/6th GR, 13 May 1915, of Basradanra, No.4 West, Satun, Nepal

NARMAN LIMBU, Rfmn 2703, 2/10th GR, 19 Sep 1915, of Parwadin, Dhankuta, Nepal

NARSING RAI, Naik 2733, 2/10th GR, 7 Aug 1915, of Likhukhola, Chainpora, Dhankuta, Nepal

NARSUBHA GURSUNG, Rfmn 1178, 1/6th GR, 1 Dec 1915, of Pakharikote, Lamjung, No.3 West, Nepal (Name wrongly shown as Narbahadur Gurung)

NARYAN SINGH, Sepoy 2045, 14th Sikhs, 31 Dec 1915, of Moom, Patiala, Punjab (Heliopolis (Port Tewfik) Memorial, Egypt)

NASHA, Bearer 2220, ABC, 108th Field Amb, 19 Jun 1915

NATHA SINGH, Havildar 2319, 14th Sikhs, 4 Jun 1915, of Boparai, Jagraon, Ludhiana, Punjab

NATHA SINGH, Sepoy 4447, 14th Sikhs, 14 May 1915, of Motemajra, Kharar, Ambala, Punjab

NAURANG SINGH, L/Nk 1527, 14th Sikhs, 19 Sep 1915, of Pendori Sidwan, Taran Taran, Amritsar, Punjab

NAWAB, Dvr 1728, Mule Corps, 26 May 1915, of Tutur, Kahuta, Rawalpindi, Punjab

NIDHAN SINGH, Sepoy 4379, 14th Sikhs, 14 May 1915, of Mehta, Bhatinda, Patiala, Punjab

NIHAL SINGH, Sepoy 4375, 14th Sikhs, 14 Jun 1915, of Taliwala, Fazilka, Ferozepore, Punjab

NIKKA SINGH, Sepoy 4157, 14th Sikhs, 4 Jun 1915, of Hiron Chhoti, Bhikhi, Patiala, Punjab

NIKKA SINGH, Sepoy 4429, 14th Sikhs, 11 Aug 1915, of Bhadaur, Barnala, Patiala, Punjab

NUR AHMAD, Dvr 1228, 27th Mountain Battery, 13 Aug 1915, of Mandroch, Abbottabad, NWF, Province

NUR ALLAH, Dvr 668, Mule Corps, 14 Aug 1915, of Balbalpari, Jhelum, Punjab

NUR MUHAMMAD, Follower, 807, S&T Corps, 19 Sep 1915

NURASANNA, Dvr 1152, Mule Corps, 19 Sep 1915, of Tawaipura Tarband, Secunderabad, Madras

NURJIT GURUNG, Rfmn 951, 1/5th GR, 22 May 1915, of Sanjop, No.2 West, Lamjung, Nepal

NUR MUHAMMAD, Bugler, 86, Patiala Infantry, 9 Sep 1915, of Khurd, Malerkotla, Punjab (Heliopolis (Port Tewfik) Memorial, Egypt)

ONSLOW, Lt Brian Walton, 11th King Edward's Own Lancers (Probyn's Horse)/ADC to Birdwood, 28 July 1915, of Crowborough, Sussex, England (Beach Cemetery, Anzac)

PADAMBAHADUR SUNWAR, Rfmn 1130, 2/10th GR, 19 Sep 1915, of Khukse, Tamarkhola, Dhankuta, Nepal

PADAMBAHADUR THAPA, Rfmn 1134, 2/10th GR, 19 Sep 1915, of Khatte, Rawakhola, Okhaldhunga, Nepal

PADAMBIR THAPA, Rfmn 664, 1/6th GR, 5 Jul 1915, of Kedri, No.5 West, Gairhung, Nepal

PADAMSING RANA, Rfmn 4728, 1/5th GR, 5 Jun 1915, of Rungdi, No.4 West, Bhirkote, Nepal

PADMA RAI, Follower, 22, 2/10th GR, 21 Aug 1915, of Nibhare, Aselukharka, Okhaldhunga, Nepal

PAHALMAN RAI, Rfmn 1097, 2/10th GR, 19 Sep 1915, of Dingding, Chainpore, Dhankuta, Nepal

PAHALMANSING GURUNG, Rfmn 4936, 1/5th GR, 3 Oct 1915, of Gumdi, Kaski, No.3 West, Nepal

PAHALSING THAPA, Rfmn 4544, 1/5th GR, 20 Sep 1915, of Sarung, No.4 West, Bhirkote, Nepal

PAHARA SINGH, Sepoy 4470, 14th Sikhs, 14 May 1915, of Sakrullapore, Kharar, Ambala, Punjab

PAHLMAN GURUNG, Rfmn 557, 1/6th GR, 22 Aug 1915, of Lumadi, No.5 West, Satun, Nepal

PAHLWAN, Dvr 1188, 26th Jacob's Battery, 12 Jun 1915, of Ram Dial, Jhelum, Jhelum, Punjab

PAKHAR SINGH, Sepoy 2201, 14th Sikhs, 8 Nov 1915, of Rajoana, Raikote, Ludhiana, Punjab

PAKHAR SINGH, Havildar 2742, 14th Sikhs, 4 Jun 1915, of Boparai, Jagraon, Ludhiana, Punjab

PAKHAR SINGH, Sepoy 4562, 14th Sikhs, 4 Jun 1915, of Bassian, Jagraon, Ludhiana, Punjab

PAL SINGH, L/Nk 1223, 14th Sikhs, 19 Sep 1915, of Makhi Kalam, Patti, Lahore, Punjab

PAL SINGH, Sepoy 4107, 14th Sikhs, 4 Jun 1915, of Madhe, Moga, Ferozepore, Punjab

PAL SINGH, Sepoy 4382, 14th Sikhs, 2 Jun 1915, of Kotli, Muktsar, Ferozepore, Punjab

PANCHANSING RAI, Jem. 2/10th GR, 7 Aug 1915, of Grekari, Dhankuta, Nepal

PANCHASOR RAI, Rfmn 3517, 2/10th GR, 19 Sep 1915, of Khena, Siktel, Bhojpore, Nepal

PANCHIAL LIMBU, Rfmn 1197, 2/10th GR, 19 Sep 1915, of Hasing, Tamarkhola, Dhankuta, Nepal

PANJBAHADUR RAI, Rfmn 1105, 2/10th GR, 19 Sep 1915, of Nigale, Panchthar, Ilam, Nepal

PANTHBIR RAI, Rfmn 1719, AMP att 1/4th GR, 17 Sep 1915, of Chotimorong, Chanbisya, Dhankuta, Nepal

PARBIR DAMAI, Rfmn 690, 1/6th GR, 30 Jun 1915, of Ada, Tansing, Nepal

PARBIR THAPA, Rfmn 4718, 1/5th GR, 4 Jun 1915, of Sarang, No.2 West, Lamjung, Nepal

PARMA RAI, Rfmn 2767, 2/10th GR, 19 Sep 1915, of Laketung, Memting, Nepal

PARMANDHOJ LIMBU, Naik 2334, 2/10th GR, 29 Jun 1915, of Numtak, Dhankuta, Nepal

PARMANSING LIMBU, Bugler, 2662, 2/10th GR, 11 Aug 1915, of Hathikharka, Chhathar, Dhankuta, Nepal

PARSIE RAI, Rfmn 1160, 2/10th GR, 19 Sep 1915, of Muwi, Chisankhu, Okhaldhunga, Nepal

PARTAB SINGH, Sepoy 1699, 14th Sikhs, 19 Sep 1915, of Hasanpore, Dine Nagar, Gurdaspore, Punjab

PARTAB SINGH, Sepoy 2977, 14th Sikhs, 5 Jun 1915, of Bhatian, Ludhiana, Punjab

PARTAB SINGH, Sepoy 3603, 14th Sikhs, 6 Jun 1915, of Dakha, Ludhiana, Punjab

PARTABSING RAI, Rfmn 1138, 2/10th GR, 19 Sep 1915, of Pabong, Gangtok, Sikkim

PARTAP SINGH, Follower, 186, S&T Corps, 19 Sep 1915

PARTAPSING RAI, Rfmn 3503, 2/10th GR, 19 Sep 1915, of Dilpa, Siktel, No.3 West, Nepal

PARTHIMAN GHARTI, Rfmn 593, 1/6th GR, 5 Jul 1915, of Dhantana, Sallyana, Sallyana, Nepal

PARTIMAN THAPA, Rfmn 4467, 1/5th GR, 7 Aug 1915, of Tankora, Piuthan, Nepal

PARTU PUN, Rfmn 322, 1/5th GR, 6 Mar 1916, of Karas, Baglung, Nepal

PASRAM THAPA, Rfmn 669, 1/6th GR, 25 May 1915, of Kokia, No.3 West, Rising, Nepal

PASSY, Maj. De Lacy Woolrich, 25th Punjabis att 8th Bn, Northumberland Fusiliers, 12 Aug 1915, of London, England (Lancashire Landing Cemetery, Helles)

PATAMBAR LIMBU, Rfmn 2891, 2/10th GR, 30 Jun 1915, of Phausing, Panthar, Dhankuta, Nepal

PAULA, Follower, 805, S&T Corps, 19 Sep 1915

PHARSAMAN RAI, Rfmn 3256, 2/10th GR, 19 Sep 1915, of Khwa, Dilpa, Bhojpore, Nepal

PHUMAN SINGH, Havildar 348, 21st Kohat Battery, 20 May 1915, of Raipore, Samrala, Ludhiana, Punjab

PHUMAN SINGH, Dvr 418, 21st Kohat Battery, 2 May 1915, of Koop, Malerkotla, Ludhiana, Punjab

PHUMAN SINGH, Sepoy 1121, 15th Ludhiana Sikhs att 14th Sikhs, 19 Sep 1915, of Abuwal, Jagraon, Ludhiana, Punjab

PHUMAN SINGH, Gnr 2917, 26th Jacob's Battery, 5 Oct 1915, of Thawana, Garh Shankar, Hoshiarpore, Punjab

PHUMAN SINGH, Havildar 3032, 14th Sikhs, 5 Jul 1915, of Dharldiwal, Dhuri, Patiala, Punjab

PHUMAN SINGH, Sepoy 4176, 14th Sikhs, 14 May 1915, of Abiwal, Jagraon, Ludhiana, Punjab

PHUMAN SINGH, Sepoy 4401, 14th Sikhs, 4 Jun 1915, of Jangpore, Jagraon, Ludhiana, Punjab

PHUMAN SINGH, Sepoy 4549, 14th Sikhs, 4 Jun 1915, of Ditarpore, Ropar, Ambala, Punjab

PHURBIR GHALE, Rfmn 880, 1/6th GR, 13 May 1915, of Jangbal, Bhatgaon, Nepal

PIAMBA SUBHA, Bearer 8946, ABC, 108th Field Amb, 24 Aug 1915, of Kotey, Charikote, No.2, Charikote, Nepal
PIRTHICHAND LIMBU, Rfmn 2113, 2/10th GR, 9 Aug 1915, of Umarjang, Dhankuta, Nepal
PIRTHIDHOJ LIMBU, Rfmn 2528, 2/10th GR, 13 Dec 1915, of Tamphula, Phedap, Dhankuta, Nepal
PIRTHIMAN GURUNG, Rfmn 1017, 1/6th GR, 4 Jun 1915, of Dabling, Gurkha, Nepal
PIRTHIMAN THAPA, Rfmn 4439, 1/5th GR, 8 Aug 1915, of Bakumi, Palpa, Parvat, Nepal
PIRTHISING LIMBU, Rfmn 959, 2/10th GR, 28 Jun 1915, of Phejon, Panchthar, Dhankuta, Nepal
PITAMBAR THAPA, Rfmn 4354, 1/5th GR, 7 Aug 1915, of Paya, No.4 West, Nawakote, Nepal
POHLA SINGH, Sepoy 4233, 14th Sikhs, 4 Jun 1915, of Madhe, Moga, Ferozepore, Punjab
POHLA SINGH, Sepoy 4466, 14th Sikhs, 4 Jun 1915, of Bhatian, Ludhiana, Punjab
PREM SINGH, Sepoy 4533, 14th Sikhs, 4 Jun 1915, of Rurki Parawali, Kharar, Ambala, Punjab
PREMNARAIN THAPA, Jem., 1/5th GR, 8 Aug 1915, of Orasti, Bahakote, Nawakote, Nepal
PREMSING GURUNG, Rfmn 3480, 2/10th GR, 19 Sep 1915, of Kopu, Kuncha, Lamjong, Nepal
PUNAHANG LIMBU, Havildar 2804, 2/10th GR, 9 Aug 1915, of Poklabung, Chainpore, Dhankuta, Nepal
PUNALANG LIMBU, Rfmn 656, 2/10th GR, 10 Sep 1915, of Hangpabo, Maiwakhola, Dhankuta, Nepal
PUNAHANG LIMBU, Havildar 2352, 2/10 GR, 10 Aug 1915 (Chunuk Bair Cemetery, Anzac)
PUNIA THAPA, Rfmn 3907, 1/5th GR, 4 Jun 1915, of Ekbing, Palpa, Nepal
PUNTHE PUN, Rfmn 4618, 1/4th GR, 27 Sep 1915, of Damri, Piuthan, Nepal
PURAN SINGH, Sepoy 4111, 14th Sikhs, 2 Jul 1915, of Lialan Meghewalian, Jagraon, Ludhiana, Punjab
PURAN SINGH, Sepoy 4328, 14th Sikhs, 9 Jul 1915, of Katari, Pail, Patiala, Punjab
PURAN SINGH, Sepoy 4352, 14th Sikhs, 4 Jun 1915, of Padiala, Sirhind, Patiala, Punjab
PURAN SINGH, Sepoy 4356, 14th Sikhs, 4 Jun 1915, of Isewal, Ludhiana, Punjab
PURAN SINGH, Sepoy 4660, 14th Sikhs, 19 Sep 1915, of Kauloke, Phul, Nabha, Punjab
PURAN SINGH, Follower, Patiala Infantry att 14th Sikhs, 9 Oct 1915, of Choonghan, Malerkotla, Punjab
PURANDAJ LIMBU, Rfmn 2038, 2/10th GR, 19 Sep 1915, of Wareni, Panthar, Dhankuta, Nepal
PURANSING GURUNG, Naik 4979, 1/6th GR, 8 Aug 1915, of Nawakote, Piuthan, Nepal
PURNABIR LIMBU, Rfmn 1214, 2/10th GR, 19 Sep 1915, of Wareni, Panchthar, Dhankuta, Nepal
PURNAHANG LIMBU, Rfmn 2493, 2/10th GR, 25 Nov 1915, of Dingla, Mewakhola, Dhankuta, Nepal
PURNAHANG LIMBU, Rfmn 5773, 14th Sikhs, 28 Oct 1915, of Serjong, Phedap, Dhankuta, Nepal
PURNIA GURUNG, Rfmn 4763, 1/5th GR, 7 Aug 1915, of Jhalbanyang, No.3 West, Tanlru, Nepal
QAIM DIN, Dvr 1333, Mule Corps, 4 Nov 1915, of Sambalgia, Kahuta, Punjab
RAGHOBIR RAI, Rfmn 1104, 2/10th GR, 19 Sep 1915, of Damku, Chisankhu, Bhojpore, Nepal
RAGUBIR PUN, Rfmn 4528, 1/6th GR, 4 Jun 1915, of Lespore, Palpa, Parvat, Nepal
RAHMAT ALI, Dvr 1256, Mule Corps, 5 Jan 1916, of Sabour, Kharian, Gujrat, Punjab
RAHMATULLAH, L/Nk 376, Mule Corps, 24 Sep 1915, of Sirin, Abbottabad, Hazara, Punjab
RAI GURUNG, Rfmn 995, 1/6th GR, 13 Jun 1915, of Nalwang, No.2 West, Lamjung, Nepal
RAIBAHADUR LIMBU, Follower, 2/10th GR, 19 Sep 1915
RAJBAHADUR LIMBU, Sub., 2/10th GR, 7 Aug 1915, of Sangapu, Phedap, Dhankuta, Nepal
RAJBAHADUR RAI, Rfmn 1153, 2/10th GR, 19 Sep 1915, of Sambin, Gangtok, Sikkim, Nepal

RAJBAL RAI, Rfmn 3160, 2/10th GR, 19 Sep 1915, of Godel, Aselukharka, No.3 West, Nepal

RAJBIR GURUNG, Rfmn 2, 1/5th GR, 28 Jun 1915, of Thana, Nawakote, No.4 West, Nepal

RAJBIR IRAI, Rfmn 3337, 2/10th GR, 27 Aug 1915, of Pauku, Tuluwa, No.3 East, Nepal

RAJDHAN RAI, Rfmn 3533, 2/10th GR, 19 Sep 1915, of Warang, Siktel, Bhojpore, Nepal

RAJMAN RAI, Jem. 2/10th GR, 2 Jul 1915, of Gairigaon, Panwa, Bhojpore, Nepal

RAJMAN RAI, Rfmn 1200, 2/10th GR, 19 Sep 1915, of Damucha, Khotang, Ramechhap, Nepal

RAJNANDA LIMBU, Rfmn 2660, 2/10th GR, 19 Sep 1915, of Obrai, Yangrup, Dhankuta, Nepal

RAJWALI, Gnr 1674, 26th Jacob's Battery, 8 May 1915, of Dhok Dani, Jhelum, Punjab

RALA SINGH, Sepoy 4353, 14th Sikhs, 4 Jun 1915, of Lachhawadi, Malerkotla, Ludhiana, Punjab

RALA SINGH, Sepoy 4416, 14th Sikhs, 4 Jun 1915, of Dakha, Ludhiana, Punjab

RALA SINGH, Sepoy 4753, 14th Sikhs, 19 Sep 1915, of Changli, Dhuri, Patiala, Punjab

RAM LAL, Follower, JhansI/117, S&T Corps, 19 Sep 1915

RAM SARAN, Follower, Lahore/185, S&T Corps, 26 Oct 1915

RAM SINGH, Jem. 26th Jacob's Battery, 12 Aug 1915, of Majra, Samrala, Ludhiana, Punjab

RAM SINGH, Sepoy 621, Patiala Infantry, att 14th Sikhs, 8 Aug 1915, of Karhalia, Patiala, Punjab

RAM SINGH, Sepoy 3394, 14th Sikhs, 4 Jun 1915, of Rangi, Ludhiana, Punjab

RAM SINGH, Sepoy 3670, 14th Sikhs, 4 Jun 1915, of Fateda Kote, Bhatinda, Patiala, Punjab

RAM SINGH, Naik 3675, 14th Sikhs, 12 Aug 1915, of Talwandi Khurd, Jagraon, Ludhiana, Punjab

RAM SINGH, Sepoy 4049, 14th Sikhs, 4 Jun 1915, of Sangatpura, Moga, Ferozepore, Punjab

RAM SINGH, Sepoy 4297, 14th Sikhs, 14 May 1915, of Burj Ladhe Wala, Faridkot, Ferozepore, Punjab

RAM SINGH, Sepoy 4406, 14th Sikhs, 4 Jun 1915, of Tahliwala, Fazilka, Ferozepore, Punjab

RAM SINGH, Follower, 14th Sikhs, 6 Oct 1915

RAM THAPA, Rfmn 84, 2/10th GR, 8 Aug 1915, of Phalikote, Bhojpore, Nepal

RAMANATH, Dvr 177, Indore Transport Corps, 19 Sep 1915, of Kasipore, Gusai Ganj, Lucknow, United Provinces

RAMBAHADUR LIMBU, Rfmn 2908, 2/10th GR, 19 Sep 1915, of Angon, Chainpore, Dhankuta, Nepal

RAMBAHADUR THAPA, Rfmn 821, 1/6th GR, 13 May 1915, of Muchur, No.2 West, Gurkha, Nepal

RAMBARAN, Follower, Jhansi/11, S&T Corps, 19 Sep 1915, of Khajuri Purri Bhaktavar Ahir, Bikapur, Fyzabad, United Provinces

RAMDIYAL, Bearer 4553, ABC, 108th Field Amb, 13 May 1915, of Dhamore, SuLtanpore, United Provinces

RAMKISHOR MISR, Sepoy 1414, 89th Punjabis, 13 May 1915, of Garyan, Ballia, United Provinces

RAMNAGHASING, Rfmn 883, 1/6th GR, 9 Dec 1915, of Rasanpore, Abmedabad, Azamgarh, United Provinces

RAMPARSHAD RAI, Naik 1577, 2/10th GR, 28 Jun 1915, of Nesam, Changi, Dhankuta, Nepal

RAMSLAL RAI, Rfmn 3372, 2/10th GR, 29 Jun 1915, of Juling, Aselukharka, Okhaldhunga, Nepal

RAMUSING RAI, Rfmn 2998, 2/10th GR, 28 Jun 1915, of Repcha, Solu, Okhaldhunga, Nepal

RANBAHADUR LIMBU, Rfmn 2/10th GR, 23 Jul 1915 (Pieta Cemetery, Malta)

RANAHANG LIMBU, Rfmn 3952, 2/10th GR, 19 Sep 1915, of Gidange, Chaubisya, Dhankuta, Nepal

RANAK SINGH, Sepoy 4644, 14th Sikhs, 8 Oct 1915, of Chak No.52, Samundri, Lyallpore, Punjab

RANBAHADUR ALE, Rfmn 911, 1/6th GR, 4 Jun 1915, of Tarle, No.4 West, Bhirkote, Nepal

RANBAHADUR GURUNG, Rfmn 4592, 1/6th GR, 6 Jun 1915, of Ghyachok, No.3 West, Kaski, Nepal

RANBAHADUR LIMBU, Rfmn 447, 2/10th GR, 29 Aug 1915, of Bhanre, Gangtok, Sikkim, Nepal

RANBAHADUR PUN, Rfmn 4869, 1/5th GR, 3 Jul 1915, Tulachun Pun, of Bachigaon, Palpa, 4000, Parvat, Nepal

RANBAHADUR RAI, Rfmn 100, 2/10th GR, 7 Aug 1915, of Dungma, Bhojpore, Nepal

RANBAHADUR RAI, Rfmn 725, 2/10th GR, 20 Aug 1915, of Madi, Chainpore, Dhankuta, Nepal

RANBAHADUR RANA, Rfmn 4410, 1/6th GR, 4 Jun 1915, of Daichap, Palpa, Gulmi, Nepal

RANBAHADUR SARKI, Rfmn 1187, 2/10th GR, 19 Sep 1915, of Rawakote, No.1 West, Nepal

RANBAHADUR THAPA, Rfmn 735, 2/10th GR, 7 Aug 1915, of Pungphung, Puwapar, Ilam, Nepal

RANBAHADUR THAPA, Rfmn 4571, 1/5th GR, 2 Jul 1915, of Dolimara, Palpa, Nepal

RANBIR ALE, Rfmn 205, 1/6th GR, 14 May 1915, of Najhung, No.3 West, Rising, Nepal

RANBIR GURUNG, Rfmn 37, 1/5th GR, 9 Aug 1915, of Okare, Lamjung, No.2 West, Nepal

RANBIR THAPA, L/Nk 4669, 1/5th GR, 7 Aug 1915, of Palikote, Palpa, Gulmi, Nepal

RANBIR THAPA, Havildar 4571, 1/6th GR, 1 Dec 1915, of Amthok, No.3 West, Rising, Nepal

RANBIR THAPA, Rfmn 4578, 1/6th GR, 4 Jun 1915, of Arge-Danra, Palpa, Palpa, Nepal

RANDHOJ LIMBU, Rfmn 252, AMP att 2/10th GR, 7 Aug 1915

RANDHOJ LIMBU, Rfmn 3611, 2/10th GR, 11 Dec 1915, of Nagi, Dhankuta, Nepal

RANDHOJ RAI, Rfmn 1372, 2/10th GR, 30 Jun 1915, of Malpar, Warpa, Nepal, Nepal

RANGALAL RAI, Rfmn 3218, 2/10th GR, 19 Sep 1915, of Kalbote, Ilam, Ilamdana, Nepal

RANGIT LIMBU, Naik 1682, 2/10th GR, 25 Aug 1915, of Barbote, Sikkim, Nepal

RANGLAL PUN, Rfmn 2673, 1/5th GR, 9 Aug 1915, of Uleri, Parvat, No.2 West, Nepal

RANGUBIR THAPA, Rfmn 1045, 1/6th GR, 4 Jun 1915, of Amalabas, Palpa, Nepal

RANIA THAPA, Rfmn 4861, 1/5th GR, 5 Jul 1915, of Malangkote, Bhirkote, Nawakote, Nepal

RANSING GURUNG, Rfmn 3848, 1/5th GR, 30 Jun 1915, of Karbria, Thapria, Nepal

RANSING THAPA, Rfmn 127, 1/5th GR, 21 Aug 1915, of Ritia, Palpa, Nepal

RANSING THAPA, Naik 3842, 1/5th GR, 4 Jun 1915, of Bahakote, Nawakote, Nepal

RANSUR GURUNG, Rfmn 79, 1/5th GR, 21 Sep 1915, of Tanar, Lamjung, No.2 West, Nepal

RANU GURUNG, Rfmn 908, 1/6th GR, 28 Jun 1915, of Bange, No.2 West, Gurkha, Nepal

RAOMAN GURUNG, Havildar 83, 1/6th GR, 13 May 1915, of Arwain, Palpa, Parvat, Nepal

RATAN DEWA, Follower, 9, ABC, 110th Field Amb, 28 Dec 1915

RATAN SINGH, L/Nk 1149, 14th Sikhs, 19 Sep 1915, of Khara, Serali, Amritsar, Punjab

RATAN SINGH, Sepoy 2771, 14th Sikhs, 4 Jun 1915, of Chhangali, Dhuri, Patiala, Punjab

RATAN SINGH, Sepoy 4410, 14th Sikhs, 4 Jun 1915, of Alam Khel, Tiral, NWF Province

RATANBAHADUR RAI, Rfmn 855, 2/10th GR, 30 Aug 1915, of Dungma, Bhojpore, Nepal

RATANBIR RANA, Rfmn 4812, 1/5th GR, 4 Jun 1915, of Parokni, Palpa, Nepal

RATANDHOJ LBIBU, Rfmn 3425, 2/10th GR, 9 Aug 1915, of Narpani Phedap, Dhankuta, Nepal

RATANSING GURUNG, Follower, 1/5th GR, 8 Nov 1915, of Barabari, Syangja, Nawakote, Nepal

RATNE RAI, Lance Havildar 77, 2/10th GR, 19 Sep 1915, of Pangnam, Dhankuta, Nepal

RATTAN SINGH, L/Nk 2012, 89th Punjabis, 13 May 1915, of Sehna, Ludhiana, Punjab

REANEY, Capt. Michael Foster, IMS att 1/5th GR, 2 Jul 1915, of London, England (Pink Farm Cemetery, Helles)

RICKETTS, Maj. Henry William Felix, 93rd Burma Infantry att 5th Bn, WiLtshire Regiment, 10 Aug 1915, of Eastbourne, Sussex, England

RIKHIDAN RAI, Rfmn 895, AMP att 1/4th GR, 21 Oct 1915, of Bansi Kora, Hatua, Bhojpore, Nepal

RINGE RAI, Rfmn 3120, 2/10th GR, 7 Aug 1915, of Majhuwa, Chisankhu, No.3 East, Nepal

ROBERTS, Second Lt John Ernest Bate, IARO att 1/5th GR, 23 Sep 1915, of London, England

RUDARBIR ALE, Rfmn 4176, 1/5th GR, 28 Jun 1915, of Gaysa, Palpa, Nepal

RUDARBIR GURUNG, Rfmn 4500, 1/5th GR, 21 Aug 1915, of Morie, Palpa, Parvat, Nepal

RUDRASING THAPA, Rfmn 280, 1/6th GR, 30 Aug 1915, of Pokhra-Danra, Palpa, Gulmi, Nepal

RULIYA SINGH, Sepoy 3758, 14th Sikhs, 4 Jun 1915, of Khadiyal, Kainthal, Karnal, Punjab

RUR SINGH, Sepoy 2077, 14th Sikhs, 16 Nov 1915, of Nanshera, Lahorimal, Amritsar, Punjab

RUSSELL, Lt James, 2/10th GR, 2 Jul 1915

SABIA GURUNG, Piper, 2105, 1/4th GR, 1 Dec 1915, of Barigaon, Dura Danra, No.2 West, Nepal

SADDA SINGH, Havildar 3006, 14th Sikhs, 4 Jun 1915, of Sekha, Barnala, Patiala, Punjab

SAGUNE RANA, Rfmn 1137, 2/10th GR, 19 Sep 1915, of Manjal, Lanjung, Pokhra, Nepal

SAHABIR PUN, Rfmn 699, 1/6th GR, 24 May 1915, of Ranepani, No.4 West, Parvat, Nepal

SAHABIR RAI, Rfmn 469, AMP att 2/10th GR, 30 Jun 1915

SAHIB DIN, Dvr 980, Mule Corps, 20 Aug 1915, of Baroo, Nowshera, Bhinber, Punjab

SAIBAHADUR RAI, Rfmn 2911, 2/10th GR, 19 Sep 1915, of Hathuwa, Chainpore, Dhankuta, Nepal

SAIBAR GURUNG, Rfmn 4901, 1/5th GR, 7 Aug 1915, of Nalma, Parewadanra, Lamjung, Nepal

SAIDA KHAN, Dvr 1810, Mule Corps, 15 Aug 1915, of Laiku, Kahuta, Rawalpindi, Punjab

SAID MUHAMMAD, Gnr 679, 21st Kohat battery, 9 May 1915, of Tharpal, Chakwal, Jhelum, Punjab (Manara Indian Muhammadan Cemetery, Egypt)

SAKHA RAM DIPA, Follower, 802, S&T Corps, 19 Sep 1915

SAKHTARAM PUN, Rfmn 909, 1/6th GR, 4 Jun 1915, of Julia, Palpa, Parvat, Nepal

SALAM DIN, Follower, 2066, Mule Corps, 19 Sep 1915

SALBAHADUR GURUNG, Rfmn 840, 2/10th GR, 9 Aug 1915, of Sekima, Terathum, Dhankuta, Nepal

SAMSHER RANA, Rfmn 4942, 1/5th GR, 15 Aug 1915, of Tagura, Piuthan, Nepal

SAMU LIMBU, Rfmn 558, 2/10th GR, 9 Aug 1915, of Purjan, Phedap, Dhankuta, Nepal

SANJAPATI LIMBU, Rfmn 2157, 2/10th GR, 19 Sep 1915, of Yemason, Yangrup, Dhankuta, Nepal

SANKHABIR LIMBU, Rfmn 3497, 2/10th GR, 19 Sep 1915, of Tunbet, Mewakhola, Dhankuta, Nepal

SANKHAMAN LIMBU, Jem. 2/10th GR, 19 Sep 1915, of Andaram, Chhathar, Dhankuta, Nepal

SANMAN SUNWAR, Rfmn 1155, 2/10th GR, 19 Sep 1915, of Rasnalu, Charikote, Ramechhap, Nepal

SANTA SINGH, Sepoy 827, 45th Rattray's Sikhs att 14th Sikhs, 4 Jun 1915, of Singh Pura, Gurdaspore, Punjab

SANTA SINGH, Sepoy 1204, 14th Sikhs, 19 Sep 1915, of Kheyala, Lopoke, Amritsar, Punjab

SANTA SINGH, Sepoy 1492, 14th Sikhs, 19 Sep 1915, of Gago Baba, Taran Taran, Amritsar, Punjab

SANTA SINGH, Sepoy 1645, 14th Sikhs, 19 Sep 1915, of Reru, Jullundur, Punjab

SANTA SINGH, Sepoy 3389, 14th Sikhs, 4 Jun 1915, of Raipore, Ludhiana, Punjab

SANTA SINGH, Sepoy 3860, 14th Sikhs, 4 Jun 1915, of Ghanaur, Malerkotla, Punjab

SANTA SINGH, Sepoy 4166, 14th Sikhs, 4 Jun 1915, of Patto, Moga, Ferozepore, Punjab

SANTA SINGH, Sepoy 4219, 14th Sikhs, 26 May 1915, of Bina Heri, Dhode, Patiala, Punjab

SANTA SINGH, Sepoy 4574, 14th Sikhs, 2 Jun 1915, of Mum, Barnala, Patiala, Punjab

SANTABIR ALE, Rfmn 4431, 1/5th GR, 4 Jun 1915, of Kaptutsoora, No.3 West, Tanh, Nepal

SANTBIR GURUNG, Rfmn 1091, 1/6th GR, 9 Oct 1915, of Chandrakote, No.3 West, Satun, Nepal

SANTBIR THAPA, Rfmn 462, 1/6th GR, 9 Aug 1915, of Pasgaun, Palpa, Nepal

SANTE RAI, Rfmn 516, 2/10th GR, 29 Jun 1915, of Panku, Tuluwa, Okhaldhunga, Nepal

SANTRAM PUN, Rfmn 4663, 1/6th GR, 9 Aug 1915, of Naugali, Baglung, Palpa, Nepal

SAPURAN SINGH, Bugler, 81, Patiala Infantry att 14th Sikhs, 7 Aug 1915, of Bakhopir, Bhawanigarh, Sunam, Patiala, Punjab

SAPURAN SINGH, Sepoy 4727, 14th Sikhs, 19 Sep 1915, of Dakhe, Ludhiana, Punjab

SARABJIT ALE, Rfmn 415, 1/6th GR, 30 Sep 1915, of Sunpore, Piuthan, Nepal

SARABJIT THAPA, Naik 4266, 1/5th GR, 27 Aug 1915, of Paryami, Palpa, Nepal

SARBADHOJ RAI, Rfmn 1149, 2/10th GR, 19 Sep 1915, of Surma, Majuwa, Okhaldhunga Nepal

SARBAN SINGH, Sepoy 4329, 14th Sikhs, 4 Jun 1915, of Parta Bhup Singh, Kainthal, Karnal, Punjab

SARBAN SINGH, Sepoy 4495, 14th Sikhs, 4 Jun 1915, of Bahini Sahib, Ludhiana, Punjab

SARBANG SINGH, L/Nk 1419, 90th Punjabis, 14 May 1915, of Chambaybat, Oryia, Sialkote, Punjab

SARBHADHOJ RAI, Rfmn 487, AMP att 2/10th GR, 7 Aug 1915

SARBIR RAI, Rfmn 2525, 2/10th GR, 7 Aug 1915, of Kengch, No.4 East, Nepal

SARE BURA, Rfmn 4989, 1/6th GR, 22 Aug 1915, of Malba, Ishma, Nepal

SARKI GURUNG, Rfmn 5, 1/5th GR, 27 Aug 1915, of Dangaon, Tanhu, No.3 West, Nepal

SARMUKH SINGH, Sepoy 3805, 14th Sikhs, 4 Jun 1915, of Gaga, Sunam, Patiala, Punjab

SARWAN SINGH, Sepoy 1024, 45th Rattray's Sikhs att 14th Sikhs, 4 Jun 1915, of Gill, Nabha, Punjab

SASHE THAPA, Rfmn 2706, 1/5th GR, 9 Dec 1915, of Chara, Palpa, Nepal

SATABIR GURUNG, Rfmn 1280, 1/6th GR, 10 Dec 1915, of Ramchya, No.1 West, Nepal (Heliopolis (Port Tewfik) Memorial, Egypt)

SATBAR GURUNG, Rfmn 4509, 1/5th GR, 5 Jul 1915, of Deorali-Khola, No.5 West, Payung, Nepal

SATBIR GURUNG, Rfmn 1280, 1/6th GR, 10 Dec 1915, of Ramche, No.4 West, Nawakote, Nepal

SAUDAGAR SINGH, Sepoy 742, 45th Rattray's Sikhs att 14th Sikhs, 4 Jun 1915, of Bandala, Kasur, Lahore, Punjab (Redoubt Cemetery, Helles)

SAWAN SINGH, Sepoy 4190, 14th Sikhs, 4 Jun 1915, of Sagakpore, Kharar, Ambala, Punjab

SAWAN SINGH, Sepoy 4381, 14th Sikhs, 4 Jun 1915, of Chanoon, Fazilka, Ferozepore, Punjab

SAYID MUHAMMAD, Gnr 679, 21st Kohat Battery, 9 May 1915, of Tharpal, Chakwal, Jhelum, Punjab

SAYID SUBHAN, Dvr 1337, Mule Corps, 18 Aug 1915, of Khalaspada, Khalaspada, Bangalore, Madras

SAYID SULIMAN, Dvr 816, Mule Corps, 30 May 1915

SEMLAL LIMBU, Rfmn 396, 2/10th GR, 9 Oct 1915, of Tamkhu, Mewakhola, Dhankuta, Nepal

SETALAL RAI, Rfmn 1073, 2/10th GR, 19 Sep 1915, of Habu, Khesang, Bhojpore, Nepal

SETE GHARTI, Rfmn 1133, 1/6th GR, 28 Jun 1915, of Papli, Piuthan, Nepal

SETE PUN, Rfmn 112, 1/6th GR, 30 Jun 1915, of Tunikharak, Piuthan, Nepal

SETU SUNWAR, Rfmn 614, 2/10th GR, 7 Aug 1915, of Sisneri, Okhaldhunga, Nepal

SEWA SINGH, Sepoy 2874, 14th Sikhs, 19 Sep 1915, of Hiron, Bhikhi, Patiala, Punjab

SEWA SINGH, Sepoy 4748, 14th Sikhs, 19 Sep 1915, of SuLtanpore, Dhuri, Patiala, Punjab

SHAH MIR, Dvr 1556, Mule Corps, 3 Jun 1915, of Kahatti, Murree, Rawalpindi, Punjab

SHAM SINGH, Dvr 1632, 26th Jacob's Battery, 10 Aug 1915, of Gobindpore, Nawan Shahar, Jullundur, Punjab

SHAM SINGH, Sepoy 4191, 14th Sikhs, 4 Jun 1915, of Gure, Jagraon, Ludhiana, Punjab

SHAM SINGH, Sepoy 4212, 14th Sikhs, 5 Jul 1915, of Majuki, Talwandi, Barnala, Patiala, Punjab

SHAM SINGH, Sepoy 4548, 14th Sikhs, 4 Jun 1915, of Khota, Moga, Ferozepore, Punjab

SHAMAT ALI, Lance Daffadar, 3, Indore Transport Corps, 3 Oct 1915, of Achod, Bawal, Nabha, Punjab

SHAMSHER, Dvr 461, Mule Corps, 19 Sep 1915

SHANKARDAS, Dvr 447, Mule Corps, 19 Sep 1915

SHEIKH MITHOO, Follower, 14th Sikhs, 23 Jun 1915 (Manara Indian Muhammadan Cemetery)

SHER BAZ, Dvr 1434, Mule Corps, 15 Jun 1915

SHER JANG, Dvr 837, 21st Kohat Battery, 8 Jul 1915, of Dhok Ranjha, Chakwal, Jhelum, Punjab

SHER KHAN, Gnr 774, 21st Kohat Battery, 27 Apr 1915, of Mattaur, Kahuta, Rawalpindi, Punjab

SHER SINGH, Naik 3102, 14th Sikhs, 23 Aug 1915, of Dosanjh, Moga, Ferozepore, Punjab

SHER SINGH, Sepoy 3163, 14th Sikhs, 23 May 1915, of Ludbanjara, Dhode, Patiala, Punjab

SHER SINGH, Sepoy 4617, 14th Sikhs, 12 Jul 1915, of Faggu, Sarsa, Hissar, Punjab

SHER ZAMAN, Dvr 1416, Mule Corps, 15 Jun 1915, of Shahder, Campbellpore, Attock, Punjab

SHER ZAMAN, Follower, 26th Jacob's Mountain Battery, 15 Jun 1915

SHERBAHADUR GURUNG, Jem. 1/5th GR, 1 Jul 1915, of Maranis, Parvat, Palpa, Nepal

SHERBAHADUR GURUNG, Rfmn 539, 1/6th GR, 9 Aug 1915, of Parbang, No.3 West, Tanhu, Nepal

SHERBAHADUR GURUNG, L/Nk 2961, 1/4th GR, 17 Oct 1915, of Tilgeni, Piuthan, Nepal

SHERBAHADUR THAPA, Rfmn 1115, 1/6th GR, 2 May 1915, of Bhargaun, Palpa, Parvat, Nepal

SHERSING CHETTRI, Havildar 664, 2/10th GR, 8 Aug 1915, of Gangkote, Tallosorad, Siliguri, Nepal

SHERSING THAPA, Havildar 370, 2/10th GR, 7 Aug 1915, of Mar, Almora, United Provinces

SHIAMDHOJ RAI, Rfmn 691, 2/10th GR, 28 Jun 1915, of Hangpabong, Chethar, Dhankuta, Nepal

SHUTTLEWORTH, Maj. Robert George, 110th Mahratta Light Infantry att 9th Bn, Royal Warwickshire Regiment, 10 Aug 1915, of Ewell, Surrey, England

SINGBAHADUR LIMBU, Rfmn 3538, 2/10th GR, 19 Sep 1915, of Parwadin, Chhathar, Dhankuta, Nepal

SINGBIR THAPA, L/Nk 506, 1/6th GR, 11 Nov 1915, of Besanga, Palpa, Nepal

SINGDHOJ GURUNG, Rfmn 1195, 2/10th GR, 19 Sep 1915, of Madi, Dhankuta, Nepal

SINGDHOJ LIMBU, Rfmn 2792, 2/10th GR, 27 Sep 1915, of Chaubisya, Dhankuta, Nepal

SIRDHOJ RAI, Rfmn 3314, 2/10th GR, 28 Jun 1915, of Semkharka, Songdel, No.3 East, Nepal

SIRIDHOJ LIMBU, Rfmn 3136, 2/10th GR, 19 Sep 1915, of Amko, Phedap, Dhankuta, Nepal

SIRIMAN THAPA, Rfmn 826, 1/6th GR, 30 Jun 1915, of Ramkote, No.3 West, Tanhu, Nepal

SOBHA SINGH, Sepoy 4300, 14th Sikhs, 4 Jun 1915, of Budh Singh Wala, Moga, Ferozepore, Punjab

SOHNA SINGH, Sepoy 3066, 14th Sikhs, 4 Jun 1915, of Fatehgarh, Dhanaula, Nabha, Punjab

SOHNA SINGH, Sepoy 4218, 14th Sikhs, 5 Jun 1915, of Sahaur, Ludhiana, Punjab

SPANKIE, Lt Montague Doulas, 14th Sikhs, 14 May 1915, of London, England (Pink Farm Cemetery, Helles)

SRIJANG RAI, Rfmn 220, 2/10th GR, 28 Aug 1915, of Sanodungma, Bhojpore, Nepal

SRIKISHOR RAI, Rfmn 220, 2/10th GR, 29 Jun 1915, of Necha, Chisankhu, Okhaldhunga, Nepal

SRIMAN RAI, Rfmn 1091, 2/10th GR, 19 Sep 1915, of Didung, Chainpore, Dhankuta, Nepal

SRIPAL LIMBU, Rfmn 2109, 2/10th GR, 7 Aug 1915, of Tembe, Mewakhola, Dhankuta, Nepal

STEVENSON, Capt, Harry Burnett, 2nd Queen Victoria's Own Rajput Light Infantry att 2/10th GR, 6 Aug 1915, of Christchurch, Hampshire, Britain

SUCHA SINGH, Dvr 1706, 21st Kohat Battery, 13 Aug 1915

SUCHA SINGH, Sepoy 2330, 14th Sikhs, 12 Nov 1915, of Barnala, Patiala, Punjab

SUCHA SINGH, Sepoy 4098, 14th Sikhs, 4 Jun 1915, of Gumti, Dhuri, Patiala, Punjab

SUCHA SINGH, Sepoy 4521, 14th Sikhs, 4 Jun 1915, of Makha, Sirsa, Hissar, Punjab

SUKAMBAR GURUNG, Rfmn 4858, 1/5th GR, 4 Jun 1915, of Barahpani, No.3 West, Rising, Nepal

SUKBAHADUR PUN, Rfmn 4586, 1/5th GR, 3 Sep 1915, of Kolo, Baglung, Charhung, Nepal

SUKH LAL, Follower, ABC, 108th Field Amb, 13 May 1915

SUKHA SINGH, Sepoy 4538, 14th Sikhs, 4 Jun 1915, of Mastura, Hangu, Kohat, NWF Province

SUKHAN SINGH, Rfmn 4854, 1/4th GR, 3 Oct 1915, of Pyapung, Phedap, Dhankuta, Nepal

SUKHI, Bearer 6457, ABC, 137th Field Amb, 30 Dec 1915, of Matmara, Chawk, Bareilly, United Provinces

SUKHMAN LAMA, Rfmn 1117, 2/10th GR, 19 Sep 1915, of Ibum, Charkhola, Ramechhap, Nepal

SUKLALGURUNG, Rfmn 3699, 1/5th GR, 7 Aug 1915, of Pawa, No.3 West, Dhor, Nepal

SULTAN KHAN, Gnr 565, 21st Kohat Battery, 1 Jun 1915, of Khumbi, Kharian, Gujrat, Punjab

SULTAN MUHAMMAD, Dvr 645, Mule Corps, 16 Nov 1915, of Sahal, Gujar Khan, Rawalpindi, Punjab

SUNBIR GURUNG, Rfmn 4537, 1/5th GR, 2 Jul 1915, of Bachha, No.5 West, Payung, Nepal

SUNDAR SINGH, Gnr 151, 21st Kohat Battery, 20 May 1915, of Barnala, Patiala, Punjab

SUNDAR SINGH, Sepoy 224, Patiala Infantry att 14th Sikhs, 22 Aug 1915, of Mithewal, Malerkotla, Punjab

SUNDAR SINGH, Naik 393, 21st Kohat Battery, 26 May 1915, of Ramgarh, Samrala, Ludhiana, Punjab

SUNDAR SINGH, Sepoy 499, Patiala Infantry att 14th Sikhs, 1 Dec 1915, of Dhaulmajra, Ludhiana, Punjab

SUNDAR SINGH, Sepoy 948, 45th Rattray's Sikhs att 14th Sikhs, 28 Aug 1915, of Chak No.30, Lyallpore, Lyallpore, Punjab

SUNDAR SINGH, Sepoy 2684, 14th Sikhs, 4 Jun 1915, of Nim Ghanaur, Kotla, Ludhiana, Punjab

SUNDAR SINGH, Naik 2976, 14th Sikhs, 4 Jun 1915, of Gill, Dhanaula, Nabha, Punjab

SUNDAR SINGH, Sepoy 3548, 14th Sikhs, 31 May 1915, of Fatehpuri, Tohana, Hissar, Punjab

SUNDAR SINGH, Sepoy 4254, 14th Sikhs, 4 Jun 1915, of Khokhar, Barnala, Patiala, Punjab

SUNDAR SINGH, Sepoy 4312, 14th Sikhs, 4 Jun 1915, of Ghudda, Bhatinda, Patiala, Punjab

SUNDAR SINGH, Sepoy 4612, 14th Sikhs, 2 Jul 1915, of Mandurian, Alzai, Kohat, NWF Province

SURABIR RAI, Rfmn 1225, 2/10th GR, 19 Sep 1915, of Apsora, Chisankhu, Okhaldhunga, Nepal

SURJAMAN RAI, Rfmn 3535, 2/10th GR, 19 Sep 1915, of Nathuwa, Chainpore, Dhankuta, Nepal

SURJAN SINGH, Sepoy 4469, 14th Sikhs, 5 Jun 1915, of Kube, Pail, Patiala, Punjab

SWINLEY, Maj. George Dighton Probyn, 14th Sikhs, 14 May 1915, of CheLtenham, Worcestershire, England (Pink Farm Cemetery, Helles)

TAKBIR PUN, Rfmn 3916, 1/5th GR, 4 Jun 1915, of Dobha, Palpa, Parvat, Nepal

TARA SINGH, Follower, 21st Kohat Battery, 14 May 1915, of Burjlittan, Ludhiana, Ludhiana, Punjab

TARABIR LIMBU, Rfmn 554, 2/10th GR, 7 Aug 1915, of Nangi, Chaubisya, Dhankuta, Nepal

TAUKE LIMBU, Rfmn 630, 2/10th GR, 10 Aug 1915, of Nalibo, Mewakhola, Dhankuta, Nepal

TEJA SINGH, Sepoy 794, 14th Sikhs, 19 Sep 1915, of Gagobowah, Lahorimal, Amritsar, Punjab

TEJA SINGH, Sepoy 1900, 89th Punjabis, 7 May 1915, of Balaschandra, Amritsar, Punjab

TEJANJE LIMBU, Sub. 2/10th GR, 28 Jun 1915, of Wokokma, Mewakhola, Dhankuta, Nepal

TEKABIR RAI, Rfmn 184, 1/5th GR, 13 Jan 1916, of Ralanchha, Bhojpore, Nepal

TEKAN RANA, Havildar 3711, 1/5th GR, 8 Aug 1915, of Rupakhara, No.4 West, Garhung, Nepal

TEKBAHADUR ALE, Rfmn 4018, 1/5th GR, 4 Jun 1915, of Tarb, Nawakote, Bhirkote, Nepal

TEKBAHADUR GURUNG, Rfmn 1187, 1/6th GR, 30 Jun 1915, of Malagiri, No.4 West, Nawakote, Nepal

TEKBIR LIMBU, Rfmn 556, 2/10th GR, 7 Aug 1915, of Purjan, Phedap, Dhankuta, Nepal

THAKAR SINGH, Sepoy 1463, 14th Sikhs, 19 Sep 1915, of Ghanieke, Dehrananak, Gurdaspore, Punjab

THAKUR SINGH, Sepoy 612, 45th Rattray's Sikhs att 14th Sikhs, 3 Jul 1915, of Gharnan, Sirhind, Patiala, Punjab

THAKURA SINGH, Havildar 2902, 14th Sikhs, 14 May 1915, of Bilai, Barnala, Patiala, Punjab

THALBIR PUN, Rfmn 795, 1/6th GR, 9 Aug 1915, of Kura, Palpa, Gulmi, Nepal

THAMAN SINGH, Bugler, 78, Patiala Infantry att 14th Sikhs, 27 Aug 1915, of Gubrra, Amargarh, Sunam, Patiala, Punjab

THAPA LIMBU, Rfmn 297, 2/10th GR, 30 Jun 1915, of Songsabo, Tamarkhola, Dhankuta, Nepal

TIKARAM RAI, Rfmn 1157, AMP att 1/4th GR, 17 Sep 1915, of Termunj, Bhojpore, Nepal

TIKARAM SUNWAR, Rfmn 848, 2/10th GR, 20 Aug 1915, of Hangpaboom, Mewakhola, Dhankuta, Nepal

TIKARAM THAPA, Naik 4862, 1/6th GR, 13 May 1915, of Arjun, Palpa, Argha, Nepal

TIKOBIR RAI, Rfmn 184, 1/5th GR, 13 Jan 1916, of Ratchunda, No. 4 East, Nepal (Heliopolis (Port Tewfik) Memorial, Egypt)

TILAKSING THAPA, Rfmn 487, 1/6th GR, 8 Aug 1915, of Majakote, Tansing, Palpa, Nepal

TILBIR THAPA, Rfmn 4817, 1/5th GR, 4 Jun 1915, of Mukal, Palpa, Nepal

TILCHAND RANA, Rfmn 2792, 1/5th GR, 7 Aug 1915, of Jaskun, Palpa, Nepal

TILOK SINGH, Bearer 4537, ABC, 108th Field Amb, 8 Aug 1915, of Akhandi, Pauri, Garhwal, United Provinces

TILOK SINGH, Sepoy 4451, 14th Sikhs, 22 Jun 1915, of Manakpore, Kharar, Ambala, Punjab

TILOKSING LIMBU, Havildar 1579, 2/10th GR, 19 Sep 1915, of Ilamke, Mewakhola, Dhankuta, Nepal

TIRTHAMAN RAI, Rfmn 2730, 2/10th GR, 7 Aug 1915, of Gaudani, Bangdel, Okhaldhunga, Nepal

TIRTHASOR RAI, Rfmn 3542, 2/10th GR, 19 Sep 1915, of Baspani, Rawakhola, Okhaldhunga, Nepal

TOMES, Capt, Geoffrey, 53rd Sikhs att 1/6th GR, 10 Aug 1915

TOTA SINGH, Jem. Patiala Infantry, att 14th Sikhs, 21 Aug 1915

TOTA SINGH, Jem. Patiala Infantry, 21 Aug 1915, of Rampora, Phul, Nabha, Punjab (Heliopolis (Port Tewfik) Memorial, Egypt)

TULARAM BURA, Rfmn 3861, 1/5th GR, 10 Aug 1915, of Mehal, Ismr, Gulmi, Nepal

TULARAM GURUNG, Rfmn 4323, 1/5th GR, 21 Aug 1915, of Bhiagote, No.3 West, Tanhu, Nepal

TULARAM THAPA, Naik 303, 2/10th GR, 7 Aug 1915, of Batera, Kangra, Punjab

TULASING THAPA, Rfmn 72, 1/6th GR, 22 May 1915, of Lunga, Khalanga, Piuthan, Nepal

TULLA SINGH, Sepoy 642, Patiala Infantry att 14th Sikhs, 8 Aug 1915, of Bhanri, Patiala, Punjab

TULMAN RAI, Rfmn 746, 2/10th GR, 7 Aug 1915, of Deosa, Okhaldhunga, Nepal

TULSA SINGH, Sepoy 1292, 69th Punjabis, 10 May 1915, of Bhagowal, Kharar, Ambala, Punjab

TULSI, Follower, 37, 2/10th GR, 29 Oct 1915, of Chauwakh, Ghauwakh, Jaunpore, United Provinces

TULSIRAM THAPA, Naik 4086, 1/5th GR, 7 Aug 1915, of Kosbari, Palpa, Nepal

TULUDHMAN RAI, Rfmn 646, 2/10th GR, 9 Aug 1915, of Sungdel, Rawakhola, Okhaldhunga, Nepal

TURNER, Capt. Gerald, 1/5th GR, 4 Jun 1915 (Pink Farm Cemetery, Helles)

UDAIBAHADUR LIMBU, Rfmn 3109, 2/10th GR, 19 Sep 1915, of Samite, Chaubisya, Dhankuta, Nepal

UDHE RAM, Bearer 4404, ABC, 108th Field Amb, 15 Jun 1915, of Aroli, Pauri, Garhwal, United Provinces

UDHE SINGH, Bearer 4607, ABC, 108th Field Amb, 15 Jun 1915, of Guilana, Pauri, Garhwal, United Provinces

UJAGAR SINGH, L/Nk 1403, 14th Sikhs, 19 Sep 1915, of Bhakhana, Thekriwala, Lyallpore, Punjab

UJIRSING GURUNG, Rfmn 1172, 1/6th GR, 9 Aug 1915, of Tholi, Dailekh, Nepal

UMRAO, Bearer 6463, ABC, 137th Field Amb, 1 May 1915, of Janspore, Jelalabad, Shahjahanpore, United Provinces

UMRAO SINGH, Bearer 4605, ABC, 108th Field Amb, 30 Dec 1915, of Gaydi, Pauri, Garhwal, United Provinces

UNDERHILL, Second Lt Hugh, IARO, att 1/6th GR, 8 Aug 1915

UNGER, Second Lt Michael, IARO, att 14th Sikhs, 20 Sep 1915

UTTAM SINGH, Sepoy 481, Patiala Infantry att 14th Sikhs, 8 Aug 1915, of Jandpore, Kharar, Ambala, Punjab

UTTAM SINGH, Sepoy 2993, 14th Sikhs, 14 May 1915, of Ghanauli, Ropar, Ambala, Punjab

UTTAM SINGH, Naik 3431, 14th Sikhs, 4 Jun 1915, of Kokribari, Moga, Ferozepore, Punjab

UTTAM SINGH, Sepoy 4140, 14th Sikhs, 4 Jun 1915, of Pamal, Ludhiana, Punjab

UTTAM SINGH, Sepoy 4145, 14th Sikhs, 4 Jun 1915, of Sehna, Ludhiana, Punjab

UTTAM SINGH, Sepoy 4553, 14th Sikhs, 4 Jun 1915, of Ditarpore, Ropar, Ambala, Punjab

UTTAMSING CHETTRI, Lance Havildar 46, 2/10th GR, 19 Sep 1915, of Neansi, Pithoragarh, Almora, United Provinces

VILLIERS-STUART, Maj. Charles, 56th Punjab Rifles/ANZAC HQ, 17 May 1915, of Castleton, Carrick-on-Suir, India (Beach Cemetery, Anzac)

WADHAWA SINGH, Sepoy 725, 45th Rattray's Sikhs att 14th Sikhs, 14 May 1915, of Dasuwal, Kasur, Lahore, Punjab

WALAYAT KHAN, Dvr 1956, Mule Corps, 19 Sep 1915, of Baran, Suddan Hotel, Poonch, Punjab

WALI MUHAMMAD, Dvr 1717, 26th Jacob's Battery, 19 Sep 1915, of Katha, Khushab, Shahpore, Punjab

WARIS, Dvr 476, Mule Corps, 21 Aug 1915

WARIS ALI, Dvr 2069, Mule Corps, 26 May 1915

WARYAM SINGH, Naik 3581, 14th Sikhs, 4 Jun 1915, of Butari, Ludhiana, Punjab

WAZIR, Follower, 804, S&T Corps, 19 Sep 1915

WAZIR KHAN, Dvr 819, Mule Corps, 15 Oct 1915, of Karkhana, Secunderabad, Madras

WAZIRSING GURUNG, Naik 4348, 1/5th GR, 7 Aug 1915, of Bhoksing, Kham, Payung, Nepal

WHITFIELD, Second Lt Gilbert, IARO att 14th Sikhs, 8 Aug 1915

WILMER, Maj. Harold, 14th Sikhs, 5 Jul 1915

WYTEHEAD, Capt. Hugh Richard Augustin, 1/6th GR, 22 May 1915, of York, Yorkshire, England (Twelve Trees Copse Cemetery, Helles)

YAKUB, Naik 1357, Mule Corps, 3 Dec 1915, of Jhubba, Mansera, Hazara, Punjab

YESHWANT NARAYAN DEUSKAR, Sub-Asst, Surgeon, (2nd Class), 322, Indian Medical Department, 2 Sep 1915, of Godhra, Panch Mahals, Gujarat, Bombay

ZORA SINGH, Naik 108, Patiala Infantry att 14th Sikhs, 8 Aug 1915, of Adampore, Dhanaula, Nabha, Punjab

Sources

ABBREVIATIONS

ADFA	Australian Defence Force Academy, Canberra
ANZ	Archives New Zealand, Wellington
ATL	Alexander Turnbull Library, Wellington
AWM	Australian War Memorial, Canberra
BL	British Library, London
CWGC	Commonwealth War Graves Commission, Maidenhead
GM	Gurkha Museum, Winchester
IWM	Imperial War Museums, London
LHCMA	Liddell Hart Centre for Military Archives, University College London
ML	Mitchell Library, Sydney
NAA	National Archives of Australia, Canberra
NAI	National Archives of India, New Delhi
NAM	National Army Museum, London
NAUK	National Archives (United Kingdom), London[1]
PLC	Peter Liddle Collection, Brotherton Library, University of Leeds
QEIIAMM	Queen Elizabeth II Army Memorial Museum, Waiourou
SLNSW	State Library of New South Wales, Sydney
SLV	State Library of Victoria, Melbourne

---

1 I refuse to abet or countenance the arrogance of the British National Archives, which has the effrontery to insist on calling itself '*The* National Archives (TNA)', as if no other nation had one.

ARCHIVAL

Australia

Australian Defence Force Academy, Special Collections
MS21, Papers of George MacMunn

Australian War Memorial, Canberra
AWM 4
    1/4, General Staff, General Headquarters, MEF
    1/17, War diary, General Staff, Headquarters, Dardanelles Army
    9/1, War diary, 29th Indian Infantry Brigade
    26/3/1, War diary, Director of Medical Services, MEF
AWM 6
    182-85, War diaries, 7th Indian Mountain Artillery Brigade
    186-87, War diary, 29th Indian Infantry Brigade
    188, War diary, 1/4th Gurkha Rifles
    189-90, War diaries, Indian Mule Cart Train
AWM 25
    399/7, 'Australians at No. 5 Indian General Hospital'
AWM 27
    370/3 [medical lecture 108th Field Ambulance]
AWM 38
    Diaries of Charles Bean, Australian official correspondent
AWM 51
    Dardanelles Commission; Statements and Evidence
AWM 140
    Official Historian's biographical cards

Private records
PR88/96, Sgt Fred Aspinall, 1st Signal Squadron, AIF
PR462, LCpl Octavius Carr, 1st Field Ambulance, AIF
1DRL203, Pte Frank Coen, 18th Battalion, AIF
1DRL221, Maj-Gen Herbert Cox, 29th Indian Infantry Brigade
MS1825, Pte Septimus Elmore, 6th Field Ambulance, AIF
3DRL3635, Maj Arthur Fergusson, 'Gallipoli 1915'
PR91/005, Pte Philip Harrison, 16th Battalion, AIF
PR360, Pte Vyner Jones, 1st Battalion, AIF
1DRL454, Sgt John McLennan, 5th Battalion, AIF
1DRL513 Lt Walter Morrice, 1st Light Horse Regiment, AIF
MSS0863, Cpl Henry Taylor, 17th Battalion, AIF

Mitchell Library, State Library of New South Wales
MLMSS 1493/Box 1, Archie Barwick
PXE 702 Leslie Hore, 'Sketches at Gallipoli, 1915'

National Archives of Australia, Canberra
A11803 Governor-General's correspondence
A11804 Governor-General's correspondence
B2455 AIF personnel files

National Library of Australia
Newspapers

State Library of Victoria
Photographs

India

United Services Institution of India, New Delhi
Books and periodicals
14th Sikhs albums (in the possession of 4th Mechanised Battalion, Indian Army)

Jawaharlal Nehru Library, New Delhi
   Newspapers

National Archives of India
Military Department, War Branch
   WWI/145/H-154/H, General War Diary, Army Headquarters, India, Vols 15-24, 1915
   WWI/286/H- 300/H, War Diary, Army Headquarters, India, Indian Expeditionary Force 'E', Vols 1-15, 1914-16
   WWI/333/H-338/H, War Diary, Army Headquarters, Indian Expeditionary Forces 'E' & 'G', Vols 13-18, 1915-16
   WWI/342/H-348/H, Casualty Appendix to War Diary, Indian Expeditionary Force 'G', Vols 1-7, 1915
   WWI/429/H-430/H, War Diary, Army Headquarters, India, Indian Mediterranean Expeditionary Force, Vols 1-2, 1915
Index to Army Department Proceedings, War 1914-1915
Foreign & Political Department
   Proceedings
   Deposits

New Zealand

Alexander Turnbull Library, Wellington
MS-Papers-2299, George Donovan
MS-Papers-1676-1, Frank Cooper

Kippenberger Military Archive, Queen Elizabeth II Army Memorial Museum, Waiouru
B1989.199, John Atkins
2003.409, Keith Little

Nga Taonga (New Zealand Archive of Film, Television and Sound) Wellington
16406, Frederick Wilson
27620, Alexander Fraser & Lazzell Davidson

United Kingdom

British Library, London
L/MIL series including war diaries, Indian Army Headquarters and reports from Force G
L/MIL/7/18921 (Collection 425/1673) 'Appreciation of assistance rendered to Australian Medical Corps by Indian ambulance men in Gallipoli'
L/MIL/L/7/5/2401, Col. Sir Bruce Seton, 'An analysis of 1000 wounds and injuries received in action', 1915

Gurkha Museum, Winchester
2-10th Gurkhas, Digest of Service 1908-1927
Research files
    Ops/137, Mihir Bose, 'Why were the heroic Gurkhas forgotten?', *Daily Telegraph*, 23 April 2005
    6GR/301-304 Cecil Allanson papers
    6GR/314 Papers relating to the death of Lt John Le Marchand
    6GR/324 Four photographs relating to Sari Bair
    'British Gurkha recruiting in Nepal: Notes on Gurkha recruitment, 1914'

Imperial War Museum, London
18517; 14/15/1, Maj Leonard Abbott, 11th Rajputs
15793; 07/12/1, Captain A.W. Bird, Hampshire Regiment
14940; 06/33/1 Lt Bartle Bradshaw, Border Regiment
797; 99/4/1, Pte Denis Buxton, Royal Army Medical Corps
16463; 08/94/1, Lt Noel Crosby, 1/5th Gurkha Rifles
584; 04/37/1, Captain W.B.S. Deverell, Army Service Corps
799; 9/10/1, Lt Patrick Duff, Royal Artillery

10048; P158, Captain Humphrey Gell, 29th Indian Infantry Brigade
11617; 01/45/1 2nd Lt Angus McCracken, Royal Artillery
P399, 9984, Lt A.M. McGrigor, Royal Gloucestershire Hussars
5537; 96/29/1, Sgt John McIlwain, Connaught Rangers
21088; 76/175/A, Captain Edward Phipson, 1/6th Gurkha Rifles
7884; 98/24/1, Captain Noel Tattersall, Royal Army Medical Corps
584; 88/56/1, Captain Aubrey Williams, South Wales Borderers
13305; 05/9/1, Pte Thomas Wilson, Royal Naval Division
6508; 97/18/1, Lt Herbert Winn, 1/5th Gurkha Rifles

Liddell Hart Centre for Military Archives, London
Ian Hamilton Papers
Alexander Godley Papers
John North Papers
Patrick Donlea Papers

National Archives, London
CAB42/3/11, Dardanelles Committee – effect on Indian opinion of withdrawal from Gallipoli
CAB45/259, Diary of Captain Clement Milward, 29th Division, 1915[2]
PRO30/57, Kitchener Papers
WO33/796, Dispatches from Lieutenant-General Sir J.G. Maxwell, February-August 1915
WO 95, Mediterranean Expeditionary Force unit war diaries
WO95/4264, General Headquarters, Mediterranean Expeditionary Force, 1915
WO95/4272, 29th Indian Infantry Brigade, 1914-16
WO95/4279, 137th Indian Combined Field Ambulance
WO95/4289, 7th Indian Mountain Artillery Brigade, 1914-16
WO95/4358, Headquarters Mule Cart Corps, 1915
WO95/4385, DAAG (Indian troops) Egypt, 1915
WO95/4423, Patiala Infantry, 1914-16
WO95/4954, Graves Registration Unit (Gallipoli), 1918-19
WO95/5474, Troops in Egypt from December 1914
WO162/72, 'Progress report on state of preparations for Dardanelles Winter campaign'

National Army Museum, London
6602-22, Allanson Papers
7603-93, Savory Papers
7407-138, Swinley Papers

---

2   This diary is wrongly described as being the diary of Captain C.A. Milnard

Liddle Collection, Brotherton Library, Leeds
Typescript recollection by Raymond Baker, Baker, Canterbury Infantry Battalion
Diary, William Malone, Wellington Infantry Battalion
Interview with Justin Westernra, Otago Mounted Rifles

Manuscripts in private hands

The Bowler papers (Murray & Elizabeth Bowler, Auckland, New Zealand)
David Cloughley, (ed.), 'The Riverton Boys' (Glenda Cloughley, Canberra)
Diary of Lt Edward King, 3rd Field Company, AIF (Terry King, Ipswich, Queensland)
Archives of His Highness the Maharaja of Patiala
History of Patiala State Forces, Part III and Album of Photos by Colonel G.S. Harika
Letters and photographs relating to Maj. Harold Wilmer (Anto O'Brien, Dublin, Ireland)

SELECTED PUBLISHED WORKS

Official Histories

Cyril Aspinall-Oglander, *Military Operations: Gallipoli*, 2 Vols, William Heinemann, London, 1929, 1932
Charles Bean, *The Story of Anzac*, 2 Vols, Angus & Robertson (Sydney: 1921 & 1922).
George MacMunn & Cyril Falls, *Military Operations Egypt & Palestine*, Vol. I., *from the outbreak of War with Germany to June 1917*, (HMSO: London, 1928).
Turkish General Staff, *A Brief History of the Çanakkale Campaign in the First World War*, Turkish General Staff Printing House (Ankara, 2004).
Fred Waite, *The New Zealanders at Gallipoli* (Auckland:Whitcombe and Tombs, 1921).

Unit Histories

Anon, *Record of the 5th (Service) Battalion The Connaught Rangers* (Privately printed, 1916).
Anon [Regimental Committee], *History of the 5th Royal Gurkha Rifles (Frontier Force) 1858-1928* (Aldershot: Gale & Polden, [1928?]).
C.T. Atkinson, *The History of the South Wales Borderers 1914-1918*, (London: Medici Society, 1931).
P.G. Bamford, *1st King George's Own Battalion, The Sikh Regiment* (Aldershot: Gale & Polden, 1948).
Walter Belford, *"Legs Eleven" Being the Story of the 11th Battalion (A.I.F.) in the Great War of 1914-1918* (Perth: Imperial Printing Company, 1940).
Bryan Cooper, *The Tenth (Irish) Division in Gallipoli* (London: Herbert Jenkins, 1918).

C.A.L. Graham, *The History of the Indian Mountain Artillery* (Aldershot: Gale & Polden, 1957).
Richard Head & Tony McClenaghan, *The Maharajas' Paltans: A History of the Indian State Forces 1888-1948* (USI/Manohar, 2013).
James Lunt, *Jai Sixth!: the Story of the 6th Queen Elizabeth's Own Gurkha Rifles, 1817-1994* (London: Leo Cooper, 1994).
Ronald Macdonell & Marcus Macaulay, *A History of the 4th Prince of Wales's Own Gurkha Rifles*, (Edinburgh: Blackwood, 1940).
Charles MacFetridge & Pat Warren, (eds), *Tales of the Mountain Gunners*, William (Edinburgh: Blackwood, 1973
R.M. Maxwell, *Desperate Encounters: Stories of the 5th Royal Gurkha Rifles (Frontier Force)* (Edinburgh: Douglas Law, 1986).
B.R. Mullaly, *Bugle and Kukri: the Story of the 10th Princess Mary's Own Gurkha Rifles*, (Edinburgh: William Blackwood, 1957).
D.G. Ryan, G.C. Strahan & J.K. Jones, *Historical Record of the 6th Gurkha Rifles*, Vol. 1. (Privately published, 1925).
F.E.G. Talbot, *The 14th King George's Own Sikhs 1846-1933* (London: RUSI, 1937).

Official Documents

Anon, *District and State Gazetteers of the Undivided Punjab*, Vol. III (Delhi: BR Publishing, 1985).
Army Headquarters, India, *Army Tables of a Battalion of Indian Infantry*, (Calcutta: Government of India Army Department, 1909).
——, *Military Handbook of General Information on India* (Simla: Government Monotype Press, 1908).
Army Department, India, *The Quarterly Indian Army List, January 1915* (Calcutta: Government Printers, 1915).
A.H. Bingley, *Sikhs: Their Origin, History, Religion, Customs, Fairs and Festivals* [1910] (New Dehli: Sumit Publications, 1984).
Government of India, Military Account Code, Government of India, Calcutta, 1896
——, *India's Contribution to the Great War*, (Calcutta: Superintendent of Government Printing, 1923).
His Majesty's Stationery Office, *London Gazette*, 1915-16
Imperial War Graves Commission, *The War Graves of the British Empire: The Register of the Names of Those who Fell in the Great War ... Hill 60 Cemetery* (London: Imperial War Graves Commission, 1925).
M.S. Leigh, *The Punjab and the War* (Lahore: Superintendent of Government Printing, 1922).
Proceedings of the Army in India Committee, 1912, Vol. II, Minutes of Evidence, (Simla, Government Central Branch Press, 1913).

Report of the Committee appointed by the Secretary of State for India on the Administration and Organization of the Army in India (Simla: Government of India, 1920).
War Office, *Field Service Regulations* (London: HMSO, 1911).
J.M. Wikeley, *Handbooks for the Indian Army: Punjabi Musalmans* (Simla: Superintendent of Government Printing, 1915).

Contemporary Published Works

H.M. Alexander, *On Two Fronts: Being the Adventures of an Indian Mule Corps in France and Gallipoli*, William (London: Heinemann, 1917).
Copy of the personal diary kept in the field by Lieut-Colonel Cecil Allanson, (Privately published, 1917).
Anon, *Patiala and the Great War: A Brief History of the Services of the Premier Punjab State* (London: Medici Society, 1923).
Anon, *Uncensored Letters from the Dardanelles* (London: William Heinemann, 1916).
A.E. Barstow, *Handbook on Sikhs* [1928] (New Dehli: Uppal Publishing House, 1989).
Ellis Ashmead-Bartlett, *Ashmead-Bartlett's Despatches from the Dardanelles* (London: George Newnes, 1915).
——, *The Uncensored Dardanelles* (London: Hutchinson & Co., 1928).
Joseph Beeston, *Five Months at Anzac* (Sydney: Angus & Robertson, 1916).
Birdwood of Anzac and Totnes, *Khaki and Gown: an Autobiography*, (London: Ward, Lock & Co., 1941).
——, *In My Time* (London: Skeffington & Son, 1945).
P.D. Bonarjee, *A Handbook to the Fighting Races of India*, Thacker (Calcutta: Spink & Co., 1899).
C.G. Bruce, *Himalayan Wanderer*, (London: Alexander Maclehose, 1934).
Charles Callwell, (ed.), *The Autobiography of General Sir O'Moore Creagh*, (London: Hutchinson & Co., ND).
——, *Small Wars: their Principles and Practice* (London: HMSO, 1906).
Edmund Candler, *The Sepoy* (London: John Murray,1919).
Valentine Chirol, *Indian Unrest* (London: Macmillan & Co., 1910).
Raymond Coker, *Incidents from a Soldier's Life* (Adelaide: Barrington Levy, [1921]).
W.R.G. Colman, (ed. Claire Woods & Paul Skrebels), *There and Back with a Dinkum* (Melbourne: Australian Scholarly Publishing, 2013).
O'Moore Creagh, *Indian Studies* (London: Hutchinson, 1919).
F.M. Cutlack, (ed.), *War Letters of General Monash* (Sydney: Angus & Robertson, 1934).
Edmund Dane, *British Campaigns in the Nearer East 1914-1918* [sic] (London: Hodder & Stoughton, 1917).
James Douie, *The Panjab, North-West Frontier Province and Kashmir*, (Cambridge: Cambridge University Press, 1916).
P.G. Elgood, *Egypt and the Army* (Oxford: Oxford University Press, 1924).

William Ewing, *From Gallipoli to Baghdad* (London: Hodder & Stoughton, 1917).
Frederick Gibbon, *The 42nd (East Lancashire) Division 1914-1918* (London: Country Life, 1920).
Ian Hamilton, *Gallipoli Diary*, 2 Vols (London: Edward Arnold, 1920).
——, *Listening for the Drums* (London: Faber & Faber, 1944).
Lord Hardinge of Penshurst, *My Indian Years 1910-1916* (London: John Murray, 1948).
John Hargrave, *At Suvla Bay* (London: Constable & Co., 1916).
Reginald Hodder, *Famous Fights of Indian Native Regiments* (London:Hodder & Stoughton, 1914).
P.P. Hypher, *Deeds of Valour Performed by Indian Officers and Soldiers During the Period from 1860 to 1925* (Simla: Liddell's Press, 1927).
Imperial War Graves Commission, *The War Graves of the British Empire: The Register of the Names of Those who Fell in the Great War ... Hill 60 Cemetery* (London: Imperial War Graves Commission, 1925).
——, *The Helles Memorial*, Gallipoli (London: Imperial War Graves Commission, 1927).
——, *The Helles Memorial Register* (London: Imperial War Graves Commission, 1929).
Dennis Jones, *Diary of a Padre at Suvla Bay*, (London: The Faith Press [1916]).
H.M. Leapman, 'Organisation in the field in France and Gallipoli', *Journal of the United Service Institute of India*, Vol. XLVI, 1917, pp. 127-36
M.S. Leigh, *The Punjab and the War* (Lahore: Superintendent of Government Printing, 1922).
Charles Lucas, *The Empire at War*, Vol. V, Humphrey (London: Milford/Oxford University Press, 1926).
R.F. Lushington, *A Prisoner with the Turks 1915-1918* (Bedford: F.R. Hockliffe, 1923).
Compton Mackenzie, *Gallipoli Memories* (London: Cassell & Co., 1929).
George MacMunn, *The Indian States and Princes* (London: Jarrolds, 1936).
——, *The Armies of India* (London: Adam & Charles Black, 1911).
——, *The Martial Races of India* (Marston: Sampson Low, 1932).
William Marshall, *Memories of Four Fronts* (London: Ernest Benn, 1929).
John Masefield, *Gallipoli* (London: William Heinemann, 1917).
Tim Moreman, *The Army in India and the Development of Frontier Warfare, 1849-1947* (Basinstoke: Macmillan, 1998).
L. McCustra, *Gallipoli Days and Nights* (London: Hodder & Stoughton, 1916).
A.H. Mure, *With the Incomparable 29*[th] (London: W&R Chambers, 1919).
Joseph Murray, *Gallipoli 1915* (London: New English Library, 1977).
Jawaharlal Nehru, *An Autobiography* (London: John Lane, 1939).
Henry Nevinson, *The Dardanelles Campaign* (London: Nisbet & Co., 1918).
Michael O'Dwyer, 'India's Man-power in the War', *Army Quarterly*, Vol. 2, No. 2, July 1921, pp. 249-66
——, *India as I Knew it 1885-1925* (London: Constable and Co., 1925).

J.H. Patterson, *With the Zionists in Gallipoli* (London: Hutchinson, 1916).
Lord Sydenham, *India and the War* (London: Hodder & Stoughton, 1915).
O. Teichman, *The Diary of a Yeomanry M.O.* (London: T. Fisher Unwin, 1921).
C.D. Webster, 'The Supply of Followers on Active Service', *Journal of the United Service Institute of India*, Vol. XLV, Jan-Oct 1916, pp. 272-76

Newspapers and Journals

Amrita Bazaar Patrika (Calcutta) 1915
Pioneer (Allahabad) 1914-15
Civil and Military Gazette (Lahore) 1915
Journal of the United Service Institution of India (Simla) 1912-40
The Jat Gazette (Rohtak) 1915
The Times (London) 1910-25

OTHER SECONDARY WORKS

George Arthur, *General Sir John Maxwell* (London: John Murray, 1932).
George Barrow, *The Life of General Sir Charles Carmichael Monro* (London: Hutchinson, 1931).
Charles Bean, *Gallipoli Mission* [1948] (Sydney: ABC Books, 1990).
Arthur Behrend, *Make me a Soldier* (London: Eyre & Spottiswood, 1961).
Lionel Caplan, *Warrior Gentlemen: 'Gurkhas' in the Western Imagination* (Lalitpur: Himal Books, 2003).
George Cassar, *Kitchener's War: British Strategy from 1914 to 1916* (Washington DC: Brassey's Inc., 2004).
Stephen Chambers, *Gully Ravine* (Barnsley: Pen & Sword, 2003).
——, *Anzac: Sari Bair* (Barnsley: Pen & Sword, 2014).
Rana Chhina, 'Their mercenary calling: the Indian army on Gallipoli, 1915', in Ashley Ekins, (ed.), *Gallipoli: a Ridge Too Far* (Wollombi: Exisle Publishing, 2013).
John Crawford and Peter Cooke, (ed.), *No Better Death: the Great War Diaries and Letters of William G. Malone* (Auckland: Exisle, 2014).
Harry Davies, *Allanson of the 6th* (Worcester: Square One Publications, 1990).
Edward Duyker & Coralie Younger, *Molly and the Rajah: Race Romance and the Raj* (Sydney: Australian Mauritian Press, 1991).
De Witt Ellinwood & S.D. Pradhan, (eds), *India and World War I* (New Delhi: Manohar, 1978).
Edward Erikson, *Ordered to Die: A History of the Ottoman Army in the First World War* (Westport, Connecticut: Greenwood Press, 2001).
Martin Farndale, *History of the Royal Regiment of Artillery*, Vol. II, *The Forgotten Fronts and the Home Base 1914-18* (Woolwich: Royal Artillery Institution, 1988).
Percival Fenwick, *Gallipoli Diary* (Auckland: Auckland Museum, ND).

5th Gurkhas Regimental Association, *Centenary of 5th Royal Gurkha Rifles (Frontier Force) 1858-1958* (London: 1958).
Rajmohan Gandhi, *Punjab: A History from Aurangzeb to Mountbatten* (New Delhi: Aleph, 2013).
John Gillam, *Gallipoli Diary* (Stevenage: Strong Oak Press & Tim Donovan Publishing, 1989).
Tony Gould, *Imperial Warriors: Britain and the Gurkhas* (London: Granta Books, 1999).
Alan Guy and others, *Soldiers of the Raj* (London: National Army Museum, 1997).
Peter Hart, *Gallipoli* (London: Profile Books, 2011).
Robert Rhodes James, *Gallipoli*, (London: Pan Books, 1965).
Raj Kumar, *Military System During the Raj, 1858 to 1947* (Delhi: Commonwealth, 2004).
John Lee, *A Soldier's Life: General Sir Ian Hamilton 1853-1947* (London: Pan Books, 2001).
Ronald Lewin, *The Standardbearer: a Biography of Field Marshal the Viscount Slim*, (London: Leo Cooper, 1976).
Peter Liddle, *Men of Gallipoli* (London: Allen Lane, 1976).
Philip Longworth, *The Unending Vigil: the History of the Commonwealth War Graves Commission* (Barnsley: Leo Cooper, 2007).
Philip Magnus, *Kitchener: Portrait of an Imperialist* (London: John Murray, 1958).
B.N. Majumdar, *History of the Army Service Corps*, Vol. III 1858-1913 (New Delhi: Sterling Publishers, 1976).
Razit Mazumder, *The Indian Army and the Making of Punjab* (New Delhi: Permanent Black, 2003).
Philip Mason, *A Matter of Honour* (London: Jonathan Cape, 1974).
Robert Maxwell, *Villiers-Stuart on the Frontier*, (Edinburgh: The Pentland Press, 1989).
——, *Villiers-Stuart at War* (Edinburgh: The Pentland Press, 1990).
S.L. Menezes, *Fidelity and Honour: The Indian Army from the Seventeenth to the Twenty-first Century* (NewDelhi: Oxford University Press, 1999).
Ministry of Defence, *Nepal and the Gurkhas* (London: HMSO, 1965).
David Omissi, *The Sepoy and the Raj: the Indian Army, 1860-1940* (London: Macmillan, 1994).
——, *Indian Voices of the Great War* (Basingstoke: Palgrave Macmillan, 1999).
——, 'The Indian Army in the First World War, 1914-1918', in Daniel Marston & Chandar Sundaram, (eds), *A Military History of India and South Asia* (Westport, Connecticut: Praeger Security International, 2007).
Peter Pedersen, *Monash as Military Commander* (Melbourne: Melbourne University Press, 1986).
F.W. Perry, *The Commonwealth Armies: Manpower and Organisation in Two World Wars* (Manchester: Manchester University Press, 1988).

——, *Order of Battle of Divisions, Part 5B Indian Army Divisions*, Ray Westlake Military Books, Newport, 1993

Richard Popplewell, *Intelligence and Imperial Defence: British Intelligence and the Defence of the Indian Empire 1904-1924* (London: Frank Cass, 1995).

Robin Prior, *Gallipoli: the End of the Myth* (Sydney: UNSW Press, 2009).

Richard Reid, *Gallipoli 1915* (Sydney: ABC Books, 2002).

John Robertson, *Anzac and Empire: The Tragedy and Glory of Gallipoli* (Melbourne: Hamlyn, 1990).

Kaushik Roy, *Brown Warriors of the Raj: Recruitment and the Mechanics of Command in the Sepoy Army, 1859-1913* (New Delhi: Manohar, 2008).

Shyam Narain Saxena, *Role of Indian Army in the First World War* (New Delhi: Bhavana Prakashan, 1987).

Anil Shorey, *A Legendary Force:1st Patiala ; 300 years of 15 Punjab (Patiala)* (New Delhi: Manas Publications, 2005).

The Sikh Regiment, *Presentation of the Regimental Colours to the Sikh Regiment*, (Meerut: 1968).

Kushwant Singh, *A History of the Sikhs*, 2 vols (New Delhi: Oxford University Press, 1977).

K. Natwar Singh, *The Magnificent Maharaja: The Life and Times of Maharaja Bhupindar Singh of Patiala* (New Delhi: Rupa & Co., 2008).

6th Gurkha Rifles, *An Abridged History of the 6th QEO Gurkha Rifles Regimental Trust Property* (London: 6th QEO Gurkha Rifles, 1987).

Andrew Skeen, *Passing it On: Short Talks on Tribal Fighting on the North-West Frontier of India* (Aldershot: Gale & Polden, 1932).

Peter Stanley, *Quinn's Post, Anzac, Gallipoli* (Sydney: Allen & Unwin, 2005).

Nigel Steel & Peter Hart, *Defeat at Gallipoli* (London: Macmillan, 1994).

Phil Taylor & Pam Cupper, *Gallipoli: A Battlefield Guide* (Sydney: Kangaroo Press, 2000).

Ahmet Tetik, Serdar Demirtaş and Sema Demirtaş, *Çanakkale Muharebeleri'nin Esirleri [Prisoners of War at the Canakkale Battles]*, Vol. I, *Testimonies and Letters* (Ankara: GenelKurmay Basimevi, 2009).

Harbans Singh Thandi, *Down the Memory Lane: Saga of Bravery and Devotion: A Leaf from the Gallipoli Campaign – 1915* (Chandigargh, Privately published, 2012).

Tim Travers, *Gallipoli 1915* (Stroud: Tempus, 2001).

Charles Chenevix Trench, *The Indian Army and the King's Enemies, 1914-1945*, (London: Thames & Hudson, 1988).

D.C. Verna, *Indian Armed Forces in Egypt and Palestine 1914-1918* (New Delhi: Rajesh Publications, 2004).

Rob Walker, *To What End Did They Die?: Officers died at Gallipoli*, Upton-upon-Severn: R.W. Walker Publishing, 1985).

Tan Tai Yong, *The Garrison State: The Military, Government and Society in Colonial Punjab, 1849-1947* (New Delhi: Sage, 2005).

Articles

Anon, 'Pharsaldhoj Rai IOM', *Bugle and Kukri*, 2011, p. 92
——, 'Summary of the more important general remarks …', *Journal of the United Service Institution of India*, Vol. XLIII, July 1914, pp. 437-47
G. Aylmer, [Lecture on Supply and Transport, Rawalpindi, 14 April 1917], *Journal of the United Service Institute of India*, Vol. XLVI, No. 207, pp. 297-311
'Chameleon', 'Regimental Spirit in the Indian Army, *Journal of the United Services Institution of India*, No. 232, July 1923
Harry Fecitt, '"Turks across the Canal!": The Suez Canal 1914-15', *Durbar: Journal of the Indian Military Historical Society*, Vol. 27, No. 1, Spring 2010, pp. 16-23
David Harding, 'Sari Bair: some key 10th Gurkha participants', *Bugle and Kukri*, 2011, pp. 74-83
T.M. Lowe, 'Gurkhas remember France and Palestine', *The Kukri*, No. 41, May 1989, p. 139
R.W.L. McAlister, 'Sari Bar – Gallipoli, 6th to 10th August 1915', *Bugle and Kukri*, 2011, pp. 63-74
A.V.A. Mercer, 'Shadows from the past history of the Gurkhas', *The Kukri*, April 19156, No. 8, pp. 51-53
J. Moore, 'Merits and demerits of the various breeds of animals used in war', *Journal of the United Service Institution of India*, Vol. L, 1921, pp. 104-68
Reginald Savory, 'Some Gallipoli Memories', *The Gallipolian*, nos. 15-21, 1974-76
Dhanna Singh, 'Sikh seeks Sikh', *The Gallipolian*, no. 27, 1978
Peter Stanley, '"An Entente … Most Remarkable": Indians at Anzac', *Sabretache*, Vol. XXII, No. 2, Apr-Jun 1981, pp. 17-21
Harbans Singh Thandi, 'A Profile in Courage', *The Gallipolian*, no. 34, 1980,
T. Vershoyle, 'The Shelling of Allanson's party on Hill Q', *The Gallipolian*, No. 38, 1982, pp. 30-31
C.D. Webster, 'The supply of followers on active service for a battalion of Indian infantry', *Journal of the United Service Institution of India*, Vol. XLV, 1916, pp. 272-76

Electronic Sources

Gordon Smith, *World War 1 at Sea – British Merchant and Fishing Vessels Lost and Damaged* <http://www.naval-history.net/WW1NavyBritishBVLSMN1507.htm>
Diary, George King, 19th Battalion, 1 September 1915 <http://users.bigpond.net.au/rhearne/gallipolli5.htm>

Theses

Ian Leask, 'The Expansion of the Indian Army during the Great War', School of Oriental and African Studies, London, 1989

Peter Liddle, 'The Dardanelles and Gallipoli experience August 1914 to January 1916', M.Litt., University of Newcastle-upon-Tyne, 1975

Field work

Turkey (Gallipoli); India (Ferozepore, Simla, Patiala); Nepal (Pokhara, Kathmandu); Egypt (Cairo); Britain (St Luke's, Chelsea: both of them)

Index

400 Plateau, 85
Abbottabad, 35, 41, 45, 46, 48, 72, 166, 169, 198, 295
Achi Baba, 117, 118, 140, 141, 158, 160
Aghyl Dere, 196, 198, 200, 201, 212
Alexander, Heber, 33, 40, 47, 48, 78, 79, 87, 88, 104, 105, 131, 162, 176, 191, 194, 233, 244, 245, 247, 254, 259, 277, 286
Alexandria, 52, 78
Ali, Hashmet (Ressaidar), 80, 88, 89, 194, 244
Ali, Hashmet (carpenter), 89
Ali, Sultan, 278
Ali, Waris, 130
Allahabad, 190
Allanson, Cecil, 179, 180-181, 192, 197, 199, 200, 205-211, 213, 215, 217, 224, 228, 232, 253, 263, 264, 265, 279, 285-286, 287, 294
Amballa, 40, 47, 292-293
Amritsar, 143, 187
Antikythera, 255-256
Anzac Cove, 86
Ashmead-Bartlett, Ellis, 158, 240
Asiatic Annie, 131
Aspinall, Fred, 109-110
Aspinall-Oglander, Cyril, 73, 301
Atatürk in Anafartalar, 300
Atkins, John, 93
Atrocities, 146-147
Australian and New Zealand Army Corps, 51, 62, 75, 76, 192
   Formations
      1st Australian Division, 87, 94, 242

2nd Australian Division, 230, 242, 260, 268
2nd Australian Brigade, 94
4th Australian Brigade, 193, 195, 197, 199, 200, 204, 212, 223, 225
New Zealand and Australian Division, 94, 105, 192
Australian units
   1st Battalion, 257
   4th Battalion, 85
   5th Light Horse, 158
   7th Light Horse, 158
   8th Light Horse, 245
   10th Light Horse, 225
   11th Battalion, 266
   16th Battalion, 92, 230
   18th Battalion, 223
Australians and Indians, 52, 55, 64-65, 71, 72, 91, 92-93, 109-113, 135, 172-173, 179-180, 200, 229-232, 257-262, 268, 284
Aylmer, Fenton, 39, 43, 47, 76, 239
Aylmer, George, 49, 78, 131, 186, 244, 258, 279

Baby 700, 90, 93, 94
Baker, Raymond, 106, 186
Bakloh, 45
Baksh, Mohammed, 257
Baldwin, Anthony, 210, 212, 213
Balkan Gun Pits, 158
Barwick, Archie, 257, 258
Bateman-Champain, Hugh, 239
Battalions; organisation and administration, xix-xx, 31

Battye, Hedley, 30
Battye, Rothney, 30, 114, 130, 130, 143-146, 162, 166, 224, 232, 249
Bauchop, Arthur, 195
Beachy Bill, 89, 94, 98, 100, 177
Bean, Charles, 42, 80, 84, 85, 93, 99, 102, 176, 215, 275
Beersheba, 59
Beeston, Joseph, 104, 128, 195, 232, 244
Behrend, Arthur, 128, 132, 266
Beville, Charles, 80
Bingley, Arthur, 27, 38, 141
Birdwood, Christopher, 30, 59, 62, 120, 138
Birdwood family, 30-31
Birdwood, William, 30, 60, 62, 72, 75, 76, 77, 79, 84, 93, 97, 164, 192, 196, 209, 225, 228, 236, 274, 277, 285
Birrell, William, 128
Bitter Lakes, 58
Bose, Mihir, 299
Bolsragon, Guy, 139
Bolton's Ridge, 90, 100, 175
Bombs, 126, 127, 153, 159, 181, 253
Bonarjee, P.D., 27
Bowler, Edmund, 77, 99
Braithwaite, Walter, 165
Braund's Hill, 90
Bridges, William, 94
British Army
  Formations
    2nd Mounted Division
    9th Corps, 271, 277
    10th Division, 193, 223
    11th Division, 193
    13th Division, 193, 195, 223
    29th Division, 43, 75, 114, 117, 134, 151, 152, 157, 192, 196, 274, 282
    39th Brigade, 212
    42nd Division, 134
    52nd Division, 209
    53rd Division, 193
    54th Division, 193, 275
    87th Brigade, 151, 248
    88th Brigade, 134
  Territorials, 52, 65, 117, 128, 134

Units
  Connaught Rangers, 223, 225, 226, 282
  Gloucestershire Regiment, 210
  Hampshire Regiment, 223
  King's Own Scottish Borderers, 124
  Lancashire Fusiliers, 134, 136
  North Staffordshire Regiment, 204
  Royal Artillery, 31
  Royal Fusiliers, 125
  Royal Gurkha Rifles, 291, 292, 301
  Royal Inniskilling Fusiliers, 120, 124, 134
  Royal Munster Fusiliers, 153
  South Lancashire Regiment, 204
  South Wales Borderers, 115, 149, 223, 253
  Warwickshire Regiment, 202, 204, 211
  Welch Regiment, 210
  Welsh Horse, 253
  West Yorkshire Regiment, 315
  Worcestershire Regiment, 136
British other ranks, 47, 87, 248-249
British troops and Indians, 115, 122, 149, 253, 257-262, 257-262
Browett, Arthur, 110
Bruce, Charles, 30, 31, 32, 33, 35, 41, 50, 53, 56, 64, 70, 73, 77, 95, 114, 115, 118, 119, 120, 122, 138, 140, 155, 160, 233, 248, 253, 285, 295
Bruce, John, 83, 108, 273

Cairo, 38, 54,
Callwell, Charles, 69, 78
Campbell, Donald, 255
Canal Defence Force, 57-68
Cape Helles Memorial, 297, 300
Carey-Evans, Thomas, 70, 101-102, 104, 165, 177, 276
Casualties; see Indian Army, casualties
Cemeteries; see Gallipoli, cemeteries
Censorship, 54, 108, 239
Ceylon Planters' Rifle Corps, 163-164
Chamberlain, Austen, 110, 142, 252, 295
Chambers, Stephen, 309

Chanda (Jemadar), 278
Channi, 297
Chapman, Perceval, 84
Chettri, Sankasing, 130
Chetwode, Phillip, 292
Chhina, Rana, 185, 301, 302, 311
'Chitiwallas', 167
Chunuk Bair, 193, 196, 199, 207-210, 299
Churches
   All Saints, Maymyo, 295
   Ferozepore, 295
   Holy Trinity, Eltham, 295
   St Luke's, Abbottabad, 295
   St Luke's, Chelsea, 295
   St Luke's, Redcliffe Square, 295
Churchill, Wandrill, 130
Churchill, Winston, 68, 179
Cloughley, George, 229
Clowes, Cyril, 100
Coen, Frank, 239, 260, 261
Commonwealth War Graves Commission, 221, 254, 290, 299, 313, 315
Connaught Ridge, 270
Cooper, Frank, 110, 178, 258
Cosby, Noel, 153, 198, 201, 202, 277
Cox, Herbert, 48, 50, 53, 56, 59, 64, 66, 67, 69, 71, 93, 95, 97, 120, 125, 125, 127, 136, 139, 143, 151, 156, 162, 165, 178, 183, 192, 196-210, 222-237, 249, 274, 285, 286, 290
Creagh, O'Moore, 29, 30, 57
Cremation; see Dead, disposal of
Cremen, Leonard, 295
Crewe, Marquess of, 43, 54, 109
Cullen, Hedley, 88, 212
Cummins, Harry, 224
Cuneo, Terence, 291
Cunliffe-Owen, Charles, 170
Cursetjee, Herajee, 137, 289
Curzon, Lord, 29

Daisy Patch, 85
Dallas, Jack, 59, 199, 236
Daniell, John, 188
Dardanelles Commission, 200, 203, 209, 280, 286

Davies, Harry, 210
Dawes, Arthur, 218-219
De Crespigny, Henry, 100
Dead, disposal of, 128-129, 299
Dehra Dun, 47, 298
Demakjelik Bair, 212, 213, 217, 242, 238-264, 262-282, 310
Derversoir, 58
Din, Bahwal, 105
Din, Fateh, 122
Din, Mohamed, 258
Dinapore, 48
Donovan, George, 110
Duff, Beauchamp, 29-30, 40, 44, 54, 75, 76, 112, 143, 157, 164, 181, 183, 188, 216, 248
Duff, Patrick, 117, 148
Dugshai, 47
Duidar, 65

Earle, Edward, 253-254
Edgerton, Granville, 209
Edmonds, James, 301
Egypt, 51-52, 53-67
El Ferdan, 58, 63, 65
Ellinwood, De Witt, xxiii, 237
Elmore, Septimus, 260
Elston, William, 92
Engledue, Ralph, 125, 136, 141, 157
Erskine, Kenneth, 127, 215, 271

Faridkot, 187, 297
Farm, The, 211, 212, 213
Fergusson, Arthur, xxiv, 70, 82, 83, 84-85, 90-91, 93, 95, 98, 100, 108, 113, 170, 176-177, 214, 227-228, 273, 275, 277, 278, 293
Ferozepore, 33, 34, 167, 187, 295, 297-298
Firth, Richard, 199, 204
Flies, 107, 158, 164, 165
Followers, xix, xx, 47, 111, 112, 132, 152, 153, 248, 260, 286
Force G see Indians troops on Gallipoli
Fusilier Bluff, 152, 155, 157

Gaba Tepe, 76, 79, 83-85, 175

Gallipoli campaign
    4 June attack, 134-143
    19 May attack, 100-104
    28 June attack, 151-156
    24 May truce, 105
    Anzac, landing at 83-113
    Anzac, fighting at, 170-178, 197
    Art depicting Indians, 132, 229, 235, 243, 245, 249, 259, 267, 272, 291, 300
    August offensive, 192-216
        6-7 August, 197-199
        7 August, 199-202
        8 August, 202-210
    Bathing, 108, 118, 133, 147, 170, 182, 273
    Cape Helles fighting, 114-169, 160-163, 196
    Cemeteries, 236, 287, 290, 298-300, 309
    Conceived, 68-69
    Dardanelles Army, 277
    Dardanelles Commission, 200, 209, 280
    Evacuation, 275-279
    J trenches fights, 154-156
    Judgment on August offensive, 214-216
    Judgment on Gallipoli, 280-282
    Judgment on Helles, 160-161
    Judgment on Hill 60, 226-228
    Krithia, 162, 193, 197
    Landings, 76-77
    Logistics, 180
    Memorials, 295-300
    Official histories, 301
    Patrolling, 125, 218-219
    Propaganda, 148, 158, 178, 187-188
    Strengths, 311-314
    Third battle of Krithia, 134-143
    Winter, 268-275
'Gallipoli Day', 291
Gallipoli guide books, 308
Gallipoli, visiting, 308-310
Galway, Edgar, 87
Gandhi, Mohandas, 293
Gell, Humphrey, 41, 49, 64, 69, 70, 114, 115, 123, 125, 139, 140, 146, 192, 228, 239

German Officer's Trench, 93
Ghadr movement, 34, 41, 45, 142
Gharti, Dhanjit, 160
Gillam, John, 130, 131, 133, 232, 247, 254
Glanville, Miss R.E., 234
Godley, Alexander, 94, 117, 192, 195, 196, 198, 209, 225, 228
Gorruckpore, 167
Govan, Douglas, 153
Graves; see Cemeteries
Green Patch Farm, 224
'Guel Bahadur', 179
Gully Ravine, 119, 134-150, 178, 187, 309
Gully Spur, 124, 151-169
Gurkha Beach, 178
Gurkha Bluff, 118-122, 124, 160
Gurkha Mule Trench, 178, 309
Gurkha Museum, Winchester, 291
Gurkhas, 25-26, 33-35, 52, 64-65, 119-122, 127, 196, 240-242
    Selected for Gallipoli, 72-75, 281
Gurkha troops, xviii, 27-28, 34-37, 120, 149
Gurkha verses, 182
Gurung, Ambare, 154
Gurung, Apai, 169
Gurung, Bebesur, 166
Gurung, Dhanbir, 82, 201
Gurung, Dhanraj, 160
Gurung, Dhansing, 139
Gurung, Dirasing, 277
Gurung, Dirgasing, 277
Gurung, Duble, 169, 291-292, 302
Gurung, Harkabir, 198
Gurung, Kulbahadur, 240-242
Gurung, Naharsing, 274
Gurung, Nandlal, 227
Gurung, Tulbir, 35, 286

Hamilton, Ian, 36, 68, 72, 74, 77, 96, 117, 120, 123, 137, 142, 143, 146, 151, 157, 162, 173, 177, 181, 185, 188, 190, 193, 196, 207, 209, 210, 214, 215, 222, 236, 271, 274, 281
Hands, wounds to; see Indian Army, self-inflicted wounds?

Hardinge, Lord, 29, 42, 43, 75, 112, 166, 169, 287, 292
Hargrave, John, 186, 244, 245, 248, 260, 262, 267, 287
Harrison, Phillip, 92
Harwood, Ross, 230-232
Helles Memorial; see Cape Helles Memorial
Higgin, James, 154
Hill 60, 221-237, 299
Hill Q, 196, 199, 200, 204, 207, 211, 295, 301
Hill 971, 196
Hogg, Rudolph, 179
Hore, Leslie, 235, 245, 249
Hospitals, 30, 143-146, 166-169, 201, 232-234, 263
Hospital ships, 234, 263
Hunter-Weston, Aylmer, 117, 118, 137, 139
Husband, George, 144
Hypher, P.P., 285

Ilahi, Fazl, 188
Imbros, 178-183, 268, 273
Imperial Service Troops, 46, 184-185
  Bharatpur, 185-186
  Bikaner Camel Corps, 59
  Gwalior, 185, 256
  Hyderabad Lancers, 65
  Indore, 185-186, 256
  See also Patiala
Imperial War Graves Commission; see Commonwealth War Graves Commission
India Gate, 295, 301
Indian Army, 28-33
  Army Bearer Corps, 104
  Army Headquarters, 40-41, 81, 163
  Bureaucracy, 27, 129, 169
  Casualties, 66, 102, 128-130, 141, 143-146, 161, 181, 188, 214-215, 236, 254-256, 263, 265, 276, 278, 289, 297
  Central Casualty Bureau, 130
  Conditions of service, 37-39, 54, 109, 133, 169, 276, 286

Decorations; recommended and awarded, 62, 112, 137, 138, 154, 158-159, 174, 181, 190, 208, 213, 214, 225, 228, 244, 274
Diet, 104, 112, 118, 129, 131, 132, 165, 170, 172, 246, 248-249, 250, 258, 268
Disloyalty; see Loyalty
Expeditionary forces, 74, 235, 252
Families, 166-167
Force G, 181
Formations
  22nd Indian Infantry Brigade, 53, 66
  28th Indian Infantry Brigade, 53, 238
  29th Indian Infantry Brigade, 43, 48, 51, 59, 66, 69, 82, 97, 113, 115, 117, 124, 134, 136-143, 143-146, 151, 157, 160, 162, 192, 194-210, 222-228, 284
Health, 54, 100, 107, 108, 131, 132, 144, 164-169, 179, 232-234, 268, 274
Indian officers, 31, 33, 160, 191
Labourers, 252
Loyalty, 56-57, 63, 73, 102, 122-124, 235, 279
Martial race theory, 26-28, 65, 125, 141, 205, 213, 224
Mobilisation, 40-43, 48-52
Pay; see Conditions of service
Pensions; see Conditions of service
Recruiting, 42, 43-45, 143, 239
Reforms, 28-33, 48, 292
Reinforcements, 157, 163-164, 180, 183-186, 223, 248-254, 256, 311-314
Relations and comparisons between Gurkhas and Sikhs, 118, 214, 240-242, 257-258, 266
Religion, 32, 129, 133
Reserve of Officers, 163-164, 220, 253
Self-inflicted wounds?, 161-162, 236, 265-266, 271
Units
  1st Brahmans, 270
  1st Mule Corps, 130
  4th Gurkhas, 30, 45, 226, 238-239,

248, 262, 276, 277, 279, 287, 301, 311
5th Gurkhas, 30, 34, 35, 44, 45, 48, 50, 53, 63, 65, 67, 82, 126, 127, 140, 148, 151, 152, 154, 161, 197, 198, 199, 213, 215, 223, 226, 250, 271, 273, 277, 278, 279, 280, 283, 284, 301
5 Indian General Hospital, 112, 233
6th Gurkhas, 31, 32, 36, 37, 41, 43, 45, 48, 49, 53, 58, 59, 62, 114, 124118, 121, 122, 123, 125, 132, 138-139, 151, 161, 164, 169, 179, 199, 202-210, 212-213, 215, 223, 228, 234, 248, 274, 277, 278, 280-281, 284, 286, 287, 288
9th Mule Corps, 105
10th Gurkhas, 34, 45, 46, 53, 62, 126, 145, 151, 152, 153, 154, 161, 162, 173, 179, 199, 201, 203-204, 211, 213, 217, 223, 225, 254, 270, 274, 276, 280, 295, 299, 301
14th Sikhs, 30, 31, 33-34, 43, 48, 49, 50, 53, 61, 62, 67, 115, 118, 124, 136-143, 144, 147, 155, 157, 161, 183-191, 194-210, 214, 223, 225, 266, 268, 276, 280, 283, 284, 285, 295, 297, 301, 313
15th Sikhs, 49, 256
19th Punjabis, 235
22nd Mule Corps, 299
22nd Punjabis, 315
23rd Pioneers, 50
24th Punjabis, 76
25th Punjabis, 315
27th Punjabis, 122
33rd Mule Corps, 88
45th Sikhs, 256
51st Sikhs
53rd Sikhs, 212
54th Sikhs, 238
56th Punjabi Rifles, 77, 100
66th Punjabis, 315
69th Punjabis, 41, 43, 48, 49, 50, 56, 57, 59, 62, 64, 69, 115, 122, 123, 124, 279

87th Punjabis, 252
89th Punjabis, 43, 48, 50, 62, 66, 122, 123, 279
93rd Burma Infantry, 315
108th Field Ambulance, 30, 59, 62, 115, 143-146, 167, 194, 263
110th Field Ambulance, 266
120th Rajputana Regiment
126th Baluchis, 56
128th Pioneers, 56
137th Combined Field Ambulance, 70, 143, 283
Assam Military Police, 180, 256
Burma Military Police, 191, 223, 252, 256
Mountain artillery – see Mountain artillery
Probyn's Horse, 41, 77
Supply & Transport Corps, 37, 40, 47, 77-82, 87-89, 112-113, 130-133, 171, 189, 194, 242-248, 260-261, 275, 277, 282
Zhob Militia, 235
See also Patiala Rajindra Infantry
Indian Medical Service, 104, 112, 128, 144-145
Indian National Congress, 28, 39, 42, 46-47, 293
Indian Soldiers Fund, 42
Indian troops on Gallipoli
  Burials, 99-100
  Casualties, 129, 164-169, 236, 311-314
  Comparisons, Sikh and Gurkha, 266
  Cremation, 99, 128-129, 288
  Frontier experience, 33-34, 73, 77-78, 118-122, 137, 139, 152, 177, 199, 201, 213
  Frostbite, 266, 268-271, 272
  Kit, 35-36, 194-195
  Memorials, 289-290, 295-300
  Morale, 182-183, 242, 251, 254, 266, 267, 283
  Imbros, 178-183, 268, 273
  'Indians in front', 92-93
  Order of battle, 303-304
  Prisoners of war, 179, 219, 240-242

Reasons for selection, 66
Sport, 179
Stretcher-bearers, 214, 268, 270, 282
Irvine, Andrew, 285
Irvine, Christopher, 127
Irwin, Neville, 254
Islington, Lord, 289
Ismailia, 55, 58, 63, 108

James, Robert Rhodes, 74, 117
Jang, Chandra Shumshere, 44
Jhelum, 48, 188
'Jhill-o! Johnnie', 261
Johnston, Francis, 193
Jones, Dennis, 248
Jones, Vyner, 234
Jopp, Arthur, 171
Jullunder, 188

Kangaroo Beach, 244
Kagan, 112
Kalka, 47
Kantara, 58, 60, 69, 164
Karachi, 45, 49
Katia, 65
Kenyon, Herbert, 106
Khan, Dulla, 84
Khan, Khan Fazl Rahman, 239
Khan, Hussain, 178
Khan, Medi, 108
Khan, Sher, 85
Khan, Mahomed Shah Aga, 56
Khud running, 35, 36
Kirkpatrick, John Simpson, 102, 273
Kirkwood, Thomas, 254
King, Charles, 179
Kirwan, Matthew, 89
Kitchener, Lord, 29, 30, 43, 68-69, 73, 95, 157, 209, 275
Koe, Frederick, 79, 80, 242
Kophamel, Waldemar, 255
KOSB Trench, 125
Krithia, 117, 118, 120, 139
Kubri, 58, 65

Lachman, 108

Lamjung, 169, 292
Lancashire Landing, 134, 205, 299
Lane, Hugh, 153, 157, 198, 199, 224
Languages, 31, 32, 72, 88, 93, 110, 145, 162, 163-164, 171, 181, 202, 229-232, 239, 242, 270
Le Marchand, John, 181, 207, 286, 290
Lemnos, 70, 72, 77, 78, 238
Lesslie, William, 98, 105
Limbu, Kamansing, 218-219
Limbu, Punahang, 299
Little, Keith, 87
Lloyd, Duncan, 218
Lone Pine, 107, 158, 197
Lorelai, 34
Lucas, Charles, 235
Lucknow, 37
Lushington, Reginald, 92-93, 219
Lutyens, Edwin, 290
Lyons, Rita, 234

Mackenzie, Compton, 128, 135, 139, 142
MacLagan, Ewen, 90, 94
MacLagan's Ridge, 85, 90
MacMunn, George, 26, 32, 268, 278, 292, 298
Maer; see Meyer
Mahomed, Jan, 176
Mahomed, Wali, 80
Maidos, 196
Mallory, George, 285
Malone, William, 56, 98, 208, 210
Manners-Smith, John, 44, 250
Marsh, Jeremy, 88
Martial race theory; see Indian Army, martial race theory
Masefield, John, 240, 268, 294
Mathew, Murray, 137
Maxwell, John, 54, 58, 60, 64, 68, 73, 74, 75, 95, 109, 117, 163-164, 181, 185, 234, 238
Mayer; see Meyer
McCay, James, 94
McDonald, Ronald, 92
Meade, Dick, 295

Mediterranean Expeditionary Force, 67, 68-82,
Mesopotamia, 77, 123, 124, 140, 235, 284
Meyer, Cyril, 72, 220-221, 277
Milward, Clement, 114, 153, 192, 203
Mohammed, Satar, 172-173
Mohammedan troops; see Musalman troops
Molloy, Henry, 30, 224, 310
Monash, John, 52, 193, 195, 199, 200, 202
Monash Valley, 107
Monro, Charles, 275, 279
Morrice, Walter, 257
Mortar Ridge, 93, 175
Mountain artillery, 31, 64, 81, 86, 97, 158, 170-178, 214, 227-228, 266, 267, 271
   at Anzac, 89-92, 97-113
   Units
      7th Brigade, 47, 67, 70, 76, 84, 89-92, 97-113, 170-178, 274, 278
      21st Kohat Battery, 47, 70, 81, 85, 100, 165, 175-178, 197, 210, 211, 214, 228, 236, 257, 265, 274, 275, 278, 291
      26th Jacob's Battery, 47, 59, 61, 83, 108, 112, 165, 197, 228, 265, 273, 274
Mudros, 70, 77
Mule Gully, 89, 235, 242, 243, 247
Mules, 47, 70, 78-80, 98, 172-173, 242-248
Mullaly, Brian, 214
Multan, 34, 163
Murphy (donkey), 102
Murray, Joe, 135, 208
Musalman troops, 32, 38, 41, 55, 56, 73, 99, 122-124, 131, 143, 148, 279, 315
Music, 172

Nabha, 188
'Nahdar', 260
National Archives of India, 38
National Army Museum, 295
Nehru, Jawaharlal, 190
Nepal, 44-45
Nevinson, Henry, 170, 294

Newfoundland Battalion, 274
New Zealand units and formations
   Canterbury Battalion, 106, 186
   New Zealand and Australian Division, 192
   New Zealand Infantry Brigade, 193, 197, 203, 205
   New Zealand Mounted Rifles, 222
   Maori Pioneer Battalion, 211, 274
   Otago Mounted Rifles, 230
   Wellington Battalion, 56, 97-98, 110, 208, 210
   Wellington Mounted Rifles, 107
New Zealander and Indians, 52, 64-65, 87, 93, 109-113, 172-173, 174-175, 201, 229-232, 257-262
Newton, Leslie, 93
No. 2 Outpost, 227, 242
No. 3 Post, 107
North-West Frontier, 33-34, 73, 77-78, 118-122, 137, 139, 152, 177, 199, 201, 213, 235

O'Dwyer, Michael, 41, 142-143, 291
Officers, British, 28, 30, 31, 65, 82, 137, 138, 70-171, 213, 224, 248, 250, 252-253
Officers, Indian, 31, 33, 160, 170-171, 191
Öktem, Tankut, 300
Omissi, David, 28, 32
Onslow, Brian, 77
Overton, Philip, 195
Palin, Philip, 31, 34, 95, 115, 141, 157, 179, 204, 214, 220, 249, 270
Parker, John, 67, 70, 84, 170, 273, 274
Patiala, 46, 184-186, 187, 285, 286, 294, 296-297
   Patiala Lancers, 62, 65
   Patiala Rajindra Infantry, 53, 184-185, 191, 204-205, 214, 222, 223, 231, 236, 252, 283, 284, 286, 297
Patiala, Maharaja, 42-43, 46, 184-186, 187, 284, 285, 286, 294, 297
Pepys, Gerald, 138, 228
Pershad, Adjudhia, 104
Peshawur, 34, 45, 48, 49

Phillips, Owen, 101
Phipson, Edward, 208, 212
Pifferpore, 94, 172, 309
Pink Farm, 299
Plugge's Plateau, 85, 90
Pope, Harold, 92
Pope's Post, 101
Port Said, 53, 55, 58, 129
Poynder, Leopold, 51, 123
Pradhan, S.D., xxiii
Prior, Robin, xxiii
Prisoners of war, 179, 219, 240-242
Propaganda, 148, 158, 178, 187-188
Pun, Gambirsing, xx, 50, 120, 154, 190, 212-213, 224, 250, 287
Pun, Hastabir, 270
Pun, Tulbir, 161
Punjab, 45, 141-143, 184-185, 302

Queensland Ridge/Point, 90
Quetta, 34, 76
Quinn's Post, 101, 105, 107, 175, 193, 195, 197, 253

Rai, Amaldhoj, 277
Rai, Bajirdhoj, 159
Rai, Joglal, 62
Rai, Kirpe, 161
Rai, Mangat, 33, 106
Rai, Nar Bahadur, 225, 227, 274
Rai, Pharalhoj, 182, 202
Rai, Sriman, 154
Ramazan, sinking of, 254-256
Rana, Chandrabin, 288
Rana, Chandra Singh, 234
Rana, Hembahadur, 166
Rana, Ranbahadur, 166
Rangasammy, 276
Ranks, xix, xxi
Rao, Ganpat, 88
Rasul, Ghulam, 105
Rations; see Indian Army, diet
Rawalpindi, 46, 84, 187, 195
Rawson, Cresswell, 95, 100, 101, 102, 106, 171, 177, 215, 228, 278
Reaney, Michael, 154

Recruiting; see Indian Army, recruiting
'Ressaldar', 39
Rhododendron Ridge, 198, 201, 215
Roberts, Lord, 69, 73
Rossiter, Frederick, 228
Royal Military Academy, Sandhurst, 295
Royal Naval Division, 69, 75, 93, 134, 135
Russell's Top, 92, 107, 175
Russo-Japanese war, 127
Ryan, Denis, 60, 62, 153, 155, 190, 250, 287

Saidullah, 94
Sari Bair Range, 175, 193, 200, 202-210
Savory, Reginald, xx, 49, 115, 116, 130, 131, 137, 157, 162, 163, 179, 186, 196, 204, 254, 258, 271, 276, 298
Scrubby Knoll, 193
Secundrabad, 37
Sedd-ul-Bahr, 87-88
Senn, Frederick, 112
Serapeum East, 62, 67
Seton, Bruce, 161
Shah, Ajib, 108, 233
Shah, Bahadur, 88, 244
Shaw, Richard, 195
Sheik Sayed, 50-51
Shewen, Rob, 181-182, 202, 280
Ships
   Ajax, 143
   Annaberg, 126
   Aragon, 128
   Bacchante, HMS, 211
   City of Manchester, 45
   Clio, HMS, 63
   Devhana, 88
   Dongala, 212
   Duke of Edinburgh, HMS, 50
   Dunluce Castle, 114
   Guildford Castle, 234
   Hessen, 70, 72
   Loyalty, 263
   Madras, 263
   Maquette, 256
   Minnewaska, 79
   Orvieto, 55

Pera, 70, 72, 82, 83
Queen Elizabeth, HMS, 78
Ramazan, 78, 80, 87, 88, 254-256, 313
River Clyde, 87
Royal Edward, 256
Sicilia, 233, 263
Swiftsure, HMS, 50, 62
Syria, 263
Talbot, HMS, 120
Teesta, 50, 53, 238
Triumph, HMS, 108
U-35, 255
Shrapnel Gully, 90, 104
Sialkote, 47
Simla, 38, 40-41, 47, 75, 81, 129
Sikh Street, 178
Sikh Walk, 278
Sikhs, 25-26, 33-35, 41-42, 52, 57, 134-143, 178, 229-231, 275
Singh, Ajat, 188
Singh, Amar, 273
Singh, Bagwan, 137
Singh, Bajinder, 80
Singh, Bhagat, 191
Singh, Bhola, 298
Singh, Bir, 88, 89, 190, 244
Singh, Chanda, 80, 233
Singh, Dulat, 104
Singh, Dhiyan, 156
Singh, Gurbaksh, 184, 204
Singh, Gurdit, 49, 188
Singh, Harban, 185, 186, 204
Singh, Harpal, 187
Singh, Hazara, 204
Singh, Hem, 278
Singh, Hukam, 236
Singh, Johahir, 108
Singh, Jwala, 112
Singh, Karam, 101-102, 112, 293-294
Singh, Kela, 294-295
Singh, Kishan, 191
Singh, Mit, 100, 188, 236
Singh, Nanak, 115, 116, 118
Singh, Narain, 67, 88, 136, 174
Singh, Nikka, 112, 188
Singh, Paktar, 110, 173-174

Singh, Phuman, 273
Singh, Piraya, 174
Singh, Prem, 177
Singh, Puran, 278
Singh, Ram, 188
Singh, Santa, 161
Singh, Sham, 191
Singh, Sher, 94
Singh, Ude, 137-138, 298
Skeen, Andrew, 62, 76, 100, 193, 215
Slim, William, 202-203
Smyth, Charles, 265, 270-271
Snipers, 104, 173, 203, 218, 219
Spankie, Montague, 134
St Dunstan's, 293-294
Strachan, Hew, 78
Stretcher-bearers, 174
Suez Canal, 57-67
    Attacks on, 60-67
Susuk Kuyu, 223, 225, 263, 310
Sutton, Francis, 34, 46, 157, 162, 183, 201, 202, 203
Swinley, George, 30, 67, 114, 124, 134

Takdah, 45
Tanga, 42
Tattersall, Noel, 212
Taylor's Gap, 198
Thandi, Harbans Singh, 137, 298
Thapa, Bahadur, 225
Thapa, Dalbadhar, 160
Thapa, Girman, 166
Thapa, Harkabir, 62
Thapa, Harkasing, 214
Thapa, Padambir, 236
Thapa, Sahibir, 154, 159
Thapa, Karbir, 161
Thapa, Kulia, 129
Thom, John, 84, 100, 101, 106, 171, 175-176, 190, 215, 228
Tillard, Arthur, 30, 31, 165, 227, 238, 239, 253, 265, 271, 278
Tillard Sap, 278
Tomes, Geoffrey, 181, 212, 217, 287, 290
Tomes, Harriet, 217, 287, 290
Travers, Tim, xxiii, 193, 208

Treloar, John, 55, 65, 95, 170
Trenchard, Guy, 101, 105, 171, 210
Truce of 23 May, 105

Unger, Michael, 255

Victoria Cross, 39, 146, 208-209, 228
Victoria Memorial, 33
Villiers-Stuart, Charles, 50-51, 62, 82, 98-99
Villiers-Stuart, William, 31, 82, 127, 162, 250, 269, 283

Walker, Harold, 76
Walker's Ridge, 94, 101, 245
War, effects of, 49, 292
Water, 173
Weekes, Henry, 161-162
Westernra, Justin, 230

Whitting, Everard, 176, 228
Widows, 37, 109, 179, 291
Willcocks, James, 105
Williams, Aubrey, 115
Wilmer, Harold, 30, 31, 51, 156, 179, 298
Wilmer, Kitty, 298
Wilmer, Violet, 156, 179, 298
Wilson, Alec, 58, 62, 66, 74, 97, 122, 164, 181, 240
Wilson, Thomas, 52
Wimbush, Norman, 132, 229, 245, 259, 272
Winn, Herbert, 49, 251, 253, 278
White Australia, 258
Woodyat, Nigel, 146, 260
Wounds, self-inflicted; see Indian Army, self-inflicted wounds?
Wreford, Reginald, 163